`TextArea(int numberRows, int maximumNumberCharacters)`	Constructor for a TextArea.
`TextArea(String initialValue)`	Constructor for a TextArea.
`TextArea(String initialValue, int numberRows, int maxNumberCharacters)`	Constructor for a TextArea.
`TextArea(String initialValue, int numberRows, int maxNumberCharacters, int Scroll)`	Constructor for a TextArea.
`TextField(int maximumNumberCharacters)`	Constructor for a TextField.
`TextField(String initialValue)`	Constructor for a TextField.
`TextField(String initialValue, int maximumNumberCharacters)`	Constructor for a TextField.

<pre>try
{
    //Statement(s) that could generate an exception
}
catch(ErrorObject errIdentifier)
{
    //Statement(s) to execute if an exception occurs
}</pre>
	Trap for exception that could occur and execute error-handling code if an exception does occur.

<pre>while(condition)
{
    //Statement(s);
}</pre>
	Loop through (repeat) statements in loop block as long as the condition evaluates true.

Programming with Java

Julia Case Bradley
Mt. San Antonio College

Anita C. Millspaugh
Mt. San Antonio College

Boston   Burr Ridge, IL   Dubuque, IA   Madison, WI   New York   San Francisco   St. Louis
Bangkok   Bogotá   Caracas   Kuala Lumpur   Lisbon   London   Madrid   Mexico City
Milan   Montreal   New Delhi   Santiago   Seoul   Singapore   Sydney   Taipei   Toronto

McGraw-Hill Higher Education

A Division of The **McGraw-Hill** *Companies*

PROGRAMMING WITH JAVA

Published by McGraw-Hill, an imprint of The McGraw-Hill Companies, Inc. 1221 Avenue of the Americas, New York, NY, 10020. Copyright © 2002, by The McGraw-Hill Companies, Inc. All rights reserved. No part of this publication may be reproduced or distributed in any form or by any means, or stored in a database or retrieval system, without the prior written consent of The McGraw-Hill Companies, Inc., including, but not limited to, in any network or other electronic storage or transmission, or broadcast for distance learning.

Some ancillaries, including electronic and print components, may not be available to customers outside the United States.

This book is printed on acid-free paper.

domestic   2 3 4 5 7 8 9 0 QPD/QPT 0 9 8 7 6 5 4 3 2
international   1 2 3 4 5 7 8 9 0 QPD/QPT 0 9 8 7 6 5 4 3 2 1
ISBN 0-07-248819-0

Senior sponsoring editor: *George Werthman*
Associate editor: *Steve Schuetz*
Developmental editor: *Craig S. Leonard*
Senior marketing manager: *Jeff Parr*
Project manager: *Christina Thornton-Villagomez*
Production supervisor: *Carol A. Bielski*
Media producer: *David Barrick*
Senior designer: *Jennifer McQueen*
Lead supplement producer: *Marc Mattson*
Cover illustrator: *Peter Sui*
Interior design: *Carla Pacilio*
Typeface: *11/13 Bodoni Book*
Compositor: *GAC Indianapolis*
Printer: *Quebecor World Dubuque Inc.*

Library of Congress Cataloging-in-Publication Data

Bradley, Julia Case.
    Programming with Java / Julia Case Bradley, Anita C. Millspaugh.
        p. cm.
    ISBN 0-07-248819-0 (alk. paper)
    1. Java (Computer program language) I. Millspaugh, A. C. (Anita C.) II. Title.
    QA76.73.J38 B675 2002
    005.13'3—dc21   2001045220

International Edition ISBN 0-07-112309-1
Copyright © 2002. Exclusive rights by The McGraw-Hill Companies, Inc. for manufacture and export.
This book cannot be re-exported from the country to which it is sold by McGraw-Hill.
The International Edition is not available in North America.

http://www.mhhe.com

InformationTechnology

At McGraw-Hill Higher Education, we publish instructional materials targeted at the higher education market. In an effort to expand the tools of higher learning, we publish texts, lab manuals, study guides, testing materials, software, and multimedia products.

At **Irwin/McGraw-Hill** (a division of McGraw-Hill Higher Education), we realize that technology has created and will continue to create new mediums for professors and students to use in managing resources and communicating information with one another. We strive to provide the most flexible and complete teaching and learning tools available as well as offer solutions to the changing world of teaching and learning.

> **Irwin/McGraw-Hill is dedicated to providing the tools for today's instructors and students to successfully navigate the world of Information Technology.**

- **Seminar series**—Irwin/McGraw-Hill's Technology Connection seminar series offered across the country every year demonstrates the latest technology products and encourages collaboration among teaching professionals.

- **Osborne/McGraw-Hill**—This division of The McGraw-Hill Companies is known for its best-selling Internet titles *Harley Hahn's Internet & Web Yellow Pages* and the *Internet Complete Reference.* Osborne offers an additional resource for certification and has strategic publishing relationships with corporations such as Corel Corporation and America Online. For more information visit Osborne at **www.osborne.com.**

- **Digital solutions**–Irwin/McGraw-Hill is committed to publishing digital solutions. Taking your course online doesn't have to be a solitary venture, nor does it have to be a difficult one. We offer several solutions that will allow you to enjoy all the benefits of having course material online. For more information visit **www.mhhe.com/solutions/index.mhtml.**

- **Packaging options**—For more about our discount options, contact your local Irwin/McGraw-Hill Sales representative at 1-800-338-3987 or visit our website at **www.mhhe.com/it.**

Preface

Java has become one of the leading development languages today. It plays a very important role in application development for business as well as a tool for Web programming.

Approach

This Java text is designed primarily for business programming students. It assume no prior programming experience and can be used for a first language course or a first course in Java.

The object-oriented approach and visual components are introduced in the first program—in Chapter 1. Most texts begin with a simple program that writes a line to the Java console. This text avoids that artificial and uninteresting output and instead begins programming with objects, in the form of visual components.

The text has been extensively classroom tested. Students enjoy using the text because it begins with an introduction to applets using a Web browser and the visual approach is fun! Students like to create output that is visually pleasing as they are introduced to the concept of classes and objects through the visual components.

The concepts of layout managers and dates are introduced much earlier than in other texts. Business students demand the ability to control the layout and presentation of an interface. The Calendar object, introduced in Chapter 2, provides a convenient method for introducing variables.

The text itself is visual. The large number of screen captures and illustrations makes it easy to understand the concepts.

The code used in the text is standard for all Java compilers. Appendixes provide step-by-step directions for several popular development environments, including Microsoft Visual J++, Inprise/Borland JBuilder, Sun Fortè, and Monash BlueJ.

All programs in the text conform to standards. As each new concept is introduced, the conventions and standards are also discussed. The complete set of standards is found in an appendix.

Features

The pedagogical features from the successful Bradley/Millspaugh *Visual Basic* books are incorporated into this Java text.

Presentation of Concepts

Within each chapter you will find explanations of concepts with small snippets of code, as well as some complete programs. The complete programs for all in-chapter code are included in the supplemental material.

Hands-on Example

Each chapter contains a hands-on programming example, complete with planning, documentation, and code. This has proved to be a very popular feature, as students can go through the entire process of creating and running a program.

Feedback

Short questions are presented throughout the chapter to reinforce learning. The answers to these feedback questions are found in an appendix at the end of the text.

Tips

Many programming tips are included, which can help students become better programmers and/or avoid common pitfalls.

Summary

Each chapter contains a review of the topics covered in the chapter.

Review Questions

Questions of varying levels of analysis are presented at the end of each chapter. Answers to the questions are included in the Instructors' Manual.

Key Terms

Lists of new terms introduced in the chapter are listed at the end of the chapter. A definition for each of the terms may be found in the glossary at the end of the text.

Programming Exercises

Each chapter has a variety of programming exercises to reinforce the concepts covered in the chapter.

Case Studies

Following the programming exercises for each chapter are two case studies that the instructor can assign. The case studies require programs for a coffee shop/newsstand and a quilt store that offers training classes.

Appendixes

The appendixes provide greater detail for some text topics, such as debugging, math functions, dealing with large decimal numbers, and creating JAR files.

Appendix A gives a step-by-step introduction to four development environments: Microsoft Visual J++, Sun Forté, Borland/Inprise JBuilder 4, and Monash BlueJ. The debugging tools for these development environments are covered in Appendix G.

Answers to feedback questions are included in Appendix D, and suggested conventions and standards are found in Appendix B. Note that all in-chapter programs follow the standards.

Book Organization

Chapter 1

The first chapter introduces the concept of an applet and using HTML to display the applet in a Web browser. The students are introduced to the history, purpose, and advantages of the Java language, the Java packages in the language, and the elements of an integrated development environment.

Object-oriented (OO) terminology is explained and applied to applets, Label components, and Font and Color objects. The syntax and punctuation for Java are explained as the students create their first program.

Chapter 2

Object-oriented concepts are further developed in relation to existing objects. Each new component is presented with a list of constructors. The Button, TextField, and TextArea visual components are demonstrated.

The text components require the use of methods to obtain data, assign text to a component, and position the cursor in a text field. The button objects require the use of Listeners and the `actionPerformed` method. Mouse listeners also are included. At this point only one button is used in each project—multiple buttons require decision statements that are covered in Chapter 6.

Variables are introduced in this chapter to aid in an understanding of the constructor options. However, other than manipulating dates, the use of variables is postponed until Chapter 4.

Chapter 3

Students are usually frustrated with the lack of control provided by the default FlowLayout manager. This chapter introduces the GridLayout, BorderLayout, and GridBagLayout. The use of multiple panels demonstrates another method for controlling the design of an interface.

Chapter 4

Java contains a large number of operators. This chapter covers the arithmetic operators and assignment operators for calculations. The concept of prefix and postfix are introduced with the increment and decrement operators.

In business programming it is desirable to control the appearance of the output and the formatting of numbers. This chapter gives a detailed coverage of the formatting objects. The concept of locales for international programming is also introduced.

Chapter 5

Now that students have a fairly clear understanding of developing applets in Java using existing classes, they are introduced to creating their own classes. The OO topics are covered in greater detail.

With the use of multiple classes, the `public` and `private` keywords are introduced. The chapter examples incorporate both class variables and instance variables.

Chapter 6

This chapter covers making decisions using the `if` statement.

Relational operators are presented and used for comparisons of numeric data types. For comparisons of String objects and other wrapper classes, methods are used in conditional statements. Nested and compound conditions provide the ability to test multiple conditions.

Input data validation is a common use of decision statements. Using business rules in one class and displaying results in the applet class introduce the students to a multi-tier approach to developing projects. Enabling and disabling buttons also can be used to control user actions.

At this point multiple buttons can be added to the user interface. Using an `if` statement in the listener event, the program can determine the source of an event and take appropriate action.

Chapter 7

Option buttons and check boxes are introduced in this chapter using both action listeners and item listeners. The `switch` statement is added as an alternative for testing multiple conditions.

Swing components from the Java Foundation Classes (JFC) are first used in this chapter. Most browsers require a plug-in to run applets containing these components, so JavaScript code is included for the HTML file to determine which browser is being used.

Chapter 8

This chapter introduces the concept of a program loop. List components are introduced, which are a common and convenient use of loops. The projects include code to add and remove items from a list and to clear all elements.

Chapter 9

Both single and multidimensional arrays are covered as well as arrays of objects. Examples include iterating through an array for lookups and calculating with array elements.

Chapter 10

Frames, dialogs, and menus are introduced using an application. The chapter demonstrates how to create a popup menu and incorporate multiple windows in an application. An example shows how to design a project that can execute as an applet or as an application.

Chapter 11

Chapter 11 introduces graphics. Although Java contains some elementary drawing objects, this chapter concentrates on images, sounds, and animation. Printing is also covered.

Chapter 12

Interfaces and inner classes are the main topics in this chapter. These features enhance the OO approach in Java.

Chapter 13

Storing information is a very important topic in business application development. This chapter introduces the concept of streams and then writes code to store and retrieve objects.

A more common way to store data in today's environment is with a database. This chapter covers using JDBC as a tool for connecting to a database and writing SQL to retrieve ResultSets. A primer on writing SQL queries and updates is included.

Chapter 14

Although JavaScript is an entirely different language from Java, many people think the two are the same. This chapter introduces the JavaScript language mainly to point out that it is really a different language.

Chapter 15

In this chapter, several more advanced Java topics are introduced. These include JavaBeans, client/server topics, and security.

Supplements

For the Instructor

An instructors manual is available that contains answers to the chapter review questions, chapter outlines, teaching suggestions, and sample exam questions.

Solutions for the programming exercises and the case studies for each chapter are available to instructors of the course.

For the Student

The text includes a CD with the sample code from the chapters, data files, and extra graphic files. JBuilder 5 Personal Edition is also included, along with Sun's SDK/JDK 1.3 and BDK 1.1.

Acknowledgements

We would like to express our appreciation to the many people who have contributed to the successful completion of this text. Most especially, we thank the students at Mt. San Antonio College who helped class-test the material and who greatly influenced the manuscript.

Many people have worked very hard to design and produce this book, including George Werthman, publisher; Steve Schuetz, associate editor; Craig Leonard, development editor; and Christina Thornton-Villagomez, project manager.

A great big thank you goes to Jaishri Mehta, who wrote a thorough technical review, classroom-tested the manuscript, and wrote the exercise solutions, Instructor's Manual, Testbank, and PowerPoint demonstration. We couldn't have done it without you.

We also want to thank our reviewers, who made many helpful suggestions: Rebecca Bruce of University of North Carolina—Asheville, Joe Daniel of Delaware Valley College, Chris Howard of DeVry Institute of Technology—Georgia, Mary Johnson of Mt. San Antonio College, Dennis Lang of DeVry Institute of Technology—Missouri, Dion Melton of Austin Community College, Derek Otieno of DeVry Institute of Technology—Georgia, Bina Ramamurthy of University of Buffalo, Steve Taylor of Bucks County Community College, Catherine Wyman of DeVry Institute of Technology—Phoenix.

Julia Case Bradley
Anita C. Millspaugh

To The Student

The best way to learn a programming language is to do it. If you enter and run the sample projects, you will be on your way to writing Java applets and applications. Reading the examples without trying to run them is like trying to learn a foreign language or mathematics just by reading about it. Enter the projects, look up your questions in Help, and make those projects *run*.

The tools in this text can help you on your way:

- Each chapter begins with a list of topics and ends with a summary. Combine these for a thumbnail review of the chapter. Understanding the terminology is an important part of learning any new language. That's also true with programming languages.

- A list of key terms appears at the end of each chapter. Each of those terms is in boldface within the chapter. You can look up the definition of the key terms in the glossary, which appears at the end of the text.

- Test yourself with the feedback questions as you work through each section of a chapter. The answers to the feedback questions appear in an appendix. The review questions at the end of each chapter can test your understanding of the topics.

- Tips are included to give programming suggestions to make you a better programmer and hopefully avoid common pitfalls.

Format Used for Java Statements

Java keywords and methods are shown in `this font`. Any values you must supply are in *italics*.

Example

```
GridLayout (int rows, int columns)
```

Programming in Java

CHAPTER

1

Introducing Java

At the completion of this chapter, you will be able to ...

1. Recognize the strengths of the Java programming language.

2. Understand the uses of Java for applets and applications.

3. Use the `import` statement to incorporate Java packages into your code.

4. Declare and add components to an interface.

5. Modify text using the Color and Font objects.

6. Write an applet and run it in a browser or applet viewer.

7. Locate and correct errors in a Java applet.

Java

Using this text you will learn to write computer programs using the Java programming language. With Java, you can write small programs, called **applets**, that run in a Web browser, such as Netscape Navigator or Internet Explorer. You also can write stand-alone programs, called **applications**, that run independently rather than in a Web browser. Your programs can be text based or have a graphical user interface (GUI), displaying components such as labels, text boxes, check boxes, buttons, and menus. Applications may run on an individual system, over a local network, or over the Internet. Figure 1.1 shows an applet running on a Web page; Figure 1.2 is an example of a stand-alone application.

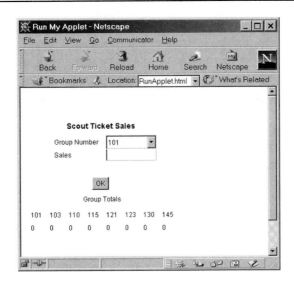

Figure 1.1

A Java applet running on an HTML page in a Web browser.

Figure 1.2

A Java application runs independently.

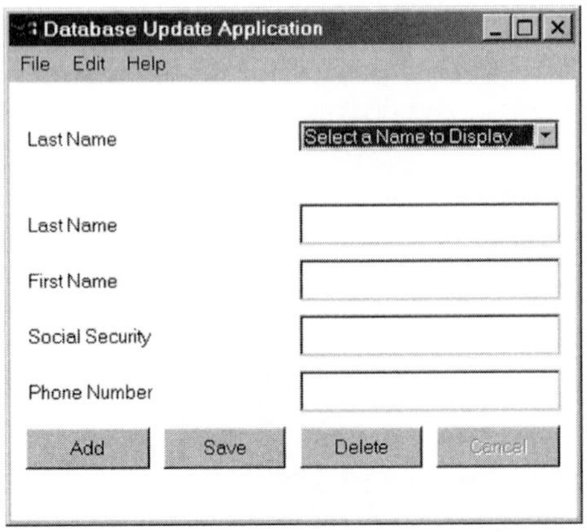

Java is a relatively new programming language, developed by Sun Microsystems in 1991. The original purpose of Java was to control small electrical appliances, which require very small, compact programs. Soon it became apparent that Java's compact code was ideal for programs that run on an HTML (hypertext markup language) page for the World Wide Web. Java was licensed for use with Netscape Navigator in August 1995.

The acceptance and use of Java has been phenomenal. This is due partly to the strengths of the language and partly to the policies of Sun Microsystems, which has made the core of Java available free. Many programmers have contributed to the quickly evolving language and many companies have created tools and extensions for Java. Although Sun Microsystems gives away the basic version of Java, it also sells more robust versions for enterprisewide and database applications.

An Official Description

When Java was first introduced, Sun Microsystems published a paper describing the language like this:

Java is a simple, object-oriented, robust, secure, portable, high-performance, architecturally neutral, interpreted, multi-threaded, dynamic language.

What a bunch of buzzwords! However this concise sentence describes the language well and rates a further look.

Simple?

If this is your first programming language, Java may not seem simple at all. But to a programmer, Java is one of the more simple languages. The language will seem very familiar to a C or C++ programmer, because Java's syntax is similar. However, Java has fewer constructs than most traditional programming languages, including C, C++, and Visual Basic.

Object Oriented

Java was conceived and developed as an object-oriented language. Although some other languages, such as C++ and Visual Basic, have been adapted for **object-oriented programming (OOP)**, Java is completely object oriented. A programmer writing in C++ or Visual Basic can choose whether to write in an object-oriented style, but a Java programmer has no choice: all programs *must* be object oriented (however, the quality of object-oriented programs can differ greatly).

In OOP, programmers create units called *classes* that contain data and the instructions for handling the data. Well-designed classes are reusable components that can be combined to create new applications. Many times a programmer can quickly create a new applet or application using existing classes.

Applets running in a browser and GUI applications do not follow a sequential logic. You, as the programmer, do not take control and determine the sequence of execution. Instead, the user can press keys and click on various buttons and boxes on the user interface (the screen). Each user action can cause an event to occur, which can trigger an event handler. For example, the user clicks on a button labeled Calculate. The clicking causes the event listener to notify your program, and the program automatically jumps to a procedure you have written to do the calculation.

Robust

A robust language contains a full set of features. Java contains the technology to work with multiple platforms, access databases, and develop client/server applications that allow one user (the client) to access information or files on another computer (the server). Java is the language of choice for many developers working with Web-based applications.

A robust application is highly reliable. Although sloppy programming can produce unreliable and buggy software, the Java tools and constructs are designed to aid the programmer and help eliminate many common programming errors. A careful programmer can produce solid reliable applications in Java.

High Performance

Performance is a relative thing. Some languages produce code that runs faster than Java; others run slower. The types of applications generally written in Java typically have user interaction, in which the user enters information, moves a mouse or pointer, and presses buttons. For highly interactive programs such as these, the speed of Java is generally sufficient. Also, a technique called *just-in-time compilation* (JIT), implemented in some later versions of Java, helps speed the execution of Java programs considerably. In the section titled "Java Programs," later in this chapter, you will learn more about JIT.

Secure

Security is a major issue in computer programs, especially with the large number of people using the Internet. Java was designed with security in mind and is more secure than most other languages. The "Security" section later in this chapter describes the various levels of security built in to Java.

Portable and Architecture Neutral

A major reason for the popularity of Java is that programs can run on many different computers without modification. It isn't necessary to compile (translate) a program for a specific computer system; all that's required is that the target computer have software called a **Java Virtual Machine (JVM)**. The JVM is embedded in most Web browsers, such as Netscape Navigator and Internet Explorer, and is available to install for stand-alone applications for most computers. Therefore, Java programs can run on most any computer, including computers running Windows, Unix, Linux, Solaris, and Macintosh OS and mainframe computers such as IBM.

You will learn more about how the JVM interprets and executes Java programs later in this chapter.

Interpreted

One big advantage of Java is that programs are portable. You can write the code once and run it on different computers and operating systems without modification. This is possible because of the way that Java is translated for the machine, using a combination of a **compiler** and an **interpreter.** Most traditional languages are compiled (translated) into machine language that is specific for each processor type (Figure 1.3). That means that a program can run only on the machine type for which it was compiled. To run the program on a different type of computer, the program must be compiled for that machine. A program that is compiled for a Windows environment will not run under Unix or on a Macintosh.

Figure 1.3

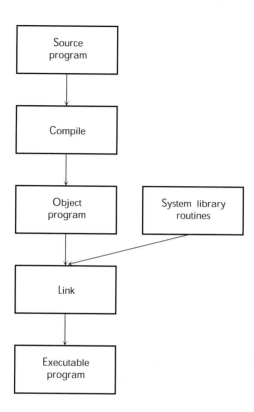

Traditional programming languages are compiled into machine code for the specific processor that will run the application.

Java achieves portability by using a multistep process. The language compiler converts the program source code into **bytecode**, which is not dependent on the type of computer that will run the program. You can transfer the bytecode to another computer, such as over an intranet or the Internet. The bytecode is then interpreted on each different system by the Java Virtual Machine for use on that particular system (Figure 1.4).

Multithreaded

Most computer systems can process multiple applications by dividing the processor time. In Java you actually can run different processes or threads within a single application. This feature is referred to as *threading*.

Dynamic

When you think of dynamic, think of constant change. Java is a very young language but is also changing at a very rapid pace. In fact you will discover that many of the newer features in the language are not yet supported by the browsers. Throughout the text you will learn about newer techniques and how to adapt your browser to use the latest technology.

Java Programs

Several steps are required to write and run a computer program, whether the language is Java or any of the hundreds of other programming languages.

Figure 1.4

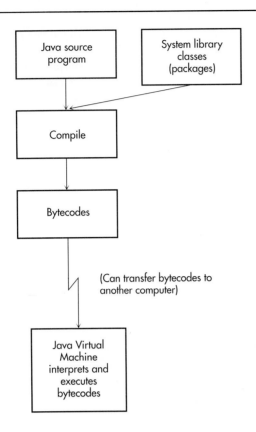

Java applets and applications are compiled into bytecodes, which are interpreted by the Java Virtual Machine.

A programmer writes a computer program using a text editor, following the rules of the programming language. Each programming language has its own set of rules for vocabulary and punctuation (called the *syntax*), just as every spoken language has a similar set of rules. This written program is called the **source program** (or source code).

A language translator program, called a *compiler* (or sometimes an *interpreter*), analyzes the source program. The compiler converts the source program into bytecode (for Java) or object code (for many other languages). If the compiler finds errors in the syntax, error messages display. In other languages, the compiled program is specific to the machine on which the program will run, since each type of processor has its own set of basic instructions that it can execute.

Java differs from other compilers. It doesn't produce compiled code for the specific processor that will run the program. Instead, it produces code, called *bytecode,* that is stored in a class file and runs on an "imaginary" (virtual) computer. The imaginary computer is JVM. The JVM software converts the bytecode into the correct object code for the specific processor.

Think of the Java Virtual Machine as a computer that exists in the memory of your computer. JVM, also known as the *Java interpreter,* understands the bytecode and translates it for the current machine. That means that a system must have a JVM installed to run any Java applets or applications. Most operating systems and browser software now include the **Java Runtime Environment (JRE)**, which includes a JVM. But the Java language is changing faster than the JVM builders can keep up.

Translating the bytecode into actions can be quite time-consuming or appear to be for someone staring at the screen waiting for something to happen. To solve this problem, a **just-in-time (JIT) compiler** translates the bytecode to the native code of the current platform and stores it in case the code is needed later. This process can speed up a program containing loops (repeated instructions) many times over the regular interpreter.

Java Development Tools

To run a Java program, you need the runtime environment (JRE). To develop or write Java applications and applets, you need the **Java Development Kit (JDK)** from Sun Microsystems, which is included with most commercial development environments.

The language has evolved quickly through different versions. The version numbers relate to the JDK from Sun Microsystems. Most browsers support JDK 1.02. Major changes to event handling and the user interface were made in 1997 with the release of version 1.1.5. In December of 1998, JDK 1.2 was released and called Java 2. And in 2000 Sun released JDK 1.3, which is a minor upgrade to 1.2 and still referred to as Java 2. This book is primarily based on Java 2; however, we'll let you know when you are using features that are not compatible with version 1.1.5.

You can download the JDK from Sun Microsystems and write and run Java programs. Or, if you are using one of the commercial development environments, the JDK will be installed automatically.

Integrated Development Environments

You can develop programs using only a text editor and the JDK. You write the Java source code in an editor such as Notepad. You then compile the program using javac, the Java compiler included in the JDK. You can run a compiled applet in a browser by creating a small HTML file that includes an applet tag. And you can run stand-alone applications as a command from the operating system prompt. But this is the hard way.

Sure, you can get by with just those tools, but it is much easier to use an integrated development environment (IDE). You may be familiar with IDEs from other languages. A development environment contains an editor for writing the source code, a compiler, and many helpful tools for executing and debugging projects.

Several IDEs are available, each with its own strengths, weaknesses, and proponents. The biggest weakness of most of the IDEs is that they require lots of memory to run, and some run very slowly. (Remember, we're talking about the speed of the development environment, not a completed Java program.) Sun Microsystems' IDE is called *Forté for Java.* Forté combines a product formerly called NetBeans with Forté's SynerJ. You can set Forté to have the look and feel of different operating systems. The Forté for Java Community Edition 1.0 is downloadable (free) from www.java.sun.com under "Products and API." Other IDEs are available, including WebGain's Visual Café, IBM's Visual Age for Java, Inprise (Borland) JBuilder, and Microsoft Visual J++ (VJ++). If you are using a computer with limited speed and/or memory, you might want to consider Kawa (www.allaire.com) or BlueJ (bluej.monash.edu). Both Kawa and

BlueJ implement a minimal IDE incorporating Sun's compiler and debugger but their own (very good) editors. You will find more details about the individual IDEs and installing the JDK in Appendix A.

Caution: Microsoft's VJtt does not conform to Sun's Java standards.

The Java Application Programming Interface

The Java **Application Programming Interface (API)** consists of classes created by Sun Microsystems and stored in library files called **packages.** You can use these classes and write programs without knowing the details of the API, but as you get more advanced in your programming, you will find it necessary to learn more about the details of some classes.

The programs in this chapter use classes from java.lang, java.awt, and java.applet. Table 1.1 shows a list of some of the common API packages.

Table 1.1

Partial List of Core Java API Packages

Package	Purpose
java.applet	Creates applets.
java.awt	Provides graphical components using abstract windows toolkit.
java.beans	Creates software components.
java.io	Handles input and output of data.
java.lang	Provides core functions of the language; automatically included.
java.math	Handles math functions, very large integers, and decimal values.
java.net	Provides networking.
java.rmi	Provides remote objects.
java.security	Manages certificates, signatures, and other security.
java.sql	Queries databases.
java.swing	Provides GUI using Java Foundation Classes.
java.text	Manipulates text including searches.
java.util	Provides utilities such as dates.

Security

Security in Java exists in several layers. Since a primary purpose of Java is to run on the Internet, security is extremely important. The biggest concern arises when a program is "sent" to another machine. This situation exists with Java applets and with client/server systems. The security of Java basically comes from five different arenas: the rules of the language, the compiler, the verifier, the ClassLoader, and the Security Manager (Figure 1.5).

After the Java compiler translates an applet or application source code into bytecode, this class file may run on the local machine, or it may be sent to another machine through a network or the Internet. When a program executes, a verifier checks the bytecode; if the classes are valid, the verifier allows them to load. The Java interpreter then translates and executes the instructions. A Security Manager also can impose local security policies as the program executes.

Figure 1.5

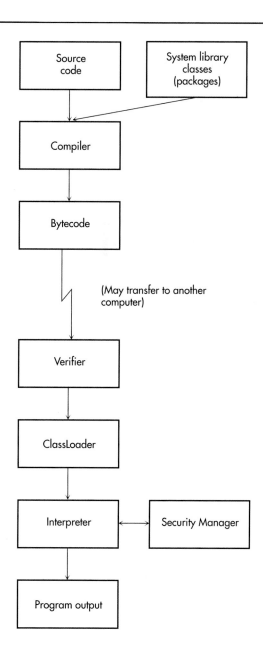

Java has several levels of security.

The Java programming language restricts applets in their access to files and the network. You usually cannot read or write files on the local machine with an applet. However, applications do not have the same restrictions. The language does not allow applets to rename, create, copy, or delete files or directories.

Feedback 1.1

1. List three advantages of using Java for developing software.
2. What makes Java secure?
3. What are JDK, JVM, and JIT?

Object-Oriented Programming

You can relate the concepts of object-oriented programming to objects in the real world. When you describe an **object**, such as a vehicle, a dog, or a ball, you can include the physical characteristics, such as size or color, and you can tell about the behaviors or actions of the object, such as move, bark, or bounce. In programming, you may describe an object such as a button that the user can click. Physical characteristics (called **properties** or **variables**) might be the size of the button and the text or image that appears on the button. Behaviors or actions (called **methods**) might be to move or change the appearance of the text or graphic as the button is clicked.

Classes and Objects

A particular type of object is called a **class.** A class is a template or blueprint for an object, but it is not the object itself. For example, we can describe the characteristics of a certain breed of dog, such as typical coloring and general size and whether the breed barks, bites, or runs fast. Such descriptions are the properties and methods of the class. But an actual dog (an **instance** of the dog class) will have a set of characteristics such as a name and a size.

Many people use a cookie analogy to describe the relationship of a class and an object. The cookie cutter is the class. You can't eat a cookie cutter, but you can use it to make cookies; the cookie is the object. When you make a cookie using a cookie cutter, you **instantiate** an object of the cookie class. You can use the same cookie cutter to make various kinds of cookies. Although all cookies will have the same shape, some may be chocolate, lemon, or vanilla; some may have frosting or colored sprinkles on top. The characteristics such as flavor and topping are the properties or variables of the object. You could refer to the properties of your cookie object as

```
Cookie1.Flavor = "Lemon"
Cookie1.Topping = "Cream Frosting"
```

What about methods? Recall that a method is an action or behavior—something the object can do or have done to it, such as move, clear, or print. Possible methods for our cookie object might be eat, bake, or crumble. Using object terminology, you can refer to object.method():

```
Cookie1.Crumble();
```

Note that when you refer to a method in Java, you must always include parentheses after the method name. Sometimes you include values, called arguments, within the parentheses to give additional information to the method. But whether or not the method needs arguments, you must include the parentheses. Although you may find this cumbersome, it's really helpful: you can always tell the difference between a property reference and a method reference, since methods have parentheses and properties don't.

Inheritance

What if you need to create a new object but don't have an appropriate class? Continuing with the cookie analogy, you need a new cookie cutter to make a different-shaped cookie. You could start from scratch and create an all new cookie cutter, including the form and the handle, and describe all the properties and methods of a cookie. Or you could say something like "I want another cookie cutter that creates cookies just like the old cookie cutter, but the shape is different. Keep all of the other properties and methods."

You are using an important concept of OOP: **inheritance.** The new class is based on an existing class. In Java, we say that the new class **extends** or **inherits** from the existing class.

Java Objects

In Java, all objects are inherited from the Object class from the lang package (java.lang.Object). The Object class is the **superclass** of all other classes, which are called **subclasses**. The Applet class, which you will use to create your own applet, inherits from the Panel class, which inherits from the Container class, which inherits from Component, which inherits from Object (Figure 1.6).

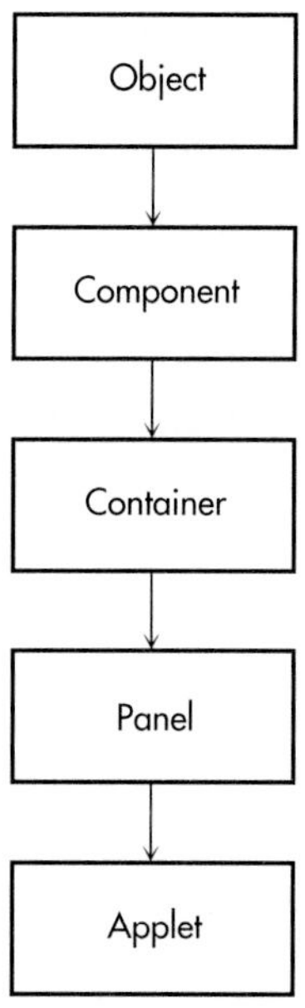

Figure 1.6

Each class inherits from its superclass. The superclass of Applet is Panel. The superclass of Panel is Container. All Java classes inherit from Object.

Encapsulation

Another important concept of OOP is **encapsulation,** which refers to the combination of characteristics of a class. You have one "package" that holds the definition of all properties and methods.

Encapsulation is often referred to as *data hiding.* The class can "expose" certain properties and methods and keep others hidden. In Chapter 5 you will learn to use the `public` and `private` keywords, which specify whether other classes can access each property and method.

Creating Your First Applet

When you begin a program, the first step is to plan. It's important that you know what you are trying to accomplish before you start. Start by sketching or describing the user interface—how your program looks and interacts with the user. Then describe any actions that the user can take and what should be your program's response. The next step is to plan the classes, methods, and properties that your program needs to carry out the tasks.

Your first applet is very simplistic: it displays the words "Hello World" on the screen. You will learn to create a new applet that displays words in a component called a *label*. For this first program, you will not have much control over the placement of the label or have any user interaction. But you will learn to write a program, compile it, and run it. And if you make any mistakes, you will learn to find and correct the errors in a process called *debugging*.

The Applet Class

Each applet is a new class, based on the existing Applet class. You make up a name for each applet. In this case, we called it HelloWorldApplet (all one word). The Applet class is actually a container, or panel, that can hold other objects. Think of the applet as an empty bulletin board to which you can attach items such as words, pictures, and your souvenirs. Each "thing" that you place on the applet is called a *component*.

The first component that you will add to your applet is an object based on the Label class. (The Label class, like the Applet class, is part of the Java API you learned about earlier.) You also must give your label a name, which you make up (following some rules you'll learn about a little later).

The planning for this first applet has already been done for you. Figure 1.7 shows the output you want to produce—the applet's user interface. Figure 1.8 shows the class diagram for the applet.

Figure 1.7

Hello World

The user interface of the Hello World applet.

Figure 1.8

The class diagram for the Hello World applet.

Class: HelloWorldApplet	
Methods	**Variables and Components**
init	lblMessage

The Applet Code

The program statements, written in the Java language, are called *code*. The Java code for your first applet appears below. Following the code listing, we will discuss each of the parts of the program. After this discussion, you will be given the opportunity to enter and run the program. Appendix A gives steps for using the JDK and several IDEs (Sun Forté, Inprise JBuilder, and Microsoft VJ++).

```
//Folder:      Ch1HelloWorld
//Programmer:  Bradley/Millspaugh
//Date:        6/2001
//ClassName:   HelloWorldApplet
//Description: Display the text "Hello World" in a label

import java.applet.Applet;
import java.awt.Label;

public class HelloWorldApplet extends Applet
{
    //Create components
    Label lblMessage = new Label("Hello World");

    public void init()
    {
        //Place component on applet panel
        add(lblMessage);
    }
}
```

Comments

Each of the lines that begin with two slashes is a comment. Java does not translate comments for the machine; the purpose of comments is documentation for the programmer or others who are trying to read the code.

Two types of comments are available in Java. The single line comment is preceded by two slashes // and may appear at the end of a line or on a line by itself.

```
//Create components
add(lblMessage);      //Display Hello World
```

An alternative style of comment is multiline comments, which begin with /* and end with */.

```
/* A Hello World Applet
   Programmed by Your Name
   Date:  */
```

A drawback of using multiline comments is that often programmers begin the comment and forget to close it. The entire program is treated as a comment, with no code to execute. If you are using an IDE, the comments display in a different color, so it's easier to spot your error.

Multiline comments are handy when you want to turn several lines into comments for testing purposes in more advanced applications.

It's a good idea to write lots of comments in programs; it's amazing how difficult it is to remember what you were trying to accomplish when you look back at a program after some time has elapsed. The comment lines at the top of the code are for identification and should always be included in your programs.

Punctuation

Java is very picky about punctuation. Every statement must be terminated by a **semicolon** (;). (You will learn about the exceptions later, as they arise.) The **braces** ({}) enclose a **block** of statements. The applet class contains a block of statements and the method inside the class contains another block.

Case Sensitivity

Java is case-sensitive, so it is critical that you observe the capitalization. Most errors on first programs are due to incorrect capitalization. A section later in this chapter discusses the types of errors that you may encounter.

Spacing and Indentation

Although Java is very strict about punctuation and case sensitivity, it is very forgiving of spacing. Although you cannot leave a space in the middle of a word, between words and lines you can leave as many spaces as you like. The following three code segments are equivalent and give the same results in Java:

```
public void init(){add(lblMessage);}

public void init()
 {
    add(lblMessage);
 }

public void init()
 {
    add (lblMessage) ;
 }
```

Use spacing and indentation freely to make your code easier to read. The spacing does not affect the translation of code.

Importing Packages

Java stores the classes that make up the language in library files called *packages*. The primary portion, or core of the language, is in a package called "lang". Your Java program can use any of the classes in the lang package without specifically naming the package. However, to use classes in any other package, you must specify the package. You can choose from two techniques to specify a package: Either include an **import statement** or fully qualify every class to which you refer, such as

```
public class HelloWorldApplet extends java.applet.Applet
```

Tip

When you add multiline comments, type the /* and */ first and type your comments between the symbols. You can use the same technique for opening and closing braces { }

and

```
java.awt.Label lblMessage = new java.awt.Label("Hello World");
```

Most programmers use `import` statements at the top of a program rather than fully qualify all classes. That is the technique used throughout this book.

The import Statement—General Format

```
import packageName;
```

The import Statement—Examples

```
import java.applet.Applet;
import java.applet.*;
import java.awt.*;
import java.awt.Label;
```

The first example calls for the Applet class from the applet package; the second example with the asterisk specifies that you can use any class in the entire applet package. The **awt** (abstract windows toolkit) package holds the classes for the visual components, such as buttons, labels, text fields, check boxes, and option buttons.

If you choose to use an asterisk (`java.awt.*`) rather than specify the actual class from the package (`java.awt.Label`), Java does not automatically load all classes. When the compiler executes, it imports only those classes from the package that you actually use.

Creating the Applet Class

The applet class name must match the name of the java source code file. Since you called the class "HelloWorldApplet", you also must save the file with that name, with an extension of .java. If you are using an IDE, the extension is automatically added; but if you are using a text editor, you must make sure to save with the .java extension rather than with .txt.

The word `public` specifies that other programs and the browser can access this program and is required for an applet.

The basic structure of a class source program is

```
public class ClassName
{
    // statements
}
```

Inheriting from the Applet Class

There is no need for us to write all of the code to create an applet. The base code exists in the Applet class, which is the superclass for your new applet. The keyword `extends` indicates that this class inherits from another class. The following class header indicates that we want to create a class called HelloWorldApplet that inherits its functionality from the Applet class.

Tip

Watch the case of the class name and the case of the file name. They must exactly match.

```
public class HelloWorldApplet extends Applet
{
    // statements
}
```

Creating Components

Each of the components that you add to an applet is based on a class from the awt package. (Later you will learn to create components from classes in other packages as well.) The label in your HelloWorldApplet class is an object based on the Label class, or an *instance* of the class. A **label** is a graphical component used to display text information.

Before you can use a component, you must declare it, using a **declaration statement.** In a declaration statement, you specify the component's class followed by the name that you will use to refer to the component in your code. This line of code declares a Label component called lblMessage.

```
Label lblMessage;
```

Naming Components

The name you give a component must follow the Java naming rules, and *should* follow additional guidelines referred to as naming conventions. And always be very careful about capitalization. Java is case-sensitive and considers the names lblMessage, LblMessage, and lblmessage to be three different elements.

Naming Rules
A Java name

- Must contain only letters, numbers, and underscores.

- Must begin with a letter or underscore.

- Cannot have any embedded spaces.

- Is case-sensitive.

- Cannot be one of Java's reserved words, such as `boolean`, `public`, or `import`. (Note that all of the Java reserved words are lowercase. If you use uppercase as part of your names, you should not have any naming conflicts.)

Naming Conventions
To create good Java names, you should

- Make all names meaningful. Do not use names such as a, b, c, or x. Always create names that a person reading your code can tell the purpose of. And do not abbreviate unless you are using a standard abbreviation that has a clearly understood meaning.

- Begin the name with a lowercase prefix that indicates the type of component.

- Begin the actual name (following the prefix) with an uppercase letter. Use mixed upper- and lowercase letters for the name, with a capital to begin each new word.

Examples

lblMessage
lblHelloWorld
fntLargeText
fntName

Naming Labels and Fonts

In this chapter, the components you must name are Labels and Fonts. Use *lbl* as the prefix for a Label and *fnt* as the prefix for a Font.

The new Keyword

The declaration statement you saw earlier:

```
Label lblMessage;
```

declares the name and component type but does not create the new object. To actually create a component called lblMessage, an object that is an instance of the Label class, you need to use the **new keyword.** You can place the two statements on separate lines, like the following:

```
Label lblMessage;
lblMessage = new Label("Hello World");
```

Or you can combine the two statements, which is the more common technique.

```
//Declare and create an instance of a Label
Label lblMessage = new Label("Hello World");
```

The previous line declares the component, gives it a name, instantiates (creates) it, and assigns the text that you want to appear in the label.

There is more than one way to create a component. For example, to instantiate an object of the Label class, you can specify the initial content of the label or you don't have to. The Label class has two different methods for constructing an instance. As you learn to use more components in Java, you often will find that a component has several methods for creating an instance of the class. You will see more of this in Chapter 2.

The Applet's init Method

When you run an applet, Java first creates the components that you name at the top of the code, then looks for an **init method.** The init method is the first method to execute. You write the code for the actions that you want to take and usually set up the user interface in the init method.

The statement

```
public void init()
```

specifies that the method is public (can be seen and used by other classes and programs, such as the browser). The keyword void means that this method does not return any value, and the empty parentheses mean that this method does not expect or pass any arguments (more about these concepts in Chapter 5).

The Applet Panel

When you create a new applet that is based on Java's Applet class, you are declaring a container called a **panel.** You can add components to the panel.

Java has additional methods for creating your own layouts and panels and determining locations and sizes. Layouts and panels are covered in Chapter 3.

Adding Components to a Panel

After you create an instance of a component, such as a label, it exists only in the computer's memory. If you want to display the label on the applet panel, you must add the component to the applet. Use the applet's **add method,** which has a single argument specifying the name of the component.

The add Method—General Format

```
add(ComponentName);
```

The add Method—Example

```
add(lblMessage);
```

The Location and Size of Components

When you place multiple labels on an applet, they appear in the order you add them.

```
add(lblTitle);
add(lblMessage);
```

The first label to appear is lblTitle, followed by lblMessage. Depending on the width of the applet panel and the widths of the two labels, the labels may appear on the same line or on two lines. Until you learn about layout managers in Chapter 3, you have very little control over the placement of the components. The best you can do for now is to control the size of the panel, which you do in the HTML file that runs your applet.

When you create a label, the value inside the quotation marks determines the size of the label.

```
Label lblMessage = new Label("Hello World");
```

The size of this label is 11 characters, including the space between the words. You can adjust the width of a label by adding spaces to the text. In Chapter 2, you learn more about setting the size of components.

```
Label lblMessage = new Label("  Hello World  ");
```

Note that the spaces and characters are not all the same size, since most fonts are proportional.

Running the Applet

You can run an applet in a browser (Figure 1.9), such as Netscape Navigator or Internet Explorer, or in a special program called an applet viewer (Figure 1.10). Most IDEs include an applet viewer, which simplifies testing your projects.

Figure 1.9

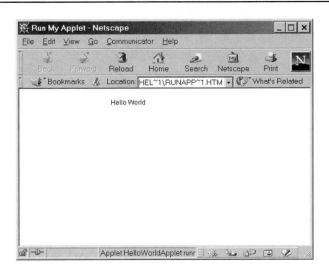

You can run an applet in a browser, such as Netscape Navigator or Internet Explorer.

Figure 1.10

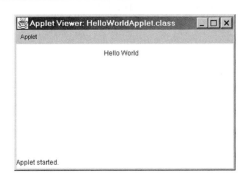

You can run an applet in an applet viewer program.

If you are using an IDE, you can usually select a *Run* command, which will compile the program and run it in applet viewer (assuming there are no errors). Appendix A gives instructions for compiling using the most popular IDEs.

If you are using the JDK, rather than an IDE, you will need to give a command to compile the program. Then you run the compiled program (with an extension of .class) from an HTML page. Appendix A gives instructions for compiling from the JDK. See the section "Using HTML to Run the Applet in a Browser" later in this chapter to display in a browser.

Hello World?

If you haven't done so already, it's time to enter the Hello World applet and make it run! See the appropriate section in Appendix A for your IDE or the

Java JDK for specific instructions. See the following sections for help in finding and correcting any program errors, which programmers like to call *bugs*.

Feedback 1.2

1. Write the statement to include the java.util package into a program.
2. Code the statement to create a label called lblCompanyName that displays "TriState Industries".
3. Create a multiline comment for the beginning of an applet containing the identifying information for a program, such as Class name, Programmer name, Date, and Description.

Finding and Fixing Errors

You already may have seen some errors as you entered the first sample project. Programming errors come in three varieties: **compile errors**, **run-time errors**, and **logic errors.**

Compile Errors

As Java attempts to convert your project code to machine language (called *compiling the code*), it may find compile errors. Compile errors occur when you break the syntax rules of Java and sometimes when you use an illegal object or property. In each case, the Java compiler is unable to translate what you wrote into bytecode.

For example, try spelling *class* as *clas* or using the word *nothing* instead of *void*. The compiler can only translate the exact spelling of a word and cannot recognize either of these words; each causes a compile error.

You also can receive a compile error if you accidentally use the wrong punctuation or place the punctuation in the wrong place. The compiler cannot understand add(lblMessage) followed by a period or placed in square brackets add[lblMessage]. (Square brackets have a different meaning in Java, which you will learn about in Chapter 9 on arrays.)

Some IDEs show you compile errors as you move off the offending line. Or you may not find compile errors until you try to compile and run the program.

After you have corrected your compile errors, you can attempt to compile and run. Sometimes you may find it necessary to "rebuild" a project. This option is available in most IDEs.

One type of compile error that is all too common for beginning programmers is the inconsistent spelling of object names. For example, if you set a label component's name to lblMessage, you must always refer to it with that exact spelling and capitalization. The following line of code will generate a compile error. Can you spot the problem?

```
add(lblMessages);
```

Run-Time Errors

If your project halts during execution, that's a run-time error. Statements that cannot execute correctly cause run-time errors. The statements are correctly formed statements that pass the syntax checking of the compiler; however, the statements fail to execute. Run-time errors can be caused by attempting to do impossible arithmetic operations such as calculate with nonnumeric data, divide by zero, or find the square root of a negative number.

Run-time errors generate "exceptions" that you can handle in your code. You will learn about exceptions in Chapter 4.

Logic Errors

With logic errors, your project runs but produces incorrect results. Perhaps the results of a calculation are incorrect or the wrong text appears or the text is okay but appears in the wrong location.

Beginning programmers often overlook their logic errors. If the project runs, it must be right—right? All too often, that statement is not correct. You may need to use a calculator to check the output. Check all aspects of the project output: computations, text, and spacing.

For example, if you forget to add the label in the `init` method, the project compiles and runs but nothing appears. That's certainly not the result that you want.

Changing Fonts and Colors

When you want to change the font used in a component, such as a label, you must declare an instance of the Font class. You can then assign the new font to the component.

The Font Class

You create a font object from the **Font class.** The Font class allows you to specify the font name, the size, and style, such as bold or italic. The Font class comes from the awt package; you must either add its name to an `import` statement or use the asterisk to include the class.

```
import java.awt.Label;
import java.awt.Font;
```

or

```
import java.awt.*; //The recommended approach
```

You then declare a name for your font object and instantiate the object, just as you did for a label.

The Font Object—General Format

```
Font(FontName, FontStyle, FontSize)
```

For the font name, you can use the actual name of a font from your system, such as Times New Roman or Arial. However, that's not a good idea if your program will run on other systems that may not have that font. The better approach is to use the generic Java font names, which will work on any system running Java. Table 1.2 lists the Java font names.

For the font style, use the constants defined by the Font class: Font.BOLD, Font.ITALIC, Font.PLAIN. These constants are actually names given to numeric values, so you can add them together: Font.BOLD + Font.ITALIC gives both attributes.

For the size argument, specify the font size in points.

The Font Object—Examples

```
Font fntName = new Font("Serif", Font.ITALIC, 14);
Font fntPhone = new Font("Sans Serif", Font.BOLD, 12);
Font fntMonospacedLarge = new Font("Monospaced", Font.PLAIN, 36);
Font fntBoldItalic = new Font("Serif", Font.BOLD + Font.ITALIC, 10)
```

Table 1.2

Java Generic Font Names

Java 1.0	Java 1.1, 1.2, and 1.3
"Courier"	"Monospaced"
"Dialog"	"Dialog"
"DialogInput"	"DialogInput"
"Helvetica"	"Sans Serif"
"Times New Roman"	"Serif"

Assigning a Font to a Component

Declaring a new font creates the object but does not apply it to any component. You need to assign the font using the **setFont method** of the component. In this chapter, you will set the fonts in the init method. In a later chapter you will learn to change the font in response to a user action.

```
lblName.setFont(fntName);        //Assign a font to lblName
lblPhone.setFont(fntPhone);      //Assign a font to lblPhone
```

To execute a method, you specify the name of the object, a period, the name of the method, and parentheses to hold the arguments (say "object–dot–method"). If you use a method name without an object, the method applies to the applet object (the entire page).

Changing the Color of Text

Other methods allow you to change the color of the text or the color of the text's background. The **setForeground method** changes the color of the letters while the **setBackground method** changes the background color.

```
setBackground(Color.cyan);          //Change the background of the page to cyan
lblPhone.setForeground(Color.red); //Change the text color of lblPhone to red
```

Notice that the name of a color is preceded by the word "Color." When you set the color, you are using the Color class. The Color class contains several constants that represent colors (Table 1.3). The capitalization of the color names must be precise. You will learn more about constants in Chapter 2.

T a b l e   1 . 3

black
blue
cyan
darkGray
gray
green
pink
lightGray
magenta
orange
red
white
yellow

Color Constants

To specify any of these colors, precede the name with "Color.".

Feedback 1.3

1. Code the statement to create a Font object called fntBold that has a 12-point boldface Dialog font.
2. Apply the font declared in question 1 to a label called lblMessage.
3. Write the statements to set the background color of the applet to gray and the label's text to dark gray.

Using HTML to Run the Applet in a Browser

In order to run your applet in a browser, you need to create an HTML file that calls the applet and then open the HTML file with the browser. Some IDEs such as Forté and Microsoft VJ++ have tools that will help with creating the HTML file. If you do not have a tool, use a text editor and save the file with an .htm or .html extension. One possible text editor is Notepad.

The purpose of this text is not to teach HTML. You can use the following code to display the FontApplet class created in the hands-on programming example. You should set the width and height to the value of your choice.

```
<HTML>
<BODY>
<Applet    code = FontApplet.class
           width = 600
           height = 200>
           </Applet>
</BODY>
</HTML>
```

The codes in HTML tags < > are not case-sensitive, but the name of the class file *is* case-sensitive. Recall that your Java source code file has a .java extension. After the compiler completes, it creates the .class file, which holds the bytecodes. The .class file name is the same as the .java file name (with the exception of the extension). Follow the applet information with the closing tag </Applet>.

Running an Applet

During design and testing, you are running your applet on your own system. In fact, unless you plan to transfer your applet to a machine set up as a Web server, for others to run from their computers, all of your applets will run from your own computer.

When applets run from a Web page over the Internet, the HTML file resides on a server machine. When a user opens a Web page that contains an applet tag, the tag causes the HTML file to obtain the Java class files from the server. Java security ensures that the bytecodes are valid. After verification, the Java Virtual Machine starts processing the statements. Any import statement in your program causes the appropriate class files to download; however, the core Java packages are part of the JVM and do not require downloading. If your program requires additional classes, all must be downloaded to the local machine before the applet's init method can run.

The Life Cycle of an Applet

The execution of an applet in a browser follows a specific cycle. Each applet always executes four methods: init, start, stop, and destroy (Table 1.4). Although you haven't written all four methods, your applet is based on Java's Applet class, which automatically creates the methods for every applet. The only method you are writing currently is the init method. As you advance in your programming knowledge, you will learn to code these other methods as the need arises.

Method	Purpose
init	Executes the first time an applet is loaded.
start	Follows the init and reexecutes each time that the page displays.
stop	Executes when the user leaves a Web page containing the applet.
destroy	Executes prior to shutdown of the browser.

Planning a Project

Planning is an important part of developing software. Although its purpose may not be obvious to you with the short programs in this chapter, planning ultimately can save many hours as your programs become more complex. The time spent in planning will be more than exceeded in reducing the debugging time as well as creating code that easily interacts with other projects.

Earlier you saw a diagram for a class that lists the methods and components. In this text, you also will use a planning tool called a *Class Design Form*. Complete one form for each class in your project. At this point, we have only one, but as additional classes are added, you also will need to plan the relationship between the classes.

Class Design Form

Class Name: _____

Properties:

Access Mode (public or private)	Variable or Component Name	Data Type or Class	Description

Methods:

Access Mode (public or private)	Return Type	Method Name (include any parameters)	Pseudocode

For each class, you list the properties and methods for that class.

Your Hands-on Programming Example

Create an applet that displays the name "Janet Lynn Jones" in one label and her phone number, "555-1111", in a second label. Change the background color of the applet to cyan. The font for the name should be 14-point italic Serif. The font for the phone is 12-point bold Sans Serif. Change the text color of the phone number to red. Figure 1.11 shows the interface in a browser.

Figure 1.11

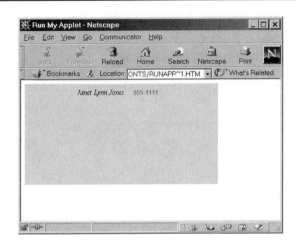

The user interface for the hands-on example applet.

Note: With your instructor's permission, you may want to use your own name and phone number for this exercise.

Planning the Project

Plan the Objects and Properties
Class: FontsApplet
Figure 1.12 shows the class diagram.

Figure 1.12

The class diagram for the hands-on example applet.

Class: FontsApplet	
Methods	**Variables and Components**
init	lblName
	lblPhone
	fntName
	fntPhone

Properties:

Access Mode (public or private)	Variable or Component Name	Data Type or Class	Description
	lblName	Label	Display the name.
	lblPhone	Label	Display the phone number.
	fntName	Font	Set font style for the name label.
	fntPhone	Font	Set font style for the phone label.

Methods:

Access Mode (public or private)	Return Type	Method Name (include any parameters)	Pseudocode
public	void	init	Set the background color to cyan.
			Set the font for the name label.
			Add the name label.
			Set the font for the phone label.
			Set the text color for the phone label.
			Add the phone label.

Write the Project

- Follow the plan to add components to the class.

- Write the appropriate statements in the init method of the class to add the components and to change the color and font as needed.

- When you complete the code, thoroughly test the project.

The Project Solution

```
//Folder:        Ch1Fonts
//Programmer:    Bradley/Millspaugh
//Date:          6/2001
//ClassName:     FontsApplet
//Description:   Display a name and phone number in a label.
//               Set fonts and colors

import java.applet.Applet;
import java.awt.*;

public class FontsApplet extends Applet
{
    //Create two label components
    Label lblName = new Label("Janet Lynn Jones");
    Label lblPhone = new Label("555-1111");
    //Create two fonts for the labels
    Font fntName = new Font("Serif", Font.ITALIC, 14);
    Font fntPhone = new Font("Sans Serif", Font.BOLD, 12);
    public void init()
    {
        //Set colors and fonts; add labels
        setBackground(Color.cyan);
        lblName.setFont(fntName);
        add(lblName);
        lblPhone.setFont(fntPhone);
        lblPhone.setForeground(Color.red);
        add(lblPhone);
    }
}
```

Summary

1. Java is a relatively new object-oriented language that is ideal for use on the Internet. It is designed for use on multiple platforms and provides more security than other languages.
2. Use Java to create full stand-alone applications or applets that run in a Web browser.
3. Source code in Java is compiled into bytecodes that can be translated and run on any platform with a Java Virtual Machine.
4. You write a Java source program using an editor. The Java compiler checks for syntax errors and produces the bytecode class file. The Java interpreter in the JVM translates the bytecode for the local machine.
5. Java 2, the most current version of Java, uses JDK version 1.2 or 1.3 from Sun Microsystems.
6. Many companies offer IDEs for developing Java applications and applets. The IDEs include an editor, compiler, tools for running and debugging programs, a way to display Java classes, and Help files.
7. The Java API is a set of classes stored in packages, which are files. You reference a package in a program using an `import` statement. The entire package may be included or just a portion.
8. Java has several layers of security, which is necessary for programs that run on the Internet.
9. Java strictly adheres to the techniques of object-oriented programming. All definitions and methods are contained in classes to encapsulate the data and actions. Inheritance allows the functionality of a class to be extended without rewriting the entire class.
10. Each new applet is a panel that extends, or inherits from, the existing Applet class.
11. Comments are used to document programs and are not translated by the compiler. Single-line comments begin with two slashes. Multiline comments begin with `/*` and end with `*/`.
12. Each Java statement ends with a semicolon. A pair of braces encloses a block of statements.
13. Java is case-sensitive.
14. You can include extra spacing in a Java source program. Spacing and indentation make a program easier to read and to follow.
15. You can use classes in the java.lang package without specifically importing them. For all other packages, you must use an `import` statement or fully qualify the name of every class.
16. The awt package holds the classes for graphical components, such as the Label class. Components must be declared and the `new` keyword used to generate an instance of the class.
17. Components that display when an applet begins are generally added in the `init` method. Use the applet's `Add` method to add components.
18. Program errors, also called bugs, may be compile errors, run-time errors, or logic errors.
19. The Font object allows you to control the point size and font style of a component. Create a Font object and assign it to the component with the `set-Font` method.
20. Change the background color of the applet panel or a component with the `setBackground` method. Set the color for text by using the

setForeground method. Use the color constants from the Color class to name the colors.

21. To run an applet in a browser, you must create an HTML file that has an applet tag. The applet tag references the class file name of your compiled applet.

22. The life cycle of an applet consists of the init, start, stop, and destroy methods. Although you may write only the init method, the Applet class, from which your applet inherits, automatically creates the other methods.

23. It's important to plan a program before beginning to write it. One important tool is the Class Design Form.

Key Terms

add method *18*

applet *2*

application *2*

Application Programming Interface (API) *8*

awt *15*

block *14*

braces *14*

bytecode *5*

class *10*

compile error *20*

compiler *4*

declaration statement *16*

encapsulation *12*

extends *11*

Font class *21*

import statement *14*

inheritance *11*

inherits *11*

init method *17*

instance *10*

instantiate *10*

interpreter *4*

Java Development Kit (JDK) *7*

Java Runtime Environment (JRE) *6*

Java Virtual Machine (JVM) *4*

just-in-time (JIT) compiler *7*

label *16*

logic error *20*

method *10*

new keyword *17*

object *10*

object-oriented programming (OOP) *3*

package *8*

panel *18*

property *10*

run-time error *20*

semicolon *14*

setBackground method *23*

setFont method *22*

setForeground method *23*

source program *6*

subclass *11*

superclass *11*

variable *10*

Review Questions

1. Why is Java considered desirable as a language for the Internet?
2. What is a JVM? What is its purpose?
3. What is bytecode and what is its purpose?
4. What is the API? How do you use the API in Java?
5. Describe OOP?
6. Define inheritance and encapsulation.

7. What statement is used to include a package in a program?
8. Explain the difference between declaring an object name and creating the object.
9. List the rules for naming objects.
10. What are naming conventions? Why are they needed?
11. Discuss the purpose of comments in a Java program. What types of comments can you use?
12. What is the purpose of the awt package?
13. What is the purpose of an HTML file? What tag must appear in the HTML file to make an applet run?
14. Name and describe the three types of bugs that may appear in a program.
15. How are the Color and Font objects used?
16. Describe how to change the color of an applet's panel and how to change the color of text that displays on the applet.
17. What is the purpose of the Class Design Form?

P r o g r a m m i n g   E x e r c i s e s

1.1. Code, test, and debug an applet that contains labels to display your name, course name, section, and meeting day and time.

1.2. Code, test, and debug an applet that displays your class schedule in labels.

1.3. Code, test, and debug an applet that displays a company name and address in labels. Test it for "ABC Electronics" located at "12134 Main Street", "Los Altos, California".

1.4. Eric and Tim's Auto Restoration would like to have a Web page that displays the title of the company along with a description of their project. They are currently restoring a 1957 Chevy station wagon. Use your own words for a brief description (substitute a different vehicle if you wish).

C A S E   S T U D I E S

R 'n R—for Reading and Refreshment

R 'n R is a newstand that sells books and periodicals and contains a coffee bar. The company would like to develop Web pages for use in their business and is considering expansion into e-commerce for their book inventory.

Code, test, and debug an applet that displays the company name, address, and a brief product list in labels. Change the font and color for a nice layout and appealing design.

Merry Pea's Quilting

Merry Pea's Quilting offers courses in quilting along with quilting supplies and ideas. The motto is "A fine stitch is worth a thousand words". Create a Web page with the company name and motto. Ms. Pea really likes red, black, and yellow.

2

Using Variables and Constants

At the completion of this chapter, you will be able to . . .

1. Use multiple forms of constructors.

2. Add buttons and text fields to an interface.

3. Use variables to store information.

4. Input data into a text field.

5. Display multiple lines of output in a text area.

6. Obtain and display the system date.

7. Capture user actions with a listener.

8. Add event handling for a button and text field.

9. Incorporate mouse events.

In the last chapter you created an applet that displayed information in a label on the applet. The output did not change during program execution. Not terribly useful! Now you will increase the usefulness of applets by requesting input from the user and processing that information.

In this chapter you will add text fields, text areas, and buttons to an applet. The applet can accept input from the user and display results. When the user clicks on a button, an event occurs. Your program code uses an event listener to determine when the button is clicked. Figure 2.1 shows an applet panel with a text field, a text area, and a button.

An applet panel with a text field,
a text area, and a button.

Classes and Methods

Each class that you use has **methods** defined to perform actions. In the last chapter you used the `init` method of the applet class as well as methods for setting colors and fonts. You often will write your own methods, which may replace a method supplied by the class. For example, in Chapter 1 you wrote an `init` method that replaced the `init` method defined in the Applet class.

You will learn to use many methods that already exist in the classes in the libraries as well as to write your own methods. One important method of each class is called a *constructor*.

Constructor Methods

As you saw in Chapter 1, you use the `new` keyword to create a new object of a class:

```
Label lblMessage = new Label("Hello World");
```

When the Label object is created, the class **constructor method** automatically executes. In this example, you are passing the string literal "Hello World" as an **argument** to the constructor method. Any values that you supply inside the parentheses are called *arguments*.

Often a class may have several different constructor methods that you may use, each with a different list of expected arguments. For example, the Label class has three constructors:

Constructor Method and Parameters	Result
Label()	Blank label.
Label(*String text*)	Label that displays the specified text.
Label(*String text*, int *Alignment*)	Label that specifies the text and the alignment; may be LEFT, CENTER, or RIGHT.

You may choose to use any of the three formats, but you must match the order of the arguments to the expected order. Each of these statements is valid in Java:

```
Label lblBlank = new Label();              //A new label with blank contents
Label lblMessage = new Label("Good Job!"); //A new label with this message
Label lblCompany = new Label("Julia's Jellybeans", Label.CENTER); //Centered text
```

However, you cannot specify the third format with the arguments reversed (Label.CENTER, "Julia's Jellybeans") without causing an error. When you specify the class name (Label) and the arguments, Java selects the correct constructor to execute based on the supplied arguments.

Strictly speaking, when you pass values to a method, those values are called *arguments;* but from the perspective of the method, the values are called **parameters**. You might say that because the Label constructor method has two parameters, you will pass it two arguments. A method's parameter list shows the data type and a value for each parameter. When you call a method, the argument values you supply are assigned to the parameter list in the order specified. Figure 2.2 shows the relationship between parameters and arguments.

F i g u r e   2 . 2

The arguments in a code declaration match the parameter list in the constructor, on a one-for-one basis.

Format of Contructor
```
Label(String text, int Alignment)
```
                              parameter list
Java Code
```
Label lblMessage = new label("Hello World", Label.RIGHT);
```
                                            arguments

Note: The terms `String` and `int` are data types, which are explained in the following section on variables and constants.

Feedback 2.1

1. Write a statement to create a Label that initially displays *Hello World*, with center alignment.
2. How does the compiler determine which constructor you want to call?

Variables and Constants

To do any useful work in a program, you must be able to store information. The data in a program may be **variable** or **constant.** Variables, as the name implies, can change value while the program is executing or from one execution to the next. Constants, on the other hand, cannot change; they keep their value.

You already have used some constants. Your first project contained "Hello World" inside of quotation marks. Anything inside of quotation marks is called a **string literal** or *string constant.* No matter how many times you execute the applet, the string literal always has the same value.

In the last chapter, the Color object had several constants, such as Color.blue, Color.cyan, and Color.green. Each of these names represents a number, which you also could use to specify the color. However, a named constant is much easier to read and easier to remember than having to use a number to represent the color.

The Label constructor also uses named constants to represent alignment options: Label.LEFT, Label.CENTER, and Label.RIGHT. These constants represent integer numbers, which could be used in place of the named constants. In Chapter 3 you will create your own named class constants.

Java Data Types

The **data type** determines the way that a program handles and stores data. Java has eight **primitive data types** (Table 2.1) that are built in to the language. Besides the primitive data types, Java supplies some classes that define additional data types to give more flexibility. Java's four integer (whole number) data types are byte, short, int, and long. Values with a decimal point (floating point numbers) use float and double data types. The two other primitive types are char, for storing a single character, and boolean, for true/false values. Table 2.1 shows the Java primitive data types, a suggested prefix for naming each type of variable, and examples of the contents of variables.

Declaring Variables

When you declare a variable, you reserve a location in memory to store information and give the variable a name. The data type determines the amount of memory and how the data are handled. The variable name is an identifier that follows the naming rules (refer to Chapter 1, page 16) and should include a prefix to indicate the data type. Table 2.2 shows some valid and invalid variable names.

Java Primitive Data Types

Data Type	Naming Prefix	Contents	Default Initial Value	Possible Values
boolean	bln	true or false	false	true or false
byte	byt	small integers	0	−128 to 127
char	chr	single character	char code 0	Unicode character—a code designed for internationalization of applications
double	dbl	double-precision floating point number	0.0	15-digit precision
float	flt	single-precision floating point number	0.0	7-digit precision
int	int	integer data	0	−2,147,483,648 to 2,147,483,647
long	lng	long integer	0	−9,223,372,036,854,775,808L to 9,223,372,036,854,775,807L
short	int	short integer	0	−32,768 to 32,767

Valid and Invalid Variable Names

Identifier	Valid or Invalid	Reason
int Person Count	invalid	No spaces allowed in a name.
int_Person_Count	valid	
chrLetter	valid	
blnIsFinished	valid	
2Times	invalid	Must begin with a letter or underscore.
fltBig#	invalid	Only letters, numbers, and underscore characters allowed. No special characters.
dblBig.Number	invalid	No periods allowed.
X	valid	Accepted by Java but is a terrible identifier since the name is not meaningful.

Declaring a Variable—General Format

```
datatype variablename;
```

Declaring a Variable—Examples

```
float fltTotalSales;
int intStudentCount;
boolean blnItemFound;
```

Notice that you capitalize the first letter of each word in a variable name. This naming convention makes the variable name easier to read. See Appendix B for a more complete list of naming conventions.

Initial Values

When you declare a variable, you also can assign an initial value using an **assignment operator** (=). The value on the right side of the operator is assigned to the memory location for the variable named on the left. The value must be the same data type as the variable.

```
int intMaximumCount = 100;
int intCount = intMaximumCount;
long lngLargeInteger = 0L;
flt fltTotalAmount = 0.0f;
```

Notice that the value on the right side can be another variable or a literal.

Forming Numeric Literals

Numeric literals can consist of the digits 0–9, a decimal point, a sign at the left, and an exponent. You also can include an upper- or lowercase letter at the right end to declare the data type of the literal. Use *F* or *f* to declare a float value; *D* or *d* to declare a double (floating point) value; and *L* or *l* to declare a long integer.

You can create numeric literals by just typing a number, such as 10 or 1.25. By default, any whole number is assigned an int data type, unless its value is larger than 2,147,483,647, in which case the number is assumed to be a long data type. Any literal that contains a decimal point or an exponent is automatically assigned to a double data type in the absence of a type-declaration suffix.

Examples

Literal	Data Type
0.0f	float
0.0	double
0d	double
1000F	float
1,000.0	illegal (no commas allowed)
−10	int
10	int
0	int
0L	long integer
0l	long integer (best to avoid lowercase *l* since it resembles numeric 1)

Literal	Data Type
$100	illegal (no special characters allowed)
1.234e6	double
1.234e-6	double

Declaring Numeric Constants

Java uses the keyword **final** to specify that a data value should remain constant during execution of the application. To follow standard naming conventions, name constants like this:

- Begin with a lowercase prefix to indicate the data type.

- Use all uppercase for the rest of the name.

- Separate words with the underscore character, to make the name easier to read.

```
final float fltTAX_RATE = 0.07f;
final int intNUMBER_POSSIBLE = 100;
```

Place the `final` keyword before the data type. You must assign a value to the constant, which cannot be altered while the program executes.

The examples above demonstrate a constant for an integer field and one for a float. You can create constants of any data type; just be sure that the literal is the same data type as the constant. The 'f' creates a float literal. To create a long constant you would use an L with the literal.

```
final long lngUPPER_LIMIT = 50000L;
```

Classes for Data Types

Java expands on the primitive data types by including classes for handling data. Each data type class has methods to help manipulate the data.

One of the most useful classes is the String class. You saw in the primitive data types that Java has a char data type, but a char variable can hold only one character. Usually you need to store several characters, such as to hold a name.

Declare String objects using the same format as for primitive data types:

```
String strName;
String strCompanyName = "Julia's Jellybeans";
```

Numeric Wrapper Classes

There are also classes for holding numeric data. These classes are sometimes referred to as **wrapper classes**, because they take a primitive data type and "wrap" it with additional functionality. Table 2.3 shows some of the wrapper classes.

When declaring objects of the wrapper classes, use the format for declaring objects:

```
Boolean blnIsValid = new Boolean (false);
```

Data Type	Naming Prefix	Contents
Boolean	Bln	true or false
Float	Flt	Floating point numeric
Integer	Int	Integer

The Float class is a wrapper for the float primitive type and Boolean for the boolean primitive. You will recognize the difference if you remember that Java is case-sensitive. The primitive data types are all lowercase, but the classes begin with an uppercase character.

Later you will find some advantages to using the wrapper classes rather than primitive data types, when you need the functionality provided by the class methods. For example, the wrapper classes have methods that convert data from one data type to another. You will take advantage of this feature in Chapter 4.

There is a big difference in the effects of declaring objects of the numeric wrapper classes and declaring variables of the intrinsic data types. When you delcare a variable of one of the intrinsic data types, you are allocating the memory for the variable; the variable actually exists. But when you declare an object of a class type, you have given the object a name but the object doesn't yet exist; you must use the new keyword to instantiate the object.

Scope and Lifetime

When you declare variables and constants, you can choose where to place the declaration statements. The placement determines where the variable or constant can be used (where it's visible), called the **scope.** The declaration's location also determines the **lifetime** of the variable or constant: how long the value remains in memory and can be used by the program.

You can place declarations inside your class block or inside a method. The variables and constants that you declare in the class are visible to all methods in the class and exist in memory as long as the object exists. However, the variables that you declare inside a method can be seen and used only inside that method. These variables, called **local variables**, are erased from memory when the method finishes. Each time the program calls the method, a new variable is created in memory.

Example

```
public class DemoVariables extends Applet
{
    //Declare variables
    long lngBigCount;              // Class scope and lifetime

    public void CalculateSomething();
    {
        //Declare local variables
        int intCount;              // Local scope and lifetime
        // ... Statements in method to calculate something
    }
}
```

The scope and lifetime rules also apply to the identifiers that you create for components such as TextFields and Labels. You generally declare the identifier and instantiate the component at the top of the class. The identifier for the component is then visible in all methods of the class. In this example, the components are declared and instantiated at the beginning of the class. Then the components can be referred to in any method of the class, including the `init` method.

Example

```
import java.applet.*;
import java.awt.*;

public class ButtonApplet extends Applet
{
    //Declare and instantiate components
    TextField txtDept = new TextField(15);
    TextField txtName = new TextField(25);

    public void init ()
    {
        //Place components on Web page
        add(txtDept);
        add(txtName);
}
. . .
```

Using Local Variables

In a class, generally most of your variables should be declared at the top of the class so the variable is visible in all methods. However, when you use a variable in only one method, declare it as a local variable inside that method.

```
public void actionPerformed(ActionEvent p1)
{
    //Actions for "Add to List"
    String strOutputLine;
    . . . rest of method statements
```

Instance Variables and Class Variables

When you declare a variable inside a class, each object created from the class contains an instance of the variable. Let's say that you have a class called *Student* that contains variables for strFirstName and strLastName. If you create three Student objects, each object has a first name and a last name variable. This is great because all students need a name of their own. These variables are referred to as **instance variables.**

However, you may want to have a variable that applies to all students, such as a count of the number of students. You want only one copy of the student count variable regardless of how many Student objects you create. You need one variable per class, not one variable per instance. You can create this type of variable, called a **class variable,** by using the keyword `static` in the declaration:

```
static int intStudentCount;
```

Table 2.4 summarizes the lifetime and scope rules for class variables, instance variables, and local variables.

Table 2.4

Scope and Lifetime of Variables

Type	Location of Declaration	Scope (Visibility)	Lifetime	Memory Allocated
Class	Inside a class but not within a method. Keyword `static`.	Visible in all methods of the class.	As long as any instance of the class exists.	One copy for the class.
Instance	Inside a class but not within a method.	Visible in all methods of the class.	As long as this specific instance of the class exists.	One copy for each object instantiated from the class.
Local	Inside a method.	Visible only inside the method where it is declared.	Until the method ends.	New copy each time the method is called.

Feedback 2.2

1. Declare a variable using the primitive data types that will hold the number of surveys returned. (Assume the number will be less than 5,000.)
2. Declare a variable using the primitive data types that will hold the number of surveys returned. (Assume the number will be more than 50,000.)
3. Declare and assign an initial value of zero to a float field for Balance.
4. Declare a variable that will contain a vendor name.
5. Declare a class variable to hold the dollars and cents sum of all transactions. Where will this declaration appear?
6. Declare an instance variable to hold the dollars and cents amount of one transaction. Where will this declaration appear?
7. When should you use a local variable? An instance variable? A class variable?

Text Components

You use text components when you want to both display and input information. Unlike a label, the user can enter information into a text component. Java contains two types of text components (Figure 2.3): the **TextField** and the **TextArea**. A TextField allows only a single line of text; a TextArea can have multiple lines of text.

Note: The layout of components in this chapter is very primitive. Java has several layout managers, which you will learn about in Chapter 3. In this chapter we are using the default layout, FlowLayout, which places one component after another.

Text Fields

Use a text field when you want the user to enter information. The component looks like a label, can display information, but also has an insertion point to allow the user to enter and edit the text. The naming prefix for a text field is "txt".

Figure 2.3

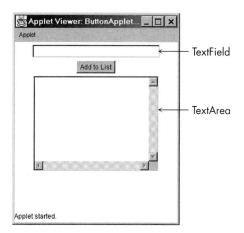

The TextField allows only one
line of text; the TextArea allows
multiple lines.

The TextField Component—Constructor Formats

```
TextField()
TextField(int maximumNumberCharacters)
TextField(String initialValue)
TextField(String initialValue, int maximumNumberCharacters)
```

Do you recognize the data types in the parameter list for the last three constructor formats? You can supply an integer length, an initial string value, or an initial string value followed by the integer length. Note that you cannot reverse the two values in the last constructor format. The sequence is critical: the compiler expects the string first and then the integer; reversing the values causes an error.

The TextField Component—Examples

```
TextField txtName = new TextField(20);
TextField txtQuantity = new TextField(5);
TextField txtZipCode = new TextField("91789");
TextField txtZipCode = new TextField("91789", 9);
```

When you specify an initial value but no length, the length of the string determines the length of the text field. Also notice that you use a text field to input string values such as a name as well as numeric values like a quantity. Any numeric digits that the user enters are treated as text. Therefore, when we work with calculations in Chapter 3, it will be necessary to convert the string value to a numeric data type.

Text Areas

Similar to a text field, a text area allows you to input data and/or display output. With a text area you can specify the number of lines plus the width. Use "txa" for the prefix.

The TextArea Component—Constructor Formats

```
TextArea()
TextArea(int numberRows, int maximumNumberCharacters)
TextArea(String initialValue)
TextArea(String initialValue, int numberRows, int maxNumberCharacters)
TextArea(String initialValue, int numberRows, int maxNumberCharacters, int Scroll)
```

The TextArea class defines several constants that you can use as values for the scroll argument: SCROLLBARS_BOTH, SCROLLBARS_VERTICAL_ONLY, SCROLLBARS_HORIZONTAL_ONLY, and SCROLLBARS_NONE. The default is a vertical scroll bar.

The TextArea Component—Examples

```
TextArea txaInvoice = new TextArea(20, 40);
TextArea txaGrades = new TextArea(15, 20);
TextArea txaGrade = new TextArea("Name Average", 15, 20);
TextArea txaGrade = new TextArea("Name Average", 15, 20,   TextArea.SCROLLBARS_BOTH);
```

Setting Initial Values for a TextArea

Notice that you can give a TextArea an initial value. Using one of the constructor formats that includes an initial value argument, enter the desired text.

```
TextArea txaOutput = new TextArea("Name           Address", 15,
20);
```

You also can use control characters to add a horizontal tab or linefeed character. See "Including Control Characters" later in this chapter.

```
TextArea txaOutput = new TextArea("Name \tAddress", 15, 20);
```

Methods for Text Components

The TextField and TextArea share many methods (Table 2.5). Both of the text components share the **getText method** for retrieving information from the graphical control. Use the **setText method** when you want to display information in a TextField, TextArea, or Label.

The getText and setText Methods

Use the getText method to retrieve the value from a text component. You then can assign its value to a variable or use the value any way you choose.

The value from a getText is always String even if the user types in a number. If you need to use the value in a calculation, you must convert it to a numeric data type. You will learn to convert the data from a text component to numeric in Chapter 4.

Method	Purpose
getText()	Returns the contents of the text component.
setText(String *value*)	Assigns the value to the text component.
append()	Adds text to the end of the contents; only available with TextArea.
selectAll()	Selects (highlights) the contents of the text component.
getSelectedText()	Returns only the text that is selected in the text component.

The getText Method—General Format

```
componentName.getText()
```

The getText Method—Example

```
strName = txtName.getText();
```

This statement places the value from txtName in a variable called strName. This is an example of an assignment statement, which assigns the value on the right side of the equal sign to that named on the left.

The setText Method—General Format

```
componentName.setText(string to be displayed)
```

You can place the text that you want to display into a text component or a label using the setText method. The string may be a variable or a literal.

The setText Method—Examples

```
lblMessage.setText("Hello World");
txtGreeting.setText(strName);
txtAnswer.setText("Hello " + txtName.getText());
txtName.setText(""); //Clear the text field
```

Notice that the third example gets the name from the txtName text field and "adds" it to the string "Hello". The plus sign (+) is used to combine string fields. This process is called **concatenation.** Any spaces inside the quotation marks of the string are included. Make sure to add spaces so that you have a space between the string literal ("Hello ") and the value from the text field.

The last example illustrates a method for clearing a text field. Note that there is no space between the two quotation marks, which is called an *empty string.*

Including Control Characters   When you create a string to display, you may want to insert special characters used for spacing. These characters, called *escape characters,* each begins with a backslash.

\n	linefeed (also called **newline**)
\t	horizontal tab (advance to the next tab stop on the line)
\f	form feed (eject a page when sending output to a printer)
\"	double quote (include double quote within a string)
\'	single quote (include single quote within a string)
\\	backslash (include a backslash within a string)

For example, you can display a string on multiple lines. The string "Hello \n World" will display on two lines, assuming that you are using a component that allows multiple lines, such as a TextArea.

You can use the \t horizontal tab to advance to the next tab stop on the line. This is similar to pressing the Tab key on the keyboard when typing. Depending on the width of the tab stops and the length of the strings to display, you may be able to align columns of data. For example, the string "Hello \tWorld \tFrom \tMe" displays as Hello   World   From   Me.

The append Method

The **append method** allows you to add information to the end of the string in a text area. You can use append to "build" your output as the information becomes available or use it to create multiple lines of output.

The append Method—General Format

```
componentName.append(string);
```

You can create multiple lines in a TextArea by including the code for a new line: \n. The following three statements produce three lines of text in one TextArea component.

The append Method—Examples

```
txaInvoice.append("Sold To: " + strName + "\n");
txaInvoice.append("Address: " + strStreet + "\n");
txaInvoice.append(" City: " + strCity);
```

The following code retrieves data from TextField components, assigns the values to string variables, and concatenates the string variables and tab characters for spacing. The concatenated string displays in a TextArea, along with a new-line code, so that the next entry will be on a new line. The TextField components are then cleared for the next entry.

```
//Retrieve strings from TextField components and assign to variables
strDept = txtDept.getText();
strName = txtName.getText();
strPhone = txtPhone.getText();

//Concatenate the variables into one long string
strOutputLine = strDept + "\t" + strName + "\t" + strPhone;

//Append the concatenated string to the TextArea
txaPhoneList.append(strOutputLine + "\n");

//Clear the screen components
txtDept.setText("");
txtName.setText("");
txtPhone.setText("");
```

You might expect to align columns of text with the preceding code, but unfortunately the different length fields do not appear in neat columns. For now, accept the misaligned columns; later you will learn to align columns of data. Most of the assignments at the end of the chapter give data of equal length, which is not an accident.

Sample Output 1

Sales	Jane	x412
Acctg	Bill	x782

Sample Output 2

Sales	Jane Smith	x412
Accounting	William Proninten	x782

You may see Java programs that use the appendText method instead of append. The appendText method was **deprecated** in Java 1.1 (replaced with the append method).

Prompts for Text Components

Each of the text boxes for user data entry should be labeled with a prompt (Figure 2.4). The prompt tells the user what to enter. You can create the prompts with labels, but those labels will not be referenced anywhere in code after they are created. If you do not plan to refer to a label after creating it, you can eliminate one step and create the component without a name.

For a named label, recall that you declared a new variable at the top of the class and added the label in a method.

```
//Declare the variable in the declarations at the top of the class
Label lblName = new Label("Howdy Doody");
. . .
//Add the label in a method
add(lblName);
```

For an unnamed label, you can just use the new keyword in the add method:

```
//Add an unnamed label; belongs in a method
add(new Label("Department: ")); //Prompt for Department
```

Tip

Avoid deprecated methods, which are methods that have been replaced with a newer version. Use the newer version instead.

Figure 2.4

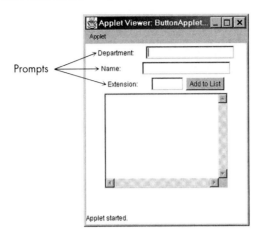

Prompts

*You can use unnamed labels for
the prompts.*

When you set up an applet panel, you usually use unnamed labels for the prompts and named components for the text fields used to enter and display data.

```
//Place components on applet panel
add(new Label("Department: ")); //Prompt for Department
add(txtDept);
add(new Label("Name: ")); //Prompt for Name
add(txtName);
add(new Label("Extension: ")); //Prompt for Phone extension
add(txtPhone);
add(btnAdd);
add(txaPhoneList);
```

Positioning the Cursor

You can control the placement of the cursor (insertion point) in a text field. The component with the cursor is said to have the **focus.** Use the `requestFocus` method of a component to place the cursor in that component. You should place the cursor when the applet begins running in the `init` method. And be sure to set the focus again after clearing the text fields for new data entry.

```
//Place the cursor in the init method
txtDept.requestFocus();
. . .

//(Later)
//Clear the screen components
txtDept.setText("");
txtName.setText("");
txtPhone.setText("");
txtDept.requestFocus(); //Place the cursor in the first field
```

Feedback 2.3

1. Declare text fields for entering a first name and a last name.
2. Code the `add` statements for the first name and last name text fields along with prompts.

3. Write the statement to set the focus to the last name text field.
4. Code the statements to get the first name and last name values and place them in the string variables strFirstName and strLastName.
5. Write a statement that displays last name followed by a comma and a space, then the first name. Display the information in txaClient.

System Dates

Frequently you need to display the current date with your information. You can easily access the system date and time using the *Calendar* class found in the Java *util* package. A getInstance method creates an instance of the Calendar class, which contains the current date and time for the default locale and time zone.

```
Calendar calCurrent = Calendar.getInstance();
```

You can retrieve the properties of the Calendar object using the get method. Use the named constants (Table 2.6) to specify which property you want. The next step is to obtain the information included in the date. Store the information separately in variables or use them directly in a label or text component.

Tip

Use the Calendar class for dates and times, not the Date class from earlier versions of Java. Date does not support internationalization.

Table 2.6

Partial List of Calendar Integer Constants

Constant	Returns
YEAR	4-digit year
MONTH	Month starting with 0
DAY_OF_MONTH	Day starting with 1
DAY_OF_YEAR	Julian date
DAY_OF_WEEK	Starts with 0 for Sunday
ERA	BC or AD
HOUR	Hour (12-hour time)
MINUTE	Minute of hour
SECOND	Seconds
HOUR_OF_DAY	Military time (24-hour clock)

This applet retrieves the date and time and displays them in an applet.

```
//Folder: Ch2Dates
//Programmer:    Bradley/Millspaugh
//Date:          6/2001
//ClassName:     CurrentDateApplet
//Description:   Gets current date and time
```

```
import java.awt.*;
import java.applet.*;
import java.util.*;

public class CurrentDateApplet extends Applet
{
    // Get the current date and time
    //Declare objects
    Calendar calCurrent = Calendar.getInstance();
    TextArea txaDate = new TextArea(5, 20);

    //Declare variables and assign initial value
    int intDay = calCurrent.get(Calendar.DATE); //gets day of month
    int intMonth = calCurrent.get(Calendar.MONTH) + 1;
    int intYear = calCurrent.get(Calendar.YEAR);

    public void init()
    {
    //Add text area
    add(txaDate);

    //Display Dates
    txaDate.append(" Date: " + intMonth + "/" + intDay + "/" + intYear + "\n");
    txaDate.append(" Time: " + calCurrent.get(Calendar.HOUR) +
        ":" + calCurrent.get(Calendar.MINUTE) + "\n");
    }
}
```

Note that the month starts with zero, *not* one. You need to add one to the month, making January one instead of zero.

Many other classes are contained in the utility package along with subclasses of Calendar. Some of these are covered in later chapters.

Buttons

Another common component is a button (refer to Figure 2.1). The user clicks on a button to request an action. You create a button object by using the Button class in the awt package and name it with a "btn" prefix. You can create a **Button component** with or without a label on top, called the button's *caption.*

The Button Component—Constructor Formats

```
Button()
Button(String label);
```

The Button Component—Examples

```
Button btnBlank = new Button()
Button btnClear = new Button ("OK");
Button btnDisplay = new Button("Display");
```

Note: We are using the button component from the awt package because all versions of Java and all browsers can use awt components. Later you will learn to use the JButton component from the swing package, which is part of Java 2. The swing components, such as JButton, JLabel, and JTextField, have more functionality than their awt counterparts. For example, you can define a hot key for a JButton and include an icon as well as text on top of the button.

Capturing an Event

When the user clicks on a button, an **event** occurs. In fact, many events occur as the mouse pointer moves around and the focus moves from one component to another. In your Java program, you want to respond to some events and ignore others. You "listen" for the events to which you want to respond by using Java listeners. You must include the listener in your program when you want to respond to an event.

Note: Earlier versions of Java include an `action` method, which has been deprecated. Use listeners instead.

The ActionListener Interface

An ActionListener detects the click of a button. To add the listener to your code, you must add another `import` statement and include the **implements** clause in the class header:

```
import java.awt.event.*;

public class Ch2Action extends Applet  implements ActionListener
```

ActionListener is an **interface,** not a class. An interface is a set of specifications for methods. You will use the methods to respond to events. To use an interface, you use the **implements** keyword rather than `import` or `extends`. You will learn more about interfaces in Chapter 5.

But more must be done to respond to a button click. You also must add the listener to the component and then write the code that executes when the event occurs.

Adding the Listener to a Component

Use the `addActionListener` method of a component to add an ActionListener for that component. The following code includes an argument called **this,** which refers to the current class. It tells the ActionListener that the current class should be notified when an event occurs for the named object (btnAdd).

```
btnAdd.addActionListener(this);
```

Coding for the Event

Once you have added an action listener, the next step is to code an **actionPerformed method**. This method executes each time the event fires—that is, the user clicks on the button. In the `actionPerformed` method, you write the statements that you want to execute when the user clicks the button.

For this chapter, an applet can have only one button. When you have several buttons, each with an action listener, the same `actionPerformed` method executes when *any* button is clicked. In Chapter 6 you will learn to use the `If` statement to make decisions and check to see which button was clicked.

The `actionPerformed` method executes when the user clicks on the Add to List button. It assigns the contents of the three TextField components to variables, concatenates the strings, appends the concatenated string to the TextArea component, clears the contents of the three TextField components, and places the cursor in the first TextField.

```
public void actionPerformed(ActionEvent event)
 {
    //Actions for "Add to List" button
    String strOutputLine;

    //Retrieve strings from TextField components and assign to variables
    strDept = txtDept.getText();
    strName = txtName.getText();
    strPhone = txtPhone.getText();

    //Concatenate the variables into one long string
    strOutputLine = strDept + " " + strName + " " + strPhone;

    //Append the concatenated string to the TextArea
    txaPhoneList.append(strOutputLine + "\n");

    //Clear the screen components
    txtDept.setText("");
    txtName.setText("");
    txtPhone.setText("");

    //Place the cursor in the first component
    txtDept.requestFocus();
 }
```

Notice that the `actionPerformed` method contains a parameter (`Action-Event event`). When the user fires an event, the system supplies a value for the `ActionEvent`. This argument indicates the component for which the event occurred. In Chapter 6 you will learn to check the value of the `ActionEvent` argument to determine which button was clicked.

Improving the Event Handling

The preceding code works great when the user clicks the applet's Add to List button. But what happens when the user presses the Enter/Return key? Most users prefer to press the Enter key after entering text, rather than reach for the mouse. You also can add an action listener to a text field, which causes your `actionPerformed` method to execute when the user presses Enter while the focus is in the text field.

```
//Add action listeners
btnAdd.addActionListener(this);   //Listen for click of the button
txtPhone.addActionListener(this); //Listen for Enter key in this component
```

Which text field should have the action listener? The last one? One of the advantages of a GUI is that the user can move the cursor from field to field in any order and return to a previous field to edit its contents. So the user might press Enter with the focus in any of the three text fields. If you want your program to respond consistently to the Enter key, you must add an action listener to all three text fields:

```
//Add action listeners
btnAdd.addActionListener(this);    //Listen for click of the button
txtDept.addActionListener(this);   //Listen for Enter key in this component
txtName.addActionListener(this);   //Listen for Enter key in this component
txtPhone.addActionListener(this);  //Listen for Enter key in this component
```

When the user clicks the button or presses Enter, your `ActionPerformed` method executes.

```
public void actionPerformed(ActionEvent event)
  {
    //Actions for "Add to List"
    //Triggered when the user clicks the button or presses the Enter
    // key in any of the text fields
    String strOutputLine; //Declare local variable

    //Assign the text fields to variables
    strDept = txtDept.getText();
    strName = txtName.getText();
    strPhone = txtPhone.getText();

    //Concatenate the variables
    strOutputLine = strDept + " " + strName + " " + strPhone;

    //Append the concatenated line to the phone list
    txaPhoneList.append(strOutputLine + "\n");

    //Clear the text fields
    txtDept.setText("");
    txtName.setText("");
    txtPhone.setText("");

    //Place the cursor in the first text field
    txtDept.requestFocus();
  }
```

Caution: If your users are accustomed to using the Enter/Return key at the end of each field rather than to select a button, do not add listeners to the text fields.

Feedback 2.4

1. What is the purpose of the `implements ActionListener` clause on the class header?
2. Write the `actionPerformed` method that captures the data from txtLastName and txtFirstName; concatenates them as first name, a space, and then last name; displays the output in txaOutput; and clears the text fields. Make sure that you include code to display multiple entries on separate lines.
3. Assume that you have written the `actionPerformed` method but nothing happens when the user clicks the button. What code must you add to the `init` method to activate the button?

Mouse Events

Many actions taken by the user cause events to occur. The user may do several things with a mouse, such as click the mouse, move it over an object, or move it away from an object. Java allows you to listen for mouse events using a **MouseListener.** The MouseListener interface requires you to include five mouse methods, even if you leave some of the methods empty. The five mouse methods are mouseClicked, mousePressed, mouseReleased, mouseEntered, and mouseExited.

To use a MouseListener, you need to import java.awt.event.* (the same package that you imported for the ActionEvent). You also must add implements MouseListener to the class header line.

In the following class, the color of the button changes when the mouse enters the text field or the command button. The color changes back when the mouse exits either component. The applet also displays a line of text in the browser's status bar, which is covered shortly in the "StatusBar" section.

When you change the color of a button, you can change the color of its caption (the foreground) or the color of the button itself (the background). In this applet we change the color of both the background and the foreground.

```java
//Folder:       Ch2MouseEvents
//Programmer:   Bradley/Millspaugh
//Date:         6/2001
//Class Name:   MouseEventsApplet
//Description: This class demonstrates the MouseListener

import java.applet.*;
import java.awt.*;
import java.awt.event.*;

public class MouseEventsApplet extends Applet
                                implements MouseListener , ActionListener
{
    //Create Controls
    TextField txtName = new TextField(35);
    Button btnCalculate = new Button(" Calculate ");

    public void init()
    {
        //Place components on the panel
        add(txtName);
        add(btnCalculate);

        //Add Listeners for components
        txtName.addMouseListener(this);
        btnCalculate.addMouseListener(this);

        btnCalculate.addActionListener(this);

        //Set focus to txtName
        txtName.requestFocus();
    }

    public void mouseClicked(MouseEvent e)
    { //Empty method
    }

    public void mousePressed(MouseEvent e)
    { //Empty method
    }

    public void mouseReleased(MouseEvent e)
    { //Empty method
    }
```

```
public void mouseEntered(MouseEvent e)
{
    //Set the button's colors to blue and cyan
    btnCalculate.setForeground(Color.blue);
    btnCalculate.setBackground(Color.cyan);

    //Show text on browser's status bar
    showStatus("Calculate");
}


public void mouseExited(MouseEvent e)
{
    //Set the button's text color to black
    btnCalculate.setForeground(Color.black);
    btnCalculate.setBackground(Color.lightGray);

    //Show text on browser's status bar
    showStatus("Ready");
}

public void actionPerformed(ActionEvent e)
{
    //Respond to a button click
    showStatus("Calculate button clicked");
}
}
```

The empty methods are required. They override methods defined in the MouseListener interface of the awt.event package. When you plan to implement an interface, such as a listener, it's a good idea to look up the definition of the interface. You can find all package classes and interfaces using the Object Browser included in most IDEs.

Other Listeners

Many other listeners are available in Java. The FocusListener has focusGained and focusLost methods, which can notify you that a component has received or lost the focus. A ComponentListener provides methods for componentHidden, componentMoved, componentResized, and componentShown. Other listeners include KeyListener, MouseMotionListener, TextListener, and WindowListener.

StatusBar

Notice the **showStatus method** in the mouse events of the previous example. This method displays a string in the status window of most browsers. If you are using the Applet Viewer, the status string appears at the bottom of the window.

```
public void mouseExited(MouseEvent e)
{
    //Set the button's forecolor to black
    btnCalculate.setForeground(Color.black);
```

```
btnCalculate.setBackground(Color.lightGray);

//Show text on browser's status bar
showStatus("Ready");
}
```

The showStatus Method—General Format

```
showStatus(String);
```

The showStatus Method—Examples

```
showStatus("Click here to Calculate");
showStatus("Invalid entry");
```

The showStatus method is a member of the Applet class, so it's always available in an applet.

Feedback 2.5

1. Why must all five mouse methods be included in the code, even if the methods are empty?
2. Code the statement to display the phrase "Clear all entries" in the status window.

Your Hands-on Programming Example

Create an applet that generates a phone list in a text area. Use prompts and text fields to allow the user to enter a department name, employee name, and telephone extension. Include a button with the caption "Add to Phone List". If the user clicks on the button or presses the Enter key, the applet adds the information from the three text fields to the phone list in a new line of output. After adding the information to the phone list, clear the text fields, and reset the focus in the first text field. Figure 2.5 shows one possible layout for this applet.

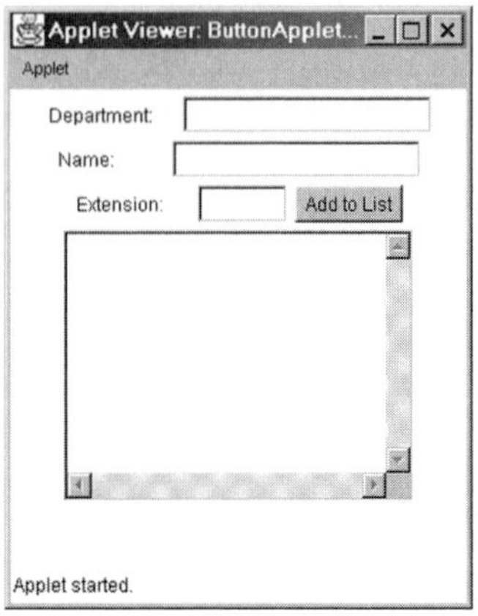

F i g u r e   2 . 5

A possible layout for the hands-on exercise.

CHAPTER 2 55

Planning the Project

Plan the Objects and Properties
Class: ButtonApplet
Figure 2.6 shows the class diagram.

Figure 2.6

Class: ButtonApplet	
Methods	**Variables and Components**
init actionPerformed	strDept strName strPhone txtDept txtName txtPhone btnAdd

The class diagram for the chapter hands-on exercise.

Properties:

Access Mode (public or private)	Variable or Component Name	Data Type or Class	Description
	txtDept	TextField	Input the department.
	strDept	String	Store the department.
	txtName	TextField	Input the name.
	strName	String	Store the name.
	txtPhone	TextField	Input the phone extension.
	strPhone	String	Store the phone extension.
	btnAdd	Button	Add to phone list and clear fields.
	txaPhoneList	TextArea	Holds a list of names and phone numbers.

Methods:

Access Mode (public or private)	Return Type	Method Name (include any parameters)	Pseudocode
public	void	init	Add the controls.
public	void	actionPerformed	Transfer data from text boxes. Concatenate the data. Append line to text area. Clear text fields. Reset the focus.

Write the Project

- Follow the plan to add components to the class.

- Write the appropriate statements in each method of the class to add the components and to change the color and the font as needed.

- When you complete the code, thoroughly test the project.

The Project Solution

```
//Folder:        Ch2Buttons
//Programmer:    Bradley/Millspaugh
//Date:          6/2001
//Class Name:    ButtonApplet
//Description:   User enters a department, name, and phone extension.
//               When the user clicks on the button, the information
//               is added to a phone list.

import java.applet.*;
import java.awt.*;
import java.awt.event.*;

public class ButtonApplet extends Applet implements ActionListener
{
    //Declare components
    TextField txtDept = new TextField(15);
    TextField txtName = new TextField(20);
    TextField txtPhone = new TextField(5);
    TextArea txaPhoneList = new TextArea(10, 30);
    Button btnAdd = new Button("Add to List");
    //Declare variables
    String strDept;
    String strName;
    String strPhone;

    public void init ()
    {
        //Place components on applet

        add(new Label("Department: "));
        add(txtDept);
        add(new Label("Name:        "));
        add(txtName);
        add(new Label("Extension:   "));
        add(txtPhone);
        add(btnAdd);
        add(txaPhoneList);
        txtDept.requestFocus();

        //Add action listeners
        btnAdd.addActionListener(this);
        txtDept.addActionListener(this);
        txtName.addActionListener(this);
        txtPhone.addActionListener(this);
        }
```

```java
public void actionPerformed(ActionEvent event)
{
    //Actions for "Add to List"
    //Triggered when the user clicks the button or presses the Enter
    // key in any of the text fields
    String strOutputLine; //Declare local variable

    //Assign the text fields to variables
    strDept = txtDept.getText();
    strName = txtName.getText();
    strPhone = txtPhone.getText();

    //Concatenate the variables
    strOutputLine = strDept + "\t" + strName + "\t" + strPhone;
    //Append the concatenated line to the phone list
    txaPhoneList.append(strOutputLine + "\n");

    //Clear the text fields
    txtDept.setText("");
    txtName.setText("");
    txtPhone.setText("");

    //Place the cursor in the first text field
    txtDept.requestFocus();
    }
}
```

Summary

1. Classes contain methods for performing actions. A constructor method executes when an object is created. A class may contain multiple constructor methods, each with different parameters.

2. A method's list of expected arguments is called its *parameter list,* made up of parameters and their data types. When information is passed to the method, the values are called *arguments.*

3. Data used in programming can be variable or constant. Many constants are predefined and named in the core Java packages.

4. Text inside quotation marks is called a *string literal* or *string constant.*

5. Data are stored in different data types. Java has eight primitive data types: byte, short, int, long, float, double, char, and boolean.

6. Variable names must follow the Java naming rules and should follow naming conventions. To follow naming conventions, include a three-character prefix on variable names to identify the data type.

7. You can declare an initial value when you declare a new variable. If you don't give the variable a value, it will hold the default value for that data type.

8. The keyword `final` declares a constant.

9. Most primitive types have wrapper classes that include methods for manipulating or converting the data.

10. The placement of the declaration determines the scope and the lifetime of variables and constants.

11. For instance variables, each object created from the class has its own set of variables. For class variables, created with the `static` keyword, only one copy of the variable exists for the entire class, regardless of the number of instances of the class.

12. The TextField and TextArea components allow the user to enter and edit data. The TextArea can hold multiple lines of output.

13. The `getText` and `setText` methods provide for retrieving and assigning values to text and label components.
14. You can join text strings using concatenation.
15. Text can be added to a TextArea using the `append` method. The "\n" character makes text go to the next line.
16. Create prompts for text fields using labels. It isn't necessary to name labels used for prompts.
17. The `requestFocus` method places the focus in the named text field.
18. Use the Calendar class to retrieve the system date and time.
19. A Button component provides a visual component that a user can click to take some action. The button can appear with or without text on top; the text is called the button's *caption*.
20. An ActionListener is needed to listen for and catch the button's click. The actionPerformed event occurs when the listener is fired.
21. Place an `implements ActionListener` clause on the class header to include the event methods; add the listener(s) to desired components in the `init` method.
22. A MouseListener allows you to listen for and catch mouse events.
23. Information can be displayed in the status bar using the `showStatus` method.

K e y   T e r m s

`actionPerformed` method *49*
`append` method *44*
argument *32*
assignment operator *36*
Button component *48*
class variable *39*
concatenation *43*
constant *34*
constructor method *32*
data type *34*
deprecated *45*
event *49*
`final` *37*
focus *46*
`getText` method *42*
`implements` *49*
instance variable *39*

interface *49*
lifetime *38*
local variable *38*
method *32*
MouseListener *51*
parameter *33*
primitive data type *34*
scope *38*
`setText` method *42*
`showStatus` method *53*
string literal *34*
`TextArea` component *40*
`TextField` component *40*
`this` *49*
variable *34*
wrapper class *37*

R e v i e w   Q u e s t i o n s

1. What is the purpose of a constructor method? When and how would you call a constructor method?
2. Give examples of constants defined in the Java awt package.
3. What is a string literal? Give an example of its use.

4. How do you create a named numeric constant?

5. Differentiate between a primitive data type and a data wrapper class.

6. Explain the differences between a class variable and an instance variable. How is each declared and used?

7. List and explain three methods available for a TextArea component.

8. Explain the purpose of concatenation? How is concatenation implemented?

9. What does it mean if you receive a message that your code is deprecated?

10. List and explain the steps you need to have your program respond to a button's click.

11. What methods must you include in your program when you implement the MouseListener?

Programming Exercises

2.1. Create an applet that inputs first name, last name, street, city, state, and zip code. In a text area, create multiple lines of output to display the information in the format of a mailing label. Append punctuation, spaces, and new line symbols as needed. Include a button with the text "Display Label" that appends the information from the text fields to the mailing label.

Test Data

Last Name:	DeVoss
First Name:	Karen
Street:	515 Rainbow Drive
City:	Montclair
State:	California
Zip Code:	91763-4321

Sample Output

Karen DeVoss
515 Rainbow Drive
Montclair, California 91763-4321

Optional: Add code to clear the text fields when the text is added to the text area.

2.2. Create an applet that prompts for your name and phone number. Add a button with the caption "Add to List" that appends one line containing the name and phone number to a text area and then clears the text fields so another name can be entered. Leave a blank line between names. Include the current date as a title.

Sample Output

Kristin	555-5678
Heather	555-7125
Lisa Ann	555-9321

2.3.   Create an applet to input a class schedule. The text fields should include student name, class, days, hours, and room. A button called "Add Class" will add a line of text to a text area with the class information and clear all of the text fields except for the student name. Use the constructor methods to set up the titles.

Sample Output

Course	Days	Time	Room
Java Prgmg	M	1:00	17-13
English 1A	TTh	8:00	26-101
Spanish 22	TTh	9:30	28-204

2.4.   Modify any of the previous programming exercise applets to change the foreground color of the labels when the mouse enters the label. Return to the startup colors when the mouse exits the label. *Optional:* Also modify the font.

CASE STUDIES

R 'n R—for Reading and Refreshment

Create an applet that inputs a book request. Include prompts and text fields for the customer name and phone number and for the title and author of the book. An "Order" button should display the customer name on one line and the phone number on the next followed by the book information. Include an identifier on each line: Customer, Phone, Title, and Author followed by colons and the appropriate information. Also clear the text fields.

Sample Output

Customer:	Tricia Mills
Phone:	555-7865
Title:	Programming in Visual Basic
Author:	Bradley and Millspaugh

Merry Pea's Quilting

Create an applet that produces a list of people who have signed up for a quilting class. Include prompts and text fields for the student name and the phone number. Include a class title "Fat Squares Class" and the current date at the top of the text area.

Include an "Add" button, which appends the name and phone number to a text area. The information for each student should display on a separate line. The button's actions should clear the text fields for the student name and phone number.

Sample Output

Fat Squares Class	09/15/01
Char	111-1111
Jane	222-2222
Anne	333-3333

3

Designing the Interface with Layout Managers

At the completion of this chapter, you will be able to . . .

1. Position components on the interface.

2. Use the `setLayout` method to select the layout manager.

3. Place equally sized components in rows and columns with the GridLayout manager.

4. Arrange components using the BorderLayout manager.

5. Create more flexible displays with the GridBagLayout and the GridBagConstraints.

6. Use Panels to combine multiple layouts on one applet.

So far the layout of components on an applet has been rather arbitrary. If you have spent much time trying to "pretty up" your applets, you probably have been disappointed and maybe a little frustrated. Each component that you add to an applet is placed in sequence, and when the user resizes the window, the component location changes. But all that is about to change; you are about to learn to control the placement of components using Java's layout managers.

Java Layout Managers

If you have done any programming in languages other than Java, you may be accustomed to specifying the exact screen locations for components. However, when you write in Java, you are expecting the program to run on many different platforms, operating systems, screen resolutions, screen sizes, and fonts. Specifying an exact location just doesn't work when the program must be transportable. What looks good on one system may be unusable on another, with components overlapping, cut off, or unreadable.

Java uses **layout managers** to dynamically determine the placement of components and containers when the program runs. These layout managers are specific for the system running your program, so the components have the correct look and spacing for that system.

An applet is actually a **container**, which can hold components and other containers. Any component that you add in a Java program *must* be in a container. You can think of the program interface as a container that changes depending on use. The layout manager determines the sequence of components in the container.

The default layout manager for an applet is the FlowLayout manager. For the applets you have written so far, you didn't specify a layout manager, so Java used the FlowLayout manager by default. Other layouts available are GridLayout, BorderLayout, CardLayout, and GridBagLayout. Because a container may hold other containers, you can place panel containers on the applet and give the new panel another layout manager, which allows you to combine layouts.

Specifying a Layout Manager

You specify the layout manager that you want to use with the **setLayout method**.

The setLayout Method—General Format

```
setLayout(new LayoutManager);
```

The setLayout Method—Examples

```
setLayout(new FlowLayout());
setLayout(new GridLayout());
```

When you do not specify a layout manager, the Applet class automatically applies the FlowLayout manager.

The FlowLayout Manager

The **FlowLayout** manager places components in the order they are added with add statements. A little extra space is added around each item. You determine the size of the components (TextFields and TextAreas) and the captions (Buttons and Labels) when you declare them.

You can use one of three constructors for the FlowLayout manager:

The FlowLayout Class—Constructors

```
FlowLayout();
FlowLayout(int Alignment):
FlowLayout(int Alignment, int horizontalGap, int verticalGap);
```

The horizontal and vertical gaps determine the minimum number of pixels to leave between components. The default is five pixels. For the alignment, use the constants FlowLayout.LEFT, FlowLayout.RIGHT, and FlowLayout.CENTER. The empty constructor format creates a flow layout with centered alignment and five-pixel gaps.

The FlowLayout Constructor—Examples

```
setLayout(new FlowLayout());

MyAppletLayout = new FlowLayout(FlowLayout.LEFT, 5, 10);
setLayout(MyAppletLayout);
```

The GridLayout Manager

The **GridLayout** manager arranges the components in rows and columns and makes all components the same size. You can specify the number of rows and columns for the grid and, optionally, the horizontal and vertical spacing. The spacing determines the gap in pixels between the components. The layout manager resizes each control to fill its cell.

The GridLayout class constructor has three forms:

The GridLayout Class—Constructors

```
GridLayout();
GridLayout(int rows, int columns);
GridLayout(int rows, int columns, int horizontalGap, int verticalGap);
```

The GridLayout Constructor—Examples

```
setLayout(new GridLayout(3, 2));
setLayout(new GridLayout(3, 2, 40, 20));
```

The preceding two examples create grid layouts with three rows and two columns. Figure 3.1 shows the result of the first example, GridLayout(3, 2), and Figure 3.2 shows the result of the second example, GridLayout(3, 2, 40, 20). Notice how different the outputs look for the same applet displayed in Internet Explorer (Figure 3.2a) and Netscape Navigator (Figure 3.2b). You should always test your applets in both browsers.

Figure 3.1

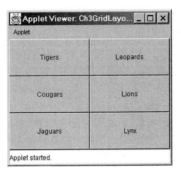

A grid of 3 rows and 2 columns. The GridLayout manager makes all components the same size.

Figure 3.2

A grid layout created with the statement GridLayout(3, 2, 40, 20). a. Displayed in Internet Explorer; b. Displayed in Netscape Navigator.

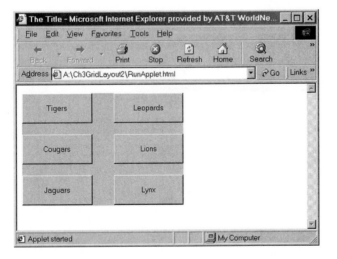

a.

b.

In an applet, you generally call the setLayout method in the init method:

```
public void init()
{
  //Set up the GridLayout Manager
  setLayout(new GridLayout(3, 2));
  //Add the components
  add(btnOne);
  add(btnTwo);
  add(btnThree);
  add(btnFour);
  add(btnFive);
  add(btnSix);
}
```

You can create a grid layout with a single row or a single column by setting either the row or the column argument to zero. For example, Figure 3.3 is created from this statement:

```
setLayout(new GridLayout(6, 0, 10, 10));
```

and Figure 3.4 is created from this statement:

```
setLayout(new GridLayout(0, 6, 10, 10));
```

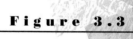

Figure 3.3

A grid layout with a single column, created with this statement: setLayout(new GridLayout(6, 0, 10, 10));

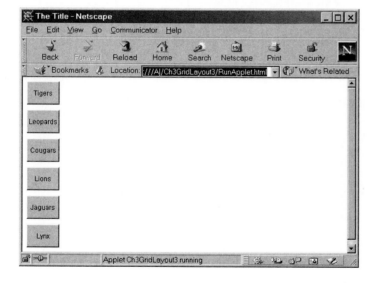

When you set the number of rows or columns to zero, Java calculates the number to use based on the number of components that you add. For example, this statement

```
GridLayout(3, 0)
```

specifies three rows and any number of columns. If you add only three components to the layout, they appear in one column. But if you add 12 components to the layout, you get three rows and four columns. And if you add 13 components, you get three rows and five columns, with only one component in the fifth column.

*A grid layout with a single row,
created from this statement:*
setLayout(new GridLayout(0, 6,
10, 10));

Tip

Set either the number of rows or
the number of columns for Grid-
Layout and set the other parameter to zero. The layout
manager will calculate
the other parameter
based on the num-
ber of components
that you add.

The BorderLayout Manager

A **BorderLayout** manager divides the container into sections based on the
compass. The sections are called *North*, *South*, *East*, *West*, and *Center* (Figure 3.5). You can add only one component to each section; the BorderLayout resizes the component to fill the section. However, as you will see later in this
chapter, you can add a new container to a section. The container can have its
own layout manager and contain additional components.

*A border layout created using the
empty constructor*
setLayout(new
BorderLayout());

The BorderLayout Class—Constructors

```
BorderLayout();
BorderLayout(int horizontalGap, int verticalGap);
```

The optional horizontal and vertical gap arguments specify the number of
pixels separating the components. The empty constructor creates the layout
shown in Figure 3.5.

The BorderLayout Constructor—Examples

```
setLayout(new BorderLayout());

BorderLayout layMyBorderLayout = new BorderLayout(10, 10);
setLayout(layMyBorderLayout);
```

Figure 3.6 illustrates the second example above, with a 10-pixel separation between components.

Figure 3.6

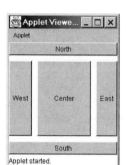

A border layout with 10 pixels between the components in both directions, created with this statement: `setLayout(new BorderLayout(10, 10));`

When you add a component to the layout, you must specify the section, using the provided constants. If you add more than one component to a section, only the last one added appears. If you omit the name of the section, the component is added to the center section. Therefore, if you omit the name of the section for multiple components, all are placed in the center, with only the last one added appearing.

Use this new form of the `add` method to add components to a border layout:

The add Method with Border constants

```
add("North", new Button ("Top"));
add("South", btnDisplay);
add("West", lblMessage);
```

This code produces the output shown in Figure 3.5.

```
//Folder:          Ch3BorderLayout1
//Programmer:      Bradley/Millspaugh
//Date:            6/2001
//Class Name:      Ch3BorderLayout1
//Description:     This class demonstrates the BorderLayout manager.

import java.applet.*;
import java.awt.*;

public class Ch3BorderLayout1 extends Applet
```

```
{
    //Declare the components
    Button btnNorth = new Button("North");
    Button btnSouth = new Button("South");
    Button btnEast = new Button("East");
    Button btnWest = new Button("West");
    Button btnCenter = new Button("Center");

    public void init()
    {
        //Set up the BorderLayout Manager
        setLayout(new BorderLayout());
        //Add the components
        add("North", btnNorth);
        add("South", btnSouth);
        add("East", btnEast);
        add("West", btnWest);
        add("Center", btnCenter);
    }
}
```

Feedback 3.1

1. Code the statement to set the layout to FlowLayout with left alignment, a vertical gap of 5 pixels, and a horizontal gap of 10 pixels.
2. Write the statements to set the layout and to add the following components to a GridLayout:
    (a) A prompt "Name:"
    (b) txtName
    (c) A prompt "Phone:"
    (d) txtPhone
3. Write the add statement to place lblCompanyName at the top of a Border-Layout.

The GridBagLayout Manager

Are you looking for more control of the layout? You can use the **GridBagLayout** manager, which is much more flexible but more complicated than the other layouts. Basically, a grid bag layout is a grid with rows and columns, but you can control the sizes and placement of components using **GridBagConstraints.**

By setting constraints, you can combine multiple cells, set the size and location of any component, and set the alignment of each component within its cell. The area inside a cell where you can place a component is called its **display area.**

You can think of the grid bag layout as a grid with as many rows and columns as you need. By default, the grid is centered in the middle of the container. The largest component determines the size of a cell. For example, a tall text area might set the height of a row, or a long text field may set the width of a column. You also can set the relative size of components by using constraints.

Remember, when you create Java layouts, you are describing how the components should be placed for a variety of systems. You are giving relative placement, telling which components may grow and shrink when the applet is resized and describing the alignment and extra spacing between components. But you are **not** specifying an absolute size or placement. The output of your layouts will vary depending on the platform, the browser, and even the size of the browser window.

Specifying a GridBagLayout

To use a grid bag layout, declare GridBagLayout and GridBagConstraints objects and attach the layout to your applet:

```
GridBagLayout gridbag = new GridBagLayout();
GridBagConstraints constraints = new GridBagConstraints();
setLayout(gridbag);
```

Setting Constraints for Components

For each component that you add to the grid bag layout, you first set an instance of the GridBagConstraints class. Then you actually add the component. Although you can set as many as 11 different data members of the GridBagConstraints object, usually you set only a few values and accept the default for the rest.

For example, the following code specifies that a label (lblDept) be aligned right (EAST) and should not expand to fill the display area. After setting the anchor and fill constraint data members, the setConstraints method assigns the instance of the constraints object to lblDept. Then the add method adds lblDept to the applet.

```
//Set constraints and add lblDept to the applet
constraints.anchor = GridBagConstraints.EAST;  //Align the label right
constraints.fill = GridBagConstraints.NONE;     //Do not expand to fill cell
gridbag.setConstraints(lblDept, constraints);
add(lblDept);
```

The GridBagConstraints object keeps the data values that you assign to it. For example, if you set the constraints for another component following the above example, the next component will have the same constraint values unless you modify them.

```
gridbag.setConstraints(txtDept, constraints);
add(txtDept);
```

In this case, txtDept also will be set to align right and not fill its display area, since the data members of the constraints object were not changed after the previous code. If you want to specify different values for the next component, you must set the data members of the constraints object before calling the setConstraints method.

```
//Set constraints and add txtDept to the applet
constraints.anchor = GridBagConstraints.WEST; //Align at left of display area
gridbag.setConstraints(txtDept, constraints);
add(txtDept);
```

The setConstraints Method—General Format

```
GridBagLayoutObject.setConstraints(Component, GridBagConstraintsObject)
```

The GridBagLayoutObject and GridBagContraintsObject are objects that you have already declared with the `new` keyword. You also must declare the component before using it in the `setConstraints` method. Usually the next statement after the `setConstraints` method is to add the component to the applet.

The setConstraints Method—Example

```
gridbag.setConstraints(txtDept, constraints);
add(txtDept);
```

Each time you use the `setConstraints` method, you assign the current data member values of the constraints object to the component. So if you want to make a setting for all components, you can set the data member once and apply it to all components. For example, this code makes two components aligned left:

```
//Set constraints once and apply to two text fields
constraints.anchor = GridBagConstraints.WEST; //Align at left of display area
gridbag.setConstraints(txtDept, constraints);
add(txtDept);
gridbag.setConstraints(txtSales, constraints);
add(txtSales);
```

Precisely Placing Components

You can place components in any cell of the grid, in any order. Use gridx to set the column and gridy to set the row; both are zero based (see Figure 3.7). Note that the grid lines do not appear on the interface; the lines are to help you visualize the layout.

F i g u r e   3 . 7

gridx = 0; gridy = 0	gridx = 1; gridy = 0	gridx =2; gridy = 0
gridx = 0; gridy = 1	gridx = 1; gridy = 1	gridx = 2; gridy = 1
gridx = 0; gridy = 2	gridx = 1; gridy = 2	gridx = 2; gridy = 2

Refer to each cell of the GridBagLayout using gridx and gridy coordinates.

This code places a label component in the second column (gridx = 1) and first row (gridy = 0):

```
constraints.gridx = 1;    //Set column
constraints.gridy = 0;    //Set row
gridbag.setConstraints(lblDept, constraints);  //Assign constraints to component
add(lblDept);             //Add component to applet
```

Setting the Alignment of Components within Cells

Use the **anchor** constraint to set the alignment of a component that is smaller than its display area. You can set the anchor to one of these constants: NORTH,

SOUTH, EAST, WEST, NORTHWEST, NORTHEAST, SOUTHWEST, SOUTHEAST, or CENTER. The default alignment is CENTER. Note that setting an anchor has no effect if the component fills its cell (its display area).

This example has only two components—the label is right-aligned and the text field is left-aligned. The GridBagLayout is automatically centered within the panel. The height and width of the single row is determined by the height and width of the applet panel, as set in the HTML. Figure 3.8 shows the layout.

Figure 3.8

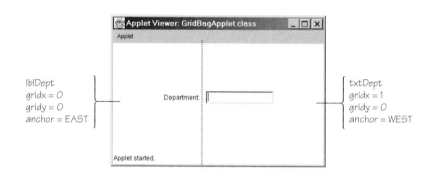

Set the anchor constraint data member to EAST or WEST to align the component right or left.

```
//Row 1 Label
constraints.gridx = 0; //Set cell position
constraints.gridy = 0;
constraints.anchor = GridBagConstraints.EAST;
gridbag.setConstraints(lblDept, constraints);
add(lblDept);

//Row 1 TextField
constraints.gridx = 1; //Column 1 (still row 0)
constraints.anchor = GridBagConstraints.WEST;
gridbag.setConstraints(txtDept, constraints);
add(txtDept);
```

Setting Insets

To control the spacing between components use an **Insets** object. You can specify the number of pixels to add as padding between a component and the edge of its cell. The arguments for the Insets constructor represent integer values for the pixel spacing for top, left, bottom, and right, in that order. This statement insets a component five pixels from the edge of the cell on all four sides:

```
constraints.insets = new Insets(5, 5, 5, 5);
```

The GridBagLayout Phone List Example

The following code adds the GridBagLayout to the phone list project from Chapter 2. Notice the alignment of the labels and text fields, which you can see in Figure 3.10. Also notice the new method, called DesignLayout. Creating a new method is discussed in the "Creating Your Own Methods" section later in this chapter.

Figure 3.9 shows a planning sketch and Figure 3.10 shows the program output.

Tip

If you encounter difficulty with smaller text fields, try reducing the size of your Inset values.

Figure 3.9

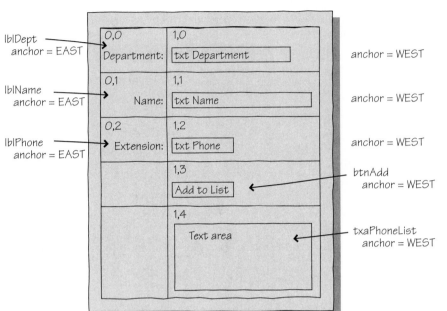

*Plan the GridBagLayout by
drawing a sketch and filling in
the necessary constraints.*

Figure 3.10

*Use a GridBagLayout and x, y
coordinates to place the
components for the phone list
applet.*

```
//Folder:        Ch3GridBagAddress1
//Programmer:    Bradley/Millspaugh
//Date:          6/2001
//ClassName:     GridBagLayoutDemo
//Description:   Use a GridBagLayout for a phone list.
//               Modifies the applet from Ch2Buttons to use a GridBagLayout.

import java.applet.*;
import java.awt.*;
import java.awt.event.*;
```

```
public class GridBagLayoutDemo extends Applet implements ActionListener
{
    //Declare components
    Label lblDept = new Label("Department:");
    Label lblName = new Label("Name:");
    Label lblPhone = new Label("Extension:");
    TextField txtDept = new TextField(15);
    TextField txtName = new TextField(25);
    TextField txtPhone = new TextField(5);
    TextArea txaPhoneList = new TextArea(10, 30);
    Button btnAdd = new Button("Add to List");

        //Declare variables
        String strDept;
        String strName;
        String strPhone;

    public void init ()
        {
        DesignLayout();        //Place components on applet
        txtDept.requestFocus()
        btnAdd.addActionListener(this);
        txtDept.addActionListener(this);
        txtName.addActionListener(this);
        txtPhone.addActionListener(this);
        }

    public void DesignLayout()
    {
        //Set the layout manager
        GridBagLayout gridbag = new GridBagLayout();
        GridBagConstraints constraints = new GridBagConstraints();
        setLayout(gridbag);
        constraints.insets = new Insets(5, 5, 5, 5);//Padding around components

    //Row 1 Label
        constraints.gridx = 0;
        constraints.gridy = 0;             //Column 0, row 0
        constraints.anchor = GridBagConstraints.EAST;
        gridbag.setConstraints(lblDept, constraints);
        add(lblDept);

    //Row 1 TextField
        constraints.gridx = 1;             //Column 1; still row 0
        constraints.anchor = GridBagConstraints.WEST;
        gridbag.setConstraints(txtDept, constraints);
        add(txtDept);

    //Row 2 Label
        constraints.gridy = 1;
        constraints.gridx = 0;             //Column 0, row 1
        constraints.anchor = GridBagConstraints.EAST;
        gridbag.setConstraints(lblName, constraints);
        add(lblName);

    //Row 2 TextField
        constraints.gridx = 1;             //Column 1, still row 1
        constraints.anchor = GridBagConstraints.WEST;
```

```
        gridbag.setConstraints(txtName, constraints);
        add(txtName);

        //Row 3 Label
        constraints.gridx = 0;
        constraints.gridy = 2;              //Column 0, row 2
        constraints.anchor = GridBagConstraints.EAST;
        gridbag.setConstraints(lblPhone, constraints);
        add (lblPhone);

    //Row 3 TextField
        constraints.gridx = 1;              //Column 1, still row 2
        constraints.anchor = GridBagConstraints.WEST;
        gridbag.setConstraints(txtPhone, constraints);
        add(txtPhone);

    //Row 4 Button
        constraints.gridy = 3;              //Column 1, row 3
        gridbag.setConstraints(btnAdd, constraints);
        add(btnAdd);

    //Row 5 TextArea
        constraints.gridy = 4;              //Column 1, row 4
        gridbag.setConstraints(txaPhoneList, constraints);
        add(txaPhoneList);
    }

    public void actionPerformed(ActionEvent p1)
    {
        //Actions for "Add to List"
        String strOutputLine;

        strDept = txtDept.getText();
        strName = txtName.getText();
        strPhone = txtPhone.getText();
        strOutputLine = strDept + "\t" + strName + "\t" + strPhone;

        txaPhoneList.append(strOutputLine + "\n");
        txtDept.setText("");
        txtName.setText("");
        txtPhone.setText("");
        txtDept.requestFocus();
    }
}
```

Using Relative Placement

You can specify relative placement and relative size for components, rather than precise grid coordinates. Using this technique, you set the gridwidth constraint to RELATIVE, which places a component in the next cell. To finish off one row and make the next component appear in the following row, set the gridwidth constraint to REMAINDER, which makes the cell fill the remainder of the row. The following code segment adds 6 buttons to a GridBagLayout using relative placement. The output appears in Figure 3.11, the complete applet appears in Ch3GridBagButtons1.

Figure 3.11

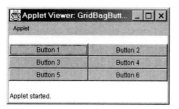

A demonstration grid bag layout with six buttons set to fill their display area.

Tip

For best results, do not mix absolute placement and relative placement.

```
public void DesignLayout()
{
    //Set the layout manager
    GridBagLayout gridbag = new GridBagLayout();
    GridBagConstraints constraints = new GridBagConstraints();
    setLayout(gridbag);
    constraints.fill = GridBagConstraints.BOTH;

    //Button 1; Start first row
    constraints.weightx = 1.0;      //Relative size of the columns
    gridbag.setConstraints(btn1, constraints);
    add(btn1);

    //Button 2; Finish first row
    constraints.gridwidth = GridBagConstraints.REMAINDER;
    gridbag.setConstraints(btn2, constraints);
    add(btn2);

    //Button 3; Start second row
    constraints.gridwidth = GridBagConstraints.RELATIVE;
    gridbag.setConstraints(btn3, constraints);
    add(btn3);

    //Button 4; Finish second row
    constraints.gridwidth = GridBagConstraints.REMAINDER;
    gridbag.setConstraints(btn4, constraints);
    add(btn4);

    //Button 5; Start third row
    constraints.gridwidth = GridBagConstraints.RELATIVE;
    gridbag.setConstraints(btn5, constraints);
    add(btn5);

    //Button 6; Finish third row
    constraints.gridwidth = GridBagConstraints.REMAINDER;
    gridbag.setConstraints(btn6, constraints);
    add(btn6);
}
```

Setting the Relative Width of Columns

You can use the weightx data member to set the relative widths of columns. You should set the column width once for each column, usually in the first row in the grid, and then use 0 for the weightx argument for all following rows. (If you forget to set weightx to 0, the last setting you used will apply to all cells after that point.)

You can use relative weights for the cells, such as making column 1 relative weight of 1 and column 2 relative weight of 3 (column 2 should be 3 times as wide as column 1). Sometimes it makes more sense to use percentages, so you might make column 1 relative weight of 25 and column 2 relative weight of 75. It doesn't really matter which way you set the weight; the layout manager adds the numbers you use and assigns the correct proportion to each cell.

In this code, column 1 has a relative size of 1; column 2 has a relative size of 3. This should make column 2 three times as large as column 1. You could get the same result by setting weightx = 25 for column 1 and weightx = 75 for column 2. Figure 3.12 shows the output for the program; the complete code is in Ch3GridBagButtons2.

Figure 3.12

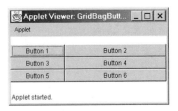

Adjust the grid column widths by setting the weightx constraint.

```
//Button 1; Start first row
constraints.weightx = 1; //Relative size of column 1
gridbag.setConstraints(btn1, constraints);
add(btn1);

//Button 2; Finish first row
constraints.weightx = 3; //Relative size of column 2
constraints.gridwidth = GridBagConstraints.REMAINDER;
gridbag.setConstraints(btn2, constraints);
add(btn2);

//Button 3; Start second row
constraints.weightx = 0; //Column widths already set by Button 1
constraints.gridwidth = GridBagConstraints.RELATIVE;
gridbag.setConstraints(btn3, constraints);
add(btn3);
```

Note: The rest of the code for Figure 3.12 is unchanged from Figure 3.11.

Controlling Placement Size, and Alignment

You will want to experiment with GridBagLayout constraints to achieve your best output. See Table 3.1 for more possibilities. Notice that you can make a component use more than one cell by setting the gridwidth and gridheight data members.

```
constraints.gridwidth 2;   //Join two cells horizontally
constraints.gridheight 2;  //Join two cells vertically
```

When you use any of the constants shown in the table, you must name the class to which it belongs (GridBagConstraints). For example, to set the fill to BOTH, you must use GridBagConstraints.BOTH.

Table 3.1

GridBagConstraint Data Members

Data Members (variables)	Value	Purpose
gridx	integer RELATIVE(default)	The grid column to place the component; first column is 0. Upper-left cell for a multicell component. Default RELATIVE specifies column to the right of last component placed.

Examples:	`constraints.gridx = GridBagConstraints.RELATIVE;//Next column`
	`constraints.gridx = 1;//Column two`	

gridy	integer RELATIVE(default)	The grid row to place the component; first row is 0. Upper-left cell for a multicell component. Default RELATIVE specifies row below last component placed.
Examples:	`constraints.gridy = GridBagConstraints.RELATIVE;` `constraints.gridy = 0;//Row one`	
gridwidth	integer Default value is 1.	Number of cells in the same row the component will use. To make this component the last in the row, use REMAINDER.

Examples:	`constraints.gridwidth = GridBagConstraints.REMAINDER;//Last cell in row`
	`constraints.gridwidth = 2;//Component uses two cells`	

gridheight	integer Default value is 1.	Number of cells in the same column the component will use. To make this component the last in the column, use REMAINDER.

Examples:	`constraints.gridheigth = GridBagConstraints.REMAINDER;//Last in column`
	`constraints.gridheigth = 2;//Component uses two cells in column`	

fill	NONE (default) HORIZONTAL VERTICAL BOTH	Resizing rules for a component smaller than its display area; HORIZONTAL makes component as wide as the display area; VERTICAL, as tall; BOTH expands it vertically and horizontally.

Examples:	`constraints.fill = GridBagConstraints.BOTH;//Fill cell height & width`
	`constraints.fill = GridBagConstraints.HORIZONTAL;//Fill cell width`	

anchor	CENTER (default) NORTH SOUTH EAST WEST NORTHWEST NORTHEAST SOUTHWEST SOUTHEAST	Alignment of component within display area.

Examples:	`constraints.anchor = GridBagConstraints.WEST;//Align component left`
	`constraints.anchor = GridBagConstraints.EAST;//Align component right`	

continued

Table 3.1

continued

Data Members (variables)	Value	Purpose
weightx	integer Default value is 0.	Determines relative width of grid column. Set weightx for one component in a column to set the relative width of the entire column. A weightx of 1 for each column makes the cells equal in width. You can use relative sizes, such as 2 or 3, or make all widths percentages. The default, 0, places all extra space at the beginning and ending of the row.

Examples:	`constraints.weightx = 1;//Relative weight`
	`constraints.weightx = 3;//Relative weight-3 times larger than 1`
	`constraints.weightx = 20;//Make this column 20% of total width of 100`
	`constraints.weightx = 80;//Make this column 80% of total width of 100`	

weighty	integer Default value is 0.	Determines relative height of grid row. Set weighty for one component in a row to set the relative height of the entire row. A weighty of 1 for each row makes the cells equal in height. You can use relative sizes, such as 2 or 3, or make all heights percentages. The default, 0, places all extra space at the beginning and ending of the column.

Examples:	`constraints.weighty = 3;//Relative weight-3 times taller than 1`
	`constraints.weighty = 20;//Make this row 20% of total height of grid of 100`
	`constraints.weighty = 80;//Make this row 80% of total height of grid of 100`	

insets	An instance of the Insets class. Default is 0,0,0,0	Sets distance in pixels from edge of display area (cell) to edge of component. Creates a blank space around the component. Includes separate values for top, left, bottom, and right.
Example:	`constraints.insets = new Insets(5, 5, 5, 5);//Padding around components`	
ipadx	integer Default value is 0.	Number of pixels to add to the width of a component on both the left and right. Will increase the component width by twice the setting, since the pixels are added on both ends.
Example:	`constraints.ipadx = 2;//Increase component width by 2 pixels on each end`	
ipady	integer Default value is 0.	Number of pixels to add to the height of a component on both the top and bottom. Will increase the component height by twice the setting, since the pixels are added on both ends.
Example:	`constraints.ipady = 2;//Increase component height by 2 pixels on top and bottom`	

Planning a GridBagLayout

It helps to draw a sketch when you plan a user interface using a GridBagLayout (see Figure 3.9). Draw a grid with the maximum number of rows and columns that you might need and then sketch the components in the cells. Remember that you can make a component take more than one cell horizontally and/or vertically. And you can make a component fill its display area, or set it to remain a fixed size and set its alignment within the display area. Also remember that the largest component determines the size for a column or row.

Creating Your Own Methods

Did you notice the `DesignLayout` method in the preceding applet? Although you could write all of the code to lay out the applet's user interface (UI) in the `init` method, it's better to organize a program by function. You can group the statements that perform a program function into a new method and call that method from the appropriate location.

To create a new method, write the statements

```
public void MethodName()
{
 //Statements in new method
}
```

Of course, you will substitute your own name for `MethodName`. Make sure to select a meaningful name—preferably a verb and an object, such as `DesignLayout`, `CalculatePay`, `SetUpScreen`, or `HandleError`.

You can call the new method from somewhere else in the program by specifying the method name:

```
MethodName();
```

Look back at the previous program listing (Ch3GridBagAddress1). The `init` method has a call to `DesignLayout`, and the `DesignLayout` method appears later in the program. When Java is executing the `init` method and comes to the `DesignLayout()`; statement, it jumps down to that method and executes the block of code inside the method. When it completes the statements in the `DesignLayout` method, Java transfers control back to the `init` method, to the statement immediately following the call to `DesignLayout` (in this case, the `txtDept.requestFocus` statement).

In Chapter 5 you will learn lots more about creating your own methods, including the meaning of the terms `public` and `void` and the empty parentheses. In fact, you will substitute other values for those terms as needed. At this point you can just write the statements as given, or look ahead if you are curious.

Creating a Method for the GridBagLayout Constraints

When you have a line or a few lines of code that must be repeated often, that's a good candidate for a separate method. In the preceding GridBagLayout program, you must execute the `setConstraints` method many times. You might want to create a method that sets the constraints and then call the method each time it is needed. However, to do so, you must pass arguments to the method. Passing arguments is covered in Chapter 5, so we'll leave that exercise for later.

Feedback 3.2

Draw a planning sketch and determine the constraints for the components in this user interface. Use a grid of four rows and four columns. Specify the constraints for these components:

   (a) txtDescription
   (b) txtPartNumber

(c) txtVendorCode
(d) lblDescription
(e) lblPartNumber
(f) lblVendorCode
(g) btnOK

Product Description:	
Part Number: [ ]	Vendor Code: [ ]

[OK]

The CardLayout Manager

The **CardLayout** is another flexible layout manager. It allows you to create multiple layouts on different "cards" and then arrange the cards as you want. You can think of the user interface as multiple cards stacked on top of each other. Place any card on the top to display it. The CardLayout manager contains methods for next(), previous(), first(), last(), and show(). With the show() method you can select a specific card to display.

Using Panels

For the greatest flexibility in laying out a user interface, you can use multiple **Panel** objects. Each Panel is a container, which you can set to any layout manager. So you can use a grid for one panel, a different grid or a border layout for another panel, and a grid bag layout for another, if you wish.

To display a panel on your applet, you must declare a new instance of a Panel class. Then set the layout manager, specify the components, and add the panel to the applet:

```
//Declare a new Panel object
Panel pnlDisplay = new Panel();
//Assign a layout manager to the panel
pnlDisplay.setLayout(new GridLayout(1, 2));
//Add components to the panel
pnlDisplay.add(new Label("Name: "));
pnlDisplay.add(txtName);
//Add the panel to the applet
add(pnlDisplay);
```

Note: Did you notice that the form of the setLayout and add methods changed for this example? In all previous programs and in the last line of this one, no object is specified. When you don't specify the object, Java assumes the current class (the applet). Therefore, the statements

```
setLayout(new GridLayout(1, 2));
```

and

```
add(new Label("Department:"));
```

actually are interpreted to mean

```
this.setLayout(new GridLayout(1, 2));
```

and

```
this.add(new Label("Department:"));
```

If you want to set a layout manager for a panel and add a component to the panel, you must specify the object:

```
pnlDisplay.setLayout(new GridLayout(1, 2));
pnlDisplay.add(new Label("Name: "));
```

The following applet modifies the Chapter 2 phone list applet to use two panels with different layout managers (Figure 3.13). An Input panel uses the GridLayout and an Output panel uses the BorderLayout manager. Be sure to notice the new methods, which aid in program organization. The layout for each panel is in its own method.

Figure 3.13

This applet uses two panels. The upper panel uses a grid layout and the lower panel uses a border layout.

```
//Folder            Ch3Panels
//Programmer:       Bradley/Millspaugh
//Date:             6/2001
//Description:      Use panels with layout managers to input department,
// name, and extension. Display a phone list in a text area.

import java.applet.*;
import java.awt.*;
import java.awt.event.*;

public class Ch3Layout extends Applet implements ActionListener
{
    //Declare components
    //Use Panels for multiple layout managers
    Panel pnlInput = new Panel();
    Panel pnlOutput = new Panel();
    TextField txtDept = new TextField(15);
    TextField txtName = new TextField(25);
    TextField txtPhone = new TextField(5);
```

```java
TextArea txaPhoneList = new TextArea(10, 30);
Button btnAdd = new Button("Add to List");

//Declare variables
String strDept;
String strName;
String strPhone;

public void init()
{
    //Create the user interface
    DesignInputPanel();
    DesignOutputPanel();
    add(pnlInput);
    add(pnlOutput);
    txtDept.requestFocus();
    btnAdd.addActionListener(this);
}

public void actionPerformed(ActionEvent p1)
{
    //Actions for "Add to List"
    String strOutputLine;

    strDept = txtDept.getText();
    strName = txtName.getText();
    strPhone = txtPhone.getText();
    strOutputLine = strDept + "\t" + strName + "\t" + strPhone;

    txaPhoneList.append(strOutputLine + "\n");
    txtDept.setText("");
    txtName.setText("");
    txtPhone.setText("");
}

public void DesignInputPanel()
{
    //Lay out the input panel
    pnlInput.setLayout(new GridLayout(3, 2, 4, 4));
    pnlInput.add(new Label("Department: "));
    pnlInput.add(txtDept);
    pnlInput.add(new Label("Name: "));
    pnlInput.add(txtName);
    pnlInput.add(new Label("Extension: "));
    pnlInput.add(txtPhone);
}

public void DesignOutputPanel()
{
    //Lay out the output panel
    pnlOutput.setLayout(new BorderLayout(4, 4));
    pnlOutput.add("North", btnAdd);
    pnlOutput.add("Center", txaPhoneList);
}
}
```

Using No Layout Manager

It isn't absolutely necessary to use a layout manager. You can turn off the default FlowLayout manager and place components precisely by specifying the actual pixel locations. Doing so gives up the great advantage of Java that allows programs to run on any system. If you know that all systems that will run your program have the same screen size and resolution, you may want to try this.

Turn off the default FlowLayout by setting the layout manager to null. Then use the setBounds method for each component to set its location, width, and height, all in pixels.

The setBounds Method—General Format

```
component.setBounds(int x, int y, int width, int height);
```

The setBounds Method—Example

```
lblDept.setBounds(10, 10, 100, 30);
```

Here is the phone list example using the null layout manager. This example was tested only on a PC running Windows with the resolution set to 1024 × 768. It likely won't look the same with any other settings. Figure 3.14 shows the output on this system.

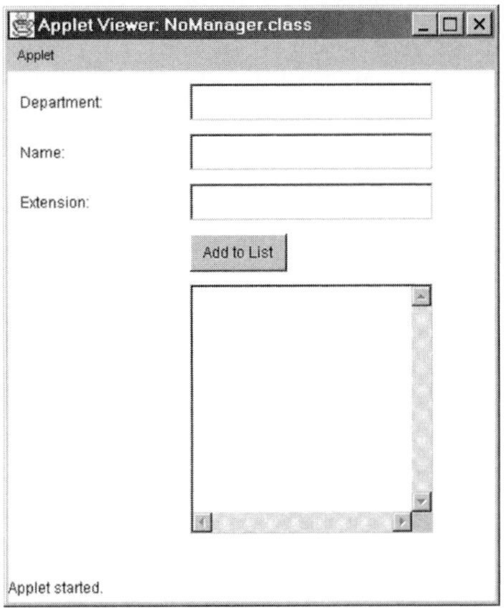

Figure 3.14

Using the null layout manager and the setBounds method, you can precisely place and size components. However, the program will no longer be portable to other systems.

```
public void DesignLayout()
{
   //Turn off the default layout manager
   setLayout(null);

   //Row 1 - Dept
   lblDept.setBounds(10, 10, 100, 30);
   add(lblDept);
   txtDept.setBounds(150, 10, 200, 30);
   add(txtDept);
```

```
//Row 2 - Name
lblName.setBounds(10, 50, 100, 30);
add(lblName);
txtName.setBounds(150, 50, 200, 30);
add(txtName);

//Row 3 - Phone
lblPhone.setBounds(10, 90, 100, 30);
add(lblPhone);
txtPhone.setBounds(150, 90, 200, 30);
add(txtPhone);

//Row 4 - Button
btnAdd.setBounds(150, 130, 80, 30);
add(btnAdd);

//Row 5 - Phone List
txaPhoneList.setBounds(150, 170, 200, 200);
add(txaPhoneList);
}
```

Your Hands-on Programming Example

Rewrite the applet from the Chapter 2 programming example using a grid bag layout. Use prompts and text fields to allow the user to enter a department name, employee name, and phone extension. A button that reads "Add to List" adds a line of output to the phone list, clears the text fields, and sets the focus to the first text field.

Figure 3.15 shows a planning sketch and Figure 3.16 shows the user interface.

Figure 3.15

Plan the user interface by drawing a grid to use for the GridBagLayout.

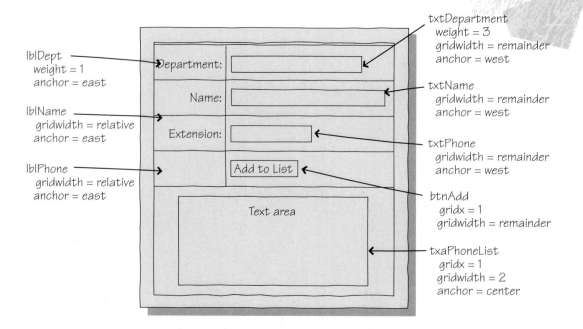

Figure   3.16

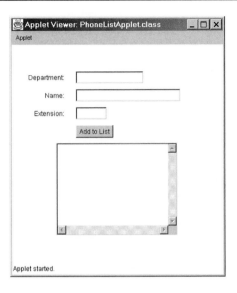

The solution to the hands-on programming example. This was created using a grid bag layout and constraints.

Planning the Project

Plan the Objects and Properties

Class: PhoneListApplet

Figure 3.17 shows the class diagram.

Figure   3.17

Class: PhoneListApplet	
Methods	**Variables and Components**
init	strDept
actionPerformed	strName
DesignInputPanel	strPhone
DesignOutputPanel	txtDept
	txtName
	txtPhone
	btnAdd
	txaPhoneList
	pnlInput
	pnlOutput

The class diagram for the chapter hands-on example.

Properties:

Access Mode (public or private)	Variable or Component Name	Data Type or Class	Description
	lblDept	Label	"Department" prompt
	lblName	Label	"Name" prompt
	lblPhone	Label	"Phone" prompt

continued

Access Mode (public or private)	Variable or Component Name	Data Type or Class	Description
	txtDept	TextField	Input the department.
	strDept	String	Store the department.
	txtName	TextField	Input the name.
	strName	String	Store the name.
	txtPhone	TextField	Input the phone extension.
	strPhone	String	Store the phone extension.
	btnAdd	Button	Add to phone list and clear fields.
	txaPhoneList	TextArea	Display holds a list of names and phone numbers.

Methods:

Access Mode (public or private)	Return Type	Method Name (include any parameters)	Pseudocode
public	void	init	Set up the user interface. Add the controls. Add action listeners. Set the focus in first text field.
public	void	actionPerformed	Transfer data from text boxes. Concatenate the data. Append line to text area. Clear text fields. Set the focus in first text field.
public	void	DesignInputPanel	Set the layout manager and add components for the input panel.
public	void	DesignOutputPanel	Set the layout manager and add components for the output panel.

Write the Project

- Follow the plan to add containers, layouts, and components to the class.
- Write the appropriate statements in the `init` method of the class to add the panels and set the focus.

- Code remaining methods.
- When you complete the code, thoroughly test the project.

The Project Solution

```
//Folder:         Ch3HandsOn
//Programmer:     Bradley/Millspaugh
//Date:           6/2001
//ClassName:      PhoneListApplet
//Description:    Create a phone list using a GridBagLayout.

import java.applet.*;
import java.awt.*;
import java.awt.event.*;

public class PhoneListApplet extends Applet implements ActionListener
{
    //Declare components
    Label lblDept = new Label("Department:");
    Label lblName = new Label("Name:");
    Label lblPhone = new Label("Extension:");
    TextField txtDept = new TextField(15);
    TextField txtName = new TextField(25);
    TextField txtPhone = new TextField(5);
    TextArea txaPhoneList = new TextArea(10, 30);
    Button btnAdd = new Button("Add to List");

    //Declare variables
    String strDept;
    String strName;
    String strPhone;

    public void init ()
    {
        DesignLayout();      //Place components on applet
        txtDept.requestFocus();
        btnAdd.addActionListener(this);
        txtDept.addActionListener(this);
        txtName.addActionListener(this);
        txtPhone.addActionListener(this);
    }

    public void DesignLayout()
    {
    //Set the layout manager
    GridBagLayout gridbag = new GridBagLayout();
    GridBagConstraints constraints = new GridBagConstraints();
    setLayout(gridbag);
    constraints.insets = new Insets(5, 5, 5, 5);//Padding around components

    //Row 1 Label
    constraints.weightx = 1.0;     //Relative size of column 1
    constraints.anchor = GridBagConstraints.EAST;
    constraints.fill = GridBagConstraints.NONE;
    gridbag.setConstraints(lblDept, constraints);
    add(lblDept);
```

```java
        //Row 1 TextField
        constraints.weightx = 3.0; //Relative size of column 2
        constraints.gridwidth = GridBagConstraints.REMAINDER;
        constraints.anchor = GridBagConstraints.WEST;
        gridbag.setConstraints(txtDept, constraints);
        add(txtDept);

        //Row 2 Label
        constraints.weightx = 0;    //Column width already set
        constraints.gridwidth = GridBagConstraints.RELATIVE;
        constraints.anchor = GridBagConstraints.EAST;
        gridbag.setConstraints(lblName, constraints);
        add(lblName);

        //Row 2 TextField
        constraints.gridwidth = GridBagConstraints.REMAINDER;
        constraints.anchor = GridBagConstraints.WEST;
        gridbag.setConstraints(txtName, constraints);
        add(txtName);

        //Row 3 Label
        constraints.gridwidth = GridBagConstraints.RELATIVE;
        constraints.anchor = GridBagConstraints.EAST;
        gridbag.setConstraints(lblPhone, constraints);
        add(lblPhone);

        //Row 3 TextField
        constraints.gridwidth = GridBagConstraints.REMAINDER;
        constraints.anchor = GridBagConstraints.WEST;
        gridbag.setConstraints(txtPhone, constraints);
        add(txtPhone);

        //Row 4 Button
        constraints.gridwidth = GridBagConstraints.REMAINDER;
        constraints.gridx = 1;      //Place button in second column
        gridbag.setConstraints(btnAdd, constraints);
        add(btnAdd);

        //Row 5 TextArea
        constraints.gridx = 0;      //Begin in first column
        constraints.gridwidth = 2; //Join two cells
        constraints.anchor = GridBagConstraints.CENTER; //Center in display area
        gridbag.setConstraints(txaPhoneList, constraints);
        add(txaPhoneList);
    }

public void actionPerformed(ActionEvent p1)
{
    //Actions for "Add to List"
    String strOutputLine;

    strDept = txtDept.getText();
    strName = txtName.getText();
    strPhone = txtPhone.getText();
    strOutputLine = strDept + "\t" + strName + "\t" + strPhone;

    txaPhoneList.append(strOutputLine + "\n");
    txtDept.setText("");
    txtName.setText("");
```

```
        txtPhone.setText("");
        txtDept.requestFocus();
    }
}
```

S u m m a r y

1. You can lay out the user interface using a layout manager, which adjusts the screen layout for the system on which the program runs.
2. Using the default layout manager, FlowLayout, components are sequenced according to the order of the add methods.
3. Use the setLayout method to assign a layout manager to an applet.
4. GridLayout allows you to specify the number of rows and columns of a grid. All components that you place on the grid are the same size.
5. BorderLayout creates sections called *North*, *South*, *East*, *West*, and *Center*. You can add one component to each of the named sections.
6. GridBagLayout allows a grid with components of varying sizes. GridBagConstraints specifies the position, size, and alignment of individual components. An inset determines the gap between components.
7. You can improve the organization of a program by grouping related statements into a new method and calling the method as needed.
8. A CardLayout may have several different "cards" that display one at a time.
9. You can add new panels to an applet. Panels are containers that may each use a different layout manager.
10. You can use a null layout manager and specify exact pixel locations and sizes for components, at the cost of making your program nontransportable.

K e y   T e r m s

anchor *70*
BorderLayout *66*
CardLayout *80*
container *62*
display area *68*
FlowLayout *63*
GridBagConstraints *68*

GridBagLayout *68*
GridLayout *63*
Insets *71*
layout manager *62*
Panel *80*
setLayout method *62*

R e v i e w   Q u e s t i o n s

1. What is the default layout when no layout manager is specified?
2. If you want to create a table appearance with each component of the same size in rows and columns, what would be the appropriate layout manager?
3. Name the sections available in a BorderLayout.

4. What is the purpose of the horizontal and vertical gap parameters?
5. How would you add a component to the top section of a border layout?
6. Explain each of the following GridBagConstraints data members:
   (a) gridx
   (b) gridheight
   (c) weightx
   (d) fill
   (e) anchor
7. Discuss the purpose of the REMAINDER and RELATIVE constants. What is the difference between using gridx versus gridheight?
8. What is the default alignment within a cell of a GridBagLayout?
9. Why would you want to use Panels?

Programming Exercises

3.1 Modify your Chapter 2 project to use an appropriate layout manager.
3.2 Create a project that generates a task list. The input fields are for task, responsible party, and deadline date. Use text areas to generate a list of the tasks. Use an appropriate layout manager.
3.3 Code a project for a potluck party. The input fields allow the user to enter the name of the person and the dish he or she plans to bring. A text area displays the names and the dishes. Include an add button that adds to the list and clears the text fields.

   Use at least two panels for the layout: one for the input fields and prompts and another one for the text area and the command button.

CASE STUDIES

R 'n R—for Reading and Refreshment

Design a layout for entering customer information. You may use panels and/or a GridBagLayout. The data entry fields are Last Name, First Name, Street, City, State, Zip Code, Phone Number, and E-mail address. Include an add button that displays the information concatenated in a text area and clears the text fields.

Display the company name across the top of the input area in a label; define a font for the label.

Merry Pea's Quilting

Design a layout for entering customer information. You may use panels and/or a GridBagLayout. The data entry fields are Last Name, First Name, Street, City, State, Zip Code, Phone Number, and E-mail address. Include an add button that displays the information concatenated in a text area and clears the text fields.

Display the company name across the top of the input area in a label; define a font for the label.

4

Performing Calculations and Formatting Numbers

At the completion of this chapter, you will be able to . . .

1. Perform calculations using the arithmetic operators.

2. Calculate and assign the result using the assignment operators.

3. Add and subtract using the increment and decrement operators.

4. Perform multiple calculations correctly based on the precedence of operators.

5. Retrieve string data from the screen and convert to numeric for calculations.

6. Convert between data types both implicitly and explicitly.

7. Find the formatting rules for the locale where an applet is run.

8. Format output for currency, percent, or decimal numbers.

9. Catch input and calculation errors by using exception handling.

10. Declare variables based on the numeric wrapper classes and perform operations using the methods of the classes.

In Chapter 2 you learned to declare and use variables and constants. In this chapter you will learn to perform calculations with variables and constants, convert data from one data type to another, and use the wrapper data classes for converting and storing data. You will learn to calculate and manipulate data using several Java operators and to format output using the formatting style for the locale in which the applet is executed.

Calculation Operators

Java has several types of operators available. The **arithmetic operators** perform basic calculations; the assignment operators and the increment/decrement operators also can perform calculations but use a shortcut notation.

Arithmetic Operators

You can perform basic calculations on primitive variables and constants with arithmetic operators: addition ($+$), subtraction ($-$), multiplication ($*$), division ($/$), and modulus ($\%$) (Table 4.1).

T a b l e   4 . 1

Arithmetic Operators

Arithmetic Operator	Purpose
+	Addition
−	Subtraction
*	Multiplication
/	Division
%	Modulus (remainder)

You generally perform a calculation in an expression on the right side of an equal sign. Java calculates the result and assigns it to the variable named on the left of the equal sign. It's important to remember that the equal sign in Java does not mean equality, such as in a math equation. Instead, the equal sign means assignment. Some people prefer to read the equal sign as "becomes" or "let the variable be replaced by." So you can read the Java statement

```
intCount = intCount + 1;
```

as "intCount becomes intCount plus one," or "Let intCount be replaced by int-Count plus one." You also can say "Assign the value intCount plus one to int-Count."

```
fltTax = fltTotalSale * fltTaxRate;
fltTotalPayroll = fltTotalPayroll + fltPay;
intCountDown = intCountDown - 1;
fltAverage = fltSum / intCount;
```

Java is more strict about data types than most programming languages. If you perform calculations with floating-point values, you get a floating-point result. If you calculate using integers, the result is an integer. And if you use mixed types, as in the previous example (fltSum / intCount), you must be careful. In this case, Java converts the value in intCount to a floating-point value (called a *promotion*) and produces a floating-point result. Later in this chapter you will see more examples of mixed types and learn to convert from one data type to another.

When you divide 3 by 2 using floating-point data types, the result is 1.5. If you use integer fields, the result is 1. Since an integer cannot hold fractional values, Java truncates (chops off) the result to produce an integer; it does not round the result. Therefore, when you divide 2 by 3, the floating point result is 0.6666666; an integer calculation produces zero.

Modulus

The one Java operator you may not be familiar with is the **modulus.** Modulus is the remainder of a division operation.

When you divide one value by another, often you are looking for a decimal result. You can just use the division operator and floating point variables. However, many times you need to know the actual remainder from a division operation.

A good example comes when you convert data that use a base other than 10, such as hours and minutes. If you want to convert 90 minutes into hours, a division operation results in a decimal answer of 1.5 but you may want one hour and 30 minutes.

```
intHours = intMinutes / 60;
```

Assuming that intMinutes contains 90, the previous calculation assigns an integer value of 1 to intHours. (The calculation does not affect the value stored in intMinutes.) You can retrieve the remainder of the calculation by using the modulus operator:

```
intMinutes = intMinutes % 60;
```

The modulus operation divides 90 by 60 and stores the remainder of 30 in the variable intMinutes.

The Order of Arithmetic Operations

The order in which operations are performed determines the result. Consider the expression 3 + 4 * 2. What is the result? If the addition is done first, the result is 14. However, if the multiplication is done first, the result is 11.

Java follows normal math hierarchy of operations, called the **precedence.** Operations inside of parentheses are performed first. Multiplication, division, and modulus operations are then calculated from left to right in the calculation expression. Finally, addition and subtraction operations are done, proceeding from left to right.

In the previous example, the multiplication is done before addition and the result is 11. To change the order of evaluation, use parentheses:

(3 + 4) * 2

which will yield 14 as the result. One set of parentheses may be used inside another set. In that case, the parentheses are said to be *nested*.

Calculation Expression	Result
(6 + 5) * 4	44
6 + 5 * 4	26
6 + 5 * 4 / 2	16
6 + 5 * 4 / 2 − 1	15
(6 + (5 * 4)) / (2 − 1)	26
((6 + 5) * 4) / 2 − 1	21

You can always use extra parentheses for clarity. The expressions

```
2 * fltCost * fltRate
```

and

```
(2 * fltCost) * fltRate
```

are equivalent, but the second may be easier to understand.

Arithmetic expressions are evaluated in this order:

1. Operations within parentheses. If parentheses are nested, operations within
   the inner parentheses are evaluated first. Multiple operations within a set
   of parentheses are performed according to the rules of precedence.
2. All multiplication and division. Multiple operations are performed from left
   to right.
3. All addition and subtraction are performed from left to right.

Exponentiation

There is no operator for **exponentiation** in Java. If you wish to raise a number
to a power, you can either write the expression using multiplication or use the
`pow` method, which is found in the java.math package.

Squaring a Number

When you want to square a number, you can multiply the number by itself,
as in

```
intYearsSquared = intYears * intYears;
```

or you can use the `pow` method. Note that the `pow` method requires double-pre-
cision, floating-point arguments.

```
dblYearsSquared = Math.pow(dblYears, 2.0);
```

The pow Method—General Format

```
Math.pow(double Number, double Power)
```

The pow Method—Example

```
dblFiveSquared = Math.pow(5.0, 2.0);
```

You will find the pow method most helpful when you need to raise a number to a power higher than 2. For example, this calculation for the future value of an annuity raises the investment value to the power of the number of years, which is a variable (dblYears).

```
dblFutureValue = dblInvestment * Math.pow((1.0 + dblRate), dblYears);
```

The Math class includes many more methods that perform such math functions as sqrt, abs, min, max; trigonometric function such as sin, asin, cos, acos, tan, toDegrees, toRadians; exponential and logarithmic functions; and constants for PI and E. See Appendix F for the definition of these methods.

Feedback 4.1

1. Write the statement to calculate a bonus amount based on 5 percent of sales.
2. Write the statements to convert ounces into pounds and ounces using integer fields. (*Hint:* There are 16 ounces per pound.)
3. Given that intNum1 = 5 and intNum2 = 3, what is the result of the following operations.
   (a) 2 + intNum1 * intNum2
   (b) intNum1 * intNum2 + 2
   (c) intNum1 / intNum2
   (d) intNum1 % intNum2
4. Write the statement to cube dblWidth. (*Hint:* Raise it to the power of 3.)

Assignment Operators

In addition to the equal sign (=), Java has several other **assignment operators** that can perform a calculation and assign the result at the same time. These "shortcut" operators are handy for accumulating totals and counts, which are very common operations in programming.

The statement

```
dblTotalPay = dblTotalPay + fltPay;
```

adds the value in fltPay to the value in dblTotalPay. You can take advantage of the shortcut assignment operator and write the statement like this, which has the same effect:

```
dblTotalPay += fltPay;
```

Any time the previous value of a variable is a factor in calculating the new value, you can use one of the assignment operators.

+=	Add and assign
−=	Subtract and assign
*=	Multiply and assign
/=	Divide and assign
%=	Modulus and assign

Each of these assignment operators works as if the variable on the left of the operator were also placed on the right. (Note that the use of these shortcut assignment operators is completely optional. Use them only if you want to.)

These examples use the assignment operators:

```
fltTotalSales += fltSales;
dblSales −= dblReturns;
intDoubleUp *= 2;
fltSubdivide /= 10;
```

And this example calculates the number of minutes using the modulus assignment operator:

```
intHours = intMinutes / 60;
intMinutes %= 60;
```

The first statement contains different variables and must use a normal arithmetic operator. The second statement uses intMinutes as a factor in the calculation and also as the result field.

The Increment and Decrement Operators

Adding one to a variable and subtracting one are such common operations that Java has special operators just to accomplish the tasks: the **increment** and the **decrement operators.**

Increment Operator

Java's increment operator (++) is another shortcut operator that you can use if you wish. Using ++ automatically adds one to a variable.

The statement

```
intCount++;
```

has the same result as

```
intCount = intCount + 1;
```

or

```
intCount += 1;
```

All three statements increase the value of intCount by one.

You can use the increment operator in a statement by itself, as in the previous example, or in an expression:

```
strOutputString = "The count is " + intCount++;
```

You also can place the increment operator in front of the variable rather than behind it, which has a little different effect:

```
strOutputString = "The count is " + ++intCount;
```

When the increment operator follows the variable, it is called a **postfix** operation, and the actual incrementing occurs *after* the variable is evaluated and concatenated to the string. If the increment operator precedes the variable, it's called a **prefix** operation, and the increment occurs *before* the variable is evaluated and concatenated to the string. This code demonstrates the difference between the two operations:

```
String strOutputString;

//Postfix
int intCount = 0;
strOutputString = "Using postfix, the count is " + intCount++;
txtOutput.append(strOutputString + "\n");

//Prefix
intCount = 0;
strOutputString = "Using prefix, the count is " + ++intCount;
txtOutput.append(strOutputString);

add(txtOutput);
```

The output of this code:

```
Using postfix, the count is 0
Using prefix, the count is 1
```

It is common in Java to include an arithmetic operation nested inside another calculation expression. Therefore, you need to choose the correct form of the increment operator, taking into account the difference between prefix and postfix operators.

Decrement Operator

The decrement operator is similar to the increment operator: it reduces the variable by 1. The statement

```
intCount--;
```

subtracts one from intCount. You also can use the decrement operator as a prefix or postfix when you include it in an expression:

```
strOutputString = "The postfix result is " + intCount--;
```

or

```
strOutputString = "The prefix result is " + --intCount;
```

The postfix example decrements after the concatenation; the prefix example decrements before the concatenation.

Feedback 4.2

1. Write the statement to add one to intCount; use the increment operator.
2. Write the statement to add five to intCount; use the assignment operator.
3. What is the difference between these two statements?

```
lblCount.setText(intNumberEmployees--);
lblCount.setText(--intNumberEmployees);
```

Converting between Data Types

Java is considered a strongly typed programming language. If you have written programs in Visual Basic or C++, you may be used to relying on the automatic conversion between data types. In Java, the compiler checks the data type of all operands and arguments and insists on the correct type. When performing calculations with mixed numeric types, some operands may be implicitly converted or "promoted," so that precision is maintained. You will find the rules for this automatic conversion in the section "Implicit Numeric Type Conversion." But you often must explicitly convert to the correct type, and you always must be aware of the data type of every value.

Converting Strings to Numeric Data Types

Java does not automatically convert strings to numeric data types; you must explicitly convert them. When the user enters data into a text field or text area, the value is a string of characters. If you need to use the entered value as a number, you must convert it.

Recall that you retrieve the text from a text field with the getText method, such as

```
String strEnteredText = txtTextField.getText();
```

You can convert the string to a float variable, for example, using one of these forms:

```
float fltEnteredNumber = Float.parseFloat(strEnteredText); //Java 1.2 and later
```

or

```
float fltEnteredNumber = Float.valueOf(strEnteredText).floatValue(); //Java 1.1 and before
```

Notice that both of these conversion statements use methods from the Float class. The Float class, like the Double class, the Integer class, and the Long class, is one of the numeric "wrapper" classes that are part of the java.lang package. Later in this chapter in the section titled "Using the Wrapper Data Classes," you will learn to create instances of each of these classes. For now, you will use the methods of the classes for converting strings to primitive numeric data types.

Note that you can nest the getText method inside the conversion method in either of the above statements:

```
//Java 1.2 and later:
float fltEnteredNumber = Float.parseFloat(txtTextField.getText());
```

or

```
//Java 1.1 and before:
float fltEnteredNumber = Float.valueOf(txtTextField.getText()).floatValue();
```

As of this writing, Java 1.1 is supported by nearly all browsers; Java 1.2 is not. If you want your applets to run in Internet Explorer 4, for example, you will have to use the more cumbersome `valueOf` and `floatValue` methods and save the nicer `parseFloat` method for later.

Here's how the conversion methods work: The `valueOf` method converts a string to a Float value (notice the uppercase Float, which means that you are converting to a data member of the Float wrapper class, not a primitive float value). The `floatValue` method converts a Float value (uppercase Float data member) to a float primitive value. So the expression

```
Float.valueOf(txtTextField.getText()).floatValue()
```

starting with the inner parentheses, means "get the text string from txtTextField, use the `valueOf` method to convert the string to a Float value, then use the `floatValue` method to convert the Float to a primitive float. So the net effect is to retrieve the string from the text field and convert it to a float value so it can be used for calculations.

Converting Strings to Various Data Types

You already have seen how to convert the text in a text field to a float value. You can use the methods of the Integer, Long, and Double classes in the same way to convert to primitive data types.

```
int intNumber = Integer.valueOf(txtNumber.getText()).intValue();
long lngValue = Long.valueOf(txtLongNumber.getText()).longValue();
double dblDoubleNumber = Double.valueOf(txtDoubleNumber.getText()).doubleValue();
```

Accuracy of Decimal Fractions

When you calculate and display decimal fractions, you sometimes see strange results that appear inaccurate. This seeming inaccuracy is due to the way that fractional values are stored in the float and double data types.

The floating-point data types store values as binary fractions and an exponent, which can represent very large and very small numbers. You can think of the values as scientific notation, with a fraction and exponent, such as $+1.234567E4$ or $0.23456789E–2$. (The values actually are stored as binary digits rather than decimal digits, but you get the idea.)

You know that in the decimal number system some values cannot be represented exactly, such as

$\frac{1}{3} = 0.33333$ (almost)

and

$\frac{2}{3} = 0.66667$ (nearly)

Fractional values stored in float and double data types are held in binary. In the binary number system, some fractions cannot be held accurately. Unfortunately, those inaccurate fractions are some like ⅒ and ⅟₁₀₀. When you display the result of floating-point arithmetic, sometimes you see an unrounded value that is close to, but not exactly right on, the expected value. For example, you may enter 0.01 but the output displays as 0.00998.

Note: Different versions of the JVM and different browsers can produce slightly different results for a single program.

The Solution for Dollars and Cents? If you need to keep accurate decimal fractions, such as for dollars and cents, you cannot use floating-point numbers. The Java solution is to use the BigDecimal class in the java.math package. You can see an example using BigDecimal in Appendix F.

Invalid Data Entry

What happens if the user enters bad data into the text area? Maybe the user enters nonnumeric values, leaves the field blank, or enters a decimal point and fractional value for a field that should be an integer. The short answer is that the valueOf method throws an exception. In the section titled "Handling Exceptions" later in this chapter, you will learn to catch the exception and display a message to the user.

Calculating with Data from the Screen

It's time to put it together. Here is a program segment that takes numeric data entry from the screen and performs calculations with the data. This code gets the pay rate and the number of hours from text fields, converts the strings to float, assigns the values to float variables, calculates the pay, and adds the pay to a total. Soon we will format and display the result of these calculations.

```
//Obtain data from text boxes and convert to float values
float fltRate = Float.valueOf(txtRate.getText()).floatValue();
float fltHours = Float.valueOf(txtHours.getText()).floatValue();

//Calculate pay and totals
float fltPay = fltHours * fltRate;      //Calculate pay
fltTotalPay += fltPay;                  //Add pay to total pay
```

Converting Numeric Fields to String

It's easy to convert a primitive data type to a string. Although Java has methods that perform conversions, you can do an automatic (implicit) conversion by concatenating a numeric field to a string. You must perform the concatenation before displaying the result of a calculation in a label or text component.

```
strPayOutput = "Pay: " + fltPay; //Convert to string
lblPayOut.setText(strPayOutput);
```

To concatenate, you need to add the numeric value to a string, but the operation works perfectly well even when the string literal is empty.

```
strPayOutput = "" + fltPay; //Convert to string
lblPayOutput.setText(strPayOutput);
```

You also can place the concatenation directly in the `setText` method and eliminate the need for a string variable.

```
lblPayOutput.setText("" + fltPay);
lblNumberProcessed.setText("" + ++intNumberProcessed);
```

Note: The `setText` method requires a string argument. If you use only the numeric expression inside the parentheses, you get an error message. You *must* convert to string.

The String.valueOf Method

You can explicitly convert a numeric field to string using the `valueOf` method of the String class. The `valueOf` method can convert any int, long, float, or double data type to string.

```
strPayOutput = String.valueOf(fltPay); //Convert float to string
```

or

```
lblPayOutput.setText(String.valueOf(fltPay));
```

Converting between Numeric Types

You always must be aware of the data type of operands in calculations. Sometimes Java will automatically convert the type for you (implicit conversion) and sometimes you must convert the data type yourself (explicit conversion).

Implicit Numeric Type Conversion

When you perform a calculation that involves multiple data types, Java attempts to maintain the greatest precision possible. Some operands may be "promoted" to a data type with greater precision. For example, if you have a calculation that contains a float and an integer, the integer is treated as a float. In an operation that involves a double and a float, the float is converted to a double value. Note that the data type of the original variable is not changed, but a converted value is used in the calculation.

- If both operands are one of the integer types (byte, short, int, or long) and one of the operands is long, the Java compiler converts the other operand to long and the result of the calculation is long. If neither operand is long, Java converts both operands to int and the result of the calculation is int.

- If both operands are one of the floating-point types (float or double) and one of the operands is double, Java converts the other operand to double and the result of the calculation is double. Otherwise, both operands are float and the result of the calculation is float.

- If one operand is an integer type and one is long, the integer is converted to long and the result of the calculation is long.

- If one operand is an integer type and one is float, the integer is converted to float and the result of the calculation is float.

Java performs these implicit type conversions without your help. You usually are not aware of the conversion unless there is a danger of losing data precision, in which case you will receive a warning message.

```
//The float value is converted to double for this calculation.
dblPayTotal = dblPayTotal + fltPay;

//The int variable is converted to long and the result of the calculation is long.
lngHugeCount = intCount3 + lngCount4;

//No conversion is done on the operands. The result of the calculation is int.
//The result is then converted to long. This could lose digits if the result is
//too large for an int.
lngBigCount = intCount1 + intCount2;
```

Explicit Numeric Type Conversion

Often you need to explicitly convert a value for calculation into the correct data type. You can convert from one numeric data type to another using **casting.**

To create a cast operator, place the name of the primitive data type within parentheses. Then place the operator in front of the value you want to convert. The cast operator has a higher precedence than the calculation operators, so it will be performed first.

This statement converts the value stored in intHours to float, converts the value of intPayRate to float, then multiplies the two values, producing a float result, and assigns the result to fltPay.

```
fltPay = (float) intHours * (float) intPayRate;
```

Note that the data type of intHours and intPayRate is not changed, but a new temporary internal variable is created for each with the correct type and value.

You can change the results of the calculation by the placement of the cast operator. This statement first multiplies the int values, producing an int result, then converts the result to float.

```
fltPay = (float) (intHours * intPayRate);
```

This statement combines an explicit and implicit type conversion. The cast converts intHours to float, then intPay rate is converted implicitly since the types are different.

```
fltPay = (float) intHours * intPayRate;
```

You can cast from any numeric type to any other, but you will receive a warning message if you convert from a data type with more precision than the new type. It's best to always cast from a smaller data type to a larger one.

```
//Cast to double for calculation and result.
dblResult = (double) intNumber * 12.5;

//Cast to long for calculation and result
lngSquaredInteger = (lng) bytLittleNumber * bytLittleNumber;
```

Feedback 4.3

1. Write the statement(s) to retrieve the text in txtAmount and assign it to a float variable.
2. Write the statement(s) to retrieve the text in txtNumber and assign it to an integer variable.
3. Write the statement(s) to display fltTotalAmount in lblTotalAmount.
4. For each of these expressions, tell what will be the data type of the result of the calculation (before the result is assigned to the variable on the left side of the equal sign).
   (a) `dblTotal += fltAmount;`
   (b) `dblTotal = fltAmount1 + fltAmount2;`
   (c) `lngNumber = intNumber * intNumber;`
   (d) `lngNumber = (long) intNumber * intNumber;`
   (e) `lngNumber = lngCount + intCount;`
   (f) `fltSum = dblAmount + intAmount;`

Formatting Numeric Output

Java is designed to work not only with multiple platforms but also with localized applications. Many countries use different formatting rules for displaying numbers. The operating system stores the rules for formatting as a **locale.** You can retrieve the formatting specifications for a locale by using subclasses of the NumberFormat class, which comes from the text package. Although you write your application in your own country, when someone in another country retrieves your applet, it displays using the local formatting styles.

The formatting classes allow you to format general numbers, currency, and percent fields. You also can specify the number of decimal positions to display.

Note: As you learned in the earlier section "Accuracy of Decimal Fractions," floating-point values are subject to rounding errors. If you need accuracy in tenths and hundredths in decimal fractions, you can use the Java BigDecimal class. See Appendix F.

The Instance Methods

The **NumberFormat class** contains methods for obtaining the proper format for a given locale. You first create an object of the NumberFormat class, get the appropriate formatting instance, and then format your number.

Note: You must include the statement

```
import java.text.*;
```

to use the NumberFormat class.

Decimal Numbers

The **getInstance method** returns the default number format for a locale. The following statement creates a NumberFormat object called *fmtDecimal* and assigns it the default number style for the computer running the applet:

```
NumberFormat fmtDecimal = NumberFormat.getInstance();
```

Once you have created the formatting object, you can refine it by setting the number of decimal positions with the **setMaximumFractionDigits method**. Numbers are automatically rounded to the maximum number of digits that you select.

```
fmtDecimal.setMaximumFractionDigits(2); //Maximum 2 digits to right of decimal point
```

This statement causes 1.789 to display as 1.79
To make sure all numbers that you format have two decimal places you also must call the **setMinimumFractionDigits method.** This method causes 1 to display as 1.00.

```
fmtDecimal.setMinimumFractionDigits(2); //Minimum 2 digits to right of decimal point
```

After setting the desired number of decimal positions, call the **format method** using the number to format as the argument. The format method returns a String value.

```
strFormat = fmtDecimal.format(fltNumber);
lblDecimal.setText(strFormat);
```

Examples

This code formats the float variable fltNumber to two decimal positions. See the output for sample values of fltNumber.

```
//Format a float value to decimal number format with 2 decimal positions.
NumberFormat fmtDecimal = NumberFormat.getInstance();
fmtDecimal.setMaximumFractionDigits(2);
fmtDecimal.setMinimumFractionDigits(2);
strFormat = fmtDecimal.format(fltNumber);
lblDecimal.setText(strFormat);
```

Program Output

fltNumber Value	Displays
1000	1,000.00
456.789	456.79
2.444	2.44
1	1.00
4.1	4.10
0.054	0.05

Besides setting the number of digits to the right of the decimal point, you can specify the minimum and maximum number of digits to the left of the decimal point with the `setMaximumIntegerDigits` and the `setMinimumIntegerDigits` methods.

Currency Formats

The **getCurrencyInstance method** retrieves the local format for currency numbers. In the United States, that format typically includes a dollar sign, two decimal positions, and commas separating the thousands. Assuming that the local format includes the number of decimal positions, you don't need to set the maximum and minimum fraction digits. Fractional values are rounded to fit the format.

Examples

This code formats the float variable fltNumber to the local currency format. See the output for sample values of fltNumber, assuming the typical U.S. currency format.

```
//Format a float value to currency number format.
NumberFormat fmtCurrency = NumberFormat.getCurrencyInstance();
strFormat = fmtCurrency.format(fltNumber);
lblCurrency.setText(strFormat);
```

Program Output

fltNumber Value	Displays
1000	$1,000.00
456.789	$456.79
2.444	$2.44
1	$1.00
4.1	$4.10
0.054	$0.05

Percent Formats

Formatting percents is similar to formatting decimal and currency. Use the **getPercentInstance method** to retrieve the local percent format. You also can set the minimum and maximum fraction digits, if you choose.

The format method converts the argument to a percent and formats it with a percent sign.

Examples

This code formats the float variable fltNumber to the local percent format. See the output for sample values of fltNumber, assuming the typical U.S. percent format.

```
//Format a float value to percent number format.
NumberFormat fmtPercent = NumberFormat.getPercentInstance();
strFormat = fmtPercent.format(fltNumber);
lblPercent.setText("" + strFormat);
```

Program Output

fltNumber Value	Displays
1	100%
.1	10%
.056	6%

```
//Folder:         Ch4Formatting
//Programmer:     Bradley/Millspaugh
//Date:           6/2001
//ClassName:      FormatDecimals
//Description:    Use formatting methods to display float numbers.

import java.applet.*;
import java.awt.*;
import java.awt.event.*;
import java.text.*; //Formatting methods

public class FormatDecimals extends Applet implements ActionListener
{
    //Declare components
    TextField txtNumber = new TextField(10);
    Label lblDecimal = new Label();
    Label lblCurrency = new Label();
    Label lblPercent = new Label();
    Button btnOK = new Button("Display Formatted");

    public void init()
    {
        PanelLayout();
        btnOK.addActionListener(this);
        txtNumber.addActionListener(this);
        txtNumber.requestFocus();
    }

    public void actionPerformed(ActionEvent evt)
    {
        //Format number to desired formats
        String strFormat;

        //Obtain data from text field
        float fltNumber = Float.valueOf(txtNumber.getText()).floatValue();

        //Set up formatting styles
        NumberFormat fmtDecimal = NumberFormat.getInstance();
        fmtDecimal.setMaximumFractionDigits(2);
        fmtDecimal.setMinimumFractionDigits(2);
        NumberFormat fmtCurrency = NumberFormat.getCurrencyInstance();
        NumberFormat fmtPercent = NumberFormat.getPercentInstance();
```

```
        //Format and display results
        strFormat = fmtDecimal.format(fltNumber);
        lblDecimal.setText(strFormat);

        strFormat = fmtCurrency.format(fltNumber);
        lblCurrency.setText(strFormat);

        strFormat = fmtPercent.format(fltNumber);
        lblPercent.setText(strFormat);
    }

    public void PanelLayout()
    {
        //Place labels and text fields on a grid layout
        setLayout(new GridLayout(5,2,10,10));
        add(new Label ("Enter a number"));
        add(txtNumber);
        add(new Label (""));//Used for spacing
        add(btnOK);
        add(new Label ("Decimal Format: "));
        add(lblDecimal);
        add(new Label ("Currency Format: "));
        add(lblCurrency);
        add(new Label ("Percent Format: "));
        add(lblPercent);
    }
}
```

Table 4.2 shows some of the methods of the NumberFormat class.

Table 4.2

Selected Methods of the NumberFormat class

Method	Purpose
format	Return a string that holds the formatted number.
getInstance	Return the default number format for the current locale.
getCurrencyInstance	Return the currency format for the current locale.
getNumberInstance	Return the general-purpose number format for the current locale.
getPercentInstance	Return the percent number format for the current locale.
getScientificInstance	Return the scientific number format for the current locale.
getAvailableLocales	Return an array of available locales on the current system.
parse	Return a number from a formatted string.
setMaximumFractionDigits	Set the maximum number of digits to the right of the decimal point.
setMaximumIntegerDigits	Set the maximum number of digits to the left of the decimal point.
setMinimumFractionDigits	Set the minimum number of digits to the right of the decimal point.
setMinimumIntegerDigits	Set the minimum number of digits to the left of the decimal point.

Specifying a Locale

To force your application to use a specific style of formatting, you can specify the locale in the getInstance method using the Locale object.

```
NumberFormat fmtDecimal = NumberFormat.getInstance(Locale.FRENCH);
```

You also can retrieve a list of available locales on the current system using the getAvailableLocales method. However, this method returns an array. Arrays are covered in Chapter 9.

Feedback 4.4

1. Write the statements to create an object that displays dollar amounts in a formatted string.
2. Code the statement(s) to create an object that can display a decimal number that rounds to three decimal places. Do not worry about the minimum number of decimal positions.
3. Write the format method to convert fltTotalSales into a formatted string.
4. Write the statement to display the formatted string created in question 3.

Handling Exceptions

Several of the operations performed in this chapter could potentially generate errors, called *exceptions* in Java. What happens if the user leaves a text box blank and you try to convert the blank to a numeric value? Or what happens if the user enters a decimal point and a fractional value and your program attempts to convert the text string to an integer? Or maybe the user enters 0 and you try to divide by that number? Each of these situations generates an **Exception object.** The correct terminology is that the operation "throws an exception"—and it's your job to "catch" the exception.

Try and Catch

To catch an exception, you first must identify the statement(s) that might cause an error, such as converting user input to numeric. Then enclose the statement(s) that may cause an error in a try block. The **try** statement has an associated **catch**. If an error occurs while the statements in the try block are executing, execution transfers to the statements in the catch block.

```
try
{
    //Get data from screen. Invalid integer or blank throws an exception.
    int intNumber = Integer.valueOf(txtNumber.getText()).intValue();
}
catch(NumberFormatException err)
{
    showStatus("Invalid data entered.");
}
```

In this program segment, you expect the statement inside the try block to execute successfully. If it does, the catch block is skipped and the statement immediately following the catch block is executed next. However, if the statement inside the try block fails, Java immediately jumps to the statement inside the catch block.

You can include multiple statements inside both the try block and the catch block. The statements inside the try block are executed in sequence. If one of the statements throws an exception, execution transfers to the first statement in the catch block (skipping any more statements in the try block).

The try and catch—General Format

```
try
{
    // The statement(s) that might generate an exception.
}
catch(ErrorObject errIdentifier)
{
    // The statement(s) to handle the exception.
}
```

After the word try, you must include the curly braces for a block. You also need curly braces for the statements in the catch block. The ErrorObject parameter is one of the predefined exception objects. Table 4.3 lists the most common exception objects. As you learn more statements in later chapters, you also will learn the exception object that each statement throws. The errIdentifier parameter is a name that you give to the exception object, which you can use within the block. For example, you can display the text of the exception error message by placing this statement in the catch block:

```
showStatus("The official message is: " + errIdentifier.getMessage());
```

using the name that you give the exception object in the catch clause.

You will find that the "official" messages are somewhat cryptic: it's usually better to write your own meaningful message.

The try and catch—Example

```
try
{
    //Integer division. Zero for intSecond throws an exception.
    intResult = intFirst / intSecond;
    lblIntegerResult.setText("" + intResult);
}
catch(ArithmeticException err)
{
    showStatus("Error in calculation");
}
```

Table 4.3

Common Exception Objects

Exception Object	Purpose
ArithmeticException	Error caused by a calculation, such as division by zero.
NumberFormatException	Problem converting a string to a number; occurs when the text field is blank or contains a fraction when an integer is required.
IllegalArgumentException	Unable to format the value passed to one of the format methods.
FileNotFoundException	File does not exist in path specified.
IOException	Failure of an input or output operation such as reading from a file.
OutOfMemoryException	Not enough memory to create an object.

Unhandled Exceptions

If an exception occurs and you do not handle it, the exception is passed up a level. If not handled there, the exception is passed up another level, and another, until it reaches the top level of the program. Depending on the error, sometimes Java will display an error message. But in an applet, often the applet will just sit there and do nothing, giving no output or any indication of the problem.

Handling Multiple Exceptions

You can handle more than one type of exception by including multiple `catch` blocks. The following program catches illegal user input (blank or a fraction for integer input) and integer division by zero. You can run this program by running Ch4Exceptions on your text CD.

Note that integer division by zero throws an exception, but floating-point division by zero does not. In a floating-point division, the result is set to *infinity* but does not cause an error to occur.

```
//Folder:        Ch4Exceptions
//Programmer:    Bradley/Millspaugh
//Date:          6/2001
//ClassName:     ExceptionDemo
//Description:   Generate error messages for bad data.

import java.applet.*;
import java.awt.*;
import java.awt.event.*;

public class ExceptionDemo extends Applet implements ActionListener
{
    TextField txtFirst = new TextField(5);
    TextField txtSecond = new TextField(5);
    Label lblIntegerResult = new Label("");
    Label lblFloatResult = new Label("");
    Button btnCalc = new Button("Calculate");
```

```
public void init()
{
    //Set up interface
    setLayout(new GridLayout(5,2,20,20));
    add(new Label("Enter first integer: "));
    add(txtFirst);
    add(new Label("Enter second integer: "));
    add(txtSecond);
    add(new Label("Integer result:"));
    add(lblIntegerResult);
    add(new Label("Floating-point result:"));
    add(lblFloatResult);
    add(new Label(" ")); //Spacing
    add(btnCalc);
    txtFirst.requestFocus();

    btnCalc.addActionListener(this);
    txtFirst.addActionListener(this);
    txtSecond.addActionListener(this);
}

public void actionPerformed(ActionEvent event)
{
    //Clear Status
    showStatus("Ready");
    try
    {
        //Get data from screen. Invalid integer or blank throws an exception.
        int intFirst = Integer.valueOf(txtFirst.getText()).intValue();
        int intSecond = Integer.valueOf(txtSecond.getText()).intValue();

        //Float division. Zero for intSecond gives infinity result.
        float fltResult = (float)intFirst / intSecond;
        lblFloatResult.setText("" + fltResult);

        //Integer division. Zero for intSecond throws exception.
        int intResult = intFirst / intSecond;
        lblIntegerResult.setText("" + intResult);
    }
    catch(ArithmeticException err)
    {
        lblIntegerResult.setText("Arithmetic Error");
        showStatus("Error in calculation");
    }
    catch(NumberFormatException err)
    {
        lblIntegerResult.setText("Input Data Error");
        lblFloatResult.setText("");
        showStatus("Invalid data entered.");
    }
}
}
```

Feedback 4.5

1. Write the try and catch to catch an integer division by zero.
2. Write the try and catch to catch a blank for user input in a text field called txtNumber.

Using the Wrapper Data Classes

Each of the primitive data types has a **wrapper class** that you can use. When you use data classes, you conform a little closer to object-oriented programming. Each variable is an object, with methods that you can use to operate on the data. Figure 4.1 shows the Integer and Float classes, with some of their methods.

Figure 4.1

*Some of the methods of the
Integer and Float classes.*

Integer Class	Float Class
`byteValue`	`intValue`
`doubleValue`	`longValue`
`equals`	`floatValue`
`floatValue`	`doubleValue`
`getInteger`	`equals`
`intValue`	`toString`
`toString`	`isInfinite`
`valueOf`	`isNaN`

When you declare an object of a data class, you must use the `new` keyword. Begin the new variable name with an uppercase letter to differentiate the variable from a primitive data type.

```
Float FltInterestRate = new Float(fltRate);
```

The Float Class

Use the Float class to store a fractional value. The Float constructors allow conversion from a double or float primitive data type or from a String.

The Float Class—Constructors

```
Float(double)     //Create a Float instance converting the double value
Float(float)      //Create a Float instance converting the float value
Float(String)     //Create a Float instance converting the string value
```

The Float Class—Examples

```
Float FltRate = new Float(txtRate.getText()); //Convert string to float
Float FltHours = new Float(txtHours.getText());
Float FltTotal = new Float(0.0f);
```

Methods

The Float class provides many methods to work with the data (Table 4.4). You can convert from one data type to another, retrieve the data in a different data type, or test the value in the Float object. The method you will use most frequently is the `floatValue` method. This method returns the value of a Float object and can be used in a calculation. The following calculation performs a multiplication operation on two Float objects; the answer is stored in a primitive data type.

```
fltPay = FltHours.floatValue() * FltRate.floatValue();
```

Method	Purpose
intValue	Returns the value of the Float as an integer.
longValue	Returns the value of the Float as a long integer.
floatValue	Returns the value of the Float as a float.
doubleValue	Returns the value of the Float as a double.
toString	Converts the float value to String.
isInfinite	Returns true if the Float value is infinity.
isNaN	Returns true if the Float value is not a number.

Table 4.4

Partial List of Float Methods

You also can set Float variables MAX_VALUE and MIN_VALUE. If you attempt to assign a value outside the range, an exception is thrown.

The Integer Class

You can use the Integer class to create an Integer object. You can create a new Integer object from a primitive int or from a String.

Integer Class—Constructors

```
Integer(int)
Integer(String)
```

Integer Class—Examples

```
Integer IntQuantity = new Integer(txtQuantity.getText());
Integer IntCount = new Integer(0);
```

The `intValue` method provides a value for use in calculations. Once again you need to convert the text field from a string into an integer.

```
int intQuantity;                           //A primitive data type
Integer IntQuantity = new Integer(txtQuantity.getText());   //Get string value
intQuantity = IntQuantity.intValue();   //Assign integer value
```

Feedback 4.6

1. Write the statements to declare a Float class called FltPrice, retrieve a value from txtPrice, and store the value in the Float class.
2. Assuming that the quantity has been retrieved and stored in IntQuantity, write the calculation statement to multiply the price in FltPrice by the value in IntQuantity and store the result in fltAmountDue.

Your Hands-on Programming Example

Create an applet that calculates and displays payroll information. Allow the user to input the employee name, hours, and rate. Include a Calculate button that multiplies the hours by the rate to calculate the pay, accumulates the total pay, and counts the number of employees processed. Format and display the total pay and count in labels. Use a text area to display a payroll report with the name and pay. Be sure to check for an exception if the user leaves either text field blank.

Note: Use currency format for the total pay. Use decimal format with two decimal positions for the pay on the payroll report.

Figure 4.2 shows a possible layout for the applet.

Figure 4.2

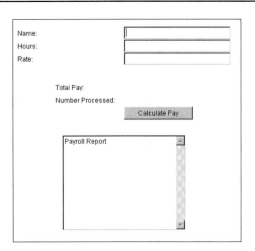

A possible layout for the chapter hands-on example.

Planning the Project

Plan the Objects and Properties
Class: PayrollApplet
Figure 4.3 shows the class diagram.

Figure 4.3

The class diagram for the chapter hands-on example.

Class: PayrollApplet	
Methods	**Variables and Components**
init	intNumberProcessed
actionPerformed	fltTotalPay
DesignInputPanel	strFormattedData
DesignOutputPanel	fltRate
	fltHours
	fitPay
	txtName
	txtRate
	txtHours
	txaPayroll
	btnCalculate
	lblPayOut
	lblNumberProcessed
	lblError
	pnlInput
	pnlOutput

Properties:

Access Mode (public or private)	Variable or Component Name	Data Type or Class	Description
	pnlInput	Panel	Panel for input components.
	pnlOutput	Panel	Panel for output components.
	txtName	TextField	Input the name.
	txtRate	TextField	Input the hourly pay rate.
	txtHours	TextField	Input the hours worked.
	txaPayroll	TextArea	Display report of names and pay.
	btnCalculate	Button	Process pay.
	lblPayOut	Label	Display total pay.
	lblNumberProcessed	Label	Display number of employees.
	lblError	Label	Display error message.
Class variables	intNumberProcessed	int	Count variable for number of employees.
	fltTotalPay	float	Accumulation variable for pay.
Local variables	strFormattedData	String	Hold formatted data for display.
	fltRate	float	Hold value from input for rate.
	fltHours	float	Hold value from input for hours.
	fltPay	float	Hold pay for one individual.

Methods:

Access Mode (public or private)	Return Type	Method Name (include any parameters)	Pseudocode
public	void	init	Call method to lay out panels. Add panels. Add text area. Set focus to the name text field. Add action listeners.
public	void	actionPerformed	Obtain input for hours and rate. Calculate pay. Add pay to total. Set formatting for local rules. Format output. Display results. Clear text fields. Set focus to first text field.
public	void	DesignInputPanel	Lay out the input fields.
public	void	DesignOutputPanel	Lay out the output fields.

Write the Project

● Follow the plan to declare components and variables.

● Code the methods.

● When you complete the code, thoroughly test the project.

The Project Solution

```
//Folder:        Ch4HandsOnPrimitives
//Programmer:    Bradley/Millspaugh
//Date:          6/2001
//ClassName:     PayrollApplet
//Description:   Input hours and rate, calculate pay, total pay,
//               and number processed. Format and display results.
//               This version uses primitive data types for variables.

import java.applet.*;
import java.awt.event.*;
import java.awt.*;
import java.text.*; //Formatting

public class PayrollApplet extends Applet implements ActionListener
{
    //Create components
    Panel pnlInput = new Panel();
    Panel pnlOutput = new Panel();
    TextField txtName = new TextField(25);
    TextField txtHours = new TextField();
    TextField txtRate = new TextField();
```

```java
TextArea txaPayroll =
    new TextArea("Payroll Report", 10, 30, TextArea.SCROLLBARS_VERTICAL_ONLY);
Button btnCalculate = new Button("Calculate Pay");
Label lblPayOut = new Label();
Label lblNumberProcessed = new Label();
Label lblError = new Label("");

//Declare class variables
int intNumberProcessed = 0;
float fltTotalPay = 0.0f;

public void init()
{
    //Create user interface
    DesignInputPanel();
    DesignOutputPanel();
    add(pnlInput);
    add(pnlOutput);
    add(txaPayroll);
    txtName.requestFocus();
    btnCalculate.addActionListener(this);
    txtHours.addActionListener(this);
    txtRate.addActionListener(this);
}

public void actionPerformed(ActionEvent evt)
{
    //Retrieve data and calculate
    //Declare local variables
    String strFormattedData;

    //Clear any previous errors
    lblError.setText("");
    showStatus("Ready");

    try
    {
        //Obtain data from text boxes
        //Convert strings to float values
        float fltRate = Float.valueOf(txtRate.getText()).floatValue();
        float fltHours = Float.valueOf(txtHours.getText()).floatValue();

        //Calculate pay and totals
        float fltPay = fltHours * fltRate;
        fltTotalPay += fltPay; //Add pay to total pay

        //Set local formatting
        NumberFormat fmtCurrency = NumberFormat.getCurrencyInstance();
        NumberFormat fmtDecimal = NumberFormat.getInstance();
        fmtDecimal.setMinimumFractionDigits(2);
        fmtDecimal.setMaximumFractionDigits(2);

        //Format and display results
        strFormattedData = fmtCurrency.format(fltTotalPay);
        lblPayOut.setText(strFormattedData);
        lblNumberProcessed.setText("" + ++intNumberProcessed);
        strFormattedData = fmtDecimal.format(fltPay);
        txaPayroll.append("\n" + txtName.getText() + "\t" + strFormattedData);
```

```java
            //Clear text fields
            txtName.setText("");
            txtHours.setText("");
            txtRate.setText("");
            txtName.requestFocus();
        }
        catch(NumberFormatException err)
        {
            lblError.setForeground(Color.red);
            lblError.setText("Invalid data entered");
            showStatus("Invalid data entered");
        }
    }

    public void DesignInputPanel()
    {
        //Lay out the input panel
        pnlInput.setLayout(new GridLayout(4,2));
        pnlInput.add(new Label("Name: "));
        pnlInput.add(txtName);
        pnlInput.add(new Label("Hours: "));
        pnlInput.add(txtHours);
        pnlInput.add(new Label("Rate: "));
        pnlInput.add(txtRate);
        pnlInput.add(lblError);
    }

    public void DesignOutputPanel()
    {
        //Lay out the output panel
        pnlOutput.setLayout(new GridLayout(4,2));
        pnlOutput.add(new Label("Total Pay:"));
        pnlOutput.add(lblPayOut);
        pnlOutput.add(new Label("Number Processed: "));
        pnlOutput.add(lblNumberProcessed);
        pnlOutput.add(new Label("")); //Spacing
        pnlOutput.add(btnCalculate);
    }
}
```

Summary

1. Perform calculations with the arithmetic operators for addition (+), subtraction (−), multiplication (*), division (/), and modulus (%).

2. The precedence of operations follows the normal math hierarchy. Operations inside parentheses are executed first and parentheses may be nested to any level.

3. Java does not have an operator for exponentiation. Use the `Math.pow` (power) method to raise to a power.

4. Use assignment operators to perform a calculation on a variable and store the result of the calculation in the same field.

5. The increment and decrement operators provide a coding shortcut for adding one or subtracting one from a number.

6. A prefix operator performs the calculation before any other action on the expression; a postfix operator causes the operation to be performed after the statement executes.

7. You must convert string input to numeric for calculation. Use the `valueOf` and `floatValue` methods of the Float wrapper class to convert from string to float.

8. Floating-point data types store values as binary fractions and may not hold tenths and hundredths accurately.

9. A numeric field must be converted to string before it can be displayed in a label or text field. You can concatenate a numeric field to a string to perform the conversion or use the `String.valueOf` method.

10. When multiple data types are combined in a single arithmetic expression, some data types may be "promoted" to a higher precision data type.

11. You can explicitly convert from one data type to another using casting. The cast operator has a higher precedence than calculation operators.

12. The formatting methods in the text package provide for formatting numbers as general numbers, currency, and percents. Formatting can default to the computer system's locale or a specific locale can be specified.

13. When an operation cannot complete successfully, it throws an exception, which is a specialized Java object. Enclose any statements that may cause an exception in a `try` block and write code to handle the exception in a `catch` block. You can use multiple `catch` blocks to handle different types of exceptions.

14. The wrapper data classes enclose a primitive data type in an object, which has methods for handling the data.

Key Terms

Review Questions

1. What are the differences between using the + and += and ++ operators?

2. What is the difference between intCount++ and ++intCount if the operation is a statement by itself?

3. When would you use a decrement operator?

4. How does precedence of operators impact your applications?

5. Why must you convert user input to a numeric data type? How is the conversion accomplished?

6. How can you convert a numeric field for display in a label?

7. How does Java handle mixed data types in a calculation?

8. How can you explicitly change the data type of a variable?

9. Describe the steps necessary to format a floating-point number for output. The number should display with exactly two decimal positions.

10. How is the locale for formatting determined? How can you indicate a specific locale?

11. What is an exception? When does an exception occur? How can you handle an exception?

12. What is a wrapper class? When would it be advantageous to use a wrapper class?

Programming Exercises

4.1. Create an applet that allows the user to type in the name of a book, the price, and the quantity desired. Calculate the total due by multiplying the price by the quantity and applying a sales tax of 8¼% and a shipping and handling fee of $1.00 per book.

Display the formatted results in a text area on separate lines as

Title:

Extended Price:

Tax:

Handling:

Total Due:

Use the keyword `final` to set the handling fee and tax rate as constants.

4.2. In retail sales, management needs to know the average inventory figure and the turnover of merchandise. Create an applet that allows the user to enter the beginning inventory, the ending inventory, and the cost of goods sold.

Input panel: Include labeled text fields for the beginning inventory, the ending inventory, and the cost of goods sold. Output panel: After calculating the answers, display the average inventory and the turnover formatted in labels. Format the average inventory as currency and the turnover as a number with one digit to the right of the decimal point. Include a Calculate button.

Formulas:

Average inventory = (Beginning inventory + Ending inventory) /2

Turnover = Cost of goods sold / Average inventory

Note: The average inventory is expressed in dollars; the turnover is the number of times the inventory turns over.

Test Data			Check Figures	
Beginning Inventory	Ending Inventory	Cost of Goods Sold	Average Inventory	Turnover
58500	47000	400000	52750.00	7.6
75300	13600	515400	44450.00	11.6
3000	19600	48000	11300.00	4.3

4.3.   A local recording studio rents its facilities for $200 per hour. Management charges only for the number of minutes used. Create an applet in which the input is the name of the group and the number of minutes it used the studio. Your program calculates the appropriate charges, accumulates the total charges for all groups, and computes the average charge and the number of groups that used the studio.

Use labeled text fields for the name of the group and the number of minutes used. The charges for the current group should be displayed formatted in a label. Create a text area for the summary information. Inside the text area, display the total charges for all groups, the number of groups, and the average charge per group. Format all output appropriately.

Use a numeric constant for the rental rate per minute. (*Hint:* Use the `final` keyword.)

Test Data		Check Figures			
Group	Minutes	Total Group Charge	Number of Groups	Average Charge	Total Charges
Pooches	95	316.67	1	316.67	316.67
Hounds	5	16.67	2	166.67	333.33
Mutts	480	1,600.00	3	644.44	1,933.33

4.4.   Create a project that determines the future value of an investment at a given interest rate for a given number of years. The formula for the calculation is

Future value = Investment amount * (1 + Interest rate) ^ Years

Use labeled text fields for the amount of investment, the interest rate (as a decimal fraction), and the number of years the investment will be held.

Display the future value in a label, formatted as currency. Include a Calculate button.

Test Data			Check Figures
Amount	Rate	Years	Future Value
2000	.15	5	$4,022.71
1234.56	.075	3	$1,533.69

4.5. Write an applet that calculates the shipping charge for a package if the shipping rate is $0.12 per ounce. Use labeled text fields for the package-identification code (a six-digit code) and the weight of the package—one box for pounds and another one for ounces. Use a label to display the shipping charge. Include a button for Calculate.

Use a constant for the shipping rate, calculate the shipping charge, and display it formatted in a label. *Calculation hint:* There are 16 ounces in a pound.

Test Data		Check Figures
ID	Weight	Shipping Charge
15496P	0 lb. 5 oz.	$0.60
J1955K	2 lb. 0 oz.	$3.84
Z0000Z	1 lb. 1 oz.	$2.04

4.6. Create an applet for the local car rental agency that calculates rental charges. The agency charges $15 per day plus $0.12 per mile.

Use text fields for the customer name, address, city, state, ZIP code, beginning odometer reading, ending odometer reading, and the number of days the car was used. Use labels to display the miles driven and the total charge. Format the output appropriately.

Include a button for Calculate.

For the calculation, subtract the beginning odometer reading from the ending odometer reading to get the number of miles traveled. Use a constant for the $15-per-day charge and the $0.12 mileage rate. (*Hint:* Use the final keyword.)

4.7. Create an applet that will input an employee's sales and calculate the gross pay, deductions, and net pay. Each employee will receive a base pay of $900 plus a sales commission of 6 percent of sales. After calculating the net pay, calculate the budget amount for each category based on the percentages given.

Pay

Base pay	900 (set as a numeric constant using `final`)
Commission	6% of sales
Gross pay	Sum of base pay and commission
Deductions	18% of gross pay
Net pay	Gross pay minus deductions

Budget

Housing	30% of net pay
Food and clothing	25% of net pay
Entertainment	10% of net pay
Savings	30% of net pay
Miscellaneous	5% of net pay

CASE STUDIES

R 'n R—for Reading and Refreshment

R 'n R—For Reading and Refreshment needs to calculate prices and discounts for books sold. The company is currently having a big sale, offering a 15 percent discount on all books. In this applet you will calculate the amount due for a quantity of books, determine the 15 percent discount, and deduct the discount, giving the new amount due—the discounted amount. In addition to calculating individual sales and discounts, management wants to know the total number of books sold, the total amount collected, and the average price per book.

The panel contains text fields for the book title, the quantity, and the price. Use two text areas: one to display the information relating to the current sale and the other to show the summary information.

Use a Calculate button called "Add to Shopping Cart" to process the information. The calculate button will

- Multiply the price by the quantity to find the extended price.

- Calculate the discount.

- Subtract the discount from the extended price giving the discounted price.

- Add the discounted price to the total sales.

- Add the quantity to the count of books sold.

- Display the book title, extended price, discount, and discounted price on separate lines in the current sale text area.

- Show the total number of books sold, the total of actual sales, and the average price per book.

- Clear the text fields.

You may use any layout you wish for the design of the screen. Do not append the information for each sale; instead, replace the output in the text areas for each sale. *Hint:* The first line of output to the text area will not be an append. Be sure to format all numbers for the text areas.

Merry Pea's Quilting   Ms. Pea would like to have an applet that creates an invoice for quilting classes. Include text fields for the customer name, the class number, the class name, and the price. Use a Calculate button to add the price to a total and add to a count of classes for which the user has signed up. Use a text area to display the names of the classes. In a separate text area, display the summary numbers: the total due, the number of classes, and the average price per class. The Calculate button also should clear the information in the class number, class name, and price text fields.

5

Creating Classes

At the completion of this chapter, you will be able to . . .

1. Understand more thoroughly the characteristics of object-oriented programming.

2. Know when to appropriately use public and private variables and methods.

3. Create your own classes.

4. Instantiate objects of your class.

5. Write methods that return values and accept input values.

So far, each of the applets that you have created is a single class. As you add more functionality to an applet, the program size could soon become very large and difficult to manage. The proper way to develop programs is to break up the tasks into small objects, each of which is responsible for a specific task.

In this chapter you will learn to break up your previous applets, separating the processing from the user interface in the applet class.

Review of Object-Oriented Programming

As you learned in Chapter 1, Java is an object-oriented language, which means that the programs you write must be object oriented. Some of the features of object-oriented programming (OOP) are encapsulation, inheritance, and polymorphism.

Encapsulation

Encapsulation refers to the combination of properties and methods in a single unit. Before object-oriented programming, computer programs handled data completely separately from the processing. The newer techniques deal with both the characteristics and the actions of each object, which makes sense, because the properties and methods relate to each other. And encapsulation allows an object to maintain integrity of the data by "hiding" it from other objects. You can think of an object as a "black box" that carries out a task. The only way to gain access to any of the properties and methods of an object is to use those properties and methods specifically declared as public. Each object keeps control of its own components, variables, and methods; this is encapsulation.

Inheritance

Using **inheritance,** you can add enhancements to an existing class without modifying the original. By creating a new class that inherits from an existing class, you can add or change class variables and methods. In each of the applets that you create, you are extending, or inheriting from, the existing Applet class. The existing class is known as the **base class** or **superclass.** The extended class is called a **subclass.** Of course, a new class can inherit from a subclass—that subclass becomes a superclass as well as a subclass. A **hierarchy** is the relationship of superclasses and subclasses.

The applets you have created are based on inheritance. The Applet class already exists in a Java package. Your new applet adds to that class but also has all of the features and functionality of the base class. When you declare variables at the beginning of your class, you are adding new properties to the class. The Applet class already has an `init` method; the `init` method that you write executes instead of the `init` method in the base class, in a process called **overriding.**

Overriding is how you modify an existing method: you write your own method with the same name as an existing method and your new method overrides the existing one. You can even achieve the effect of deleting a method by overriding it with a method that contains no code. When the empty method is called from the subclass, nothing happens. *Note:* You already have written empty methods for mouse events in Chapter 2. You had to override all of the methods in the MouseListener interface but any unwanted methods did not contain any statements.

Interfaces and Inner Classes

A class in Java can inherit from only one superclass. If you have programmed in C++, you have seen multiple inheritance, which is not allowed in Java. However, Java has two other features that can assist you when you need characteristics from more than one class: interfaces and inner classes.

An **interface** is similar to a class; it exposes a set of methods. However, you must override all of the methods in any interface you use and you cannot instantiate an object from an interface. You already have used interfaces in your programming: the ActionListener interface and the MouseListener interface. You use the `implements` keyword on your class header to use an interface:

```
public class MyApplet extends Applet implements ActionListener, MouseListener
```

When you implement the ActionListener interface, you must write an `actionPerformed` method, which overrides the (only) method in the interface. And when you implement the MouseListener interface, you must override five methods: `mouseClicked`, `mousePressed`, `mouseReleased`, `mouseEntered`, and `mouseExited`. As you saw in Chapter 2, you can leave empty any methods for which you don't want to take any action, but all of the methods must appear in your code.

When you implement an interface, you are guaranteeing that your class will contain each of the specified methods. Any other class that uses your class can be assured that the methods exist. In fact, the Java compiler enforces this restriction and generates error messages if you implement an interface and do not code every method of the interface.

Although one class can have only one superclass, it can implement many interfaces. This gives a class access to many methods in addition to those in the superclass.

You can create your own interface in the same manner as you create a class. You replace the keyword `class` with `interface`. An interface can contain methods and constants (`final` keyword) but no variables.

An **inner class** is a class defined within another class. Inner classes were introduced with Java 1.1. You will learn more about interfaces and inner classes in Chapter 12.

Abstract Classes

Closely related to an interface is an **abstract class.** An abstract class is a class written solely for the purpose of inheritance: to be a superclass of more than one related subclass. An abstract class contains methods that do not contain any statements, called *abstract methods.* You cannot instantiate an object from an abstract class; instead you inherit from an abstract class. You may wonder what the purpose of this could be. When several types of objects have similar characteristics, you may create a superclass and subclasses that inherit from the superclass. This allows some methods and class variables to be the same among the subclasses. An example of this situation is the Component class in Java, which is an abstract class. Label, TextField, TextArea, and Button are subclasses of Component.

See Chapter 12 for an example using interfaces and abstract classes.

Polymorphism

An additional feature of OOP languages is **polymorphism.** The term *polymorphism* actually means the ability to take on many shapes or forms. As applied to OOP, polymorphism refers to method names having identical names but having different implementations, depending on the situation. For example, several classes may have a `getItem` method. In each case, the `getItem` method operates appropriately for its class. Also, one class can have several methods with the same name, each with a different set of arguments. Each of the identically named methods performs its tasks in a slightly different way from the other methods.

One way that polymorphism is implemented is to have method names that are the same in a superclass and its subclasses. For example, the Applet class has an `init` method. When you write your own `init` method in a subclass (a class that extends Applet), your `init` method overrides the superclass's `init` method. Each of the methods has the same name, but the implementation is different.

For an example of polymorphism, consider the Component class, which is the superclass for both the Label and the TextComponent classes. Each of these classes has `setText` and `getText` methods that work appropriately for objects of the particular class. And TextComponent is the superclass for both the TextField and the TextArea classes. Therefore, all objects that are instances of Label, TextField, or TextArea have methods that use the same names but may not perform in exactly the same way.

Objects

Although all of our programs so far have been object oriented—that's the only choice in Java—they haven't been designed to take advantage of the features of OOP. The main idea behind OOP is to create reusable items that can be accessed from any project that might require such an object.

An **object** is a "thing" that has characteristics and behaviors. All of the components you have used are objects. The text fields have a value and have actions such as `getText`, `setText`, `setForeground`, and `setBackground`. The button has a label property that displays on the button and has methods such as `getLabel` and `setLabel`.

To create these component objects, you use the `new` keyword with a preexisting type known as a *class*.

```
Button btnDisplay = new Button("Display");
```

This statement declares the object btnDisplay as an **instance** of the Button class. When you **instantiate** an object from a class, the **constructor method** in the class executes. In the case of btnDisplay, when the object is created, the text "Display" is assigned to the label property. Of course, you can instantiate more button objects from the Button class, each with its own name and own label property. Also, you can declare a button with no label:

```
Button btnMystery = new Button();
```

which illustrates an important point: A class may have more than one constructor method, just as we earlier saw more than one `format` method. If you supply the label when you create a button, one constructor method executes; if you don't supply the label, a different constructor method executes. This concept is called **overloading.**

Your Own Objects

Just as you use the Button class and the TextField class to create multiple objects, you can create your own class and instantiate multiple objects from the class. The class describes the characteristics of the object with variables and the actions of the object with methods. In this chapter you will create your own classes and instantiate objects from the classes.

Feedback 5.1

1. In your own words, give an example of
   (a) Encapsulation.
   (b) Inheritance.
2. Define the following terms:
   (a) Object.
   (b) Instance.
   (c) Instantiate.

Creating a New Class

Your project can have multiple classes. You create a separate file for each class and save it using the class name and file extension of .java. For example, a new Interest class should be saved as Interest.java. When it is compiled, the compiler saves the bytecode as Interest.class.

If you are using an IDE, the IDE handles keeping all the files in the same folder so that one class can reference another. If you are using an editor and the JDK, you need to make sure to store all files in the same folder.

Create a new class file just as you would a new applet:

```
//Comments to identify the class

public class ClassName
{
    //Declare variables
    //Code methods
}
```

Public versus Private

As you start working with multiple classes, the concept of **public** or **private** access becomes more important. Your applet classes and the methods inside the classes have all been public. Because you had only one class, the distinction has not been critical.

Recall the concept of encapsulation, which also means data hiding. A well-designed class keeps its details hidden from other classes as much as possible.

For example, when you declare an object of the Button class, you cannot directly access the label property (`btnDisplay.label` is an illegal reference), but you can use the `getLabel` or `setLabel` method. The Button class hides the label property but allows access only through the "get" or "set" methods. Inside the Button class, label is declared as a private variable; the `getLabel` and `setLabel` methods are declared as public methods.

Inside a class, you can declare variables to be public or private. You also can declare methods to be public or private. Public variables and methods can be referenced by an object instantiated from the class. Only statements within the class itself can reference variables and methods declared as private. Good programming practice is to declare all class variables private and allow access to the variables only through public methods. To accomplish this, use a method (usually called the setxxx method, where xxx is the name of the property).

The following code segment comes from a class called Interest, which creates a private class variable called fltRate. An object outside of the class cannot access this variable directly.

```
private float fltRate;

public void setRate(float fltNewRate)
{
    //Assign new value to the rate property
    fltRate = fltNewRate;
}
```

Another class that instantiates an object from the Interest class can set the rate property with code like this:

```
Interest myInterest = new Interest();
myInterest.setRate(fltRate);
```

The `setRate` method in the Interest class can just assign the value, as you saw above, or it can validate the new value. Sometimes a setxxx method will check to make sure that data are valid before assigning the value to the property.

Feedback 5.2

1. Create a Product class with private class variables for Description, Quantity, and Cost.
2. Code the statement to instantiate an object called currentProduct from the Product class.
3. Write the public `setCost` method to store a new float value in the Cost variable.
4. Code the statement(s) to pass the value in txtCost to the `setCost` method of the currentProduct object.

Returning Values from a Method

The methods you have written so far do not return any value to the code that calls the method. For example, the statement

```
public void DesignInputPanel()
```

begins a method that holds a series of statements. When a statement in another location (init, in this case) calls this method with the statement

```
DesignInputPanel();
```

it means "Go execute the statements in the method and come back when you're through, but don't bring me anything." The keyword **void** in the method header means that the method does not return a value.

A method also can return a value to the statement that calls the method. If so, the return value must have a data type. The return type of a method precedes the name of the method in the method header.

A Method Header—General Format

```
public|private ReturnType MethodName(Arguments)
```

A Method Header—Examples

```
public float getRate()
public String getDescription()
public float calculateInterest(float fltPrincipal, float fltRate; float fltTime)
private void doSomething()
```

The return Statement

A method that returns a value must contain a **return statement.** Before the method terminates, you must return a value of the type named on the method header. The value may be a variable, a constant, or an expression.

The return Statement—General Format

```
return Value;
```

The return Statement—Examples

```
return fltRate;
return "Really big deal";
return intCount;
return 15;
return fltHours * fltRate;
```

The following method has public access and returns a float value:

```
public float calculateInterest()
{
    //Calculate the interest
    return fltPrincipal * fltRate * fltTime;
}
```

Tip

Always include a return type or void. If you omit the return type, the default type of integer is assumed. You receive an error message if you don't return an integer.

Passing Arguments to a Method

Often a method needs values on which to operate. You can declare on the method header that it is expecting arguments, and then pass the arguments when you call the method.

Technically, on the method header, the expected values are called *parameters*. When you call the method and supply values for the parameters, the values are called *arguments*.

On the method header, you must specify the number of parameters, their data types, and their sequence. Then, when calling the method, the arguments must match *exactly*. The number, data type, and sequence are critical, since Java passes the values to the method in sequence.

The next example shows a public method that returns a float value. The parameter list contains an integer value and a float value.

```
public float calculateExtendedPrice(int intQuantity, float fltPrice)
{
    //Calculate the extended price
    return intQuantity * fltPrice;
}
```

To call this method from another method in the class, use this statement:

```
fltExtendedPrice = calculateExtendedPrice(intNumber, fltUnitPrice);
```

Notice that the names of the arguments in the calling statement do not match the names in the method's parameter list. But the arguments match in number, type, and sequence. Java passes one integer and one float value, in sequence. Inside the called method, the passed values are local variables—the names are not passed, only the values. In this case, the `calculateExtendedPrice` method multiplies the two passed values and returns the result to the calling statement.

Dividing an Applet Class

In this example, we'll create an applet project with two classes—one that calculates interest from the input fields for principal, rate, and time (Figure 5.1). The items and functions that relate to the user interface should remain in the Applet class. The variables and methods for calculating the interest go in a separate class. The project will have two .java source files: one for the applet and one for the new Interest class.

Figure 5.1

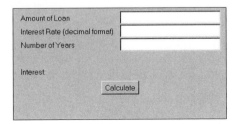

This applet uses an Interest object to calculate the interest from the input fields.

The Applet Class

Begin the project by deciding which items relate to the user interface, which includes any graphical item such as labels, buttons, and text fields. Even though the text fields for entering principal, rate, and time may sound like interest-related items, they are the graphical components for getting the data.

The `init` and `actionPerformed` methods belong in the Applet class.

Class Name: InterestApplet

Properties:

Access Mode (public or private)	Variable or Component Name	Data Type or Class	Description
	txtPrincipal	TextField	Input the amount of the loan.
	txtRate	TextField	Input the interest rate.
	txtTime	TextField	Input the years of the loan.
	lblOutput	Label	Display the calculated interest.
	btnCalculate	Button	Activate `actionPerformed`.

Methods:

Access Mode (public or private)	Return Type	Method Name (include any parameters)	Pseudocode
public	void	init	Add components. Set focus to principal text field. Add action listeners.
public	void	actionPerformed	Create Interest object. Obtain input from text fields. Set Interest properties. Calculate interest. Display results.

InterestApplet Code

```
//Folder:       Ch5Interest
//Programmer:   Bradley/Millspaugh
//Date:         6/2001
//ClassName:    InterestApplet
//Description:  Input principal, rate, and time and calculate simple interest.
```

```java
import java.applet.*;
import java.awt.event.*;
import java.awt.*;

public class InterestApplet extends Applet implements ActionListener
{
    //Create components
    TextField txtPrincipal = new TextField(5);
    TextField txtRate = new TextField(5);
    TextField txtTime = new TextField(5);
    Button btnCalculate = new Button("Calculate");
    Label lblOutput = new Label(" ");

    public void init()
    {
        //Create the user interface
        Panel pnlLayout = new Panel(new GridLayout(5, 2));
        pnlLayout.add(new Label("Amount of Loan "));
        pnlLayout.add(txtPrincipal);
        pnlLayout.add(new Label("Interest Rate (decimal format)"));
        pnlLayout.add(txtRate);
        pnlLayout.add(new Label("Number of Years "));
        pnlLayout.add(txtTime);
        pnlLayout.add(new Label(" ")); //Spacing
        pnlLayout.add(new Label(" ")); //Spacing
        pnlLayout.add(new Label("Interest:"));
        pnlLayout.add(lblOutput);
        add(pnlLayout);
        add(btnCalculate);
        txtPrincipal.requestFocus();
        btnCalculate.addActionListener(this);
        txtPrincipal.addActionListener(this);
        txtRate.addActionListener(this);
        txtTime.addActionListener(this);
    }

    public void actionPerformed(ActionEvent evt)
    {
        //Retrieve data and calculate
        Interest myInterest = new Interest(); //Instantiate an Interest object

        try
        {
            float fltPrincipal = Float.valueOf(txtPrincipal.getText()).floatValue();
            float fltRate = Float.valueOf(txtRate.getText()).floatValue();
            float fltTime = Float.valueOf(txtTime.getText()).floatValue();
            myInterest.setPrincipal(fltPrincipal);
            myInterest.setRate(fltRate);
            myInterest.setTime(fltTime);

            lblOutput.setText("" + myInterest.calculateInterest());
        }
        catch(NumberFormatException e)
        {
            lblOutput.setText("Invalid Data");
        }
    }
}
```

The Interest Class

You need to create an Interest class, to process the data you obtain from the user.

Class Name: Interest

Properties:

Access Mode (public or private)	Variable or Component Name	Data Type or Class	Description
private	fltPrincipal	float	Amount of the loan.
private	fltRate	float	Interest rate.
private	fltTime	float	Years of loan.

Methods:

Access Mode (public or private)	Return Type	Method Name (include any parameters)	Pseudocode
public	void	setPrincipal	Assign new principal value to property.
public	void	setRate	Assign new rate value to property.
public	void	setTime	Assign new time value to property.
public	float	calculateInterest	Multiply principal by rate by time. Return result.

Interest Class Code

```
//Folder:        Ch5Interest
//Programmer:    Bradley/Millspaugh
//Date:          6/2001
//ClassName:     Interest
//Description:   Contains private class variables for principal, rate, and time.
//               Methods: Assign values to private variables and calculate interest.

public class Interest
{
    //Class variables
    private float fltPrincipal;
    private float fltRate;
    private float fltTime;

    public void setPrincipal(float fltNewPrincipal)
    {
        //Assign value to class variable
        fltPrincipal = fltNewPrincipal;
    }
```

```
public void setRate(float fltNewRate)
{
    //Assign value to class variable
    fltRate = fltNewRate;
}

public void setTime(float fltNewTime)
{
    //Assign value to class variable
    fltTime = fltNewTime;
}

public float calculateInterest()
{
    //Calculate the interest
    return fltRate * fltTime * fltPrincipal;
}
}
```

Constructors

A constructor is a very important method of a class. You have used constructors when you created objects from existing classes such as Button, TextField, and Label. For example, these two statements use two different constructors of the Button class:

```
Button btnOK = new Button("OK")
Button btnEmpty = new Button();
```

In the first statement, the text string "OK" is passed to the constructor and the new button object displays "OK". In the second statement, no text string is passed, so a different constructor of the Button class executes and the button does not display any text.

A constructor is a method that is automatically called when a new object is created from the class. Constructors must follow these rules:

A constructor method

● has the same name as the class.

● cannot return a value and therefore has no return type.

● must be public. (Remember, this method is called as a new object is instantiated.)

Use constructor methods to perform actions that are necessary when an object is created, such as initializing data members or opening up databases and data files. Recall that creating a class creates a blueprint for a type of object; it does not create a memory location for an actual object. You actually allocate the memory when you use the new keyword to create an instance of the class. If you are using class variables, such as for totals, you cannot assign any values to those variables until you create an object. The constructor is the place to perform all such initialization tasks.

Adding a Constructor

You could use a different technique for passing the input values to the Interest class that you saw in the previous section. Rather than assign each input value from the related text box, you could create a constructor for your class so that you can create an object and assign all values at once.

To create a constructor method, name the method the same as the class, without using the `public` or `private` keyword. A constructor must be public, which is the default. The constructor method should be the first method in the Interest class, right after declaring the class variables.

```
//Constructor
Interest(float fltNewPrincipal, float fltNewRate, float fltNewTime)
{
    //Assign passed values to data variables
    fltPrincipal = fltNewPrincipal;
    fltRate = fltNewRate;
    fltTime = fltNewTime;
}
```

Using this constructor, you can create an object with the arguments that are passed. The following code goes in the applet and replaces the code in the `actionPerformed` method from the previous applet listing.

```
public void actionPerformed(ActionEvent evt)
{
    //Retrieve data and calculate
    try
    {
        float fltPrincipal = Float.valueOf(txtPrincipal.getText()).floatValue();
        float fltRate = Float.valueOf(txtRate.getText()).floatValue();
        float fltTime = Float.valueOf(txtTime.getText()).floatValue();

        Interest myInterest = new Interest(fltPrincipal, fltRate, fltTime);
        lblOutput.setText("" + myInterest.calculateInterest());
    }
    catch(NumberFormatException e)
    {
        lblOutput.setText("Invalid Data");
    }
}
```

Although you could write the Interest constructor to expect three strings and pass the strings using the `getText` method directly, that's not a very good idea. As you know, when you convert an input string to numeric, Java throws an exception if the string is empty or an invalid numeric value. You cannot have the Interest class display an error message to the user; all user interaction must be done in the applet. You should plan to convert from string to numeric variables in the applet and pass the validated numeric values to the Interest class.

Obtaining Values from Private Class Variables

Sometimes you may want to keep a class variable private but still allow an object of the class to retrieve the data. Create a public method to retrieve the information. This method is usually given a name containing the prefix *get*. The following Interest class has been modified to include a private float variable called `fltInterest`. The constructor automatically calls the `calculateInterest` method (which is now private).

The `getInterest` method returns the value in fltInterest.

```
//Folder:        Ch5Gets
//Programmer:    Bradley/Millspaugh
//Date:          6/2001
//ClassName:     Interest
//Description:   Contains private class variables for principal, rate, and time.
//               Methods: Assign values to private variables and calculate interest.


public class Interest
{
    //Class variables
    private float fltRate;
    private float fltPrincipal;
    private float fltTime;
    private float fltInterest;

    Interest(float fltNewPrincipal, float fltNewRate, float fltNewTime)
    {
        //Constructor
        fltPrincipal = fltNewPrincipal;
        fltRate = fltNewRate;
        fltTime = fltNewTime;
        calculateInterest();
    }

    public float getInterest()
    {
        //Return interest value of the private class variable
        return fltInterest;
    }

    private void calculateInterest()
    {
        //Calculate the interest
        fltInterest = fltRate * fltTime * fltPrincipal;
    }
}
```

Notice that the `calculateInterest` method is now private but `getInterest` is public. Remember the Applet class only can access the methods and variables that are public.

Using a Class Variable for a Total

The next example returns to the payroll example from the previous chapters. In this chapter we are going to separate the applet (user interface) from the payroll processing by creating a Payroll class. For each new employee, we will create a new Payroll object to calculate the pay. In addition, we need to accumulate a count of the number of employees processed and the total pay for all employees.

A problem here is that each employee you process is a separate object. Each employee has an instance of hours and an instance of rate. That's easy enough; we can just make a property for each value. But what about the count and the total pay? If you create a regular property in the Payroll class, the property is recreated for each instance (these are called instance variables).

In Chapter 2 you learned about the concept of a **class variable,** but we have not yet used one. Now is our chance. When you declare a class variable, only one copy of the variable exists, no matter how many objects are instantiated from the class. Use the `static` keyword to declare a class variable. Note that `static` can appear before or after `public` or `private`.

```
static private double dblTotalPay;
static private int intNumberProcessed;
```

or

```
private static double dblTotalPay;
private static int intNumberProcessed;
```

Since these variables are private, you need a *get* method for each to return the value to the class that creates a payroll object. Make sure the return type matches the data type, int for the count and double for the total.

```
public double getTotalPay()
{
    //Retrieve and return value from private variable
    return dblTotalPay;
}

public int getNumberProcessed()
{
    //Retrieve and return value from private variable
    return intNumberProcessed;
}
```

The calculations for the total and count are done each time the pay is calculated for a single object.

```
public float CalculatePay()
{
    //Calculate the pay
    float fltPay;
    fltPay = fltHours * fltRate; //Calculate pay
    dblTotalPay += fltPay; //Add pay to total
    intNumberProcessed ++; //Add 1 to count
    return fltPay;
}
```

Creating a Class for Formatting

In Chapter 4 you learned to get the local formatting and apply the formatting to general numbers and currency values. It takes quite a few statements to perform these operations, which you likely will want to include in many programs. This sounds like a perfect candidate for a new class: the LocalFormat class.

We are going to write this general-purpose class to format float or double values, so we need at least two `FormatCurrency` methods. And it would be helpful for future applications to allow a default of two decimal positions, but to allow a program to specify a different number of decimal positions. For this we need more methods, one for each way that the `FormatCurrency` method may be called. Here are the four method headers for the `FormatCurrency` method (without the coding for the methods). After instantiating an object of the class, a program can call the `FormatCurrency` method with any of these argument lists. (However, an error will result if the arguments don't exactly match one of these headers.)

```
public String FormatCurrency (float fltNumber)
public String FormatCurrency (float fltNumber, int intDecimalPos)
public String FormatCurrency (double dblNumber)
public String FormatCurrency (double dblNumber, int intDecimalPos)
```

The LocalFormat class constructor can retrieve the formatting for the locale, which only must be done once. Then, each call to FormatCurrency will apply the format to the argument and return a formatted string.

```
//Folder:        Ch5Payroll
//Programmer:    Bradley/Millspaugh
//Date:          6/2001
//ClassName:     LocalFormat
//Description:   Get format for locale and format numbers for display

import java.text.*;

public class LocalFormat
{
    //Instance variables
    private NumberFormat fmtCurrency;
    private NumberFormat fmtDecimal;

    //Class constructor
    LocalFormat()
    {
        //Get formatting for default locale
        fmtCurrency = NumberFormat.getCurrencyInstance();
        fmtDecimal = NumberFormat.getInstance();
    }
```

Here we will show only one of the formatting methods. You can use this one as a pattern to write the others, or see them all done in Ch5Payroll.

```
public String FormatCurrency (float fltNumber)
{
```

```
//Format as currency, 2 decimal positions
fmtCurrency.setMinimumFractionDigits(2);
fmtCurrency.setMaximumFractionDigits(2);
String strFormattedData = fmtCurrency.format(fltNumber);
return strFormattedData;
}
```

In the applet, when you want to format output, you must create an instance of the LocalFormat class and then call the correct method to format numeric output.

```
//Set up local formatting
LocalFormat fmtLocal = new LocalFormat();
strFormattedData = fmtLocal.FormatCurrency(myPayroll.getTotalPay());
lblPayOut.setText(strFormattedData);
```

Your Hands-on Programming Example

Modify the Payroll project from Chapter 4 to contain a Payroll class. In the applet, perform only the user-interface tasks; perform all calculations in the Payroll class. Create a constructor to assign the float input values to the Payroll private class variables for hours and rate. Instantiate an object of the Payroll class in the applet class.

Figure 5.2 shows a possible layout for the user interface.

The user interface for the hands-on example.

Planning the Project

Plan the Objects and Properties

Classes: PayrollApplet, Payroll, and LocalFormat

Figure 5.3 shows the class diagrams for this project.

Figure 5.3

The class diagrams for the hands-on example.

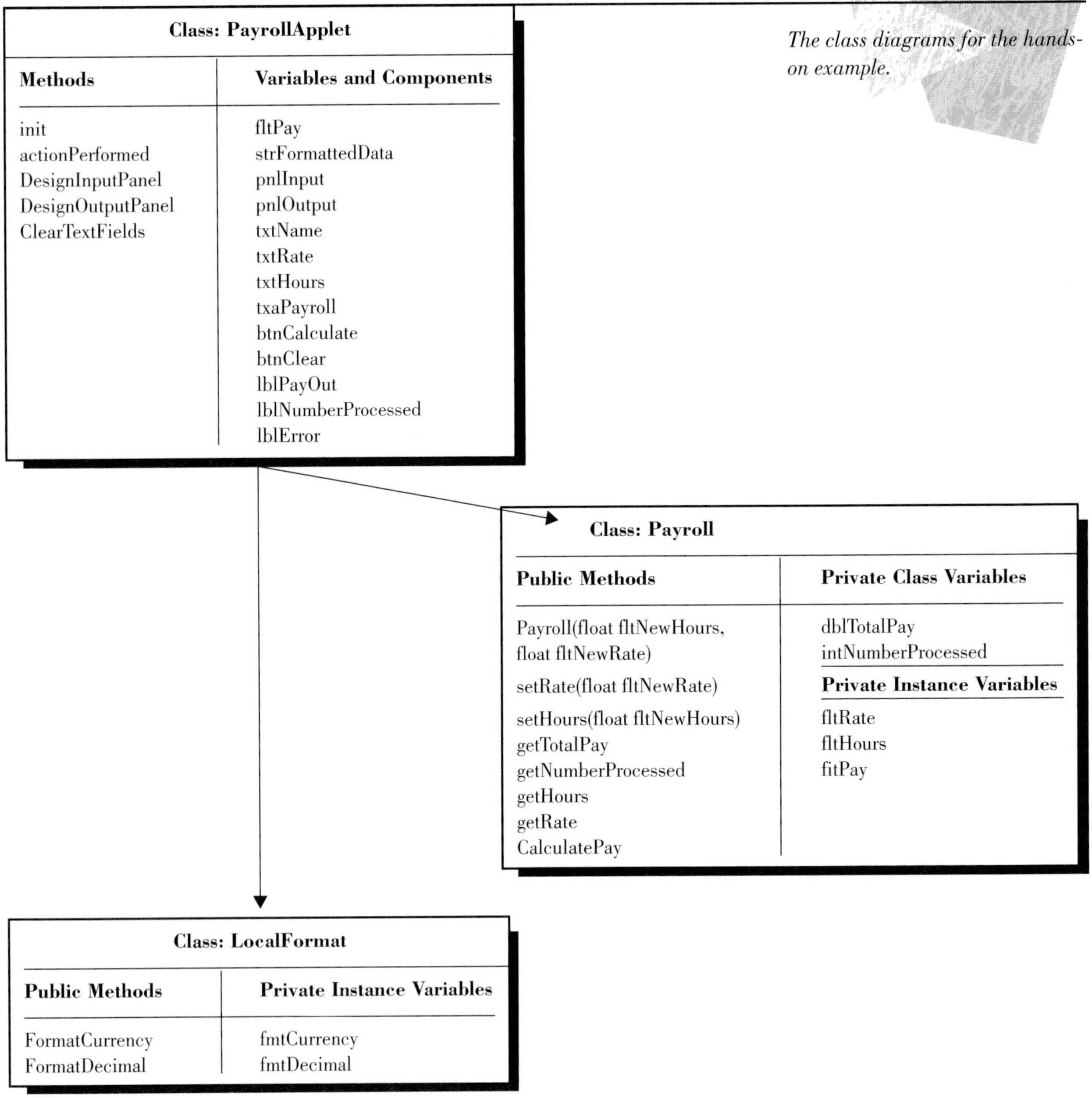

Class: PayrollApplet	
Methods	**Variables and Components**
init	fltPay
actionPerformed	strFormattedData
DesignInputPanel	pnlInput
DesignOutputPanel	pnlOutput
ClearTextFields	txtName
	txtRate
	txtHours
	txaPayroll
	btnCalculate
	btnClear
	lblPayOut
	lblNumberProcessed
	lblError

Class: Payroll	
Public Methods	**Private Class Variables**
Payroll(float fltNewHours, float fltNewRate)	dblTotalPay
	intNumberProcessed
setRate(float fltNewRate)	**Private Instance Variables**
setHours(float fltNewHours)	fltRate
getTotalPay	fltHours
getNumberProcessed	fitPay
getHours	
getRate	
CalculatePay	

Class: LocalFormat	
Public Methods	**Private Instance Variables**
FormatCurrency	fmtCurrency
FormatDecimal	fmtDecimal

Class: PayrollApplet

Components and Variables:

Access Mode (public or private)	Variable or Component Name	Data Type or Class	Description
	txtName	TextField	Input the name.
	txtRate	TextField	Input the hourly pay rate.
			continued

Access Mode (public or private)	Variable or Component Name	Data Type or Class	Description
	txtHours	TextField	Input the hours worked.
	lblPayOut	Label	Display total pay.
	lblNumberProcessed	Label	Display number of employees.
	txaPayroll	TextArea	Display report of names and pay.
	btnCalculate	Button	Process pay.
	pnlInput	Panel	Panel for input components.
	pnlOutput	Panel	Panel for output components.
(local)	fltPay	float	Variable for individual pay.
(local)	strFormattedData	String	Hold formatted output.

Methods:

Access Mode (public or private)	Return Type	Method Name (include any parameters)	Pseudocode
public	void	init	Call method to lay out panel. Add panels. Add text area. Set focus to the name text field. Add action listeners.
public	void	actionPerformed	Obtain input for hours and rate. Create a Payroll object. Calculate pay and totals. Format output. Display results.
public	void	ClearTextFields	Clear text fields. Set focus in first text field.
public	void	DesignInputPanel	Lay out the input fields.
public	void	DesignOutputPanel	Lay out the output fields.

Class: Payroll

Components and Variables:

Access Mode (public or private)	Variable or Component Name	Data Type or Class	Description
private	fltHours	float	Private property for hours.
private	fltRate	float	Private property for rate.
private static	intNumberProcessed	int	Variable to count number of employees.
private static	dblTotalPay	double	Accumulate total pay.
(local)	fltPay	float	Variable for individual pay.

Methods:

Access Mode (public or private)	Return Type	Method Name (include any parameters)	Pseudocode
		`Payroll(float fltNewHours, float fltNewRate)`	Set the hours and rate variables.
public	float	`CalculatePay`	Multiply hours by rate. Add to count. Add to total.
public	void	`setRate(float fltNewRate)`	Assign value to private variable fltRate.
public	void	`setHours(float fltNewHours)`	Assign value to private variable fltHours.
public	double	`getTotalPay`	Return total pay.
public	int	`getNumberProcessed`	Return number processed.
public	float	`getHours`	Return hours.
public	float	`getRate`	Return rate.
public	float	`CalculatePay`	Calculate pay = hours * rate. Add pay to total pay. Add 1 to number processed. Return pay.

Class: LocalFormat

Components and Variables:

Access Mode (public or private)	Variable or Component Name	Data Type or Class	Description
private	fmtCurrency	NumberFormat	Format currency for locale.
private	fmtDecimal	NumberFormat	Format decimal for locale.

Methods:

Access Mode (public or private)	Return Type	Method Name (include any parameters)	Pseudocode
		`LocalFormat()`	Constructor with no parameters. Get formatting for locale.
public	String	`FormatCurrency(float fltNumber)`	Set fractional digits to 2. Format number as currency. Return formatted number.
public	String	`FormatCurrency(float fltNumber, int intDecimalPos)`	Set fractional digits to decimal pos. Format number as currency. Return formatted number.
public	String	`FormatCurrency(double dblNumber)`	Set fractional digits to 2. Format number as currency. Return formatted number.
public	String	`FormatCurrency(double dblNumber, int intDecimalPos)`	Set fractional digits to decimal pos. Format number as currency. Return formatted number.
public	String	`FormatDecimal(float fltNumber)`	Set fractional digits to 2. Format number as decimal. Return formatted number.
public	String	`FormatDecimal(float fltNumber, int intDecimalPos)`	Set fractional digits to decimal pos. Format number as decimal. Return formatted number.

Write the Project

● Create the classes.

● Follow the plan to declare components and variables.

● Code the methods.

● When you complete the code, thoroughly test the project.

The Project Solution

PayrollApplet.java

```java
//Folder:        Ch5Payroll
//Programmer:    Bradley/Millspaugh
//Date:          6/2001
//ClassName:     PayrollApplet
//Description:   Input hours and rate; calculate pay, total pay,
//               and number processed. Format and display results.

import java.applet.*;
import java.awt.event.*;
import java.awt.*;

public class PayrollApplet extends Applet implements ActionListener
{
    //Create components
    Panel pnlInput = new Panel();
    Panel pnlOutput = new Panel();
    TextField txtName = new TextField(25);
    TextField txtHours = new TextField();
    TextField txtRate = new TextField();
    TextArea txaPayroll =
        new TextArea("Payroll Report", 10, 30, TextArea.SCROLLBARS_VERTICAL_ONLY);
    Button btnCalculate = new Button("Calculate Pay");
    Label lblPayOut = new Label();
    Label lblNumberProcessed = new Label();
    Label lblError = new Label(" ");

    public void init()
    {
        //Create user interface
        DesignInputPanel();
        DesignOutputPanel();
        add(pnlInput);
        add(pnlOutput);
        add(txaPayroll);
        txtName.requestFocus();
        btnCalculate.addActionListener(this);
        txtHours.addActionListener(this);
        txtRate.addActionListener(this);
    }

    public void actionPerformed(ActionEvent evt)
    {
        //Retrieve data and calculate
        //Declare local variables
        float fltPay;
        String strFormattedData;

        //Clear any previous error messages
        lblError.setText("");
        showStatus("Ready");

        try
        {
            //Obtain data from text boxes
```

```
            float fltRate = Float.valueOf(txtRate.getText()).floatValue();
            float fltHours = Float.valueOf(txtHours.getText()).floatValue();

            //Instantiate a new Payroll object
            Payroll myPayroll = new Payroll(fltHours, fltRate);
            fltPay = myPayroll.CalculatePay();

            //Set up local formatting
            LocalFormat fmtLocal = new LocalFormat();

            //Format and display results
            strFormattedData = fmtLocal.FormatDecimal(fltPay);
            txaPayroll.append("\n" + txtName.getText() + "\t" + strFormattedData);
            strFormattedData = fmtLocal.FormatCurrency(myPayroll.getTotalPay());
            lblPayOut.setText(strFormattedData);
            lblNumberProcessed.setText("" + myPayroll.getNumberProcessed());
            ClearTextFields();
        }

        catch(NumberFormatException e)
        {
            lblError.setForeground(Color.red);
            lblError.setText("Invalid data entered");
            showStatus("Invalid data entered");
        }
    }

    public void DesignInputPanel()
    {
        //Lay out the input panel
        pnlInput.setLayout(new GridLayout(4, 2));
        pnlInput.add(new Label("Name: "));
        pnlInput.add(txtName);
        pnlInput.add(new Label("Hours: "));
        pnlInput.add(txtHours);
        pnlInput.add(new Label("Rate: "));
        pnlInput.add(txtRate);
        pnlInput.add(lblError);
    }

    public void DesignOutputPanel()
    {
        //Lay out the output panel
        pnlOutput.setLayout(new GridLayout(4, 2));
        pnlOutput.add(new Label("Total Pay:"));
        pnlOutput.add(lblPayOut);
        pnlOutput.add(new Label("Number Processed: "));
        pnlOutput.add(lblNumberProcessed);
        pnlOutput.add(btnCalculate);
    }

    public void ClearTextFields()
    {
        //Clear text fields
        txtName.setText("");
        txtHours.setText("");
        txtRate.setText("");
        txtName.requestFocus();
    }
}
```

Payroll.java

```
//Folder:          Ch5Payroll
//Programmer:      Bradley/Millspaugh
//Date:            6/2001
//ClassName:       Payroll
//Description:     Input hours and rate; calculate pay, total pay, and number processed.

public class Payroll
{
    //Class variables
    private static double dblTotalPay;
    private static int intNumberProcessed;

    //Instance variables
    private float fltHours;
    private float fltRate;

    //Constructor
    Payroll(float fltNewHours, float fltNewRate)
    {
        setHours(fltNewHours);
        setRate(fltNewRate);
    }

    //Public methods
    public void setRate(float fltNewRate)
    {
        //Assign new value to private variable
        fltRate = fltNewRate;
    }

    public void setHours(float fltNewHours)
    {
        //Assign new value to private variable
        fltHours = fltNewHours;
    }

    public double getTotalPay()
    {
        //Retrieve and return value from private variable
        return dblTotalPay;
    }

    public int getNumberProcessed()
    {
        //Retrieve and return value from private variable
        return intNumberProcessed;
    }

    public float getHours()
    {
        //Retrieve and return value from private variable
        return fltHours;
    }

    public float getRate()
    {
        //Retrieve and return value from private variable
        return fltRate;
    }
```

```java
    public float CalculatePay()
    {
        //Calculate the pay
        float fltPay;
        fltPay = fltHours * fltRate; //Calculate pay
        dblTotalPay += fltPay;      //Add pay to total
        intNumberProcessed++;       //Add 1 to count
        return fltPay;
    }
}
```

LocalFormat.Java

```java
//Folder:        Ch5Payroll
//Programmer:    Bradley/Millspaugh
//Date:          6/2001
//ClassName:     LocalFormat
//Description:   Get format for locale and format numbers for display.

import java.text.*;

public class LocalFormat
{
    //Instance variables
    private NumberFormat fmtCurrency;
    private NumberFormat fmtDecimal;

    //Class constructor
    LocalFormat()
    {
        //Get formatting for default locale
        fmtCurrency = NumberFormat.getCurrencyInstance();
        fmtDecimal = NumberFormat.getInstance();
    }

    //Methods
    public String FormatCurrency (float fltNumber)
    {
        //Format as currency, 2 decimal positions
        fmtCurrency.setMinimumFractionDigits(2);
        fmtCurrency.setMaximumFractionDigits(2);
        String strFormattedData = fmtCurrency.format(fltNumber);
        return strFormattedData;
    }

    public String FormatCurrency (float fltNumber, int intDecimalPos)
    {
        //Format as currency, variable number of decimal positions
        fmtCurrency.setMinimumFractionDigits(intDecimalPos);
        fmtCurrency.setMaximumFractionDigits(intDecimalPos);
        String strFormattedData = fmtCurrency.format(fltNumber);
        return strFormattedData;
    }

    public String FormatCurrency (double dblNumber)
    {
        //Format as currency, 2 decimal positions
        fmtCurrency.setMinimumFractionDigits(2);
        fmtCurrency.setMaximumFractionDigits(2);
        String strFormattedData = fmtCurrency.format(dblNumber);
```

```
        return strFormattedData;
    }

    public String FormatCurrency (double dblNumber, int intDecimalPos)
    {
        //Format as currency, variable number of decimal positions
        fmtCurrency.setMinimumFractionDigits(intDecimalPos);
        fmtCurrency.setMaximumFractionDigits(intDecimalPos);
        String strFormattedData = fmtCurrency.format(dblNumber);
        return strFormattedData;
    }

    public String FormatDecimal (float fltNumber)
    {
        //Format as decimal, 2 decimal positions
        fmtDecimal.setMinimumFractionDigits(2);
        fmtDecimal.setMaximumFractionDigits(2);
        String strFormattedData = fmtDecimal.format(fltNumber);
        return strFormattedData;
    }

    public String FormatDecimal (float fltNumber, int intDecimalPos)
    {
        //Format as decimal, variable number of decimal positions
        //Set decimal positions
        fmtDecimal.setMinimumFractionDigits(intDecimalPos);
        fmtDecimal.setMaximumFractionDigits(intDecimalPos);
        String strFormattedData = fmtDecimal.format(fltNumber);
        return strFormattedData;
    }
}
```

Summary

1. Java is an object-oriented programming language supporting encapsulation, inheritance, and polymorphism.
2. Encapsulation is the process of combining data and methods into a single unit called a class and hiding the data from outside the class.
3. The `extends` keyword provides inheritance in Java. A subclass is based on a superclass or base class.
4. In subclasses you write classes that override a method of the same name in the superclass.
5. Each class can inherit from only one superclass but can implement many interfaces. An interface exposes a set of methods, which are abstract methods, and must be overridden.
6. An inner class is a class within a class.
7. An abstract class is a class with abstract methods that you can use as a superclass.
8. Polymorphism refers to multiple methods that are called the same name but act differently depending on the situation.
9. An object is created from a class using the `new` keyword. The process of creating an object is called instantiation. When an object is instantiated, the constructor method of the class executes automatically.
10. A project can contain multiple classes. Each class is a separate file with a .java extension and should be in the same folder as the rest of the project.

11. Private members of a class can be used only by the methods in the class. Objects instantiated from a class type have access to public members of the class.

12. Instance variables should be declared as private, with public `set` methods to assign values to the variables.

13. To return a value from a method, declare the data type of the return value on the method header and use a `return` statement within the method.

14. To pass values to a method, include parameters on the method header. The parameter list must include the number of parameters, their data type, and the sequence. To call the method, the argument list must exactly match the parameter list.

15. An applet should handle only the user-interface tasks. The processing tasks should be included in a separate class. In the applet you instantiate an object of your separate class.

16. A constructor is a method with the same name as the class. There can be multiple constructor methods, each with a different argument list.

17. Write a `get` method to allow an object to retrieve the value of a private property.

18. A class variable, declared with the `static` keyword, has only one instance, even though there may be multiple instances of the class. Use class variables to accumulate totals and counts.

Key Terms

abstract class *127*	object *128*
base class *126*	overloading *129*
class variable *139*	overriding *126*
constructor method *128*	polymorphism *128*
encapsulation *126*	private *129*
hierarchy *126*	public *129*
inheritance *126*	`return` statement *131*
inner class *127*	subclass *126*
instance *128*	superclass *126*
instantiate *128*	`void` *131*
interface *127*	

Review Questions

1. List and define the basic concepts of object-oriented programming.
2. Explain the relationship between a superclass and a subclass.
3. What is an abstract class? An interface?
4. What is an object? How is it created?
5. What is the effect of making a data member private? A method private?
6. Where is the data type for a method's return value specified?
7. How is a value returned from a method?
8. When would you use the return type `void`?
9. What is a method's parameter list and how does it relate to arguments in a method call?

10. What items properly belong in an applet class? What items properly belong in a separate class?
11. Explain how the compiler can recognize that a method is a constructor method.
12. How can an object of a class retrieve the value of a private property?
13. What is a class variable and how does it differ from an instance variable?
14. Why might a class have multiple methods with the same name but different parameter lists?

Programming Exercises

5.1 Rewrite your project from Chapter 4 to use three classes. Instantiate an object of your new class in the applet class.

5.2 Create a Student class that contains the student name, student ID, phone, and number of units completed. Include a constructor that assigns values to the private class variables. Create an applet to input data and assign it to the class variables. Create methods in the Student class to get the name from the private class variables. Display the student name, student ID, phone, and number of units completed in the text area.

5.3 Create a Course class containing the course name, course number, and number of units. Include a constructor that assigns values to the private class variables and methods that return the course name (getCourse-Name) and number of units (getUnits).

Create an applet class called ClassApplet that inputs the data and assigns the values to the class variables. Use the get methods to display the course name and units. (Although you could do these directly from the input fields, we are preparing for Chapter 7 when you will learn to perform searches.)

CASE STUDIES

R 'n R—for Reading and Refreshment

Modify the project in Chapter 4 to contain a separate class for processing sales. The processing must be divided into separate methods for each item that is displayed. For example, an addToTotalBooks method will add the quantity to the number of books sold and an addToTotalSales adds the amount due to the total of all sales. Make the price and quantity fields private and use a constructor to transfer the values to the sales class.

Merry Pea's Quilting

Divide the applet from Chapter 4 into multiple classes. Create a .java class for processing information about quilting courses. The applet class should contain the visual components and instantiate an object for the quilting courses. You will need to use a class variable (static) for the totals.

CHAPTER

6

Decisions and Conditions

At the completion of this chapter, you will be able to . . .

1. Read and create flowcharts that show the logic of a selection process.

2. Use `if` statements to control the flow of logic.

3. Understand and use nested `if`s.

4. Evaluate conditions using the relational operators.

5. Combine conditions using the logical operators.

6. Perform validation on numeric fields.

7. Determine the event that caused the `actionPerformed` method to be called.

8. Understand the precedence and relationship of assignment, arithmetic, logical, and relational operators.

This chapter introduces decision statements, which allow you to test conditions and perform different actions depending on the outcome of the condition.

All of the applets you have created so far have a single command button. If you include multiple buttons, you must determine in the `actionPerformed` method which button was clicked. You need a decision statement to do that.

With decision statements, you can compare values in variables and constants using relational and logical operators. You can keep track of sales separately for different classes of employees, different sections of the country, or different departments. You may want to check the value entered by the user to make sure it is valid and display an error message for inappropriate values.

Decision Statements

A powerful asset of the computer is its ability to make decisions and to take alternate courses of action based on the outcome. A decision made by the computer is formed as a question: Is a given condition true or false? If it is true, do one thing; if it is false, do something else.

if the sun is shining (condition)
    go to the beach;   (action to take if condition is true)
else
    go to class;   (action to take if condition is false)

(See Figure 6.1.)

Figure 6.1

The logic of an if *statement in flowchart form.*

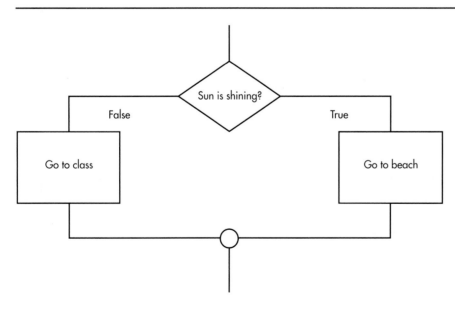

or

if you don't succeed (condition)
    try, try again;   (action)

(See Figure 6.2.)

Figure 6.2

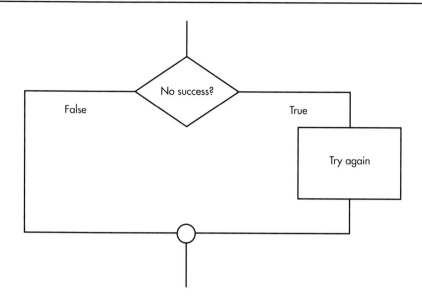

The logic of an if *statement without an* else *action in flowchart form.*

Notice in the second example that no action is specified if the condition is not true.

In an **if statement**, when the condition is true, only the statement(s) after the if executes. When the condition is false, only the statements following the **else**, if present, execute.

The if Statement—General Format

```
if (condition)
    statement;
[else
    statement;]
if (condition)
{
    statement(s);
}
[else
{
    statement(s);
}]
```

The if Statement—Examples

```
if (fltHours > 40.0f)
{
    CalculateOvertime();
}
```

continued

```
if (intGrade >= 70)
{
    lblGrade.setText("Pass");
}
else
{
    lblGrade.setText("No Pass");
}

if (intAge < 12)
    CalculateDiscount();
```

In the first of the preceding examples, the `CalculateOvertime` method executes only when fltHours exceeds 40. If fltHours is less than or equal to 40, execution will continue with the statement following the brace. The second example displays "Pass" in the label if the condition is true. "No Pass" displays when the condition is false.

Note: If you omit the *f* for float on the 40.0f constant of the condition, you do not get an error. However, it is better programming practice to always make sure that the data type is the same on both sides of a relational operator.

When you have only one statement to execute for a condition, you can omit the braces. For example, you can write this statement as

```
if (intAge < 12)
    CalculateDiscount();
```

or

```
if (intAge < 12)
{
    CalculateDiscount();
}
```

It's a good practice to always use the braces.

```
intAge = 12;

if (intAge < 12)
    CalculateDiscount();
CalculateTotal();
```

In this example, the `CalculateTotal` statement is not part of the `if` statement and will execute whether the `if` condition evaluates true or false. Since the condition (intAge < 12) evaluates false, the `CalculateDiscount` statement does not execute, but `CalculateTotal` does execute. Execution continues with the statement following the `if`.

You must be very careful about the semicolon. If you place a semicolon after the `if` statement, you will not get a syntax error; instead, the Java interpreter just terminates the `if`. The next statement will execute whether or not the condition is true.

Notice also that you must enclose the condition in parentheses, which is different from many other programming languages.

Always indent the statements under the `if` and `else` clauses, which greatly aids the readability and clarity of your program. Although the Java interpreter ignores the indentation, humans can read and understand indented code much better.

```
if (intAge < 12)
{
    CalculateDiscount();
    DisplayDiscount();
}
else
{
    CalculateFullPrice();
    DisplayFullPrice();
}
CalculateTotal();
```

Any statements following the `else` clause execute if the condition evaluates false. The `else` clause is optional but may contain any statement, including another `if`.

Remember it's always better to use the braces when coding an `if` or an `else`. The braces make certain all desired statements are included in the `if` statement. You will be less likely to make a mistake and the logic of your program will be clearer.

Flowcharting *if* Statements

A flowchart is a useful tool for showing the logic of an `if` statement. It has been said that one picture is worth a thousand words. Many programmers find that a flowchart helps them organize their thoughts and design projects more quickly.

The symbols used in this text are a subset of the available flowcharting symbols. The diamond-shape symbol (called a *decision symbol*) represents a condition. The two branches from the symbol indicate which path to take when the condition evaluates true or false. (See Figure 6.3.)

Figure 6.3

The programming symbols used for program decisions and processes.

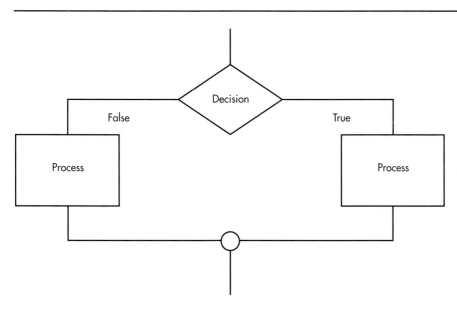

Conditions

The test in an `if` statement is based on a **condition** used to compare values. The result of the comparison is either true or false. You can use relational operators on numeric or character fields. However, the operators do not work with the String class, which contains its own methods for comparisons.

Relational Operators

You can use **relational operators** to compare values. The operators can test for equality or if a value is greater or less than another value. The relational operators in Java are shown in Table 6.1.

Table 6.1

Relational Operators

Relational Operator	Condition
<	Less than
>	Greater than
==	Equal
!=	Not equal
<=	Less than or equal
>=	Greater than or equal

You can form conditions with numeric variables and constants, character (char) variables and constants, and arithmetic expressions. Notice that the list does not include Strings, which are objects and handled differently. Comparisons for Strings are covered in the section "Comparing Strings."

The relational operator for equality is two equal signs. A single equal sign is the assignment operator. If you attempt to use the assignment operator in a conditional expression, you receive an error that a boolean is required. Also notice the != represents the not equal relationship.

Tip

If you are a C++ programmer, you may be familiar with using an assignment within the conditional expression. The security rules of the Java compiler do not allow this.

Comparing Numeric Variables and Constants

When numeric values are involved in a test, an algebraic comparison is made; that is, the sign of the number is taken into account. Therefore, negative 20 is less than 10, and negative 2 is less than negative 1.

For example, the condition

```
if (fltPrice == fltMaximum)
```

means "Is the current numeric value stored in fltPrice equal to the value stored in fltMaximum?"

More Examples

```
fltHours > 40.0f    //Test for greater than 40 hours
intQuantity == 0;   //Test for equal to 0
```

Sample Comparisons

Given:

```
int intAlpha = 5;
int intBravo = 4;
int intCharlie = -5;
```

Condition	Evaluates
intAlpha == intBravo	false
intCharlie < 0	true
intBravo > intAlpha	false
intCharlie <= intBravo	true
intAlPha >= 5	true
intAlpha != intCharlie	true

Comparing Character Data

You can use the relational operators to compare character data stored in the char data type. As you recall, char variables hold only a single character. For longer strings of text, you normally create objects from the String class to store character data.

The determination of which character is less than another is based on the code used to store characters internally in the computer. Java stores characters using the 16-bit Unicode, which is designed to hold characters in any language, such as Japanese and Chinese. However, the Latin alphabet, numerals, and punctuation have the same values in Unicode as they do in the ANSI and ASCII codes. The code has an established order (called the collating sequence) for all letters, numbers, and special characters. Note in Table 6.2 that A is less than B, L is greater than K, and all numeric digits are less than all letters. Some special symbols are lower than the numbers and some are higher, and the blank space is lower than the rest of the characters shown.

You can compare a char variable to a literal, another char variable, an escape sequence, or the code number. You enclose char literals in single quotes, which then compares to the value of the literal. Without the quotes, you are comparing the char literal to a code number (from the code chart).

```
(chrSex == 'F')     //Compare to the uppercase letter 'F'
(chrCode != '\0')   //Compare to a null character (character 0)
(chrCode == '9')    //Compare to the digit 9
(chrCode == 9)      //Compare to code 9 (the Tab character)
```

Table 6.2

Selected Unicode Codes

Code	Value	Code	Value	Code	Value
0	Null	38	&	60	<
8	Backspace	39	'	61	=
9	Tab	40	(	62	>
10	Linefeed	41	)	63	?
12	Form Feed	42	*	64	@
13	Carriage Return	43	+	65–90	A–Z
27	Escape	44	,	91	[
32	Space	45	-	92	\
33	!	46	.	93	]
34	"	47	/	94	^
35	#	48–57	0–9	95	_
36	$	58	:	96	`
37	%	59	;	97–122	a–z

Examples

```
char chrUpperCase = 'C';
char chrLowerCase = 'c';
```

The condition (`chrLowerCase > chrUpperCase`) is true because the ASCII code for 'C' is 67 while the code for 'c' is 99.

```
char chrQuestionMark = '?';
char chrExclamation = '!';
```

The condition (`chrQuestionMark < chrExclamation`) is false because the code for '?' is 63 while the code for '!' is 33.

You can compare individual characters in a string by obtaining a single character with the `charAt` method. The first character in the string has an index of 0. The following statement uses relational operators to compare the first letter of the string object.

```
(strName.charAt(0) == 'A')
```

Note: You enclose char literals in single quotes. Double quotes are used for String literals.

Comparing Numeric Wrapper Classes

The Integer and Float classes both have an `equals` method. You get the same result using the `equals` method as comparing the values with the == relational operator.

```
Float FltBalance = new Float(0.0f);
Float FltAmount = new Float(0.0f);
```

After declaring these two Float objects, the following conditions are equivalent:

```
(FltBalance.equals(FltAmount.floatValue()))
(FltBalance.floatValue() == FltAmount.floatValue())
```

Note that you can use any of the relational operators when comparing the value of a numeric object. For example, if you want to compare for *greater than*, use

```
(FltBalance.floatValue() > FltAmount.floatValue())
```

Comparing Strings

You can use the methods of the String class to compare String objects to other String objects or String literals enclosed in quotation marks. If you are testing for equality, use the `equals` or the `equalsIgnoreCase` method. However, when you need to compare for *less than* or *greater than*, such as arranging strings alphabetically, you will use the `compareTo` method.

The equals Method

The String class `equals` method returns true if the strings are the same and false if they differ.

```
(strName.equals(strInput))
(strName.equals("Bill"))
```

The comparison begins with the leftmost character and proceeds one character at a time from left to right. As soon as a character in one string is not equal to the corresponding character in the second string, the comparison is terminated and the condition returns false.

Example

```
String strName = new String("Joan");
String strName2 = new String("John");
```

The condition

```
(strName.equals(strName2))
```

evaluates to false. The *a* in Joan is lower ranking than the *h* in John.

The equalsIgnoreCase Method

The `equalsIgnoreCase` method is similar to the `equals` method but does not differentiate between uppercase and lowercase.

```
String strName = new String("Joan");
String strName2 = new String("JOAN");
```

The condition

```
(strName.equals(strName2)
```

evaluates false, but the condition

```
(strName.equalsIgnoreCase(strName2)
```

evaluates true.

The compareTo Method

Use the `compareTo` method to determine *less than* or *greater than*. The `compareTo` method returns an integer with one of three possible values.

```
strString1.compareTo(strString2)
```

If the two strings are equal, the method returns zero; when strString1 is greater than strString2, a positive number returns. A negative number is returned when strString2 is greater than strString1. To use this method effectively, you can set up a condition using the return value and a relational operator.

```
(strString1.compareTo(strString2) == 0) //Are the strings equal?
(strString1.compareTo(strString2) != 0) //Are the strings different?
(strString1.compareTo(strString2) > 0)  //Is strString1 greater than strString2?
```

Example

```
String strWord = new String("Hope");
String strWord2 = new String("Hopeless");
//Compare the strings
if (strWord.compareTo(strWord2) < 0)
    //Display a message -- What will it be?
```

How will the preceding comparison test, true or false? Before reading any further, stop and figure it out.

Ready? When one string is shorter than the other, the comparison proceeds as if the shorter string is padded with blanks to the right of the string, and the blank space is compared to a character in the longer string. So the comparison `"Hope     " < "Hopeless"` is true.

```
String strCar = new String("300ZX");
Label lblCar = new Label("Porsche");
```

The condition

```
(strCar.compareTo(lblCar.getText()) > 0)
```

evaluates false. When the number 3 is compared to the letter *P*, the 3 is lower; all numbers are lower than all letters.

Additional String Methods

The String class has many other useful methods that you may want to try. Table 6.3 shows a few of the methods; you can find more in Java's Help.

Method	Purpose
charAt(int *position*)	Returns the character at the given position.
compareTo(String *value*)	Compares contents of the String with the String argument. Returns negative number, zero, or positive number.
concat(String *value*)	Appends the String argument to the String object.
endsWith(String *value*)	Checks if the String object ends with the specified characters. Returns true or false.
equals(Object)	Compares the String to the specified object. Returns true or false.
equalsIgnoreCase(String)	Compares the String to the String argument. Returns true or false.
length()	Returns the number of characters in the String as an integer.
replace(char oldCharacter, char newCharacter)	Replaces all occurrences of the old character with the new character.
startsWith(String *value*)	Checks if the string begins with the specified characters. Returns true or false.
toLowerCase()	Converts the String to lowercase.
toUpperCase()	Converts the String to uppercase.
trim()	Removes spaces from both ends of the String.

Feedback 6.1

Evaluate the following expressions as true or false.

1. Given:

```
float fltTotalSales = 0.0f;
int intCount = 5;
```

Evaluate:

```
(fltTotalSales == intCount)
```

2. Given:

```
char chrCode = 'A';
char chrLimit = 'J';
```

Evaluate:

```
(chrCode <= chrLimit)
```

continued

3. Write the conditional expression to test `intNumberCorrect`. The condition should evaluate true for a value greater than or equal to 90.

4. Determine which conditions will evaluate true and which ones will evaluate false.

   Given:

   ```
   int intCountOne = 5;
   int intCountTwo = 5;
   intCountThree = -5;
   String strOne = new String("Bit");
   String strTwo = new String("Bite");
   String strNumber = new String("2");
   String strDollar = new String("$");
   ```

   (a) `(intCountOne >= intCountTwo)`
   (b) `(intCountThree < 0)`
   (c) `(intCountThree <= intCountTwo)`
   (d) `(intCountOne != intCountTwo)`
   (e) `(intCountOne + 2 . intCountTwo + 2)`
   (f) `(strOne.charAt(0) == strTwo.charAt(0))`
   (g) `strNumber.equals("Two");`
   (h) `strDollar.equals("?");`

5. Write the statements necessary to compare txtApples.getText() and txtOranges.getText(). Display in lblMost which has more, the apples or the oranges.

6. Write the statements that test the current value of fltBalance. When fltBalance is greater than 0, set fltBalance back to 0 and increment intCounter by 1.

Testing Boolean Values

You can form a condition using a Java boolean primitive data type, which contains either a true or false value. You also can use the Boolean wrapper class, which has the same values.

The statement

```
if (blnSuccessfulOperation == true)
```

is equivalent to

```
if (blnSuccessfulOperation)
```

The Logical Operators

You can test for multiple conditions using **logical operators** to combine conditions. Table 6.4 shows three of the logical operators.

Table 6.4

Logical Operators

Logical Operator	Meaning	Evaluates
&&	And	Both conditions must be true for the entire condition to be true.
||	Or	Either condition or both conditions must be true for the entire condition to be true.
!	Not	Reverse the truth of a condition.

With the && operator, both conditions must be true for the condition to evaluate to true. Only one condition needs to be true with the || operator, but both may be true.

```
(fltBalance > 5000.0f || intCount == 0)
```

This **compound condition** consists of two separate conditions. The first, fltBalance > 5000.0f, evaluates either true or false. The second condition, intCount == 0, evaluates true or false. Then, the entire compound condition evaluates true if either of the conditions is true. Of course, the compound condition is also true if both conditions are true.

You can create compound conditions by combining two or more conditions with the logical operators && or ||.

Precedence of Logical Operators in Compound Conditions

You may combine the && and || operators in the same condition when you are testing more than two conditions. The && operator has a higher precedence and the conditions around the && are tested first. To alter the order of evaluation, use parentheses around your conditions.

Compound Condition Examples

Given:

```
int intAlpha = 5;
int intBravo = 4;
int intCharlie = -5;
```

Condition	Evaluates
(intAlpha <= 5 || intCharlie == 0)	true
(intAlpha <= 5 && intCharlie == 0)	false
(intAlpha <=5 || intCharlie == 0 && intBravo < 10)	true
(intAlpha <= 5 && intCharlie == 0 || intBravo < 10)	true
(intAlpha <= 5 && intCharlie == 6 && intBravo < 10)	false

Beware: Some compilers are considered "smart," which means that once the compiler can determine that a condition is false, the evaluation process is terminated. This may affect your results if you have embedded an increment operator in a conditional expression. For example, look at this statement:

```
if (blnSuccessfulOperation && intCount++ > 10)
```

If blnSuccessfulOperation is false, intCount may not get incremented, which may or may not be what you intended. If you reverse the two conditions, you can make sure that intCount will always be incremented.

Nested if Statements

In many situations, another if statement is one of the statements to be executed when a condition tests true or false. An if statement that contains additional if statements is said to be a **nested if statement**. The following example shows a nested if statement in which the second if occurs in the true portion of the first if (Figure 6.4).

Figure 6.4

Flowcharting a nested if statement.

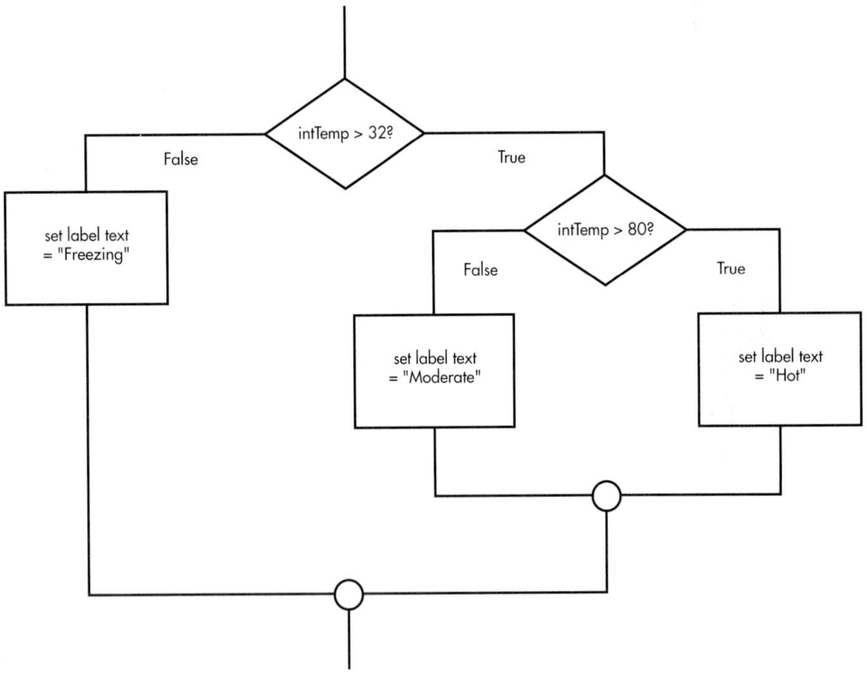

```
if (intTemp > 32)
{
    if (intTemp > 80
    {
        lblComment.setText("Hot");
```

```
    }
    else
    {
        lblComment.setText("Moderate");
    }
}
else
{
    lblComment.setText("Freezing");
}
```

To nest `if` statements in the `else` portion, you may use either of the following approaches; however, your code is simpler if you use the second method (using `else if`).

First Method

```
if (intTemp <= 32)
{
    lblComment.setText("Freezing");
}
else
{
    if (intTemp > 80)
    {
        lblComment.setText("Hot");
    }
    else
    {
        lblComment.setText("Moderate);
    }
}
```

Second Method

```
if (intTemp <= 32)
{
    lblComment.setText("Freezing");
}
else if (intTemp > 80)
{
    lblComment.setText("Hot");
}
else
{
    lblComment.setText("Moderate);
}
```

Notice that in the second format using the `else  if`, the indentation changes and you use one less set of brackets.

You may nest `if`s in both the true and false actions. In fact, you may continue to nest `if`s within `if`s. However, projects become very difficult to follow (and may not perform as intended) when `if`s become too deeply nested.

Feedback 6.2

Assume that intFrogs = 10, intToads = 5, and intPolliwogs = 6. What will be displayed for each of the following statements?

```
1.  if (intFrogs > intPolliwogs)
        lblResult.setText("It's the frogs");
2.  if (intFrogs > intToads + intPolliwogs)
        lblResult.setText("It's the frogs");
    else
        lblResult.setText("It's the toads and the polliwogs");
3.  if (intPolliwogs > intToads && intFrogs != 0 || intToads == 0)
        lblResult.setText("It's true");
    else
        lblResult.setText("It's false");
```

The Conditional Operator

You also can write decisions using Java's **conditional operator**, which is a shortcut version of an if/else. You write the condition, then a question mark (?), the result if true, a colon (:), and the result if false.

The Conditional Operator—General Format

```
(condition) ? TrueResult : FalseResult
```

The Conditional Operator—Examples

```
fltRate = (fltSales < 10000f) ? .05f : .1f;
fltCommission = (fltSales < 10000f) ? fltSales * .05f : fltSales * .1f;
```

The first example tests the condition (fltSales < 10000); if the condition evaluates true, .05 is assigned to fltRate; if the condition evaluates false, .1 is assigned to fltRate. The second example calculates the commission and assigns it to fltCommission: If the sales are less than 10,000, the commission is 5 percent (.05) of sales; otherwise it is 10 percent (.1) of sales.

You never have to use the conditional operator as a replacement for an if statement, but some find it easier to read and to write. The choice is yours.

Note: Java does not require the *f* for float on the constant in a condition, but it does require the data type to be correct for assignment and calculations. Good programming practice requires that you always specify the correct data type.

Feedback 6.3

1. Write the following statement using an if:

    ```
    chrGrade = (fltScore >= 85.0f) ? 'A' : 'C';
    ```

2. Code a statement using the conditional operator that sets intQuota to 1000 if chrCode is '1'; otherwise the quota is 2000.

Validating User Input

Careful programmers check the values entered into text fields by the user before beginning the calculations. Validation is a form of self-protection; it is better to reject bad data than to spend hours (and sometimes days) trying to find an error only to discover that the problem was caused by a "user error." Finding and correcting the error early often can keep the program from producing erroneous results, halting with a run-time error, or just halting with no error and no indication of the reason.

Checking to verify that appropriate values were entered is called **validation**. The validation may include making sure that data are numeric, checking for specific values, checking a range of values, or making sure that required items are entered.

In object-oriented programming, you generally separate the user interface code from the code to handle processing. It makes sense to check for nonnumeric input in the applet (the UI), but check for business rules, such as valid values for a specific field, in a class designed to perform the processing.

In Chapter 4 you learned to handle exceptions that are thrown when you attempt to convert nonnumeric text data to a numeric field. In this chapter, you will learn to validate data using if statements.

Checking Business Rules

Often you must check an input value to make sure that it follows **business rules**. A business rule may specify that the rate of pay, a check amount, or the hours worked cannot exceed a predefined number, or that input values must match a list of acceptable values. The following code checks to make sure that the number of hours is not greater than fltMAX_HOURS, which is defined as a constant.

```
if (fltHours > fltMAX_HOURS)
{
    showStatus("Invalid Hours field"); //Display an error status message
    txtHours.selectAll();   //Select the text in the field in error
    txtHours.requestFocus();      //Return the focus to the field in error
}
```

Validating in a Class

You can check the validity of input data in an applet, but the preferred technique is to check business rules in a class that handles the data. You may choose to validate in a calculation method or in methods that set the values of instance variables (the recommended approach). In the following segment from the Payroll class, the setRate method checks the validity before assigning the new value to the instance variable. Notice that for invalid data, the code sets fltRate to a negative number. You will see another way to indicate bad data using a boolean in a section to follow.

Code in Payroll Class

```java
// Instance variables
private float fltRate;
//Constants
private final float fltMAX_RATE = 100.0f;

//Constructor
Payroll(float fltNewHours, float fltNewRate )
{
    setHours(fltNewHours);
    setRate(fltNewRate);
}


    //Public methods
    public void setRate(float fltNewRate)
    {
        //Check range for valid data
        if (fltNewRate > fltMAX_RATE || fltNewRate < 0.0)
        {
            fltRate = -1.0f; //Indicate bad data
        }
        else
        {
            fltRate = fltNewRate; //Good data
        }
    }

    public float getRate()
    {
        return fltRate;
    }
```

In the applet that instantiates the Payroll class, you can check the value of the instance variable to determine whether the data passed the validation.

Code in the Applet Class

```java
try
{
    float fltHours = Float.valueOf(txtHours.getText()).floatValue();
    float fltRate = Float.valueOf(txtRate.getText()).floatValue();
    Payroll myPayroll = new Payroll(fltHours, fltRate ); //Instantiate the class
    if (myPayroll.getRate() < 0) //Rate failed validation
    {
        txtRate.requestFocus();
        txtRate.selectAll();
        showStatus("Invalid Rate");
    }
    //(More processing here)
}
catch(Exception err) //Catch nonnumeric data here
{
    showStatus("Hours and Rate must be numeric.");
}
```

Using this technique, you properly separate the user interface components from the business rules and calculations. The applet takes care of displaying messages, but the rules are checked in the Payroll class. You will find the complete program showing this business-rule validation in the chapter hands-on example.

Note that both this example and the one that follows check only the Rate variable. You likely would check both Hours and Rate. In fact, the programs on your CD do validate both variables. This example was simplified to clarify the concept.

Passing Variables as Arguments of a Method

When you set up a class, you must decide whether to assign the class instance variables in the class constructor or pass the variables as arguments of a method. There are good reasons for choosing each technique.

The previous example used the constructor to pass the data values, which makes sense in OOP: you instantiate an object of the Payroll class using the desired data. The one drawback is that you cannot return any value from a constructor. That's why we set the instance variable (fltRate) to −1 when the validation failed, choosing a value that cannot possibly be correct for calculations. The applet must then use a `get` method (`myPayroll.getRate()`) to see the value of the variable.

The following code passes the values fltHours and fltRate as arguments of the `CalculatePay` method, rather than use the constructor. Notice also the use of boolean variables to indicate whether input values pass the business-rule validation.

Code in Payroll Class

```
// Instance variables
private float fltRate;
//Constants
private final float fltMAX_RATE = 100.0f;

//Public instance variables
public boolean blnInvalidRate;    //Property to indicate if Rate passed validation

//Public methods
public void setRate(float fltNewRate)
{
    //Check range for valid data
    if (fltNewRate > fltMAX_RATE || fltNewRate < 0.0)
    {
        blnInvalidRate = true;    //Bad data
    }
    else
    {
        fltRate = fltNewRate;
        blnInvalidRate = false;   //Good data
    }
}

//Calculate the pay
public float CalculatePay(float fltHours, float fltRate)
{
    setRate(fltRate);
    if (blnInvalidRate) //Bad data
    {
        return −1.0f;
```

```
        }
    else //Data passed validation
        {
            //(Perform the calculations here)
            return fltPay;
        }
    }
```

The code in the applet can check the boolean variable to determine whether a field passed validation.

Code in the Applet Class

```
if (myPayroll.blnInvalidRate) //Rate did not pass validation
    {
    txtRate.requestFocus();
    txtRate.selectAll();
    showStatus("Invalid Rate");
    }
```

You can find the complete program that uses boolean values and passes the input values as arguments to the method on your student CD as Ch6Payroll-Booleans.

Checking for Numeric Values

In most cases, the best way to check for nonnumeric data is by catching exceptions, as you saw in Chapter 4. You also can use the isNaN method (is "not a number") of the Double and Float wrapper classes. The boolean isNaN method returns true if the argument is not numeric.

```
if (FltHours.isNaN())
    {
    lblError.setText("The Hours field must contain a number");
    showStatus("Invalid data in the Hours field");
    }
```

This code must appear in an applet class, since you cannot set a label or status message in a class called by an applet. However, you can use the isNaN method in a class if you return a value that indicates the data were bad. In this example, a CalculatePay method returns the calculated pay if the data are good, or −1 (negative one) if the data are bad.

```
public float CalculatePay(FltHours, FltRate)
    {
    //Check for good data
    if (FltHours.isNaN() || FltRate.isNaN())
        {
        return -1.0f;
        }
    else
        {
        fltPay = FltHours.floatValue() * FltRate.floatValue();
        return fltPay
        }
    }
```

Programming for Multiple Button Objects

When a project contains more than one button, you still have only one `action-Performed` method. The event for any component that has an actionListener assigned triggers the same `actionPerformed` method. Therefore, inside the method you must determine which object caused the call.

The `actionPerformed` method header looks like this:

```
public void actionPerformed(ActionEvent myEvent)
```

Java passes an ActionEvent object as an argument to the method. You give the argument a name (myEvent, in this example), which you use to refer to the object in code. You can use the methods of the ActionEvent class to determine the object that triggered the event.

The `getSource` method returns the name of the object that caused the event. You can declare a generic object using the Object class and assign it the return value from the `getSource` method:

```
Object objSource = myEvent.getSource();
```

The next step is to use a condition to compare the object with the names of your components.

```
if (objSource == btnCalculate)
{
    Calculate();
}
else if (objSource == btnClear)
{
    Clear();
}
```

It's best to write a separate method for each of the buttons, rather than write all of the processing code in the `actionPerformed` method. Call the `Calculate` method when the object is `btnCalculate`; otherwise execute the `Clear` method.

In the following code, action listeners were assigned to the two text fields as well as the buttons. When the user presses the Enter key in one of the text fields, you want to simulate pressing the Calculate button. In this method, evt is the name of the ActionEvent object.

```
public void actionPerformed(ActionEvent evt)
{
    //Determine the object calling this method
    Object objSource = evt.getSource();

    if (objSource == btnCalculate
        || objSource == txtHours
        || objSource == txtRate)
    {
        CalculatePay();
    }
    else
    {
        ClearTextFields();
    }
}
```

When you have several event sources, you may find the code easier to read with individual `if` statements with no braces.

```
if(objSource == btnAdd)
    Add();
if (objSource == txtHours || objSource == txtRate)
    Add();
if(objSource == btnClear)
    Clear();
if(objSource == btnCount)
    Count();
if(objSource == btnRemove)
    Remove();
```

Disabling and Enabling Buttons

You can help direct a user's actions by selectively enabling and disabling buttons. For example, do not allow the user to click on a Summarize button before entering any transactions, or do not enable a Calculate button until an entry appears in the appropriate text field.

In Java you can disable a button, which makes it appear grayed (Figure 6.5). You also can hide a button, which makes it disappear. In most cases, you should not make buttons appear and disappear—it confuses and frustrates the user. Instead, make a button appear disabled when it shouldn't be clicked. Use the **setEnabled method** to enable and disable buttons or the **setVisible method** to show and hide buttons.

Figure 6.5

Disable the Clear button by setting `btnClear.setEnabled(false);`

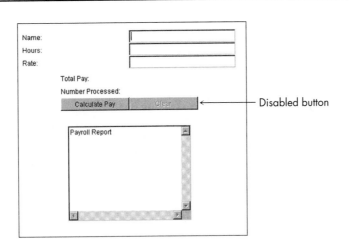

— Disabled button

The setEnabled Method—General Format

```
object.setEnabled(booleanValue);
```

Set the boolean value to true (the default) to make the object enabled or false to disable it.

The setEnabled Method—Examples

```
btnCalculate.setEnabled(true);
btnClear.setEnabled(false);
```

These examples make btnCalculate appear enabled and btnClear appear disabled. When a button is disabled, the user cannot select it.

You can use the setVisible method in a similar way as the setEnabled method. Remember though that you shouldn't make buttons invisible unless you have a very good reason.

You can find an example applet that disables and enables buttons on your text CD. The folder is called Ch6PayrollDisabled.

Precedence of Assignment, Logical, and Relational Operators

Combining expressions and operators in Java can lead to very complex statements. Not only must you understand the precedence among arithmetic operators and logical operators, you also must know what occurs when you mix operators. The sequence of evaluation of operators is sometimes called **binding.** Table 6.5 contains the relationship of the operators you have learned. Notice the association: you must read some operators from left to right and others from right to left. All of the operators in a row have the same precedence.

Table 6.5

Precedence of Operators

Operator	Association
++ −− * / %	left to right*
+ −	left to right
< > <= >=	left to right
== !=	left to right
&&	left to right
||	left to right
? :	right to left
= *= += /= %= −=	right to left

*Increment and decrement operators read right to left.

You may never combine these operators, but you need to be aware of the consequences. This example should give you a better feel for the evaluation of expressions. First, a combination of math operators:

```
int intClass1Count = 0, intClass2Count = 10, intResult = 0;

intResult += -intClassCount1++ - ++intClassCount2;
```

This statement is evaluated in the following order:

1. intClassCount2 has a prefix increment, which is performed first.
2. The result is then subtracted from the negative value of intClassCount1.
3. The result is added to intResult;
4. intClassCount1 is incremented, due to the postfix operator.

The following example combines an increment operator, a relational operator, and a logical operator.

```
int intOne, intTwo;

intOne = intTwo = 1;

if (intOne == 1 || intTwo++ > 1)
    lblMessage.setText("True");
```

The first condition is true, so a smart compiler does not evaluate the second condition. The increment operation does not occur.

Feedback 6.4

What displays when the following code segments execute?

```
1.  intCount = 0;
    if (intCount++ < 1)
    {
        lblMessage.setText("Increment is after comparison");
    }
2.  intCount = 6;
    if(--intCount < 5)
    {
        lblMessage.setText ("Less");
    }
    else
    {
        lblMessage.setText ("Not less");
    }
3.  if('J' == 'j')
    {
        lblMessage.setText ("The letters are equal");
    }
4.  float fltLimit = 1000.0f;
    float fltAmount = 1400.0f;
    if (fltAmount >= fltLimit);
    {
        lblMessage.setText ("Limit exceeded");
    }
```

Your Hands-on Programming Example

Modify the Payroll project from Chapter 5 to incorporate overtime calculations. Calculate overtime at time and a half for all hours over 40.

Include a Calculate button and a Clear button. The Calculate button should display the results for the current employee. The Clear button clears the information for the text fields and the results for the current employee.

Display a message in the status line for nonnumeric values, as well as any input values that do not pass business rules. The hours may be zero and cannot exceed 80; the rate may be zero and cannot exceed 100. Neither field should accept a negative number as input. When a field value is in error, select that field and set focus to the field.

Figure 6.5 shows a possible layout for the user interface.

Planning the Project

Plan the Objects and Properties

Classes: **PayrollApplet, Payroll, and LocalFormat**

Figure 6.6 shows the class diagrams for this project.

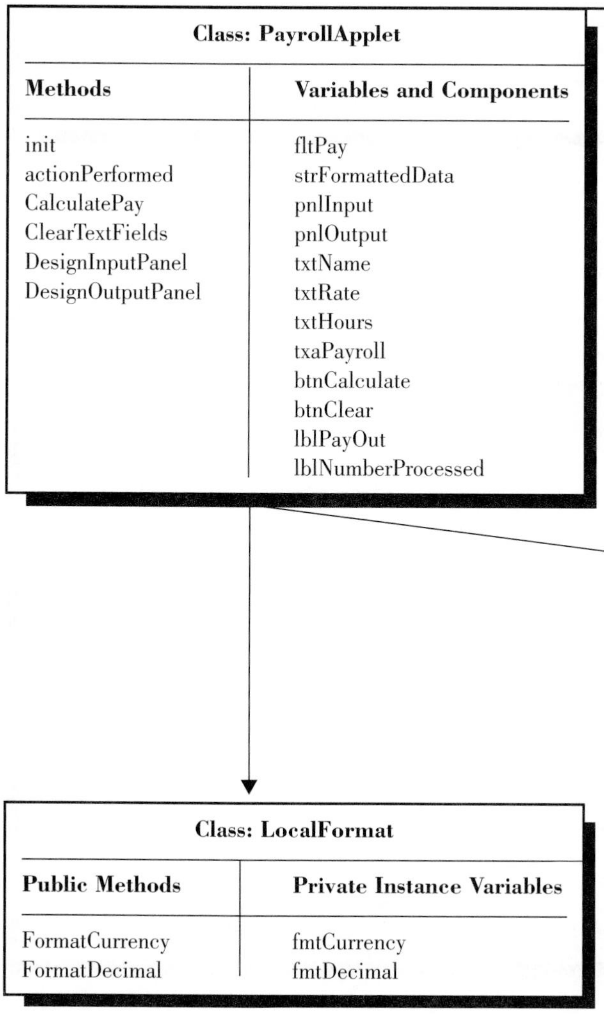

Figure 6.6

The class diagrams for the hands-on example.

Class: PayrollApplet

Methods	Variables and Components
init	fltPay
actionPerformed	strFormattedData
CalculatePay	pnlInput
ClearTextFields	pnlOutput
DesignInputPanel	txtName
DesignOutputPanel	txtRate
	txtHours
	txaPayroll
	btnCalculate
	btnClear
	lblPayOut
	lblNumberProcessed

Class: Payroll

Public Methods	Private Class Variables
Payroll(float fltNewHours, float fltNewRate)	dblTotalPay
	intNumberProcessed
setRate(float fltNewRate)	**Private Instance Variables**
setHours(float fltNewHours)	fltPay
getTotalPay	fltRate
getNumberProcessed	fltHours
getHours	
getRate	
CalculatePay	

Class: LocalFormat

Public Methods	Private Instance Variables
FormatCurrency	fmtCurrency
FormatDecimal	fmtDecimal

Class: PayrollApplet

Components and Variables:

Access Mode (public or private)	Variable or Component Name	Data Type or Class	Description
	pnlInput	Panel	Panel for input components.
	pnlOutput	Panel	Panel for output components.
	txtName	TextField	Input the name.
	txtHours	TextField	Input the hours worked.
	txtRate	TextField	Input the hourly pay rate.
	txaPayroll	TextArea	Display report of names and pay.
	btnCalculate	Button	Process pay.
	btnClear	Button	Clear text boxes.
	lblPayOut	Label	Display total pay.
	lblNumberProcessed	Label	Display number of employees.
	fltPay	float	Variable for individual pay.
	strFormattedData	String	Hold formatted output.

Methods:

Access Mode (public or private)	Return Type	Method Name (include any parameters)	Pseudocode
public	void	init	Call method to lay out panels. Add panels. Add text area. Set focus to the name text field. Add action listeners.
public	void	actionPerformed	Test for event. If btnCalculate or text field CalculatePay. else ClearTextFields.
public	void	CalculatePay	Clear previous status message. Obtain input for hours and rate. Create payroll object. If hours fails validation Show error message. Select hours text and set focus. else if rate fails validation

Access Mode (public or private)	Return Type	Method Name (include any parameters)	Pseudocode
			Show error message. Select rate text and set focus. else (passed all validation) Create LocalFormat object. Format and display total pay. Format and display number processed. Format and display name and pay.
public	void	ClearTextFields	Clear text fields. Set focus in first text field.
public	void	DesignInputPanel	Lay out the input fields.
public	void	DesignOutputPanel	Lay out the output fields.

Class: Payroll

Components and Variables:

Access Mode (public or private)	Variable or Component Name	Data Type or Class	Description
private static	dblTotalPay	double	Hold total pay.
private static	intNumberProcessed	int	Hold number processed.
private	fltPay	float	Hold pay for one individual.
private	fltRate	float	Hold value for rate.
private	fltHours	float	Hold value for hours.

Methods:

Access Mode (public or private)	Return Type	Method Name (include any parameters)	Pseudocode
		Payroll(float fltNewHours, float fltNewRate)	Set the hours and rate variables.
public	void	setRate(float fltNewRate)	If rate within good range Assign value to fltRate. else Assign −1 to fltRate.
public	void	setHours(float fltNewHours)	If hours within good range Assign value to fltHours. else Assign −1 to fltHours.

continued

Access Mode (public or private)	Return Type	Method Name (include any parameters)	Pseudocode
public	double	getTotalPay	Return total pay.
public	int	getNumberProcessed	Return number processed.
public	float	getHours	Return hours.
public	float	getRate	Return rate.

public	float	CalculatePay	If hours or rate < 0
			    Return -1.
			else
			    If overtime
			        Calculate pay $=$ (rate $* 40 +$
			        (hours $- 40$) $* (1.5 *$ rate)).
			    else
			        Calculate pay $=$ hours $*$ rate.
			Add pay to total pay.
			Add 1 to number processed.
			Return pay.

Class: LocalFormat

Components and Variables:

Access Mode (public or private)	Variable or Component Name	Data Type or Class	Description
private	fmtCurrency	NumberFormat	Format currency for locale.
private	fmtDecimal	NumberFormat	Format decimal for locale.

Methods:

Access Mode (public or private)	Return Type	Method Name (include any parameters)	Pseudocode
		LocalFormat()	Constructor with no parameters. Get formatting for locale.
public	String	FormatCurrency(float fltNumber)	Set fractional digits to 2. Format number as currency. Return formatted number.
public	String	FormatCurrency(float fltNumber, int intDecimalPos)	Set fractional digits to decimal pos. Format number as currency. Return formatted number.
public	String	FormatCurrency(double dblNumber)	Set fractional digits to 2. Format number as currency. Return formatted number

Access Mode (public or private)	Return Type	Method Name (include any parameters)	Pseudocode
public	String	`FormatCurrency(double dblNumber, int intDecimalPos)`	Set fractional digits to decimal pos. Format number as currency. Return formatted number.
public	String	`FormatDecimal(float fltNumber)`	Set fractional digits to 2. Format number as decimal. Return formatted number.
public	String	`FormatDecimal(float fltNumber, int intDecimalPos)`	Set fractional digits to decimal pos. Format number as decimal. Return formatted number.

Write the Project

- Create the classes.

- Follow the plan to declare components and variables.

- Code the methods.

- When you complete the code, thoroughly test the project.

The Project Solution

PayrollApplet.java

```
//Folder:        Ch6Payroll
//Programmer:    Bradley/Millspaugh
//Date:          6/2001
//ClassName:     PayrollApplet
//Description:   Input Hours and Rate for Payroll. Format and display results.

import java.applet.*;
import java.awt.event.*;
import java.awt.*;

public class PayrollApplet extends Applet implements ActionListener
{
    //Create components
    Panel pnlInput = new Panel();
    Panel pnlOutput = new Panel();
    TextField txtName = new TextField(25);
    TextField txtHours = new TextField();
    TextField txtRate = new TextField();
    TextArea txaPayroll = new TextArea("Payroll Report", 10, 30);
    Button btnCalculate = new Button("Calculate Pay");
    Button btnClear = new Button("Clear");
    Label lblPayOut = new Label();
    Label lblNumberProcessed = new Label();
```

```java
public void init()
{
    //Create Interface
    DesignInputPanel();
    DesignOutputPanel();
    add(pnlInput);
    add(pnlOutput);
    add(txaPayroll);
    txtName.requestFocus();
    btnCalculate.addActionListener(this);
    btnClear.addActionListener(this);
    txtHours.addActionListener(this);
    txtRate.addActionListener(this);
}

public void actionPerformed(ActionEvent evt)
{
    //Determine object calling this method
    Object objSource = evt.getSource();
    if (objSource == btnCalculate
        || objSource == txtHours
        || objSource == txtRate)
    {
        CalculatePay();
    }
    else
    {
        ClearTextFields();
    }
}

private void CalculatePay()
{
    //Retrieve data and calculate
    //Declare variables
    float fltPay;
    String strFormattedData;

    //Clear any previous status message
    showStatus("");
    try
    {
        float fltHours = Float.valueOf(txtHours.getText()).floatValue();
        float fltRate = Float.valueOf(txtRate.getText()).floatValue();
        Payroll myPayroll = new Payroll(fltHours, fltRate);
        if (myPayroll.getHours() < 0) //Hours failed validation
        {
            txtHours.requestFocus();
            txtHours.selectAll();
            showStatus("Invalid Hours");
        }
        else if (myPayroll.getRate() < 0) //Rate failed validation
        {
            txtRate.requestFocus();
            txtRate.selectAll();
            showStatus("Invalid Rate");
        }
        else //Passed all business rule validations
        {
```

```
            fltPay = myPayroll.CalculatePay();

            //Format and display output
            LocalFormat fmtLocal = new LocalFormat();
            strFormattedData = fmtLocal.FormatCurrency(myPayroll.getTotalPay());
            lblPayOut.setText(strFormattedData);
            lblNumberProcessed.setText("" + myPayroll.getNumberProcessed());
            strFormattedData = fmtLocal.FormatDecimal(fltPay);
            txaPayroll.append("\n" + txtName.getText() + "\t" + strFormattedData);
        }
    }

    catch(Exception err)
    {
        showStatus("Hours and Rate must be numeric.");
    }
}

private void ClearTextFields()
{
    //Clear text fields
    txtName.setText("");
    txtHours.setText("");
    txtRate.setText("");
    txtName.requestFocus();
}

private void DesignInputPanel()
{
    //Lay out the input panel
    pnlInput.setLayout(new GridLayout(3, 2));
    pnlInput.add(new Label("Name: "));
    pnlInput.add(txtName);
    pnlInput.add(new Label("Hours: "));
    pnlInput.add(txtHours);
    pnlInput.add(new Label("Rate: "));
    pnlInput.add(txtRate);
}

private void DesignOutputPanel()
{
    //Lay out the output panel
    pnlOutput.setLayout(new GridLayout(4, 2));
    pnlOutput.add(new Label("Total Pay:"));
    pnlOutput.add(lblPayOut);
    pnlOutput.add(new Label("Number Processed: "));
    pnlOutput.add(lblNumberProcessed);
    pnlOutput.add(btnCalculate);
    pnlOutput.add(btnClear);
    }
}
```

Payroll.Java

```
//Folder:        Ch6Payroll
//Programmer:    Bradley/Millspaugh
//Date:          6/2001
//ClassName:     Payroll
//Description:   Input hours and rate; calculate pay, total pay, and number
//               //processed. Format and display results.
```

```java
public class Payroll
{
    //Class variables
    private static double dblTotalPay;
    private static int intNumberProcessed;

    // Instance variables
    private   float fltPay;
    private float fltRate;
    private float fltHours;

    //Constants
    private final float fltMAX_HOURS = 80.0f;
    private final float fltMAX_RATE = 100.0f;

    //Constructor
    Payroll(float fltNewHours, float fltNewRate)
    {
        setHours(fltNewHours);
        setRate(fltNewRate);
    }

    //Public methods
    public void setRate(float fltNewRate)
    {
        //Check range for valid data
        if (fltNewRate > fltMAX_RATE || fltNewRate < 0.0)
        {
            fltRate = -1.0f;//Indicate bad data
        }
        else
        {
            fltRate = fltNewRate; //Good data
        }
    }

    public void setHours(float fltNewHours)
    {
        //Check range for valid data
        if (fltNewHours > fltMAX_HOURS || fltNewHours < 0.0)
        {
            fltHours = -1.0f;        //Indicate bad data
        }
        else
        {
            fltHours = fltNewHours; //Good data
        }
    }

    public double getTotalPay()
    {
        return dblTotalPay;
    }

    public int getNumberProcessed()
    {
        return intNumberProcessed;
    }
```

```java
    public float getHours()
    {
        return fltHours;
    }

    public float getRate()
    {
        return fltRate;
    }

    public float CalculatePay()
    {
        if (fltHours < 0 || fltRate < 0) //Bad data
        {
            return -1.0f;
        }
        else //Data passed validation
        {
            //Calculate and return the amount of pay
            if (fltHours > 40.0f) //Overtime
            {
                fltPay=fltRate * 40.0f
                            + (fltHours - 40.0f) * 1.5f
                            * fltRate;
            }
            else       //No overtime
            {
                fltPay = fltHours * fltRate;
            }
            dblTotalPay += fltPay;
            intNumberProcessed++;
            return fltPay;
        }
    }
}
```

LocalFormat.Java

```java
//Folder:        Ch6Payroll
//Programmer:    Bradley/Millspaugh
//Date:          6/2001
//ClassName:     FormatCurrency
//Description:   Get format for locale and format numbers for display.

import java.text.*;

public class LocalFormat
{
    //Instance variables
    private NumberFormat fmtCurrency;
    private NumberFormat fmtDecimal;

    //Class constructor
    LocalFormat()
    {
```

```java
        //Get formatting for default locale
        fmtCurrency = NumberFormat.getCurrencyInstance();
        fmtDecimal = NumberFormat.getInstance();
    }


    //Methods
    public String FormatCurrency (float fltNumber)
    {
        //Format as currency, 2 decimal positions
        fmtCurrency.setMinimumFractionDigits(2);
        fmtCurrency.setMaximumFractionDigits(2);
        String strFormattedData = fmtCurrency.format(fltNumber);
        return strFormattedData;
    }


    public String FormatCurrency (float fltNumber, int intDecimalPos)
    {
        //Format as currency, variable number of decimal positions
        fmtCurrency.setMinimumFractionDigits(intDecimalPos);
        fmtCurrency.setMaximumFractionDigits(intDecimalPos);
        String strFormattedData = fmtCurrency.format(fltNumber);
        return strFormattedData;
    }


    public String FormatCurrency (double dblNumber)
    {
        //Format as currency, 2 decimal positions
        fmtCurrency.setMinimumFractionDigits(2);
        fmtCurrency.setMaximumFractionDigits(2);
        String strFormattedData = fmtCurrency.format(dblNumber);
        return strFormattedData;
    }


    public String FormatCurrency (double dblNumber, int intDecimalPos)
    {
        //Format as currency, variable number of decimal positions
        fmtCurrency.setMinimumFractionDigits(intDecimalPos);
        fmtCurrency.setMaximumFractionDigits(intDecimalPos);
        String strFormattedData = fmtCurrency.format(dblNumber);
        return strFormattedData;
    }


    public String FormatDecimal (float fltNumber)
    {
        //Format as decimal, 2 decimal positions
        fmtDecimal.setMinimumFractionDigits(2);
        fmtDecimal.setMaximumFractionDigits(2);
        String strFormattedData = fmtDecimal.format(fltNumber);
        return strFormattedData;
    }


    public String FormatDecimal (float fltNumber, int intDecimalPos)
    {
        //Format as decimal, variable number of decimal positions
        //Set decimal positions
```

```
        fmtDecimal.setMinimumFractionDigits(intDecimalPos);
        fmtDecimal.setMaximumFractionDigits(intDecimalPos);
        String strFormattedData = fmtDecimal.format(fltNumber);
        return strFormattedData;
    }
}
```

Summary

1. A conditional expression evaluates to true or false.
2. If a condition on an `if` statement evaluates true, the statement or statement block following the `if` executes. If false, any statements following the `else`, if present, execute.
3. Relational operators allow you to test the relationship ($>$, $<$, $==$, $!=$, $>=$, $<=$) between two values.
4. Flowcharts are useful visual tools for planning and viewing the logic of `if` statements.
5. Numeric variables are compared by value; characters are compared by their order in a code table, such as ASCII.
6. Wrapper classes contain methods for performing comparisons.
7. To compare strings, use the `equals` or `equalsIgnoreCase` method of the String class. To test for greater or less than, use the `compareTo` method of the String class.
8. You can test a boolean variable for true or false in a condition.
9. You can create compound conditions by combining multiple conditions using logical operators.
10. The not `!` operator reverses the boolean result of an evaluation.
11. An `if` statement may be nested by placing an `if` inside of an `if` block or an `else` block.
12. The conditional operator is a shortcut for an `if` statement; the operator uses a question mark and a colon.
13. Checking user input is called *validation*. Business rules define ranges or specific values for fields. These rules should be checked in a class, rather than in the applet.
14. An applet that has multiple buttons has only one `actionPerformed` method. In that method you must use a decision statement to determine the source of the event.

Key Terms

binding *175*

business rule *169*

compound condition *165*

condition *158*

conditional operator *168*

else *155*

if statement *155*

logical operator *164*

nested if statement *166*

relational operator *158*

setEnabled method *174*

setVisible method *174*

validation *169*

Review Questions

1. Give an example of a situation that would require the use of a decision statement.
2. Explain the effect of using an assignment operator (=) instead of the equality operator (==) in the expression (fltAmount = 0.0f).
3. Explain the differences between logical operators and relational operators.
4. What is meant by *boolean expression*?
5. How does the use of a Float object differ from a float variable?
6. Why can relational operators be used for char variables but not String objects?
7. Give the expression to compare whether strString1 is equal to strString2
   (a) Using the equals method.
   (b) Using the compareTo method.
8. What is the purpose of the conditional operator? How does it work?
9. Why is it important to discuss operator precedence when dealing with decision statements?
10. What is validation?
11. Give some examples of business rules.
12. What additional processing is required in an actionPerformed method when an applet has more than one button with actionListeners?

Programming Exercises

6.1. Create a project to compute your checking account balance. Use a text field to indicate the type of transaction. Give instructions to the user to type a letter: D, for deposit, C, for check, or S, for service charge. Another text field will allow the user to enter the amount of the transaction. Display the new balance in a label. Calculate the balance by adding deposits and subtracting service charges and checks. Include buttons for *Calculate* and *Clear*.

6.2. Add validation to project 6.1 by verifying that the user typed an appropriate letter for the transaction. Display a message if the new balance would be a negative number. If there is not enough money to cover a check, do not deduct the check amount. Instead, display a message "Insufficient Funds" and deduct a service charge of $10.

6.3. Modify project 6.2 by adding a Summary button that will display the total number of deposits, the total dollar amount of deposits, the number of checks, the dollar amount of the checks, the number of service charges, and the dollar amount of the service charges in a text area. Do not include checks that were returned for insufficient funds, but do include the service charges. Disable the Summary button until after a transaction is entered.

6.4. Piecework workers are paid by the piece. Workers who produce a greater quantity of output are often paid at a higher rate. Use text fields to obtain the person's name and the number of pieces completed. Include a Calculate button to display the dollar amount earned. You will need a Summary button to display the total number of pieces, the total pay, and the average pay per person. A *Clear* button should clear the name and the number of pieces for the current employee.

Include validation to check for missing data. If the user clicks on the *Calculate* button without first entering a name and number of pieces, display a message. Also, you need to make sure not to display a summary before any data are entered; you cannot calculate an average when no items have been calculated. You can check the number of employees in the Summary method or disable the Summary button until the first transaction is calculated.

Pieces Completed	Price Paid per Piece for All Pieces
1–199	0.50
200–399	0.55
400–599	0.60
600 or more	0.65

CASE STUDIES

R 'n R—for Reading and Refreshment

Modify the project in Chapter 5, allowing a customer to purchase multiple books. Entering a quantity of 10 or more of one title gives the customer an additional 10 percent discount for that title. Add text fields for the customer's name, customer number, and credit card number. (This information should remain for the entire process.)

All sales receive a 15 percent discount; any single book title with more than 10 copies entered at one time receives a 25 percent discount. *Note:* We will assume that every customer has an account with us and a six-character account number. Do not worry about new customers.

Merry Pea's Quilting

Discounts are offered for quilting students who have taught courses for the store or who belong to a quilting guild. Place two additional text fields on the input area for your Chapter 5 applet: one labeled *Guild Name* and one *Staff (Y/N)*.

In your processing, test to see if there is a value in the guild name field. Test for 'y' (upper- or lowercase) in the Staff field. Discount the class by 15 percent for staff and 10 percent for guild members. If a person is both a staff member and a guild member, the discount is 25 percent.

Display class information in a text area and summary information in a second text area.

For class information, display the name and price of the class. If there is a discount, display the discount amount and the balance.

For summary information, display the total due for all classes, the number of classes, and the average price per class.

7

Making Selections with Check Boxes and Option Buttons

At the completion of this chapter, you will be able to . . .

1. Allow the user to enter yes/no responses using check boxes.

2. Combine check boxes in a group to act as option buttons.

3. Test integer conditions with a `switch` statement.

4. Incorporate Swing components into an applet.

Now that you are familiar with decision statements, you can incorporate some additional components into your applets. Option buttons (also called *radio buttons*) and check boxes (Figure 7.1) allow the user to make selections; both types of components are based on the Checkbox class. When you place check boxes in groups, check boxes turn into option buttons. In Chapter 8, you learn about another selection method: lists from which the user can select choices.

Figure 7.1

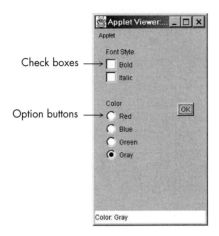

Check boxes and option buttons.

Check Boxes and Option Buttons

You use check boxes and option buttons on a user interface when you want to give the user a yes/no choice, also referred to as true/false or on/off. When the screen holds several check boxes, each operates independently; that is, the user can select none, one, or any number of the boxes. Option buttons, on the other hand, operate in groups. The user can select only one button at a time; selecting a new button deselects the previous selection.

Creating Check Boxes

Creating a check box is very similar to creating the other components you have used, such as text fields and buttons. You declare a variable of the Checkbox class, instantiate it with the new keyword, and add it to the layout. The Checkbox class constructors allow you also to create a label, which appears to the right of the box (refer to Figure 7.1).

The Checkbox Component—Constructors

```
Checkbox()
Checkbox(String label)
Checkbox(String label, CheckboxGroup groupName, boolean state)
Checkbox(String label, boolean state, CheckboxGroup groupName)
```

The default **state** (on or off) of a check box is "off" (false). If you want the check box to appear checked initially, set the state to true. The groupName parameter is used only for option buttons. When you want to create a check box (no group name) and set the initial state, set the groupName argument to null.

The Checkbox Component—Examples

```
Checkbox chkBold = new Checkbox("Bold");
Checkbox chkItalic = new Checkbox("Red", null, true);
```

This code adds two check boxes to an applet:

```
//Declare components
Checkbox chkBold = new Checkbox("Bold");
Checkbox chkItalic = new Checkbox("Italic");
//In the init method
add(chkBold);
add(chkItalic);
```

Creating Option Buttons

When a check box is a member of a group, the check box looks and acts as an option button. Each check box in a group is round rather than square, and only one component in the group can be selected at a time.

Create option buttons by first declaring a CheckboxGroup. Then you can name the group when you declare the buttons.

The CheckboxGroup—Constructor

```
CheckboxGroup()
```

The CheckboxGroup—Example

```
CheckboxGroup cbgColor = new CheckboxGroup();
```

This code creates a check box group and then creates four option buttons inside the group.

```
//Declare components
CheckboxGroup cbgColor = new CheckboxGroup();
Checkbox optRed = new Checkbox("Red", cbgColor, false);
Checkbox optBlue = new Checkbox("Blue", cbgColor, false);
Checkbox optGreen = new Checkbox("Green", cbgColor, false);
Checkbox optGray = new Checkbox("Gray", cbgColor, true);
```

When you add the components to the layout, you add the option buttons, not the group.

```
//In the init method
add(optRed);
```

```
add(optBlue);
add(optGreen);
add(optGray);
```

Notice the prefixes in the previous examples. Use *chk* as a prefix for a check box, *opt* for an option button, and *cbg* for a CheckboxGroup.

Checking the State of Check Boxes and Option Buttons

You can determine whether a check box or option button is selected by using the **getState method**. The statement chkItalic.getState() returns a boolean value: true if the box (or option button) is "on" or false for "off".

The following code segment sets the applet's background color to red if the option button for red is selected and displays the color name in the status bar. It also sets the font to italic or plain based on the state of the Italic check box.

```
if(optRed.getState())
{
    setBackground(Color.red);
    showStatus("Color: Red");
}
if(chkItalic.getState())
    lblFontStyle.setFont(fntItalic);
else
    lblFontStyle.setFont(fntPlain);
```

Testing Multiple Check Boxes

If you have multiple check boxes that are not in a group, each box works independently. Therefore, you use separate if statements to test each box.

```
//Font check boxes
if(chkItalic.getState())
    lblFontStyle.setFont(fntItalic);
if(chkBold.getState())
    lblFontStyle.setFont(fntBold);
```

However, in the case of fonts, if you want to be able to apply both bold and italic, you need a separate statement that checks for both.

```
if (chkBold.getState() && chkItalic.getState())
    lblFontStyle.setFont(fntBoldItalic);
```

For a group of option buttons, the components work as a unit. Use a single if/else statement to test the buttons.

```
//Color option buttons
if(optRed.getState())
    setBackground(Color.red);
else if(optBlue.getState())
    setBackground(Color.blue);
else if(optGreen.getState())
    setBackground(Color.green);
else
    setBackground(Color.lightGray);
```

Check Box and Option Button Program

The following program demonstrates the check boxes and option buttons. The check boxes and option buttons were added to a panel, in order to line up the components. You can refer back to Figure 7.1 for the applet layout.

Note: When you are first experimenting with check boxes and option buttons, you may want to omit the panel and just use a default flow layout with the code segments that appeared earlier in the chapter.

```java
//Folder:        Ch7CheckboxGroup
//Programmer:    Bradley/Millspaugh
//Date:          6/2001
//ClassName:     OptionButtons
//Description:   Demo check boxes and option buttons (check box groups).

import java.applet.*;
import java.awt.*;
import java.awt.event.*;

public class OptionButtons extends Applet implements ActionListener
{
    //Declare components
    CheckboxGroup cbgColor = new CheckboxGroup();
    Checkbox optRed = new Checkbox("Red", cbgColor, false);
    Checkbox optBlue = new Checkbox("Blue", cbgColor, false);
    Checkbox optGreen = new Checkbox("Green", cbgColor, false);
    Checkbox optGray = new Checkbox("Gray", cbgColor, true);
    Checkbox chkBold = new Checkbox("Bold");
    Checkbox chkItalic = new Checkbox("Italic");
    Font fntItalic = new Font("Times New Roman", Font.ITALIC, 12);
    Font fntBold = new Font("Times New Roman", Font.BOLD, 12);
    Font fntBoldItalic = new Font("Times New Roman",
        Font.BOLD + Font.ITALIC, 12);
    Font fntPlain = new Font("Times New Roman", Font.PLAIN, 12);
    Label lblFontStyle = new Label("Font Style");
    Button btnOK = new Button("OK");

    public void init()
    {
        //Add controls
        setBackground(Color.lightGray);
        Panel pnlChoices = new Panel();
        pnlChoices.setBackground(Color.lightGray);
        pnlChoices.setLayout(new GridLayout(10,0));
        pnlChoices.add(lblFontStyle);
        pnlChoices.add(chkBold);
        pnlChoices.add(chkItalic);
        pnlChoices.add(new Label(" "));
        pnlChoices.add(new Label("Color "));
        pnlChoices.add(optRed);
        pnlChoices.add(optBlue);
        pnlChoices.add(optGreen);
        pnlChoices.add(optGray);
        add(pnlChoices);
        add(btnOK);
        btnOK.addActionListener(this);
    }
```

```java
public void actionPerformed(ActionEvent action)
{
    //OK button clicked
    //Take action depending on the state of the check boxes
    // and option buttons

    //Font style check boxes
    lblFontStyle.setFont(fntPlain);//Set to plain to begin
    if (chkBold.getState())
        lblFontStyle.setFont(fntBold);
    if (chkItalic.getState())
        lblFontStyle.setFont(fntItalic);
    if (chkBold.getState() && chkItalic.getState())
        lblFontStyle.setFont(fntBoldItalic);

    //Color option buttons
    if(optRed.getState())
    {
        setBackground(Color.red);
        showStatus("Color: Red");
    }
    else if(optBlue.getState())
    {
        setBackground(Color.blue);
        showStatus("Color: Blue");
    }
    else if(optGreen.getState())
    {
        setBackground(Color.green);
        showStatus("Color: Green");
    }
    else
    {
        setBackground(Color.lightGray);
        showStatus("Color: Gray");
    }
}
}
```

Checkbox Methods

Table 7.1 shows some of the methods available for the Checkbox class.

Table 7.1

Selected Checkbox Methods

Method	Purpose
getCheckboxGroup()	Returns the name of the group or null if there is no group.
getState()	Returns true or false depending on whether the component is on or off (selected or deselected).
setCheckboxGroup (CheckboxGroup *group*)	Sets the group for a check box. Can be set to null for no group. If the check box was already in a group and is given a new group, it is removed from the previous group.
setState(boolean *value*)	Sets the component to true or false (on or off).

Feedback 7.1

1. Code the statement(s) to create a check box for "Return Customer".
2. Code the statement(s) to create option buttons for Male or Female.
3. Write the statement to determine if the Male option is selected.

The ItemListener

You can determine a change in the state of check box components by using an item listener. An item listener is similar to an action listener: You can add the item listener to each check box or option button that you want to check. Then an event (the itemStateChanged event) occurs each time the component changes state.

Like action listeners, you must first implement the **ItemListener** interface and add a listener to one or more components. Then write code for the **item-StateChanged method**.

```
public class Listen extends Applet implements ItemListener
...
    //In the init method
    add(chkBold);
    chkBold.addItemListener(this);

    //Method to respond to a change of state
    public void itemStateChanged(ItemEvent item)
    {
        //Test state of Bold check box
        if (chkBold.getState())
            lblFontStyle.setFont(fntBold);
        else
            lblFontStyle.setFont(fntPlain);
    }
```

When the user clicks in a check box component, the code in the `item-StateChanged` method is executed immediately. If you add item listeners to several components, you can use the `getSource` method of the ItemEvent argument to determine the control that changed state.

```
public void itemStateChanged(ItemEvent item )
{
    //Get the object that caused the event
    Object eventSource = item.getSource();
    //Is the source the Bold check box?
    if (eventSource == chkBold)
    ...
```

Check boxes and option buttons change state when clicked, which may mean the control is selected or deselected. You usually need to check the source of the event as well as whether its state is true or false.

```
//Is the source the Red option button and is it selected?
if (eventSource == optRed && optRed.getState())
{
    setBackground(Color.red);
    showStatus("Color: Red");
}
```

The ItemListener Program

This program responds to clicks in option buttons and check boxes as they occur. Notice in Figure 7.2 that there is no button control in this applet. You should be aware that it is not a good programming practice to take action when the user clicks an option button or check box. Generally, you should take action when the user clicks a button, such as OK or Apply. In the section "Using a switch to Check Option Buttons" later in this chapter, you will see an example that uses an item listener and the `itemStateChanged` method along with a button.

*These check boxes and option
buttons cause actions to occur
when they are clicked.*

```
//Folder:        Ch7ItemListener
//Programmer:    Bradley/Millspaugh
//Date:          6/2001
//ClassName:     ListenApplet
//Description:   Demo check boxes and option buttons (check box groups)
//               using an ItemListener.

import java.applet.*;
import java.awt.*;
import java.awt.event.*;

public class ListenApplet extends Applet implements ItemListener
{
    //Declare components
    CheckboxGroup cbgColor = new CheckboxGroup();
    Checkbox optRed = new Checkbox("Red", cbgColor, false);
    Checkbox optBlue = new Checkbox("Blue", cbgColor, false);
    Checkbox optGreen = new Checkbox("Green", cbgColor, false);
    Checkbox optGray = new Checkbox("Gray", cbgColor, true);
    Checkbox chkBold = new Checkbox("Bold");
    Font fntBold = new Font("Times New Roman", Font.BOLD, 12);
    Font fntPlain = new Font("Times New Roman", Font.PLAIN, 12);
    Label lblFontStyle = new Label("Font Style");
```

```
public void init()
{
    //Add controls
    setBackground(Color.lightGray);
    Panel pnlChoices = new Panel();
    pnlChoices.setBackground(Color.lightGray);
    pnlChoices.setLayout(new GridLayout(9, 0));
    pnlChoices.add(lblFontStyle);
    pnlChoices.add(chkBold);
    pnlChoices.add(new Label(" "));
    pnlChoices.add(new Label("Color "));
    pnlChoices.add(optRed);
    pnlChoices.add(optBlue);
    pnlChoices.add(optGreen);
    pnlChoices.add(optGray);
    add(pnlChoices);
    chkBold.addItemListener(this);
    optRed.addItemListener(this);
    optBlue.addItemListener(this);
    optGreen.addItemListener(this);
    optGray.addItemListener(this);

}


public void itemStateChanged(ItemEvent item)
{
    //A check box or option button changed state. Check to see which
    // item changed and take action.

    //Get the object that caused the event
    Object eventSource = item.getSource();

    //Test for the Bold check box
    if (eventSource == chkBold)
    {
        if (chkBold.getState())
            lblFontStyle.setFont(fntBold);
        else
            lblFontStyle.setFont(fntPlain);
    }

    //Test for the color option buttons
    if (eventSource == optRed && optRed.getState())
    {
        setBackground(Color.red);
        showStatus("Color: Red");
    }
    if (eventSource == optBlue && optBlue.getState())
    {
        setBackground(Color.blue);
        showStatus("Color: Blue");
    }
    if (eventSource == optGreen && optGreen.getState())
    {
        setBackground(Color.green);
        showStatus("Color: Green");
    }
```

```
    if (eventSource == optGray && optGray.getState())
    {
        setBackground(Color.lightGray);
        showStatus("Color: Gray");
    }
  }
}
```

Feedback 7.2

Differentiate between using an ActionListener and an ItemListener for a check box.

The switch Statement

In Chapter 6 you learned to test a condition and take alternate courses of action using the `if` statement. Whenever you want to test a single variable or expression for multiple values, the **switch statement** provides a flexible and powerful solution. The `switch` statement, which is often referred to by programmers as the *case structure*, might be useful when you have a code that may have several possible values, each requiring a different action. The logic of a `switch` statement is usually more clear and easier to read than nested `if` statements.

The Java `switch` statement works only with int, char, short, or byte expressions. Therefore, you can check for an integer or a single character.

The switch Statement—General Format

```
switch(expression)
{
    case ConstantValue:
        statements;
    [case Constantvalue:
        statement(s);]
    ...
    [default:
        statement(s);]
}
```

The expression in a `switch` statement is usually an int or char variable, although it can be an expression, such as (`intCounter - 1`). The body of the `switch` statement must be in braces.

A **case statement** holds the constant value that you want to match, followed by a colon (:). The constant value must be the same data type as the expression in the `switch` statement.

The switch Statement—Example

```
switch(intChoice)
{
    case 1:
        HandleChoice1();
        break;
    case 2:
        HandleChoice2();
        break;
    case 3:
        HandleChoice3();
        break;
    default:
        showStatus("Choice must be 1, 2, or 3");
}
```

The **default statement** is optional. It is used only when none of the `cases` produces a match. If you omit the `default` statement and none of the `cases` match, execution passes through the `switch` block without executing anything. The purpose of the `break` statements will become clear when you understand how Java executes the `switch` statement.

When the Java interpreter comes to a `switch` statement, it first evaluates the expression. Next Java starts checking the `case` statements looking for a match for the expression. As soon as a match is found, Java jumps to the next statement following the match and continues executing all following statements. Therefore, in the preceding example, if the `break` statements are omitted and the expression evaluates to 1, Java would find a match at `case 1:`, execute the `HandleChoice1` method, then fall right through the rest of the statements, executing `HandleChoice2` and `HandleChoice3` and then displaying the error message in the status bar.

The **break statement** jumps out of the current block of code to the first statement following the closing brace. Notice that there are no extra braces inside the `switch` block.

If you want to execute the same method for more than one value, you can place the `case` statements together. When a match is found for either value, Java executes the next statement following the `case` statements.

```
switch(chrLetter)
{
    case 'a':
    case 'A':
        Advertising();
        break;
    case 's':
    case 'S':
        Sales();
}
```

Using a switch to Check Option Buttons

Earlier you learned that actions should not take place until the user clicks an OK button. This applet sets an integer class variable whenever the user selects an option button, but does not make any changes to the color. When the user clicks the OK button, the actionPerformed method uses a switch statement based on the current value of intColor.

```
//Folder:        Ch7Switch
//Programmer:    Bradley/Millspaugh
//Date:          6/2001
//ClassName:     SwitchesApplet
//Description:   Demo check boxes and option buttons (check box groups)
//                    using an ItemListener and a switch statement.

import java.applet.*;
import java.awt.*;
import java.awt.event.*;

public class SwitchesApplet extends Applet implements ActionListener, ItemListener
{
    //Declare components
    CheckboxGroup cbgColor = new CheckboxGroup();
    Checkbox optRed = new Checkbox("Red", cbgColor, false);
    Checkbox optBlue = new Checkbox("Blue", cbgColor, false);
    Checkbox optGreen = new Checkbox("Green", cbgColor, false);
    Checkbox optGray = new Checkbox("Gray", cbgColor, true);
    Checkbox chkBold = new Checkbox("Bold");
    Font fntBold = new Font("Times New Roman", Font.BOLD, 12);
    Font fntPlain = new Font("Times New Roman", Font.PLAIN, 12);
    Label lblFontStyle = new Label("Font Style");
    Button btnOK = new Button("OK");

    //Declare variables
    int intColor;
    public void init()
    {
        //Add controls
        setBackground(Color.lightGray);
        Panel pnlChoices = new Panel();
        pnlChoices.setBackground(Color.lightGray);
        pnlChoices.setLayout(new GridLayout(9, 0));
        pnlChoices.add(lblFontStyle);
        pnlChoices.add(chkBold);
        pnlChoices.add(new Label(" "));
        pnlChoices.add(new Label("Color "));
        pnlChoices.add(optRed);
        pnlChoices.add(optBlue);
        pnlChoices.add(optGreen);
        pnlChoices.add(optGray);
        add(pnlChoices);
        add(btnOK);

        optRed.addItemListener(this);
        optBlue.addItemListener(this);
        optGreen.addItemListener(this);
        optGray.addItemListener(this);
        btnOK.addActionListener(this);
    }

    public void itemStateChanged(ItemEvent item)
    {
        //Determine which option button is selected
        if (optRed.getState())
```

```
            intColor = 1;

        else if (optBlue.getState())
             intColor = 2;
        else if (optGreen.getState())
             intColor = 3;
        else if (optGray.getState())
             intColor = 4;
    }

    public void actionPerformed(ActionEvent action)
    {
        //OK button clicked. Make settings for option buttons
        // and check box.

        //Change color depending on intColor
        switch(intColor)
        {
        case 1:
            setBackground(Color.red);
            showStatus("Color: Red");
            break;
        case 2:
            setBackground(Color.blue);
            showStatus("Color: Blue");
            break;
        case 3:
            setBackground(Color.green);
            showStatus("Color: Green");
            break;
        case 4:
            setBackground(Color.lightGray);
            showStatus("Color: Gray");
            break;
        default:
            showStatus("Select a color");
        }

        //Set font depending on setting of check box
        if (chkBold.getState())
            lblFontStyle.setFont(fntBold);
        else
            lblFontStyle.setFont(fntPlain);
    }
}
```

Feedback 7.3

Write a switch statement to replace the following nested if statement.

```
if(intAisle == 1)
    lblComment.setText("Books");
else if(intAisle == 2)
    lblComment.setText("Software");
else if(intAisle == 3)
    lblComment.setText("Toys")
else
    lblComment.setText("General Merchandise");
```

Swing Components

From the first chapter you have been using graphical components. The AWT classes allow you to create a user interface that has the "**look and feel**" of the platform that you are using. The AWT graphical components are based on the platform in which they are running. Unfortunately, they do not always work well when moved to another platform. They also tend to inherit problems related to the platform.

Java 1.2 introduced the **Java Foundation Classes (JFC)**, another set of components often referred to as **Swing components**. These newer components are less dependent on the platform and have more capabilities than AWT components. Some people refer to AWT components as heavyweight and Swing components as lightweight, because the newer components user fewer system resources.

Swing components build the graphical component from library classes instead of from the underlying operating system. The classes have distinct "look-and-feel" options available. You can select a Windows look, a **Motif** look based on Sun's Unix interface appearance, a **Metal** look designed for Java, and, on Macintosh systems, a Macintosh look. The default look is called the Basic look and feel.

If you are running Java 2, the JFC is available. You can add JFC to a JDK 1.1 system by downloading the JFC package at http://www.javasoft.com.

Most of the components with which you are familiar have corresponding Swing components (Table 7.2). However, the Swing components generally have more options and capabilities. For example, buttons may have keyboard shortcuts (often called *accelerator keys* or *hotkeys*); you can add icons to buttons and labels and choose the alignment of labels on check boxes, radio buttons, and panels.

Eventually the Swing components will become more commonplace than AWT components. It's a matter of time until all systems can handle the newer JDK.

Note: As of this writing, Microsoft does not support the JFC in Visual J++. Instead, they provide their own Windows Foundation Classes (WFC), which contain a different set of components.

T a b l e   7 . 2

*Swing Components and
Corresponding AWT Components*

Swing Component	AWT Component
JApplet	Applet
JButton	Button
JLabel	Label
JPanel	Panel
JTextField	TextField
JTextArea	TextArea
JCheckBox	Checkbox
JRadioButton	Checkbox (in a group)
ButtonGroup	CheckboxGroup

Swing components are based on the Container class from the java.awt package. Therefore, you must still import the AWT package. Swing components can use the familiar AWT events or events from the Swing event package.

Running the SwingSet Sample

The jdk1.3 directory contains many sample programs. It is a good idea to look at these samples when you want to learn more about programming in Java. As an introduction to Swing, take a few minutes to look at a sample that contains lots of "cool" Swing components called the SwingSet. The application is stored in a jar (Java Archive) file called SwingSet2.jar. The folder position may vary on your system.

STEP 1: With Windows Explorer or your systems file browser, open the jdk1.3/ demo/jfc/SwingSet2 folder.

STEP 2: Open the SwingSet2.jar file. The SwingSet program opens and runs. Trouble? To run a jar file, your computer must be set up to run the correct application. In Windows, use the Windows Explorer or My Computer, `View` menu, `Folder` Options, `File Types` tab, and set the JAR extension to c:\jdk1.3\bin\javaw.exe - jar, or to the location of the file on your system.

STEP 3: Change the look and feel using the Look & Feel menu (Figure 7.3).

Figure 7.3

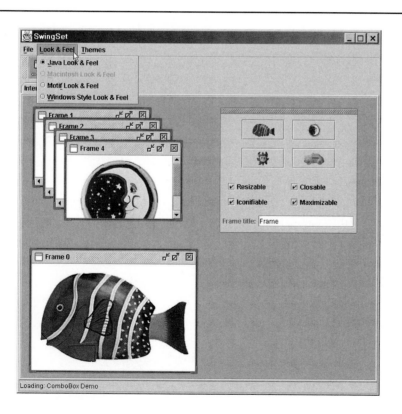

The Look & Feel menu of the Java SwingSet program example. You can change the look and feel of each of the Swing components.

STEP 4: Select the various buttons to look at the sample Swing components. Make sure to pause your pointer to look at ToolTips and to change the look and feel on different panels to see how the components look.

You can click on the `Source` tab to see the Java source files used to create the Swing components; it's interesting to see how the programming was done for this clever sample application.

This chapter introduces you to some of the Swing components; others are introduced throughout the next several chapters.

Note: You will learn to create jar files in Chapter 12.

Multiple Panes

A big advantage of Swing components over AWT involves the layering of panels. With AWT, sometimes one component is hidden behind another component or container. With Swing you can achieve the visual effect of placing an item on top of another through the use of multiple panes.

The basic pane is the **Content Pane**. Over that you may have a Layered Pane and/or a Glass Pane. You use a separate pane for the Menubar. You can think of the Content Pane as a sheet of white paper and the Layered Pane and Glass Pane as sheets of clear, transparent plastic that lie on top of the Content Pane.

You add most components to the Content Pane. When you want something to appear on top of another component, you use a Layered Pane or Glass Plane.

Setting the Content Pane

The Content Pane must be a container. One way to set up an applet is to declare a panel, add components to the panel, and set the panel as the Content Pane. Use the `setContentPane` method to set the panel as the Content Pane.

```
//Declare Swing components
JPanel pnlPane = new JPanel(); //Panel for Content Pane
JLabel lblHello = new JLabel("Hello World");

//In the init method:
//Add component to the panel
pnlPane.add(lblHello);
//Make the panel the Content Pane
setContentPane(pnlPane);
```

An alternative is to skip creating the panel and add components directly to the Content Pane. You can use the `getContentPane` method, which returns the object that is the Content Pane. For example, the statement

```
getContentPane().add(lblHello);
```

adds the label directly to the Content Pane.

Using the Swing Components

To use Swing components, you must import both java.awt.* and javax.swing.* (note the *x* in javax).

The Swing HelloWorld Applet

Here is the Hello World applet, now using Swing components.

Tip

Although you can mix AWT and Swing components in one program, it's best not to. Sometimes the results are not what you expected if you use both types of components.

```
//Folder:        Ch7SwingHelloApplet
//Programmer:    Bradley/Millspaugh
//Date:          6/2001
//ClassName:     SwingApplet
//Description:   Hello World using Swing components.

import javax.swing.*;
import java.applet.*;
import java.awt.*;

public class SwingApplet extends JApplet
{
    // Declare Swing Components
    JPanel pnlPane = new JPanel();
    JLabel lblHello = new JLabel("Hello World");

    public void init()
    {
        //Add component to the panel
        pnlPane.add(lblHello);
        //Make the panel the Content Pane
        setContentPane(pnlPane);
    }
}
```

Running a Swing Applet in a Browser

It's easy to run an applet with Swing components in the Applet Viewer, but running in a browser is a different story. Development of the Java language has occurred faster than the ability of the browsers to keep up. Hopefully the new release of each browser will include a Java Virtual Machine that includes JFC.

Both Netscape Navigator/Communicator (NN) and Microsoft Internet Explorer (IE) can run applets that include Swing components, if they have a plug-in installed. The plug-in has to be downloaded only once on a computer, and then applets can run in either browser, assuming that the paths are set correctly so that the browsers can find the plug-in files. The plug-in causes the browser to use the Java Runtime Environment in the JDK folder rather than the browser JVM.

The Student Data files on the text CD (or Website download) hold a file called RunSwingApplet.htm, which has a JavaScript to run an applet with Swing components. The html file checks to see which browser you are using (IE or NN), downloads the plug-in if necessary, and tells the browser where to find the plug-in files. You can insert your own class name into the file and run your Swing applet in either browser.

Using Enhanced Properties of Swing Components

Some of the reasons for using Swing components rather than AWT components are

● Swing has a more complete set of components.

● Swing components have more functionality.

- Swing components require fewer system resources.

- Swing components more nearly have the look and feel of the destination system.

With most Swing components, you can add icons, ToolTips, and keyboard shortcuts and control the look of the borders. You will learn to declare and use icons in Chapter 11. Figure 7.4 shows a ToolTip, a keyboard shortcut, and a raised border.

F i g u r e   7 . 4

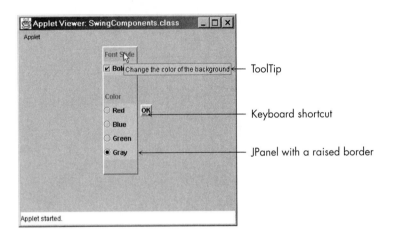

Using Swing components, you can display ToolTips and keyboard shortcuts and control the look of borders.

ToolTips

To add a **ToolTip** (the text line that pops up when you pause the mouse pointer over a component), use the `setToolTipText` method:

```
btnOK.setToolTipText("Make changes depending on settings");
chkBold.setToolTipText("Change the font of the Font Style label");
```

Keyboard Shortcuts

Keyboard shortcuts, also called *access keys* or *hotkeys*, allow the user to select an option using the keyboard rather than the mouse. Use the `setMnemonic` method to set the single letter used for keyboard access.

```
btnOK.setMnemonic('o');
```

In this example, the *O* of *OK* on the button's label appears underlined. The user can select the button by pressing Alt + *O* (uppercase or lowercase).

Borders

To add a border to your component, you must import the border package:

```
import javax.swing.border.*;
```

You can choose from among several types of borders. Table 7.3 shows some of the possibilities.

```
pnlChoices.setBorder(new BevelBorder(BevelBorder.RAISED));
```

```
btnOK.setBorder(new EtchedBorder());
btnOK.setBorder(new LineBorder(Color.black, 3));
```

Table 7.3

Selected Swing Component Border Types

Border Type	Options Available	Example
BevelBorder	The type of bevel (raised or lowered) and the colors for highlight and shadow.	`BevelBorder(BevelBorder.RAISED)`
EtchedBorder	The type of etch (raised or lowered) and the colors for the highlight and shadow.	`EtchedBorder() //Defaults to lowered` `EtchedBorder(EtchedBorder.LOWERED)`
LineBorder	Color and width of the line.	`LineBorder(Color.blue, 3)`
MatteBorder	A tile icon, width of insets, and a color.	`MatteBorder(10,10,10,10,Color.green)`

Radio Buttons

One of the extra Swing components is a **radio button**, also called an *option button*. Instead of using a check box, as in AWT, you can use the Swing JRadioButton. You create groups for radio buttons using the ButtonGroup class.

```
ButtonGroup grpColor = new ButtonGroup();
JRadioButton optRed = new JRadioButton ("Red");
JRadioButton optBlue = new JRadioButton ("Blue");
JRadioButton optGreen = new JRadioButton ("Green");
JRadioButton optGray = new JRadioButton ("Gray");
```

Initializing Radio Buttons

When you use radio buttons, you should initialize their state (true or false) in the init method. If you fail to initialize buttons, they will appear deselected initially and Java generates warning error messages, so it's best to always initialize the components. Of course, you should set the initial state to true for any option that appears selected when the program begins.

You also add radio buttons to their group in the init method.

```
//Initialize components
optRed.setSelected(false);
optBlue.setSelected(false);
optGreen.setSelected(false);
optGray.setSelected(true); //Color initially gray

//Add option buttons to the group
grpColor.add(optRed);
```

```
grpColor.add(optBlue);
grpColor.add(optGreen);
grpColor.add(optGray);
```

A Swing Applet

This example modifies the check box and option button project to use Swing
components. Note that although this example does not use an item listener, you
can specify an item listener for Swing components in the same way as with
AWT components.

```java
//Folder:        Ch7SwingDemo
//Programmer:    Bradley/Millspaugh
//Date:          6/2001
//ClassName:     SwingComponents
//Description:   Use Swing components in an applet.

import java.applet.*;
import java.awt.*;
import java.awt.event.*;
import javax.swing.*;
import javax.swing.border.*;

public class SwingComponents extends JApplet implements ActionListener
{
    //Declare components
    JCheckBox chkBold = new JCheckBox("Bold");
    ButtonGroup grpColor = new ButtonGroup();
    JRadioButton optRed = new JRadioButton("Red");
    JRadioButton optBlue = new JRadioButton("Blue");
    JRadioButton optGreen = new JRadioButton("Green");
    JRadioButton optGray = new JRadioButton("Gray");
    JButton btnOK = new JButton("OK");

    JLabel lblFontStyle = new JLabel(" Font Style ");
    JPanel pnlAppletPanel = new JPanel(); //Panel for Content Pane
    Font fntBold = new Font("Arial", Font.BOLD, 12);
    Font fntPlain = new Font("Arial", Font.PLAIN, 11);

    public void init()
    {
        //Set up interface
        //Initialize components
        optRed.setSelected(false);
        optBlue.setSelected(false);
        optGreen.setSelected(false);
        optGray.setSelected(true); //Color initially gray
        chkBold.setSelected(true); //Font initially bold
        btnOK.setMnemonic('o');

        //Add option buttons to the group
        grpColor.add(optRed);
        grpColor.add(optBlue);
        grpColor.add(optGreen);
        grpColor.add(optGray);

        //Set up interior panel for selections
        JPanel pnlChoices = new JPanel();
```

```
    pnlChoices.setBackground(Color.lightGray);
    pnlChoices.setLayout(new GridLayout(9,0));
    pnlChoices.add(lblFontStyle);
    pnlChoices.add(chkBold);
    pnlChoices.add(new JLabel(" "));
    pnlChoices.add(new JLabel(" Color "));
    pnlChoices.add(optRed);
    pnlChoices.add(optBlue);
    pnlChoices.add(optGreen);
    pnlChoices.add(optGray);

    //Set up applet panel
    pnlAppletPanel.add(pnlChoices);
    pnlAppletPanel.add(btnOK);
    pnlAppletPanel.setBackground(Color.lightGray);

    //Format the components
    btnOK.setToolTipText("Make changes depending on settings");
    chkBold.setToolTipText(
        "Change the font of the Font Style label");
    pnlChoices.setToolTipText("Change the color of the background");
    pnlChoices.setBorder(new BevelBorder(BevelBorder.RAISED));
    btnOK.setBorder(new BevelBorder(BevelBorder.RAISED));

    //Make the applet panel the Content Pane
    setContentPane(pnlAppletPanel);

    //Add listener
    btnOK.addActionListener(this);
}

public void actionPerformed(ActionEvent action)
{
    //OK button clicked. Make settings for option buttons
    // and check box.

    //Test the font check box
    if (chkBold.isSelected())
        lblFontStyle.setFont(fntBold);
    else
        lblFontStyle.setFont(fntPlain);
    pnlAppletPanel.repaint(); //Force any font change to appear

    //Test the option buttons
    if (optRed.isSelected())
    {
        pnlAppletPanel.setBackground(Color.red);
        showStatus("Color: Red");
    }
    else if (optBlue.isSelected())
    {
        pnlAppletPanel.setBackground(Color.blue);
        showStatus("Color: Blue");
    }
    else if (optGreen.isSelected())
    {
        pnlAppletPanel.setBackground(Color.green);
        showStatus("Color: Green");
    }
```

```
        else if (optGray.isSelected())
        {
            pnlAppletPanel.setBackground(Color.lightGray);
            showStatus("Color: Gray");
        }
    }
}
```

Your Hands-on Programming Example

Modify the Payroll project from Chapter 6 to incorporate salaried and hourly employees. The company has three pay levels for hourly employees and two for salaried, as shown below. Overtime applies only to hourly employees.

Use constants in the Payroll class for the various pay rates. Add a check box called Hourly to the applet and delete the text field for rate. Display option buttons for the levels depending on whether or not hourly is selected. Notice from the salary tables that you will need three option buttons for hourly employees and only two for salaried and that the levels are labeled differently.

In calculating the pay for non-Hourly, divide the salary by 52 to determine the weekly pay.

Note: The Payroll class does not recognize the applet's check box, so you must "pass" the value to the Payroll class and modify the constructor appropriately.

Salaried Payroll Levels

Level	Salary
A	27,000
B	42,000

Hourly Pay Levels

Level	Hourly Rate
1	6.25
2	8.15
3	10.85

Figure 7.5 shows a possible layout for the user interface.

Figure 7.5

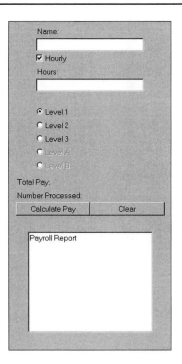

Planning the Project

Plan the Objects and Properties

Classes: **PayrollApplet, Payroll, and LocalFormat**

Figure 7.6 shows the class diagrams for this project.

The class diagram for the hands-on example.

PayrollApplet Class	
Methods	**Variables and Components**
init	pnlInput
actionPerformed	pnlOutput
itemStateChanged	txtName
CalculatePay	txtHours
ClearUI	txaPayroll
DesignInputPanel	btnCalculate
DesignOutputPanel	btnClear
InitalizeHourly	lblPayOut
InitiatizeSalaried	lblNumberProcessed
	lblErrorMessage
	chkHourly
	cbgSalary
	cbgHourly
	optLevelA
	cptLevelB
	optLevel1
	optLevel2
	optLevel3

LocalFormat Class	
Methods	**Variables and Components**
Public Methods	**Private Instance Variables**
FormatCurrency	fmtCurrency
FormatDecimal	fmtDecimal

Payroll Class	
Methods	**Variables and Components**
Public Methods	**Private Class Variables**
setHours	dblTotalPay
getTotalPay	intNumberProcessed
getNumberProcessed	**Private Instance Variables**
getHours	fltPay
CalculatePay	fltHours
	blnHourly
	chrPayLevel
	fltRate
	Private Constants
	fltLEVEL_A
	fltLEVEL_B
	fltLEVEL_1
	fltLEVEL_2
	fltLEVEL_3
	fltMAX_HOURS

Class: PayrollApplet

Components and Variables:

Access Mode (public or private)	Variable or Component Name	Data Type or Class	Description
	pnlInput	Panel	Panel for input components.
	pnlOutput	Panel	Panel for output components.
	txtName	TextField	Input the name.
	txtHours	TextField	Input the hours worked.
	chkHourly	Checkbox	Hourly or Salaried.
	cbgLevel	Checkbox group	Hold Level option buttons.
	optLevel1	Checkbox	Pay level option.
	optLevel2	Checkbox	Pay level option.
	optLevel3	Checkbox	Pay level option.
	optLevelA	Checkbox	Pay level option.
	optLevelB	Checkbox	Pay level option.
	lblPayOut	Label	Display total pay.
	lblNumberProcessed	Label	Display number of employees.
	lblErrorMessage	Label	Display error message.
	txaPayroll	TextArea	Display report of names and pay.
	btnCalculate	Button	Process pay.
	btnClear	Button	Clear text fields and check boxes.
	chrLevel	char	Hold selection from Level option.
	fltPay	float	Hold pay for one individual.
	fltHours	float	Hold hours for one individual.
	strFormattedData	String	Hold formatted output.

Methods:

Access Mode (public or private)	Return Type	Method Name (include any parameters)	Pseudocode
public	void	init	Call method to lay out panels. Add panels. Add text area. Set focus to the name text field. Add action listeners. Add item listeners for options. Initialize elements for hourly.
public	void	actionPerformed	If event caused by Calculate button or text field 　　Calculate pay. else 　　Clear UI.
public	void	itemStateChanged	If Hourly option selected 　　Initialize elements for hourly. else 　　Initialize elements for salaried.
public	void	CalculatePay	Set chrLevel for correct option button. Clear any previous message. If hourly 　　Get Hours from screen. else 　　Set Hours to 0. Create payroll object. If Hours fails validation 　　Display error message. 　　Select text and set focus. else 　　Calculate pay. 　　Create LocalFormat object. 　　Format and display total pay. 　　Format and display number processed. 　　Format and display name and pay.
public	void	ClearUI	Clear text boxes. Initialize screen for hourly.
public	void	DesignInputPanel	Lay out the input fields.
public	void	DesignOutputPanel	Lay out the output fields.
public	void	InitializeHourly	Enable Hours text field. Set background and clear text. Enable Hourly option buttons. Disable Salaried option buttons. Set the focus in first text field.
public	void	InitializeSalaried	Disable Hours text field. Set background and clear text. Enable Salaried option buttons. Disable Hourly option buttons. Set the focus in first text field.

Class Name: Payroll

Components and Variables:

Access Mode (public or private)	Variable or Component Name	Data Type or Class	Description
private static	dblTotalPay	double	Holds total pay.
private static	intNumberProcessed	int	Holds number processed
private	fltPay	float	Holds pay for one individual.
private	blnHourly	boolean	Holds value of chkHourly.
private	chrPayLevel	char	Letter or number of pay option.
private	fltRate	float	Pay rate.
private	fltLEVEL_A	float	Constant for salary level A.
private	fltLEVEL_B	float	Constant for salary level B.
private	fltLEVEL_1	float	Constant for hourly level 1.
private	fltLEVEL_2	float	Constant for hourly level 2.
private	fltLEVEL_3	float	Constant for hourly level 3.
private	fltMAX_HOURS	float	Constant for maximum hours.

Methods:

Access Mode (public or private)	Return Type	Method Name (include any parameters)	Pseudocode
		`Payroll(float fltNewHours, boolean blnNewHourly, char chrNewLevel)`	(Constructor.) Set variables to argument values.

public	void	`setHours(float fltNewHours)`	If hours > max
			    Set hours to −1.
			else
			    Set fltHours to hours.

public	double	`getTotalPay`	Return total pay.
public	int	`getNumberProcessed`	Return number processed.
public	float	`getHours`	Return hours.
public	float	`CalculatePay`	If hours invalid Return −1. Determine pay rate. If hourly

continued

Access Mode (public or private)	Return Type	Method Name (include any parameters)	Pseudocode

			If overtime
			    Calculate pay = (rate * 40 +
			        ((hours − 40) * (1.5 * rate).
			else
			    Calculate pay = hours * rate.
			else (salaried employee)
			    Calculate pay = rate / 52.
			Add pay to total pay.
			Add 1 to number processed.
			Return pay.

Class: LocalFormat

Components and Variables:

Access Mode (public or private)	Variable or Component Name	Data Type or Class	Description
private	fmtCurrency	NumberFormat	Format currency for locale.
private	fmtDecimal	NumberFormat	Format decimal for locale.

Methods:

Access Mode (public or private)	Return Type	Method Name (include any parameters)	Pseudocode
		LocalFormat()	Constructor with no parameters. Get formatting for locale.
public	String	FormatCurrency(float fltNumber)	Set fractional digits to 2. Format number as currency. Return formatted number.
public	String	FormatCurrency(float fltNumber, int intDecimalPos)	Set fractional digits to decimal pos. Format number as currency. Return formatted number.
public	String	FormatCurrency(double dblNumber)	Set fractional digits to 2. Format number as currency. Return formatted number.
public	String	FormatCurrency(double dblNumber, int intDecimalPos)	Set fractional digits to decimal pos. Format number as currency. Return formatted number.
public	String	FormatDecimal(float fltNumber)	Set fractional digits to 2. Format number as decimal. Return formatted number.
public	String	FormatDecimal(float fltNumber, int intDecimalPos)	Set fractional digits to decimal pos. Format number as decimal. Return formatted number.

Write the Project

- Create the classes.

- Follow the plan to declare components and variables.

- Code the methods.

- When you complete the code, thoroughly test the project.

The Project Solution

PayrollApplet.java

```
//Folder:        Ch7Payroll
//Programmer:    Bradley/Millspaugh
//Date:          6/2001
//ClassName:     PayrollApplet
//Description:   Input Hours and Rates for Payroll using check boxes
//               and option buttons. Format and display the results.

import java.applet.*;
import java.awt.event.*;
import java.awt.*;

public class PayrollApplet extends Applet
         implements ActionListener, ItemListener
{
    //Create components
    Panel pnlInput = new Panel();
    Panel pnlOutput = new Panel();
    TextField txtName = new TextField(25);
    TextField txtHours = new TextField();
    TextArea txaPayroll = new TextArea("Payroll Report",10, 30);
    Button btnCalculate = new Button("Calculate Pay");
    Button btnClear = new Button("Clear");
    Label lblPayOut = new Label();
    Label lblNumberProcessed = new Label();
    Label lblErrorMessage = new Label(" ");
    Checkbox chkHourly = new Checkbox("Hourly",true);
    CheckboxGroup cbgLevel = new CheckboxGroup();
    Checkbox optLevelA = new Checkbox("Level A",cbgLevel,false);
    Checkbox optLevelB = new Checkbox("Level B",cbgLevel,false);
    Checkbox optLevel1 = new Checkbox("Level 1",cbgLevel,false);
    Checkbox optLevel2 = new Checkbox("Level 2",cbgLevel,false);
    Checkbox optLevel3 = new Checkbox("Level 3",cbgLevel,false);

    public void init()
    {
        //Create Interface
        DesignInputPanel();
        DesignOutputPanel();
        add(pnlInput);
        add(pnlOutput);
        add(txaPayroll);
        btnCalculate.addActionListener(this);
```

```java
        btnClear.addActionListener(this);
        txtHours.addActionListener(this);
        chkHourly.addItemListener(this);
        InitializeHourly();
    }

    public void actionPerformed(ActionEvent evt)
    {
        //Determine object calling this method
        Object objSource = evt.getSource();
        if (objSource == btnCalculate
                || objSource == txtHours)
        {
            CalculatePay();
        }
        else
        {
            ClearUI();
        }
    }

    public void itemStateChanged(ItemEvent event)
    {
        //Display the options based on the pay level
        if(chkHourly.getState()) //Hourly selected
            InitializeHourly();
        else
            InitializeSalaried();
    }

    public void CalculatePay()
    {
        //Retrieve data and calculate
        //Declare variables
        char chrLevel;
        float fltPay;
        float fltHours;
        String strFormattedData;

        //Determine which option button is selected
        if (chkHourly.getState())
        {
            if(optLevel1.getState())
                chrLevel = '1';
            else if (optLevel2.getState())
                chrLevel = '2';
            else if(optLevel3.getState())
                chrLevel = '3';
            else
                chrLevel = '0';
        }
        else
        {
            if(optLevelA.getState())
                chrLevel = 'A';
            else if(optLevelB.getState())
```

```
                chrLevel = 'B';
            else
                chrLevel = '0';
        }


    try
    {
        lblErrorMessage.setText("");   //Clear any previous message
        if (chkHourly.getState())      //Hourly
            fltHours = Float.valueOf(txtHours.getText()).floatValue();
        else
            fltHours = 0;                   //Salaried. Hours don't count.
        Payroll myPayroll = new Payroll(fltHours,
                    chkHourly.getState(), chrLevel);
        if (myPayroll.getHours() < 0) //Hours failed validation
        {
            txtHours.requestFocus();
            txtHours.selectAll();
            lblErrorMessage.setText("Invalid Hours");
        }
        else //Passed business rule validation
        {
            //Calculate pay
            fltPay = myPayroll.CalculatePay();

            //Format and display output
            LocalFormat fmtLocal = new LocalFormat();
            strFormattedData = fmtLocal.FormatCurrency
                                    (myPayroll.getTotalPay());
            lblPayOut.setText(strFormattedData);
            lblNumberProcessed.setText("" +
                                    myPayroll.getNumberProcessed());
            strFormattedData = fmtLocal.FormatDecimal(fltPay);
            txaPayroll.append("\n" + txtName.getText() + "\t"
                                    + strFormattedData);
        }
    }


    catch(Exception err)
    {
        lblErrorMessage.setText("Hours must be numeric");
        txtHours.requestFocus();
        txtHours.selectAll();
    }
}

public void ClearUI()
{
    //Reset the user interface
    txtName.setText("");
    txtHours.setText("");
    chkHourly.setState(true);
    InitializeHourly();
}

public void DesignInputPanel()
{
```

```java
        //Lay out the input panel
        pnlInput.setLayout(new GridLayout(11,0));
        pnlInput.add(new Label("Name: "));
        pnlInput.add(txtName);
        pnlInput.add(chkHourly);
        pnlInput.add(new Label("Hours: "));
        pnlInput.add(txtHours);
        lblErrorMessage.setForeground(Color.red);
        pnlInput.add(lblErrorMessage);
        pnlInput.add(optLevel1);
        pnlInput.add(optLevel2);
        pnlInput.add(optLevel3);
        pnlInput.add(optLevelA);
        pnlInput.add(optLevelB);
    }

    public void DesignOutputPanel()
    {
        //Lay out the output panel
        pnlOutput.setLayout(new GridLayout(4,2));
        pnlOutput.add(new Label("Total Pay:"));
        pnlOutput.add(lblPayOut);
        pnlOutput.add(new Label("Number Processed: "));
        pnlOutput.add(lblNumberProcessed);
        pnlOutput.add(btnCalculate);
        pnlOutput.add(btnClear);
    }

    public void InitializeHourly()
    {
        //Initialize the interface for an hourly employee
        txtHours.setEnabled(true);
        txtHours.setBackground(Color.white);
        txtHours.setText("");
        lblErrorMessage.setText("");
        optLevel1.setEnabled(true);
        optLevel2.setEnabled(true);
        optLevel3.setEnabled(true);
        optLevel1.setState(true);
        optLevelA.setEnabled(false);
        optLevelB.setEnabled(false);
        txtName.requestFocus();
    }

    public void InitializeSalaried()
    {
        //Initialize the interface for a salaried employee
        txtHours.setEnabled(false);
        txtHours.setBackground(Color.gray);
        txtHours.setText("");
        lblErrorMessage.setText("");
        optLevel1.setEnabled(false);
        optLevel2.setEnabled(false);
        optLevel3.setEnabled(false);
        optLevelA.setEnabled(true);
        optLevelB.setEnabled(true);
        optLevelA.setState(true);
        txtName.requestFocus();
    }
}
```

Payroll.Java

```
//Folder:       Ch7Payroll
//Programmer:   Bradley/Millspaugh
//Date:         6/2001
//ClassName:    Payroll
//Description:  Input hours and pay class; calculate pay, total pay,
//              and number processed. Format and display results.

public class Payroll
{
    //Class variables
    private static double dblTotalPay;
    private static int intNumberProcessed;

    //Instance variables
    private   float fltPay;
    private float fltHours;
    private boolean blnHourly;
    private char chrPayLevel;
    private float fltRate;  //Determined by pay level

    //Constants
    private final float fltLEVEL_A = 27000f;
    private final float fltLEVEL_B = 42000f;
    private final float fltLEVEL_1 = 6.25f;
    private final float fltLEVEL_2 = 8.15f;
    private final float fltLEVEL_3 = 10.85f;
    private final float fltMAX_HOURS = 80.0f;

    //Constructor
    Payroll(float fltNewHours, boolean blnNewHourly, char chrNewLevel)
    {
        setHours(fltNewHours);
        blnHourly = blnNewHourly;
        chrPayLevel = chrNewLevel;
    }

    //Public methods
    public void setHours(float fltNewHours)
    {
        //Check range for valid data
        if (fltNewHours > fltMAX_HOURS || fltNewHours < 0.0)
            fltHours = -1.0f;           //Indicate bad data
        else
            fltHours = fltNewHours;     //Good data
    }

    public double getTotalPay()
    {
        return dblTotalPay;
    }

    public int getNumberProcessed()
    {
        return intNumberProcessed;
    }
```

```java
public float getHours()
{
    return fltHours;
}


public float CalculatePay()
{
    //Calculate and return the amount of pay
    if (fltHours < 0)   //Bad data
        return -1.0f;    //Exit the class

    //Find rate
    switch(chrPayLevel)
    {
        case 'A':
            fltRate = fltLEVEL_A;
            break;
        case 'B':
            fltRate = fltLEVEL_B;
            break;
        case '1':
            fltRate = fltLEVEL_1;
            break;
        case '2':
            fltRate = fltLEVEL_2;
            break;
        case '3':
            fltRate = fltLEVEL_3;
            break;
        default:
            fltRate = 0.0f;
    }
    if (blnHourly)              //Hourly employee
    {

        if (fltHours > 40.0f)  //Overtime
        {
            fltPay = fltRate * 40.0f
                             + (fltHours - 40.0f) * 1.5f
                             * fltRate;
        }
        else                   //No overtime
        {
            fltPay = fltHours * fltRate;
        }
    }
    else                       //Salaried employee
    {
        fltPay = fltRate / 52.0f;
    }
    dblTotalPay += fltPay;
    intNumberProcessed++;
    return fltPay;
    }
}
```

LocalFormat.Java

```
//Folder:        Ch6Payroll
//Programmer:    Bradley/Millspaugh
//Date:          6/2001
//ClassName:     LocalFormat
//Description:   Get format for locale and format numbers for display.

import java.text.*; //Formatting methods

public class LocalFormat
{
    //Instance variables
    private NumberFormat fmtCurrency;
    private NumberFormat fmtDecimal;

    //Class constructor
    LocalFormat()
    {
        //Get formatting for default locale
        fmtCurrency = NumberFormat.getCurrencyInstance();
        fmtDecimal = NumberFormat.getInstance();
    }

    //Methods
    public String FormatCurrency (float fltNumber)
    {
        //Format as currency, 2 decimal positions
        fmtCurrency.setMinimumFractionDigits(2);
        fmtCurrency.setMaximumFractionDigits(2);
        String strFormattedData = fmtCurrency.format(fltNumber);
        return strFormattedData;
    }

    public String FormatCurrency (float fltNumber, int intDecimalPos)
    {
        //Format as currency, variable number of decimal positions
        fmtCurrency.setMinimumFractionDigits(intDecimalPos);
        fmtCurrency.setMaximumFractionDigits(intDecimalPos);
        String strFormattedData = fmtCurrency.format(fltNumber);
        return strFormattedData;
    }

    public String FormatCurrency (double dblNumber)
    {
        //Format as currency, 2 decimal positions
        fmtCurrency.setMinimumFractionDigits(2);
        fmtCurrency.setMaximumFractionDigits(2);
        String strFormattedData = fmtCurrency.format(dblNumber);
        return strFormattedData;
    }

    public String FormatCurrency (double dblNumber, int intDecimalPos)
    {
        //Format as currency, variable number of decimal positions
        fmtCurrency.setMinimumFractionDigits(intDecimalPos);
        fmtCurrency.setMaximumFractionDigits(intDecimalPos);
```

```java
        String strFormattedData = fmtCurrency.format(dblNumber);
        return strFormattedData;
    }

    public String FormatDecimal (float fltNumber)
    {
        //Format as decimal, 2 decimal positions
        fmtDecimal.setMinimumFractionDigits(2);
        fmtDecimal.setMaximumFractionDigits(2);
        String strFormattedData = fmtDecimal.format(fltNumber);
        return strFormattedData;
    }

    public String FormatDecimal (float fltNumber, int intDecimalPos)
    {
        //Format as decimal, variable number of decimal positions
        //Set decimal positions
        fmtDecimal.setMinimumFractionDigits(intDecimalPos);
        fmtDecimal.setMaximumFractionDigits(intDecimalPos);
        String strFormattedData = fmtDecimal.format(fltNumber);
        return strFormattedData;
    }
}
```

Summary

1. A check box component is used to make a selection. The component can have a true/false, yes/no, or on/off value.
2. Checkbox components placed in a group look and act like option buttons; only one component in the group can be selected.
3. The value of a check box or option button is called its state and can be tested with the getState method.
4. Check boxes operate independently and generally should be tested with separate if statements. Option buttons operate as a group and usually should be tested with a nested if statement.
5. You can assign an ItemListener to a component. As soon as the state of the item changes, the itemStateChanged method executes.
6. A switch statement provides an alternative for decisions when multiple comparisons must be made with the same integer or character field.
7. Test each possible value in a switch statement using a case statement.
8. The default clause is executed when no match occurs for a switch statement.
9. Once a value in a switch evaluates to true, all of the following statements in the block execute unless a break statement is used.
10. The JFC of Java 2 hold a set of components called *Swing* components. Swing components have more capabilities than their AWT counterparts, and as well take fewer system resources and have a more consistent look and feel.

11. A Swing applet has multiple panes that can be layered to allow one component on top of another. The primary pane is the Content Pane.

12. Current browsers do not support Swing components in their virtual machine. In order to run a Swing applet in a browser, you must write code in your html file to tell the browser where to find the Swing components. A sample html file is included with the Student Data for this text.

13. Using Swing components, you can add icons, ToolTips, and keyboard access keys and control the borders of components.

Key Terms

break statement *201*	look and feel *204*
case statement *200*	Metal *204*
Content Pane *206*	Motif *204*
default statement *201*	radio button *209*
getState method *194*	state *193*
ItemListener *197*	Swing components *204*
itemStateChanged method *197*	switch statement *200*
Java Foundation Classes (JFC) *204*	ToolTip *208*
keyboard shortcut *208*	

Review Questions

1. How does the action of a check box in a group differ from one that is not in a group?
2. How does the appearance of a check box in a group differ from one that is not in a group?
3. List and explain the constructors available for the Checkbox class.
4. Describe the format of a `switch` statement.
5. What is the purpose of the `default` statement in a `switch`?
6. What are some advantages of using Swing components over AWT components?
7. What are some disadvantages of using Swing components?

P r o g r a m m i n g   E x e r c i s e s

7.1 Create an applet for purchasing widgets. Data entry includes the buyer's name, address, and credit card number. This information will be entered only once, even though the user may purchase multiple widgets.

● Allow the user to select the color of the widget—blue, red, or yellow—using option buttons.

● Use a text field to allow the buyer to enter the quantity desired.

● A check box allows the users to select having the widget engraved.

● Include an "Add to Shopping Cart" button that displays a line in a text area for the current widget information and then clears the option buttons, check box, and quantity fields.

● A "Purchase" button totals all of the costs and displays the entire purchase.

● The Purchase button is disabled until the first item is added to the shopping cart.

Widget Prices:

Blue	10.00
Red	14.00
Yellow	12.00
Engraving:	4.00 per widget

7.2 Tricia's Travels needs an applet for displaying tour prices. Their current packages offer both 7-day and 14-day deals. The destinations are the Caribbean, the Mediterranean, and Alaska. Include option buttons for the number of days and for the destination. Use a check box for First Class. Set defaults to 7 days and no First Class. Display the appropriate price in a label when the user selects options.

Package Prices:

Days	Destination	Standard Price	First Class Price
7	Caribbean	3250	5000
14	Caribbean	6000	9000
7	Mediterranean	4250	7999
14	Mediterranean	7999	11999
7	Alaska	3800	5250
14	Alaska	7200	10500

7.3   Kenna's Kandles offers candles in various shapes, scents, and colors. Create an applet that includes a text field for quantity; options for TeaLight, Votive, or Pillar; a check box for scented; and options for colors: federal blue, sunflower yellow, Christmas red, and lily white.

Allow the user to enter his or her name and credit card number. You need two buttons: Add to Shopping Cart and Sale Complete.

Calculate the price for a candle based on the options selected and clear the options and quantities when the Add button is clicked. The Sale Completed button should add a sales tax of 8 percent and a shipping fee of 3 percent.

Prices	Base Price	Scented
TeaLight	5.75	0.75
Votive	7.50	1.25
Pillar	12.25	1.75

You will need a label to display the price of each item ordered and a text area to display an invoice with a list of items, the subtotal, tax, shipping, and total.

7.4   Use a `switch` statement to calculate a letter grade based on a numeric average up to 100. Allow the numeric score to be entered in a text field. A Grade button will display the corresponding letter grade in a label. Grading policy:

    90–100   A
    80–89   B
    70–79   C
    60–69   D
    < 60   F

Hint: You can divide the grade by 10 and store the result in an integer field. Use the integer in your `switch` statement.

7.5   Create an applet that displays a grading report in a text area. Text fields include student name, three project grades, two quiz grades, and a final exam grade. The projects are worth 50 percent of the grade and the quiz and final are worth 25 percent each.

A Process button should place the numeric average, the letter grade, and the student's name on a line in the text area as well as clear the text fields. See exercise 7.4 for a hint on finding the letter grade.

7.6   Modify exercise 7.5 by adding a Complete button that will display the overall average for the class and the number of students processed.
Optional: Also display the name of the student with the highest grade.

7.7   Write any of the preceding exercises using Swing components. Include keyboard shortcuts and ToolTips on the components. Make sure that your applet will run in both Internet Explorer and Netscape Navigator.

7.8   Modify the hands-on example in this chapter to use Swing components. Include keyboard shortcuts and ToolTips on the components.

CASE STUDIES

R 'n R—for Reading and Refreshment

Add a check box for Gold Customers and one for Plat-

Modify your program from Chapter 6.

inum Customers. Gold customers receive an additional discount of 5 percent; Platinum customers receive an 8 percent discount.

Merry Pea's Quilting

Chapter 6, replacing the text fields for guild name and

Modify your program from

staff with check boxes. Make sure that the program still properly credits the discounts. Make the prompt of the Guild Check box say "Guild Member."

8

Using Lists, Choices, and Looping

At the completion of this chapter, you will be able to . . .

1. Create and use a List object.

2. Update lists by using the `add`, `remove`, and `removeAll` methods.

3. Determine which item in a list is selected.

4. Use the `getItemCount` method to determine the number of items in a list.

5. Display a selected item from a list.

6. Use the Choice class to create a drop-down list.

7. Create program loops using `do`, `while`, and `for` statements.

8. Use the JList and JComboBox Swing components.

Lists

The AWT List and Choice components allow you to set up a list of items from which the user can make a selection. Figure 8.1 shows three Lists and two Choice components. Notice that the widths of the components vary depending on the widths of the items you add to the lists and that scroll bars appear if the list is longer or wider than the allocated space. As a programmer, you do not have to be concerned about the location of the scroll box in the scroll bar; the scrolling is handled automatically.

F i g u r e   8 . 1

List and Choice components.

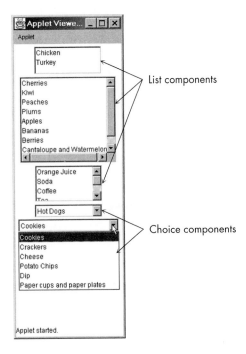

Similar to the other components you have used, the AWT components are more limited than their Swing counterparts. Later in this chapter you will learn to use the JList and JComboBox Swing components, which provide more functionality.

The items in a list are numbered internally with an index that starts with zero. When a user selects an item from the list, you can retrieve the selected item or the selected index. You can assign an item listener and/or an action listener to a List and respond whenever an item is selected, if you wish.

The List Component—Constructors

Use the **List class** to create a Java list box.

```
List()
List(int rows)
List(int rows, boolean mode)
```

The *rows* parameter specifies the number of rows that are visible before adding a scroll bar. If you use the empty constructor, the default is 4 rows. The *mode* specifies whether the user is allowed to select multiple items from the list: set to true for multiple selections; the default is false.

All of the lists include a scroll bar if the list holds more entries than the number of visible rows.

The List Component—Examples

```
List lstSelection = new List();
List lstDepartments = new List(5);
List lstSchools = new List(10, true);
```

Adding Items to a List

After you declare a List component, you usually add items to the list. You may want to hard code the list elements in your program code or add items as the program executes. You use the **add method** to add list items either during program design or execution. (Earlier versions of Java used the deprecated addItem method.)

The add Method—General Formats

```
add(String item);
add(String item, int position);
```

The item you add can be a string expression, a variable, or a literal. The first form of the add method adds the new item to the end of the list. With the second format, you can specify the position of the new element. Position 0 is the first list item. If the number you specify is greater than the number of elements in the list, the new element is added at the end of the list. You can use a value of -1 to add an item to the end of the list.

The add Method—Examples

```
lstDepartments.add("Accounting");
lstDepartments.add(strDepartment);
lstDepartments.add(strDepartment, 0);
lstDepartments.add(txtDepartment.getText());
```

The following code checks for user entry in txtAdd and adds the new item to the list. If txtAdd doesn't have an entry, it displays a message to the user rather than add a blank entry to the list. Figure 8.2 shows the applet screen, which comes from the Ch8ListUpdate program.

```
public void addItem()
{
    //Add string in text field to list box
    String strAdd = new String(txtAdd.getText());
    if(strAdd.compareTo("") == 0)
    {
        lblMessage.setText("Enter Dept to add");
        txtAdd.requestFocus();
    }
    else
    {
        lstDepartments.add(strAdd);
        txtAdd.setText("");
    }
}
```

Figure 8.2

*The applet screen for
Ch8ListUpdate. The user can add
a new element to the list.*

Clearing the List

In addition to adding items during run time, you also can clear all items from a list. Use the **removeAll method** to empty a list.

The removeAll Method—General Format

```
List.removeAll();
```

The removeAll Method—Example

```
lstDepartments.removeAll();
```

The getSelectedIndex Method

When a project is running and the user selects (highlights) an item from the list, you can retrieve the index number of the selected item by using the **getSelectedIndex method**. Recall that the index of the first item in the list is 0. If no list item is selected, the method returns –1 (negative 1).

```
if (lstDepartments.getSelectedIndex() == -1)
    lblMessage.setText("Select an item from the list");
```

The getItemCount Method

You can use the **getItemCount method** of a list component to find the number of items in the list. The item count is always one more than the highest index, since indexes begin with 0. For example, in a list with four elements, the item count is four and the indexes for the elements are 0, 1, 2, and 3.

```
public void displayCount()
{
    //Display the number of items in the list
    String strCount;

    strCount = new String("Count: " + lstDepartments.getItemCount());
    lblCount.setText(strCount);
}
```

Displaying One Element from a List

If you need to display a single item from a list, you can refer to the text of an element using the **getItem method** or the **getSelectedItem** method. The getItem requires an index; the getSelectedItem retrieves the currently selected item. This technique can be useful if you need to display a list item in a label in another location.

The getItem Method—General Format

```
getItem(int index)
```

The getSelectedItem Method—General Format

```
getSelectedItem()
```

The getSelectedItem Method—Examples

```
lblManager.setText(lstManagers.getSelectedItem());

String strDeptName;
strDeptName = lstDepartments.getSelectedItem();
```

> **Tip**
>
> When your list allows multiple items to be selected, use the getSelectedIndexes and getSelectedItems methods.

Removing an Item from a List

In addition to clearing all elements from a list, you can remove individual elements. Use the **remove method** to remove a single item from a list.

The remove Method—General Formats

```
remove(int index);
remove(String item);
```

The index specifies which element to remove by its index number. If you specify a string to remove, the string must exactly match one of the elements in the list. If the string appears more than once, the first occurrence is removed, and if no match for the string is found, an exception occurs.

The remove Method—Examples

```
lstDepartments.remove(5);
lstDepartments.remove("Accounting");
lstSchools.remove(intSchoolIndex);
lstSchools.remove(strSchoolName);
```

The following method checks to make sure the user has selected an item from the list. If an item is selected, it is removed. If no item is selected, a message displays for the user.

```
public void removeItem()
{
    //Remove selected item
    int intIndex = lstDepartments.getSelectedIndex();

    if(intIndex == -1) //No item is selected
    {
        lblMessage.setText("Select item to remove");
    }
    else
    {
        lstDepartments.remove(intIndex);
    }
}
```

Deselecting All List Elements

Sometimes you need to reset a list so that no elements are selected. You can do that with a combination of the `deselect` method and the `getSelectedIndex` method:

```
lstDepartments.deselect(lstDepartments.getSelectedIndex());
```

Note: Java AWT does not have a combo box component. Combo boxes combine the features of a text box with a list. Swing has a JComboBox component, which is covered later in this chapter.

The Choice Class

The **Choice class** provides a drop-down list of items. Choice components are also referred to as *popup menus*. Figure 8.3 shows the interface for this applet, which you will find in Ch8ChoiceClass.

Figure 8.3

a.   b.

The applet screen for Ch8ChoiceClass. A Choice class allows the user to make a selection from a list. a. As the Choice list initially appears; b. The Choice list dropped down.

```
//Create an applet with a Choice menu
Choice chcActions = new Choice();
```

You can use the Choice class to create a menu rather than use a series of buttons.

```
public void fillMenu()
{
    //Add items to the menu

    chcActions.add("Add New Department");
    chcActions.add("Display List Count");
    chcActions.add("Clear List");
    chcActions.add("Remove Selected Item");
}
```

Use an ItemListener to respond when the user makes a selection. You can use the Choice component's index to determine which option the user selects.

```
public void itemStateChanged(ItemEvent event)
{
    //Take action based on index of Choice menu

    switch(chcActions.getSelectedIndex())
    {
        case 0:
            addItem();
            break;
        case 1:
            displayCount();
            break;
        case 2:
            clearList();
            break;
        case 3:
            removeItem();
    }
}
```

Using Choice for a Drop-Down List

You also can use an object of the Choice class to work as a drop-down list for selection. The advantage of using a drop-down list rather than a regular list is that the drop-down takes less screen space and can make a cleaner user interface.

The Choice class has many of the same methods as the List class, so you can allow the user to select an item from the drop-down list and use the same logic in your programs. Table 8.1 shows some of the methods for both the Choice and List classes.

Table 8.1

Selected Members of the Choice and List Classes

Method	Purpose
add(String *value*)	Add an element to the list.
addItem(String *value*)	Add an element to the list. (Method deprecated, so should be avoided.)
getItem(int *position*)	Return the element at the specified index position.
getItemCount()	Return the number of elements in the list.
getSelectedIndex()	Return the index of the selected item (starts with 0).
getSelectedItem()	Return the string value of the selected item.
insert(String *value*, int *position*)	Insert the string value at the specified position in the list.
remove(int *position*)	Remove the element at the specified index position.
removeAll()	Clear the list.
select(int *position*)	Select (highlight) the element at the specified position.
select(String *value*)	Select (highlight) the element that matches the specified string.

This program substitutes a drop-down list for a list. Figure 8.4 shows the user interface; the program is Ch8DropDownList.

Figure 8.4

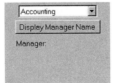

The applet screen for Ch8DropDownList. The Choice component takes less screen space than a List and allows the user to select a department name from the list.

```
//Folder:          Ch8DropDownList
//Programmer:      Bradley/Millspaugh
//Date:            6/2001
//ClassName:       ListBoxApplet
//Description:     Displays a list using the Choice class
//                 for selecting the department name.

import java.applet.*;
import java.awt.*;
import java.awt.event.*;

public class ListBoxApplet extends Applet implements ActionListener
{
    //Create components
    Choice chcDepartments = new Choice();
    Button btnDisplay = new Button("Display Manager Name ");
    Label lblManager= new Label(" ");

    public void init()
    {
        //Place components on panel
        add(chcDepartments);
        add(btnDisplay);
        add(new Label("Manager:"));
        add(lblManager);
        btnDisplay.addActionListener(this);

        //Fill List box
        chcDepartments.add("Accounting");
        chcDepartments.add("Human Resources");
        chcDepartments.add("Information Systems");
        chcDepartments.add("Marketing");
        chcDepartments.add("Sales");
    }

    public void actionPerformed(ActionEvent event)
    {
        //Find the manager for the selected department
        String strManager, strMessage;
        Manager myManager = new Manager(); //Instantiate Manager class

        //Pass the index of selected department to class method
        strManager = myManager.getManager(chcDepartments.getSelectedIndex());
        lblManager.setText(strManager);
    }
}

//Folder:          Ch8DropDownList
//Programmer:      Bradley/Millspaugh
//Date:            6/2001
//ClassName:       Manager
//Description:     Returns the name of a manager from the department number.

public class Manager
{
    public String getManager(int intDepartment)
    {
```

```java
//Find department
switch (intDepartment)
{
    case 0:    //Accounting
        return "Jones";
    case 1:    //Human Resources
        return "Lee";
    case 2:    //Information Systems
        return "Nguyen";
    case 3:    //Marketing
        return "Gonzales";
    case 4:    //Sales
        return "De Voss";
    default:
        return "Not Found";
}
}
}
```

Loops

Until now, there has been no way to repeat the same steps in a method without calling them a second time. The computer is capable of repeating a group of instructions many times for each new set of data. The process of repeating a series of instructions is called *looping*. The group of repeated instructions is called a **loop.** An **iteration** is a single execution of the statement(s) in the loop. In this section you will learn about the do and while loops. Later in this chapter you will learn about another type of loop: a for loop.

The while and do Loops

Both the do and while loops terminate based on a condition that you specify. Execution of the loop continues *while* a condition is true. Place the condition at the top of the loop for a while loop or at the bottom of the loop for a do loop. Use either of these loops when the exact number of iterations is unknown (when you do know the exact number of iterations, you usually use a for loop, which you will learn about soon).

The while Loop—General Formats

```java
while(condition)
    statement;

while(condition)
{
    statement(s);
}
```

You create a while loop very much like an if statement. You specify a condition, and only one statement is considered the body of the loop unless you use braces.

Java tests for completion at the top of the loop. Each time execution reaches the `while` statement, the condition is tested. If the condition tests true, the statement(s) inside the loop are executed again. When the condition tests false, the next statement following the loop is executed. If the condition tests false the first time it is tested, the statements inside the loop will never be executed.

```
intTotal = 0;
while (intTotal == 5)
{
    //Statements in loop
}
```

Since intTotal is zero the first time the condition is tested, the condition is false and the statements inside the loop will not execute. Control passes to the statement following the closing brace.

The while Loop—Examples

```
while(intCount > 0)
    statement;

while(intCount > 0)
{
    statement(s);
}
```

The do Loop—General Formats

```
do
    statement;
while(condition);

do
{
    statement(s);
}
while(condition);
```

The `do` loop tests for completion at the bottom of the loop, which means that statements inside the loop will *always* execute at least once. Changing the earlier example, you can see the difference:

```
intTotal = 0;
do
{
    //Statements in loop
}
while (intTotal == 5);
```

In this case, the statements inside the loop will execute at least once. Assuming the value for intTotal does not change inside the loop, the condition (intTotal == 5) tests false the first time it is tested and control passes to the first statement following the closing brace. Figure 8.5 shows flowcharts of `while` and `do` loops.

Tip

Be careful not to place a semicolon at the end of the `while` statement. This would terminate the loop.

Figure 8.5

Flowcharts of the logic for while *loops and* do *loops.*

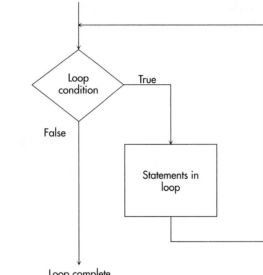

a. A while loop

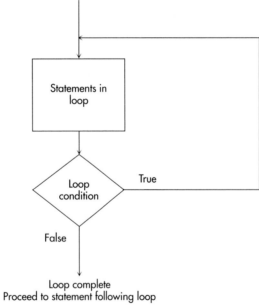

b. A do loop

The do Loop—Examples

```
do
    statement;
while (intCount > 0);
do
{
```

```
    statement(s);
}
while (intCount > 0);
```

The boolean Data Type Revisited

In Chapter 6 you learned about the boolean primitive data type, which holds only the values true or false. You will find boolean variables very useful when setting and testing conditions for a loop. You can set a boolean variable to false when a specific circumstance occurs and then write a loop condition to continue while the variable is true.

An example of using a boolean variable is when you want to search through a list for a specific value. The item may be found or not found, and you want to quit looking when a match is found.

Using a boolean variable is usually a three-step process. First you must declare a variable and set its initial value (or use the default setting of false). Then, when a particular situation occurs, set the variable to true. A loop condition can then check for true.

```
boolean blnItemFound = false;
while (!blnItemFound) //Continues as long as condition tests false
...
```

A boolean variable is always in one of two states: true or false. Many programmers refer to boolean variables as *switches* or *flags*. Switches have two states: on or off; flags are considered either up or down.

Using a Loop with a List Box

This small example combines a boolean variable with a loop. The loop searches through the list to see if the element already exists before adding it to the list. Inside the loop, each element of the list is compared to txtAdd for a match. The loop terminates if a match is found or when all elements have been tested. Follow through the logic to see what happens when there is a match, when there isn't a match, when the match occurs on the first list element, and when the match occurs on the last list element. (The following code comes from Ch8LoopSearch.)

```
public boolean findDuplicate(String strFind)
{
    //Look for a match between the text box and list elements
    boolean blnItemFound = false;
    int intItemIndex = 0;
    int intNumberItems = lstDepartments.getItemCount();
    String strListElement;

    while(!blnItemFound && intItemIndex < intNumberItems)
    {
        strListElement = lstDepartments.getItem(intItemIndex++);
        if (strFind.equalsIgnoreCase(strListElement))
            blnItemFound = true;
    }
    return blnItemFound;
}
```

Feedback 8.1

Explain the purpose of each line of the following code:

```
boolean blnItemFound = false;
int intItemIndex = 0;

while(!blnItemFound && intItemIndex == lstItems.getItemCount())
{
    if (txtNewItem.getText().equals(lstItems.getItem(intItemIndex)))
    {
        blnItemFound = true;
    }
    intItemIndex ++;
}
if (blnItemFound)
{
    lblMessage.setText("Item is in the list");
}
else
{
    lblMessage.setText("Item is not is the list");
}
```

The for Loop

When you want to repeat the statements in a loop a specific number of times, the **for loop** is ideal. The for loop has a counter variable, called the loop index, that determines the number of times the statements inside the loop will execute. The for statement includes an initialization clause, a condition, and an action statement (Table 8.2).

```
int intLoopIndex, intMaximum;
intMaximum = lstSchools.getItemCount() - 1
```

```
for(intLoopIndex = 0; intLoopIndex < intMaximum;intLoopIndex++)
```

```
{
    // The statements inside of the loop are indented
    // and referred to as the body of the loop
}
```

When the for statement is reached during program execution, several things occur. The first expression sets intLoopIndex to 0, and the condition (intLoopIndex < intMaximum) is evaluated. If the condition is true, the body of the loop executes, and then the third expression processes. In this example, intLoopIndex is presumably less than the maximum, so the statements inside the loop execute and then intLoopIndex increments. At this point the condition is tested again and the process repeats as long as the condition is true.

When the condition is evaluated and the loop index is greater than the final value, control passes to the statement immediately following the closing brace.

Table 8.2

Parts of the for *Statement*

Element	Purpose	Example
Initialization code	Set initial value of loop index variable. Can also initialize additional variables here.	`intCounter = 0`
Boolean expression	Condition to test for completion of loop.	`intCounter < 10`
Update code	Statement(s) to execute after each iteration of the loop. After the update code executes, the boolean condition is again evaluated.	`intCounter++`

The for Loop—General Form

```
for(initializationStatement; Expression; updateCode)
    statement;

for(initializationStatement; Expression; updateCode)
{
    statement(s);
}
```

A `for` loop has three elements separated by semicolons (see Figure 8.6 for a flowchart of `for` loop logic):

1. Initialization statement(s).
2. Condition.
3. Update statement(s) to execute after each time the statements inside the loop execute.

The for Loop—Examples

```
for(intCount = 0; intCount <= 10; intCount++)
{
    statement(s);
}
```

```
for(intCount = 0, fltTotal = 0.0f; intCount < 10; intCount++, fltTotal += fltBalance)
{
    statement(s);
}
```

Figure 8.6

A flowchart of the logic of a for *loop.*

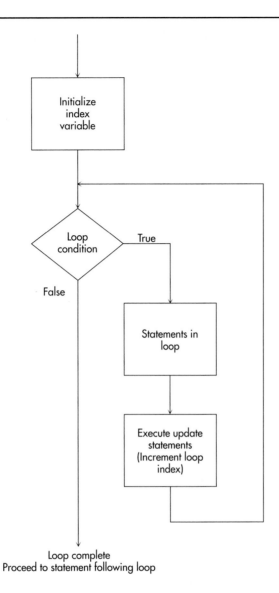

As you can see in the second of the previous examples, you can have multiple statements for initialization and/or update separated by commas. In addition, you can leave any of the three parts of the for statement blank, but you must include the semicolon as a placeholder.

Examples

```
for(; fltSum < 1000.0f;)
for(fltTotal = 0.0f; fltTotal <= fltMaximum;)
```

Using a for Loop

The following code uses the for loop to sum a series of numbers. The user enters the start and end numbers in text boxes. The for statement sets the loop counter to the value of the first text box and sets the ending value to the number in the second text box. Each number is added to a total. Notice that it is legal to declare a new integer variable for the loop index inside the for expression.

```
public void actionPerformed(ActionEvent event)
{
    //Add the numbers between the start and end
    int intStart = Integer.valueOf(txtStart.getText()).intValue();
    int intEnd = Integer.valueOf(txtEnd.getText()).intValue();
    int intTotal = 0;

    for(int intCount = intStart; intCount <= intEnd; intCount++)
        intTotal+= intCount;
    lblMessage.setText("Total: " + intTotal);
}
```

Notice that the preceding for loop also could be written like this:

```
for(int intCount = intStart; intCount < intEnd;intCount++,
    intTotal += intCount);
lblMessage.setText("Total: " " intTotal);
```

You may have missed one important difference in the two previous versions of the for statement. Can you see the difference in the conditions in the two statements? Don't read the next sentence until you look for the difference and figure out why the condition must be different.

Ready? The condition in the first for statement tests intCount <= intEnd; the second for statement left out the equal sign (intCount < intEnd). The reason? By including intTotal += intCount as part of the for statement, rather than inside the body of the loop, the operation adding intCount to intTotal occurs at the end of each iteration, before the condition is tested. When intCount is exactly equal to intEnd, intCount is added to intTotal, as it should be. If the condition allows one more test (as in intCount <= intEnd), intCount is again incremented, intCount is added to intTotal, and then the condition is tested. At that time the condition tests false and the loop terminates, but the extra number (one past intEnd) has already been added to intTotal.

Condition Satisfied before Loop Entry

At times the final value will be reached before entry into the loop. In that case the statements in the body of the loop will not be executed at all.

```
//An unexecutable loop
int intFinal = 5;
for(intIndex = 6; intIndex < intFinal; intIndex++)
{
    //The execution will never reach here
}
```

Endless Loops

Changing the value of a variable inside a loop not only is considered poor practice but also may lead to an endless loop. Your code could get into a loop that is impossible to exit. Consider the following examples; when will the loop end?

```
// Poor Programming
for(intIndex = 1; intIndex < 10; intIndex++)
{
    intIndex = 1;
}
```

or

```
for(;;)
```

Exiting Loops

In the previous examples of endless loops, you will have to break the program execution manually. You can click on your browser or applet viewer's close box or use the browser menu bar to stop the program. If you prefer, on a Windows system you can close the application through Explorer (Ctrl + Alt + Del).

Usually, loops should proceed to normal completion. However, on occasion you may need to terminate a loop before the loop index reaches its final value. You can use the break statement, which you used with the switch statement, to exit a loop early.

```
for (int intIndex = 1; intIndex < 100; intIndex++)
{
    String strInput = txtInput.getText();
    if (strInput = "")
    {
        showStatus("Enter input value");
        break;
    }
    // . . . Rest of statements in the body of the loop
}
```

Feedback 8.2

1. What, if anything, is wrong with the following for loops?
   (a) `for(intCount = 0, intCount < 10, intCount++)`
       `{ // body of loop}`
   (b) `for(intCount = 0; intCount < 10; intCount++);`
       `{ // body of loop}`
2. How many times will the body of the loop be executed for each of these examples? What will be the value of the loop index *after* normal completion of the loop?
   (a) `for(intCounter = 2; intCounter < 11, intCounter += 3)`
   (b) `for(intCounter = 10; intCounter > 1; intCounter--)`
   (c) `for(fltCounter = 3.0f; fltCounter < 6.0f; fltCounter += .5)`
   (d) `for(intCounter = 5; intCounter > 1; intCounter++)`
3. Write a for loop that will display the even numbers from 0 to 20 in txaNumbers, using a variable called intIndex.
4. What will the output be in the following?
   ```
   for(intNum = 5; intNum > 0; intNum--)
   {
       txaOutput.appendText ("" + intNum + "\n");
   }
   ```
5. What will the loop do?
   ```
   for(;;)
   {
       lblMessage.setText("Let's loop");
   }
   ```

Swing Lists

The Swing components in JFC contain a list as well as a combo box. You will find that the Swing lists (**JList** and **JComboBox**) have some significant advantages over the AWT lists (List and Choice).

Setting List Values

One really nice addition to lists in Swing is that you can directly add items to the list. This technique uses an array, something you learn more about in Chapter 9. Notice the following code creates a string variable with square brackets. This technique allows us to specify several strings with the same variable name. We then pass the variable name strVegetables as an argument when creating the list.

```
String strVegetables[] = {"Broccoli", "Cauliflower",
                          "Eggplant", "Lima Beans", "Potatoes"};
JList lstVegetables = new JList(strVegetables);
```

Another advantage of Swing lists over those in AWT is the ability to have nonstring elements. In the AWT components, you are restricted to adding only string values to the list.

Take a look at the following program that displays both a JList and a JComboBox. Figure 8.7 shows the user interface for this applet, which is Ch8SwingListApplet.

Figure 8.7

A Swing applet that uses JList and JComboBox components.

```
//Folder:       Ch8SwingListApplet
//Programmer:   Bradley/Millspaugh
//Date:         6/2001
//ClassName:    SwingListApplet
//Description:  Display a list and combo box using Swing components.

import java.applet.*;
import java.awt.*;
import javax.swing.*;
```

```
public class SwingListApplet extends JApplet
{
    //Create components
    String strVegetables[] = {"Broccoli", "Cauliflower", "Eggplant",
            "Lima Beans", "Potatoes", "Carrots", "Celery",
            "Peas", "Beans"};
    JList lstVegetables = new JList(strVegetables);
    String strFruits[] = {"Apples", "Bananas", "Cherries", "Peaches", "Pears",
            "Plums", "Apricots", "Kiwi", "Lemons", "Limes", "Oranges"};
    JComboBox cboFruit = new JComboBox(strFruits);

    public void init()

    {
        //Place components on panel
        Container AppletPanel = getContentPane();
        AppletPanel.setSize(300, 200);
        AppletPanel.setLayout(new FlowLayout());
        lstVegetables.setVisibleRowCount(2);
        AppletPanel.add(lstVegetables);
        AppletPanel.add(cboFruit);
        cboFruit.setEditable(true);
    }
}
```

Editing the Text in a Combo Box

The JComboBox looks like a drop-down list. However, you also can set the text
portion of the list to allow the user to enter a new value. To make the combo box
editable, call the setEditable method.

```
cboFruit.setEditable(true);
```

Note that by making the combo box editable, you allow the user to type an
entry in the text portion, but that does not automatically add a new entry to the
list. If you want to add the new entry to the list, you must add code to make it
happen. You can add a button for adding to the list or assign an action listener
to the combo box, which will fire an actionPerformed event when the user
presses the Enter key on the list. The following code, found in Ch8AddList,
uses both approaches: it adds a button *and* an action listener for the list. But
since it checks for duplicates, it adds a new entry only once.

```
//Folder:        Ch8SwingAddList
//Programmer:    Bradley/Millspaugh
//Date:          6/2001
//ClassName:     SwingListApplet
//Description:   Display a list and combo box using Swing components.

import java.applet.*;
import java.awt.*;
import javax.swing.*;
import java.awt.event.*;
```

```java
public class SwingListApplet extends JApplet implements ActionListener
{
    //Create components
    JPanel pnlPane = new JPanel();
    String strFruits[] = {"Apples", "Bananas", "Cherries", "Peaches", "Pears",
                          "Plums", "Apricots", "Kiwi", "Lemons", "Limes", "Oranges"};
    JComboBox cboFruit = new JComboBox(strFruits);
    JButton btnAdd = new JButton("Add Fruit to List");

    public void init()
    {
        //Place components on panel
        setContentPane(pnlPane);
        pnlPane.add(cboFruit);
        cboFruit.setEditable(true);
        pnlPane.add(btnAdd);
        cboFruit.addActionListener(this); //Causes event when Enter pressed on list
        btnAdd.addActionListener(this);   //Causes event when button clicked
    }

    public void actionPerformed(ActionEvent event)
    {
        //Add new fruit to the list
        //Make sure it's not a duplicate
        if (event.getSource() == btnAdd)
        {
            String strNewFruit = String.valueOf(cboFruit.getSelectedItem());
            boolean blnDuplicate = findDuplicate(strNewFruit);
            if (blnDuplicate)
                showStatus("Duplicate fruit not added to list");
            else
            {
                cboFruit.addItem(strNewFruit);
                showStatus(strNewFruit + " added to the list");
            }
        }
    }

    public boolean findDuplicate(String strNewItem)
    {
        //Look for a match between the new item and the list elements
        boolean blnItemFound = false;
        int intItemIndex = 0;
        int intNumberItems = cboFruit.getItemCount();
        String strListElement;

        while (!blnItemFound && intItemIndex < intNumberItems)
        {
            strListElement = String.valueOf(cboFruit.getItemAt(intItemIndex));
            if (strNewItem.equals(strListElement))
                blnItemFound = true;
            intItemIndex++;
        }
        return blnItemFound;
    }
}
```

Scrolling Lists

The AWT components List and Choice automatically add a scroll bar when the number of list elements exceeds the number of visible rows. In Swing, a JComboBox automatically adds a scroll bar, but for a JList, you must do some extra programming to add a scroll bar. (Figure 8.8 shows a Swing user interface with scrolling list and combo box.)

Figure 8.8

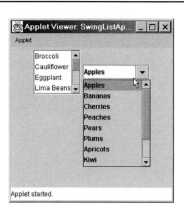

Add scroll bars and set the number of visible lines for a JList component. The JComboBox component automatically adds scroll bars when needed.

```
//Set up lstVegetables for scrolling
lstVegetables.setVisibleRowCount(4);
JScrollPane scrollList = new JScrollPane();
scrollList.setViewportView(lstVegetables);
pnlUI.add(scrollList); //Add lstVegetables in a viewport
```

Notice that you add the list to the scroll bar pane using the `setViewportView` method. You then add the scroll bar pane (JScrollPane) to the Content Pane, rather than directly adding the list component. You set the number of visible rows using the `setVisibleRowCount` method of the list component.

Feedback 8.3

1. Write the statements to create a combo box called cboEmployees that contains Employee names (Mary Jones, Kim Le, Jerry Altman, and Yvonne Gonzales).
2. Code the statement to create an editable field for the combo box.

Your Hands-on Programming Example

Create an applet that contains a list of departments. Allow the user to update the list by adding or removing elements. Also give the option of displaying the number of departments in the list. Display error messages if the user tries to add an empty element or attempts to delete an element before selecting the item to delete.

Planning the Project

Plan the User Interface

Figure 8.9 shows a possible layout for the user interface.

Figure 8.9

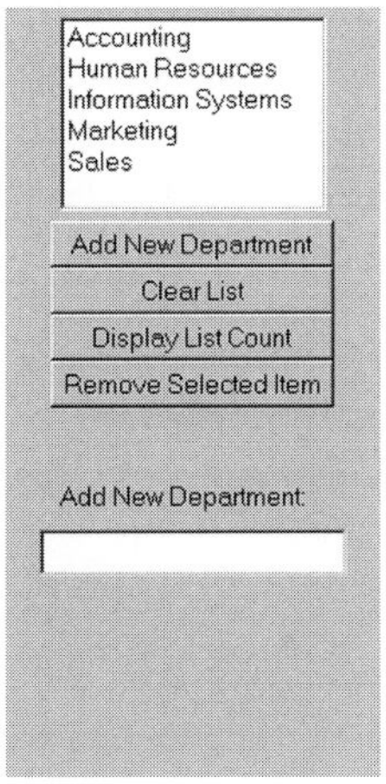

A possible user interface for the chapter hands-on example.

Plan the Objects and Properties

Figure 8.10 shows the class diagram.

Figure 8.10

The class diagram for the hands-on example.

Class: ListBoxApplet	
Methods	**Variables and Components**
init	lstDepartments
addComponents	btnAdd
fillList	btnClear
actionPerformed	btnCount
clearList	btnRemove
addItem	lblCount
removeItem	txtAdd
displayCount	lblMessage
findDuplicate(String strFind)	pnlButtons

Class Name: Ch8LoopSearch

Properties:

Access Mode (public or private)	Variable or Component Name	Data Type or Class	Description
	lstDepartments	List	List of department names.
	btnAdd	Button	Add element to list.
	btnClear	Button	Clear the list.
	btnCount	Button	Display number of elements in the list.
			continued

Access Mode (public or private)	Variable or Component Name	Data Type or Class	Description
	btnRemove	Button	Remove selected item from the list.
	lblCount	Label	Display number of elements in the list.
	txtAdd	TextField	Data entry field for the name of department to be added to list.
	lblMessage	Label	Display error messages.

Methods:

Access Mode (public or private)	Return Type	Method Name (include any parameters)	Pseudocode
public	void	`init`	Call `addComponents` method. Call `fillList` method.
public	void	`addComponents`	Add components. Set lblMessage foreground to red. Add listeners.
public	void	`fillList`	Add department names to lstDepartments.
public	void	`actionPerformed`	Clear any previous message and count. Test source of event and execute correct method based on button clicked.
public	void	`clearList`	Clear the list.
public	void	`addItem`	Call `findDuplicate` to see if element exists. If element does not exist, add to list.
public	void	`removeItem`	If no item selected, display message. Remove selected element from the list.
public	void	`displayCount`	Display the current number of elements in the list.
public	boolean	`findDuplicate (String strFind)`	Search the list for a match with the txtAdd text field. Return true for match, false for no match.

Write the Project

- Follow the plan to add components to the class.

- Code the methods to perform the planned actions.

- When you complete the code, thoroughly test the project.

The Project Solution

```
//Folder:         Ch8LoopSearch
//Programmer:     Bradley/Millspaugh
//Date:           6/2001
//ClassName:      ListBoxApplet
//Description:    Displays and updates a list box for department names.
//                Does not allow duplicate names.

import java.applet.*;
import java.awt.*;
import java.awt.event.*;

public class ListBoxApplet extends Applet implements ActionListener
{
    //Create components
    List lstDepartments = new List(6);
    Button btnAdd = new Button("Add New Department");
    Button btnClear = new Button("Clear List");
    Button btnCount = new Button("Display List Count");
    Button btnRemove = new Button("Remove Selected Item");
    Label lblCount = new Label(" ");
    TextField txtAdd = new TextField(20);
    Label lblMessage = new Label("                          " );

    public void init()
    {
        //Initialize the screen
        addComponents();
        fillList();
    }

    public void actionPerformed(ActionEvent event)
    {
        //Determine object that caused the event
        Object objSource = event.getSource();

        lblMessage.setText("");    //Clear any previous message
        lblCount.setText("");

        if(objSource == btnAdd)
            addItem();
        if(objSource == btnClear)
            clearList();
        if(objSource == btnCount)
            displayCount();
        if(objSource == btnRemove)
            removeItem();
    }

    public void addComponents()
    {
        //Place components on panel
        add(lstDepartments);
        Panel pnlButtons = new Panel(new GridLayout(4, 0));
        pnlButtons.add(btnAdd);
        pnlButtons.add(btnClear);
        pnlButtons.add(btnCount);
        pnlButtons.add(btnRemove);
```

```java
        add(pnlButtons);
        add(lblCount);
        add(new Label("Add New Department:"));
        add(txtAdd);
        add(lblMessage);
        lblMessage.setForeground(Color.red);
        btnAdd.addActionListener(this);
        btnRemove.addActionListener(this);
        btnClear.addActionListener(this);
        btnCount.addActionListener(this);
    }

public void fillList()
{
    //Fill List box
    lstDepartments.add("Accounting");
    lstDepartments.add("Human Resources");
    lstDepartments.add("Information Systems");
    lstDepartments.add("Marketing");
    lstDepartments.add("Sales");
}

public void addItem()
{
    //Add string in text field to list box
    String strAdd = new String(txtAdd.getText());

    if(strAdd.compareTo("") == 0)
    {
        lblMessage.setText("Enter department to add");
        txtAdd.requestFocus();
    }
    else
    {
        //See if item is already on the list
        boolean blnFound = findDuplicate(strAdd);
        if(blnFound)
        {
            //Item is already in the list
            lblMessage.setText("Duplicate Department");
        }
        else
        {
            //Item does not already exist, so add to the list
            lstDepartments.add(strAdd);
            txtAdd.setText("");
        }
    }
}

public boolean findDuplicate(String strFind)
{
    //Look for a match between the text box and list elements
    boolean blnItemFound = false;
    int intItemIndex = 0;
    int intNumberItems = lstDepartments.getItemCount();
    String strListElement;
```

```
    while(!blnItemFound && intItemIndex < intNumberItems)
    {
        strListElement = lstDepartments.getItem(intItemIndex++);
        if (strFind.equalsIgnoreCase(strListElement))
            blnItemFound = true;
    }
    return blnItemFound;
}

public void clearList()
{
    //Clear the list box
    lstDepartments.removeAll();
}

public void displayCount()
{
    //Display the number of items in the list
    String strCount;

    strCount = new String("Count: " + lstDepartments.getItemCount());
    lblCount.setText(strCount);
}

public void removeItem()
{
    //Remove selected item
    int intIndex = lstDepartments.getSelectedIndex();
    if(intIndex == -1)
    {
        lblMessage.setText("Select item to remove");
    }
    else
    {
        lstDepartments.remove(intIndex);
    }
}
}
```

Summary

1. The AWT List and Choice classes create objects that contain a list of elements.
2. The elements in a list are referred to by an index, which begins with zero.
3. A list that has more elements than are visible will automatically have a scroll bar. You can set the number of visible rows for the list.
4. A list can be updated at run time with the add, remove, and removeAll methods.
5. The getSelectedIndex method returns the index number of the selected item or −1 if nothing is selected.
6. The getItemCount method returns the number of elements in a list.

7. To return the text of the selected list item, use the `getSelectedItem` method. If you want to return an item by index number, use the `getItem` method.

8. The Choice class can be used to create objects that resemble drop-down lists, also called *popup menus*.

9. Use the `getSelectedIndex` method and a `switch` statement to branch execution when using the Choice as a menu.

10. A loop allows a statement or series of statements to be repeated. Java supports the `do` loop, `while` loop, and `for` loop constructs. Use a `do` or `while` loop when the number of iterations is unknown; use a `for` loop for a specific number of iterations.

11. A `while` loop tests the condition at the top of the loop; a `do` loop tests the condition at the bottom of the loop.

12. A `for` statement has three parts: initialization, condition, and update code.

13. Java Foundation Classes support the JList and the JComboBox Swing components. The JComboBox can be set to contain an editable field.

14. Swing components contain a constructor that allows the values for the list to be added with the constructor using an array.

15. A JList component does not automatically display a scroll bar and must be programmed to scroll.

Key Terms

`add` method *233*	iteration *240*
Choice class *236*	JComboBox *249*
`for` loop *244*	JList *249*
`getItem` method *235*	List class *232*
`getItemCount` method *235*	loop *240*
`getSelectedIndex` method *234*	`remove` method *235*
`getSelectedItem` method *235*	`removeAll` method *234*

Review Questions

1. Describe the constructors available for the List class.
2. List and explain the methods used to update a List object.
3. What methods are used to find
   (a) The number of items in a list?
   (b) The index of the selected item?
   (c) The text of the selected item?
   (d) The text for the item at index 5?
4. How can you tell whether or not the user has selected an item from a list?
5. Can elements be added to a Choice object at run time? If yes, how?
6. Differentiate between a `do` loop and a `while` loop in terms of the position of the condition and the effect in the program.
7. Why is it important to include braces when coding a loop?
8. Name the three parts of a `for` loop expression.
9. Give an example that could result in a continuous loop.

10. Specify at least two differences between the AWT list components and the Swing list components.

11. What is the advantage of using a constructor that contains an array for a list component?

Programming Exercises

8.1 Modify exercise 7.1 to create an applet for purchasing widgets. Data entry includes the buyer's name, address, and credit card number. This information will be entered only once, even though the user may purchase multiple widgets.

- Use a list to allow the user to select the color of the widget: blue, red, or yellow.
- Use a text field to allow the buyer to enter the quantity desired.
- A check box allows the users to select having the widget engraved.
- Include an "Add to Shopping Cart" button that displays a line in a text area for the current widget information and then clears the list selection, check box, and quantity fields.
- A "Purchase" button totals all of the costs and displays the entire purchase.
- The Purchase button is disabled until the user adds the first item to the shopping cart.

Rates:

Blue	10.00
Red	14.00
Yellow	12.00
Engraving:	4.00 per widget.

8.2 Modify exercise 7.3 to include two lists.

Kenna's Kandles offers candles in various shapes, scents, and colors. Create an applet that includes a text field for quantity, a list for the candle type—TeaLight, Votive, or Pillar; a check box for scented; and a list for colors: federal blue, sunflower yellow, Christmas red, and lily white.

Allow the user to enter his or her name and credit card number. You need two buttons: Add to Shopping Cart and Sale Complete.

Calculate the price for a candle based on the selected style from the list, deselect the list item, and clear the options and quantities when the Add button is clicked. The Sale Completed button should add a sales tax of 8 percent and a shipping fee of 3 percent.

Prices	Base Price	Scented
TeaLight	5.75	0.75
Votive	7.50	1.25
Pillar	12.25	1.75

You will need a text area to display an invoice with a list of items, their prices, the subtotal, tax, shipping, and total.

8.3 Modify any of your previous projects replacing the command buttons with a drop-down list of options (a Choice component).

8.4 Maintain a list of bagel types for Bradley's Bagels. Use a list box to hold the bagel types and a text field for entering new types. Use buttons or menu choices to *Add Bagel Type, Remove Bagel Type, Clear Bagel List, and Display Bagel Type Count.*

Do not allow a blank type or a duplicate type to be added to the list. Display an error message if the user selects Remove without first selecting a bagel type.

Here are some suggested bagel types. You can make up your own list.

Plain	Poppy seed
Egg	Sesame seed
Rye	Banana nut
Salt	Blueberry

CASE STUDIES

R 'n R—for Reading and Refreshment

Modify the program for Chapter 7 by removing the text field for the book title and replacing it with a list of books. Place at least 10 books on your list. Also, replace the command buttons with a Choice component and modify the action listeners to respond to the choices as a menu selection.

Merry Pea's Quilting

Modify the program for Chapter 7 by removing the text fields for the class name, class number, and price and substituting a list. Each element of the list should hold a class number and class name. Use an `if` or `switch` statement to determine the price based on the position in the list. Continue to place the name of the quilting class on the course list along with the price and to add the appropriate price to the total.

Classes		
TAW	Trip around the World	35
SRF	Split Rail Fence	25
LNS	Lone Star	35
SMP	Sampler (4 sessions)	80

9

Arrays

At the completion of this chapter, you will be able to . . .

1. Establish an array of variables and refer to individual elements in the array with variable subscripts.

2. Use a `for` loop to step through an array.

3. Use a loop to look up a matching value in an array.

4. Accumulate totals using array elements.

5. Distinguish between direct access and indirect access of a table.

6. Combine the advantages of list objects with arrays.

7. Store data in multidimensional arrays.

8. Create and use an array of objects.

Arrays

An **array** is a series (or list) of values that all have the same data type and all have the same name. You can think of an array as a list without the box, or visual representation. Any time you need to keep a series of items for later processing, such as reordering, calculating, or printing, you need to set up an array. An array can be a list of variables or a list of objects. This section covers arrays of variables; later in this chapter you will learn to create an array of objects.

Consider an example of an applet for entering product information, one product at a time. After the user finishes entering many products, you need to calculate some statistics and perhaps use the information in different ways. Of course, each time the user enters the data for the next product, the previous contents of the text fields are replaced. You could assign the previous values to variables, but they also would be replaced for each new product. Another approach might be to create multiple variables, such as strProduct1, strProduct2, strProduct3, and so on. This approach might be reasonable for a few entries, but what happens when you need to store 50 or 500 products?

When you need to store multiple values, use an array. An array is a series of individual variables, all referenced by the same name. Sometimes arrays are called *lists*, **tables**, or **subscripted variables**. You refer to each individual element within the array using a subscript, which represents the position within the array. In an array for storing names, you may have strName[0], strName[1], strName[2], and so on. Notice that the first element has a subscript of zero. The subscripts are enclosed in square brackets.

Each individual variable is called an **element** of the array. The individual elements are treated the same as any other variable and may be used in any statement, such as an assignment or a setText. The **subscript** (which also may be called an *index*) inside the brackets is the position of the element within the array. Figure 9.1 illustrates an array of 10 elements with subscripts from 0 to 9.

Figure 9.1

strName[] array

[0]	Janet Baker
[1]	George Lee
[2]	Sue Li
[3]	Samuel Hoosier
[4]	Sandra Weeks
[5]	William Macy
[6]	Andy Harrison
[7]	Ken Ford
[8]	Denny Franks
[9]	Shawn James

An array of string variables with 10 elements. Subscripts are 0 through 9.

Note: Some other programming languages allow subscripts beginning with 1 instead of 0; Java does not. If you are used to using subscripts beginning with 1, you need to take extra care to be aware of the 0 element as you program.

Also note: Most other programming languages use parentheses to hold subscripts, rather than square brackets. The Java developers chose brackets to more clearly differentiate an array reference from a method reference.

Subscripts

The real advantage of using an array comes when you use variables for subscripts in place of the constants.

```
strName[intIndex] = "";
lblName.setText(strName[intIndex]);
```

Subscripts may be constants, variables, or numeric expressions. Although subscripts must be integers, Java will round any noninteger subscript.

A question has probably occurred to you by now: how many elements are there in the strName array? The answer is that you must either specify the number of elements in a declaration statement or initialize the array when you declare it.

Declaring an Array

You can choose one of several techniques for declaring an array. One way is to first declare an array variable and later instantiate the array using the new keyword (similar to instantiating an object).

```
float fltPayment[];
```

or

```
float[] fltPayment;
```

The square brackets declare that the variable (fltPayment) is an array variable. Notice that you can place the brackets on either the variable name or the data type.

Declaring the array variable does not actually create the array. You must use the new keyword to declare the number of elements in the array and actually allocate the storage for the array.

You also can use a shortcut and combine the two statements, declaring the array variable and instantiating it at the same time:

```
fltPayment = new float[50];
```

You also can use a shortcut and combine the two statements, declaring the array variable and instantiating it at the same time:

```
float[] fltPayment = new float [50];
```

Using the new Keyword to Create an Array—General Format

```
DataType VariableName[] = new DataType [size];
DataType[] VariableName = new DataType[size];
```

Using the new Keyword to Create an Array—Examples

```
int intEmployeeCount[] = new int[50];
float[] fltTotal = new float[10];
String strName[] = new String[25];
```

The declaration statement allocates storage for the specified number of elements and initializes each element to the default value for the data type. For example, all numeric variables are initialized to 0 and all String variables are initialized to an empty string.

When you declare an array of 10 elements, the valid subscripts are 0 through 9. Some programmers prefer to ignore the 0 element and use only the elements beginning with 1. For example, if you need to refer to elements 1 through 100, you could declare an array of 101 elements, leave the 0 element unused, and use subscripts of 1 through 100. The alternative is to declare an array of 100 elements and use subscripts 0 through 99, which can be confusing in some situations.

Initializing an Array at Declaration

For primitive data types and Strings, you can give initial values to array elements as you declare an array. This shortcut technique does not allow you to specify the size of the array and you do not use the new keyword.

Using an Initializer to Create an Array—Examples

```
int intDepartmentNumber[] = {423, 633, 672, 981};
String strDepartmentNames[] =    {"Accounting", "Information Systems", "Marketing",
                                   "Sales"};
```

More on Subscripts

A subscript must reference a valid element of the array. If a list contains 10 names, it wouldn't make sense to ask: What is the 15th name on the list? *or* What is the 2½th name on the list? Java rounds fractional subscripts and throws an exception for invalid subscripts.

Feedback 9.1

```
String strName[] = new String[20];
final int intValue = 10;
```

After execution of the preceding statements, which of the following are valid subscripts?

1. strName[20]
2. strName[intValue]
3. strName[intValue * 2]

```
4.   strName[intValue * 3]
5.   strName[0]
6.   strName[intValue — 20]
7.   strName[intValue / 3]
8.   strName[intValue / 5 — 2]
```

Iterating through an Array

You can use a `for` loop to iterate through all of the elements in an array. The following loop initializes a loop index to 0 to access the first element in the fltSales array. As intIndex is incremented, each element is added to the total.

```
for(int intIndex = 0; intIndex < 10; intIndex++)
{
    fltTotal += fltSales[intIndex];
}
```

Another example using a loop illustrates displaying all of the elements in the array in a text area. The `append` statement displays the index for the group followed by a total and the new-line character.

```
public void Report()
{
    //Iterate through intTotal array and display in text area

    txaReport.setText("Summary\n\n");
    txaReport.append("Group # \t\tSales\n");
    for(int intIndex = 0; intIndex < 8; intIndex++)
    {
        txaReport.append(intIndex + "\t\t" + intTotal[intIndex] + "\n");
    }
}
```

Using Array Elements for Accumulators

Array elements are regular variables and perform in the same ways as all variables used so far. You may use the subscripted variables in any way you choose such as for counters or total accumulators.

To demonstrate the use of array elements as total accumulators, eight totals will be accumulated. For this example, eight scout troops, numbered 1 through 8, are selling raffle tickets. A separate total must be accumulated for each of the eight groups. Each time a sale is made, the number of tickets must be added to the correct total. The statement

```
int intTotal[] = new int[8];
```

creates the eight accumulators.

Adding to the Correct Total

Assume that your user inputs a group number into txtGroup and the number of tickets sold into txtSale. The sales may be input in any order, with multiple sales for each group. Your problem is to add each ticket count to the correct total (0 to 7).

Since the group numbers are 1 through 8 and the subscripts must be 0 through 7, you will subtract one from the group number to use as the subscript. Using the subscript, you can add to the correct total. If the first sale of 10 tickets is for group 4, the 10 must be added to intTotal[3]. (Figure 9.2 shows the applet and the variables used for this example.)

F i g u r e   9 . 2

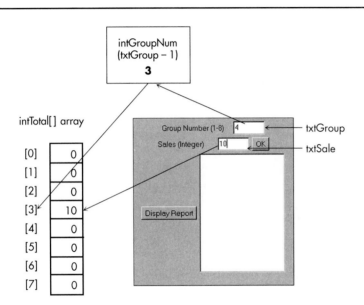

The group number is entered in the txtGroup text field. Subtract one from its value to use as a subscript to add to the correct intTotal array element.

```
//Get the user input
int intGroupNum = Integer.valueOf(txtGroup.getText()).intValue();
int intSale = Integer.valueOf(txtSale.getText()).intValue();

//Add to the appropriate total
intGroupNum--;        //Subtract 1 from group number to use for subscript
intTotal[intGroupNum] += intSale;
```

Catching User Input Errors

Of course, there is always the danger that the user will enter an incorrect group number and foul up your program.

Since Java throws an exception if you use an out-of-range subscript, the group number must be validated. You can either check the range using an `if` statement or catch the exception.

```
if(intGroupNum >=0 && intGroupNum <=7)
{
    //Valid group; add to total
    intTotal[intGroupNum] += intSale;
}
```

```
else
{
    lblMessage.setText("Invalid group number");
}
```

If you choose to catch an exception rather than test with an if statement, check for an ArrayIndexOutOfBoundsException.

```
try
{
    //Add to appropriate total
    int intGroupNum = Integer.valueOf(txtGroup.getText()).intValue();
    int intSale = Integer.valueOf(txtSale.getText()).intValue();
    intGroupNum--;   //Subtract 1 from group number to use for subscript

    //Add to correct total
    intTotal[intGroupNum] += intSale;
}

catch(ArrayIndexOutOfBoundsException exc)
{
    //Invalid group number
    lblMessage.setText("Invalid group number ");
    showStatus("Group numbers must be 1 - 8");
}
```

Using the group number as an index to the array is a technique called *direct reference*. The groups are assigned numbers from 0 through 7 (or 1 through 8), which you can use as the subscripts of the array.

Table Lookup

Things don't always work out so neatly as having sequential group numbers that can be used to access the table directly. Sometimes you will have to do a little work to find (look up) the correct value. Reconsider the eight scout troops and their ticket sales. Now the groups are not numbered 1 through 8, but 101, 103, 110, 115, 121, 123, 130, and 145. The group number and the number of tickets sold are still input and the number of tickets must be added to the correct total. But now you must do one more step: determine to which array element to add the ticket sales.

The first step in the project is to declare the arrays. You will need a second array to hold the group numbers. The elements in the group number array correspond to the elements in the intTotal array (Figure 9.3).

```
//Create the lookup table array
int intGroupNumArray[] = {101, 103, 110, 115, 121, 123, 130, 145};
```

During program execution, the user still enters the group number and the number of tickets sold into text boxes.

Figure 9.3

intGroupNumArray[ ]

[0]	101
[1]	103
[2]	110
[3]	115
[4]	121
[5]	123
[6]	130
[7]	145

intTotal[ ] array

[0]	0
[1]	0
[2]	0
[3]	0
[4]	0
[5]	0
[6]	0
[7]	0

Each element in the intGroupNumArray corresponds to one element of the intTotal array. Look up the group number in the first array and add the sale to the corresponding element in the second array.

The technique used to find the subscript is called a ***table lookup***. In this example, the object is to find the element number (0 through 7) of the group number and use that element number as a subscript to the total table. If the user enters the third group number (110), the sale is added to the third total. If the seventh group number (130) is entered, the sale is added to the seventh total, and so on. Hence, you need a way, given the group number in txtGroup, to find the corresponding subscript of the intGroup array.

When Java executes the statement

```
intTotal[intGroupNum] += intSale;
```

the value of intGroupNum must be a number in the range 0 through 7. The task for the lookup operation is to find the number to place in intGroupNum, based on the value of txtGroup. Figure 9.4 shows the variables used for the lookup. Figure 9.5 shows the flowchart of the lookup logic.

Figure 9.4

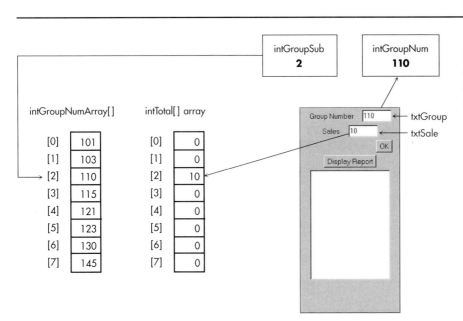

A lookup operation: The group number is looked up in intGroupNumArray; the correct subscript is found and used to add the sale to the correct intTotal.

Figure 9.5

A flowchart of the logic of a lookup operation.

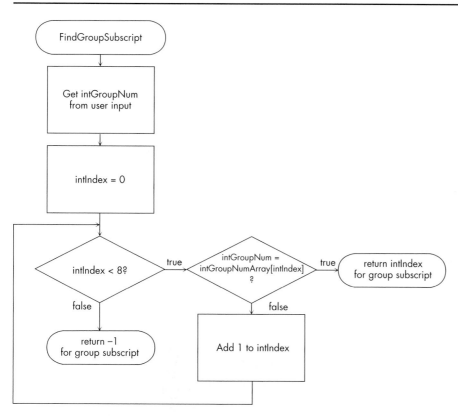

Coding a Table Lookup

For a table lookup, you will find that a `while` loop works better than a `for` loop. As you compare to each element in the array and eventually find a match, you need to know the subscript of the matching element and quit when a match is found.

```
public int FindGroupSubscript()
{
    //Look up group number
    int intGroupNum = Integer.valueOf(txtGroup.getText()).intValue();
    int intIndex = 0;

    while(intIndex < 8)
    {
        if(intGroupNum == intGroupNumArray[intIndex])
            return intIndex;                //Match found
        intIndex++;
    }
    return -1; //No match was found
}
```

This method returns the subscript of the matching element or –1, to indicate that no match was found. If the user enters an invalid group number, you should display a message.

```
int intGroupSub = FindGroupSubscript();
int intSale = Integer.valueOf(txtSale.getText()).intValue();
if(intGroupSub != -1)
{
    //Valid group; add to total
    intTotal[intGroupSub] += intSale;
}
else
{
    //Invalid group number
    lblMessage.setText("Invalid group number   ");
}
```

The table-lookup technique will work for any table, numeric or string. It isn't necessary to arrange the fields being searched in any particular sequence. The comparison is made to one item in the list, then the next, and the next—until a match is found. In fact, for a very large table, you can save processing time by arranging the table with the most-often-used entries at the top so that fewer comparisons must be made.

Using Lists with Arrays

In the previous example of a lookup, the user had to type some information into a text field, which was used to look up the information in an array. A more efficient and friendly solution might be to substitute a List or Choice component for the text field. You can store the eight group numbers in a list and allow the user to select from the list (Figure 9.6).

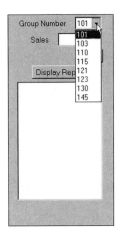

Figure 9.6

Allow the user to select the group number from a Choice list.

The initial list can contain the values 101, 103, 110, 115, 121, 123, 130, and 145.

```
Choice chcGroup = new Choice();

public void fillList()
{
    //Add group numbers to the list
    chcGroup.add("101");
    chcGroup.add("103");
    chcGroup.add("110");
    chcGroup.add("115");
    chcGroup.add("121");
    chcGroup.add("123");
    chcGroup.add("130");
    chcGroup.add("145");
}
```

You probably have already realized that you can use the `getSelectedIndex` method to determine the array subscript. Remember that the `getSelectedIndex` method holds the position or index of the selected item from the list. You can use this index as a subscript to add to the correct group total.

In place of the lookup operation, we can use this code:

```
//Add to appropriate total
int intGroupSub = chcGroup.getSelectedIndex();
int intSale = Integer.valueOf(txtSale.getText()).intValue();
if(intGroupSub >=0 && intGroupSub <=7)
{
    //Valid group; add to total
    intTotal[intGroupSub] += intSale;
}
```

To print the group numbers on the report, you use the `getItem` method.

```
public void Report()
{
    //Iterate through intTotal array and display in text area

    txaReport.setText("\tSummary\n\n");
    txaReport.append("Group # \t\tSales\n");
    for(int intIndex = 0; intIndex < 8; intIndex++)
    {
        txaReport.append(chcGroup.getItem(intIndex) + "\t\t" +
            intTotal[intIndex] + "\n");
    }
}
```

Multidimensional Arrays

You may need to use two or more subscripts to identify tabular data, where data are arranged in rows and columns.

Many applications of **two-dimensional tables** quickly come to mind: insurance rate tables, tax tables, addition and multiplication tables, postage rates, foods and their nutritive value, population by region, rainfall by state.

To define a two-dimensional array or table, the declaration statement specifies the number of rows and columns in the array. The row is horizontal and the column is vertical. The following table has three rows and four columns:

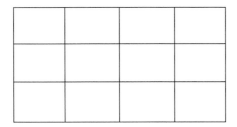

The Declaration Statement for Two-Dimensional Arrays—General Format

```
DataType ArrayName[][];
```

The Declaration Statement for Two-Dimensional Arrays—Examples

```
String strName[][] = new String[3][4];
float fltRate[][] = {{1.0f, 1.5f, 1.65f, 1.85f},
                     {1.58f, 2.0f, 2.4f, 3.05f},
                     {1.71f, 2.52f, 3.10f, 4.0f},
                     {2.04f, 3.12f, 4.0f, 5.01f},
                     {2.52f, 3.75f, 5.10f, 7.25f}};
```

The first table (strName) has three rows and four columns. The second table (fltRate) uses an initializer to set values, one row at a time.

You must always use two subscripts when referring to individual elements of the table. Specify the row with the first subscript and the column with the second subscript.

(0,0)	(0,1)	(0,2)	(0,3)
(1,0)	(1,1)	(1,2)	(1,3)
(2,0)	(2,1)	(2,2)	(2,3)

The elements of the array may be used in the same ways as any other variable: in accumulators, counts, and reference fields for lookup; in statements like assignment and displaying text; and as conditions. Some valid references to the tables include

```
strName[1][2] = "Value";
strName[intRowIndex][intColIndex] = "Value";
lblDisplay.setText(strName[1][2]);
lblDisplay.setText(strName[intRowIndex][intColIndex]);
```

Invalid references for the strName table would include any value greater than 2 for the first subscript or greater than 3 for the second subscript.

Initializing Two-Dimensional Arrays

You can initialize multidimensional arrays as you create them. The values are placed inside braces; the values for each row are inside another set of braces, with a comma separating the rows. *Note:* You do not need to fill all values; use the brace to show the end of the values for a row.

```
int intValue[][] = {{1, 1},
                    {2, 2},
                    {3, 3}};
```

If you do not initialize the array, numeric array elements are initially set to 0 and string elements are set to empty strings. Some situations may require you to initialize all elements to some other value. You can use nested `for` loops to set each array element to a value.

Nested for Loop Example

The assignment statement in the inner loop will be executed 12 times, once for each element of strName.

```
for(int intRow = 0; intRow < 3; intRow++)
    for (int intColumn = 0; intColumn < 4, intColumn++)
        strName[intRow][intColumn] = ""; //Initialize each element
```

Summing a Two-Dimensional Table

You can find the sum of a table in various ways. You may sum either the columns or the rows of the table; or, as in a cross-foot, you may sum the figures in both directions and double-check the totals.

To sum the array in both directions, each column needs one total field and each row needs one total field. Two one-dimensional arrays will work well for the totals. Figure 9.7 illustrates the variables used in this example.

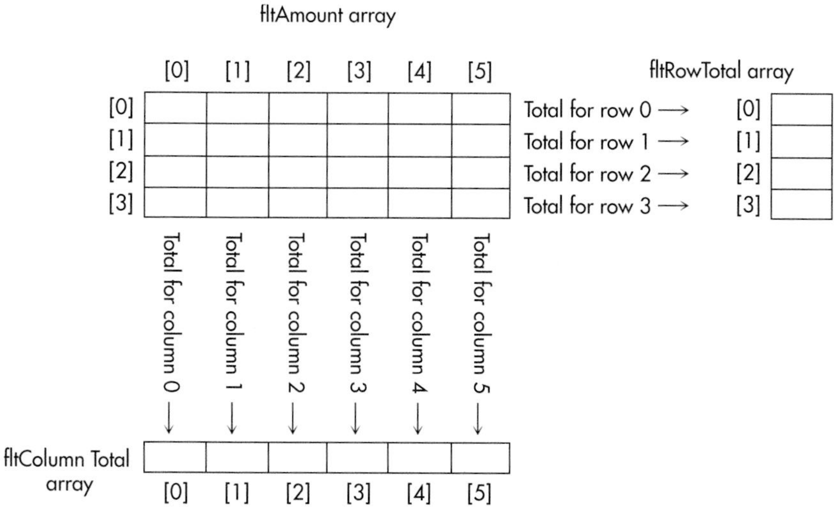

Figure 9.7

Two one-dimensional arrays hold totals for the two-dimensional array.

```
for(int intRowIndex = 0; intRowIndex < 4; intRowIndex++)
   for(int intColumnIndex = 0; intColumnIndex < 6; intColumnIndex++)
   {
       fltRowTotal[intRowIndex] += fltAmount[intRowIndex][intColIndex];
       fltColumnTotal[intColumnIndex] += fltAmount[intRowIndex][intColIndex];
   }
```

Feedback 9.2

Write statements to do the following:

1. Declare a table called intTemperature with five columns and three rows.
2. Set each element in the first row to 0.
3. Set each element in the second row to 75.
4. For each column of the table, add together the elements in rows 1 and 2, placing the sum in row 3.

Lookup Operation for Two-Dimensional Tables

When you look up items in a two-dimensional table, you can use the same techniques discussed with single-dimensional arrays: direct reference and table lookup. The limitations are the same.

● To use a direct reference, row and column subscripts must be readily available. For example, you can tally the hours used for each of five machines (identified by machine numbers 1 through 5) and each of four departments (identified by department numbers 1 through 4).

```
int intRowIndex = Integer.valueOf(txtMachine.getText()).intValue;
int intColumnIndex = Integer.valueOf(txtDepartment.getText()).intValue;
float fltHours = Float.valueOf(txtHours.getText()).floatValue;
fltMachineTotal[intRowIndex] [intColumnIndex] += fltHours;
```

● A table lookup is the most common lookup technique.

Many two-dimensional tables used for lookup require additional one-dimensional arrays or lists to aid in the lookup process. For an example, use a shipping rate table (Figure 9.8) to look up the rate to ship a package. The shipping rate depends on the weight of the package and the zone to which it is being shipped. You could design the project with the weight and zones in a list or drop-down list (Choice), or you could use a text box and let the user input the data.

Using List Components

In this example, one list holds the weight limits and another list holds the zones. The values for the two lists are filled at design time. Figure 9.8 shows the applet for this example.

Figure 9.8

This shipping rate table in a two-dimensional array can be used to look up the correct shipping charges.

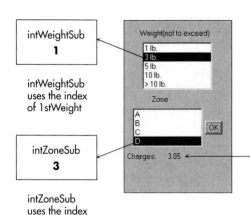

Shipping Rate Table
fltRate array

Weight (not to exceed)	Zone A	Zone B	Zone C	Zone D
1 lb.	1.00	1.50	1.65	1.85
3 lb.	1.58	2.00	2.40	3.05
5 lb.	1.71	2.52	3.10	4.00
10 lb.	2.04	3.12	4.00	5.01
>10 lb.	2.52	3.75	5.10	7.25

```
List lstZone = new List(4);
List lstWeight = new List(5);

public void fillLists()
{
    //Fill Zone and Weight lists
    lstZone.add("A");
    lstZone.add("B");
    lstZone.add("C");
    lstZone.add("D");
    lstWeight.add("1 lb.");
    lstWeight.add("3 lb.");
    lstWeight.add("5 lb.");
    lstWeight.add("10 lb.");
    lstWeight.add("> 10 lb.");
}
```

The five-by-four rate table is two dimensional, and the values are pre-loaded through initialization.

```
//Array for lookup
float fltRate[][] = {{1.0f, 1.5f, 1.65f, 1.85f},
                     {1.58f, 2.0f, 2.4f, 3.05f},
                     {1.71f, 2.52f, 3.10f, 4.0f},
                     {2.04f, 3.12f, 4.0f, 5.01f},
                     {2.52f, 3.75f, 5.10f, 7.25f}};

    public void actionPerformed(ActionEvent event)
    {
        // Display Charges
        int intWeightSub = lstWeight.getSelectedIndex();
        int intZoneSub = lstZone.getSelectedIndex();
        if (intWeightSub != -1 && intZoneSub != -1)
            lblCharges.setText("" + fltRate[intWeightSub][intZoneSub]);
        else
            lblCharges.setText("Select the weight and zone");
    }
```

Using Text Fields

If you are using text fields for data entry rather than lists, the input requires more validation. You must validate and look up both the weight and the zone entries before you can find the correct rate. The valid zones and weight ranges can be stored in two separate one-dimensional arrays. The first step in the project is to establish and fill the two arrays. The five-by-four rate table is two dimensional, and the values should be preloaded, as in the previous example.

```
//Arrays for lookup
float fltRate[][] = {{1.0f, 1.5f, 1.65f, 1.85f},
                     {1.58f, 2.0f, 2.4f, 3.05f},
                     {1.71f, 2.52f, 3.10f, 4.0f},
                     {2.04f, 3.12f, 4.0f, 5.01f},
                     {2.52f, 3.75f, 5.10f, 7.25f}};
int intWeight[] = {1, 3, 5, 10};
String strZone[] = {"A", "B", "C", "D"};
```

Notice that the zones are placed in a String array so that you can compare to the input entered by the user. You also might consider a char array, but that complicates the lookup, since you cannot compare String to char data without conversion.

```
//Folder:        Ch9ShippingTextFields
//Programmer:    Bradley/Millspaugh
//Date:          6/2001
//ClassName:     ShippingApplet
//Description:   Look up shipping charge based on a zone and a weight entered in
//               text fields. Uses a two-dimensional table.

import java.applet.*;
import java.awt.*;
import java.awt.event.*;

public class ShippingApplet extends Applet implements ActionListener
{
    //Declare components and variables
    TextField txtZone = new TextField(3);
    TextField txtWeight = new TextField(3);
    Label lblCharges = new Label("        ");
    Button btnOK = new Button("OK");

    //Arrays for lookup
    float fltRate[][] = {{1.0f, 1.5f, 1.65f, 1.85f},
                         {1.58f, 2.0f, 2.4f, 3.05f},
                         {1.71f, 2.52f, 3.10f, 4.0f},
                         {2.04f, 3.12f, 4.0f, 5.01f},
                         {2.52f, 3.75f, 5.10f, 7.25f}};
    int intWeight[] = {1,3,5,10};
    String strZone[] = {"A", "B", "C", "D"};

    public void init()
    {
        //Add components to Panel
        add(new Label("Zone: "));
        add(txtZone);
```

```java
        add(new Label("Weight(not to exceed): "));
        add(txtWeight);
        add(btnOK);
        add(new Label("Charges: "));
        add(lblCharges);
        btnOK.addActionListener(this);
        txtZone.addActionListener(this);
        txtWeight.addActionListener(this);
        txtZone.requestFocus();
    }

public void actionPerformed(ActionEvent event)
{
    // Display Charges
    boolean blnWeightFound = false;
    boolean blnZoneFound = false;
    int intIndex = 0;
    int intWeightSub = 0;
    int intZoneSub = 0;

    try
    {
        //Look up the weight to find the intWeightSub
        int intWeightInput = Integer.valueOf(txtWeight.getText()).intValue();

        while(!blnWeightFound && intIndex < 4)
        {
            if(intWeightInput <= intWeight[intIndex])
            {
                    intWeightSub = intIndex;
                    blnWeightFound = true;
            }
            intIndex++;
        }
        if(!blnWeightFound) //Weight exceeds 10 pounds
            intWeightSub = 4;

        //Look up the zone to find the intZoneSub
        intIndex = 0;
        String strZoneInput = txtZone.getText();

        while(!blnZoneFound && intIndex <= 3)
        {
            //Check next zone entry from table
            if (strZoneInput.equalsIgnoreCase(strZone[intIndex]))
            {
                    intZoneSub = intIndex;
                    blnZoneFound = true;
            }
            intIndex++;
        }

        //Display the appropriate rate
        if (blnZoneFound)
        {
            lblCharges.setText("" + fltRate[intWeightSub][intZoneSub]);
            //Clear text boxes
            txtZone.setText("");
            txtWeight.setText("");
```

```
            txtZone.requestFocus();
        }
        else
        {
            lblCharges.setText("Invalid zone");
            txtZone.selectAll();
            txtZone.requestFocus();
        }
    }

    catch(NumberFormatException exc)
    {
        //Exception in converting the weight to integer
        lblCharges.setText("Weight must be integer");
        txtWeight.selectAll();
        txtWeight.requestFocus();
    }
    }
}
```

Creating an Array of Objects

You also can create arrays of classes. Using a class requires the keyword new to create an array of objects. You can create an array of a class that you create as well as arrays of Java classes, such as components.

```
Course Courses[] = new Course[3];
Label lblGroupNumber[] = new Label[8];
```

The objects in the array are not automatically instantiated. Use a loop to instantiate each object, once again using the keyword new. Usually you place the following code in the init method.

```
// Instantiate the array
for(int intIndex = 0; intIndex < 3; intIndex++)
{
    Courses[intIndex] = new Course();
}
```

The next example creates an array of Course objects. In the "An Array of Components" section later in this chapter, the example uses two arrays of Label components.

An Array of Course Objects

The following example has a Course class that has variables for the course number, room, and units (Figure 9.9). The applet class creates an array of Courses, initializes the array values, and then uses a lookup to find the information for an input course number (Figure 9.10).

Notice in the Course class, the instance variables are public. Using this technique, it isn't necessary to use "get" methods. Instead, you can refer to objectName-dot-variableName (Courses[0].strRoom).

Figure 9.9

Class: Course	
Methods	**Public Variables**
setValues	strDesc
	strRoom
	fltUnits

The Courses class diagram.

Figure 9.10

FindCourseApplet looks up the course number in the Courses array and fills in the room and unit information

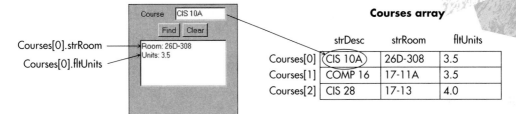

Course Class

```
//Folder:        Ch9CourseSearch
//Programmer:    Bradley/Millspaugh
//Date:          6/2001
//ClassName:     Course
//Description:   Object that contains variables for the course description,
//               room, and number of units.

public class Course
{
    String strDesc;
    String strRoom;
    float fltUnits;

    public void setValues(String strDescIn, String strRoomIn,
                float fltUnitsIn)
    {
        strDesc = strDescIn;
        strRoom = strRoomIn;
        fltUnits = fltUnitsIn;
    }
}
```

FindCourseApplet

```
//Folder:        Ch9CourseSearch
//Programmer:    Bradley/Millspaugh
//Date:          6/2001
//ClassName:     FindCourseApplet
//Description:   Look up course number to find the room and number
//               of units. Creates an array of Course objects.
```

```java
import java.applet.*;
import java.awt.*;
import java.awt.event.*;

public class FindCourseApplet extends Applet implements ActionListener
{
    // Declare variables and components
    Course Courses[] = new Course[3];
    TextField txtDesc = new TextField(10);
    Button btnFind = new Button("Find");
    Button btnClear = new Button("Clear");
    TextArea txaInfo = new TextArea(4,20);

    public void init()
    {
        // Place components on form
        add(new Label("Course "));
        add(txtDesc);
        add(btnFind);
        add(btnClear);
        add(txaInfo);
        txtDesc.requestFocus();
        btnFind.addActionListener(this);
        btnClear.addActionListener(this);
        txtDesc.addActionListener(this);

        // Instantiate the array
        for(int intIndex = 0; intIndex < 3; intIndex++)
        {
            Courses[intIndex] = new Course();
        }

        //Set the values of the array elements
        Courses[0].setValues("CIS 10A", "26D-308", 3.5f);
        Courses[1].setValues("COMP 16", "17-11A", 3.5f);
        Courses[2].setValues("CIS 28", "17-13", 4.0f);
    }

    public void actionPerformed(ActionEvent action)
    {
        //Execute correct method based on button clicked
        Object eventSource = action.getSource();

        if(eventSource == btnFind || eventSource == txtDesc)
            findCourse();
        if(eventSource == btnClear)
            clearFields();
    }

    public void findCourse()
    {
        //Look up the course number to find the room information

        boolean blnFound = false;
        int intIndex = 0;
        String strDescToFind;

        strDescToFind = txtDesc.getText();
```

```
    while(intIndex < 3 && !blnFound)
    {
        if(strDescToFind.equalsIgnoreCase(Courses[intIndex].strDesc))
        {
            blnFound = true;
            txaInfo.append("Room: " + Courses[intIndex].strRoom);
            txaInfo.append("\n" + "Units: " + Courses[intIndex].fltUnits + "\n");
        }
        intIndex++;
    }
    if(!blnFound)
    {
        txaInfo.append("Course not on File \n");
    }
}

public void clearFields()
{
    //Clear text fields
    txtDesc.setText("");
    txaInfo.setText("");
    txtDesc.requestFocus();
}
}
```

An Array of Components

You also can create arrays of components. This technique can be handy when you need several components of the same type, especially if you need to reference the components with an index.

This example modifies the earlier eight-group ticket sale program. Instead of displaying a summary of sales in a text area, this version displays current totals for the eight groups in labels (Figure 9.11). You need two arrays of Labels: one to hold the group numbers and one to hold the totals. Declare the arrays at the top of the program:

Figure 9.11

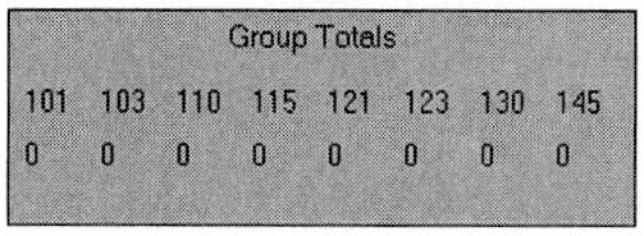

Use two arrays of Labels to display the group numbers and the total for each group.

Group Totals							
101	103	110	115	121	123	130	145
0	0	0	0	0	0	0	0

```
//Declare components
Label lblGroupNumber[] = new Label[8];
Label lblGroupTotal[] = new Label[8];
```

Then in the `init` method, after filling the Choice list, instantiate the 16 labels and add them to the layout.

```
fillList();
//Set up group totals
add(new Label("Group Totals"));
```

```
        for (int intIndex = 0; intIndex < 8; intIndex++)
        {
            //Instantiate the group number labels and add to the layout
            lblGroupNumber[intIndex] = new Label("     ");
            lblGroupNumber[intIndex].setText(chcGroup.getItem(intIndex));
            add(lblGroupNumber[intIndex]);
        }
        for (int intIndex = 0; intIndex < 8; intIndex++)
        {
            //Instantiate the total labels and add to the layout
            lblGroupTotal[intIndex] = new Label("0");
            add(lblGroupTotal[intIndex]);
        }

public void fillList()
{
    //Add group numbers to the list
    chcGroup.add("101");
    chcGroup.add("103");
    chcGroup.add("110");
    chcGroup.add("115");
    chcGroup.add("121");
    chcGroup.add("123");
    chcGroup.add("130");
    chcGroup.add("145");
}
```

When you add a sale to the array that holds the totals, you also can display the total in the corresponding label.

```
        //Group selected from drop-down list; add to total
        int intGroupSub = chcGroup.getSelectedIndex();
        intTotal[intGroupSub] += intSale;
        lblGroupTotal[intGroupSub].setText("" + intTotal[intGroupSub]);
```

Java Arrays for C++ and Visual Basic Programmers

If you have programmed in C++ or Visual Basic, you probably have noticed some differences between arrays in Java and arrays in the other languages.

Arrays in Java must have defined limits or bounds, differing from those in C++. This feature enhances the security of Java programs by not allowing arrays to exceed the allocated memory size. Also, Java does not allow pointer arithmetic to access array elements—again a security feature. Dropping these two "features" of C++ eliminates the majority of strange program bugs.

In Visual Basic you can declare an array with subscripts beginning with any number, such as (1 through 10) or (−10 through 10), which Java does not allow. Visual Basic also has dynamic arrays, which can be resized during program execution.

Vectors

In reality, Java does have resizable or dynamic arrays—they are called *vectors*. A **Vector** is a class that is similar to an array. It holds multiple values and is referenced by an index. In addition, a vector automatically grows when more elements are needed. The Vector class has many methods to aid in creating the elements, adding and removing elements, and searching for particular elements. You can find information about vectors in the Java online Help.

Note: Sun advises against using vectors as they are being deprecated.

Your Hands-on Programming Example

Create an applet to keep track of ticket sales for eight scout troops. The troops are numbered 101, 103, 110, 115, 121, 123, 130, and 145.

For each sale, the user chooses the troop number from a drop-down list, enters the number of tickets sold (an integer), and clicks the OK button. Any number of sales may occur for each troop, entered in any order. The applet must add the sale to the correct total and display a summary of the sales for each group.

Use a Choice component for the troop numbers, an array of integers to hold the group totals, and two arrays of Labels to display the group numbers and group totals on the applet.

Planning the Project

Figure 9.12 shows one possible layout for the applet.

Figure 9.12

A possible user interface for the chapter hands-on example.

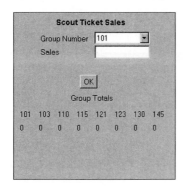

Plan the User Interface

Figure 9.13 shows the class diagram.

Figure 9.13

The class diagram for the hands-on example.

Class: ArraysApplet	
Methods	**Variables and Components**
init	intTotal[8]
setupLayout	chcGroup
fillList	txtSale
actionPerformed	btnOK
calculateSale	lblTitle
	fntTitle
	lblMessage
	pnlInput
	pnlTotals
	lblGroupNumber[8]
	lblGroupTotal[8]

Plan the Objects and Properties

Class Name: ArraysApplet

Properties:

Access Mode (public or private)	Variable or Component Name	Data Type or Class	Description
	chcGroup	Choice	Drop-down list to display the group numbers.
	txtSale	TextField	For user to enter the number of tickets sold.
	btnOK	Button	OK button.
	lblTitle	Label	Display the title on the applet.
	fntTitle	Font	Set the font of lblTitle.
	lblMessage	Label	Display error message for invalid data.
	pnlInput	Panel	Hold the input components.
	pnlTotals	Panel	Hold the group totals.
	lblGroupNumber[]	Label array	Display group numbers.
	lblGroupTotal[]	Label array	Display group totals.
	intTotal[]	int array	Hold group totals.

Methods:

Access Mode (public or private)	Return Type	Method Name (include any parameters)	Pseudocode
public	void	init	Set up layout. Add action listeners. Set the focus to the text field.
public	void	setupLayout	Fill List. Set font of lblTitle. Add lblTitle to applet. Create new panel and set layout manager. Add components to panel. Add panel to applet. Add button and lblMessage. Set foreground of lblMessage to red. Add label for group totals. Instantiate the group number labels, fill with values, and add to the panel. Instantiate the group total labels, fill with 0, and add to the panel. Add the panel to the applet.
public	void	fillList	Add the group numbers to the Choice list.
public	void	actionPerformed	Clear any previous message. Calculate sale.

Access Mode (public or private)	Return Type	Method Name (include any parameters)	Pseudocode

public	void	`calculateSale`	Get index of selected group.
			Get integer input for sale.
			If index valid
			    Add sale to correct total.
			    Display total in correct label.
			    Clear the text field.
			    Reset the focus.
			Catch NumberFormatException.
			    Display error message in label.
			    Display status message.

Write the Project

- Follow the plan to add components to the class.

- Write the appropriate statements to set up the user interface.

- Write the methods to accomplish each task, following the pseudocode in the plan.

- When you complete the code, thoroughly test the project. Add multiple sales for each group and enter bad (noninteger) values for the sales.

The Project Solution

```
//Folder:        Ch9HandsOn
//Programmer:    Bradley/Millspaugh
//Date:          6/2001
//ClassName:     ArraysApplet
//Description:   Accumulate ticket sales for eight groups; group numbers are
//               not direct subscripts. Uses a Choice list to display group numbers
//               and arrays of Labels.

import java.applet.*;
import java.awt.*;
import java.awt.event.*;

public class ArraysApplet extends Applet implements ActionListener
{
    //Declare components
    Choice chcGroup = new Choice();
    TextField txtSale = new TextField(5);
    Button btnOK = new Button("OK");
    Label lblTitle = new Label("  Scout Ticket Sales  ");
    Font fntTitle = new Font("Arial", Font.BOLD, 14);
    Label lblMessage = new Label("             ");
    Label lblGroupNumber[] = new Label[8];
    Label lblGroupTotal[] = new Label[8];

    //Declare array
    int intTotal[] = new int[8];
```

```java
public void init()
{
    //Set up applet layout
    setupLayout();
    btnOK.addActionListener(this);
    txtSale.addActionListener(this);
    txtSale.requestFocus();
}

public void setupLayout()
{
    //Add components to Panel
    fillList();
    lblTitle.setFont(fntTitle);
    add(lblTitle);
    Panel pnlInput = new Panel(new GridLayout(3, 2));
    pnlInput.add(new Label("Group Number"));
    pnlInput.add(chcGroup);
    pnlInput.add(new Label("Sales"));
    pnlInput.add(txtSale);
    add(pnlInput);
    add(new Label("        ")); //Spacing
    add(btnOK);
    add(lblMessage);
    lblMessage.setForeground(Color.red);

    //Set up group totals
    add(new Label("Group Totals"));
    Panel pnlTotals = new Panel(new GridLayout(2, 8));
    for (int intIndex = 0; intIndex < 8; intIndex++)
    {
        //Instantiate the group number labels and add to the layout
        lblGroupNumber[intIndex] = new Label("    ");
        lblGroupNumber[intIndex].setText(chcGroup.getItem(intIndex));
        pnlTotals.add(lblGroupNumber[intIndex]);
    }
    for (int intIndex = 0; intIndex < 8; intIndex++)
    {
        //Instantiate the total labels and add to the layout
        lblGroupTotal[intIndex] = new Label("0");
        pnlTotals.add(lblGroupTotal[intIndex]);
    }
    add(pnlTotals);
}

    public void fillList()
{
    //Add group numbers to the list
    chcGroup.add("101");
    chcGroup.add("103");
    chcGroup.add("110");
    chcGroup.add("115");
    chcGroup.add("121");
    chcGroup.add("123");
    chcGroup.add("130");
    chcGroup.add("145");
}
```

```java
public void actionPerformed(ActionEvent event)
{
    //Call the appropriate method
    lblMessage.setText("");    //Clear any previous message
    calculateSale();
}

public void calculateSale()
{
    //Add to appropriate total
    try
    {
        int intGroupSub = chcGroup.getSelectedIndex();
        int intSale = Integer.valueOf(txtSale.getText()).intValue();
        if(intGroupSub >= 0 && intGroupSub <= 7)
        {
            //Valid group; add to total
            intTotal[intGroupSub] += intSale;
            lblGroupTotal[intGroupSub].setText("" + intTotal[intGroupSub]);

            //Clear field
            txtSale.setText("");
            txtSale.requestFocus();
        }
    }

    catch(NumberFormatException exc)
    {
        //Invalid data entered
        lblMessage.setText("Invalid data entered ");
        showStatus("Sales must be integer");
    }
}
```

Summary

1. A series of variables with the same name and data type is called an array. The individual values are referred to as elements, and each element is accessed by its subscript, which is a position number.
2. You can declare an array variable, instantiate the array using the new keyword, and fill the array elements as three separate steps. You also can combine the declaration and the new keyword into one statement. Another way to declare an array is to give it initial values, in which case you do not use the new keyword.
3. Arrays can be used like any other variables or objects; they can be used to accumulate a series of totals or store values for a lookup procedure.
4. Using an invalid subscript causes Java to throw an exception. If a user may enter a value that will be used for a subscript, you must validate the input or catch the exception.
5. The elements in arrays may be accessed directly by subscript, or a table lookup may be used to determine the correct table position.

6. Arrays may be multidimensional. A two-dimensional table contains rows and columns and is processed similarly to a one-dimensional array. Access of a multidimensional array frequently requires the use of nested loops.
7. You can declare an array based on a class. Use the new keyword to declare the array name. You also must use the new keyword to instantiate each object in the array.

Key Terms

array *262*

direct reference *267*

element *262*

subscript *262*

subscripted variable *262*

table *262*

table lookup *268*

two-dimensional table *271*

Vector *282*

Review Questions

1. Define the following terms:
   (a) array
   (b) element
   (c) subscript
   (d) subscripted variable
2. Describe the logic of a table lookup.
3. Name some situations in which it is important to perform validation when working with subscripted variables.
4. Explain the use of the braces in initializing values in a two-dimensional table.

Programming Exercises

9.1 Create a project that looks up the phone extension for a department and displays it in a label. Use a List or Choice for the department names.

Department	Extension
Accounting	4123
Human Resources	1334
Information Technology	7654
Marketing	9807
Production	7689

9.2   Create a project to keep track of concert ticket sales by your club. Ticket prices are based on the section of the auditorium in which the seats are located. Your program should calculate the price for each sale, accumulate the total number of tickets sold in each section, display the ticket price schedule, and display a summary of all sales.

Use a List (or Choice) with the sections for seating. After the user selects a section, display the price per seat in a label. Also include a text field to enter the quantity. An Order button will display the total due for the order and clear the List selection and the quantity text field.

Section	Price
Orchestra	40.00
Mezzanine	27.50
General	15.00
Balcony	10.00

9.3   (Two-dimensional array) Create a project that looks up the driving distance between two cities. Use two drop-down lists that contain the names of the cities. Label one list *Departure* and the other *Destination*. Use an OK button to find and display the distance. Include a Clear button to clear the selection.

	Boston	Chicago	Dallas	Las Vegas	Los Angeles	Miami	New Orleans	Toronto	Vancouver	Washington, DC
Boston	0	1004	1753	2752	3017	1520	1507	609	3155	448
Chicago	1004	0	921	1780	2048	1397	919	515	2176	709
Dallas	1753	921	0	1230	1399	1343	517	1435	2234	1307
Las Vegas	2752	1780	1230	0	272	2570	1732	2251	1322	2420
Los Angeles	3017	2048	1399	272	0	2716	1858	2523	1278	2646
Miami	1520	1397	1343	2570	2716	0	860	1494	3447	1057
New Orleans	1507	919	517	1732	1858	860	0	1307	2734	1099
Toronto	609	515	1435	2251	2523	1494	1307	0	2820	571
Vancouver	3155	2176	2234	1322	1278	3447	2734	2820	0	2887
Washington, DC	448	709	1307	2420	2646	1057	1099	571	2887	0

9.4   (Two one-dimensional arrays or a two-dimensional array) Create a project that will allow the user to look up state names and their two-letter abbreviations. The user can enter either the state name or the abbreviation and click a button to look up the other value. In the event that a match cannot be found for the input, print an appropriate error message.

AL	Alabama	MT	Montana
AK	Alaska	NE	Nebraska
AS	American Samoa	NV	Nevada
AZ	Arizona	NH	New Hampshire
AR	Arkansas	NJ	New Jersey
CA	California	NM	New Mexico
CZ	Canal Zone	NY	New York
CO	Colorado	NC	North Carolina
CT	Connecticut	ND	North Dakota
DE	Delaware	OH	Ohio
DC	District of Columbia	OK	Oklahoma
FL	Florida	OR	Oregon
GA	Georgia	PA	Pennsylvania
GU	Guam	PR	Puerto Rico
HI	Hawaii	RI	Rhode Island
ID	Idaho	SC	South Carolina
IL	Illinois	SD	South Dakota
IN	Indiana	TN	Tennessee
IA	Iowa	TX	Texas
KS	Kansas	TT	Trust Territories
KY	Kentucky	UT	Utah
LA	Louisiana	VT	Vermont
ME	Maine	VA	Virginia
MD	Maryland	VI	Virgin Islands
MA	Massachusetts	WA	Washington
MI	Michigan	WV	West Virginia
MN	Minnesota	WI	Wisconsin
MS	Mississippi	WY	Wyoming
MO	Missouri		

9.5   Modify exercise 9.4 to help keep the user out of trouble. Add option buttons to allow the user to select which text box and button should be enabled and have the focus. Disable the other set so that the user isn't tempted to enter values in both boxes.

9.6   Modify exercise 9.4 or 9.5 to include an array of a class. Store the state abbreviations and state names in elements of a class array and use that class array for the lookup operation.

9.7   The Plain Wrap Auto Parts Company sells its own brand of spark plugs. To cross-reference to major brands, it keeps a table of equivalent part numbers.

Create an applet to look up part numbers. The user should be able to enter the part number and brand and look up the corresponding Plain Wrap part number. You may allow the user to select the brand (Brand A, Brand C, or Brand X) from a List or Choice component.

Store the part numbers in a two-dimensional table.

Plain Wrap	Brand A	Brand C	Brand X
PR214	MR43T	RBL8	14K22
PR223	R43	RJ6	14K24
PR224	R43N	RN4	14K30
PR246	R46N	RN8	14K32
PR247	R46TS	RBL17Y	14K33
PR248	R46TX	RBL12-6	14K35
PR324	S46	J11	14K38
PR326	SR46E	XEJ8	14K40
PR444	47L	H12	14K44

CASE STUDIES

R 'n R—for Reading and Refreshment

Modify the project for Chapter 8 to automatically fill in the price of a book after the user selects the book title, rather than type in the price. Store the prices in an array in which the prices correspond to the titles in the list. Use the index of the book selected from the list to find the corresponding price. Test that all calculations still work correctly.

Merry Pea's Quilting   Modify the project in Chapter 8 to store the class prices in an array. Use the index of the selected class to find the corresponding price.

10

Applications, Frames, Menus, and Dialogs

At the completion of this chapter, you will be able to . . .

1. Write a Java application.

2. Use a Frame object to create a window.

3. Add a menu bar, menus, and menu items to a frame.

4. Place separators between menu items.

5. Disable menu items at design time.

6. Use the CheckboxMenuItem to allow a menu item to contain a check mark.

7. Create submenus.

8. Handle menu events.

9. Exit an application.

10. Display a dialog.

11. Use multiple frames.

12. Create a popup menu.

13. Write a Swing application.

14. Convert an applet into a program that can run as an application or an applet.

Up to this point, all of your projects have been applets, which run inside a browser application. You can also use Java to create applications, which run independent of a browser. In this chapter you will use Frame objects to create windows and add menu bars, menus, and menu items. You will also create popup menus, which you can add to an applet or application.

Applications

A Java **application** runs from the operating system in stand-alone mode, rather than running from a browser. After you compile an application, you can run it using the Java interpreter from the operating system prompt, if you wish. Or if you are using a Java IDE, such as JBuilder, J++, or Forté, you can also run the application using the *Run* command in the IDE.

There are several other major differences between applications and applets. An application begins execution with a method called `main`, rather than `init`. And an applet is a panel, which is a container. An application has no such container already built in. For a graphical application, you must create a container in which to place components. Usually you will use a Frame object as a container. You will also see examples of applications that use an applet as the container. In fact, such applications sometimes have both an `init` method and a `main` method and can be run either as an applet or as an application. You will see one such example later in this chapter.

Frames

A **Frame** object is a container that you can display from an application. A frame is actually a window that resembles all windows in the operating system you are using. Figure 10.1 shows a frame running in Windows 98.

Figure 10.1

A Frame object running in Windows.

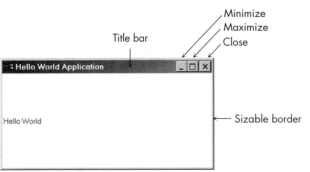

Your program can define multiple frames and display them as needed. Each frame has a title bar, a minimize box, a maximize/restore box, and a close box. However, as you will see later, you must do some programming to make the close box function. The Frame class is defined in Java's AWT package and inherits from the Window and Container classes (Figure 10.2).

Figure 10.2

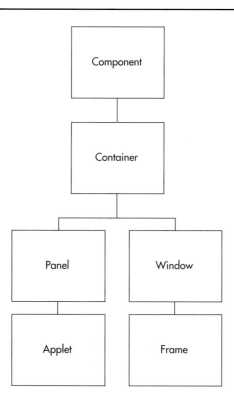

The Frame class inherits from Window, which inherits from Container. An applet is a container since the Applet class inherits from Panel, which inherits from Container.

Tip to Visual Basic programmers: Think of a frame as a VB form.

The Frame Class—Constructors

```
Frame()
Frame(String title)
```

The title appears in the title bar of the frame. If you omit the title, the frame's title bar appears with no text.

The Frame Class—Examples

```
Frame frmStartup = new Frame();
Frame frmHello = new Frame("Hello World Application");
```

Using Layout Managers with Frames

You may recall that a panel automatically defaults to the FlowLayout. The default layout for a frame is the BorderLayout. You will recall that the Border-Layout allows you to add components to each section by specifying "North", "South", "East", "West", or "Center", and defaults to center if you omit the region. If you prefer, you can set the form's layout to a FlowLayout, or add a panel to any of the sections of the BorderLayout and set the layout for the panel to the layout manager of your choice.

A Simple Application

Every application must have a **main method**. The main method header looks like this:

```
public static void main(String args[])
```

The string argument array parameter must be included. This parameter is used to pass arguments to an application, but does nothing if no arguments are required.

Creating and Showing a Frame

To create a new Frame object, declare a variable type of Frame. You can set a layout manager for the frame, if you wish, and add components to the frame. You must use the `setSize` method to give the frame a size and the `show` method to display the frame.

```
frmHello.setSize(400, 200); //Set width and height in pixels
frmHello.show();
```

The Hello World Application

You can see the output from this Hello World application in Figure 10.3. Notice that the Hello World label appears in the center section of the border layout.

Figure 10.3

The Hello World application. The Hello World label displays in a Frame object.

```
//Folder:       Ch10Frames
//Programmer:   Bradley/Millspaugh
//Date:         6/2001
//ClassName:    FrameApp
//Description:  A stand-alone Hello World application to display a
//              message in a new window.

import java.awt.*;

public class FrameApp
{
    public static void main(String args[])
    {
        //Create the frame and components
        Frame frmHello = new Frame("Hello World Application");
```

```
        Label lblHello = new Label("Hello World");
        frmHello.add(lblHello);
        frmHello.setSize(400, 200);
        frmHello.show();
    }
}
```

Running and Stopping an Application

If you are using an IDE, you can easily run this application using the *Run* command. Then test your application window: the minimize button and the maximize/restore buttons should work as expected, and the resizable borders allow you to resize the window.

Stopping the application is another story. When you see a window with a close box, you expect to be able to close the window by clicking on the box. However, closing a frame in Java requires some programming. What do you want to do when the user clicks on the close box? Just stop? Clean up? Save something? At this point, we really do want to just stop, but we are required to say so.

Until we program for the close box, you must stop the application by using the IDE's *End* command or the operating system's *Close* command.

Closing a Window

To allow the user to close your window using the close box, you must add a listener to the frame. The code for the window listener resembles the mouse listener we used in Chapter 2.

Your application must import java.awt.event.*, implement the WindowListener interface, and add a window listener to the form.

```
import java.awt.event.*;

public class FrameApp implements WindowListener
{
    ...//Other statements...
    frmHello.addWindowListener(this);
```

To implement an interface, you must write methods for every method in the interface. In this case, you must write windowClosing, windowClosed, windowDeiconified, windowIconified, windowOpened, windowActivated, and windowDeactivated. Just as you did for the mouse methods, you can write empty methods for any events to which you don't care to respond.

The one event for which you want to write code is the windowClosing event. The statement that closes the window and exits to the operating system is

```
    System.exit(0); //Exit to the operating system
```

DO NOT use this statement if you are writing an applet that will run in a browser.

Declaring an Instance of an Application

As soon as you write an application with more than one method, you need to modify the structure of the application. A main method can refer directly only to static variables and methods, which is very limiting. Instead, you will use the `main` method to declare a new instance of your application. Then all references to variables and methods will reference the instance variables.

Here is one way (not a very good way) to declare components and reference them in a `main` method. The `main` method declares a new instance of the application (using the class name, FrameApp). Then all references to variables and methods must include the instance name.

```java
public class FrameApp
{
    //Create components
    Frame frmHello = new Frame("Hello World Application");
    Label lblHello = new Label("Hello World");

    public static void main(String args[])
    {
        FrameApp myFrameApp = new FrameApp(); //Declare an instance of the app
        myFrameApp.frmHello.add(myFrameApp.lblHello);
        myFrameApp.frmHello.setSize(400, 200);
        myFrameApp.frmHello.show();
    }
}
```

A Better Structure

A better way to structure an application is to move most of the code out of the `main` method into other methods. Then you can call the other methods from `main`. The other methods can refer to variables, components, and methods without the extra instance name, since all variables and methods refer only to the one instance. Here is the recommended structure for an application along with the code to listen for the windowClosing event.

```java
//Folder:        Ch10CloseableFrame
//Programmer:    Bradley/Millspaugh
//Date:          6/2001
//ClassName:     FrameApp
//Description:   A stand-alone Hello World application to display a
//               message in a new window. The window's close box closes
//               the window.

import java.awt.*;
import java.awt.event.*;

public class FrameApp implements WindowListener
{
    //Declare the components
    Frame frmHello = new Frame("Hello World Application");
    Label lblHello = new Label("Hello World");

    public static void main(String args[])
    {
        FrameApp myFrameApp = new FrameApp();
        myFrameApp.createInterface();
    }
```

```
public void createInterface()
{
    //Set up the user interface
    frmHello.addWindowListener(this);
    frmHello.add(lblHello);
    frmHello.setSize(400, 200);
    frmHello.show();
}

public void windowClosing(WindowEvent event)
{
    //Exit to the operating system
    System.exit(0);
}

public void windowClosed(WindowEvent event)
{}
public void windowDeiconified(WindowEvent event)
{}
public void windowIconified(WindowEvent event)
{}
public void windowOpened(WindowEvent event)
{}
public void windowActivated(WindowEvent event)
{}
public void windowDeactivated(WindowEvent event)
{}

}
```

A Shortcut to Closing a Window

If you don't want to code all of the methods for the WindowListener interface,
here's a shortcut: Instead of implementing the interface, you can extend a class
called WindowAdapter, which is a class already defined with methods for each
of the classes in the interface. By extending WindowAdapter, you need to override only the method(s) you want and can ignore the rest.

```
//Folder:        Ch10CloseableAdapter
//Programmer:    Bradley/Millspaugh
//Date:          6/2001
//ClassName:     FrameApp
//Description:   A stand-alone Hello World application to display a
//               message in a new window. The window's close box closes
//               the window. Uses WindowAdapter.

import java.awt.*;
import java.awt.event.*;

public class FrameApp extends WindowAdapter
{
    //Declare the components
    Frame frmHello = new Frame("Hello World Application");
    Label lblHello = new Label("Hello World");
```

```java
public static void main(String args[])
{
    FrameApp myFrameApp = new FrameApp();
    myFrameApp.createInterface();
}

public void createInterface()
{
    //Set up the user interface
    frmHello.addWindowListener(this);
    frmHello.add(lblHello);
    frmHello.setSize(400, 200);
    frmHello.show();
}

public void windowClosing(WindowEvent event)
{
    //Exit to the operating system
    System.exit(0);
}
}
```

Feedback 10.1

1. Code the statement to create a Frame, placing your name in the title bar.
2. Explain the difference between implementing the WindowListener interface and extending the WindowAdapter class.
3. Write the statement(s) to close a window and exit back to the operating system.

Menus

When you write applications with frames, you can include a menu bar with menus and menu items (sometimes called menu commands). Figure 10.4 shows an application with a menu bar, menus, menu items, and a submenu.

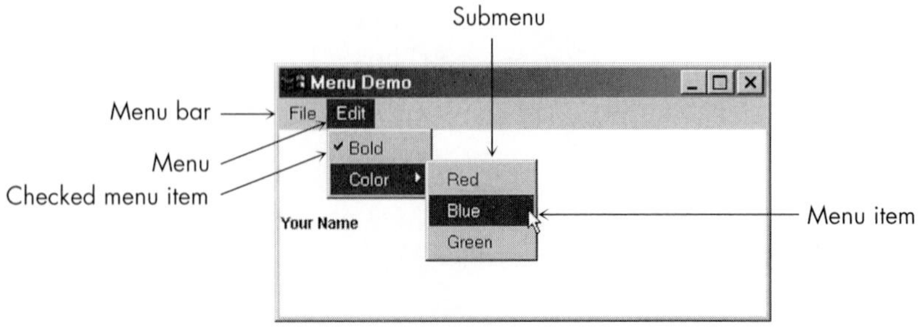

An application with a menu bar, menus, menu items, and a submenu.

You should make your menus follow the standards for the operating system. For example, you should have a File menu with menu items such as New,

Open, Save, and Exit. If you have a Help menu, it should be the rightmost menu. The Help menu usually contains an About menu item, which displays information about the application.

To add a menu bar to a window, you first create the menu bar and then add menus to the menu bar. The next step is to add menu items to each menu. You can make the menu items appear checked or disabled, and you can separate items with a separator line. After the visual portion of the menu is in place, you add the event handling, so that your program can respond when the user selects a menu item.

Creating a Menu Bar

You create a menu bar by declaring an instance of the **MenuBar class**. The class has only a single constructor with no arguments.

The MenuBar Class—Constructor

```
MenuBar()
```

The MenuBar Class—Example

```
MenuBar mnuMain = new MenuBar();
```

Use the `setMenuBar` method to attach a menu bar to a frame:

```
Frame frmMain = new Frame("Menu Demo");
MenuBar mnuMain = new MenuBar();
frmMain.setMenuBar(mnuMain);
```

The Menu Class

Of course, you will want to place some menus on the menu bar. Each drop-down section of a menu bar is considered a menu. Three constructors are available for the **Menu class**. The most common one supplies a label for the menu. Some implementations of AWT allow a menu to be "torn off" from the menu bar. The only constructor that supports a tear-off menu contains a boolean value that is set to true for the tear-off option. The tear-off option is a feature available for applications running under Motif (not for Microsoft Windows).

The Menu Class—Constructors

```
Menu()
Menu(String label)
Menu(String label, boolean tearOff)
```

The Menu Class—Examples

```
Menu mnuFile = new Menu("File");
Menu mnuEdit = new Menu("Edit");
```

After you create your menus, you must add them to the menu bar.

```
//Menu components
Menu mnuFile = new Menu("File");
mnuMain.add(mnuFile);
Menu mnuHelp = new Menu("Help");
mnuMain.add(mnuHelp);
```

Menu Items

You create the menu items with the **MenuItem class**. Once again, you can choose from several constructors. A menu item created with an empty constructor does not have a label (text to appear on the menu) or a keyboard shortcut. The second constructor creates a menu item with a label, and the third option defines both a label and a keyboard shortcut.

The MenuItem Class—Constructors

```
MenuItem()
MenuItem(String label)
MenuItem(String label, MenuShortCut keycode)
```

The MenuItem Class—Examples

```
MenuItem mnuFileSave = new MenuItem("Save");
MenuItem mnuFileExit = new MenuItem("Exit");
MenuItem mnuHelpAbout = new MenuItem("About");
mnuFile.add(new MenuItem("Save"));        //Create an unnamed menu item
```

Notice the naming conventions for naming menus and menu items. Use "mnu" as the prefix for a menu bar and a menu. For a menu item, use the menu name with the menu item name appended. For example, mnuFileExit indicates an Exit menu item that appears on the File menu.

You must add each menu item to the correct menu.

```
MenuItem mnuFileExit = new MenuItem("Exit");
mnuFile.add(mnuFileExit);
MenuItem mnuHelpAbout = new MenuItem("About");
mnuHelp.add(mnuHelpAbout);
```

Creating Unnamed Menu Items

It isn't necessary to always give a menu item a name. In the event handling for menu events, you usually add an action listener to the entire menu and check the label of the selected menu item rather than the name of the item. You can create an unnamed object using the `add` method of the Menu object. This statement creates an Exit menu item and adds it to the File menu:

```
mnuFile.add(new MenuItem("Exit"));
```

Adding a Separator

The Menu class has an **addSeparator method** for creating separator lines between menu items to logically separate the items into groups. Notice in Figure 10.5 that the separator line in the File menu appears between the Save and Exit menu items.

Figure 10.5

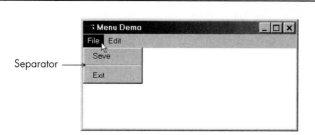

```
//Add menu items to File menu
mnuFile.addActionListener(this);
mnuFile.add(new MenuItem("Save"));
mnuFile.addSeparator();
mnuFile.add(new MenuItem("Exit"));
```

Disabling Menu Items

Many menus call for menu items to be disabled until an appropriate time. You may want to include an item on your menu but have it disabled until a certain condition exists. If you plan to modify the property of a menu item during execution, the item must have a name. Use the **setEnabled** (`boolean value`) **method** for setting the state of a menu item.

```
MenuItem mnuFileSave = new MenuItem("Save");
mnuFile.add(mnuFileSave);
mnuFileSave.setEnabled(false);
```

Note: Earlier versions of Java included `disable` and `enable` methods that have been deprecated.

Checked Menu Items

You can declare a menu item that appears checked to indicate that it is selected or active. To create such a menu item, you use a class called the ***CheckboxMenuItem.*** When you create an object of the CheckboxMenuItem class, you can use its `setState` and `getState` methods to set or check the status of the check mark.

The CheckboxMenuItem Class—Constructors

```
CheckboxMenuItem()
CheckboxMenuItem(String label)
CheckboxMenuItem(String label, boolean state)
```

The state is false by default. If you want the item to appear checked initially, use the third constructor and set the state to true. Figure 10.6 shows a Bold menu item that appears checked.

Use the CheckboxMenuItem class to create a menu item that can appear checked.

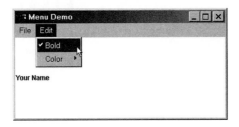

The CheckboxMenuItem Class—Example

```
mnuEdit.add(new CheckboxMenuItem("Bold", true));
```

Submenus

A **submenu** is actually a menu that is placed on a menu. The following lines of code create a Color menu, which is added to the Edit menu. The Color menu contains three menu items: Red, Green, and Blue.

```
//Add the Color submenu to the Edit menu
Menu mnuEditColor = new Menu("Color");
mnuEditColor.addActionListener(this);
mnuEdit.add(mnuEditColor);
mnuEditColor.add("Red");
mnuEditColor.add("Blue");
mnuEditColor.add("Green");
```

Event Handling for Menu Items

When the user clicks a menu item, you want to respond by executing a method. You listen for events for menu items by adding an action listener to the menu object and writing code in the `actionPerformed` method. To listen for events in a submenu, you must also add an action listener to the submenu object.

If you want to listen for events for a check box menu item, you add an item listener to the item (similar to using a Checkbox component). To respond to an event of an object with an item listener, you must write an `itemStateChanged` method.

The actionPerformed Method

The actionPerformed method appears much the same as in the applets you have written. However, for menus, you usually compare the label of the menu item to see which item the user selected. The getActionCommand method of the ActionEvent object returns a string containing the label.

```
public void actionPerformed(ActionEvent event)
    {
        //Determine which menu item was selected
        String strMenuItem = event.getActionCommand();
```

After these statements execute, strMenuItem holds the label of the selected menu item. You can use a series of if statements to determine which item was selected.

```
public void actionPerformed(ActionEvent event)
{
    //Determine which menu item was selected
    String strMenuItem = event.getActionCommand();

    if (strMenuItem.equals("Exit"))
        System.exit(0); //Exit to the operating system
    else if (strMenuItem.equals("Red"))
        lblName.setForeground(Color.red);
    else if (strMenuItem.equals("Blue"))
        lblName.setForeground(Color.blue);
    else if (strMenuItem.equals("Green"))
        lblName.setForeground(Color.green);
}
```

Note: If you are using VJ++, you may need to use a repaint method after selecting a new color.

Checkbox Menu Items

When you are working with a check box menu item, you must use an item listener instead of an action listener. Therefore, you must add the item listener to the implements clause for the class and add an itemStateChanged method to the class.

```
public class MenuApp extends WindowAdapter implements ActionListener, ItemListener

    public void itemStateChanged(ItemEvent event)
    {
        //Determine state of Checkbox menu item
        int intState = event.getStateChange();

        if (intState == event.SELECTED)
            lblName.setFont(fntBold);
        else
            lblName.setFont(fntPlain);
    }
```

There are a few new items for you to notice in this code segment. The state for the menu item is stored as an integer, accessible with the event.getStateChange method. The ItemEvent class contains the constants SELECTED and DESELECTED, which you can use in your conditional expression.

Tip

Always double-check your implements clauses. It's very easy to forget to add implements ActionListener and implements ItemListener to a program, and the error messages don't really tell you what's wrong.

The Menu Application

Here is the completed menu application. Figures 10.4 and 10.6 show the user
interface for this program.

```
//Folder:        Ch10Menu
//Programmer:    Bradley/Millspaugh
//Date:          6/2001
//ClassName:     MenuApp
//Description:   An application with a menu bar, menu items, a submenu,
//               and a Checkbox menu item.

import java.awt.*;
import java.awt.event.*;

public class MenuApp extends WindowAdapter implements ActionListener, ItemListener
{
    //Declare components
    Frame frmMenu = new Frame("Menu Demo");
    Label lblName = new Label("Your Name");
    Font fntBold = new Font("Times New Roman", Font.BOLD, 12);
    Font fntPlain = new Font("Times New Roman", Font.PLAIN, 12);

    //Menu components
    MenuBar mnuMain = new MenuBar();
    Menu mnuFile = new Menu("File");
    Menu mnuEdit = new Menu("Edit");
    Menu mnuEditColor = new Menu("Color");

    //Menu items
    MenuItem mnuFileSave = new MenuItem("Save");
    MenuItem mnuFileExit = new MenuItem("Exit");
    CheckboxMenuItem mnuEditBold = new CheckboxMenuItem("Bold", true);

    public static void main(String args[])
    {
        MenuApp myMenuApp = new MenuApp();
        myMenuApp.createInterface();
    }

    public void createInterface()
    {
        //Create the menu bar
        //File menu
        mnuMain.add(mnuFile);
        mnuFile.addActionListener(this);
        mnuFile.add(mnuFileSave);
        mnuFileSave.setEnabled(false);
        mnuFile.addSeparator();
        mnuFile.add(mnuFileExit);

        //Edit menu
        mnuMain.add(mnuEdit);
        mnuEdit.addActionListener(this);
        mnuEdit.add(mnuEditBold);
        mnuEditBold.addItemListener(this);
        mnuEdit.add(mnuEditColor);
```

```
    mnuEditColor.addActionListener(this);
    mnuEditColor.add("Red");
    mnuEditColor.add("Blue");
    mnuEditColor.add("Green");

    //Attach the menu bar to the frame
    frmMenu.setMenuBar(mnuMain);

    //Set up the components and the frame
    lblName.setFont(fntBold);
    frmMenu.add(lblName);
    frmMenu.addWindowListener(this);
    frmMenu.setSize(400, 200);
    frmMenu.show();
}

public void actionPerformed(ActionEvent event)
{
    //Determine which menu item was selected
    String strMenuItem = event.getActionCommand();

    if (strMenuItem.equals("Exit"))
        System.exit(0); //Exit to the operating system
    else if (strMenuItem.equals("Red"))
        lblName.setForeground(Color.red);
    else if (strMenuItem.equals("Blue"))
        lblName.setForeground(Color.blue);
    else if (strMenuItem.equals("Green"))
        lblName.setForeground(Color.green);
}

public void itemStateChanged(ItemEvent event)
{
    //Determine state of checkbox menu item
    int intState = event.getStateChange();

    if (intState = = event.SELECTED)
        lblName.setFont(fntBold);
    else
        lblName.setFont(fntPlain);
}

public void windowClosing(WindowEvent event)
{
    //Exit to the operating system
    System.exit(0);
}
}
```

Updating Menu Options at Run Time

You can modify a menu while a program is running. You may want to add new menu items, delete existing items, or enable or disable an item. You can make various changes using the methods in the MenuBar class, the Menu class, or the MenuItem class.

Class	Method	Purpose
MenuBar	add(MenuComponent *mnuName*)	Add a menu to the menu bar.
	getMenu(int *position*)	Return the menu at the specified position on the menu bar.
	getMenuCount()	Return the number of menus on the menu bar.
	remove(int *position*)	Remove the menu at the given position.
	remove(MenuComponent *mnuName*)	Remove a menu by name.
	setHelpMenu(Menu *mnuName*)	Set the menu specified as the Help menu. This menu will be positioned to the right of the menu bar.
Menu	add(MenuItem *mnuItemName*)	Add a named menu item to the menu.
	add(String *label*)	Add a menu item with a string label.
	addSeparator()	Add a separator line.
	getItem(int *position*)	Get the menu item at the given position.
	getItemCount()	Return the number of menu items on the menu.
	insert(MenuItem *mnuItemName*, int *position*)	Insert a new menu item at the given position.
	insert(String *label*, int *position*)	Insert a new menu item with the label at the given position.
	insertSeparator(int *position*)	Insert a separator at the given position.
	isTearOff()	Determine if this menu is a tear-off menu.
	remove(int *position*)	Remove the menu item at the given position.
	remove(MenuItem *mnuItemName*)	Remove the specific menu item.
	removeAll()	Remove all menu items from this menu.
MenuItem	addActionListener(*ActionListener*)	Assign an action listener for menu events.
	getLabel(*MenuItem*)	Return the label for the menu item.
	isEnabled(*MenuItem*)	Return boolean based on enabled state.
	removeActionListener()	Remove the action listener for the menu item.
	setEnabled(boolean *state*)	Set the state for the menu item. A false value displays as a "grayed out" menu item.
	setLabel(String *label*)	Assign a label to the menu item.

Feedback 10.2

1. Write the statements to create the following menu.

    Insert
        Break
        Page Numbers
        Date and Time

2. Add the menu created in question 1 to a menu bar called mnuFrameMain.

3. Code the statement(s) to add an action listener for all items on the Insert menu.

4. Create a menu item labeled Normal that will initially appear with a check mark.

5. Modify the code in question 1, setting the Break menu item to disabled.

Dialogs

You can use the **Dialog class** to create windows that pop up during program execution. Dialogs are useful for displaying information that you want the user to view and respond to, such as warnings and error messages. A dialog can be either modal or nonmodal. If a dialog is modal, the user must respond to the dialog before continuing execution of the application. A nonmodal dialog does not prevent the user from responding to other items before dealing with the dialog.

A dialog always belongs to a parent frame; therefore, you usually display dialogs from applications rather than applets. You cannot display a dialog from an applet unless you first display a frame.

When you create a dialog, it is not visible until you set its size and show it using the setSize and show methods.

Figure 10.7 shows a dialog that displays from an application's Help / About menu item.

Figure 10.7

An About dialog, which displays from an application's Help/About menu.

The Dialog Class—Constructors

```
Dialog(Frame parent)
Dialog(Frame parent, boolean modal)
Dialog(Frame parent, String title)
Dialog(Frame parent, String title, boolean modal)
```

Notice that each constructor requires the parent frame. You can also specify modal/nonmodal and the title, which appears in the title bar of the dialog.

The Dialog Class—Example

```
Dialog dlgAbout = new Dialog(frmMain, "About My Application", true);
```

Creating an About Dialog

To use the Dialog class, you usually create a new class that extends from the Dialog class.

```
public class AboutDialog extends Dialog implements ActionListener
```

In your new class, you must create a constructor to specify any actions that must occur when an object is instantiated from the class. Recall that a constructor method is automatically called when an object is created. The name of the constructor method is the same as the name of the class.

```
public AboutDialog (Frame frmParent)
{
    //Constructor
    //Call the parent's constructor
    super(frmParent, "About My Application", true);
    setLayout(new FlowLayout());
    add(lblProgrammer);
    add(btnOK);
    btnOK.addActionListener(this);
    setSize(220, 100);
    show();
}
```

The keyword super allows you to call the constructor method of the superclass (the Dialog class). This is necessary to pass the name of the parent frame to the constructor of the superclass. Notice that the constructor of AboutDialog contains an argument for the parent frame, which you pass to the superclass.

Responding to a Dialog's OK Button

When the user clicks the OK button, you want the dialog to disappear. The OK button has an action listener, so code for its click in the actionPerformed method. Use the dialog's dispose method to destroy the dialog.

```
public void actionPerformed(ActionEvent event)
{
    //Destroy the dialog when OK is pressed
    Object objSource = event.getSource();

    if(objSource == btnOK)
        dispose();    //Destroy the dialog
}
```

Responding to a Dialog's Close Button

If you want the user to be able to click the dialog window's close button, you need another new technique. Recall that earlier in this chapter you used two techniques for responding to a close button: (1) implement the WindowListener interface and code all seven possible window events or (2) extend (inherit from) the WindowAdapter class and code only the `windowClosing` method. Although you could use technique 1 for the dialog, you cannot extend from WindowAdapter *and* extend from Dialog, since Java allows inheriting from only one class. To get around this restriction, we are going to introduce another shortcut to save some coding.

You can use a shortcut technique called an *anonymous inner class*, which is introduced in Chapter 12, to create an instance of WindowAdapter inside your AboutDialog class.

```
//Listen for close box
addWindowListener(new WindowAdapter()
{
    public void windowClosing(WindowEvent event)
    {
        dispose(); //Destroy the dialog
    }
});
```

Notice that all of the code for the WindowAdapter is inside the parentheses for the `addWindowListener` method. For a complete description of how this works, see Chapter 12.

The AboutDialog Class

Now we can put together all of the pieces for the AboutDialog class, which inherits from the Java Dialog class and displays the About box for an application.

```
//Folder:        Ch10HelpMenu
//Programmer:    Bradley/Millspaugh
//Date:          6/2001
//ClassName:     AboutDialog
//Description:   Dialog box to display info about the application.

import java.awt.*;
import java.awt.event.*;

public class AboutDialog extends Dialog implements ActionListener
{
    //Create components
    Button btnOK = new Button("OK");
    Label lblProgrammer = new Label(" Programmer: Bradley/Millspaugh ");

    //Constructor
    public AboutDialog(Frame frmParent)
    {
        //Call the parent's constructor
        super(frmParent, "About My Application", true);
        setLayout(new FlowLayout());
        add(lblProgrammer);
        add(btnOK);
        btnOK.addActionListener(this);
```

```java
        //Listen for close box
        addWindowListener(new WindowAdapter()
        {
            public void windowClosing(WindowEvent event)
            {
                dispose(); //Destroy the dialog
            }
        });
        setSize(220, 100);
        show();
    }

    public void actionPerformed(ActionEvent event)
    {
        //Destroy the dialog when OK is pressed
        Object objSource = event.getSource();

        if(objSource == btnOK)
            dispose();//Destroy the dialog
    }
}
```

Displaying the About Dialog

You display the About dialog from an application's Help menu. You can see the entire application in Ch10HelpMenu. Here is the code segment that displays the dialog.

```java
public void actionPerformed(ActionEvent event)
{
    //Determine which menu item was selected
    String strMenuItem = event.getActionCommand();

    //Additional code to check for each menu item...

    //Check for the Help/About menu item
    if (strMenuItem.equals("About"))
    {
        //Pass the name of the frame from this app as the argument
        AboutDialog frmAbout = new AboutDialog(frmMenu);
    }
}
```

Displaying a Dialog with Error Messages

You can create your own dialog class to display error messages to the user when validating input data (Figure 10.8). Extend your new class from Dialog and allow the program to pass a message string and the title to the new class.

Figure 10.8

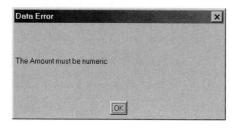

A new MsgDialog class based on Dialog. This dialog displays an error message and customized title.

Creating the MsgDialog Class

```java
//Folder:          Ch10MsgBox
//Programmer:      Bradley/Millspaugh
//Date:            6/2001
//ClassName:       MsgDialog
//Description:     Dialog box to display a message to the user.

import java.awt.*;
import java.awt.event.*;

public class MsgDialog extends Dialog implements ActionListener
{
    //Create components
    Button btnOK = new Button("OK");

    //Constructor
    public MsgDialog(Frame frmParent, String strMessage, String strTitle)
    {
        //Call the parent's constructor
        super(frmParent, strTitle, true);

        //Set up dialog box
        add("Center", new Label(strMessage));
        Panel pnlButtons = new Panel(new FlowLayout());
        pnlButtons.setLayout(new FlowLayout());
        pnlButtons.add(btnOK);
        add("South", pnlButtons);
        btnOK.addActionListener(this);

        //Listen for close box
        addWindowListener(new WindowAdapter()
        {
            public void windowClosing(WindowEvent event)
            {
                dispose(); //Destroy the dialog
            }
        });
        setSize(400,200);
        show();
    }

    public void actionPerformed(ActionEvent event)
    {
        //Destroy the dialog when button is pressed
        dispose();
    }
}
```

Displaying the Dialog for Invalid Data

In the main application, when the user clicks on the OK button, you can validate the data. For any bad input data, you can pass an error message and the dialog title, as well as the application's frame, and display the MsgDialog dialog box. Note that you can see this entire application in Ch10Msgbox.

```java
public void actionPerformed(ActionEvent event)
    {
        //Validate data and calculate
        String strMessage;
```

```
    try
    {
        if (txtName.getText().equals(""))
        {
            strMessage = "The Name is a required entry";
            MsgDialog msgBox = new MsgDialog(frmMain, strMessage, "Data Error");
            txtName.selectAll();
            txtName.requestFocus();
        }
        else
        {
            fltAmount = Float.valueOf(txtAmount.getText()).floatValue();
            if (fltAmount < 0)
            {
                    strMessage = "The Amount must be positive";
                    MsgDialog msgBox = new MsgDialog(frmMain, strMessage, "Data Error");
                    txtAmount.selectAll();
                    txtName.requestFocus();
            }
            else //Passed the validation
            {
                    fltAmountTotal += fltAmount;
                    lblAmountTotal.setText("" + fltAmountTotal);
                    txtName.setText("");
                    txtAmount.setText("");
                    txtName.requestFocus();
            }
        }
    }

    catch(NumberFormatException exc)
    {
        strMessage = "The Amount must be numeric";
        MsgDialog msgBox = new MsgDialog(frmMain, strMessage, "Data Error");
        txtAmount.selectAll();
        txtAmount.requestFocus();
    }

}
```

Feedback 10.3

1. What statement(s) belong in the constructor for a new class extended from Dialog?
2. Write the statement to make a dialog appear and to make it disappear.
3. What is the default visibility of a dialog?
4. Why can't you write a dialog class that extends WindowAdapter?

Multiple Frames

An application can display more than one frame. You may want to allow the user to make a menu choice that switches to a different window.

```
Frame frmMain = new Frame("Main ");
Frame frmTwo = new Frame("Frame Two");
```

You generally declare all of your frame objects and then call a `show` method for the one that you wish to display. Notice in the following `action-Performed` method that the Display Frame Two menu item calls a method that formats and displays the second frame. The OK button on the second frame is used to return to the first. You can use another menu on the second frame, if you prefer.

```java
public void actionPerformed(ActionEvent event)
{
    //Determine which menu item was selected
    String strMenuItem = event.getActionCommand();

    //Additional code to check for other menu items...

    if (strMenuItem.equals("Display Frame Two"))
        showFrameTwo();

    if (event.getSource() == btnClose)
        frmTwo.dispose();    //Delete second frame
        //To hide the frame use frmTwo.toBack();
}

public void showFrameTwo()
{
    //Set up and display the second frame
    frmTwo.setLayout(new FlowLayout());
    frmTwo.add(btnClose);
    btnClose.addActionListener(this);
    frmTwo.setSize(400, 200);
    frmTwo.show();
}
```

You can find the complete program showing this code in Ch10Multiple-Frames.

Popup Menus

Java 2 has an additional type of menu: the popup menu. A popup menu, also called a *shortcut menu* or a *context menu*, appears when the user right-clicks on a component (Figure 10.9). The **PopupMenu class** is a subclass of the Menu class.

Figure 10.9

A popup menu appears when the user right-clicks on the component.

You create a popup menu by first declaring the menu, adding menu items to the menu, and adding the menu to the component for which the menu should appear. You must also add a mouse listener to the component. In the mouse event method, you check to see if the user clicked the right mouse button. If so, you display the popup menu.

Creating the Menu

Add your menu items to the popup menu in the same way you do for a menu bar. The following code segment demonstrates the use of an array to add the menu items.

```
public void DesignMenu()
{
    //Add items to the popup menu
    String[] strMenuLabels = new String[]{"Red","Blue","Green"};

    for(int intIndex = 0; intIndex < strMenuLabels.length; intIndex++)
    {
        MenuItem mnuItem = new MenuItem(strMenuLabels[intIndex]);
        mnuPopup.add(mnuItem);
    }
}
```

Adding the Menu and a MouseListener

Since you only want to have the menu display for a given component, you must add the menu to the component. Also be sure to add the mouse listener to the component and add `implements MouseListener` to the class declaration.

```
//Add the menu to the component
lblMessage.add(mnuPopup);

//Add the mouse listener to the component
lblMessage.addMouseListener(this);

//Add the action listener to the menu
mnuPopup.addActionListener(this);
```

Showing the Popup Menu

A popup menu usually displays with a right-click of the mouse. However, a system can be set for different mouse actions. The mouse event's isPopupTrigger property is set for the current operating system so that you can check for the right mouse button. Show the popup menu when the isPopupTrigger property of the MouseEvent is true. Note that isPopupTrigger is set for the mouseReleased event, but not for the other mouse events, such as mousePressed or mouseClicked.

```
public void mouseReleased(MouseEvent event)
{
    //Check for right mouse button
    if (event.isPopupTrigger())
        mnuPopup.show(lblMessage, event.getX(), event.getY());
}
```

Notice that the show method has three arguments. The first argument indicates the component; the second and third are the *x* and *y* positions on the screen where the menu should appear. In this case we want to find out where the mouse is and display the menu in the same location.

Remember that we are implementing the MouseListener interface, so we must code each of the mouse events, even those we aren't using.

```
//Folder:         Ch10PopupMenu
//Programmer:     Bradley/Millspaugh
//Date:           6/2001
//ClassName:      PopupMenuApplet
//Description:    Demonstrate a popup menu.

import java.applet.*;
import java.awt.*;
import java.awt.event.*;

public class PopupMenuApplet extends Applet implements ActionListener, MouseListener
{
    PopupMenu mnuPopup = new PopupMenu();
    Label lblMessage = new Label("Right click on this label");

    public void init()
    {
        DesignMenu();
        add(lblMessage);
        lblMessage.add(mnuPopup);
        lblMessage.addMouseListener(this);
        mnuPopup.addActionListener(this);
    }

    public void DesignMenu()
    {
        //Add items to the popup menu
        String[] strMenuLabels = new String[]{"Red" "Blue" "Green"};

        for(int intIndex = 0; intIndex < strMenuLabels.length; intIndex++)
        {
            MenuItem mnuItem = new MenuItem(strMenuLabels[intIndex]);
            mnuPopup.add(mnuItem);
        }
    }

    public void actionPerformed(ActionEvent event)
    {
        //Determine which menu item was selected
        String strMenuItem = event.getActionCommand();

        if (strMenuItem.equals("Red"))
            lblMessage.setForeground(Color.red);
        else if (strMenuItem.equals("Blue"))
            lblMessage.setForeground(Color.blue);
        else if (strMenuItem.equals("Green"))
            lblMessage.setForeground(Color.green);
    }
```

```
public void mouseReleased(MouseEvent event)
{
    //Check for right mouse button
    if (event.isPopupTrigger())
        mnuPopup.show(lblMessage, event.getX(), event.getY());
}
public void mousePressed(MouseEvent event)
{}
public void mouseClicked(MouseEvent event)
{}
public void mouseEntered(MouseEvent event)
{}
public void mouseExited(MouseEvent event)
{}
}
```

A Swing Application

You can easily create an application using Swing components. Instead of extending JApplet, as you did for an applet, you can extend JFrame or JPanel.

```
public class SwingApplication extends JFrame
```

Adding Swing Components

Declare your Swing components at the top of the class, as you normally do. When you add the components to the user interface, you must add them to the content pane. You can either declare a container to be the content pane and add components to the container or use the getContentPane method to add directly to the content pane.

```
//Declare a container to use for content pane
Container conContentPane = getContentPane();
conContentPane.add(lblMessage, "Center");
```

or

```
//Add directly to the content pane
getContentPane().add(lblMessage, "Center");
```

The following lines of code apply to the frame. The title appears in the title bar of the window.

```
setTitle("Swing Application");
setSize(250, 350);
setVisible(true);
```

In the main method, instantiate an object of your class.

```
public static void main(String args[])
{
    SwingApplication Demo = new SwingApplication();
    Demo.createUI();
}
```

Using the Swing JTabbedPane

Using the JTabbedPane component, you can add tabbed panes to an application. Tabbed panes, also sometimes called *tabbed dialogs* or *tabbed pages*, allow you to display different information on different pages. Each page has a notebook-style tab that the user can use to select the page. The JTabbedPane allows you to choose the location of the tabs (top, bottom, left, or right). Figure 10.10 shows a Swing application with tabs at the top.

Figure 10.10

a.   b.

The Swing JTabbedPane creates tabs that allow the user to switch pages.

To use a JTabbedPane, first declare an instance of the class. Use the SwingConstants to specify the location of the tabs.

```
JTabbedPane tabs = new JTabbedPane(SwingConstants.TOP);
```

Then add the individual tabs to the JTabbedPane and add the pane to the content pane. The addTab method allows you to specify the label that you want to appear on the tab and the component that you want to appear on the tab page. In this case, we are adding one label to the page, but you could define a panel with many components and add that instead.

```
tabs.addTab("Hello", lblHello);
tabs.addTab("Goodbye", lblGoodbye);
Container conContentPane = getContentPane();
conContentPane.add(tabs, "Center");
```

The JTabbedPane Swing Application

Here is the code for the entire application. Figure 10.10 shows the output.

```
//Folder:      Ch10SwingApplication
//Programmer:  Bradley/Millspaugh
//Date:        6/2001
```

```
//ClassName:      SwingApplication
//Description     Use a JFrame and a JTabbedPane to create tabbed panes.

import javax.swing.*;
import java.awt.*;
import java.awt.event.*;

public class SwingApplication extends JFrame
{
    //Declare components
    private JLabel lblHello = new JLabel("Hello World!");
    private JLabel lblGoodbye = new JLabel("Goodbye!");
    JFrame frmMain = new JFrame("Swing Application");

    //Declare tabs
    JTabbedPane tabs = new JTabbedPane(SwingConstants.TOP);

    public static void main(String args[])
    {
        SwingApplication Demo = new SwingApplication();
        Demo.createUI();
    }

    private void createUI()
    {
        frmMain.addWindowListener(new WindowAdapter()
        {
            public void windowClosing(WindowEvent event)
            {
                System.exit(0);
            }
        });
        tabs.addTab("Hello", lblHello);
        tabs.addTab("Goodbye", lblGoodbye);
        Container conContentPane = getContentPane();
        conContentPane.add(tabs, "Center");
        setTitle("Swing Application");
        setSize(250,350);
        setVisible(true);
    }
}
```

Running as an Application or an Applet

At times you may want to write one program that can be run as either an applet or an application. Perhaps your user doesn't have access to the Internet and wants to run without a browser. Or maybe you want to write a program for some users that prefer applets and other users that do not have browsers.

Converting an Applet to an Application

It's generally easier to convert an applet to an application, rather than the other way around. Some things you can do with frames you simply cannot do with applets, such as display a menu bar.

Remember that an applet is a panel that contains its components. In an application's `main` method, you can create an instance of an applet and add the applet to a frame, essentially displaying the applet panel in a window.

In the following example, we will convert the Ch10PopupMenuApplet to a program that can run as either an applet or an application. We will add a static boolean variable to indicate whether the program is running as an applet or an application, and add a `main` method. When you run the program as an application, the `main` method executes; when you run as an applet, execution begins with the `init` method.

```
static boolean blnApplet = true; //Indicate whether running as applet
```

Later you can test the value of the boolean variable. For example, the `showStatus` method is valid only for an applet, and you can close a window only in an application.

```
if (blnApplet)
{
    showStatus ("Color changed to " + strMenuItem);
}
```

The main Method

In the `main` method, you set blnApplet to false, to indicate that the program is running as an application. You also declare a frame for the application window, create an instance of the applet, and add the applet to the frame:

```
public static void main(String args[])
{
    blnApplet = false;
    Frame frmMain = new Frame("Popup Menu Application");
    PopupMenuApplet aplPopup = new PopupMenuApplet();
    frmMain.add("Center", aplPopup);
```

The next step is to add a WindowAdapter to make the window's close box operational:

```
    frmMain.addWindowListener(new WindowAdapter()
    {
        public void windowClosing(WindowEvent event)
        {
            System.exit(0);
        }
    });
```

Next, set the size of the frame:

```
    frmMain.setSize(300, 300);
```

Execute the method to start the applet running:

```
    aplPopup.init();
```

And finally, show the frame:

```
    frmMain.show();
}
```

The Applet/Application Program

Here is the complete code of the program, which you can run as an application
or as an applet.

```
//Folder:        Ch10AppApplet
//Programmer:    Bradley/Millspaugh
//Date:          6/2001
//ClassName:     PopupMenuApplet
//Description:   An applet that can also be run as an application.
//               Displays a popup menu.

import java.applet.*;
import java.awt.*;
import java.awt.event.*;

public class PopupMenuApplet extends Applet implements ActionListener, MouseListener
{
    PopupMenu mnuPopup = new PopupMenu();
    Label lblMessage = new Label("Right click on this label");
    static boolean blnApplet = true;

    public void init()
    {
        DesignMenu();
        add(lblMessage);
        lblMessage.add(mnuPopup);
        lblMessage.addMouseListener(this);
        mnuPopup.addActionListener(this);
    }

    public static void main(String args[])
    {
        blnApplet = false;
        Frame frmMain = new Frame("Popup Menu Application");
        PopupMenuApplet aplPopup = new PopupMenuApplet();
        frmMain.add("Center", aplPopup);
        frmMain.addWindowListener(new WindowAdapter()
        {
            public void windowClosing(WindowEvent event)
            {
                System.exit(0);
            }
        });
        frmMain.setSize(300, 300);
        aplPopup.init();
        frmMain.show();
    }

    public void DesignMenu()
    {
        //Add items to the popup menu
        String[] strMenuLabels = new String[]{"Red","Blue","Green"};
```

```
        for(int intIndex = 0; intIndex < strMenuLabels.length; intIndex++)
        {
            MenuItem mnuItem = new MenuItem(strMenuLabels[intIndex]);
            mnuPopup.add(mnuItem);
        }
    }

    public void actionPerformed(ActionEvent event)
    {
        //Determine which menu item was selected
        String strMenuItem = event.getActionCommand();

        if (strMenuItem.equals("Red"))
            lblMessage.setForeground(Color.red);
        else if (strMenuItem.equals("Blue"))
            lblMessage.setForeground(Color.blue);
        else if (strMenuItem.equals("Green"))
            lblMessage.setForeground(Color.green);
        if (blnApplet)
        {
            showStatus ("Color changed to " + strMenuItem);
        }
    }

    public void mouseReleased(MouseEvent event)
    {
        //Check for right mouse button
        if (event.isPopupTrigger())
            mnuPopup.show(lblMessage, event.getX(), event.getY());
    }
    public void mousePressed(MouseEvent event)
    {}
    public void mouseClicked(MouseEvent event)
    {}
    public void mouseEntered(MouseEvent event)
    {}
    public void mouseExited(MouseEvent event)
    {}
}
```

Understanding Execution

The app/applet program has both an `init` method and a `main` method. When the program runs as an applet, execution begins with the `init` method. When run as an application, execution begins with the `main` method. Notice that the `main` method calls the `init` method, so an application executes both methods. However, when running as an applet, the `main` method does not execute. Verify this by following the execution path as an applet and as an application.

Running an Application from the Command Line

After you compile a Java application, you can run it from the command line using Sun's java command. In Windows, open an MS-DOS Prompt window. The format of the command is

```
java -cp ClassPath Classname
```

For example, to run the Ch10AppApplet project as an application, type this command in a MS-DOS prompt window:

```
java -cp a:\CH10AppApplet PopupMenuApplet
```

Your Hands-on Programming Example

Create an application that contains a menu bar. There should be menus for
File, Edit, and Help. The File menu items are Save (disabled), a separator line,
and Exit. Edit contains a Bold check box menu item and a submenu called
Color. The Color submenu has three menu items: Red, Green, and Blue. The
only item on the Help menu is About.

Make all of the menu items active except for Save. Make the Exit option
terminate the application. The window's close box should also terminate the
application.

Place a label on the frame that contains your name in a Bold font. The color
options will change the color of the text in the label. The Bold menu item will
be checked initially and then will change state each time it is selected. When
the Bold menu item is checked, the label should be in bold.

The About option on the Help menu will display a dialog that contains
identifying information about the application, including your name.

Planning the Project

Figure 10.11 shows one possible layout for the applet.

Figure 10.11

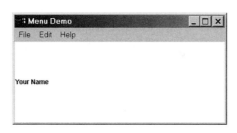

A possible user interface for the
chapter hands-on example.

Plan the User Interface

Figure 10.12 shows the class diagram.

Figure 10.12

The class diagram for the hands-
on example.

Class: MenuApp	
Methods	**Variables and Components**
init	frmMenu
createInterface	lblName
actionPerformed	fntBold
itemStateChanged	fntPlain
windowClosing	mnuMain
	mnuFile
	mnuEdit
	mnuHelp
	mnuEditColor
	mnuFileSave
	mnuFileExit
	mnuEditBold
	myMenuApp
	frmAbout

Class: AboutDialog	
Methods	**Variables and Components**
Public Methods	**Instance Variables**
AboutDialog	btnOK
actionPerformed	lblProgrammer

Plan the Objects and Properties

Class Name: MenuApp

Properties:

Access Mode (public or private)	Variable or Component Name	Data Type or Class	Description
	frmMenu	Frame	Main window.
	lblName	Label	Display the name.
	fntBold	Font	Times New Roman bold font.
	fntPlain	Font	Times New Roman plain font.
	mnuMain	MenuBar	Menu bar for main window.
	mnuFile	Menu	File menu.
	mnuEdit	Menu	Edit menu.
	mnuHelp	Menu	Help menu.
	mnuEditColor	Menu	Color submenu.
	mnuFileSave	MenuItem	File / Save menu item.
	mnuFileExit	MenuItem	File / Exit menu item.
	mnuEditBold	CheckBoxMenuItem	Menu option to change the font style.
	myMenuApp	MenuApp	Instance of this application.
	frmAbout	AboutDialog	About dialog to display from Help / About.

Methods:

Access Mode (public or private)	Return Type	Method Name (include any parameters)	Pseudocode
public	static void	`main(String args[])`	Create an instance of the application. Create the user interface.
public	void	`createInterface()`	Create the menu bar, menus, and menu items. Add action listeners to menus. Attach menu bar to the frame. Add the components to the frame. Add a window listener to the frame. Set the size and show the frame.

continued

Access Mode (public or private)	Return Type	Method Name (include any parameters)	Pseudocode
public	void	actionPerformed(ActionEvent)	Determine event that caused the action. If Exit, terminate the program. If Color, set the appropriate text color for the label. If About, display the About dialog.
public	void	itemStateChanged(ItemEvent)	If Bold selected Set label to bold. else Set label to plain font.
public	void	windowClosing	Exit to the operating system.

Class Name: AboutDialog

Properties:

Access Mode (public or private)	Variable or Component Name	Data Type or Class	Description
	lblProgrammer	Label	Display the programmer's name.
	btnOK	Button	Button to close the dialog.

Methods:

Access Mode (public or private)	Return Type	Method Name (include any parameters)	Pseudocode
public		AboutDialog(Frame)	Call the parent constructor. Set the layout manager. Add components. Add the action listener for the button. Set the size and show the dialog.
public	void	actionPerformed(ActionEvent)	If OK button is clicked destroy the dialog.

Write the Project

- Follow the plan to create the two classes and add components to the classes.

- Write the appropriate statements in each method.

- When you complete the code, thoroughly test the project.

The Project Solution

The MenuApp Class

```
//Folder:        Ch10HelpMenu
//Programmer:    Bradley/Millspaugh
//Date:          6/2001
//ClassName:     MenuApp
//Description:   An application with a menu bar, menu items, a submenu,
//               a Checkbox menu item, and a Help menu that displays
//               an About dialog.

import java.awt.*;
import java.awt.event.*;

public class MenuApp extends WindowAdapter implements ActionListener, ItemListener
{
    //Declare components
    Frame frmMenu = new Frame("Menu Demo");
    Label lblName = new Label("Your Name");
    Font fntBold = new Font("Times New Roman", Font.BOLD, 12);
    Font fntPlain = new Font("Times New Roman", Font.PLAIN, 12);

    //Menu components
    MenuBar mnuMain = new MenuBar();
    Menu mnuFile = new Menu("File");
    Menu mnuEdit = new Menu("Edit");
    Menu mnuHelp = new Menu("Help");
    Menu mnuEditColor = new Menu("Color");

    //Menu items
    MenuItem mnuFileSave = new MenuItem("Save");
    MenuItem mnuFileExit = new MenuItem("Exit");
    CheckboxMenuItem mnuEditBold = new CheckboxMenuItem("Bold", true);

    public static void main(String args[])
    {
        //Instantiate the application
        MenuApp myMenuApp = new MenuApp();
        myMenuApp.createInterface();
    }

    public void createInterface()
    {
        //Create the menu bar
        //File menu
        mnuMain.add(mnuFile);
        mnuFile.addActionListener(this);
        mnuFile.add(mnuFileSave);
        mnuFileSave.setEnabled(false);
        mnuFile.addSeparator();
        mnuFile.add(mnuFileExit);

        //Edit menu
        mnuMain.add(mnuEdit);
        mnuEdit.addActionListener(this);
        mnuEdit.add(mnuEditBold);
```

```java
        mnuEditBold.addItemListener(this);
        mnuEdit.add(mnuEditColor);
        mnuEditColor.addActionListener(this);
        mnuEditColor.add("Red");
        mnuEditColor.add("Blue");
        mnuEditColor.add("Green");

        //Help menu
        mnuMain.add(mnuHelp);
        mnuHelp.addActionListener(this);
        mnuHelp.add(new MenuItem("About"));

        //Attach the menu bar to the frame
        frmMenu.setMenuBar(mnuMain);

        //Set up the components and the frame
        lblName.setFont(fntBold);
        frmMenu.add(lblName);
        frmMenu.addWindowListener(this);
        frmMenu.setSize(400, 200);
        frmMenu.show();
    }

    public void actionPerformed(ActionEvent event)
    {
        //Determine which menu item was selected
        String strMenuItem = event.getActionCommand();

        if (strMenuItem.equals("Exit"))
            System.exit(0); //Exit to the operating system
        else if (strMenuItem.equals("Red"))
            lblName.setForeground(Color.red);
        else if (strMenuItem.equals("Blue"))
            lblName.setForeground(Color.blue);
        else if (strMenuItem.equals("Green"))
            lblName.setForeground(Color.green);
        else if (strMenuItem.equals("About"))
        {
            AboutDialog frmAbout = new AboutDialog(frmMenu);
        }
    }

    public void itemStateChanged(ItemEvent event)
    {
        //Determine state of Checkbox menu item
        int intState = event.getStateChange();

        if (intState == event.SELECTED)
            lblName.setFont(fntBold);
        else
            lblName.setFont(fntPlain);
    }

    public void windowClosing(WindowEvent event)
    {
        //Exit to the operating system
        System.exit(0);
    }
}
```

The AboutDialog Class

```java
//Folder:        Ch10HelpMenu
//Programmer:    Bradley/Millspaugh
//Date:          6/2001
//ClassName:     AboutDialog
//Description:   Dialog box to display info about the application.

import java.awt.*;
import java.awt.event.*;

public class AboutDialog extends Dialog implements ActionListener
{
    //Create components
    Button btnOK = new Button("OK");
    Label lblProgrammer = new Label(" Programmer: Bradley/Millspaugh ");

    //Constructor
    public AboutDialog(Frame frmParent)
    {
        //Call the parent's constructor
        super(frmParent, "About My Application", true);
        setLayout(new FlowLayout());
        add(lblProgrammer);
        add(btnOK);
        btnOK.addActionListener(this);

        //Listen for close box
        addWindowListener(new WindowAdapter()
        {
            public void windowClosing(WindowEvent event)
            {
                dispose(); //Destroy the dialog
            }
        });
        setSize(220, 100);
        show();
    }

    public void actionPerformed(ActionEvent event)
    {
        //Destroy the dialog when OK is pressed
        Object objSource = event.getSource();

        if(objSource == btnOK)
            dispose();//Destroy the dialog
    }
}
```

Summary

1. An application runs from the operating system, rather than from a browser.
2. An application begins execution with a `main` method, rather than `init`.
3. A graphical application must create its output in a container. Usually the container is a frame, which is a top-level window with a title bar, borders, and minimize, maximize/restore, and close buttons.

4. The default layout manager for a frame is the BorderLayout.

5. To make a frame's close button function, you must use a listener and close the window. You can implement the WindowListener interface or extend the WindowAdapter class to listen for the windowClosing event.

6. It's best to declare an instance of an application in the `main` method so that all variables and methods refer to the current instance.

7. A frame can contain a menu bar, which consists of individual menus. In turn, each menu contains menu items.

8. Menu items may be disabled at design time or run time.

9. To represent a check mark on a menu item, a special class of menu item called a CheckboxMenuItem is used.

10. Use the `addSeparator` method to add a separator line to a menu.

11. A submenu is a menu added to another menu.

12. The events for a menu are handled by an action listener. The action listener can be added to an individual menu item or to an entire menu. Check box menu items use an item listener.

13. Menus can be modified during program execution. It is possible to add menus or menu items, remove menus or menu items, change the enabled state, or check the state of a menu item.

14. A dialog is a popup window that is commonly used for messages. The dialog can be modal, requiring the user to respond to the dialog before continuing on with the program, or nonmodal. Nonmodal dialogs do not require a response from the user prior to working with other windows.

15. A dialog belongs to a parent frame.

16. An application can selectively display multiple frames.

17. A popup menu is a shortcut menu that appears when the user right-clicks a component. Create a popup menu using the PopupMenu class and adding menu items to the menu. You add a mouse listener and check the isPopup-Trigger property to display the popup menu.

18. A Swing application uses the Swing components JFrame and JPanel. The JTabbedPane will create tabbed pages that can have different content.

19. To convert an applet to an application, you must add a `main` method. You can create one program that will run as either an applet or an application if it has both an `init` and a `main` method.

Key Terms

`addSeparator` method *303*	Menu class *301*
application *294*	MenuBar class *301*
CheckboxMenuItem *303*	MenuItem class *302*
Dialog class *309*	PopupMenu class *315*
Frame *294*	`setEnabled` method *303*
`main` method *296*	submenu *304*

Review Questions

1. What are the differences between applications and applets?
2. What method runs initially in a stand-alone application?

3. What is the purpose of the array of strings argument in the `main` method?
4. What are the differences between using a frame and using a panel?
5. Describe two ways to listen for and respond to the user's clicking a window's close box.
6. Distinguish between a menu bar, a menu, and a menu item.
7. How can you create a disabled menu item? A checked menu item?
8. How do you create a submenu?
9. What does the term *popup menu* mean? How is one created?
10. What is a dialog? Give an example of when a dialog would be useful.
11. Describe how you could convert an applet into an application.

Programming Exercises

10.1 Create an application that displays your name, address, and phone number in a window. Include a menu bar with these menu choices:

File	Help
Exit	About

Include a popup menu that allows the user to change the color of the text of your name and address information. Make sure that the window closes when the user clicks the window's close box.

10.2 Create an application that calculates the amounts due for repairs at Pat's Auto Repair Shop.

The main menus:

File	Process	Help
Exit	Calculate	About
	Clear	

The window must have text fields for the user to enter the job number, customer name, amount charged for parts, and the hours of labor. Include labels to display output for Parts, Labor, SubTotal, Sales Tax, and Total.

The Calculate menu item finds the charges and displays the result in labels. Sales tax is charged only on parts, not on labor. The tax rate and the hourly labor charge should be set up as named constants so that they can be easily modified if either changes. Current charges are $30 per hour for labor and 8 percent (0.08) for the sales tax rate.

10.3 Modify project 10.2 to maintain summary information for the total dollar amount for parts, labor, sales tax, and total for all customers.

Add a Summary menu item under the Process menu with a separator bar between the two menu items. When the user selects the Summary item, display the summary information in a text area or a summary area at the bottom of the window.

10.4 Modify project 10.3 to include multiple frames. Place the summary on a separate frame.

10.5 A battle is raging over the comparative taste of Prune Punch and Apple Ade. Each taste tester rates the two drinks on a scale of 1 to 10 (10 being best). The proof of the superiority of one over the other will be the average score for the two drinks. Create an application with these menus:

The menus:

File	Help
Summary	About
Exit	

Input the test results for each drink. Include an OK button and a Cancel button.

When the user clicks the OK button, add the score for each type of drink to the drink's total, clear the text boxes, and reset the focus. If either score is blank when the OK button is pressed, display a message in a dialog box and reset the focus to the box for the missing data. (*Hint:* Use separate try/catch blocks.)

Summary menu item:

The Summary command displays a frame that contains the current results of the taste test. It should display the winner, the total number of taste testers, and the average rating for each drink. Include an OK button that returns to the startup frame. (The user will be able to display the summary at any time and as often as desired.)

The About dialog:

The About dialog should display information about the program and the programmer. Include an OK button that returns the user to the main form.

CASE STUDIES

R 'n R—for Reading and Refreshment

1. Modify your case project so that it can be executed as a stand-alone application or as an applet in a browser.

or

2. Convert your case project into an application with a frame and menu bar. Remove the Choice menu and make the commands available from menu commands. Include a Help / About menu item that displays an About dialog.

Merry Pea's Quilting

1. Modify your case project so that it can be executed as a stand-alone application or as an applet in a browser.

or

2. Convert your case project into an application with a frame and menu bar. Remove the Calculate button and make the command available from a menu command. Include a Help / About menu item that displays an About dialog.

11

Multimedia in Java: Images, Sounds, and Animation

At the completion of this chapter, you will be able to . . .

1. Enhance your applet with graphics and sound.

2. Draw graphics on a container using the `paint` method.

3. Load an image file into a project.

4. Generate sounds with the `play` method.

5. Create animation using multiple images, moving images, and animated .gif files.

Many programmers think of the primary purpose of Java as incorporating animation and sound on Web pages. Although Java contains graphics methods for primitive drawing, this chapter concentrates on techniques for incorporating multimedia files into your projects. You will learn how to use the `paint` method to write to the screen. You will also load images and sounds from files and create animation.

Graphics

The term *graphics* in Java refers to any text, drawing, image, or icon that you display on the screen. Each time an applet or a window displays, is resized, or is moved, the object's `paint` method executes. So far, in all applets and applications, we have allowed the container's `paint` method to execute automatically. But in this chapter we will override the `paint` method so we can place graphic objects on the screen for each repaint.

To create a Graphics object, you must include the java.awt.Graphics package. You usually create an object of the Graphics class, set any color or font properties you want, and specify the text and/or drawing in the **paint method.**

The paint Method

Whether you write an applet or an application, the `paint` method executes automatically and draws the screen. For an applet, `paint` executes after `init`; for an application, `paint` runs after `main`. Then every time the window is resized, maximized, minimized, moved, or uncovered, `paint` executes again. Any components that you placed on the container (applet or window) are redrawn automatically. But if you draw graphics on the screen, say in the `init` or `main` method, those are not redrawn by the `paint` method. If you want graphics to redraw every time the container is painted, you must override the `paint` method and place your graphics in your new `paint` method.

The paint Method Header

The `paint` method requires a Graphics object as an argument. You can name the argument anything you want.

```
public void paint(Graphics myGraphicObject)
```

```
public void paint(Graphics gr)
```

Drawing Text

You can create text on a Graphics object using the **drawString method** of the Graphics class. You specify the string to print and the location (*x* and *y* coordinates). The *x* and *y* coordinates are relative to the upper-left corner of the container.

The Graphics drawString Method—Format

```
drawString(String ValueToPrint, int x, int y )
```

The Graphics drawString Method—Examples

```
gr.drawString("Hi There", 1, 1);
myGraphicObject.drawString("Hello World!", 100, 150);
graScreen.drawString(strCompanyName, intXpos, intYpos);
```

Place the drawString method in the paint method of your applet or application.

The drawString method draws the text in the current font and color. You can use the Font and Color classes that you learned in Chapter 1 to change the font and/or color before drawing the text.

```
myGraphicObject.setFont(fntBigBold);
myGraphicObject.setColor(Color.red);
```

The Hello World Applet Revisited

This applet uses the drawString method to write "Hello World!" on the screen twice (Figure 11.1). The first occurrence uses the default font and color. For the second string, the font and color are changed.

Figure 11.1

Use the drawString *method to draw text directly on the container.*

```
//Folder:         Ch11HelloApplet
//Programmer:     Bradley/Millspaugh
//Date:           6/2001
//ClassName:      HelloApplet
//Description:    Use the paint method to display the Hello World message.

import java.applet.*;
import java.awt.*;

public class HelloWorld extends Applet
{
    //Declare a font
    Font fntBigBold 5 new Font("Arial", Font.BOLD, 20);

    public void init()
    {
        //Set the size of the applet panel
        resize(300, 250);
    }
```

```
public void paint(Graphics myGraphicObject)
{
    //Place a string on the graphics object
    myGraphicObject.drawString("Hello World!", 80, 100);

    //Change the font and color and draw text again
    myGraphicObject.setFont(fntBigBold);
    myGraphicObject.setColor(Color.red);
    myGraphicObject.drawString("Hello World!", 100, 150);
}
}
```

Drawing Graphics

You can also use methods of the Graphics object to draw primitive rectangles, ovals, polygons, and lines. However, most graphics in today's programs incorporate images from files, rather than primitive shapes. See Table 11.1 for a list of the Graphics methods, which specify the shape to draw and its location. You can set the color before drawing and/or filling a shape. This small example draws an open circle and a filled rectangle (Figure 11.2).

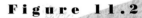

Figure 11.2

Primitive graphics shapes created with the Graphics methods.

```
public void paint(Graphics myGraphicObject)
{
    //Draw a circle in the default color (black)
    //Upper-left "corner": x=80, y=100; Radius=50
    myGraphicObject.drawOval(80, 100, 50, 50);
    //Change the color to blue
    myGraphicObject.setColor(Color.blue);
    //Draw a blue filled rectangle
    //Upper-left corner: x=200, y=100, width=100, height=50
    myGraphicObject.fillRect(200, 100, 100, 50);
}
```

Check the Java documentation for more detail if you desire to draw graphics in this way.

Table 11.1

Selected Methods from the Graphics Class

Method	Purpose
`clearRect(int x, int y, int width, int height)`	Clear a rectangular area by setting it to the container's background color.
`draw3DRect(int x, int y, int width, int height, boolean raised)`	Draw a 3D rectangle.
`drawArc(int x, int y, int width, int height, int startAngle, int arcAngle);`	Draw an arc.
`drawImage(Image img, int x, int y, int width, int height, ImageObserver observer)`	Draw the specified image.
`drawLine(int x1, int y1, int x2, int y2)`	Draw a line from one point to another.
`drawOval(int x, int y, int width, int height)`	Draw an oval.
`drawPolygon(int xPoints[], int yPoints[], int npoints)`	Draw a polygon with nPoints number of points, using arrays to store the points.
`drawRect(int x, int y, int width, int height)`	Draw a rectangle.
`drawRoundRect(int x, int y, int width, int height, int arcWidth, int arcHeight)`	Draw a rectangle with rounded corners.
`drawString(String str, int x, int y)`	Draw a string of text.
`fill3DRect(int x, int y, int width, int height, boolean raised)`	Draw a filled 3D rectangle.
`fillArc(int x, int y, int width, int height, int startAngle, int arcAngle)`	Draw a filled arc.
`fillOval(int x, int y, int width, int height)`	Draw a filled oval.
`fillPolygon(int xPoints[], int yPoints[], int nPoints)`	Draw a filled polygon.
`fillRect(int x, int y, int width, int height)`	Draw a filled rectangle.
`fillRoundRect(int x, int y, int width, int height, int arcWidth, int arcHeight)`	Draw a filled rounded rectangle.
`setColor(Color c)`	Set the color to use for future methods.
`setFont(Font font)`	Set the font to use for future methods.

Feedback 11.1

1. Describe where, on the applet panel, the text will appear for this statement:

   ```
   myGraphicObject.drawString("ABC Company", 10, 50);
   ```

continued

2. Write the statement(s) to draw your name in 14-point, blue, Arial font in approximately the center of an applet panel that is 300 × 300.
3. In what method should the statement(s) from question 2 appear?

Using Image Files

For most graphics in Java, you will use **image files**. An image file usually holds a picture, icon, or text stored in one of the graphic file formats. Java can load image files in .gif or .jpg format.

You can create your own image files or use any that you have available. You can use a draw or paint program to create a drawing, use clip art files, scan pictures using a scanner, or take photos with a digital camera. In each case, you must save the image as a separate file in .gif or .jpg format.

Obtaining the Picture

Use the applet's **getImage method** to retrieve an image file. For this method you can specify the absolute location in the form of an URL object or specify the location and file name separately (the recommended practice).

The getImage Method—General Format

```
getImage(URL)
getImage(URL location, String FileName)
```

The getImage Method—Examples

```
getImage("http://www.site.com/picture.gif")
getImage(getDocumentBase(),"Cup.jpg");
```

The **getDocumentBase method** returns the name of the current folder—the one from which the HTML document was loaded. You can make your projects portable if you always store your image files and applet in the same folder as your HTML document and use the getDocumentBase method to point to the correct location. This technique works whether your applet is running from a local disk, a network, or a Website.

Note: You can also use the getCodeBase method, which returns the location from which the applet was loaded.

It's best to store an image in an **Image object.** You can name the Image object and assign its file name, and then use the image anywhere in the applet. Place the getImage method in your init method.

```
Image imgHello;

public void init()
{
    //Load the image file
    imgHello = getImage(getDocumentBase(),"Hello.gif");
}
```

Displaying the Image

Use the **drawImage method** of the Graphics class to display an image. In each
of the drawImage method formats, you must specify the image, the coordinates
for the upper-left corner, and the object to which the ImageObserver reports.
Your other options include setting the width and the height and/or the background color.

The Graphics drawImage Method—Formats

```
drawImage(Image imgName, int x, int y, ImageObserver this)
drawImage(Image imgName, int x, int y, int width, int height, ImageObserver this)
drawImage(Image imgName, int x, int y, Color backgroundColor, ImageObserver this)
drawImage(Image imgName, int x, int y, int width, int height, Color backgroundColor,
    ImageObserver this)
```

The Graphics drawImage Method—Examples

```
grapicsObject.drawImage(imgCup, 0, 0, this);
graphicsObject.drawImage(imgCup, 100, 75, 75, 75, this);
```

The following program displays an image at full size on the applet panel.
Figure 11.3 shows the applet's output.

Figure 11.3

The drawImage *method displays
a graphic. This graphic was
created with Microsoft's WordArt
program.*

```
//Folder:        Ch11Image
//Programmer:    Bradley/Millspaugh
//Date:          6/2001
//ClassName:     ImageApplet
//Description:   Display an image from a file.

import java.applet.*;
import java.awt.*;

public class ImageApplet extends Applet
```

```
{
   //Declare variables
   Image imgHello;

   public void init()
   {
      //Load the image file
      imgHello = getImage(getDocumentBase(),"Hello.gif");
   }

   public void paint(Graphics screen)
   {
      //Display the image
      screen.drawImage(imgHello, 50, 20, this);
   }
}
```

Your project can contain as many images as you wish, all displaying at once or as events occur.

Adjusting the Size of an Image

You can change the size of an image when you display it by specifying the width and height (Figure 11.4).

```
screen.drawImage(imgHello, 50, 20, 100, 30, this);
```

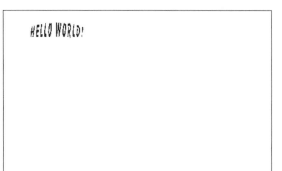

If you want the image to retain its aspect ratio, keep the relative sizes the same as the original. Be aware that the quality of a resized image will never be as good as the original size, because the image is made of a series of dots. When dots must be removed or added, you can't expect to have nice smooth edges. (You can usually improve the quality of a resized image in a graphics application and save the image in the size you want to use.)

The repaint Method

On some occasions you may need to display images other than when the applet starts. You may want to display an image as an event occurs or you may wish to allow the user to select the image. As you know, the `paint` method automatically follows the `init` method as the applet begins. You can cause the screen to redraw at any time by calling the **repaint method.** The `repaint` method requests the **update method** to execute. The `update` method clears the screen and calls the `paint` method.

The following code segment allows the user to select an image from a list. A `switch` statement selects the image to display, and the `repaint` method displays the selected image.

```
public void itemStateChanged(ItemEvent event)
{
    //Check picture choice
    int intChoice = lstPictures.getSelectedIndex();

    switch(intChoice)
    {
        case 0:
            imgChoice = imgCanal;
            break;
        case 1:
            imgChoice = imgColumbia;
            break;
        case 2:
            imgChoice = imgForest;
    }

    repaint();
}
```

Note: You can find this code in the CH11MultipleImages project.

Avoiding Screen Flicker

Sometimes when you draw images on the screen, you see an annoying flicker. The flicker is due to the interaction of the `paint`, `repaint`, and `update` methods. You can write code to avoid the flicker.

The `repaint` method calls the `update` method, which by default clears the container and calls the `paint` method. It's the clearing the screen before calling `paint` that causes the flicker. You can avoid this behavior by writing your own `update` method to override the default method. In your own `update` method, you just call `paint` without first clearing the screen.

```
public void update(Graphics gr)
    {
        //Call the paint method
        paint(gr);
    }
```

Note: Another technique for avoiding screen flicker, called *double-buffering*, uses a second graphics object. You draw graphics to the second object in memory and then when the drawing is complete, paint it to the screen. If you need to totally eliminate the flicker, you will want to research and apply this advanced technique.

Obtaining Images in Applications

Retrieving images in an application is a little different from accessing them in an applet. Since an application does not extend the Applet class, the application cannot use the `Applet.getImage` method. You must use the toolkit that comes from the java.awt.Toolkit class. The toolkit returns platform-specific information about the environment in which the application is running. You must import either java.awt.Toolkit or java.awt.*.

```
imgMove = Toolkit.getDefaultToolkit().getImage("MyPicture.gif");
```

The `getDefaultToolkit` method retrieves the default information for the current system and is required to successfully retrieve an image.

If you write a program that runs as either an applet or application, you must use the correct `getImage` method. Using the toolkit for an applet causes a security violation.

```
if (blnInApplet)
    imgMove = getImage(getDocumentBase(), "MyPicture.gif");
else
    imgMove = Toolkit.getDefaultToolkit().getImage("MyPicture.gif");
```

Deploying Applets with Images

When you deploy an application that includes image files, you must make sure that the images are available. One way to do this, as well as cut down on the number of files that must be transmitted, is to store your applet's class files and image files in a JAR (Java ARchive) file. See Appendix E for information about creating JAR files.

Feedback 11.2

1. Write the statement to load the picture "Winter.jpeg" into imgWinter. Assume that the file is located in the project folder.
2. Code the instruction to display imgWinter when the graphics object is named *gr*. (The image should display as soon as the applet begins.)
3. Write the statement(s) to display imgWinter during program execution, in response to a user action.
4. How can you keep the screen from flickering when you display an image during program execution?

Sound

Like images, sounds also are stored in files, which are referred to as ***audio clips***. Java 2 supports several sound formats: Sun audio files (.au), Windows Wave files (.wav), Macintosh AIFF files (.aif or .aiff), and Musical Instrument Digital Interface (MIDI) files (.mid or .rmi). If you are using an earlier Java version, such as Java 1.1 or Microsoft Visual J++, you are limited to .au files.

Loading and Playing an Audio Clip

Loading and playing an audio clip file is very similar to loading and displaying an image file. You declare an instance of a Java **AudioClip object** to store your sound and use the **getAudioClip method** to retrieve the file into the object. The AudioClip class is part of the applet package, so you must use one of these two statements:

```
import java.applet.*;
```

or

```
import java.applet.AudioClip;
```

Just as with images, you load the sound files during the initialization process.

```
AudioClip sndBong;

public void init()
{
    //Load sound file
    sndBong = getAudioClip(getDocumentBase(),"Bong.wav");
    ...
```

An audio clip object has three methods: **play, loop**, and **stop**. The play and stop do what you would think. The loop plays the sound continuously until stopped.

You could make an applet begin with a sound by placing the play method in the init method.

```
sndBong = getAudioClip(getDocumentBase(),"Bong.wav");
sndBong.play();
```

Stopping an Audio Clip

Make sure that you stop an audio clip after starting it, especially if you started it with the loop method. If the applet is running in a browser and the user switches to another page, the sound does not automatically stop. As you can imagine, your user probably will not appreciate the music.

You can override the applet's stop method, which executes when the applet is no longer active. Stop any sound clips that may be running. *Note:* You can safely stop a sound clip even if it wasn't already running; no error occurs.

```
public void stop()
{
    //Stop the sound clip if it's running
    sndDemo.stop();
}
```

A Sound Applet

The following applet plays a sound file. The applet contains buttons for Play and Stop (Figure 11.5). However, the play button actually calls the loop

method so that the sound plays continuously until stopped. This demo applet
uses an .au sound file so that you can run it with any version of Java. If you are
using Java 2, you can replace the sound file with any .wav, .aif, .midi, or .rmi
format file.

Figure 11.5

*Start and stop the audio clip with
this applet.*

```
//Folder:        Ch11Sounds
//Programmer:    Bradley/Millspaugh
//Date:          6/2001
//ClassName:     SoundApplet
//Description:   Play an audio clip from a file.

import java.applet.Applet;
import java.applet.AudioClip;
import java.awt.*;
import java.awt.event.*;

public class SoundApplet extends Applet implements ActionListener
{
    //Declare variables and components
    AudioClip sndDemo;
    Button btnPlay = new Button("Play");
    Button btnStop = new Button("Stop");

    public void init()
    {
        //Load sound file
        sndDemo = getAudioClip(getDocumentBase(),"spacemusic.au");

        //Set up interface
        add(btnPlay);
        add(btnStop);
        btnPlay.addActionListener(this);
        btnStop.addActionListener(this);
    }

    public void actionPerformed(ActionEvent event)
    {
        //Check for object that caused the event
        Object objSource = event.getSource();

        if (objSource == btnPlay)
            sndDemo.loop();
        else if (objSource == btnStop)
            sndDemo.stop();
    }

    public void stop()
    {
        //Stop the sound clip if it's running
        sndDemo.stop();
    }
}
```

Responding to Mouse Events

You can modify the code for the sound applet so that a mouse event causes the sound to play. Remember that when you implement the MouseListener interface, you must include all five mouse event methods, even if they do not contain any code.

```
public void mouseEntered(MouseEvent event)
{
    // Play the sound
    sndDemo.play(); //Or use loop to play continuously
}

public void mouseExited(MouseEvent event)
{
    //Stop the sound
    sndDemo.stop();
}
```

The mouse listener for this code can be placed on a component. In Ch11MouseEvents, the sound plays when the mouse enters the text field and stops when the mouse exits the text field.

Feedback 11.3

1. Write the statement(s) to declare an object to hold a sound clip. Name the object *sndWelcome*.
2. Write the statement(s) to load and play the sound "WelcomeHome.wav", using the object declared in question 1.

Using the Graphics Object to Print

You can produce printed output by sending a Graphics object to a printer. You can print from either an applet or an application, with some restrictions. It's easy to print from an applet running in the Applet Viewer, but to print from a browser causes a security violation on most systems. Although the security permission levels can be set for each system, by default an applet running in a browser cannot queue a print job. The Java developers felt that allowing an applet to print opened a security hole that would allow a person to print sensitive information.

Applications are not bound by the same security rules as applets and are allowed to print. However, to use the print toolkit that you need, your application must extend Applet. This concept is similar to the programs that you wrote in Chapter 10 that can run as an application or an applet. In the demo print application that follows, the class extends Applet but runs as an application.

Take a look at the code to print the contents of an applet panel on the printer. Each statement is explained in the sections that follow.

```
//Create a print job
PrintJob printer = getToolkit().getPrintJob(frmForPrinting, "Print Demo", null);
if(printer != null)              //Print job not canceled by the user...
{
    //Create a Graphics object to print
    Graphics grPrintPage = printer.getGraphics();
    printAll(grPrintPage); //Print the applet panel as a graphic image
    grPrintPage.dispose(); //Send the page to the printer
    printer.end();         //End the print job
}
```

Note: Printing is broken in the JDK version 1.3.0-C (which comes with JBuilder 4 Foundation). Printing works well in earlier and later versions of the JDK. To change the JDK version for JBuilder 4 Foundation, see Appendix A.

Starting a Print Job

A print job must reference a frame as well as a Graphics object. If you are printing from an applet, you must declare a Frame object, although it isn't necessary to display the frame—it won't be used for any other purpose.

To print, you must create an object from the **PrintJob class**, which comes from the AWT package. This object then calls the getPrintJob method accessed through the AWT toolkit.

```
PrintJob printer = getToolkit().getPrintJob(frmAny, "Job Name", null);
```

The getPrintJob Method—General Format

```
getPrintJob(Frame frameName, String Title, Properties value)
```

The getPrintJob method has three parameters. The first parameter is a frame, the second is a string value for the job title, and the third is for print properties. If you are not setting special print properties, set the third argument to null (empty).

The getPrintJob Method—Examples

```
getPrintJob(frmForPrinting, "", null)
getPrintJob(frmMain, "Print Demo", null)
```

Capturing the Graphics

After you create the print job, you declare a Graphics object and assign it as the object associated with the print job by using the print job's **getGraphics method**.

```
Graphics grPrintPage = printer.getGraphics();
```

Beginning the Print Job

The statement

```
PrintJob printer = getToolkit().getPrintJob(frmForPrinting, "Print Demo", null);
```

begins the print job, gives the job a name, and displays the Print dialog box to the user. If the user clicks the Cancel button, the getPrintJob method returns null instead of a PrintJob object, so you need to test for that before printing:

```
if(printer != null)
{
    Graphics grPrintPage = printer.getGraphics();
```

Printing a Page

You can print a container and all of its components using the container's **print-All method**. This is the method to use to print out an applet panel or the contents of an application's frame.

The printAll Method—General Format

```
container.printAll(Graphics graphicsObject)
```

If you are printing the applet panel, you can omit the container name, or use this instead.

The printAll Method—Examples

```
printAll(grPrintPage);   //Print the current applet panel
this.printAll(grMyPage); //Print the current applet panel
frmMain.printAll(grPrintPage);  //Print the frame called frmMain
```

Sending a Page to the Print Queue

To actually send a page to the print queue, you use the **dispose method** of the Graphics object. The Java documentation says that dispose "flushes" the page. Flushing sends the page off to the print queue and then clears the Graphics object. If you wanted to print multiple pages, you would set up one page, dispose it, set up the next page, and dispose that one.

```
grPrintPage.dispose();    //Send the page to the printer
```

Ending the Print Job

After you have printed all of the pages you want to print, terminate the print job by calling its **end method**.

```
printer.end();    //End the print job
```

Printing Text and Graphics

As you learned earlier in this chapter, you can use methods of the Graphics object to place text and primitive drawing shapes on the Graphics object. If you want to print text, use the `drawString` method of the Graphics object after creating the object but before calling the `dispose` method. Note that, in this case, you are setting up the Graphics object and printing that, rather than printing a container as you did with the `printAll` method.

```
//Create a print job
PrintJob printer = getToolkit().getPrintJob(frmForPrinting, "Print Demo", null);

if(printer != null)                        //Print job not canceled by the user...
{
    //Create a Graphics object to print
    Graphics grPrintPage = printer.getGraphics();

    //Add text to the Graphics object
    grPrintPage.setFont(new Font("Sans Serif", Font.PLAIN, 14));
    grPrintPage.drawString("This is new text", 100, 100);
    grPrintPage.drawString("Second line of text", 100, 120);
    grPrintPage.dispose();         //Send the page to the printer
    printer.end();                 //End the print job
}
```

A Printing Applet

The following applet will print either the applet panel or text, depending on which button the user clicks (Figure 11.6). Notice the `try`/`catch` block, which checks for a security violation. This applet prints when run from the Applet Viewer but displays a message on the status line when run from a browser.

Figure 11.6

Applet can print the current contents of the screen or text, depending on which button the user clicks.

```
//Folder:        Ch11PrintApplet
//Programmer:    Bradley/Millspaugh
//Date:          6/2001
//ClassName:     PrintApplet
//Description:   Print the applet panel as a graphic or print text.

import java.applet.*;
import java.awt.*;
import java.awt.event.*;

public class PrintApplet extends Applet implements ActionListener
{
    //Declare variables and components
    Image imgHello;
```

```
Frame frmForPrinting = new Frame();
Button btnPrintScreen = new Button("Print Screen");
Button btnPrintText = new Button("Print Text");

public void init()
{
    //Load the image file
    imgHello = getImage(getDocumentBase(),"Hello.gif");

    //Lay out the applet panel
    setBackground(Color.white);
    add(btnPrintScreen);
    add(btnPrintText);
    btnPrintScreen.addActionListener(this);
    btnPrintText.addActionListener(this);
}

public void paint(Graphics screen)
{
    //Display the image
    screen.drawImage(imgHello, 50, 50, this);
}

public void actionPerformed(ActionEvent event)
{
    try
    {
        //Create a print job
        PrintJob printer = getToolkit().getPrintJob(frmForPrinting, "Print Demo", null);
        if(printer != null) //Print job not canceled by the user...
        {
            //Create a Graphics object to print
            Graphics grPrintPage = printer.getGraphics();

            //Determine which Print button was clicked
            if (event.getSource()== btnPrintScreen)
            {
                printAll(grPrintPage);    //Print the applet panel as a graphic image
                //Note: Could be written as this.PrintAll(grPrintPage);
            }
            else if (event.getSource()== btnPrintText)
            {
                //Add text to the Graphics object
                grPrintPage.setFont(new Font("Sans Serif", Font.PLAIN, 14));
                grPrintPage.drawString("This is new text", 100, 100);
                grPrintPage.drawString("Second line of text", 100, 120);
            }
            grPrintPage.dispose();              //Send the page to the printer
            printer.end();                      //End the print job
        }
    }

    catch(SecurityException exc)
    {
        showStatus("Printing not allowed by security manager.");
    }
}
}
```

A Printing Application

This demo printing application can print either the application's frame or text,
depending on which menu item the user selects (Figure 11.7). Notice that even
though this is an application, it must extend Applet to use the printer toolkit.

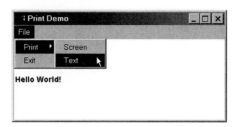

Figure 11.7

*A menu application that can print
the current contents of the screen
or text, depending on which menu
item the user selects.*

```
//Folder:       Ch11PrintMenuApplication
//Programmer:   Bradley/Millspaugh
//Date:         6/2001
//ClassName:    PrintApp
//Description:  A menu application that can print the screen or print text.
//              The extends Applet clause is necessary to use the print toolkit.

import java.awt.*;
import java.awt.event.*;
import java.applet.Applet;

public class PrintApp extends Applet implements ActionListener
{
    //Declare components
    Frame frmMain = new Frame("Print Demo");
    Label lblMessage = new Label("Hello World!");
    Font fntPlain = new Font("Sans Serif", Font.PLAIN, 14);
    Font fntBold = new Font("Sans Serif", Font.BOLD, 14);

    //Menu components
    MenuBar mnuMain = new MenuBar();
    Menu mnuFile = new Menu("File");
    Menu mnuFilePrint = new Menu("Print"); //Submenu
    MenuItem mnuFileExit = new MenuItem("Exit");
    MenuItem mnuFilePrintScreen = new MenuItem("Screen");
    MenuItem mnuFilePrintText = new MenuItem("Text");

    public static void main(String args[])
    {
        PrintApp myPrintApp = new PrintApp();
        myPrintApp.createInterface();
    }

    public void createInterface()
    {
        //Create the menu bar
        mnuMain.add(mnuFile);
        mnuFile.addActionListener(this);
```

```java
        mnuFile.add(mnuFilePrint);
        mnuFilePrint.addActionListener(this);
        mnuFilePrint.add(mnuFilePrintScreen);
        mnuFilePrint.add(mnuFilePrintText);
        mnuFile.add(mnuFileExit);
        frmMain.setMenuBar(mnuMain);

        //Set up the components and the frame
        lblMessage.setFont(fntBold);
        frmMain.add(lblMessage);
        frmMain.addWindowListener(new WindowAdapter()
        {
            public void windowClosing(WindowEvent event)
            {
                System.exit(0);
            }
        });
        frmMain.setSize(400, 200);
        frmMain.show();
    }

    public void actionPerformed(ActionEvent event)
    {
        //Determine which menu item was selected
        String strMenuItem = event.getActionCommand();

        if (strMenuItem.equals("Screen"))
            printScreen();
        else if (strMenuItem.equals("Text"))
            printText();
        else if (strMenuItem.equals("Exit"))
            System.exit(0);                    //Exit to the operating system
    }

    public void windowClosing(WindowEvent event)
    {
        //Exit to the operating system
        System.exit(0);
    }

    private void printScreen()
    {
        //Print the content of the screen as a graphic
        PrintJob printer = getToolkit().getPrintJob(frmMain, "Print Demo", null);
        if (printer ! = null)                //Print job not canceled by the user
        {
            //Create a Graphics object for printing
            Graphics grPrintPage = printer.getGraphics();
            frmMain.printAll(grPrintPage);//Print the form and its components
            grPrintPage.dispose();          //Send the page to the printer
            printer.end();                  //End the print job
        }
    }

    private void printText()
    {
        //Print text as a graphic
        PrintJob printer = getToolkit().getPrintJob(frmMain, "Print Demo", null);
```

```
if (printer ! = null)              //Print job not canceled by the user
{
    //Create a Graphics object for printing
    Graphics grPrintPage = printer.getGraphics();
    grPrintPage.setFont(fntPlain);
    grPrintPage.drawString("This is any string of text that you care to print.",
                           100, 100);
    grPrintPage.drawString("Second line of text.", 100, 120);
    grPrintPage.dispose();         //Send the page to the printer
    printer.end();                 //End the print job
}
}
}
```

Feedback 11.4

1. What actions occur when a `getPrintJob` method executes?
2. Write the statement(s) to capture and print the contents of an applet panel.
3. Write the statement(s) to print your name in text on the printer.
4. Why is it necessary to use the `extends Applet` clause if you are writing an application?

Animation

You can create animation in Java in several different ways. You can quickly display images that differ slightly from each other to give the visual impression of animation, much like the frames of a motion picture. (However, the images on the computer screen display *much* more slowly than those in a movie.) You can move an image across the screen by erasing the image and redrawing it in a new position. Another very easy way to include animation on the screen is to display an animated .gif file, which has the animation built in. Or you can use the Java Media Framework to display animations that can include full-motion video and sound.

To create animation in a Java program that does *anything* besides displaying an animated image, you must learn about threads. **Threads** allow a program to do more than one thing at a time.

Threads

To make your Java applet or application display an animated image and do some other task at the same time, you set up a separate thread for the animation. A program may have several threads running at the same time. What actually happens is that a thread runs for a short time and suspends operation (goes to sleep) so the program can switch to another thread. Each thread has its own code to execute the desired operations, and the computer switches rapidly from one to the next, so it appears that all are executing simultaneously.

Multitasking versus Multithreading

You should be aware of the differences between the terms **multitasking** and **multithreading**. Multitasking allows your computer to appear as though it is running several programs at once. Actually, each program, called a *process*, gets a share of the processor time. Each process executes in a separate area of memory and requires substantial computer resources. A process requires a complete copy of a program's code and data. However, within a single program, you may have multiple tasks to perform. Each of the tasks in the one program can be set up as a *thread*. A thread uses less resources than a process because the thread does not require its own copy of the code and all data. However, the programmer must be very careful about what each thread is doing and with which data items.

You may want to have multiple threads for several reasons. If you want your applet to display animation and also have the user enter information and perform other processing, you can place each task in a separate thread. Some methods, such as connecting to a network or a database, may have to wait for a response. Methods that wait for a response are called *blocking methods*. A blocking method should be placed in a separate thread so that if a problem occurs with the connection, you can interrupt just the thread rather than the entire applet or application.

You can choose from two techniques to set up multiple threads. You can inherit your class from the Thread class or implement the Runnable interface.

The Thread Class

When you extend the Thread class, your program can use any of the methods from the class.

```
public class MyClass extends Thread
```

Perhaps you can see why this technique is not very popular. Because Java does not allow multiple inheritance, you cannot inherit from the Thread class and also from the Applet class. Fortunately there is another way—the Runnable interface.

The Runnable Interface

The solution for avoiding multiple inheritance is to use an interface. Fortunately Java has an interface for threading. You must implement the **Runnable interface**, which allows you to instantiate Thread objects in your class.

```
public class MyApplet extends Applet implements Runnable
```

The Thread Class—Constructors

```
Thread()    //Automatically generates a thread name
Thread(String threadName)
```

The Thread Class—Examples

```
Thread StartupThread;
Thread ImageThreads[];
```

In an applet, declare Thread objects as instance variables at the top of the class. This technique makes the Thread object available in all methods of the applet's class. However, you don't want to use the new keyword to instantiate the thread until you are ready for the thread to begin running.

A thread has a run method that executes when the thread starts. You code the contents of the run method to perform whatever actions you wish. The following method puts the animation thread to sleep while other tasks are being performed.

```
public void run()
    {
        //Keep putting the thread to sleep to allow other processing to occur
        while(true)          //Loop continuously
        {
            try
            {
                //Handle the processing for the thread
                animationThread.sleep(100);       //Pause 100 milliseconds (1/10 second)
                if(intImage > 8)                  //8 images to display
                {
                        intImage = 0;
                }
                repaint();                        //Repaint the screen
            }
            catch(Exception error)
            {
            }
        }
    }
```

Notice the try and catch in this code. For thread processing, you must include exception handling even if you do not code any actions for the error condition.

Thread Methods

The Thread methods that you will use most are run, start, stop, and sleep. Table 11.2 shows other Thread methods.

As already mentioned, the actions that you want to perform in a thread belong in the run method. You can start a thread any time you choose, such as in response to a user action or when an applet begins.

```
//Start the thread for the animation
animationThread = new Thread(this);
animationThread.start();
```

You should stop a thread's execution when the applet ends. Of course, you can stop the thread at any time you choose in response to a user action.

```
//Stop the thread
animationThread.stop();
```

The `sleep` method pauses a thread the specified number of milliseconds. If your program has more than one operation occurring, such as animation and user input, you need to pause so that the other actions can occur. And if you are performing animation, the pause helps to slow the animation so that each image can display and the eye can view each image.

```
animationThread.sleep(1000);     //Pause 1000 milliseconds (1 second)
```

Table 11.2

Selected Thread methods

Method	Purpose
`activeCount()`	Returns number of threads running (currently not stopped).
`currentThread()`	Returns a reference to the thread currently running.
`destroy()`	Ends the thread without cleanup.
`getName()`	Returns the name of the current thread.
`getPriority()`	Returns the priority level of a thread.
`isAlive()`	Determines if the string is still there.
`join()`	Waits for a thread to die. An int or long can be used to indicate the time interval to wait.
`run()`	Contains code that occurs when the thread is executing.
`setName(String threadName)`	Assigns a name to the thread.
`setPriority(int PriorityLevel)`	Assigns the priority level. Constants for priority are MAX_PRIORITY, MIN_PRIORITY, and NORM_PRIORITY.
`sleep(long Interval)`	Specifies a time in milliseconds for the thread to be inactive.
`start()`	Begins execution of a thread.
`stop()`	Halts execution of a thread.
`yield()`	Temporarily halts execution of a thread for other threads to execute.

Note: Java has another type of thread called a *daemon thread*. This type of thread performs its task and then becomes inactive. If only daemon threads are executing, the Java interpreter terminates the project.

Synchronization

Because all threads have access to data, you may find it necessary to coordinate execution so the threads do not **collide**—try to access the data simultaneously. When you **synchronize** the threads, only one thread can deal with the data at a time.

The synchronization can apply to a series of statements or to an entire method. When you place the `synchronized` qualifier on a block of statements, the block is called a *critical section.*

Critical Section

```
synchronized (txaReport)
{
    //Statements modifying txaReport
    //Only one thread can alter txaReport at a time
}
```

Synchronized Method

```
synchronized void methodName()
{
    //Only one thread can be executing this method at one time
}
```

Animating Images

To make an image appear animated, you can display a series of images, each slightly different from the last. One way to implement the series of images is to create an array.

```
Image imgCollection[] = new Image[8];
```

The next step is to load the images into the array elements. You usually do this in an applet's `init` method, so that it occurs only once in the life of the applet.

```
//Load the image files
imgCollection[0] = getImage(getDocumentBase(),"Bird1.gif");
imgCollection[1] = getImage(getDocumentBase(),"Bird2.gif");
imgCollection[2] = getImage(getDocumentBase(),"Bird3.gif");
imgCollection[3] = getImage(getDocumentBase(),"Bird4.gif");
imgCollection[4] = getImage(getDocumentBase(),"Bird5.gif");
imgCollection[5] = getImage(getDocumentBase(),"Bird6.gif");
imgCollection[6] = getImage(getDocumentBase(),"Bird7.gif");
imgCollection[7] = getImage(getDocumentBase(),"Bird8.gif");
```

Just as with single images, you display the image in the `paint` method.

```
public void paint(Graphics gr)
{
    //Display the image and increment the index for the next image
    gr.drawImage(imgCollection[intImage++], 80, 100, this);
}
```

The following applet demonstrates the use of threads and an array of images (Figure 11.8). The applet also contains a text field and a button. When the animation thread is sleeping, the processor is free to work on the text and the button actions.

Figure 11.8

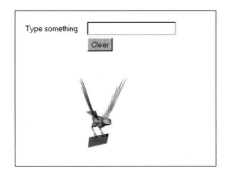

This animation applet displays eight different bird images to give the appearance of a bird in flight.

```
//Folder:          Ch11AnimateImage
//Programmer:      Bradley/Millspaugh
//Date:            6/2001
//ClassName:       AnimationApplet
//Description:     Create animation from multiple images.
//                 The animation runs in a separate thread, so that additional
//                 processing can occur.
//                 The images come from www.mediabuilder.com.

import java.applet.*;
import java.awt.*;
import java.awt.event.*;

public class AnimationApplet extends Applet implements Runnable, ActionListener
{
    //Declare variables and components
    Image imgCollection[] = new Image[8];
    int intImage = 0;
    Thread animationThread;
    TextField txtInput = new TextField(20);
    Button btnClear = new Button("Clear");

    public void init()
    {
        //Load the image files
        imgCollection[0] = getImage(getDocumentBase(),"Bird1.gif");
        imgCollection[1] = getImage(getDocumentBase(),"Bird2.gif");
        imgCollection[2] = getImage(getDocumentBase(),"Bird3.gif");
        imgCollection[3] = getImage(getDocumentBase(),"Bird4.gif");
        imgCollection[4] = getImage(getDocumentBase(),"Bird5.gif");
        imgCollection[5] = getImage(getDocumentBase(),"Bird6.gif");
        imgCollection[6] = getImage(getDocumentBase(),"Bird7.gif");
        imgCollection[7] = getImage(getDocumentBase(),"Bird8.gif");

        //Set up for any other tasks desired
        add(new Label("Type something"));
        add(txtInput);
        add(btnClear);
```

```java
        btnClear.addActionListener(this);
        setBackground(Color.white);
        txtInput.requestFocus();
    }

public void start()
{
    //Start the thread for the animation
    animationThread = new Thread(this);
    animationThread.start();
}

public void stop()
{
    //Stop the thread at the end of the applet
    animationThread.stop();
}

public void run()
{
    //Keep putting the thread to sleep to allow other processing to occur
    while(true)
    {
        try
        {
            animationThread.sleep(100);       //Pause 100 milliseconds (1/10 second)
            intImage++;
            if(intImage >= 8)                 //8 images to display
            {
                    intImage = 0;
            }
            repaint();                        //Repaint the screen (call Update method)
        }

        catch(Exception error)
        {
        }
    }
}

public void paint(Graphics gr)
{
    //Display the image
    gr.drawImage(imgCollection[intImage], 80, 100, this);
}

public void update(Graphics gr)
{
    //Override the update method,
    // so that the screen is not cleared between images.
    paint(gr);
}

public void actionPerformed(ActionEvent event)
{
    //Clear the text box
    txtInput.setText("");
    txtInput.requestFocus();
}
}
```

Waiting for Images to Load

If you have several image files to load, or are loading from a remote location over a slow connection, your program may attempt to display images before they are completely loaded. The getImage method begins retrieving the image and returns; it does not wait for the process to complete. Overall, this is a good thing, since the program can continue with other processing while the image loads. But the resulting animation can look pretty bad if partial images display. (The bird flying in the previous applet looks terrible until the images finish loading.)

You can use the **MediaTracker** object to wait for completion and/or check to see if the images have finished loading. You declare an object of the Media-Tracker class and attach each image that you want to track to the object. Then you can use the object's waitForAll method or the checkAll method to either wait or check the status.

Setting up a MediaTracker

To use a MediaTracker, declare an object of the class. You will also need a boolean variable to indicate whether the images have finished loading.

```
MediaTracker trackLoad;    //Track the image file loading
boolean blnImagesLoaded = false;
```

After the getImages (in the init method), instantiate the MediaTracker and add each image to the new object.

```
//Instantiate the MediaTracker
trackLoad = new MediaTracker(this); //"this" refers to the applet
//Add the images to the MediaTracker
for (int intIndex = 0; intIndex <= 7; intIndex++)
{
    trackLoad.addImage(imgCollection[intIndex], 0);
}
```

You will need to modify the run and paint methods to successfully wait for the images to load. In this example (Ch11MediaTracker), the paint method displays "Loading Images . . ." until all images are loaded. After that, the animation proceeds exactly the same as in the previous applet.

Recall that the animation thread's run method begins as soon as the applet starts. You will need to repaint once, to force the "Loading Images . . ." message to display, and then use the MediaTracker's waitForAll method. Several types of errors can occur when loading images, so rather than try to "catch" them all, use the MediaTracker's isErrorAny method to check for errors after the operation completes. (However, you still must enclose the statements in a try/catch block to catch an InterruptedException.)

```
public void run()
    {
        //Display loading message
        repaint();
```

```
//Wait for images to finish loading
try
{
    trackLoad.waitForAll();              //Wait for all images to load
    if (!trackLoad.isErrorAny())         //No errors occurred
        blnImagesLoaded = true;
}

catch (InterruptedException exc)
{ }
// Rest of code to display animation goes here.
// (Unchanged from previous program)
```

In the `paint` method, display the *Loading* message if the images haven't finished loading yet.

```
public void paint(Graphics gr)
{
    if (blnImagesLoaded)
        //Display the image and increment the index for the next image
        gr.drawImage(imgCollection[intImage++], 80, 100, this);
    else
        //Images not yet finished loading
        gr.drawString("Loading images . . .", 90, 110);
}
```

The MediaTracker Applet

You can see the entire MediaTracker applet in the folder Ch11MediaTracker. This is the same applet as Ch11AnimateImage, with the addition of the Media-Tracker. Try running both applets; you will see how much better the animation looks when you use the MediaTracker.

Moving an Image

Another way to animate an image is to move it across the screen. You can do this by redrawing the image in a new spot, calculating new values for the *x* and *y* coordinates. As you already have learned, the `repaint` method automatically calls the `update` method, which clears the container and calls `Paint`. You could rely on the `update` to erase the previous image before drawing the new one, but you already know the drawback—screen flicker.

The usual way to create a moving image is to erase the previous image and draw a new one. You can erase an image by drawing a rectangle of the background color over the image, using the `fillRectangle` method of the Graphics class.

```
public void paint(Graphics gr)
    {
        //Erase previous image
        gr.setColor(getBackground());   //Set the color to the current background color
        gr.fillRect(intXPos, intYPos, 40, 40); //Draw a filled rectangle over previous image
```

After erasing the previous image, calculate the new position and draw the image in its new location.

```
    intXPos += 10;                        //Increment position for image
    gr.drawImage(imgCar, intXPos, intYPos, this); //Draw image in new spot
}
```

You may want to allow the image to move across the panel and disappear from view, or check for the edge and either restart the animation or reverse its direction. You can check for the edges of the applet panel using the getsize method and the width or height properties. For example, getSize().width returns the width of the applet panel.

```
if (intXPos > getSize().width)    //Check for right edge of applet panel
    intXPos = 0;                  //Start at left edge again
```

This applet moves an image of a car across the applet panel (Figure 11.9). When the car reaches the right edge of the panel, it restarts again at the left edge. The animation is performed in a thread so that the applet can perform other processing as well.

Figure 11.9

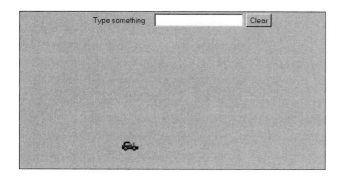

This animation applet moves the car across the screen by erasing the previous image and drawing it in a new location.

```
//Folder:         Ch11MovingImage
//Programmer:     Bradley/Millspaugh
//Date:           6/2001
//ClassName:      AnimationApplet
//Description:    Creates animation by moving an image across the applet panel.
//                The animation runs in a separate thread, so that additional
//                processing can occur.
//                The image comes from www.mediabuilder.com.

import java.applet.*;
import java.awt.*;
import java.awt.event.*;

public class AnimationApplet extends Applet implements Runnable, ActionListener
{
    //Declare variables and components
    Image imgCar;
    Thread animationThread;
    int intXPos = 0;
    int intYPos = 220;
    TextField txtInput = new TextField(20);
    Button btnClear = new Button("Clear");
```

```java
public void init()
{
    //Load image file
    imgCar = getImage(getDocumentBase(),"Auto.gif");

    //Set up for any other tasks desired
    add(new Label("Type something"));
    add(txtInput);
    add(btnClear);
    btnClear.addActionListener(this);
    txtInput.requestFocus();
}

public void start()
{
    //Start the thread for the animation
    animationThread = new Thread(this);
    animationThread.start();
}

public void stop()
{
    //Stop the thread at the end of the applet
    animationThread.stop();
}

public void run()
{
    //Keep putting the thread to sleep to allow other processing to occur
    while(true)
    {
        try
        {
            animationThread.sleep(200);      //Pause 200 milliseconds (2/10 second)
            //To speed up animation, pause for a shorter time.
            repaint();                       //Repaint the screen (calls Update method)
        }

        catch(Exception error)
        {
        }
    }
}

public void paint(Graphics gr)
{
    //Erase previous image and draw new one
    gr.setColor(getBackground());      //Set the color to the current background color
    gr.fillRect(intXPos, intYPos, 40, 40); //Draw a filled rectangle over previous image
    intXPos += 10;                          //Increment position for image
    if (intXPos > getSize().width)          //Check for right edge of applet panel
        intXPos = 0;                        //Start at left edge again
    gr.drawImage(imgCar, intXPos, intYPos, this); //Draw image in new spot
}

public void update(Graphics gr)
{
    //Override the update method,
    // so that the screen is not cleared between images.
```

```
        paint(gr);
    }

    public void actionPerformed(ActionEvent event)
    {
        //User clicked Clear button; clear the text box
        txtInput.setText("");
        txtInput.requestFocus();
    }
}
```

Animation the Easy Way

The easiest way to display animation on the screen is to display an **animated .gif** file. These files have the animation built in. You don't need a separate thread for the animation, since you don't have to control the display of images after first displaying it. This applet displays an animated .gif image and allows other processing to occur (Figure 11.10).

Figure 11.10

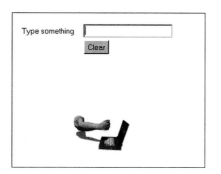

Create animation by displaying an animated .gif image.

```
//Folder:        Ch11SimpleAnimation
//Programmer:    Bradley/Millspaugh
//Date:          6/2001
//ClassName:     AnimationApplet
//Description:   Creates animation from a single .gif file.
//               Graphic comes from www.mediabuilder.com

import java.applet.*;
import java.awt.*;
import java.awt.event.*;

public class AnimationApplet extends Applet implements ActionListener
{
    Image imgAnimationGif;
    TextField txtInput = new TextField(20);
    Button btnClear = new Button("Clear");

    public void init()
    {
    //Load image file
        imgAnimationGif = getImage(getDocumentBase(),"Disgruntled.gif");
```

```
        //Set up for any other tasks desired
        add(new Label("Type something"));
        add(txtInput);
        add(btnClear);
        btnClear.addActionListener(this);
        txtInput.requestFocus();
        setBackground(Color.white);
    }

    public void paint(Graphics gr)
    {
        //Display the image
        gr.drawImage(imgAnimationGif, 100, 150, this);
    }

    public void actionPerformed(ActionEvent event)
    {
        //User clicked Clear button; clear the text box
        txtInput.setText("");
        txtInput.requestFocus();
    }
}
```

For some exciting examples and ideas for creating animation see, http://java.sun.com/applets/index.html. And for some great graphics, see http://www.mediabuilder.com.

Feedback 11.5

1. Why use threads?
2. In what method do you code the actions for a specific thread to execute?
3. Describe how to create an animation.

Swing Components

If you are using Swing, you have some additional options for images. You can add images to buttons and tabbed panes and you can substitute the Swing ImageIcon class for the Image. The ImageIcon works very much like the Image, except that ImageIcon automatically searches the default directory for an image. This means that you do not have to use the `getDocumentBase` method.

```
ImageIcon imgOne = new ImageIcon("One.gif");
ImageIcon imgTwo = new ImageIcon("Two.gif");
```

Adding Images to a JButton

In Chapter 7 you learned that you can add an image to a Swing button (but you didn't learn *how* to do it—that comes now). The JButton actually has several constructors that allow you to add text, an image, or both text and an image.

The following statements declare buttons with images, which go nicely on a toolbar.

```
JButton btnOne = new JButton(imgOne);
JButton btnTwo = new JButton(imgTwo);
```

Using ImageIcons in a Toolbar

The JToolbar is another great graphical Swing component. You can declare a JToolbar component, add buttons to it, and add it to an application's ApplicationPane.

```
private JToolBar toolbar = new JToolBar();

    //Add the toolbar buttons
    toolbar.add(btnOne);
    toolbar.add(btnTwo);
    ApplicationPane.add(toolbar, BorderLayout.NORTH);
```

Notice that the toolbar is added to the North section of the border layout. A border layout works well for a toolbar. You can also make a toolbar float by using the `setFloatable(true)` method.

The Swing Toolbar Application

This Swing application displays a toolbar, which consists of buttons with icons (Figure 11.11).

Figure 11.11

This toolbar consists of JButtons with ImageIcons.

```
//Folder:          Ch11Toolbars
//Programmer:      Bradley/Millspaugh
//Date:            6/2001
//ClassName:       Toolbars
//Description:     Display a toolbar with images using Swing components.

import javax.swing.*;
import java.awt.*;
import java.awt.event.*;
```

```java
public class Toolbars extends JFrame implements ActionListener
{
    //Declare components and variables
    private JLabel lblCompany = new JLabel("ABC Incorporated");
    private ImageIcon imgOne, imgTwo;
    private JButton btnOne, btnTwo;
    private JToolBar toolbar = new JToolBar();

    public Toolbars()
    {
        //Class constructor
        //Set up the application pane
        Container ApplicationPane = getContentPane();
        ApplicationPane.setLayout(new BorderLayout());
        ApplicationPane.add(BorderLayout.WEST, new JLabel("    "));
        ApplicationPane.add(BorderLayout.CENTER, lblCompany);

        //Set up toolbar
        imgOne = new ImageIcon("One.gif");
        imgTwo = new ImageIcon("Two.gif");
        btnOne = new JButton(imgOne);
        btnTwo = new JButton(imgTwo);
        btnOne.setToolTipText("One");
        btnTwo.setToolTipText("Two");
        toolbar.add(btnOne);
        toolbar.add(btnTwo);
        ApplicationPane.add(toolbar, BorderLayout.NORTH);

        btnOne.addActionListener(this);
        btnTwo.addActionListener(this);
        setTitle("Swing Image Application");
        setVisible(true);
    }

    public void actionPerformed(ActionEvent event)
    {
        //Determine which button was pressed
        Object objSource = event.getSource();

        if(objSource == btnOne)
            lblCompany.setText("You selected one");
        else if(objSource == btnTwo)
            lblCompany.setText("You selected two");
    }

    public static void main(String args[])
    {
        //Create an instance of the application
        Toolbars Demo = new Toolbars();

        Demo.addWindowListener(new WindowAdapter()
        {
            public void windowClosing(WindowEvent event)
            {
                System.exit(0);
            }
        });
    }
}
```

Feedback 11.6

1. Write the statement(s) to declare an ImageIcon object to hold the file Hello.gif, which is stored in the same folder as the applet.
2. Write the statement(s) to place the image from question 1 on a new button called btnGreeting.

Your Hands-on Programming Example

Create a program for Tricia's Travel Agency that displays an image moving across the window. The image must be displayed using two types of animation—an animated .gif file that moves across the window. Assume that the program will be adapted to do some other useful work, so the animation must be in its own thread.

Make the program run as either an applet or an application. When running as an application, include a File menu with menu items to print the screen and exit the program.

Planning the Project

Figure 11.12 shows a possible layout for the project.

Figure 11.12

A possible user interface for the chapter hands-on example.

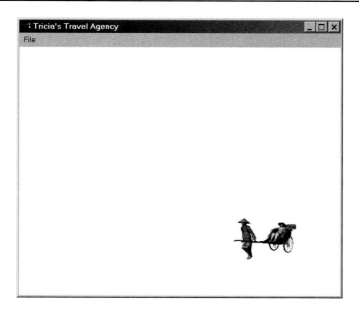

Plan the User Interface

Figure 11.13 shows the class diagram.

Figure 11.13

The class diagram for the hands-on example.

Class: TravelApp	
Methods	**Variables and Components**
main	frmMain
init	animationTread
start	blnImageLoaded
stp[	imgMove
createFrame	intXPos
actionPerformed	blnInApplet
printScreen	mnuMain
run	mnuFile
paint	mnuFilePrint
update	mnuFileExit
	trackLoad

Plan the Objects and Properties

Class: TravelApp

Properties:

Access Mode (public or private)	Variable or Component Name	Data Type or Class	Description
	frmMain	Frame	Main frame for application.
	animationThread	Thread	Control thread for animation.
	blnImageLoaded	boolean	Indicate whether image has finished loading.
	blnInApplet	boolean	Indicate whether running as applet or application.
	intXPos	int	Holds *x* coordinate for image.
	intYPos	int	Holds *y* coordinate for image.
	mnuMain	MenuBar	Menu bar for frmMain.
	mnuFilePrint	MenuItem	Menu item for File / Print.
	mnuFileExit	MenuItem	Menu item for File / Exit.
	trackLoad	MediaTracker	Watch for completion of image loading.

Methods:

Access Mode (public or private)	Return Type	Method Name (include any parameters)	Pseudocode
public static	void	`main(String args[])`	Declare an instance of the applet. Call the `createFrame` method. Set `blnInApplet = false`. Call the applet's `init` and `start` methods.
public	void	`init`	Retrieve the image file. Set up the MediaTracker to watch loading.
public	void	`start`	Start the animation thread.
public	void	`stop`	Stop the animation thread.
public	void	`createFrame(TravelApp)`	Add the File menu to the menu bar. Add an action listener to the File menu. Add the menu items to the File menu. Add a listener for the window's close button. Add the applet to the frame. Show the frame.
public	void	`actionPerformed(ActionEvent)`	If selected menu item = Print Call `printScreen` method. Else if selected menu item = Exit Exit the program.
public	void	`printScreen`	Create print job. If job not canceled by user Create graphics page. Print the page. Send the page to the print queue. End the print job.
public	void	`run`	Repaint to display the "loading" message. Wait for image to load. If no error during load Set `blnImageLoaded = true`. Set initial x-coordinate for image. Loop Make thread sleep. Repaint the screen.
			continued

Access Mode (public or private)	Return Type	Method Name (include any parameters)	Pseudocode

public	void	paint(Graphics)	If image not finished loading
			    Display "loading" message.
			Else
			    Erase "loading" message.
			    Erase previous image.
			    Calculate the next *x*-coordinate.
			    If image off left edge of window
			        Reset *x*-coordinate to right edge.
			    Draw image in new position.

public	void	update(Graphics)	Call paint method.

Write the Project

- Follow the plan to add components to the class.

- Create the methods following the pseudocode in the plan.

- When you complete the code, thoroughly test the project, running as both an applet and an application.

The Project Solution

```
//Folder:        Ch11HandsOn
//Programmer:    Bradley/Millspaugh
//Date:          6/2001
//ClassName:     TravelApp
//Description:   A program for Tricia's Travel Agency.
//               Creates animation by moving an animated .gif image across the screen.
//               Runs as either an applet or an application.
//               When run as an application, a menu item prints the screen.

import java.awt.*;
import java.awt.event.*;
import java.applet.*;

public class TravelApp extends Applet implements Runnable, ActionListener
{
    //Declare components and variables
    Thread animationThread;
    MediaTracker trackLoad;        //Track the image file loading
    boolean blnImageLoaded = false;
    Image imgMove;
    int intXPos;
    int intYPos = 300;
    boolean blnInApplet = true;

    //Declare application components
    Frame frmMain = new Frame("Tricia's Travel Agency");
```

```
//Menu components
MenuBar mnuMain = new MenuBar();
Menu mnuFile = new Menu("File");
MenuItem mnuFilePrint = new MenuItem("Print...");
MenuItem mnuFileExit = new MenuItem("Exit");

public void init()
{
    //Retrieve and track the image file
    if (blnInApplet)
        imgMove = getImage(getDocumentBase(), "rickshaw.gif");
    else
        imgMove = Toolkit.getDefaultToolkit().getImage("rickshaw.gif");
    trackLoad = new MediaTracker(this);
    trackLoad.addImage(imgMove, 0);
}

public void start()
{
    //Start the animation thread
    animationThread = new Thread(this);
    animationThread.start();
}

public void stop()
{
    //Stop the animation thread when the applet stops
    animationThread.stop();
}

public static void main(String args[])
{
    //Declare an instance of the application
    TravelApp myApp = new TravelApp();
    myApp.createFrame(myApp);
    myApp.blnInApplet = false;
    myApp.init();
    myApp.start();
}

public void createFrame(TravelApp myApp)
{
    //Create the menu bar
    mnuMain.add(mnuFile);
    mnuFile.addActionListener(this);
    mnuFile.add(mnuFilePrint);
    mnuFile.add(mnuFileExit);
    frmMain.setMenuBar(mnuMain);

    //Add listener for close button
    frmMain.addWindowListener(new WindowAdapter()
    {
        public void windowClosing(WindowEvent event)
        {
            System.exit(0);
        }
    });
```

```java
        //Display the frame
        frmMain.add("Center", myApp);
        frmMain.setSize(600, 500);
        frmMain.show();
    }

    public void actionPerformed(ActionEvent event)
    {
        //Determine which menu item was selected
        String strMenuItem = event.getActionCommand();

        if (strMenuItem.equals("Print..."))
            printScreen();
        else if (strMenuItem.equals("Exit"))
        {
            System.exit(0);                   //Exit to the operating system
        }
    }

    private void printScreen()
    {
        //Print the content of the screen as a graphic
        PrintJob printer = getToolkit().getPrintJob(frmMain, "TravelPrint", null);
        if (printer != null)        //Print job not canceled by the user
        {
            //Create a Graphics object for printing
            Graphics grPrintPage = printer.getGraphics();
            frmMain.printAll(grPrintPage); //Print the frame and its components
            grPrintPage.dispose();          //Send the page to the printer
            printer.end();                  //End the print job
        }
    }

    public void run()
    {
        //Display loading message
        repaint();

        //Wait for image to finish loading
        try
        {
            trackLoad.waitForAll();
            if (!trackLoad.isErrorAny())
                blnImageLoaded = true;
        }

        catch (InterruptedException exc)
        {}

        //Set initial position for image
        intXPos = getSize().width;

        //Keep putting the thread to sleep to allow other processing to occur
        while(true)
        {
```

```
        try
        {
            animationThread.sleep(100);          //Pause
            repaint();
        }

        catch(Exception error)
        {}
    }
}

public void paint(Graphics gr)
{
    //Draw the graphics on the screen
    if (!blnImageLoaded)
        //Image not yet finished loading
        gr.drawString("Loading image . . .", 200, 200);
    else
    {
        //Erase previous image
        gr.clearRect(200, 175, 120, 50);          //Clear Loading message
        gr.clearRect(intXPos, intYPos, 125, 85); //Clear image
        //Calculate new position and draw image
        intXPos -= 2;
        if (intXPos <= -125)                      //Image off left edge of panel
            intXPos = getSize().width;            //Restart animation
        gr.drawImage(imgMove, intXPos, intYPos, this);
    }
}

public void update(Graphics gr)
{
    //Reduce flicker by calling paint without clearing the container
    paint(gr);
}
}
```

Summary

1. Java contains a Graphics object that you can use for drawing, writing text, and displaying images. You display the Graphics object in the `paint` method.

2. The `paint` method executes after the `init` method of an applet. You usually include the Graphics methods in the `paint` method.

3. To display text on the screen, use the `drawString` method of the Graphics class.

4. You can use Graphics methods to draw primitive shapes, such as ovals, rectangles, and lines.

5. Images can be loaded into a Graphics object with the `getImage` method of the Applet object. Java handles both .gif and .jpeg files. Use the `getDocumentBase` method to point to the folder from which the applet was loaded.

6. The `drawImage` method displays an image on a Graphics object.

7. You can cause the screen to repaint by calling the `repaint` method. The `repaint` method calls the `update` method, which clears the screen and calls the `paint` method.

8. To avoid screen flicker when displaying graphic images, override the `update` method to simply call `paint` without first clearing the screen.

9. To retrieve images in an application, use the `getImage` method of the default toolkit.

10. Sounds, known as audio clips, are accessed with the `getAudioClip` method. An AudioClip object has `play`, `stop`, and `loop` methods.

11. You can send a Graphics object to a printer, which allows you to print the current screen or send text to the printer. The `getPrintJob` method begins the print job and displays the Print dialog box for the user. The `getGraphics` method assigns the Graphics object to the print job; a container's `printAll` method sends the container's contents to the Graphics object; the `dispose` method flushes the page and sends it to the print queue; and the `end` method ends the print job.

12. Java can perform multiple actions at the same time using threads. Processing on one thread takes place while another thread sleeps. You must implement the Runnable interface to use threads in an applet.

13. Threads make it possible to run an animation at the same time as data entry and other events are being processed.

14. The main action of a thread is coded in its `run` method. Other thread methods are `start`, `stop`, and `sleep`. `Sleep` pauses the thread so that other actions can occur.

15. Animation can be created by displaying a series of images, each slightly different from the last.

16. You can wait for all images to load or check their status using a MediaTracker object.

17. An image can be moved across the screen by erasing the image and redrawing it in a new location. Draw a filled rectangle in the background color to erase an image.

18. An animated .gif file contains the animation built in. You can simply display the image to achieve animation.

Key Terms

animated .gif *363*   AudioClip object *343*
audio clip *342*   collide *356*

Review Questions

1. Describe the steps needed to write "ABC, Inc" at the top of the screen in Red, using Graphics methods rather than a label component.
2. When does the paint method run?
3. What types of image files can Java handle?
4. How is an image loaded into an Image object? How is the image displayed?
5. How is a sound file loaded? Into what type of object is it loaded?
6. What methods are available for use with audio clips?
7. Explain three ways to generate animation.

Programming Exercises

11.1 Rewrite the Ch11MultipleImages applet using an array for the images. You may use as many images as you would like.

11.2 Modify the hands-on exercise in the chapter (ch11HandsOn) to add a second moving image. Make the second image move from left to right across the screen. Note that if you add both images to the MediaTracker, it will wait for both images to finish loading.

11.3 Add an animated image to one of your previous projects.

CASE STUDIES

R 'n R—for Reading and Refreshment

Add an introductory sound file to your last case project that plays as your applet begins. You may use a sound file of your choice or create one with a microphone and an appropriate application.

Merry Pea's Quilting

Find or create an appropriate logo; display it on the screen of your last case project.

12

More OOP, Interfaces, and Inner Classes

At the completion of this chapter, you will be able to . . .

1. Create your own interfaces.

2. Identify the types of inner classes available in Java.

3. Understand and use inner classes.

Since Chapter 1 you have been writing object-oriented programs, which include the concepts of encapsulation, inheritance, and polymorphism. In this chapter you learn some additional features of Java that will expand your OOP capabilities.

You have been implementing interfaces, such as the ActionListener and MouseListener, since Chapter 2. In this chapter you will learn to create your own interfaces. You will also learn about inner or nested classes.

OOP Review

Although you have been using OOP techniques for this entire book, a little review of the concepts is in order before expanding on the Java OOP techniques.

Encapsulation

The term *encapsulation* refers to the fact that all methods and variables are declared inside of a class. Each class is in charge of its own data, which it can hide or expose as necessary. When you declare variables and methods as private, no other classes have access to the data.

Later in this chapter, you learn to code a new class inside of another class.

Inheritance

Inheritance provides the ability to create a class that is based on another class. You have inherited from a superclass (also called a base class) such as Applet and then added your own features. You gain all of the functionality of the superclass and can also add your own functionality.

One superclass can have several subclasses that inherit from it. In fact, the superclass never knows about the subclasses. A subclass, on the other hand, can inherit from only a single superclass. Consider a hierarchy, such as Figure 12.1, and notice that a single class, such as Applet, can be a subclass of Panel and also be a superclass to another class, such as MyNewApplet.

Later in this chapter we look at inheriting from your own classes.

Polymorphism

You recall learning about polymorphism in Chapter 5 and have seen examples of polymorphism in your programming. Remember, polymorphism means that many methods may have identical names but have different implementations, depending on the situation. One class can have several methods with the same name, each with a different set of arguments, and a superclass and its subclasses may have identically named methods. An example of polymorphism is the setText for a label or for a text component. Keeping names consistent makes programming easier when you can anticipate what methods you might expect. When you are looking for a method, you probably have a good idea what it might be called.

Figure 12.1

A hierarchy of classes. Each class can become the superclass of multiple subclasses, but a subclass can have only one superclass.

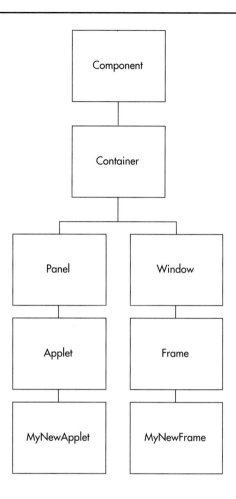

In designing your programs, you should strive to accomplish something similar. Try to make your methods and variables similar to those in the language. You also can create your own interfaces to assure that any class based on the interface will have the same method names.

Inheriting from Your Own Classes

So far you have used inheritance on classes that already exist in the Java language, such as

```
public class MyNewApplet extends Applet
```

or

```
public class MyFrameApp extends WindowAdapter
```

Let's consider why you might want to create a new class that extends another class you have written. One basic thought is "If it ain't broke, why fix it?" Applied to programming, you may find that you want to add new features to an application, but you already have a class that works fine. Consider creating your new class as an extension or subclass of your original.

Often the technique of inheritance is used intentionally at the design stage to keep similar objects with a single superclass.

Consider the Swing radio button. The component has many features in common with a check box. Notice in Figure 12.2 that the two classes are based on the same superclass. This same concept can work for you.

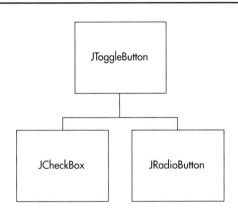

The Swing check box and radio button classes both inherit from the same superclass since they share so many functions.

Have you ever thought about how many times you need to repeat the same type of data, such as first name, last name, street, city, state, ZIP code, phone number, email, and so on? This duplication occurs every time you need a class for a person, whether the class represents a customer, an employee, or maybe even a vendor. Wouldn't it be easier to have one superclass such as Person and then inherit subclasses for employee, customer, and vendor (Figure 12.3)?

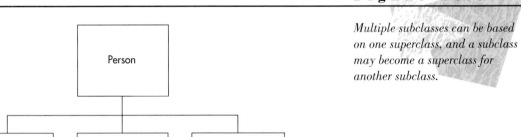

Multiple subclasses can be based on one superclass, and a subclass may become a superclass for another subclass.

```java
public class Person
{
    public String strLastName;
    public String strFirstName;
    public String strStreet;
    public String strCity;
    public String strState;
    public String strZipCode;
    public String strPhone;
    public String strEmail;
}
```

Protected Variables

Private variables are not inherited. If you plan to inherit from a class, you should make the variables public—or a second choice is ***protected.*** Variables declared as protected act as private in the superclass but can be inherited by a subclass.

```
public class Person
{
    protected String strLastName;
    protected String strFirstName;
    protected String strStreet;
    protected String strCity;
    protected String strState;
    protected String strZipCode;
    protected String strPhone;
    protected String strEmail;
}
```

Now to create subclasses, you can extend the superclass and add any additional fields that you need.

```
public class Student extends Person
{
    private float fltGPA;
}
```

The Student class contains all of the name and address information as well as the GPA.

```
public class Vendor extends Person
{
    private String strCompany;
}

public class Customer extends Person
{
    private String strAccountNumber;
}
```

Interfaces

Interfaces are Java's answer to its lack of multiple inheritance. Recall that Java does not allow a class to have more than one superclass, so an extends clause can name only a single class. But the implements clause can list several interfaces. Your program can have access to the methods and constants in many interfaces, which you have taken advantage of in past programs:

```
public class AnimationApplet extends Applet
    implements Runnable, ActionListener, MouseListener
```

Interfaces share several similarities with classes. You write each in a separate file saved with a .java extension. Both contain coding to declare variables and methods. But certain limitations apply to interfaces:

- Methods do not contain a body.

- All variables must be declared as `final` (constants).

Abstract Classes and Methods

You will recall from Chapter 5 that an **abstract class** is a class written strictly for inheritance. You cannot instantiate an object of an abstract class, but you can inherit from the class. Abstract classes may contain methods with code along with other methods that are empty, which are called ***abstract methods.*** This requires a subclass to **override** an empty class by including a method with the same name. You also have the option of overriding any of the other (nonabstract) methods in the base class.

You can declare a class to be abstract by adding the keyword `abstract` to the class header. If you include any abstract (empty) methods in a class, the class *must* be declared `abstract`. An easy error to generate in Java is to accidentally place a semicolon at the end of the line declaring a new method. Java considers this an abstract method and warns you that you must declare the class as `abstract`.

Interface Abstract Methods

In an interface, all methods are abstract. Think of the interfaces you have used, such as the listeners. You had to override the methods in your class. The ActionListener requires you to override the `actionPerformed` method, while the MouseListener requires you to override five methods.

All interfaces must be declared `public`. The methods in an interface are public by default, whether or not you include the `public` keyword. All fields will be `public`, `final`, and `static`, whether or not you include the keywords. However, it's best to always include the keywords, as a reminder to yourself and any other programmer implementing the interface.

Creating an Interface

To create your own interface, you use the keyword `interface` rather than `class`.

```
public interface InterfaceName
{
    //Declare constants and methods
}
```

This handy interface sets up constants that you can use in many applications.

```
public interface CompanyInformation
{
    static final String COMPANY_NAME = "ABC Incorporated";
    static final String URL = "www.ABCInc.net";
}
```

You now can refer to the constants in any application or applet that implements the interface.

```
//Folder:        Ch12Interfaces
//Programmer:    Bradley/Millspaugh
//Date:          6/2001
//ClassName:     Ch12Interfaces
//Description:   Create and implement an interface.

import java.applet.*;
import java.awt.*;
import java.awt.event.*;

public class Ch12Interfaces extends Applet
                            implements CompanyInformation
{
    Label lblMessage = new Label(COMPANY_NAME);

    public void init()
    {
        add(lblMessage);
    }
}
```

Feedback 12.1

1. Write the code to declare a Payroll interface. Just include empty braces for the contents of the interface.
2. What is meant by the phrase "an interface is automatically abstract"?

Inner Classes

An **inner class** is a class that is declared inside another class, just as you probably deduced from the name. Some refer to this feature as a **nested class.** Java introduced inner classes in Java 1.1.

Why would you want to declare a class inside of another? The most common reason is to organize code. (However, there are those who feel its primary purpose is to make code look more complex.) You can also take advantage of the scoping rules for variables and methods: code within the inner class can directly reference variables and methods within the scope of the class and code in the outer (enclosing) class can directly reference variables and methods inside the inner class.

An important thing to remember is that writing inner classes is merely a different style of coding; you can always achieve the same results without nesting. You will appreciate knowing how the technique works so that you can read code that embeds nested classes. And you may even decide that you prefer to code in this style.

You can create several different types of inner classes: static member classes (and interfaces), member classes, local classes, and anonymous classes (Table 12.1). Notice that you can also nest an interface inside a class, but only as a static member class. Another important point is that Java programmers have not yet standardized the terminology for inner classes. For example, some people call static member classes *top-level nested classes* (or *interfaces*). Figure 12.4 shows how inner classes fit into a top-level (containing) class.

T a b l e   1 2 . 1

Inner Classes

Type of Inner Class	Applies to	Declared	Can Be Used
Static member	Classes and interfaces	Inside a class as static	By any class
Member (non-static)	Classes	Inside a class (non-static)	Within the member class
Local (named)	Classes	Inside a method	Within the method
Anonymous (local unnamed)	Classes	Inside a method with no name	Within the method

F i g u r e   1 2 . 4

Inner classes can be static member classes, member classes, local, or anonymous.

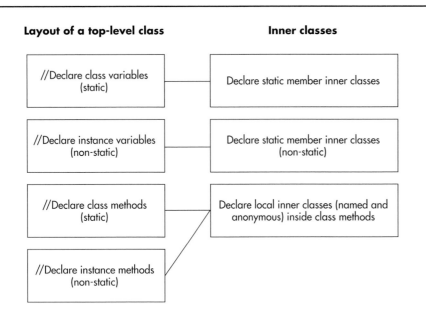

Layout of a top-level class   **Inner classes**

| //Declare class variables (static) |——| Declare static member inner classes |

| //Declare instance variables (non-static) |——| Declare static member inner classes (non-static) |

| //Declare class methods (static) |——| Declare local inner classes (named and anonymous) inside class methods |

| //Declare instance methods (non-static) |

Static Member Classes and Interfaces

Static member classes have a lot in common with static member variables. You declare static variables to be class variables; that is, the class contains only one copy of the variable, not one copy per instance. You generally use static variables to hold data that you want to accumulate for multiple instances, such as an item count or running total, as well as (final static) constants that you want to be available for all instances of the class.

You can declare an inner member class to be static. Just as with class variables, the outer (containing) class has only one copy of the inner class, not one copy per instance. Therefore, you can use the static inner class to keep summary information.

A static member class follows the scoping rules for class and instance variables. That is, you declare the inner class at the top level (not within a method), and it can be referenced by code anywhere inside the class. A static member class can access all of the static members of its containing class, including private members.

In Chapter 6, the hands-on example demonstrated a payroll project that contained three top-level classes: PayrollApplet, Payroll, and LocalFormat (for formatting output). In the Ch12InnerMemberClass example, the Payroll class is moved inside the PayrollApplet class as a static member class. (You may recall that the Payroll class maintained summary totals for the number processed and the total pay, and therefore must be static.) The LocalFormat class is also moved inside the PayrollApplet class as a (non-static) member class, which is discussed in the next section.

```
public class PayrollApplet extends Applet implements ActionListener
{
    //Create the Payroll class
    public static class Payroll
    {
        //Code for Payroll class
    }
    //Complete the Payroll applet code including instantiating a Payroll object
}
```

Note: You can find the complete program listing in Ch12PayrollMemberClass.

Although you can always use separate classes, some programmers think that nested classes can lead to more organized code. In a program with many methods, it can be difficult to determine the ones that are overriding methods from an interface and/or a superclass and those that belong specifically to your class. If you create a Payroll class inside of your PayrollApplet class, then all of the methods that belong to the Payroll class are delineated from those in the applet.

Member Classes

A **member class** is an inner class that is not declared as static and also is not declared inside a method. A member class has a lot in common with instance variables and instance methods: one copy exists for each instance of the outer class. The inner class exists only for the use of the outer class and cannot be used by other top-level classes. The nested class has access to all instance and class variables and objects of the outer class or any other inner classes, including members declared as private. And the outer class has access to all variables and methods in the inner class.

An inner class declared in an applet has access to all of the components. Therefore, you don't have to explicitly pass the contents of components to the member class. For example, in the following code segment, the Payroll class has access to the txtHours text field.

```
public class PayrollApplet extends Applet implements ActionListener
{
    //Declare components
    TextField txtHours;

    //Create the inner Payroll class
    public class Payroll
    {
        //Code for Payroll class
        //Can refer directly to txtHours
    }

    //Complete the Payroll applet code including instantiating a Payroll object
}
```

You can see another example of an inner member class in the Ch12InnerMemberClass example. As mentioned previously, this example includes a static member class (Payroll). In addition, the LocalFormat class is included as a member class. Part of the code is shown here. Note that you can code the LocalFormat inner class either before or after the method that uses the class.

```
//Method from Ch12InnerMemberClass

private void CalculatePay()
{
    //Retrieve data and calculate
    //Declare variables
    float fltPay;
    String strFormattedData;

    //Clear any previous status message
    showStatus("");
    try
    {
        float fltHours = Float.valueOf(txtHours.getText()).floatValue();
        float fltRate = Float.valueOf(txtRate.getText()).floatValue();
        Payroll myPayroll = new Payroll(fltHours, fltRate);

        if (myPayroll.getHours() < 0) //Hours failed validation
        {
            txtHours.requestFocus();
            txtHours.selectAll();
            showStatus("Invalid Hours");
        }
        else if (myPayroll.getRate() < 0) //Rate failed validation
        {
            txtRate.requestFocus();
            txtRate.selectAll();
            showStatus("Invalid Rate");
        }
        else //Passed all business rule validations
        {
            fltPay = myPayroll.CalculatePay();

            //Format and display output
            LocalFormal fmtLocal = new LocalFormat();
            strFormattedData = fmtLocal.FormatCurrency(myPayroll.getTotalPay());
```

```
            lblPayOut.setText(strFormattedData);
            lblNumberProcessed.setText("" + myPayroll.getNumberProcessed());
            strFormattedData = fmtLocal.FormatDecimal(fltPay);
            txaPayroll.append("\n" + txtName.getText() + "\t" + strFormattedData);
        }
    }

    catch(Exception err)
    {
        showStatus("Hours and Rate must be numeric.");
    }
}


public class LocalFormat
//Member inner class
{
    //Instance variables
    private NumberFormat fmtCurrency;
    private NumberFormat fmtDecimal;

    //Class constructor
    LocalFormat()
    {
        //Get formatting for default locale
        fmtCurrency = NumberFormat.getCurrencyInstance();
        fmtDecimal = NumberFormat.getInstance();
    }

    //Methods
    public String FormatCurrency (double dblNumber)
    {
        //Format as currency, 2 decimal positions
        fmtCurrency.setMinimumFractionDigits(2);
        fmtCurrency.setMaximumFractionDigits(2);
        String strFormattedData = fmtCurrency.format(dblNumber);
        return strFormattedData;
    }

    public String FormatDecimal (float fltNumber)
    {
        //Format as decimal, 2 decimal positions
        fmtDecimal.setMinimumFractionDigits(2);
        fmtDecimal.setMaximumFractionDigits(2);
        String strFormattedData = fmtDecimal.format(fltNumber);
        return strFormattedData;
    }
}
```

Local Classes

A **local inner class** is an inner class declared inside a method. Local inner classes are closely related to local variables, which have local scope and can be used only within that method. A common use of a local inner class is to implement an event-handling interface or extend another class, such as a Mouse-Adapter or WindowAdapter.

In this example, the local inner class ButtonListener implements Action-Listener. Then the new ButtonListener class is assigned to the button as well as the text fields (this so that the `actionPerformed` method responds to the Enter key in the text fields as well as a button click). Since the code for the event handling appears in only one method, it makes sense to code it as a local inner class.

```java
//Folder:        Ch12InnerLocalClass
//Programmer:    Bradley/Millspaugh
//Date:          6/2001
//Class Name:    LocalClassApplet
//Description:   Convert Ch2Buttons to use a local inner class.
//               Inputs three fields, responds to a button click,
//                 and adds text to a text area.

import java.applet.*;
import java.awt.*;
import java.awt.event.*;

public class LocalClassApplet extends Applet
{
    //Declare components
    TextField txtDept = new TextField(20);
    TextField txtName = new TextField(20);
    TextField txtPhone = new TextField(5);
    TextArea txaPhoneList = new TextArea(10, 30);
    Button btnAdd = new Button("Add to List");

    //Declare variables
    String strDept;
    String strName;
    String strPhone;

    public void init ()
    {
        //Place components on applet
        add(new Label("Department: "));
        add(txtDept);
        add(new Label("Name:   "));
        add(txtName);
        add(new Label("Extension: "));
        add(txtPhone);
        add(btnAdd);
        add(txaPhoneList);
        txtDept.requestFocus();

        class ButtonListener implements ActionListener
        //Local inner class
        {
            public void actionPerformed(ActionEvent p1)
            {
                //Actions for "Add to List"
                //Triggered when the user clicks the button or presses the Enter
                // key in any of the text fields
                String strOutputLine; //Declare local variable
```

```
                    //Assign the text fields to text area
                    strDept = txtDept.getText();
                    strName = txtName.getText();
                    strPhone = txtPhone.getText();
                    strOutputLine = strDept + "\t" + strName + "\t" + strPhone;
                    txaPhoneList.append(strOutputLine + "\n");

                    //Clear the text fields
                    txtDept.setText("");
                    txtName.setText("");
                    txtPhone.setText("");

                    //Place the cursor in the first text field
                    txtDept.requestFocus();
            }
        }

        //Add listeners using new ButtonListener class
        ActionListener AddListener = new ButtonListener();
        btnAdd.addActionListener( AddListener );

        txtDept.addActionListener( AddListener );

        txtName.addActionListener( AddListener );

        txtPhone.addActionListener( AddListener );
    }
}
```

Anonymous Classes

An **anonymous class** is a local class that you define without giving it a name.
You can declare an anonymous inner class as an expression, which may be an
argument for a method call or assigned to a variable.

If you declare a local class (with a name), you define the class and then instantiate an object of that class. With an anonymous class, you won't be referring to the class object by name, so you can combine the two steps (definition
and instantiation). You used this technique in Chapters 10 and 11 to generate
the action for closing a window.

```
frmMain.addWindowListener(new WindowAdapter()
{
    public void windowClosing(WindowEvent event)
    {
        //Action for window close box
        System.exit(0);
    }
});
```

When you look closely at this code, you see that a WindowAdapter is created without a name. The new class overrides the `windowClosing` method for
the adapter. You need a set of braces for the method and another set for the inner class. Notice the parenthesis after the closing brace: this terminates the
anonymous use of the class.

The following example uses an anonymous class to implement the event
handling for a button click. This example is very much like the previous
program that created a named inner class. However, in this example the event

handling applies only to the button (not the text fields). If you declare the inner class as anonymous, you cannot assign it to any other component since it doesn't have a name.

```java
//Folder:        Ch12AnonymousClass
//Programmer:    Bradley/Millspaugh
//Date:          6/2001
//Class Name:    AnonymousClassApplet
//Description:   Converts Ch2Buttons to use an anonymous inner class.
//               Inputs three fields, responds to a button click,
//               and adds text to a text area.

import java.applet.*;
import java.awt.*;
import java.awt.event.*;

public class AnonymousClassApplet extends Applet
{
    //Declare components
    TextField txtDept = new TextField(20);
    TextField txtName = new TextField(20);
    TextField txtPhone = new TextField(5);
    TextArea txaPhoneList = new TextArea(10,30);
    Button btnAdd = new Button("Add to List");

    //Declare variables
    String strDept;
    String strName;
    String strPhone;

    public void init ()
    {
        //Place components on applet
        add(new Label("Department: "));
        add(txtDept);
        add(new Label("Name:   "));
        add(txtName);
        add(new Label("Extension: "));
        add(txtPhone);
        add(btnAdd);
        add(txaPhoneList);
        txtDept.requestFocus();

        //Declare new anonymous (unnamed) inner class
        btnAdd.addActionListener (new ActionListener()
        {
            public void actionPerformed(ActionEvent event)
            {
                //Actions for "Add to List"
                String strOutputLine; //Declare local variable

                //Assign the text fields to text area
                strDept = txtDept.getText();
                strName = txtName.getText();
                strPhone = txtPhone.getText();
                strOutputLine = strDept + "\t" + strName + "\t" + strPhone;
                txaPhoneList.append(strOutputLine + "\n");
```

```
                        //Clear the text fields
                        txtDept.setText("");
                        txtName.setText("");
                        txtPhone.setText("");

                        //Place the cursor in the first text field
                        txtDept.requestFocus();
                    }
                });
            }
        }
```

Distributing Inner Classes

When you distribute an applet or application that uses inner classes, you must make sure to include all .class files. Although you write one class inside another, the compiler produces separate .class files for each class. For example, the PayrollApplet shown earlier in this chapter has only one .java file—PayrollApplet.java—but the compiler generates two .class files: PayrollApplet.class and PayrollApplet$Payroll.class.

Feedback 12.2

1. What are the differences between a static member class and a member class? When would you use static?
2. When would you use a local inner class rather than a member class?
3. What are the differences between a local inner class and an anonymous inner class?

Your Hands-on Programming Example

Create a program that uses inner classes: a member class, a local class, and an anonymous class. Begin with the Ch10AppApplet project, which displays a popup shortcut menu and can run as either an applet or an application. Remove the implements ActionListener, MouseListener from the class header and write inner classes. Use a local class (named) for the ActionListener. Remove the MouseListener and write a member class that extends MouseAdapter instead. Recall that MouseAdapter is a class that implements MouseListener. Using the MouseAdapter, you don't have to write code for any mouse events that you are not using.

The program already has an anonymous class. Identify the class and write comments to explain the use of the class.

Add a second label to the user interface and allow the user to pop up the shortcut menu for both labels. This requires that you give your new mouse adapter class a name and assign an object of the class to both labels. Make sure you can pop up the menu for both labels and change the color of the selected label in response to the user's selection from the shortcut menu.

Planning the Project

Figure 12.5 shows a possible layout for the project.

Figure 12.5

A possible user interface for the
chapter hands-on example.

Plan the User Interface

Figure 12.6 shows the class diagram.

Figure 12.6

The class diagram for the hands-
on example.

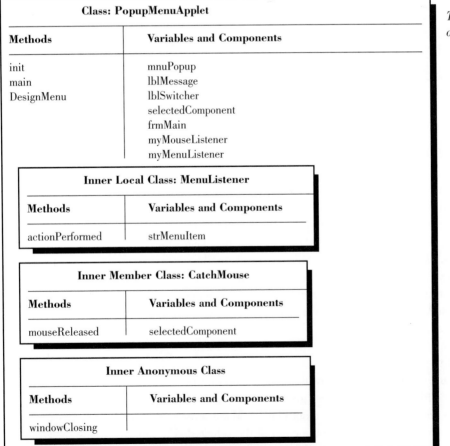

Class: PopupMenuApplet	
Methods	**Variables and Components**
init	mnuPopup
main	lblMessage
DesignMenu	lblSwitcher
	selectedComponent
	frmMain
	myMouseListener
	myMenuListener

Inner Local Class: MenuListener	
Methods	**Variables and Components**
actionPerformed	strMenuItem

Inner Member Class: CatchMouse	
Methods	**Variables and Components**
mouseReleased	selectedComponent

Inner Anonymous Class	
Methods	**Variables and Components**
windowClosing	

Plan the Objects and Properties
Class: PopupMenuApplet

Components and Variables:

Access Mode (public or private)	Variable or Component Name	Data Type or Class	Description
	mnuPopup	PopupMenu	Shortcut menu.
	lblMessage	Label	Display message.
	lblSwitcher	Label	Display a second message.
	blnApplet	boolean	Running as applet or application.
	selectedComponent	Component	Store name of selected component.
	frmMain	Frame	Frame for application.
	myMouseListener	CatchMouse	Listen for right-clicks for shortcut menus.
	myMenuListener	ActionListener	Listen for selections from shortcut menus.

Methods:

Access Mode (public or private)	Return Type	Method Name (include any parameters)	Pseudocode
public	void	`init`	Call method to design shortcut menu. Add labels. Add popup menu to labels. Create MouseListener object. Assign MouseListener to labels. Declare MenuListener class. Create MenuListener object. Add MenuListener to menu.
public static	void	`main(String args[])`	Set blnApplet to false. Declare frame. Declare instance of applet. Add applet to frame. Add WindowListener (anonymous inner class). Show frame. Call `init` and `start` methods of applet.
public	void	`DesignMenu`	Declare strings for menu items. Add each string to the popup menu.

Inner Local Class: MenuListener

Local to the `init` method.

Components and Variables:

Access Mode (public or private)	Variable or Component Name	Data Type or Class	Description
	strMenuItem	String	Holds label of selected menu item.

Methods:

Access Mode (public or private)	Return Type	Method Name (include any parameters)	Pseudocode
public	void	`actionPerformed(ActionEvent)`	Change foreground of selected component to selected color.

Inner Member Class: CatchMouse

Components and Variables:

Access Mode (public or private)	Variable or Component Name	Data Type or Class	Description
	selectedComponent	Component	Declared in outer class, to hold name of selected component.

Methods:

Access Mode (public or private)	Return Type	Method Name (include any parameters)	Pseudocode
public	void	`mouseReleased(MouseEvent)`	If right-mouse button clicked Save name of selected component. Show popup menu.

Write the Project

- Open the Ch10AppApplet project.

- Remove the `implements` clauses.

- Add a second label.

- Declare the two new inner classes.

- Modify the code to use the inner classes.

- When you complete the code, thoroughly test the project. You should be
  able to right-click either label, select a color, and change the color of the
  selected label.

The Project Solution

```
//Folder:          Ch12HandsOn
//Programmer:      Bradley/Millspaugh
//Date:            6/2001
//ClassName:       PopupMenuApplet
//Description:     An applet/application that displays a popup menu.
//                 Uses a member inner class, a local inner class, and
//                 an anonymous inner class.
//                 Based on Ch10AppApplet.

import java.applet.*;
import java.awt.*;
import java.awt.event.*;

public class PopupMenuApplet extends Applet
{
    PopupMenu mnuPopup = new PopupMenu();
    Label lblMessage = new Label("Right click on this label.");
    Label lblSwitcher = new Label("Choose me instead.");
    static boolean blnApplet = true;
    Component selectedComponent; //Save the name of the selected component

    public void init()
    {
        DesignMenu();
        add(lblMessage);
        add(lblSwitcher);
        lblMessage.add(mnuPopup);
        lblSwitcher.add(mnuPopup);

        //Create an instance of the member class
        CatchMouse myMouseListener = new CatchMouse();

        //Assign instance of class as the mouse listener for both labels
        lblMessage.addMouseListener(myMouseListener);
        lblSwitcher.addMouseListener(myMouseListener);

        //Create a new local inner class
        class MenuListener implements ActionListener
        {
            public void actionPerformed(ActionEvent event)
            {
                //Determine which menu item was selected
                String strMenuItem = event.getActionCommand();

                //Change the color of the selected component
                if (strMenuItem.equals("Red"))
                        selectedComponent.setForeground(Color.red);
                else if (strMenuItem.equals("Blue"))
                        selectedComponent.setForeground(Color.blue);
```

```
                else if (strMenuItem.equals("Green"))
                        selectedComponent.setForeground(Color.green);
            }
        }

        //Create an instance of my new MenuListener class
        ActionListener myMenuListener = new MenuListener();

        //Assign the instance of my class as the action listener
        mnuPopup.addActionListener(myMenuListener);
    }

    public static void main(String args[])
    {
        blnApplet = false;
        Frame frmMain = new Frame("Popup Menu Application");
        PopupMenuApplet aplPopup = new PopupMenuApplet();
        frmMain.add("Center", aplPopup);

        //Create an anonymous (unnamed) inner class as an expression
        frmMain.addWindowListener(new WindowAdapter()
        {
            public void windowClosing(WindowEvent event)
            {
                System.exit(0);
            }
        });
        frmMain.setSize(300, 300);
        aplPopup.init();
        frmMain.show();
    }

    public void DesignMenu()
    {
        //Add items to the popup menu
        String[] strMenuLabels = new String[]{"Red", "Blue", "Green"};

        for(int intIndex = 0; intIndex < strMenuLabels.length; intIndex ++)
        {
            MenuItem mnuItem = new MenuItem(strMenuLabels[intIndex]);
            mnuPopup.add(mnuItem);
        }
    }

    //Create a new member class for MouseAdapter
    class CatchMouse extends MouseAdapter
    {
        public void mouseReleased(MouseEvent event)
        {
            //Check for right mouse button
            if (event.isPopupTrigger())
            {
                selectedComponent = event.getComponent();//Save component name
                mnuPopup.show(selectedComponent, event.getX(), event.getY());
            }
        }
    }
}
```

Summary

1. A class that you have written can become a superclass to another subclass. To be inherited, variables must be declared public or protected.
2. Although one class cannot inherit from multiple classes, a class can implement interfaces to incorporate additional variables and methods.
3. An interface is similar to a class but is automatically abstract. All interface methods must be overridden when the interface is implemented. All fields in an interface must be `public static final`.
4. Interfaces are created with the keyword `interface` rather than `class`.
5. Java 1.1 introduced inner classes—the ability to define a class inside another class.
6. Inner classes can be static member classes, member classes, local classes, or anonymous classes. The location of the inner class determines the scope of the class and its variables.
7. A member class has access to the other members of the class including members that are declared as `private`.
8. The Java compiler produces one .class file for each class declared in the .java file.

Key Terms

abstract class   *382*   member class   *385*
abstract method   *382*   nested class   *383*
anonymous class   *389*   override   *382*
inner class   *383*   protected   *381*
interface   *381*   static member class   *384*
local inner class   *387*

Review Questions

1. What is an interface?
2. Differentiate between a class and an interface.
3. When would it be desirable to create an interface rather than a class?
4. What is meant by an abstract method?
5. Name and describe the four types of inner classes.
6. Specify a situation in which it is necessary to use an inner class.
7. Differentiate between a local inner class and an anonymous inner class.
8. How can you distinguish in code between a static member class and a member class?
9. Discuss the relationship of a member class with other members of the outer class.

Programming Exercises

12.1 Rewrite a previous project replacing the `actionPerformed` method with an anonymous inner class.

12.2 Rewrite a previous project replacing the `actionPerformed` method with a local inner class.

12.3 Rewrite a previous project replacing the `actionPerformed` method with a member inner class.

CASE STUDIES

R 'n R—for Reading and Refreshment

Rewrite your project assignment from Chapter 5 to use inner classes.

Merry Pea's Quilting

Rewrite your project assignment from Chapter 5 to use inner classes.

13

Storing Information, Object Serialization, and JDBC

At the completion of this chapter, you will be able to . . .

1. Understand the purpose of streaming classes.

2. Use the System class for input and output to standard devices.

3. Save an object to a file.

4. Retrieve an object from a file.

5. Retrieve information from a database using the JDBC API.

6. Write SQL Select statements to create a ResultSet.

7. Use SQL action queries to update an existing database.

In this chapter you learn how to store information from one execution of a project until the next execution. It is possible to use an object, store it, and then recreate the object exactly as it existed at a later time.

Streams

The most basic of input/output with Java is done with streams. Think of a **stream** as a flow of data, which can be an input stream or an output stream (Figure 13.1). The stream can flow from the program to the screen, from a keyboard to the program, to/from a disk file or other storage media, to a printer, or even to a network or the Web. The stream commands enable you to write to a disk file or to the output screen.

Figure 13.1

*An input stream flows from an
external device or file into the
program; an output stream flows
from the program to an external
device or file.*

First you will set up a basic output stream by writing to the screen. Then you will learn to use one of the newest features of Java: writing an object to a disk file.

Output to the Screen

You can send an output stream to the "standard output device" or read an input stream from the "standard input device." Although these devices can be redirected on most systems, the **standard input device** is normally the keyboard and the **standard output device** is your monitor. This concept is another of the many carryovers from C and C++.

Java's System class contains utilities for reading from the standard input device and writing to the standard output device. You can choose from two methods for sending output: the **print method** and the **println method.** Both methods send text to the screen; `println` automatically adds a carriage return while `print` does not.

Typically, Java textbooks start with elementary programs that use the output stream to display text on the screen. But this boring technique writes to a text output area in the IDE or a Java window much like the MS-DOS screen. (We hope that you agree that using a graphical user interface is much more fun and more useful.)

```
//Folder:        Ch13OutputStream
//Programmer:    Bradley/Millspaugh
//Date:          6/2001
//ClassName:     PrintStream
//Description:   Demonstrate printing to an output stream.
```

```
public class PrintStream
{
    public static void main(String args[])
    {
        //Write to standard output device
        System.out.println("Hello World");
    }
}
```

Java, like C and C++, has three standard IO (input/output) objects: *in*, *out*, and *err*. You generally display error messages on the standard output device using the err object.

```
System.err.println("No connection to database");
```

Feedback 13.1

1. Code the statement(s) to print your name on the standard output device.
2. Code the `try/catch` statements to display the message "Arithmetic Error" when an ArithmeticException occurs.

Saving an Object in a File

A common term in programming is **persistence.** How can you make data persist, or still be available, from one run of the program to the next? If you want to save data from one program execution to the next, you must have some way to store the data.

From its inception, Java has been able to store bytes of information and the contents of individual variables into a disk file. Using this technique, the programmer is responsible for writing all data into a disk file and reading it again for the next program execution. This tedious method is seldom used in industry; usually information such as this is stored in a database. You will learn to read and write database files later in this chapter.

Applets versus Applications

You will recall that the Security Manager for applets guards against damage to the local machine. Although you can perform disk reading and writing from some versions of the Applet Viewer, you cannot access disk files from an applet running in a browser. For this reason, the programs in this chapter are coded as applications rather than applets.

Object Serialization

Beginning with JDK 1.1, Java added a powerful tool for persisting an entire object as a single unit. Using **object serialization,** you can use an output stream for writing objects.

When you store an object, you need to keep the contents of the variables but not the methods. You can create a file that stores the contents of the class variables for multiple instances of a class. The program that later inputs the information from the file can read the values for the class variables into an instance, or multiple instances, of the class, one for each object stored in the file.

In the examples that follow, we create an Employee class. One program allows the user to enter the data for multiple employees and saves the data for each employee object in a file. The second program reads the employee data back in from the data file and displays them on the screen.

Note: If your object contains a reference to another object, you also must store the data of the referenced object.

Creating a Serializable Class

When you write a class that you want to persist, the class doesn't look much different from any other class. You declare class variables (generally private) and write get methods to retrieve the variables' values. You must import java.io.*.

```
//Folder:        Ch13ObjectSerialization
//Programmer:    Bradley/Millspaugh
//Date:          6/2001
//ClassName:     Employee
//Description:   Store the data for one employee object.

import java.io.*;

public class Employee implements Serializable
{
    private String strName;
    private String strHireDate;

    Employee(String strNameIn, String strHireDateIn)
    {
        //Assign property values
        strName = strNameIn;
        strHireDate = strHireDateIn;
    }

    public String getName()
    {
        //Retrieve employee name
        return strName;
    }

    public String getHireDate()
    {
        //Retrieve hire date
        return strHireDate;
    }
}
```

Writing an Object

The steps for writing an object are

● Create a FileOutputStream object.

● Create an ObjectOutputStream object.

- Obtain the data from the text fields (after the user enters them).

- Create an event for storing the data for one object.

- After all objects have been stored, close the FileOutputStream and ObjectOutputStream objects.

The FileOutputStream Object

The **FileOutputStream** class establishes a link from the program to an actual disk file. If the file does not already exist, this class creates the file.

Declare the output object at the class level.

```
FileOutputStream outputEmployee;
```

Instantiate the object and assign the file name in a method inside the application.

```
outputEmployee = new FileOutputStream("Employee.txt");
```

You must place this statement in a `try`/`catch` block, catching `Exception`.

You can use any file name that you wish. An extension of .txt makes it a little easier to look at the file while you are learning. Although the file appears to contain a lot of gibberish, you can also find your text strings embedded in the file.

The ObjectOutputStream Object

You can use the FileOutputStream object for any type of output stream. To save an object using the stream, you must also set up an **ObjectOutputStream** class. Once again you declare the object as a class variable and then assign the ObjectOutputStream object in a class method. The argument for the ObjectOutputStream constructor is the name of a FileOutputStream object.

```
//Declare the object output stream
ObjectOutputStream objSaveEmployee;

//Instantiate the object stream and associate it to the file stream
objSaveEmployee = new ObjectOutputStream(outputEmployee);
```

Obtaining the Data

The example contains text fields for the name and the hire date (Figure 13.2). The user presumably will type in the information and then press the Save button.

Figure 13.2

The user enters the employee information for one Employee object, which is saved in the disk file.

```
TextField txtEmployeeName = new TextField(25);
TextField txtHireDate = new TextField(10);
Button btnSave = new Button("Save");
```

Event for Storing Data

The Save button creates a new employee object (refer to page 402) by passing the data values from the text fields. The **writeObject method** of the ObjectOutputStream class saves the contents of the named object.

```
public void actionPerformed(ActionEvent event)
{
    //Save employee object
    try
    {
        Employee empCurrent = new Employee
            (txtEmployeeName.getText(),txtHireDate.getText());
        objSaveEmployee.writeObject(empCurrent);
        objSaveEmployee.flush();
        txtEmployeeName.setText("");
        txtHireDate.setText("");
        txtEmployeeName.requestFocus();
    }
    catch(Exception error)
    {
        System.err.println("Error writing to file");
    }
}
```

This method also clears the text fields if the save is successful. Any errors display an error message.

Note that you must enclose all statements that access the disk file in try/catch blocks.

Closing the Streams

When you are finished with the FileOutputStream and the ObjectOutputStream, you should close both. This flushes any data remaining in the buffer and releases any resources used by the streams.

```
objSaveEmployee.close(); //Close the object output stream
outputEmployee.close();  //Close the file output stream
```

The EmployeeWrite Application

Here is the application that writes the Employee objects into the Employee.txt file. Note that the Employee class file must be in the same folder as this application or the system class path must be set to include the folder holding the class. Also notice that the application must import java.io.*.

```
//Folder:        Ch13ObjectSerialization
//Programmer:    Bradley/Millspaugh
//Date:          6/2001
//ClassName:     EmployeeWriteApp
//Description:   Use a stream to store an Employee object.
```

```java
import java.awt.*;
import java.awt.event.*;
import java.io.*;

public class EmployeeWriteApp extends Frame implements ActionListener
{
    //Declare stream objects
    FileOutputStream outputEmployee;    //Stream to create file
    ObjectOutputStream objSaveEmployee; //Stream to save an object

    //Declare components
    TextField txtEmployeeName = new TextField(25);
    TextField txtHireDate = new TextField(10);
    Button btnSave = new Button("Save");

    public static void main(String args[])
    {
        //Declare an instance of this application
        EmployeeWriteApp thisApp = new EmployeeWriteApp();
        thisApp.openStream();
        thisApp.createInterface();
    }

    public void openStream()
    {
        try
        {
            //Create file and object output streams
            outputEmployee = new FileOutputStream("Employee.txt");
            objSaveEmployee = new ObjectOutputStream(outputEmployee);
        }

        catch(Exception error)
        {
            System.err.println("Error opening file");
        }
    }

    public void closeStream()
    {
        try
        {
            objSaveEmployee.close(); //Close the object output stream
            outputEmployee.close();  //Close the file output stream
        }

        catch (IOException error)
        {
            System.err.println("Error closing file");
        }
    }

    public void createInterface()
    {
        //Set up user interface for this frame

        setTitle("Save Employee Objects");
```

```
        addWindowListener(new WindowAdapter()
        {
            public void windowClosing(WindowEvent event)
            {
                closeStream();
                System.exit(0);
            }
        });
        setLayout(new FlowLayout());
        add(new Label("Employee Name "));
        add(txtEmployeeName);
        txtEmployeeName.requestFocus();
        add(new Label("Hire Date "));
        add(txtHireDate);
        add(btnSave);
        btnSave.addActionListener(this);
        txtEmployeeName.addActionListener(this);
        txtHireDate.addActionListener(this);
        setSize(400, 300);
        setVisible(true);
    }

    public void actionPerformed(ActionEvent event)
    {
        //Save Employee object
        try
        {
            Employee empCurrent = new Employee(txtEmployeeName.getText(),
                                    txtHireDate.getText());
            objSaveEmployee.writeObject(empCurrent);
            objSaveEmployee.flush();
            txtEmployeeName.setText("");
            txtHireDate.setText("");
            txtEmployeeName.requestFocus();
        }

        catch(Exception error)
        {
            System.err.println("Error writing to file");
        }
    }
}
```

Reading an Object

The procedure for reading information back from a file is very similar to writing it, but uses input streams instead of output streams.

The steps for reading an object are

- Create a FileInputStream object.

- Create an ObjectInputStream object.

- Obtain the data for one object from the file.

- Create an event to display the object's data in text fields.

The FileInputStream and ObjectInputStream Objects

The **FileInputStream** object associates the project with a file, and the **ObjectInputStream** enables you to read the entire object with one read command. Just as you did for the output stream, declare the FileInputStream and ObjectInputStream objects as class variables. Then instantiate the objects in a class method.

```java
//Declare stream objects (as class variables)
FileInputStream inputEmployee;
ObjectInputStream objGetEmployee;

public void openStream()
{
    try
    {
        //Create file and object input streams
        inputEmployee = new FileInputStream("Employee.txt");
        objGetEmployee = new ObjectInputStream(inputEmployee);
    }

    catch(Exception error)
    {
        System.err.println("Error opening file");
    }
}
```

Event for Displaying Data

When the user clicks the Display button, you create an Employee object and read the information from the disk file. Read the information using the readObject method of the ObjectInputStream; you must cast the result into an Employee object. Then you can use the Employee object's get methods to display the data to the screen.

You can check for the end of file by catching an EOFException.

```java
public void actionPerformed(ActionEvent event)
    {
        try
        {
            //Retrieve employee object
            Employee empCurrent;
            empCurrent = (Employee) objGetEmployee.readObject();
            txtEmployeeName.setText(empCurrent.getName());
            txtHireDate.setText(empCurrent.getHireDate());
            txtEmployeeName.requestFocus();
        }

        catch(EOFException eof)
        {
            //End of file
            txtEmployeeName.setText("End of File");
            txtHireDate.setText("");
        }
        catch(Exception error)
        {
            System.err.println("Error reading file");
        }
    }
```

Closing the Input Streams

Closing both input streams releases the resources used by the streams.

```
objGetEmployee.close(); //Close the object input stream
inputEmployee.close();  //Close the file input stream
```

The EmployeeRead Application

This is the complete listing of the application that reads back the employee information from the Employee.txt file (Figure 13.3). Note that the Employee class file must be in the same folder as this application or the system class path must be set to include the folder holding the class. This application must also import java.io.*.

Figure 13.3

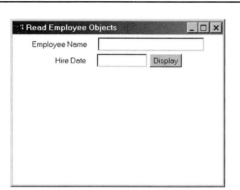

When the user clicks on the Display button, one Employee object is read from the disk file and the fields displayed for the user.

```
//Folder:        Ch13ObjectSerialization
//Programmer:    Bradley/Millspaugh
//Date:          6/2001
//ClassName:     EmployeeReadApp
//Description:   Use an input stream to read objects previously stored.

import java.awt.*;
import java.awt.event.*;
import java.io.*;

public class EmployeeReadApp extends Frame implements ActionListener
{
    //Declare stream objects
    FileInputStream inputEmployee;
    ObjectInputStream objGetEmployee;

    //Declare components
    TextField txtEmployeeName = new TextField(25);
    TextField txtHireDate = new TextField(10);
    Button btnDisplay = new Button("Display");

    public static void main(String args[])
    {
        //Declare an instance of this application
        EmployeeReadApp thisApp = new EmployeeReadApp();
        thisApp.openStream();
        thisApp.createInterface();
    }
```

```java
public void openStream()
{
    try
    {
        //Create file and object input streams
        inputEmployee = new FileInputStream("Employee.txt");
        objGetEmployee = new ObjectInputStream(inputEmployee);
    }

    catch(Exception error)
    {
        System.err.println("Error opening file");
    }
}

public void closeStream()
{
    try
    {
        objGetEmployee.close(); //Close the object input stream
        inputEmployee.close();  //Close the file input stream
    }

    catch (IOException error)
    {
        System.err.println("Error closing file");
    }
}

public void createInterface()
{
    //Set up user interface for this frame
    setTitle("Read Employee Objects");
    addWindowListener(new WindowAdapter()
    {
        public void windowClosing(WindowEvent event)
        {
            closeStream();
            System.exit(0);
        }
    });
    setLayout(new FlowLayout());
    add(new Label("Employee Name "));
    add(txtEmployeeName);
    txtEmployeeName.requestFocus();
    add(new Label("Hire Date "));
    add(txtHireDate);
    add(btnDisplay);
    btnDisplay.addActionListener(this);
    txtEmployeeName.addActionListener(this);
    txtHireDate.addActionListener(this);
    setSize(400, 300);
    setVisible(true);
}

public void actionPerformed(ActionEvent event)
{
    try
    {
        //Retrieve Employee object
```

```
            Employee empCurrent;
            empCurrent = (Employee) objGetEmployee.readObject();
            txtEmployeeName.setText(empCurrent.getName());
            txtHireDate.setText(empCurrent.getHireDate());
            txtEmployeeName.requestFocus();
        }

        catch(EOFException eof)
        {
            //End of file
            txtEmployeeName.setText("End of File");
            txtHireDate.setText("");
        }
        catch(Exception error)
        {
            System.err.println("Error reading file");
        }
    }
}
```

Feedback 13.2

1. Code the statements to allow an object called objPayroll to write to Payroll.txt located on the A drive.
2. Code the statements to allow the objPayroll to read from Payroll.txt.

Database Connection with the JDBC API

You can access data files in Java using **Java Database Connectivity (JDBC).** The JDBC API is a set of classes available in JDK 1.1 or higher, in the java.sql package. The classes and methods allow Java applets and applications to interface with data that are stored in many formats including relational, hierarchical, and network databases.

Note: JDK 1.2 (Java 2) greatly improved database handling, providing many additional features, such as scrollable recordsets.

Many issues can complicate accessing databases in Java. If you are using an applet, security is an issue. You can easily access a database on the local machine, but to access a database on a server, you must properly set up security and sign the applet (see Chapter 15). For optimal database performance on the Web, you must download and install drivers that are specific to the database format. Refer to these sites for further information:

JDBC FAQ (frequently asked questions):
   http://java.sun.com/products/jdbc/faq.html
JDBC drivers: http://java.sun.com/products/jdbc/drivers

JDBC

The JDBC classes handle communication between your Java program and a database driver. Most companies that produce database software provide JDBC drivers, and many other companies sell drivers to access various database formats. Java 2 comes with JDBC, but not the manufacturer-specific database drivers. The only driver that *does* come with Java is the JDBC-ODBC Bridge, which we will use in this chapter.

The JDBC-ODBC Bridge takes advantage of **Open DataBase Connectivity (ODBC),** which is Microsoft's implementation of universal data access for diverse database formats. Nearly all database formats provide ODBC drivers. Therefore, if an ODBC driver is available to access a database format, files in that format also can be accessed from Java.

Note: According to this quote from Sun's official Website (http://java.sun.com/products/jdbc/faq.html), you should use manufacturer-specific drivers for "real" production work: ". . . we do not recommend using the Bridge except for experimental purposes or when you have no other driver available."

The following sections introduce you to JDBC and SQL (structured query language). If you are already familiar with SQL and ODBC, you will be very comfortable working with JDBC.

Setting up a DSN

A **Data Source Name (DSN)** creates a link between a physical data file and a name that you use in a program. Before using JDBC in a Windows environment, you must create a DSN, which registers your database file on the computer. You use the ODBC icon on the control panel to register databases.

STEP 1: From the `Start` menu, select `Settings/Control Panel`.

STEP 2: Access the ODBC Database Administrator window by double-clicking on the icon for ODBC Data Sources (32 bit).

STEP 3: On the `User DSN` tab, click on the Add button.

STEP 4: The Create New Data Source window appears. Select the database type. Our file is a Microsoft Access database, so you only need to click on Finish.

Note that different versions of Windows have slightly different words on the dialog box.

STEP 5: Type in the Data Source Name, which is a name that you make up. You will use this name in your program to refer to the file. (Your dialog box may say "Data Source Name" or "DataBase Access Name".)

For the examples in this chapter, type "MerryPeas" for the Data Source Name. (Do not enter the quotes.)

STEP 6: Use the Select (or Browse) button to locate the database file, then close the dialog boxes.

You set up the DSN only once for a database file in a given location. (You can refer to the same DSN from many projects.) For testing purposes you may wish to place a copy of the database in your project folder. If so, you must create a DSN for each copy of the database.

Loading the JDBC-ODBC Bridge Driver

In your code, you must connect to the driver using the `Class.forName` method. Connect to Sun's JDBC-ODBC Bridge driver using this statement:

```
Class.forName("sun.jdbc.odbc.JdbcOdbcDriver");
```

If you are using Microsoft's VJ++ or Internet Explorer, you cannot load Sun's driver but must load Microsoft's version of the Bridge instead:

```
Class.forName("com.ms.jdbc.odbc.JdbcOdbcDriver");
```

If you need to be able to load either driver, you can use try/catch blocks and attempt to load one driver. If that fails, load the other one. If both fail, a Class-NotFound exception occurs.

```
try
{
    //Load the MicroSoft drivers
    Class.forName ("com.ms.jdbc.odbc.JdbcOdbcDriver");
}

catch (ClassNotFoundException error)
{
    try
    {
        //Load the Sun drivers
        Class.forName ("sun.jdbc.odbc.JdbcOdbcDriver");
    }

    catch (ClassNotFoundException err)
    {
        //No drivers found
        System.err.println("Driver did not load properly");
    }
}
```

Connecting to the Database

Your next step is to connect to the database using the name that you registered as a DSN. This name is included in a string literal. For example, if we registered the DSN as MerryPeas, the string becomes "jdbc:odbc:MerryPeas". Use this string with the DriverManager.getConnection method and assign it to a **Connection object.**

```
//Declare a Connection object
Connection conEmployees;

//Connect to the database
try
{
    conEmployees = DriverManager.getConnection("jdbc:odbc:MerryPeas");
}

catch(SQLException error)
{
    showStatus("No connection to database");
}
```

Notice that the connection is placed inside of a Try block, to test for an SQLException.

Creating a ResultSet

A **ResultSet object** contains a collection of records from the database. To create a ResultSet, you must declare a **Statement object** and call the Connection object's createStatement method. Then you can use the Statement object to create a query.

```
Statement cmdEmployees;
ResultSet rsEmployees;
```

You create a ResultSet with an SQL query. SQL is covered later in this chapter.

The following example selects all fields and all records in the Employees table of the MerryPeas database (Figure 13.4). The SQL string is

```
Select * from Employees
```

Figure 13.4

Last Name	First Name	SSN	Phone Number
Gunn	Chad	123-45-6666	(626) 225-0000
Chunchick	Sherry	588-09-9987	(949) 123-5678
Rigner	Michele	765-12-3445	(714) 456-7888

The Employees table in the MerryPeas database.

Use this SQL string as an argument for the **executeQuery method** of the Statement object.

```
try
{
    //Connect to the database
    conEmployees = DriverManager.getConnection("jdbc:odbc:MerryPeas");

    //Create a ResultSet
    Statement cmdEmployees = conEmployees.createStatement();
    ResultSet rsEmployees = cmdEmployees.executeQuery("Select * from Employees");
}
catch(SQLException error)
{
    System.err.println("Error: " + error.toString());
}
```

Once again, you must place the statements within a try/catch block. This is true for any statements that access a database.

You can create an SQL statement to create a ResultSet that matches a given condition. For example, this query will create a ResultSet that holds only the record(s) where the Last Name field contains "Rigner".

```
ResultSet rsEmployees = cmdEmployees.executeQuery(
            "Select * from Employees Where [Last Name] = 'Rigner'");
```

You can allow the user to enter the desired name and substitute the literal name with a string variable.

```
ResultSet rsEmployees = cmdEmployees.executeQuery(
            "Select * from Employees Where [Last Name] = '" + strLastName + "'");
```

In Java you create queries in the program code, as you have just seen. Or you can create a PreparedStatement outside of Java and call it from the Java code.

Retrieving a Record

When you first open a ResultSet, the current-record pointer is located just prior to the first record. You call the ResultSet's next method, which has a dual purpose. The next method moves the current-record pointer (also called the *cursor*) to the first record and returns boolean true or false. A true means that the next record exists and a false means that no more records exist in the ResultSet (the operation was successful or unsuccessful).

You must have a current record before you can access the data fields in a record. This code moves to the first (next) record and adds the contents of the Last Name field to a List component called lstNames. The getString method retrieves the data for the specified string field.

```
try
{
    rsEmployees.next();
    lstNames.add(rsEmployees.getString("Last Name"));
}
catch (SQLException error)
{
    System.err.println("Error: " + error.toString());
}
```

Make sure to enclose the next method in a try/catch block.

Looping through a ResultSet

You can step through all records in a ResultSet using a loop. Use while (rsResultSet.next()) to control the loop execution. The boolean condition (rsResultSet.next()) tests true as long as records remain in the ResultSet, and tests false when no more records remain.

The following code segment loops through all of the records in the Result-Set and adds the last names to a List.

```
try
{
    //Fill last name list
    while(rsEmployees.next())
        lstNames.add(rsEmployees.getString("Last Name"));
}
catch (SQLException error)
{
    System.err.println("Error: " + error.toString());
}
```

Displaying the Fields from a Record

This example retrieves one record from the ResultSet and displays each of the
three fields in text fields.

```
try
{
    //Display information
    if(rsEmployees.next()) //If more records remain
    {
        lblFirstName.setText(rsEmployees.getString("First Name"));
        lblSSN.setText(rsEmployees.getString("SSN"));
        lblPhone.setText(rsEmployees.getString("Phone Number"));
    }
    else
        System.err.println("No more records");
}
catch (SQLException error)
{
        System.err.println("Error: " + error.toString());
}
```

Accessing the Data Fields

Access the data in database fields by using the appropriate method for the data
type. Use **getString** for string fields; use getFloat or getInt for float or int
fields. You must give the correct field name, including spacing.

```
lblFirstName.setText(rsEmployees.getString("First Name"));
lblSSN.setText(rsEmployees.getString("SSN"));
lblPhone.setText(rsEmployees.getString("Phone Number"));
```

To retrieve a numeric field from a database, use the getFloat or getInt
method. Then convert the value to a string and/or format it to display the value
in a label or text field.

```
//Set formatting for numeric Cost Value
NumberFormat fmtCurrency = NumberFormat.getCurrencyInstance();

strFormattedCost = fmtCurrency.format (rsVehicles.getFloat("CostValue"));
txtCostValue.setText(strFormattedCost);
```

Caution

Even if you declare a ResultSet object at the class level, you cannot access the
ResultSet in any method other than the one in which it was created. You must
actually pass the ResultSet to any other method that needs to reference the
data. Failure to do this results in a null pointer error.

```
    //Create a ResultSet
    Statement cmdEmployees = conEmployees.createStatement();
    ResultSet rsEmployees = cmdEmployees.executeQuery("Select * from Employees");
    LoadNames(rsEmployees);
}
```

```java
public void LoadNames(ResultSet rsEmployees)
{
    try
    {
        //Fill last name list box
        while(rsEmployees.next())
            lstNames.add(rsEmployees.getString("Last Name"));
    }
    catch (SQLException error)
    {
        System.err.println("Error in display record");
    }
}
```

Closing the Connection

Make sure that the database connection is closed at the termination of the program. Place the statements in the `stop` method of an applet. If you are writing an application, place the code in your exit routine. You can avoid an exception for attempting to close a connection that doesn't exist by testing for null.

```java
public void stop()
{
    try
    {
        //Terminate the connection
        if (conEmployees != null)
            conEmployees.close();
    }
    catch(SQLException error)
    {
        System.err.println("Unable to disconnect");
    }
}
```

Sample Program

This application combines the code segments you have seen. It opens a connection to the database, creates a ResultSet of all records, and adds the last names to a list. When the user selects a last name from the list, a new Result-Set is created of only the record that matches the last name. The fields from the record are displayed in text fields on the screen.

In order to run this application, you must first create a DSN called Merry-Peas that points to the MerryPeas.mdb database file. The application should run in JBuilder, Microsoft VJ++, or any other IDE.

Note: This application can also be written as an applet. See Ch13JDB-CApplet and Ch13JDBCAppletMS (for the Microsoft driver version) on your CD.

```java
//Folder:        Ch13JDBCApp
//Programmer:    Bradley/Millspaugh
//Date:          6/2001
//ClassName:     JDBCApp
//Description:   An application to display information from an Access database.
//                   Uses the JDBC-ODBC Bridge.
```

```java
import java.sql.*;
import java.awt.*;
import java.awt.event.*;

public class JDBCApp extends Frame implements ItemListener
{
    //Declare database variables
    Connection conEmployees;
    Statement cmdEmployees;
    ResultSet rsEmployees;
    boolean blnSuccessfulOpen = false;

    //Declare components
    Choice lstNames = new Choice();
    Label lblFirstName = new Label("                      ");
    Label lblSSN = new Label("                  ");
    Label lblPhone = new Label("                    ");
    Label lblInstructions = new Label("Select Name to Display Record");

    public static void main(String args[])
    {
        //Declare an instance of this application
        JDBCApp thisApp = new JDBCApp();
        thisApp.createInterface();
    }

    public void createInterface()
    {
        //Load the database and set up the frame
        loadDatabase();
        if (blnSuccessfulOpen)
        {
            setTitle("Display MerryPea's Database");
            addWindowListener(new WindowAdapter()
            {
                public void windowClosing(WindowEvent event)
                {
                        stop();
                        System.exit(0);
                }
            });
            setLayout(new FlowLayout());
            add(new Label("Last Name"));
            add(lstNames);
            lstNames.addItemListener(this);
            add(lblInstructions);
            add(new Label("First Name"));
            add(lblFirstName);
            add(new Label("Social Security #"));
            add(lblSSN);
            add(new Label("Phone Number"));
            add(lblPhone);
            setSize(250,250);
            setVisible(true);
        }
        else
        {
            stop();           //Close any open connection
            System.exit(-1); //Exit with error status
        }
    }
}
```

```java
public void loadDatabase()
{
    try
    {
        //Load the MicroSoft drivers
        Class.forName ("com.ms.jdbc.odbc.JdbcOdbcDriver");
    }
    catch (ClassNotFoundException error)
    {
        try
        {
            //Load the Sun drivers
            Class.forName ("sun.jdbc.odbc.JdbcOdbcDriver");
        }
        catch (ClassNotFoundException err)
        {
            //No drivers found
            System.err.println("Driver did not load properly");
        }
    }
    try
    {
        //Connect to the database
        conEmployees = DriverManager.getConnection("jdbc:odbc:MerryPeas");

        //Create a ResultSet
        cmdEmployees = conEmployees.createStatement();
        rsEmployees = cmdEmployees.executeQuery("Select * from Employees;");
        loadNames(rsEmployees);
        blnSuccessfulOpen = true;
    }
    catch(SQLException error)
    {
        System.err.println("Error: " + error.toString());
    }
}

public void loadNames(ResultSet rsEmployees)
{
    try
    {
        //Fill last name list box
        while(rsEmployees.next())
            lstNames.add(rsEmployees.getString("Last Name"));
    }
    catch (SQLException error)
    {
        System.err.println("Error in display record");
    }
}

public void itemStateChanged(ItemEvent event)
{
    //Display the selected record

    lblInstructions.setText("");
    String strLastName = lstNames.getSelectedItem();
    try
    {
```

```
        Statement cmdEmployees = conEmployees.createStatement();
        ResultSet rsEmployees = cmdEmployees.executeQuery(
            "Select * from Employees where [Last Name] = '" + strLastName + "';");
        DisplayRecord(rsEmployees);
    }
    catch(SQLException error)
    {
        System.err.println("Error in recordset");
    }
}

public void DisplayRecord(ResultSet rsEmployees)
{
    try
    {
        //Display information
        if(rsEmployees.next()) //If more records remain
        {
            lblFirstName.setText(rsEmployees.getString("First Name"));
            lblSSN.setText(rsEmployees.getString("SSN"));
            lblPhone.setText(rsEmployees.getString("Phone Number"));
        }
        else
            System.err.println("No more records");
    }
    catch (SQLException error)
    {
        System.err.println("Error in display record");
    }
}

public void stop()
{
    try
    {
        //Terminate the connection
        if (conEmployees != null)
            conEmployees.close();
    }
    catch(SQLException error)
    {
        System.err.println("Unable to disconnect");
    }
}
}
```

SQL

Java's JDBC uses **Structured Query Language (SQL)** to create a ResultSet. SQL (pronounced either "sequel" or "S, Q, L") is an industry-standard language that you can use to access data in nearly every relational database format. Although the basic SQL statements are standardized, some vendors include extensions that are nonstandard. In this chapter you will learn to create basic SQL statements that should work for all databases. You will see several ways to use an SQL statement in code to create a ResultSet or to directly update a database.

In the previous program example, you saw two examples of SQL statements, each of which used the executeQuery method to create a new ResultSet:

```
ResultSet rsEmployees = cmdEmployees.executeQuery("Select * from Employees;");

ResultSet rsEmployees = cmdEmployees.executeQuery(
   "Select * from Employees where [Last Name] = '" + strLastName + "';");
```

Types of SQL Statements

SQL Select statements select data from a database and return those data to the program. You can specify which fields from which table or tables, and select only certain records based on criteria.

You can also write SQL statements that perform actions on the database rather than just select data. The actions that you can perform include inserting records and deleting and updating records, as well as modifying the structure of a database, such as adding tables and fields.

This next section provides a brief tutorial on writing Select statements. Later in the chapter you will learn to write SQL statements that perform an action.

Writing SQL Select Statements

This section shows the syntax that you need to write your own SQL Select statements.

The SQL Select Statement—General Format

```
SELECT [Distinct] Field(s) FROM Table(s) [IN Database]
   [WHERE Criteria]
   [GROUP BY Field(s)]
   [HAVING GroupCriteria]
   [ORDER BY Field(s)];
```

For the field(s), you can list the field names or use an asterisk to indicate all fields from the named table(s). Multiple-word field names must be enclosed in square brackets or accent grave marks (`).

The optional Distinct drops out duplicates so that no two records are alike.

The SQL Select Statement—Examples

```
SELECT [Last Name], [First Name], Phone FROM Patient
   ORDER BY [Last Name], [First Name];
SELECT DISTINCT `Last Name` FROM Patient
   ORDER BY `Last Name`;
SELECT * FROM Patient
   WHERE [Last Name] = "'" + txtSearch.getText() + "';"
SELECT * FROM Patient, Insurance
   WHERE Patient.[Insurance Company Code] = InsuranceCompany.Code;
```

Note that the last example joins the Patient and Insurance tables so that the actual name of the company, not just the Code, is included in the results. This easy method for joining tables creates a ResultSet that is nonupdateable and does not include any patients without a matching entry in the Insurance-Company table, including those with no insurance. To make a joined ResultSet updateable and complete, you must use the Join clause of the SQL Select statement.

Note: The closing semicolon (;) is specified in the SQL standards. Many versions of SQL do not require the semicolon, but some do. You cannot go wrong by always including it.

SQL Queries

Here are a few simple SQL queries.

```
SELECT [Last Name], [First Name] FROM Employee;
```

The ResultSet created from this SQL statement will include only the Last Name and First Name fields from the Employee table.

```
SELECT * FROM Employee;
```

This ResultSet will include all fields (* = all fields) from the Employee table.

```
SELECT Employee.[Last Name], Employee.[First Name],
    InsuranceCompany.Name
  FROM Employee, InsuranceCompany
  WHERE Employee.[Insurance Company Code] = InsuranceCompany.Code;
```

This ResultSet will include three fields: Last Name and First Name from the Employee table and the Name field from the InsuranceCompany table. It joins the two tables in order to retrieve the company name that matches the Insurance Company Code field from the Employee table.

Note: For field names that contain a space, you must enclose the name within either square brackets or the accent grave symbol (`).

```
SELECT `Last Name`, `First Name`
  FROM Employee;
```

The Where Clause

You can use a Where clause to join tables:

```
"WHERE Employee.[Insurance Company Code] = InsuranceCompany.Code"
```

You can also use a Where clause to select only those records that meet specific criteria:

```
"WHERE Employee.[Insurance Company Code] = 'ABC'"
"WHERE Employee.[Insurance Company Code] = '" + strSelectedCompany + "'"
```

You can include multiple conditions in a Where clause:

```
"WHERE Employee.[Insurance Company Code] = InsuranceCompany.Code " +
  "AND Employee.[Insurance Company Code] = '" + strSelectedCompany + "'"
```

Comparing Database Fields to Java Fields

The syntax of the criteria in a Where clause depends on the location of the data. You must specify database fields differently from program variables. And string fields must be compared only to string data; numeric fields compared only to numeric data. Otherwise your program will fail.

```
//Compare a string field to a string variable
"WHERE [Last Name] = '" + strName + "'"

//Compare a string field to a string from a text component
"WHERE [Last Name] Like '" + txtSearchName.getText() + "'"

//Compare a string field to a string constant
"WHERE [Last Name] = 'Jones'"

//Compare a numeric field to a numeric variable
"WHERE [Duration] = " + intSearchMinutes

//Compare a numeric field to a property
"WHERE [Duration] = " + Float.valueOf(txtNumber.getText()).floatValue()

//Compare a numeric field to a numeric constant
"WHERE [Duration] = 15"
```

The Order By Clause

It is incredibly easy to sort your ResultSet in SQL—just use the Order By clause. You can order by one or more fields, in ascending or descending sequence. If you don't specify the direction, ascending is assumed.

```
"ORDER BY [Last Name], [First Name]"
"ORDER BY InsuranceCompany.Name ASC"
"ORDER BY DateDue DESC"
```

Feedback 13.3

1. Write the statement to set up the drivers for a database with the DSN "ABCInc".
2. What statement connects the Java program to the database?
3. Write the SQL statement that selects the First Name and Phone fields from the Employee table.
4. Code the Java statement to execute the SQL query in question 3.

Updating a Database

You can also update a database from a Java program. You use the Statement object's **executeUpdate method,** which works with SQL statements.

Many different errors can occur while updating a database. If you get a "null pointer exception," it is likely that the update or query has failed. With an update, this could be a result of many different factors: a mandatory or key field left blank, duplicate records, incorrect data type, or not a valid format. You can use your validation techniques from Chapter 6 to avoid some of the problems; other problems may not be easy to find.

SQL Updates

So far, our database programs use only SQL Select statements that produce a ResultSet. In this section you will see a different way to program, using methods to directly update a database. You will write SQL action queries, such as **Insert**, **Delete**, and **Update**, and execute the actions using the execute-Update method of the Statement object.

Action queries operate directly on the database, not on any open ResultSet. To execute an SQL action query on a database, you must have an open Connection, but you don't need to have an open ResultSet.

The following examples develop an update program (Figure 13.5). The user can add new records, delete records, or edit (modify) existing records. For the delete and edit options, the user first displays the desired record and then clicks the appropriate button.

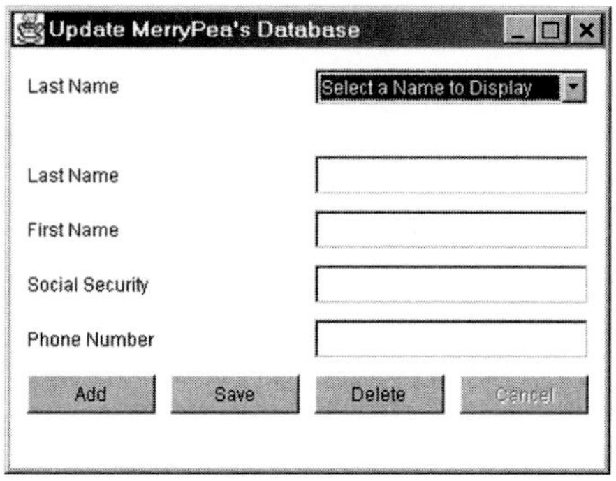

Figure 13.5

The user interface for the update program.

Note: You can see the entire program in the hands-on example at the end of this chapter.

Adding a Record

Adding a record is a two-step process. When the user clicks the Add button, you must clear the text fields for data entry and set the focus in the first text field. After the user enters the data for the new record, he or she will click the OK (or Cancel) button. To actually add a new record to the database, you use the SQL Insert statement.

The SQL Insert Statement—General Format

```
Insert Into TableName (Fieldlist) VALUES (ListOfValues);
```

The SQL Insert Statement—Examples

```
Insert Into Employees ([Last Name], [First Name]) Values ('Berry', 'Terry');

strSQL = "Insert Into Employees ([Last Name], [First Name]) "
       + "VALUES ('"+ txtLastName.getText() + "', '"
       + txtFirstName.getText() + "');"
```

The Add Method

In the Add method, you must clear the contents of the text fields so that the user can enter new values. Also, it's a good idea to give the user only two choices once the Add operation starts: OK (which saves the new record) or Cancel (in case of a mind change). We will use the Add button for a dual purpose: Once the Add is in progress, the button's caption changes to "OK". After the user clicks OK or Cancel, the caption of the Add button changes back to "Add".

```
public void Add()
{
    //Add a new record
    lblMessage.setText("              ");    //Clear previous message
    setTextToEditable();                     //Unlock the text fields
    ClearTextFields();                       //Clear text field contents
    txtLastName.requestFocus();

    //Set up the OK and Cancel buttons
    btnAdd.setLabel("OK");
    btnCancel.setEnabled(true);

    //Disable the Delete and Edit buttons
    btnDelete.setEnabled(false);
    btnEdit.setEnabled(false);
}
```

This program displays all of the employee names in a list box, just as in the earlier display-only program. So when the user adds a new employee to the database, the record's Last Name field must also be added to the list of names. The Social Security Number is a mandatory field because it is the primary key of the Employee table. And the Last Name field is required to avoid a null pointer when loading names into the list.

The Save Method

The Save method, which is executed when the user clicks OK at the end of an Add, must perform validation. If the data pass the validation, then the record is added. Use the Statement object's executeUpdate method to execute the SQL Insert Into statement.

```
public void Save()
{
    //Save the new record
    //Activated when the Add button has an "OK" label
    if (txtLastName.getText().length() == 0 || txtSSN.getText().length() == 0)
        lblMessage.setText("The Last Name or Social Security is blank");
    else
    {
        try
        {
            cmdEmployees.executeUpdate("Insert Into Employees "
                + "([Last Name], [First Name], SSN, [Phone Number]) "
                + "Values('"
                + txtLastName.getText() + "', '"
                + txtFirstName.getText() + "', '"
                + txtSSN.getText() + "', '"
                + txtPhone.getText() + "')");
```

```
          //Add to name list
          lstNames.add(txtLastName.getText());

          //Reset buttons
          Cancel();
       }
       catch(SQLException error)
       {
          lblMessage.setText("Error: " + error.toString());
       }
    }
  }
}

public void Cancel()
{
   //Enable the Delete and Edit buttons
   btnDelete.setEnabled(true);
   btnEdit.setEnabled(true);

   //Disable the Cancel button
   btnCancel.setEnabled(false);

   //Change caption of button
   btnAdd.setLabel("Add");

   //Clear the text fields and status bar
   ClearTextFields();
   lblMessage.setText("");
}
```

Tip

Watch the spaces between elements when you concatenate SQL statements.

Modifying an Existing Record

To allow users to modify an existing record, you need to display the record's current contents and allow them to make changes. In the example program, the user selects a Last Name from the list and the field contents display in the text fields—so far it's exactly the same as the Display program. Then the user should be able to change the contents of the fields and click the Save button. You use the SQL Update statement to save the changes in the database.

The SQL Update Statement—General Format

```
Update TableName
   Set FieldName = FieldValue, FieldName = FieldValue,. . .
   Where Criteria;
```

The SQL Update Statement—Examples

```
Update Employee
   Set [Last Name] = 'Bowser'
   Where [Employee Number] = 500;
```

continued

```
Update Visit
    Set Date = #1/1/2000#
    Where Date = #1/1/1900#;

strSQL = "Update Employees " +
    "Set [Last Name] = '" + txtLastName.getText() + "', " +
        "[First Name] = '" + txtFirstName.getText() + "', " +
    "Where [SSN] = " + txtSSN.getText();
```

The Edit Method

The Edit method executes when the user clicks the Save button after making changes to an existing record. After checking to make sure that the user didn't click Save without first displaying a record, save the record. Use the execute-Update method of the Statement object, passing it an SQL Update statement.

This simplified update shows how the statements execute. In a robust application, you would perform additional validation before saving the changes.

```java
public void Edit()
{
    //Save the modified record
    int intIndex = lstNames.getSelectedIndex();
    if(intIndex == 0)                //Make sure a record is selected
        //Position 0 holds a text message, not a name
        lblMessage.setText("Please select the record to change");
    else
    {
        String strLastName = lstNames.getSelectedItem();
        try
        {
            cmdEmployees.executeUpdate("Update Employees "
                + "Set [Last Name] = '" + txtLastName.getText() + "', "
                + "[First Name] = '" + txtFirstName.getText() + "', "
                + "SSN = '" + txtSSN.getText() + "', "
                + "[Phone Number] = '" + txtPhone.getText() + "' "
                + "Where [Last Name] = '" + strLastName + "';");
        }
        catch(SQLException error)
        {
            lblMessage.setText("Error during Edit. " + "Error: " + error.toString());
        }
    }
}
```

Deleting a Record

Deleting a record is similar to modifying an existing record. The user must display the record to delete and then click the Delete button. You use the SQL Delete statement to delete the record from the database; the Delete statement requires a Where clause that specifies which record(s) to delete.

The SQL Delete Statement—General Format

```
Delete From TableName
    Where Criteria;
```

The SQL Delete Statement—Examples

```
Delete From Employees
    Where [Social Security] = 555571234;              //Field defined as numeric.

Delete From Employees
    Where [Last Name] = 'Berry';

strSQL = "Delete From Employees Where [Last Name] = '"
            + txtLastName.getText() + "';"
```

The Delete Method

When writing the routine for handling the delete, consider the tasks:

● Delete the record from the database.

● Delete the name from the list.

● Clear the record from the text fields.

To delete the record from the database, use the executeUpdate method of the Statement object to execute an SQL Delete statement.

```
public void Delete()
{
    //Delete the current record
    int intIndex = lstNames.getSelectedIndex();
    String strLastName = lstNames.getSelectedItem();

    if(intIndex == 0)                //Make sure a record is selected
        //Position 0 holds a text message, not a name
        lblMessage.setText("Please select the record to be deleted");
    else
    {
        //Delete the record from the database
        try
        {
            cmdEmployees.executeUpdate(
                "Delete from Employees where [Last Name] = '" + strLastName + "';");
            ClearTextFields();                        //Delete from screen
            lstNames.remove(intIndex);                //Delete from list
            lblMessage.setText("Record deleted");     //Display message
        }
        catch(SQLException error)
        {
            lblMessage.setText("Error during Delete."
                                + "Error: " + error.toString());
        }
    }
}
```

Joins

One of the primary characteristics of relational databases is that data are stored in multiple tables that are related to each other by common fields. Data can be stored once and used in many places by using the relationships between tables. You often will want to select some fields from one table and other fields from another related table, maybe even fields from several related tables.

Although you can join tables using the Where clause, the resulting Result-Set is not updateable. If you want the user to be able to update the data, you must use a **Join** clause in the SQL Select statement. Joins are of three types: **inner join**, **left join**, and **right join**. Table 13.1 shows the three types of joins. *Note:* The left join and right join are often called *left outer join* and *right outer join*.

Table 13.1

SQL Joins

Join Type	Selects
Inner join	Only records that have matching records in both tables.
Left join	All records from the first table and only the matching records from the second table.
Right join	All records from the second table and only the matching records from the first table.

The Join Clause

To code a Join clause, name only the first table in the From clause (this becomes the left table). Then specify the join type and the second table name; then write the relationship for the join using the On clause.

```
Select [Last Name], [First Name], [Insurance Company Code], Name From Patient
    Left Join InsuranceCompany
        On Patient.[Insurance Company Code] = InsuranceCompany.Code;
```

Feedback 13.4

Assume that the user will enter data into text fields on the screen and click a Save button or Delete button to carry out the action. The text fields are txtPartNumber, txtDescription, and txtVendor. The corresponding database fields are Part Number, Description, and Vendor Code.

1. Write the statement to add a new record to the Product table, based on the contents of the text fields entered by the user.
2. Write the statement that would save a modified record in the Product table.
3. Write the SQL statement(s) to delete a record in the Product table. The user will enter the part number into txtPartNumber and you will delete the record that matches the part number.

Your Hands-on Programming Example

Create an application that updates the Employee table of the MerryPeas database file. Allow the user to add, edit, delete, or display a record in the table. Label the buttons "Add", "Save", "Delete", and "Cancel". Keep the Cancel button disabled except during an Add.

The fields in the Employee table are

> Last Name
> First Name
> SSN
> Phone Number

Load all names into a list box. Display a record when a name is selected from the list.

Add: When Add is selected, clear the text fields and allow the user to enter the data for the new record. The only buttons available during the Add operation should be OK and Cancel. Disable the Edit and Delete buttons, enable the Cancel button, and change the caption on the Add button to "OK".

Save: When the user clicks Save, validate the record. The Last Name and Social Security fields are required. Save a good record in the database. Then reset the buttons to their default (initial) settings.

Delete: The user must select and display a record before it can be deleted.

Edit: The user must select and display a record before it can be changed.

Note: As always, this entire program is stored on your CD. You can also find an applet version, called Ch13JDBCUpdateApplet.

Planning the Project

Figure 13.6 shows a possible layout for the project.

Figure 13.6

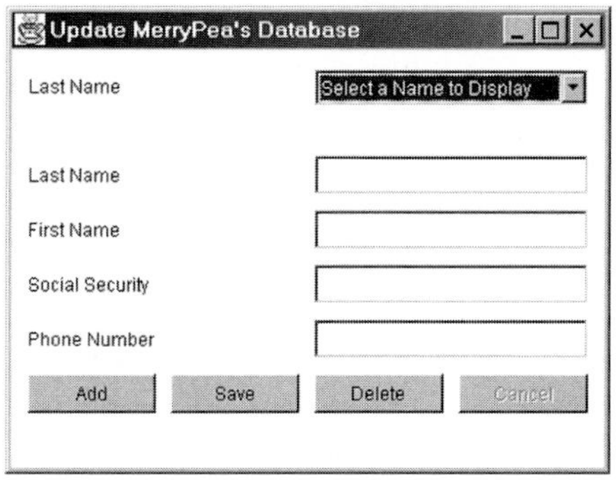

A possible user interface for the hands-on exercise.

Plan the User Interface

Figure 13.7 shows the class diagram.

Class: JDBCUpdateApp	
Methods	**Variables and Components**
main	conEmployees
createInterface	cmdEmployees
loadDatabase	rsEmployees
loadNames	blnSuccessfulOpen
itemStateChanged	lstNames
displayRecord	txtLastName
actionPerformed	txtFirstName
setTextToNotEditable	txtSSN
setTextToEditable	txtPhone
clearTextFields	btnAdd
Add	btnCancel
Save	btnEdit
Delete	btnDelete
Cancel	lblMessage
Edit	
stop	

The class diagram for the hands-on exercise.

Plan the Objects and Properties

Class: JDBCUpdateApp extends Frame

Components and Variables:

Access Mode (public or private)	Variable or Component Name	Data Type or Class	Description
	conEmployees	Connection	Connect to Employee database.
	cmdEmployees	Statement	Access to database methods.
	rsEmployees	ResultSet	Store the resulting records from a database query.
	blnSuccessfulOpen	boolean	Indicate whether ResultSet opened properly.
	lstNames	Choice	Store a list of last names from the Employee table.
	txtLastName	TextField	Display/enter last name.
	txtFirstName	TextField	Display/enter first name.
	txtSSN	TextField	Display/enter Social Security Number.
	txtPhone	TextField	Display/enter phone number.
	btnAdd	Button	Add a record.
			continued

Access Mode (public or private)	Variable or Component Name	Data Type or Class	Description
	btnCancel	Button	Cancel an Add operation.
	btnEdit	Button	Save changes to a record.
	btnDelete	Button	Delete a record.
	lblMessage	Label	Display messages to user

Methods:

Access Mode (public or private)	Return Type	Method Name (include any parameters)	Pseudocode
public static	void	`main(String args[])`	Declare an instance of the application. Create the interface.
public	void	`createInterface`	Load the database into the list of names. If successful Set up frame title, layout, listener. Add visual components. Lock the text fields. Display frame.
public	void	`loadDatabase`	Load the drivers. Connect to the database. Create a result set of all records. Call the method to load the names into the list. Set `blnSuccessfulOpen = true`.
public	void	`loadNames`	Fill last name list box.
public	void	`itemStateChanged`	Query to get record that matches selected name. Call `displayRecord`. Unlock the text fields.
public	void	`displayRecord`	Display the selected record.
public	void	`actionPerformed`	Determine event for button selected. Call `Add`, `Save`, `Edit`, `Delete`, or `Cancel`.
public	void	`setTextToNotEditable`	Lock the text boxes.
public	void	`setTextToEditable`	Unlock the text boxes.
public	void	`clearTextFields`	Clear all the text fields.

continued

Access Mode (public or private)	Return Type	Method Name (include any parameters)	Pseudocode
public	void	Add	Clear any previous message. Unlock the text boxes. Clear text fields. Change label of button to OK. Enable the Cancel button. Disable the Delete and Edit buttons.
public	void	Save	Check if last name or SSN is blank. If not Insert record in database. Add name to the list. Call Cancel to reset buttons.
public	void	Delete	Check that record is selected. If so Delete record from database. Delete name from list of names. Display deleted message.
public	void	Cancel	Enable the Delete and Edit buttons. Disable the Cancel button. Change the caption from OK to Add. Clear the text fields. Remove any messages.
public	void	Edit	Check that record is selected. If so Update the database.
public	void	stop	Close the connection.

Write the Project

● Follow the plan to add components to the class.

● Code the appropriate methods.

● When you complete the code, thoroughly test the project.

The Project Solution

```
//Folder:        Ch13JDBCUpdateApp
//Programmer:    Bradley/Millspaugh
//Date:          6/2001
//ClassName:     JDBCUpdateApp
//Description:   An application to update an Access database.
//               Uses the JDBC-ODBC Bridge and SQL statements to update data.

import java.sql.*;
import java.awt.*;
import java.awt.event.*;
```

```
public class JDBCUpdateApp extends Frame implements ItemListener, ActionListener
{
    //Declare database variables
    Connection conEmployees;
    Statement cmdEmployees;
    ResultSet rsEmployees;
    boolean blnSuccessfulOpen = false;

    //Declare components
    Choice lstNames  = new Choice();
    TextField txtLastName = new TextField(10);
    TextField txtFirstName = new TextField(10);
    TextField txtSSN = new TextField(9);
    TextField txtPhone = new TextField(14);
    Button btnAdd = new Button("Add");
    Button btnEdit = new Button("Save");
    Button btnCancel = new Button("Cancel");
    Button btnDelete = new Button("Delete");
    Label lblMessage = new Label("               ");

    public static void main(String args[])
    {
        //Declare an instance of this application
        JDBCUpdateApp thisApp = new JDBCUpdateApp();
        thisApp.createInterface();
    }

    public void createInterface()
    {
        //Load the database and set up the frame
        loadDatabase();
        if (blnSuccessfulOpen)
        {
            //Set up frame
            setTitle("Update MerryPea's Database");
            addWindowListener(new WindowAdapter()
            {
                public void windowClosing(WindowEvent event)
                {
                        stop();
                        System.exit(0);
                }
            });
            setLayout(new BorderLayout());

            //Set up top panel
            Panel pnlTop = new Panel(new GridLayout(2, 2, 10, 10));
            pnlTop.add(new Label("Last Name"));
            lstNames.insert("Select a Name to Display", 0);
            lstNames.addItemListener(this);
            pnlTop.add(lstNames);
            pnlTop.add(new Label("                    "));
            add(pnlTop, "North");

            //Set up center panel
            Panel pnlMiddle = new Panel(new GridLayout(5, 2, 10, 10));
            pnlMiddle.getInsets();
```

```java
            pnlMiddle.add(new Label("Last Name"));
            pnlMiddle.add(txtLastName);
            pnlMiddle.add(new Label("First Name"));
            pnlMiddle.add(txtFirstName);
            pnlMiddle.add(new Label("Social Security"));
            pnlMiddle.add(txtSSN);
            pnlMiddle.add(new Label("Phone Number"));
            pnlMiddle.add(txtPhone);
            setTextToNotEditable();
            Panel pnlLeftButtons = new Panel(new GridLayout(0, 2, 10, 10));
            Panel pnlRightButtons = new Panel(new GridLayout(0, 2, 10, 10));
            pnlLeftButtons.add(btnAdd);
            btnAdd.addActionListener(this);
            pnlLeftButtons.add(btnEdit);
            btnEdit.addActionListener(this);
            pnlRightButtons.add(btnDelete);
            btnDelete.addActionListener(this);
            pnlRightButtons.add(btnCancel);
            btnCancel.addActionListener(this);
            btnCancel.setEnabled(false);
            pnlMiddle.add(pnlLeftButtons);
            pnlMiddle.add(pnlRightButtons);
            add(pnlMiddle, "Center");

            //Set up bottom panel
            add(lblMessage, "South");
            lblMessage.setForeground(Color.red);

            //Display the frame
            setSize(400, 300);
            setVisible(true);
        }
    }
    else
    {
        stop ();              //Close any open connection
        System.exit(-1);      //Exit with error status
    }

    public Insets insets()
    {
        //Set frame insets
        return new Insets(40, 15, 15, 15);
    }

    public void loadDatabase()
    {
        try
        {
            //Load the Sun drivers
            Class.forName("sun.jdbc.odbc.JdbcOdbcDriver");
        }
        catch (ClassNotFoundException err)
        {
                try
                {
                        //Load the Microsoft drivers
                        Class.forName("com.ms.jdbc.odbc.JdbcOdbcDriver");
                }
                catch (ClassNotFoundException error)
```

```
                    {
                            lblMessage.setText("Drivers did not load properly");
                    }
            }
        try
        {
            //Connect to the database
            conEmployees = DriverManager.getConnection("jdbc:odbc:MerryPeas");

            //Create a ResultSet
            cmdEmployees = conEmployees.createStatement();
            rsEmployees = cmdEmployees.executeQuery("Select * from Employees;");
            loadNames(rsEmployees);
            blnSuccessfulOpen = true;
        }

        catch(SQLException error)
        {
            lblMessage.setText("Error: " + error.toString());
        }
    }

public void loadNames(ResultSet rsEmployees)
{
    //Fill last name list box
    try
    {
        while(rsEmployees.next())
            lstNames.add(rsEmployees.getString("Last Name"));
    }
    catch (SQLException error)
    {
        lblMessage.setText("Error in Display Record."
        + "Error: " + error.toString());
    }
}

public void itemStateChanged(ItemEvent event)
{
    //Retrieve and display the selected record
    String strLastName = lstNames.getSelectedItem();

    lblMessage.setText(""); //Delete instructions
    try
    {
        rsEmployees = cmdEmployees.executeQuery(
            "Select * from Employees where [Last Name] + '"
            + strLastName + "';");
        txtLastName.setText(strLastName);
        displayRecord(rsEmployees);
        setTextToEditable();
    }
    catch(SQLException error)
    {
        lblMessage.setText("Error in result set. "
        + "Error: " + error.toString());
    }
}
```

```java
public void displayRecord(ResultSet rsEmployees)
{
    //Display the current record
    try
    {
        if(rsEmployees.next())
        {
            txtFirstName.setText(rsEmployees.getString("First Name"));
            txtSSN.setText(rsEmployees.getString("SSN"));
            txtPhone.setText(rsEmployees.getString("Phone Number"));
            lblMessage.setText("");
        }
    }
    catch (SQLException error)
    {
        lblMessage.setText("Error: " + error.toString());
    }
}

public void actionPerformed(ActionEvent event)
{
    //Test the command buttons
    Object objSource = event.getSource();
    if(objSource == btnAdd && event.getActionCommand () == "Add")
        Add();
    else if (objSource == btnAdd)
        Save();
    else if(objSource == btnEdit)
        Edit();
    else if(objSource == btnDelete)
        Delete();
    else if(objSource == btnCancel)
        Cancel();
}

public void setTextToNotEditable()
{
    //Lock the text fields
    txtLastName.setEditable(false);
    txtFirstName.setEditable(false);
    txtSSN.setEditable(false);
    txtPhone.setEditable(false);
}

public void setTextToEditable()
{
    //Unlock the text fields
    txtLastName.setEditable(true);
    txtFirstName.setEditable(true);
    txtSSN.setEditable(true);
    txtPhone.setEditable(true);
}

public void clearTextFields()
{
    //Clear the text fields
    txtLastName.setText("");
    txtFirstName.setText("");
    txtSSN.setText("");
    txtPhone.setText("");
}
```

```
public void Add()
{
    //Add a new record
    lblMessage.setText("     ");              //Clear previous message
    setTextToEditable();                      //Unlock the text fields
    clearTextFields();                        //Clear text field contents
    txtLastName.requestFocus();

    //Set up the OK and Cancel buttons
    btnAdd.setLabel("OK");
    btnCancel.setEnabled(true);

    //Disable the Delete and Edit buttons
    btnDelete.setEnabled(false);
    btnEdit.setEnabled(false);
}

public void Save()
{
    //Save the new record
    // Activated when the Add button has an "OK" label
    if (txtLastName.getText().length() == 0 || txtSSN.getText().length() == 0)
        lblMessage.setText("The Last Name or Social Security is blank");
    else
    {
        try
        {
            cmdEmployees.executeUpdate("Insert Into Employees "
                    + "([Last Name], [First Name], SSN, [Phone Number]) "
                    + "Values('"
                    + txtLastName.getText() + "', '"
                    + txtFirstName.getText() + "', '"
                    + txtSSN.getText() + "', '"
                    + txtPhone.getText() + "')");

            //Add to name list
            lstNames.add(txtLastName.getText());

            //Reset buttons
            Cancel();
        }
        catch(SQLException error)
        {
            lblMessage.setText("Error: " + error.toString());
        }
    }
}

public void Delete()
{
    //Delete the current record
    int intIndex = lstNames.getSelectedIndex();
    String strLastName = lstNames.getSelectedItem();

    if(intIndex == 0)              //Make sure a record is selected
        //Position 0 holds a text message, not a name
        lblMessage.setText("Please select the record to be deleted");
```

```java
        else
        {
            //Delete the record from the database
            try
            {
                cmdEmployees.executeUpdate(
                        "Delete from Employees where [Last Name] = '" + strLastName + "';");
                clearTextFields();                              //Delete from screen
                lstNames.remove(intIndex);                      //Delete from list
                lblMessage.setText("Record deleted");           //Display message
            }
            catch(SQLException error)
            {
                lblMessage.setText("Error during Delete."
                        + "Error: " + error.toString());
            }
        }
    }

    public void Cancel()
    {
        //Enable the Delete and Edit buttons
        btnDelete.setEnabled(true);
        btnEdit.setEnabled(true);

        //Disable the Cancel button
        btnCancel.setEnabled(false);

        //Change caption of button
        btnAdd.setLabel("Add");

        //Clear the text fields and status bar
        clearTextFields();
        lblMessage.setText("");
    }

    public void Edit()
    {
        //Save the modified record
        int intIndex = lstNames.getSelectedIndex();
        if(intIndex == 0)                       //Make sure a record is selected
            //Position 0 holds a text message, not a name
            lblMessage.setText("Please select the record to change");
        else
        {
            String strLastName = lstNames.getSelectedItem();
            try
            {
                cmdEmployees.executeUpdate("Update Employees "
                        + "Set [Last Name] = '" + txtLastName.getText() + "', "
                        + "[First Name] = '" + txtFirstName.getText() + "', "
                        + "SSN = '" + txtSSN.getText() + "', "
                        + "[Phone Number] = '" + txtPhone.getText() + "' "
                        + "Where [Last Name] = '" + strLastName + "';");
                if (!strLastName.equals(txtLastName.getText()))
                {
                    //Last name changed; change the list
                    lstNames.remove(intIndex);                  //Remove the old entry
                    lstNames.add(txtLastName.getText());        //Add the new entry
                }
```

```
        }
        catch(SQLException error)
        {
            lblMessage.setText("Error during Edit. "
                                 + "Error: " + error.toString());
        }
    }
}

public void stop()
{
    //Terminate the connection
    try
    {
        if (conEmployees != null)
            conEmployees.close();
    }
    catch(SQLException error)
    {
        lblMessage.setText("Unable to disconnect");
    }
}
```

Summary

1. A stream is a flow of data to or from any device. The Java core language contains stream classes for reading and writing data.

2. The standard output device is the screen and the standard input device is the keyboard.

3. The System class contains methods for inputting and outputting to the standard devices.

4. Objects can be written using object serialization. This technique is handy for storing the state of an object from one execution of an applet or application until the next time the program runs.

5. An object must implement the Serializable interface in order to work with the Object streams.

6. To store an object, you must create a FileOutputStream and an ObjectOutputStream and use the `writeObject` method.

7. To read back a stored object, you must create a FileInputStream and an ObjectInputStream and use the `readObject` method.

8. Java contains the JDBC (Java Database Connectivity) API in the sql package.

9. JDBC uses a bridge to ODBC to connect your Java code to database files.

10. The Java JDBC API interfaces with database files. Generally, each database vendor supplies a JDBC driver for use with their database. You can use the JDBC-ODBC Bridge driver to access any database that has an ODBC driver. Nearly every relational database has an ODBC driver.

11. To access a database using the JDBC-ODBC driver in Windows, you must register a DSN on the computer on which you will run the program.

12. Before accessing records, it is necessary to load the drivers for the bridge and make a connection to the database file. Microsoft uses a different JDBC-ODBC driver from Sun's driver, which is used by most other vendors.

13. A ResultSet object is used to store the records that result from an SQL Select query.

14. Use the Statement object's `executeQuery` method to execute an SQL Select query.

15. The ResultSet's `next` method moves the record cursor to the next record and returns true for a successful move and false for end-of-file.

16. To refer to fields in the ResultSet, use the `getxxx` methods, such as `getString`, `getFloat`, and `getInt`.

17. You can add, change, and delete records in a database using the SQL Update Action commands.

18. To add a record, use the SQL Insert statement and the Statement object's `executeUpdate` method.

19. To save changed data, use the SQL Update statement and the Statement object's `executeUpdate` method.

20. To delete a record, use the SQL Delete statement and the Statement object's `executeUpdate` method.

21. To join tables and produce an updateable ResultSet, you must use the SQL Join clause rather than the Where clause.

Key Terms

Connection object *412*

Data Source Name (DSN) *411*

Delete *423*

`executeQuery` method *413*

`executeUpdate` method *422*

FileInputStream *406*

FileOutputStream *403*

`getFloat` *415*

`getInt` *415*

`getString` *415*

inner join *428*

Insert *423*

Java Database Connectivity
    (JDBC) *410*

Join *428*

left join *428*

object serialization *401*

ObjectInputStream *406*

ObjectOutputStream *403*

Open DataBase Connectivity
(ODBC) *411*

persistence *401*

`print` method *400*

`println` method *400*

`readObject` method *407*

ResultSet object *413*

right join *428*

SQL Select statement *420*

standard input device *400*

standard output device *400*

Statement object *413*

stream *400*

Structured Query Language
    (SQL) *419*

Update *423*

`writeObject` method *404*

Review Questions

1. Describe a stream, its purpose, and methods.
2. Differentiate between the `print` and `println` methods.
3. What is meant by *object serialization*?
4. List the steps required to store an object to a disk file.

5. Describe the steps for reading an object from a disk file.
6. What is JDBC? ODBC?
7. What must be done to register a database on a Windows system?
8. Describe the objects, the methods, and the sequence to read an entire table from a database, including setting up the drivers, connecting to the database, and returning a ResultSet.
9. What is SQL? What are some of the statements in the language?
10. Describe the three action queries in SQL that can be used with the `execu-teUpdate` method.

Programming Exercises

13.1 Write an application that prints your class schedule to the standard output device.

13.2 Create an application or applet that stores student information in Student.txt using object serialization. The student object should contain the

- Student Name
- Major
- Student ID
- Number of Units Completed

13.3 Create an application or applet that reads and displays the information stored in Student.txt. (*Note:* You must do exercise 13.2 before exercise13.3).

13.4 Write an application or applet that stores payroll information using object serialization. Base your program on the hands-on exercise in Chapter 6 (Ch6Payroll).

13.5 Write an applet or application to display the data in the Vehicle table of JNAAuto.mdb, which is an Access database file found on your CD. Use the JDBC-ODBC bridge or native Java Access drivers, if you have them.

Create a drop-down list that contains the InventoryID for all vehicles. Allow the user to select a number and display the Manufacturer, ModelName, Year, VehicleID, and CostValue.

Structure of JNAAuto.mdb

Vehicle Field Name	Data Type	Length
InventoryID (primary key)	Text	8
Manufacturer	Text	20
ModelName	Text	20
Year	Integer	
VehicleID	Text	17
CostValue	Currency	

13.6 Modify exercise 13.5 to allow updates of the Vehicle table. Allow the user to add vehicles, modify existing vehicle records, and delete vehicle records. For an Add operation, give the user only the options to save the record or cancel the operation.

CASE STUDIES

R 'n R—for Reading and Refreshment

1. Write an applet or application to display the data in the Books table of RnRBooks.mdb, which is an Access database file found on your CD. Use the JDBC-ODBC Bridge or native Java Access drivers, if you have them.

Create a drop-down list that contains the ISBN numbers of all books. Allow the user to select a number and display the Title, Author, and Publisher.

Although the RnRBooks.mdb file holds two tables, this exercise deals only with the Books table.

Structure of RnRBooks.mbd

Books

Field Name	Data Type	Length
ISBN (primary key)	Text	13
Title	Text	50
Author	Text	30
Publisher	Text	30
Subject_Code	Text	3

Subjects

Field Name	Data Type	Length
SubjectCode (primary key)	Text	3
Subject	Text	13

2. Modify exercise 1 to also display the subject—the full subject name (from the Subjects table), not just the code. *Hint:* Your SQL statement must include a Where clause: `Where Books.Subject_Code = Subjects.SubjectCode`.

3. Modify exercise 2 to allow updates of the Books table. Allow the user to add books, modify existing book records, and delete book records. For an Add operation, give the user only the options to save the record or cancel the operation.

Merry Pea's Quilting

Write an application that updates the Employee file in the MerryPeas database file. Use a menu for the update options: Add, Save

Changes, and Delete. You may use either Swing or AWT components.

Note: This project is a modification of the hands-on exercise in this chapter.

14

JavaScript

At the completion of this chapter, you will be able to . . .

1. Differentiate between Java and JavaScript.

2. Use JavaScript in an HTML file.

3. Hide your scripting from browsers that do not support JavaScript.

4. Determine information about the browser and operating system that is executing your JavaScript code.

5. Create links to other Websites.

JavaScript and Java are two entirely different programming languages. Although similarities exist between the two languages, that also can be said about many other languages.

You have already used JavaScript in your HTML file for Swing components in Chapter 7. In this chapter you will see the similarities and differences between Java and JavaScript and learn to develop a short JavaScript project.

Scripting

Netscape and Sun developed the JavaScript language for generating interactive and dynamic Web pages. Originally the language was created at Netscape and called LiveScript, followed by LiveWire when database connectivity was added. JavaScript, sometimes referred to as *JS*, works well for developing Web pages but cannot be used for stand-alone applications.

Frequently, coding in JavaScript is referred to as **scripting** rather than programming. Other scripting languages are CGI (Common Gateway Interface) and VBScript (Visual Basic Script). CGI is a server-side scripting language, meaning that the script resides on the Web server rather than on the user's machine. JScript and VBScript come from Microsoft; JScript resembles Java and VBScript resembles Visual Basic.

Not all Web browsers recognize JavaScript. Netscape, beginning with Navigator 2, and Internet Explorer 3 and above can read JavaScript code. Only the newer browsers support some features of JavaScript.

Writing a Script

You can create a script as a separate file or embedded in an HTML file, which is the more common practice. To place the script in an HTML file, you enclose the script in *script* **tags**. Note that the tags are not case-sensitive.

```
<Script language = JavaScript>
script goes here
</Script>
```

A problem can occur if a user attempts to display the HTML page in a browser that does not support JavaScript. Although Netscape 2 and Internet Explorer 3 support JavaScript, some features don't work correctly on these early versions. JavaScript runs best on at least version 4 of both Netscape and IE.

You can solve the compatibility problem by hiding the script when necessary. You just include tags that turn the script into HTML comments, and a browser that doesn't recognize the script ignores those lines. One tag "<!--" begins the hiding and another "-->" terminates it.

```
<Script language = JavaScript>
<!--          Hide JavaScript
script goes here
// Terminate JavaScript hiding -->
</Script>
```

If you are using a JavaScript feature from a later version, you should include the JavaScript version number in the code.

```
<Script language = "JavaScript 1.2">
   . . .
</Script>
```

Comments

As you saw in the previous section, you can create comments in HTML code using opening and closing tags. Inside a JS script you write comments by using the Java comment symbols for single-line or multiline comments.

JavaScript Comments

```
// Single line
/*. . . . . .
   multiple lines
*/
```

The document.write Method

Each Web page is considered a document object. An easy way to display information on a Web page is to use the Document's **write method.** Enclose the information to display in quotes.

```
document.write("Hello World");
```

Note: The trailing semicolon is not required in JavaScript but is used by many Java and C++ programmers.

You may have noticed that JavaScript is more lenient than Java. You will find that to be true in many situations, including how you specify literals. In JavaScript you can use either single or double quotes, such as "Hello World" or 'Hello World'. However, you must be consistent within the same literal. But be aware that JavaScript statements are case-sensitive; it's only the HTML tags that are not.

More Tags

You can include HTML tags inside JavaScript code. For example, to make a literal appear in bold font, use the HTML <b> </b> tags inside the literal.

```
document.write("<b>Hello World</b>");
```

Enclose each tag in brackets <>. Tags work as a pair, with the closing tag including a slash (/). See Table 14.1 for other formatting tags that you may want to use in your JS scripts.

Enclosing a Quote in a Literal

Your literal can contain a quotation mark, with some restrictions. Since the computer translates very precisely, the literal:

```
"Ann said "Hi Mom""
```

actually only contains the text from the first quote to the second (Ann said).

Table 14.1

Some HTML Tags

Tag	Purpose
a href	alert and reference—for links.
b	bold
h*n*	A header style; *n* can be from 1 to 6.
i	italics
p	paragraph
u	underline

The rest of the text is meaningless. To make the inner quote read as a quotation mark, precede it with a backslash, like an escape sequence in Java.

```
"Ann said \"Hi Mom\""
```

The solution is the same when you use single quotes:

```
'Anna\'s Favorite Links'
```

Concatenation

JavaScript uses + (a plus sign) for combining multiple elements in a literal. The elements can be of any data type.

```
document.write("Five plus six equals " + (5 + 6));
```

The Navigator Object

You can learn many interesting facts using the **navigator object,** which is part of the JS language. Using methods of the navigator object, you can return the browser type, the version of the browser, and the operating system. You can even determine the language used by the Web browser, that is, English, Spanish, or Chinese. Table 14.2 shows some of the navigator's methods.

Example

```
document.write("You are using " + navigator.platform);
```

might return

```
You are using Win32
```

Table 14.2

Selected Properties of the Navigator Object

Property	Returns
appName	Name of the Web browser.
appVersion	Version number of the Web browser.
language	Language used by the Web browser.
platform	Operating system.

Feedback 14.1

1. What tag begins a script in HTML?
2. Write the JavaScript statement that prints your name in bold and italics.
3. What does this statement do?

   ```
   document.write("<H3>Hello</H3>");
   ```

4. Code the JavaScript statement(s) to produce the following output:

   Browser: xxxxxxxxx

   Version: xx

   OS: xxxx

Creating Your First JavaScript Program

You can use any text editor to create the HTML page and your JavaScript source code. Although you can use a word processor, you have to be very careful to store the information as a text file with the appropriate extension. The following sample uses Notepad. Figure 14.1 shows the completed Web page.

Figure 14.1

The Web page produced by the step-by-step example.

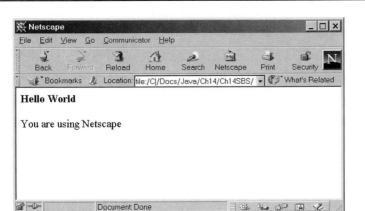

Enter the Source Code

STEP 1: Open Notepad from the Windows `Programs / Accessories` menu item, or the editor of your choice.

STEP 2: Type in the following script.

```
<Script language = JavaScript>
<!-- Hide script from incompatible browsers
document.write("<b>Hello World</b>");
document.write("<br><br>");
document.write("You are using " + navigator.appName);
// Terminate hiding -->
</Script>
```

STEP 3: Save the file as *Hello.htm*.

STEP 4: Close the file.

Run Your Script in Internet Explorer

STEP 1: Open Internet Explorer.
STEP 2: Select `File / Open`.
STEP 3: Browse to your Hello.htm file.
STEP 4: Click OK.

The JavaScript program should run and produce the requested output.

Run Your Script in Netscape Navigator

STEP 5: Open Netscape.
STEP 6: Select `File / OpenPage`.
STEP 7: Click on `Choose File` and locate your Hello.htm file.
STEP 8: Click on `Open`.

The JavaScript program should run and produce the requested output.

Correct Any Errors

If your script does not run in the browser, double check the source code. Also make sure that the file is saved as a text file with the .htm or .html extension.

The Object Model

You display items on a Web page using the JavaScript **document object model** (Figure 14.2). The top level of the hierarchy is the **window object**, which exists when a browser is open even if no document is showing. You can also create additional window objects, known as *subwindows*. The window contains a document, which is the Web page. The window can also contain other objects, such as history and location.

Figure 14.2

Selected parts of JavaScript's document object model.

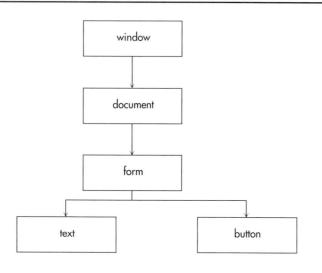

The Document Object

Earlier you used this statement:

```
document.write("String to write")
```

This statement is a call to the `write` method of the document object.

Documents can contain forms, links, and images. The forms, in turn, contain input fields, buttons, check boxes, and radio buttons (option buttons). To refer to a component in code, you must give the fully qualified name (the window can be omitted unless it is a subwindow). The following code refers to the value contained in txtName located on frmMain.

```
document.frmMain.txtName.value
```

You can use the lastModified property of a document object. This property holds the date that the file was last saved.

```
document.write("This page was last updated on: " + document.lastModified);
```

Functions

A **function** in JavaScript is a procedure, just like a method in Java. You can embed a function in the script or place the function in the HTML Head section and call it as an event occurs. Most JavaScript events begin with the prefix "on", such as `onClick` and `onLoad`.

When you write a function, you give it a name. Then, elsewhere in code, you can call the function by specifying that name. Begin a function with the keyword `function` followed by the name. Include brackets for the block of code inside the function, just as you do for a method in Java.

The `alert` statement in the following function pops up a message box that displays the specified text.

```
function Monday()
{
    //Display Monday task
    alert("Contract Meeting 1pm");
}
```

You can call the function in an HTML object tag. The following line of code creates a **button** called *btnMonday*. The Value specifies the text that appears on the button. When the button is clicked (the onClick event), the `Monday` function executes.

```
<Input Type = "button" Value = "Monday" Name = "btnMonday" onClick = "Monday()">
```

Notice that when you call a function, you must include the parentheses, which indicate that the name is a function.

Calling a Function as a Web Page Appears

You can call a function at startup by specifying the `onLoad` event in the HTML Body tag.

```
<Body onLoad = "Greetings()">
```

The Functions Script

This script uses the Greetings and Monday functions. It also displays the last-modified date using the lastModified property of the document object. Figure 14.3 shows the Web page produced. This code is available in Ch14JSFunctions.

Figure 14.3

The output of the Functions script. The Welcome message displays on the document's onLoad event.

```
<Html>
<Head>
<Script Language = "JavaScript">
<!--

function Monday()
{
   //Display Monday task
   alert("Contract Meeting 1pm");
}

function Greetings()
{
   //Display at startup
   alert("Greetings and Welcome to this page");
}

//-->
</Script>
</Head>

<Body onLoad = "Greetings()">
<Form Name = "converter">
<Center>
<Input Type = "button" Value = "English" onClick = 'window.alert("Hello")'>
<Input Type = "button" Value = "French" onClick = 'window.alert("Bonjour")'>
<Input Type = "button" Value = "Spanish" onClick = 'window.alert("Hola")'>
<Br>
<Br>
<Input Type = "button" Value = "Monday" Name = "btnMonday" onClick = "Monday()">
```

```
</Center>
<Br>
<HR>
<Script Language = "JavaScript">
<!--
    document.write("<font size = 1>" +
        "<Center>This page was last updated on: " +
        "<b>" + document.lastModified + "</b></Center>" +
        "</font>");
//-->
</Script>
</Form>
</Body>
</Html>
```

> **Tip**
>
> **H**TML tags are not case-sensitive. JavaScript code *is* case-sensitive.

Special Buttons

When you place a button on a Web page, you can choose from three types: the regular button, which you just saw in the previous script; the **submit button**; or the **reset button**. HTML and JavaScript have special buttons called *submit* and *reset*. Submit and reset buttons look the same as regular buttons but they perform special actions.

A reset button clears all text fields and options selected on a form.

```
<INPUT TYPE="reset" NAME="btnClear" VALUE="Clear">
```

A submit button is used to submit the contents of the form's fields to a CGI script on the server.

Feedback 14.2

1. Code the statement to create a button called *btnOK* labeled "OK" that calls the Calculate function.
2. Write a function that displays an alert for this important message: "Call your mother!" Code the statement that creates a button labeled "Urgent" that calls the function.

Variables

Declaring variables in JavaScript is a little different from Java. In JS you use the keyword `var` for all variables; you do not specify a data type.

```
var numValue;
var strYourName;
```

Scope

JavaScript variables have scope, just like those in Java. Any variable that you declare inside a function is local to that function. If you declare a variable outside a function, the variable's scope is the entire document. And if you give the same name to a local variable as a document-level variable, the local variable "hides" the document-level variable when the function is executing. That is, inside the function, code refers to the local variable; outside the function, code refers to the document-level variable.

Just as in Java, you should declare variables with the narrowest scope possible, consistent with the need for the variable.

Control Structures

The basic control structures in JavaScript are the same as those in Java. Because you already know how to loop, make decisions, and create arrays, you already know how to do those things in JavaScript.

The if Statement

```
if (btnClicked == "Add")
{
    //Add the two values
    result = numValueOne + numValueTwo;
}
```

The for Statement

```
for(var monthNum = 0; monthNum < 12; monthNum++)
{
    monthsString = monthsString + monthsArray[monthNum];
    if(monthNum < 11)
        monthsString = monthsString + ", ";
    else
        monthsString = monthsString + ".";
}
document.write(monthsString);
```

The Entire Listing

Here is the HTML for the entire Web page (Figure 14.4). This script demonstrates variables, control structures, and arrays.

Figure 14.4

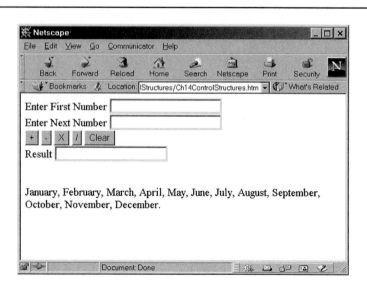

The Web page for the variables and control structures script.

```
<!--
    File:           Ch14JSControlStructures
    Programmer:     Millspaugh/Bradley
    Date:           8/2000
    Description:    Demonstrate variables, control structures, and arrays
-->

<Html>
<Head>
<Script Language = "JavaScript">
<!-- hide from non JS Browsers

function calculate(btnClicked)
{
    //Variables function for calculator
    var numValueOne = parseFloat(document.calculator.txtValueOne.value);
    var numValueTwo = parseFloat(document.calculator.txtValueTwo.value);
    var result;

    if(btnClicked == "Add")
    {
        //Add the two values
        result = numValueOne + numValueTwo;
    }
    else if(btnClicked == "Subtract")
    {
        //Subtract the two values
        result = numValueOne - numValueTwo;
    }
    else if(btnClicked == "Multiply")
    {
        //Multiply the two values
        result = numValueOne * numValueTwo;
    }
    else if(btnClicked == "Divide")
    {
        //Divide the two values
        result = numValueOne / numValueTwo;
    }
    //Return the result
    document.calculator.txtResult.value = result;
}

function writeMonths()
{
    //Declare a string that concatenates the months, display

    var monthsArray = new Array("January", "February", "March", "April",
        "May", "June", "July", "August", "September", "October",
        "November", "December");
    var monthsString = "<Br>"; //Start a new line
    for(var monthNum = 0; monthNum < 12; monthNum++)
    {
        monthsString = monthsString + monthsArray[monthNum];
        if(monthNum < 11)
            monthsString = monthsString + ", ";
        else
            monthsString = monthsString + ".";
    }
    document.write(monthsString);
```

```
}
//-->
</Script>
</Head>
<Body>
<!--Create a calculator -- Enter the numbers-->
<Form Name = "calculator">

Enter First Number
<Input Type = "text" Name = "txtValueOne" >
<Br>
Enter Next Number
<Input Type = "text" Name = "txtValueTwo">
<Br>

<!--Calculation buttons-->
<Input type = "button" Value = " + " onClick = 'calculate("Add")'>
<Input type = "button" Value = " - " onClick = 'calculate("Subtract")'>
<Input type = "button" Value = " X " onClick = 'calculate("Multiply")'>
<Input type = "button" Value = " / " onClick = 'calculate("Divide")'>
<Input type = "reset" Name = btnClear Value = "Clear"
<Br>

<!--Result-->
<Br>
Result <Input Type = "text" Name = "txtResult">
<Br>
<Br>
<Br>

Months:
<Script Language = "JavaScript">
<!-- hide from non JS Browsers
writeMonths()
// --End hiding-->
</Script>
</Form>
</Body>
</Html>
```

Fun with JavaScript—Image Rollovers

Most of the JavaScript that you find on Web pages produces the fun or action on the page. In this section you will create images that change as the user moves the mouse over them. For each image, you store two graphics. The default graphic displays until the user moves the mouse over the image, and then you display the second graphic and change the text in the status bar. When the mouse moves off the image, you again display the first graphic, and the status bar text changes back to the default.

Store the Images

Before you begin, store all the graphics in a process called *precaching* the images. For each image, create an object and assign the graphic file as its source

(.src). You will declare two images for each of the objects: one in the default color (red) and the other in the selected color (yellow).

Older browsers do not support the Image object. You can check for this error condition by testing the images property of the document object, which returns boolean true for browsers that can handle graphics.

```
//Precache the images
if (document.images)
{
    carRental              = new Image(85, 31);
    carRental.src          = "carRentals1.gif";
    carRental2             = new Image(85, 31);
    carRental2.src         = "carRentals2.gif";
    hotels                 = new Image(101, 31);
    hotels.src             = "hotels1.gif";
    hotels2                = new Image(101, 31);
    hotels2.src            = "hotels2.gif";
    entertainment          = new Image(108, 31);
    entertainment.src      = "entertainment1.gif";
    entertainment2         = new Image(108,31);
    entertainment2.src     = "entertainment2.gif";
}
```

Mouse Events

The mouse events in JavaScript include onMouseOver and onMouseOut. For each image you need an <A> tag, since each image is a link to a different page. You must include the mouse events within the <A> </A> tags. When the mouse is over the image, you change the image, change the status bar message, and then return true for the event. For the onMouseOut event, you only need to change the image; the status bar message automatically changes back to the default message that you set in the onload event in the Body tag.

```
<A HREF="carRentalInformation.htm"
   onMouseOver="cars.src = carRental2.src;
      window.status='Car Rental Information';
      return true;"
   onMouseOut="cars.src = carRental.src">
<IMG src="carRental2.gif" WIDTH=85 HEIGHT=31 BORDER=0 NAME = "cars"></IMG></A>
```

Note: Internet Explorer can handle the mouse events in either the image tag or the A tag, but Netscape only recognizes the mouse events in the A tag. The moral of this story: Place the mouse events in the A tag.

The Image Rollovers Script

This script produces the image rollover effect. Figure 14.5 shows the Web page output. Try entering and running this script. It's fun!

The Web page for the image rollovers script. Notice that the image changes along with the text in the status bar.

```
<HTML>
<!---------------------------- -->
<!--                           -->
<!-- Millspaugh /Bradley       -->
<!--                           -->
<!--                           -->
<!-- Rollovers                 -->
<!---------------------------- -->
<HEAD>

<TITLE>Tricia's Travels</TITLE>

<SCRIPT LANGUAGE="JavaScript">
<!--
//Precache the images
if (document.images)
{
    carRental            = new Image(85, 31);
    carRental.src        = "carRentals1.gif";
    carRental2           = new Image(85, 31);
    carRental2.src       = "carRentals2.gif";
    hotels               = new Image(101, 31);
    hotels.src           = "hotels1.gif";
    hotels2              = new Image(101, 31);
    hotels2.src          = "hotels2.gif";
    entertainment        = new Image(108, 31);
    entertainment.src    = "entertainment1.gif";
    entertainment2       = new Image(108,31);
    entertainment2.src   = "entertainment2.gif";
}
//-->
</SCRIPT>
</HEAD>

<BODY onLoad="window.defaultStatus='Tricia\'s Travels'">
<FONT SIZE=6><CENTER>
<b>Tricia's Travels</b><br>
```

```
</CENTER></FONT>
<BR><BR><BR>
<A HREF="carRentalInformation.htm"
    onMouseOver="cars.src=carRental2.src;
        window.status='Car Rental Information';
        return true;"
    onMouseOut="cars.src=carRental.src">
<IMG src="carRentals1.gif" WIDTH=85 HEIGHT=31 BORDER=0 NAME = "cars"></IMG></A>
<BR>
<A HREF="hotels.htm"
    onMouseOver="sleep.src=hotels2.src;
        window.status='Places to Stay';
        return true;"
    onMouseOut="sleep.src=hotels.src">
<IMG src="hotels1.gif" WIDTH=101 HEIGHT=31 BORDER=0 Name = "sleep"></IMG></A>
<BR>
<A HREF="entertainment.htm"
    onMouseOver="entertain.src = entertainment2.src;
        window.status='Local Amusements';
        return true;"
    onMouseOut="entertain.src=entertainment.src">
<IMG src="entertainment1.gif" WIDTH=108 HEIGHT=31 BORDER=0 Name = "entertain"></IMG></A>
</BODY>
</HTML>
```

S u m m a r y

1. JavaScript and Java are two different languages. JavaScript is used in HTML files to create a more dynamic Web page.
2. Script code is placed inside of <Script> </Script> tags.
3. You can hide JavaScript statements from a browser that doesn't support the code by using an opening <!–– tag and a closing ––> tag.
4. Use the `document.write` method to display information on the Web page. You can include HTML tags within the text that you write.
5. JavaScript code itself resembles Java in the keywords and control structures. The terminating semicolon on a statement is optional in JS.
6. The navigator object can provide information about the platform, browser, version, and language.
7. In the JS object model, the top level is a window, which exists when the browser is open. The Web page is a document object, which belongs to the window. A document can contain other objects, such as forms, links, and images and components such as buttons.
8. A JS function corresponds to a Java method. You can call a function in a script or execute the function in response to a button's onClick event or the document's onLoad event.
9. An alert pops up a message box for the user.
10. JS has three types of buttons you can display on a Web page: regular buttons, submit buttons, and reset buttons.
11. Variables of all types are defined with the `var` keyword. The value can be changed to a specific type with functions such as `parseInt` or `parseFloat`.

12. Events in JS are usually preceded with the prefix "on", such as onClick, onLoad, and onSubmit.

13. Control structures, such as decisions and loops, are coded the same in JavaScript as in Java.

14. You can store multiple images and choose which one to display based on the mouseOver and mouseOut events.

Key Terms

button *449*	scripting *444*
document object *445*	submit button *451*
document object model *448*	tags *444*
function *449*	window object *448*
navigator object *446*	write method *445*
reset button *451*	

Review Questions

1. Explain the differences and similarities between Java and JavaScript. What company developed each language?
2. What is a tag?
3. Discuss the use of quotation marks in literals.
4. Describe three properties of the navigator object.
5. Explain the relationship of objects in the object model.
6. How do variables in JavaScript differ from those in Java?
7. What is the format of an if statement in JavaScript? A for statement?

Programming Exercises

14.1 Create a script that displays your name, the date, and your course name on a Web page.

14.2 Create a script to display information to the user about their operating system, their browser, the version of the browser, and the last-modified date.

14.3 Add an image and Web page for Restaurants to the image rollover example. You can use the Restaurants1.gif and Restaurants2.gif files that are in the project folder, or create your own graphics. The existing graphics are 90 × 31 pixels.

   Use any editor to create the new HTML document. The Restaurants image must link to the new page.

14.4 Create your own graphic images using a graphics program or WordArt. Make two versions of the graphics so that you can display a second image when the mouse moves over the image.

   Note: To use Microsoft WordArt in Word, open a new HTML document and use Insert / Object / Microsoft WordArt. When you save the HTML document, Word saves each graphic as a separate .gif file, which you can rename.

15

Advanced Features of Java

At the completion of this chapter, you will be able to . . .

1. Recognize the importance of component-based development.

2. Use the BeanBox to display and modify existing JavaBeans.

3. Add events to connect multiple beans.

4. Create your own JavaBean components and run them in the BeanBox.

5. Recognize the importance of RMI and CORBA to client/server applications.

6. Understand how the Java Native Interface (JNI) allows Java programs to use methods written in other languages.

7. Be aware of issues affecting the internationalization of programs.

8. Know the options available to make software more accessible to individuals with disabilities.

9. Explain the parts of the java.security package and how applets can be signed.

In today's computing environment, information frequently must travel from one computer system to another. Often you must maintain an application on one system and access the application from other systems. The main system is often called the *server* and those systems that access the application are called the *clients*.

Java has many features that aid in this multisystem approach to application development. One such feature is component development with JavaBeans. Other features include methods for handling remote systems, such as Remote Method Invocation (RMI) and Common Object Request Broker Architecture (CORBA). In addition to RMI and CORBA, this chapter introduces you to the concepts of Java Native Interface (JNI), security, and internationalization.

Software Development Using Components

The ideal situation in application development is for you to write applications or components that can run on any platform, work with any operating system, and interface with any language. One goal is to be able to create software by assembling components like building blocks, much like building other physical projects.

Think of software components like components in an audio/video system. You can plug together components from different manufacturers because the interfaces are standard. You choose the components that are designed to work together, purchase the correct cables, and create your own unique system.

Another good analogy that works well for component development is Lego blocks. You can build almost anything from the components that all have a common interface. You can purchase special-purpose components, such as pulleys, motors, and wheels, that you can use to assemble a new object, due to the standardized way that the parts fit together. And you might like to create your own new component, which can then be combined with others. You might even supply your new component to other Lego builders, who could use your new specialized component in the objects they create.

JavaBeans

You may have heard the expression ***JavaBeans*** or just ***beans*** and wondered what they are. Beans are components that you can add to an applet or application, similar to the components that you already use, such as text areas, choice lists, and buttons. In fact, if you use IBM's Java IDE, Visual Age for Java, you find that *all* components are referred to as beans.

The term *JavaBean* generally refers to components written to extend the Java language. You can compare JavaBeans to Microsoft's ActiveX components or COM. These components are self-contained and can be incorporated into applications or can sometimes run by themselves. **Enterprise JavaBeans** refer to a model for creating beans for a distributed multitier environment.

When you create your own new components (beans), they must be generic, and they must include any other necessary components so that they can function by themselves. A developer should be able to use your bean following standard interface conventions.

Many components are visual; others are not. Some components may serve solely to produce a result to be used by other components. For example, consider a component that processes payroll or calculates commissions. Most likely these components do not have a visual interface of their own, but are used by other components that *do* have a visual interface.

You define a JavaBean as a class, which can include data fields or properties, methods, events, and storage (persistence). A **property** is a data field that contains a value. Examples are color, size, position, employee name, or hours. A **method** refers to the actions, such as `setColor`, `getEmployeeName`, or `calculateOvertime`.

For a program to be built from a set of components, some visual and some not, the components must have a way to send messages to each other. The communication between components is called ***event transmission.*** A component that fires an event is called an ***event source***; the component that catches the event is an ***event listener***.

The values of the properties of a component are often called the ***state*** of the component. Preserving the state of an object from one execution to another is **persistence**. When you create JavaBeans, you need to provide for persistence of properties.

Introspection, BeanBoxes, and the BeanInfo Class

A JavaBean is a component that you can use in your applications or supply to others to use in theirs. Each component exposes certain properties, methods, and events, that can be accessed by other components. Java uses a technique called ***introspection*** to look at a component and determine the properties, methods, and events that are available to other components or applications.

The java.beans.Introspector class handles the introspection process. If you use the proper naming conventions for methods that retrieve and assign property values, the Introspector class can determine the exposed properties. You will see more of the conventions and introspection a little later, but the primary rule is to name methods that access properties using get and set, such as `setHours`, `getPay`, `setFont`, and `getFont`.

Several vendors supply a tool, called a ***BeanBox*** *tool*, that you can use to test JavaBeans. You can add your bean into the bean box container, along with other beans with which your bean must interact. When you add your bean to the bean box, the tool handles the introspection by identifying the exposed properties, methods, and events. Before you can add your bean to the bean box, you must create a JAR (Java ARchive) file for the project.

If you don't follow naming conventions for your bean, introspection cannot determine the exposed properties and methods. In that case, you must create a **BeanInfo class** to specify the interface information. The BeanInfo class contains FeatureDescriptor objects and subclasses for each feature including a BeanDescriptor, PropertyDescriptor, MethodDescriptor, and EventSetDescriptor.

Another application that is sometimes used to pass data between components is **InfoBus.** You can use InfoBus to define the interface of components and pass data, including arrays and rows of a dataset, from one bean to another.

For more information about InfoBus see:
http://java.sun.com/products/javabeans/infobus/

Using the BeanBox Tool

You can use any one of several BeanBox tools to test beans. Some IDEs include
a BeanBox, so if you have been using a particular IDE, you may want to investigate its BeanBox. The JBuilder 4 Foundation Edition does not provide tools for
creating beans—those are reserved for the Professional and Enterprise Editions.
The examples in this chapter use Sun's **Bean Development Kit (BDK),**
which you can download and install on your system. The BDK is available in
versions for Windows, NT, and Solaris at:
http://java.sun.com/products/ javabeans/software/bdk_download.html

Downloading and Installing the BDK

Download the correct version of BDK for your system. For Windows, the file is
bdk1_1-win.exe. Run the program to install the BDK on your system (Figure
15.1). For Windows, make sure to change the default location to a folder beneath the root.

Figure 15.1

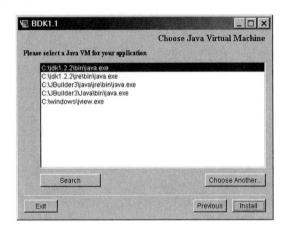

*Tell BDK which version of the
JDK to use. Your list will show the
JDK versions installed on your
system.*

*Caution: Do not allow the setup procedure to install BDK in the default lo-
cation.* The default location on a Windows system is beneath the Program Files
folder. Unfortunately, event handling in the BeanBox cannot work correctly if
any folders in the path have a space in their name. If you accidentally install
the BDK in the default location, you will have a Bdk1.1 folder under Program
Files. You can safely move the entire folder to a new location, such as beneath
the root.

The Bdk1.1 folder contains several examples as well as the BeanBox
program.

Running the BDK

Once you have installed the BDK, you can run the program in Windows by
double-clicking on the run.bat file in the BDK1.1\beanbox folder. For Unix and
Solaris systems, use the run.sh script.

Note: If you have trouble running the program, make sure that the Autoexec.bat on your system includes a path to your JDK. If you have installed the JDK with default directories, the path should include C:\JDK1.3\bin. You can view the current path by typing

```
path
```

at the MS-DOS prompt. You can modify the path by adding this `path` statement to your Autoexec.bat file and rebooting:

```
path = %path%;C:\JDK1.1.3\bin
```

You can also add the `path` statement to run.bat just before the line that runs the program, to change the path temporarily. However, you also need to have the JDK folder in your path to create JAR files, later in this chapter. The best solution is to modify Autoexec.bat.

Warning: The BDK requires that Sun's JDK 1.3 be installed and used at the root level.

The BDK User Interface

The BeanBox has several windows including the ToolBox, the BeanBox, and the **Properties Sheet** (Figure 15.2). The **ToolBox** contains the beans that are stored in the Bdk1.1\jars folder. When you create your own beans, you place their JAR files in this folder and the beans automatically appear in the ToolBox. Use the BeanBox to create instances of beans and test their operation.

Figure 15.2

Sun's BeanBox tool from the BDK.

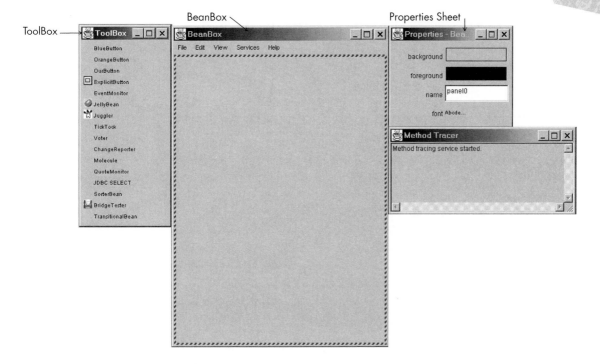

Adding Beans to the BeanBox—Step by Step

STEP 1: Execute either run.bat (Windows) or run.sh (Solaris) to run the BDK application. Your screen should resemble Figure 15.2. Note that you can resize and move each of the windows.

STEP 2: Click on the Juggler bean in the ToolBox; a cross-hair pointer appears.

STEP 3: Click in the BeanBox. This creates an instance of the bean in the BeanBox.

The Juggler bean appears with a border to indicate that it is selected and the Properties Sheet displays the properties of the selected bean (Figure 15.3).

STEP 4: Add two instances of the OurButton bean, below the Juggler bean (Figure 15.4).

Figure 15.3

The Properties Sheet shows the properties for the selected bean, or for the container if no bean is selected.

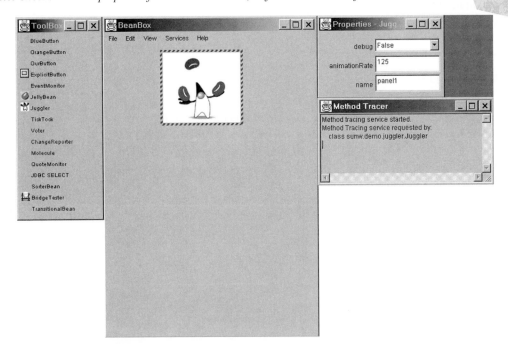

Figure 15.4

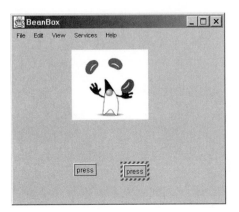

Add two OurButton beans below the Juggler bean.

Try clicking from one bean to another and on the BeanBox itself. Notice that the Properties Sheet changes to display the properties of the selected item. When no beans are selected, the Properties Sheet displays the properties of the container (the BeanBox).

Properties

You can change the values in the Properties Sheet (also called the *Properties window* or the *Properties palette*). For text values, just type a new value. If the property is a color, you can double-click on the color and an input box appears.

Changing Property Values—Step by Step

STEP 1: Select the first OurButton component. In the Properties Sheet change the Label property to "Start". When you press Enter, the label on top of the button changes to match the property.

STEP 2: Select the second button and change its Label property to "Stop".

You can experiment with changing the font, background, and foreground of the bean, if you wish. Double-click on the color block to change the background or foreground color.

Firing and Responding to Events—Step by Step

Beans can fire events and respond to events. And the BeanBox is designed to allow you to design a user interface and test bean events at the same time. (It's a little like being in design time and run time simultaneously.)

In this continuation of the chapter step-by-step example, you will specify which method of the Juggler to execute when the user clicks one of the buttons.

STEP 1: Select the Start button and then choose `Events/action/actionPerformed` from the `Edit` menu.

A stretchy line appears from the button to the mouse pointer. (Try moving the pointer around the BeanBox to see the effect.)

STEP 2: Move the mouse pointer to the Juggler bean and click.

The dialog box that appears shows the events that are defined for the target component (the Juggler).

STEP 3: From the EventTargetDialog box, select *startJuggling* (Figure 15.5) and then click OK. A dialog box appears indicating "Generating and compiling adaptor class".

Figure 15.5

Select `startJuggling` *from the list of available methods for the bean.*

Note: The dialog box should disappear quickly. If it doesn't, you may have missed a step when you installed the BDK. If any folder in the BDK's path has a space in its name, the events in the BeanBox cannot connect correctly. Return to "Downloading and Installing the BDK" in this case.

STEP 4: Repeat for the Stop button. Select the button and choose `Events/action/actionPerformed` from the `Edit` menu.

STEP 5: Move the line to the Juggler bean and click.

STEP 6: From the EventTargetDialog box, select *stopJuggling* and click OK.

STEP 7: Test the events by clicking on the Stop button and then the Start button. If the juggler doesn't stop and start, go back through the steps to see what you missed.

STEP 8: Save your work by selecting `File/Save` from the menu; call the BeanBox file *StartStopJuggling*. (The file extension doesn't matter and you can save the file anywhere you choose—just remember the location.)

To test that it's really saved, choose `File/Clear` to clear the BeanBox and then select `File/Load` and reload your BeanBox file.

What Happened?

When you connect an OurButton bean to the Juggler bean, the BeanBox generates code for the `actionPerformed` method of the button. You tell the BeanBox to write code that calls the Juggler's `stopJuggling` method in the button's `actionPerformed` method.

Designing Beans

When you design a new JavaBean, you follow a procedure similar to that for any other class. First you must determine what your component should do, then you should

- List the properties.
- Determine what events the component must respond to or must fire.
- Identify which properties, methods, and events are public.
- Decide if there are any initial property values that should be set.

Inheritance in Beans

Each new graphical bean that you design is based on some other component. You can choose to create a bean that inherits from a Panel or a Canvas, or use a more specialized component such as a Label or a TextArea. You can base a bean on AWT components, Swing components, or any other components that you have available. The new bean inherits all properties and methods of the superclass. Therefore, a new bean has a set of properties and methods that you get "for free." For example, if you create a bean that inherits from the Label class, your new bean has properties for text, background, and foreground, and methods such as `getText` and `setAlignment`.

Properties

To create a new property for a JavaBean, you usually declare a private variable to hold the value and a pair of public "get" and "set" methods. If you follow this pattern, the introspection process can identify the bean's properties. It's good practice to declare the methods as synchronized, in case the bean is used in a multithreaded application.

```
private double dblMiles;

public synchronized double getMiles()
{
    //Retrieve the current value of Miles property
    return dblMiles;
}

public synchronized setMiles (double dblMilesNew)
{
    //Set value for Miles property
    dblMiles = dblMilesNew;
}
```

Note in this example that the property name is "Miles". The Introspector determines the name from your get and set methods, not from the name of the private variable used to hold the property value. You can name the variable anything you want (following good coding guidelines, of course). You should name the property with a friendly, easy-to-understand name; this is the name used by other components.

Saving Property Values

Each time you add an object to the BeanBox (or to the interface of an applet or application), you declare a new instance of the class. You can change the properties of each object independently. For example, each button has its own label property. Each of those button objects must somehow save the set of changed properties so that the next time it is displayed, the correct values appear.

JavaBeans use object serialization to store the property values of an object. Each time the bean is displayed, the saved property values are restored. And each time the bean disappears from view, such as when the window is covered by another window, the property values are saved.

When you create a new bean, you must import java.io.Serializable and implement the Serializable interface. You don't have to write any code to perform the saving and restoring, however. All that is handled by the Serializable interface.

Indexed Properties

Properties may contain a single value or multiple values. A property with multiple values is called an indexed property. Indexed properties are similar to an array; you can get and set individual elements using an integer subscript.

Bound Properties

A property of a bean may be bound to a property of another component. If a change is made to the value of a bound property, the component to which it is bound is notified. Bound properties are implemented similarly to action listeners. You must add a PropertyChangeListener to the component to be notified. In the bean's class, when the value of a bound property changes, you must initiate the action to notify all components that have registered a listener.

Constrained Properties

A constrained property is a property that cannot be changed without first checking with another component. You must add a VetoableChangeListener and a `vetoableChange` method in the component that gives permission for the change. The code in the bean's class must notify the component of any changes in a property, which can be overridden by the component.

Methods

When you create a new bean class, you should always create a constructor method with no arguments. Although this practice is not mandatory, it is accepted as good programming style and is necessary for the BeanBox to instantiate an object of the class from the Toolbox.

You can also create any other methods that you wish. You will need property accessor methods (the set and get methods), along with any other methods needed to implement the functions of the bean.

Events

The objects that you create from your new classes can generate events, which the applet or application can respond to (or ignore). For example, if a condition exists in an object and the user should be notified, your object *should not* display a message to the user; the user interface must display the message. Your object must either fire an event or throw an exception, to which the applet or application can respond.

An object that generates or raises an event is called the *event source*. The object that responds to an event is called an *event listener*. For example, when the user clicks a button, the ActionListener captures the event and the `actionPerformed` method executes—the button is the event source and the ActionListener is the event listener.

Creating a JavaBean

When you create a bean, keep in mind the elements that allow a class to be a JavaBean:

1. You must be able to instantiate the class. This means that the bean cannot be an abstract class or an interface.
2. You should include a constructor with no parameters. You can also include additional constructors that do have parameters, if necessary.
3. The class must import java.io.Serializable and implement the Serializable interface. You used this interface in Chapter 13 for object serialization. Here you need it for persistence.
4. You should follow the naming patterns to provide for introspection (get and set methods). Otherwise, you must create a BeanInfo class to expose the properties and methods.

A Step-by-Step Example

The following step-by-step example creates a JavaBean that is based on a Panel component. The Panel has a black background and contains a single label. The label displays the company name ("ABC Inc.") on a blue background. Create a new property, called companyName, to hold the name of the company. Figure 15.6 shows the completed bean in the BeanBox.

Figure 15.6

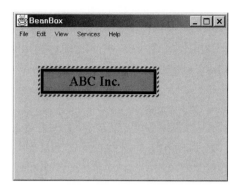

The completed CompanyBean for the step-by-step example.

You will perform the following steps to create the bean:

● Write the code.

  You can use Notepad or any editor to enter the code.

● Compile the code to a class file.

  In this example, we will use the javac compiler from the MS-DOS prompt.

● Create a manifest file.

  You can use Notepad or any editor to create the manifest file.

● Create a JAR file that includes a manifest.

  This step uses the jar utility from the JDK.

Write the Code

STEP 1: Create a folder called Ch15*CompanyBean*. You can make this folder on a diskette or the hard drive.
  Note: Your file and folder names cannot contain blank spaces. Make sure that no folder in the path of your new folder includes a space, such as "My Documents".

STEP 2: Type your code using an editor. You can use Notepad to create the file, but make sure to use .java for the extension. Notepad tries to add .txt to text files unless you specify a different extension. You can also use the editor in your favorite IDE to enter the code.

```
//Folder:        Ch15CompanyBean
//Programmer:    Your Name
//Date:          Today's Date
//ClassName:     CompanyBean
//Description:   A simple bean to display a company logo.

import java.awt.*;
import java.io.Serializable;

public class CompanyBean extends Panel implements Serializable
{
    Font fntName = new Font("SansSerif", Font.BOLD, 24);
    Label lblCompanyName = new Label("  ABC Inc.  ");
```

```
//Constructor
public CompanyBean()
{
    //Set up visible interface
    setSize(60, 100);
    setBackground(Color.black);
    lblCompanyName.setBackground(Color.blue);
    lblCompanyName.setFont(fntName);
    lblCompanyName.setAlignment(Label.CENTER);
    add(lblCompanyName);
}

public String getCompanyName()
{
    //Retrieve the value of the CompanyName property
    return lblCompanyName.getText();
}

public void setCompanyName(String strCompanyNameNew)
{
    //Assign a value to the CompanyName property
    lblCompanyName.setText(strCompanyNameNew);
}
}
```

STEP 3: Save the file as CompanyBean.java in your Ch15CompanyBean folder.

Compile the Class

You are going to use the JDK compiler, javac, for this project. The path of JDK must be in your Autoexec.bat file for this procedure to work. You can check the path and temporarily change it using the `path` command at the MS-DOS prompt.

Check the path:

```
path
```

Change the path to add a directory to the current path:

```
path = %path%;C:\JDK1.1.3\bin
```

Note: This example is based on the default location for the JDK. You must substitute the path on your system if it doesn't match the example. It's important that no folder in the path of the JDK has a space in its name. For example, JDK1.3 should not be stored in the Program Files folder.

STEP 1: Using the MS-DOS prompt, change to the Ch15CompanyBean folder. The actual command depends on the location of the folder on your system.

```
cd A:\Ch15CompanyBean
```

STEP 2: Type in the `javac` command followed by the name of the java file.

```
javac CompanyBean.java
```

Here, no news is good news. If the CompanyBean class compiles successfully, you receive another prompt and no messages (Figure 15.7). If you receive any error messages, you must carefully check the code in your CompanyBean.java file, correct any errors, and compile again.

Figure 15.7

Good news. No error message means a successful compile.

Write the Manifest file

All JavaBeans run from a JAR file. When you create the JAR, you must also create a manifest file to list the classes in the JAR and specify that this is a bean.

STEP 1: Using Notepad or some other editor, type these two lines in the file:

```
Name: CompanyBean.class
Java-Bean: True
```

Note: Be sure to add a carriage return (Enter key) to the last line of the file (Java-Bean: True). If you omit the carriage return, the jar utility ignores the entire manifest file. It is also important to include the space after each of the two colons.

STEP 2: Save the file as Manifest.txt in your CompanyBean folder.

Note: Actually you can use any name for this file; using a .txt extension simplifies editing in Notepad.

Create the Archive File

STEP 1: Use the jar utility at the system prompt (Figure 15.8). (The folder for the JDK must be in your path for this to work.)

```
jar cfmv CompanyLogo.jar Manifest.txt CompanyBean.class
```

This statement creates a JAR file called CompanyLogo.jar in the current folder. The *c* means to create a JAR file. The *f* parameter states that the JAR's file name (CompanyLogo.jar) appears. The *m* specifies that a manifest file is included (Manifest.txt). The *v* means *verbose*; it requests the detailed console output for the command. The final parameter specifies the name of the class file to include, CompanyBean.class. For more information on creating JAR files, see Appendix E.

Figure 15.8

Run the jar utility from the system prompt.

Note: The order of the parameters is important. The JAR file name and the manifest file name must appear in the same order as the *f* and *m* in the command's parameters.

Trouble? If you receive a message that you have an invalid header field, it could be caused by specifying the files in the wrong order on the jar command. The error also could be caused by incorrect spacing or lines that are too long in the manifest file. The "Name:" and "Java-Bean:" headers must each be followed by a space. And each line cannot be longer than 72 bytes. Some editors may create lines that are too long.

Move the Archive File

The easiest and best way to make a JavaBean appear in the ToolBox of the BeanBox is to place the JAR file in the Bdk1.1\Jars folder before running the BeanBox application. (This assumes that you installed the BDK in the location specified earlier in this chapter.) You also can use the `File/LoadJar` menu command of the BeanBox to retrieve a bean's JAR file.

STEP 1: Using any utility, such as the Windows Explorer, move the CompanyLogo.jar file to the Bdk1.1\Jars folder.

Test the JavaBean

STEP 1: Run the BeanBox utility again. Your bean, CompanyBean, should appear in the ToolBox (Figure 15.9).

Trouble? If the bean does not appear in the ToolBox, the most likely cause is the manifest file. Make sure that the manifest file has a carriage return at the end of the last line and that a space appears after the colon on each of the two lines. After making corrections to the manifest, run the jar utility again and move the JAR file to the correct folder.

STEP 2: Add a CompanyBean to the BeanBox. The Properties Sheet shows the properties for your bean (Figure 15.10).

STEP 3: Try changing the companyName property.

Note: To be truly useful, this bean should resize itself when the companyName property changes.

Figure 15.9

*Your new bean, CompanyBean,
appears in the ToolBox.*

Figure 15.10

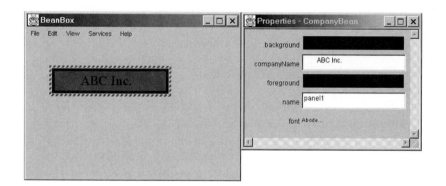

*The Properties Sheet shows the
properties for the new
CompanyBean.*

Feedback 15.1

1. What is a JavaBean?
2. Name a utility that you can use to demonstrate and test beans.
3. Explain the concepts of properties, methods, and events in relation to a bean.

Client/Server Applications

Today's computing environment requires applications to run on multiple systems. Often the application and/or library files reside on one computer, called the **server**. The system from which the user is working is called the **client**. The following sections describe several Java features that facilitate client/server computing.

RMI

Remote Method Invocation (RMI) allows you to use an object that exists on a different computer. The remote system can even call the methods of the object, just as if the object existed on the local machine. This technique is used extensively in client/server applications. The java.rmi package contains the classes to implement RMI.

For more information and a tutorial about RMI, check the Sun Website, http://java.sun.com/products/jdk/rmi/index.html

CORBA

Many client/server systems rely on **Common Object Request Broker Architecture (CORBA)** for implementation. Java can work with CORBA.

The basis of CORBA relies on an **Object Request Broker (ORB).** The ORB can call methods from objects in any language that has an **Interface Design Language (IDL).** The IDL is *not* a programming language but is used to define the interface for objects. The Java IDL defines the remote methods and attributes for the interface.

CORBA creates a client/server environment with objects. Since the objects can be remote, a system can create objects from a class defined on another system. With ORB, the programmer does not need to know the actual location of the class declaration or the language used to create the class.

CORBA has several services to expedite client/server applications. These services are Event, LifeCycle, Naming, Object Querying, Persistence, Properties, and Transactions (Table 15.1).

The Naming service is one of the most critical services because it handles the association of the object name and the location of the object. The LifeCycle service assists by making the location of the object transparent for the application programmer. An Event refers to the messaging or event handling of the objects. A supplier sends the event and a consumer receives the event. Persistence allows you to store an object and retrieve it again later. Object Querying allows a query on a field other than the name of the object.

Table 15.1

CORBA Services

Service	Purpose
Event	Messaging for objects.
LifeCycle	Create and update objects while keeping the location transparent.
Naming	Associate a name of an object with the network address.
Object Querying	Allow queries by fields other than the object name.
Persistence	Store an object for later retrieval.
Properties	Store information about another object.
Transaction	Control the operation over multiple objects.

Transaction processing in CORBA controls the operation over multiple objects using such techniques as locking, commit, and rollback.

DCOM

Distributed Component Object Model (DCOM) is Microsoft's component architecture. At times you may need to use CORBA to work with a system that uses DCOM. In that situation, you can connect a DCOM client to communicate with a CORBA server by using the Microsoft's DCOM-to-CORBA bridge.

JNI

Java Native Interface (JNI) allows Java programs to use methods that were created in another programming language. Prior to the introduction of JNI into Java, both Netscape and Microsoft generated their own techniques for incorporating "native" code into a Java application. The current JNI most closely resembles the Netscape version.

There are many obvious advantages to having JNI. It allows a program to use existing code (often called **legacy code**) regardless of the format in which it exists. The ability to interface with other systems also is enhanced.

There is also a downside to JNI. If the original program is an applet, the security on a browser may stop the program from running with native methods. In addition, the incorporation of JNI into an application eliminates the cross-platform advantages of Java.

So what exactly does JNI allow a programmer to do?

- Pass primitive data or objects to a native method.

- Return data from the method.

- Allow the native method to access, create, and update Java objects.

- Allow the native method to throw and catch exceptions.

- Incorporate run-time type checking in the native method.

- Provide synchronization for multithreading in the native method.

Java Servlets

A Java servlet provides a way to create interactive Web applications written in Java. A servlet is like an applet that runs on the server side and is platform-independent. The servlet can allow a Web developer to access existing business applications. In addition to the JDBC API, servlets have access to libraries of HTTP-specific calls.

Third-party servlet containers are available for Microsoft IIS, Apache Web Server, and iPlanet Web Server (Netscape Enterprise Server).

XML

In addition to HTML, another markup language, **XML** is gaining popularity. XML is designed for portability and cross-platform handling of data over the

Internet. Sun has announced plans to develop a Java standard extension for XML.

Jini

Jini technology is both a hardware and a software concept, covered here because it is used for connectivity. Basically the Jini concept is that devices should be easy to connect without a concern about drivers, operating system problems, or unusual cables.

The Jini concept of a community allows you to connect office equipment for sharing resources or your home appliances for central control. Jini communities must be able to adjust to changes and must be available on demand when needed. Using Jini, a device should be available immediately, as soon as it is plugged into a network.

Feedback 15.2

1. List three methods for implementing client/server architecture in Java.
2. Describe CORBA functions.

Internationalization

If you are developing applets for the Web, the applets may well be accessed from anywhere in the world. You may be writing applications for an international market. The issue of **internationalization** can only increase in importance in the future.

Internationalization issues include formatting, language, and even alphabets. In Chapter 2 you learned how to format numbers following local rules. The Locale object allows a program to produce different results when executed in different countries.

Java uses Unicode, rather than ASCII, to store characters. Unicode provides flexibility and the ability to store large character sets needed for some languages.

You also must consider the language displayed for the user. The text prompts and messages should display in the local language. Rather than "hard code" into the program the text strings for captions, labels, and messages, you can keep the text separate from the program and retrieve it at run time. This is accomplished with the ResourceBundle class, which is contained in the java.util package.

You can download a toolkit to help with internationalization from Sun at: http://java.sun.com/products/jilkit/

Accessibility

Java contains support for people with disabilities. These "assistive technologies" include screen readers, screen magnifiers, and speech recognition. The

Accessibility API works with JFC and AWT components. The assistive features allow programs to meet federal regulations and the needs of a large market. You can download the Java Accessibility Utilities from Java's Website: http://java.sun.com/products/jfc/index.html#download-access

Security

One of the advantages of Java, which you have seen since Chapter 1, is the security provided with the language. **Security** includes the validity of classes as well as the voluminous exception handling incorporated into the code. Another area of security is the resource restrictions placed on applets running in a browser, such as access to local files and printers. Several classes allow the programmer and the user more flexibility over these restrictions.

The Java compiler enforces many of the security rules. One important difference between Java and C++ is that Java does not allow pointer arithmetic. A pointer references a memory address; this restriction is to protect data in a system's memory. Unlike C++, Java checks the boundaries of arrays. If you try to access an area of memory outside of defined areas, Java creates an exception (error condition). And network connections are limited to the host machine where an applet came from.

Security is also provided by the JVM, which contains a verifier and a class loader. The class loader locates all classes used by an applet. A verifier tests classes so that only appropriate classes are loaded. The goal is to determine that a hostile compiler cannot generate dangerous bytecode. There are several steps in verification: the general format, Java conventions, bytecode verification, and the existence of classes. Tests for syntactic accuracy avoid such problems as overflows. Any untrusted classes are not allowed to execute or use system resources.

The security package in Java allows a program to check a digital signature from the developer. This theoretically determines that the program has not been altered and does not contain any viruses or malicious operations. However, if the application has complete control over the client machine and something does go wrong, the only thing you have is the ID from the signature of the perpetrator.

Finally, the Java API contains a Security Manager class for defining the tasks that an application can perform. Each company can create its own security policies and apply them to code with the Security Manager class.

The Security Class

The java.security class provides the ability to create signed applets and javakeys. The security APIs support hashing, digital signatures, and generating certificates. Table 15.2 shows the classes included in java.security.

Digitally Signed Applets

Although security is tight when running an applet from a browser, it's possible to allow an applet to do anything an application can. The applet must be recognized as coming from a trusted provider. To indicate that the source of the applet is safe, the applet can have a **digital signature** called a *certificate*. The certificate, guaranteed by a trusted third party, verifies the originator of the certificate (the programmer) and that the code in the file has not been altered since it was signed.

A company that provides verified certificates is called a *certificate authority* (CA). The two main companies that provide this service are

- VeriSign—http://www.verisign.com/developer/index.html

- Thawte—http://www.thawte.com/

Unfortunately, Netscape and Microsoft have implemented digital signing in two different ways. If you want to run on both Netscape and Internet Explorer, you must obtain a certificate for each and include both with your applet. As of this writing, VeriSign charges for each certificate and Thawte provides both types of certificates for one price.

For testing purposes, you can create a test certificate that allows your applet to run only on your system (or others that you specifically enable).

The security for signed applets consists of a private key and a public key. The developer keeps the private key secret; the public key is distributed with the software along with the certificate.

To create the private and public keys and the certificate, you must

- Use the JDK keytool application to create the public and private key files. The **keytool** application requests information about you and your organization, such as your name, organization, city, state or province, and country. This information is encoded into the key files. Use the `-certreq` option of the `keytool` command to generate a certification request file.

- Send the certification request file to the certification authority. Each company has its own procedures and will inform you how to submit your request. The CA does research to verify that you are who you say you are and satisfy themselves that you are trustworthy. When you pass their tests, they send you back a certificate file, which is encrypted.

- Include the encrypted certificate file in the JAR file for your applet and send the public key to the potential user of your applet.

- When your user attempts to access the digitally signed applet, a message appears. The user must then decide whether to trust this applet. If the user decides to trust the programmer, he or she uses the JDK **jarsigner** tool to add the software developer's public key to the list of trusted programmers.

Creating digital signatures at this time is browser specific. For Internet Explorer you must download the Microsoft Software Development Kit at http://www.microsoft.com/java/download.htm.

For Netscape you can find the Netscape Signing Tool at: http://developer.netscape.com/software/signedobj/jarpack.html.

Note: Digital signatures are recognized by Netscape Navigator 4.0 or later and by Internet Explorer 4.0 or later (on Windows only, not the Mac). If a user is using an earlier version of either browser, the digital signatures are not recognized.

Additional Resources

On the Sun Website you can find signed applet examples for both JDK 1.1 and JDK 1.2. The Microsoft, Netscape, and Sun Websites all have considerable documentation on signed applets. In addition, an excellent guide is located at http://www.suitable.com/Doc_CodeSigning.shtml.

Table 15.2

Security Class Members

Class	Purpose
java.security.acl	Restrict access to system resources.
java.security.cert	Identity certification.
java.security.interfaces	DSA authentication.
java.security.spec	Support for encoding.

Other Security Options

Many packages are available to extend security. The following list introduces you to some of the acronyms.

- JAAS, Java Authentication and Authorization Service. This package is a supplement to Java for authenticating users and controlling access. It implements a standard called the Pluggable Authentication Module (PAM) architecture.

- JCE, Java Cryptography Extension. This package, which is an extension of the JDK 1.2 software, cannot be exported outside of the United States and Canada.

- JSSE, Java Secure Socket Extension. JSSE is an optional package for Java 2 that provides Secure Socket Layer (SSL) and Transport Layer Security (TLS). Using this package, data can be made secure as they pass between a client and a server using HTTP, Telnet, NNTP, and FTP over TCP/IP.

Your Hands-on Programming Example

Create a JavaBean that converts miles to kilometers. It also should be able to clear the current values from the screen. The bean should have a Miles property and methods for `convertMilesToKilometers` and `clear`.

The user can enter the number of miles and click the Convert button; your bean will calculate the correct number of kilometers and display the result in a label. *Hint:* Multiply the miles by 1.609 to find kilometers.

Make your class extend a Panel and add a text field for the miles and a label for kilometers. You also need to include labels indicating miles and kilometers.

Add your bean to the ToolBox and test it with two OurButton beans. Make one button's label "Convert" and connect its `actionPerformed` event to the

`calculate` method of the conversion bean. Change the other button's label to
"Clear" and connect it to the `clear` method of the conversion bean.

Planning the Project

Plan the User Interface

Figure 15.11 shows a possible layout for the bean.

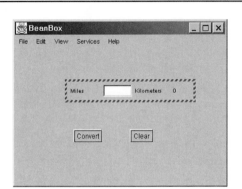

One possible layout for the bean
in the hands-on example.

Plan the Objects and Properties

Class Name: MilesConversionBean extends Panel

Components and Variables:

Access Mode (public or private)	Variable or Component Name	Data Type or Class	Description
	txtMiles	TextField	Input the miles.
	lblKilometers	Label	Display kilometers.
private	fltMiles	float	Hold the Miles property.

Methods:

Access Mode (public or private)	Return Type	Method Name (include any parameters)	Pseudocode
public	void	`constructor`	Set size and background. Add labels and text field.
public	void	`convertMilesToKilometers`	Calculate kilometers. Display the result.
public	void	`clear`	Clear txtMiles and lblKilometers.

Access Mode (public or private)	Return Type	Method Name (include any parameters)	Pseudocode
public	float	getMiles	Retrieve the Miles property.
public	void	setMiles	Set the Miles property.

The Project Solution

MilesConversionBean

```
//Folder:        Ch15MilesJavaBean
//Programmer:    Bradley/Millspaugh
//Date:          6/2001
//ClassName:     MilesConversionBean
//Description:   A bean for converting miles to kilometers.

import java.awt.*;
import java.io.Serializable;

public class MilesConversionBean extends Panel implements Serializable
{
    //Declare components
    TextField txtMiles = new TextField(5);
    Label lblKilometers = new Label("0 ");

    //Declare instance variable (property)
    private float fltMiles;

    //Constructor
    public MilesConversionBean()
    {
        //Set up UI for bean
        setSize(300,100);
        setBackground(Color.lightGray);
        add(new Label("Miles  "));
        add(txtMiles);
        add(new Label("Kilometers "));
        add(lblKilometers);
        txtMiles.requestFocus();
    }

    public void convertMilesToKilometers()
    {
        //Convert from miles into kilometers
        try
        {
            fltMiles = Float.valueOf(txtMiles.getText()).floatValue();
            float fltKM = fltMiles * 1.609f;
            lblKilometers.setText("" + fltKM);
        }

        catch(Exception exc)
        {}
    }
```

```
public void clear()
{
    //Clear fields
    txtMiles.setText("");
    lblKilometers.setText("0 ");
}

public float getMiles()
{
    //Retrieve the current value of the Miles property
    return fltMiles;
}

public void setMiles(float fltMilesNew)
{
    //Assign a value to the Miles property
    fltMiles = fltMilesNew;
}
}
```

S u m m a r y

1. Today's computing environment requires applications that run on multiple systems. The computer containing the actual application or library files is called the server computer. The system from which the user is working is called the client.

2. The ideal for program development is to create components and assemble those components to develop applications.

3. One way to develop components that can be used in other applications is to create the components as JavaBeans. A bean may contain properties, methods, and events.

4. You should define the properties of a bean following the established pattern so that the introspection process can determine the properties.

5. The Beans Development Kit (BDK) is an application for testing JavaBeans. You can add beans to the BeanBox container, connect the events of one bean to the methods of another bean, and test the bean's operation.

6. A JavaBean class must be instantiable, implement the Serializable interface, and contain a default (no parameter) constructor. It is good practice to follow the design patterns for naming methods.

7. To create a new bean, you must enter and compile a class, and create a manifest file and a JAR file. Place the JAR file into the BDK's Jars folder to make the bean appear in the ToolBox.

8. Client/server applications can be implemented in Java using RMI (Remote Method Invocation) or CORBA (Common Object Request Broker Architecture). DCOM systems can incorporate a bridge from DCOM to CORBA.

9. Java programs can incorporate methods written in other languages with JNI, the Java Native Interface.

10. Java servlets are similar to applets but run on the server.

11. XML is a cross-platform markup language for specifying data.

12. Jini is a concept to aid connectivity that uses a community metaphor.

13. Thought should be given to internationalization issues when developing projects. With the Internet, it is likely that an applet may be run in other countries and languages, and you should consider the needs of every netizen.

14. Java assistive technologies provide support for people with disabilities.

15. Java contains security classes to provide a safer environment for running software. An applet can be given the same capabilities as an application if the applet has a digital signature and is accepted as coming from a trusted provider.

Key Terms

Bean Development Kit (BDK)   462
BeanBox   461
BeanInfo class   461
beans   460
certificate   478
client   473
Common Object Request Broker Architecture (CORBA)   474
digital signature   478
Enterprise JavaBeans   460
event listener   461
event source   461
event transmission   461
InfoBus   461
Interface Design Language (IDL)   474
internationalization   476
introspection   461

jarsigner   478
Java Native Interface (JNI)   475
JavaBeans   460
keytool   478
legacy code   475
method   461
Object Request Broker (ORB)   474
persistence   461
Properties Sheet   463
property   461
Remote Method Invocation (RMI)   474
security   477
server   473
state   461
ToolBox   463
XML   475

Review Questions

1. How can components aid in program development?
2. What is a JavaBean?
3. How does a JavaBean relate to an ActiveX component?
4. What is a BeanBox? How is it used with JavaBeans?
5. How do you declare and name a new property for a bean?
6. What is the purpose of RMI and CORBA?
7. What is the purpose of JNI?
8. How can a program be made usable in different countries?
9. Explain the parts of the java.security package.
10. What is a digital signature and how is it used in applets?

Programming Exercises

15.1   Add a molecule bean to an empty BeanBox and test it. You can press the mouse button and drag to rotate the molecule diagram and change the molecule displayed by changing its moleculeName property.

15.2   Add a blueButton bean to an empty BeanBox and experiment with changing its properties. Double-click on a color property (background or foreground) to change it; double-click on the font to change that property; and change the label property.

15.3   Use the BeanBox to connect three beans. Add a JellyBean and two button beans. Make one button say *"Hide"* and the other button say *"Show."* Connect the action events of the buttons to the correct methods of the JellyBean to make the bean hide and show. Test the buttons to make sure the bean works.

15.4   Modify the chapter hands-on exercise to also convert kilometers to miles. You can substitute a text field for the lblMiles, or add a new set of labels. You also can set up a layout manager for the panel to control the placement of the components.

15.5   Create a new bean that allows the user to enter the length and the width of a room in feet and then calculates the square footage. Test the bean in the BeanBox with buttons to Calculate and Clear.

Using an IDE

Experienced Java programmers disagree about which IDE (integrated development environment) to use and even whether to use an IDE at all. An IDE typically includes an editor to write and edit code, a run-time environment that allows the programmer to run applets and applications, options for setting project properties, a debugger to aid in program testing and debugging, and an object browser.

Many IDEs also allow you to visually design the user interface of an applet or application. Using a visual designer, you usually can drag-and-drop a component onto a container surface and then change properties of the component. The IDE then automatically writes the necessary code to declare the component, change the properties, and display it. You may want to experiment with a visual designer after you learn to write Java code.

Choosing an IDE

Choosing an IDE can be difficult. Each of the available Java IDEs has some advantages and disadvantages. Both Sun's Forté and Borland/Inprise's JBuilder 4.0 Foundation are available on the Web for free download. The biggest drawback to both IDEs is that they require considerable RAM to run and run very slowly with the minimum memory size. Both really need 256 MB to run well. And even with maximum memory, Forté is still very slow.

Microsoft's Visual J++ (VJ++) is a very good IDE with the fastest compiler of the bunch, but it has severe compatibility problems. Microsoft has chosen to support the Windows components (WFC—Windows Foundation Classes) rather than Java Foundation Classes (Swing components). Although you can write VJ++ applets and applications using only AWT components, you must be careful to not include Microsoft extensions if you want to create programs that run cross-platform. VJ++ is the most comfortable IDE for most Windows programmers, as it closely resembles Visual Basic and Visual C++ and follows Microsoft's Windows conventions. VJ++ was part of Visual Studio 6.0; however, Microsoft has announced that VJ++ will not be included in VS 7.0 (.NET).

IBM's VisualAge for Java (VAJ) has strong proponents and detractors. Supporters of VAJ say that it has great tools, runs quickly, and represents objects in an organized way. Windows programmers have a more difficult time learning to use VAJ than the other IDEs due to its very different style and analogies.

An IDE to consider is BlueJ, which was developed at Monash University especially for teaching a first course in Java. BlueJ has an editor, compiler, and debugger; takes minimal memory, and runs quickly. Two unique features make BlueJ especially useful for learning Java: a visual representation of the classes using universal modeling language (UML) notation and the ability to instantiate and inspect objects without running the entire application. And the biggest advantage: BlueJ is free. See http://bluej.monash.edu/.

One disadvantage of BlueJ is its minimal implementation. Students accustomed to smart editors that pop up with lists of available variables and methods may miss the extra help. But BlueJ's editor does help by coloring various components for easier identification and is much easier to use than a plain editor, such as Notepad. Another disadvantage of BlueJ is that its debugging tools work only on applications, not applets.

Forté

The Forté IDE, formerly called NetBeans, is produced by Sun and written entirely in Java. Versions of Forté run on Windows, Solaris, Linux, and Unix. You can download and freely use their Community Edition. The Internet Edition and the Enterprise Edition, which contain advanced features, must be purchased. At the time of this writing, the current version is release 1, update 2, and can be found at www.sun.com/forte/ffj/ce/index.html. Forté is an open-source application that can be customized.

The primary drawback of Forté is that it requires at least 128 MB to run. It really needs at least 256 MB, and even then it runs very slowly. (*Note*: See the Forté documentation for Windows system modifications that allow Forté to run in 64 MB. This is not recommended.)

Another drawback of Forté may be more important to you if you are using the IDE in a shared lab or classroom. Forté stores the information about each project in a folder in its own workspace (forte4j/system/Projects). As of release 1, update 2, Forté does not have a Remove Project or Delete Project command. (The FAQ file says that the next release may have such a command.) Unfortunately, this means that Forté shows the project files for all projects that have been written on that particular machine. If the .java and .class files are on the computer's hard drive (as opposed to a diskette that has been removed), the project is available to run and/or copy. This "feature" alone may make you reconsider using Forté. However, you can write programs in Forté and avoid using projects.

Although Forté can run with JDK 1.1, 1.2, or 1.3, you should download and install JDK 1.3 before installing Forté. The 1.3 debugger is far superior to the earlier versions. Also, the 1.3 code is more compact and quicker, according to Sun.

The Forté Environment

As installed, the Forté user interface (UI) uses the Java look and feel. You can change the look and feel to Windows or Motif, if you wish, by modifying a setting in Forté's startup file. See "Changing the look and feel" in the User's Guide (*Help / Documentation / User's Guide*).

When you close Forté, the IDE saves the current state of all windows. The next time you open the IDE, it opens in the same state in which it was left. For a single-user system, this feature can save you lots of time. However, in a shared lab or classroom, it may mean that Forté begins in a strange configuration, even with someone else's project appearing. You will need to learn to switch modes and add and remove directories from the Filesystem. These topics are covered a little later in this appendix.

Figure AF.1 shows the Forté IDE as it first appears, right after the software is loaded. Notice that your desktop is visible in the background, which may be confusing if you have other windows open. As you work in Forté, multiple windows appear, which may overlap each other and might cover the desktop. You can always tell that the Forté environment is active by looking at the title bar. Also, in Windows you can check the task bar to determine the current application.

Referring to Figure AF.1, notice that the Forté IDE has a menu bar and several toolbars. (Note that depending on your screen resolution, the toolbars may appear on more lines than in the figure and you can customize the toolbar sizes and locations.) At the bottom of the toolbars you see the Workspace tabs: *Editing*, *GUI Editing*, *Browsing*, *Running*, and *Debugging*. The tabs represent the different tasks and windows in the development environment. As you move through the process of developing an application, you use the various tabs. Sometimes the tabs appear to change by themselves. For example, if you are writing a program in the editing environment and want to test the application, you may click the *Run* toolbar button. Forté automatically switches to the *Running* tab and the Execution window displays. When you are ready to return to the editor to view your source code, you can click on the *Editing* tab or chose *Editor Window* from the *View* menu.

F i g u r e   A F . 1

The Forté IDE as it first appears.

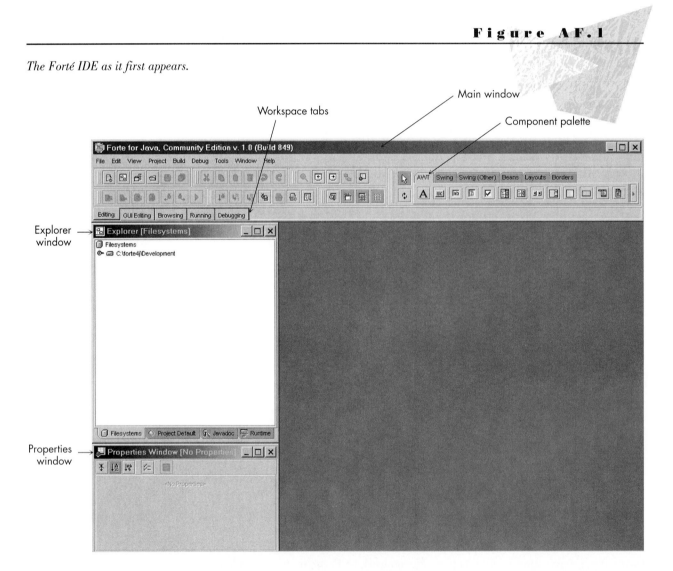

You hide and display windows using the *View* menu.

Forté has extensive context menus—those shortcut menus that pop up when you click the right mouse button. You will find it easy to point and right-

click to see your options at any time. You also can point at an object and press
F1 for context-sensitive help.

Forté's Notion of a Project

A project in Forté is a collection of files that you want to work with together.
When you create a new project, the project appears as a folder underneath the
Forté installation folder. You cannot choose the location for the project and can-
not move it. In fact, in the current version, you cannot even delete a project.

It's best to *not* use Forté projects for any of your Java programs. The key is
to create a folder for your program files. You should mount the folder in Forté's
Filesystem—all files inside the folder will appear in the Explorer. When you
finish working on your program, remove the folder from the Filesystem display
(you'll see how to do this in the tutorial that follows).

Writing the Chapter 1 HelloWorldApplet—Step by Step

Before you can enter and run the HelloWorldApplet in Chapter 1, you must set
up Forté to recognize your folders. Note that in some locations Forté refers to
folders as *directories* and sometimes as *packages*.

If you plan to write, test, and run all of your programs on a single computer,
you can set up a folder on the hard drive to hold your projects. However, if you
plan to move from computer to computer, it's best to store your programs on a
diskette. This step-by-step tutorial uses a diskette in the A: drive on a Windows
system.

Create a Folder

STEP 1: Outside of Forté, create a folder called *Ch1HelloWorld* (no spaces) on
your diskette.

For example, in Windows use the Windows Explorer. Click on the
icon for 3½ Floppy (A:), select *File / New / Folder* and type the name of
the new folder. Then minimize or close Windows Explorer.

STEP 2: Return to Forté.

Mount the Folder in Forté

STEP 1: If the Forté Explorer window is not visible, select *Explorer Window* from
the *View* menu.

STEP 2: Right-click on *Filesystems* in the Explorer window. The shortcut menu
appears.

STEP 3: Select *Add Directory* from the shortcut menu.

STEP 4: In the Add Directory dialog box, switch to your Ch1HelloWorld folder
on the A: drive (or the folder on your hard drive that you want to use).

STEP 5: Click on Add.

Add a New Class

STEP 1: Right-click on the Ch1HelloWorld icon and choose *New From Template
/ Classes / Empty*. The New From Template wizard begins.

STEP 2: Type HelloWorldApplet (no spaces) for the class name (Figure AF.2).
Click Finish.

Remember: The name of the class is also the name of the Java source code file.

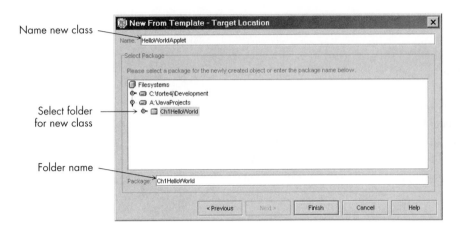

Name the class HelloWorldApplet. Forté will add the .java extension.

Note: Forté has several templates that you can use to provide a framework or skeleton of a program. The contents of each depend on the type of project. Although an applet is included, learn the basics of Java and then later you can let the templates work for you.

Type in the Java Applet Code

The Editing tab should be selected and the Edit window appears, where you can type the Java code.

STEP 1: Type the code for the HelloWorldApplet, pressing Enter at the end of each line (Figure AF.3).

Forté's dynamic completion feature helps you type your code faster. When you type a period, Forté quickly pops up a list of available entries. You can select an item from the list and press Enter to accept it, then continue with any more text on the line.

Be especially careful to note capitalization and punctuation. These two features trip up more Java programmers than any other.

Note that Forté adds line numbers at the left. These numbers, which can be turned off, can help you later to locate the line where an error occurs.

Set up for Applet Execution

STEP 1: In the Explorer window, right-click on HelloWorldApplet to display the shortcut menu. Select *Properties*.

STEP 2: In the Properties window, select the *Execution* tab at the bottom of the window.

STEP 3: Click on the entry for Executor, drop down the list, and choose *Applet Execution* (Figure AF.4). Close the Properties window.

Note: If you ever get the message `java.lang.NoSuchMethodError: main`, you will know that you forgot this step. The `main` method executes first in an application; the `init` method executes first in an applet. By default, Forté tries to run each program as an application unless you tell it to run as an applet.

Type the code for HelloWorldApplet in the Editing window.

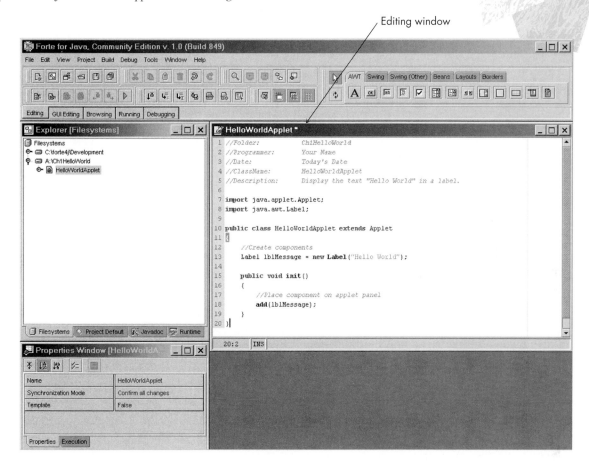

Editing window

Figure AF.4

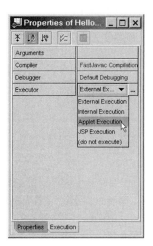

Select Applet Execution so that your class will execute as an applet rather than an application. This dialog box appears only the first time you run the project.

Compile and Run the Applet

STEP 1: Click the Execute toolbar button (▶) or select *Project / Execute Project*. The applet will first compile. And if no errors are found, it will execute.

STEP 2: Check for errors.

If Forté found any syntax errors, a Compiler window will appear with error messages. You can double-click on a message and the offending line will appear highlighted. However, often the actual error occurs on a line that comes before the highlighted line.

Correct any errors and execute again. The Applet Viewer window should appear with your Hello World applet.

STEP 3: Notice in the Explorer window that a new file appears with the same name as your applet but a different icon. This is a an HTML file with an applet tag, used to execute your applet in either the Applet Viewer or a browser.

STEP 4: Stop execution by closing the Applet Viewer window.

You can return to the Editor by clicking on the *Editing* tab.

Save and Reload a Program

STEP 1: Save your program by clicking either the Save or Save All toolbar button, or select *File / Save All*. These commands are enabled if you have made any changes since the project was last saved or loaded.

STEP 2: If you are leaving the computer, right-click on the folder name under Filesystems and choose *Remove Filesystem* from the shortcut menu.

STEP 3: To reopen a program, its folder must be mounted in the Filesystems (Explorer window). Usually, on the same machine, you will find the folder already mounted. To open the program's folder on another computer, right-click on Filesystems and choose *Add Directory* from the shortcut menu.

STEP 4: In the Explorer window, open the entry for your folder. Then double-click on the name of your Java class file.

Using the Object Browser

A useful and powerful feature of Forté is its Object Browser. Click on the *Browsing* tab to display a list of packages (Figure AF.5). Click on your project name to see the list of objects in the package (folder). Then click on your HelloWorldApplet object to display the members of the class. If you click on one of the members, such as lblMessage, you will see the properties of the component in the Properties window.

You can quickly jump to the code for one of the members by double-clicking on its entry. For example, double-click on "init"; the Editing window opens with the `init` method displaying.

Exploring Forté

Explore Forté's *Help* menu. Choose *Getting Started* for a good quick-start tutorial. More detailed tutorials are found under *Tutorials*, and a complete guide to using the UI can be found under *Documentation / User's Guide*.

The Forté Object Browser.

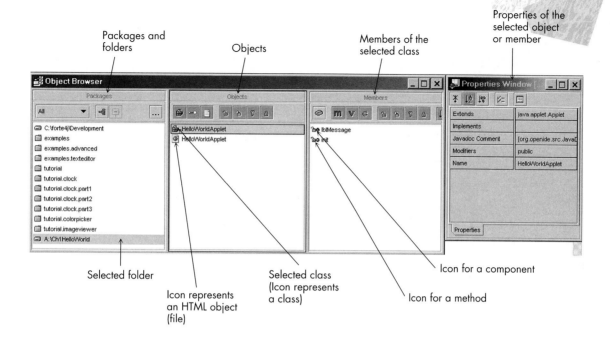

Packages and folders

Objects

Members of the selected class

Properties of the selected object or member

Selected folder

Icon represents an HTML object (file)

Selected class (Icon represents a class)

Icon for a method

Icon for a component

JBuilder 4 Foundation Edition

Note: As this text went to press, JBuilder 5 was announced by Inprise/Borland. The Personal Edition of JBuilder 5, included on the text CD, is the upgrade to JBuilder 4 Foundation. Although it was too late to change the text, the instructions in this appendix and appendix G (Debugging) should not change significantly. If you prefer, you can download JBuilder 4 Foundation from http://www.inprise.com/jbuilder/foundation/.

JBuilder, created by Borland/Inprise, is available in three versions. The basic level is called the Foundation and is available as a free download. The Professional and Enterprise versions, which have more advanced features, must be purchased.

JBuilder, like Forté, is written entirely in Java. Therefore, it is generic and can run on any platform that runs Java. Unfortunately, it also needs considerable memory (128 MB) and runs fairly slowly.

JBuilder can run with JDK 1.1, 1.2, or 1.3. You should download and install the JDK before installing JBuilder.

Download the JBuilder IDE from
http://www.inprise.com/jbuilder/foundation/

The JBuilder 4 Environment

You can choose the look and feel of JBuilder (*Tools / IDE Options / Browser / Look and feel*). The screens in this appendix use the Windows look and feel; other choices are Metal and Motif.

When you close JBuilder, the IDE saves the current configuration, including any open projects as well as the state of all windows. If you are working on your own computer, you will like this feature. But if you are using shared computers in a lab or classroom, you must be prepared to find a strange configuration when you open JBuilder.

Figure AJ.1 shows the JBuilder IDE with a project open. Underneath the menu bar and toolbar, you see that the main area of the screen is divided in two. The left side of the window displays the information about the project and its files in the Project pane. Below the Project pane is the Structure pane, which you can use to view all components of your project as well as Java classes.

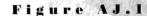

Figure AJ.1

The JBuilder 4 environment.

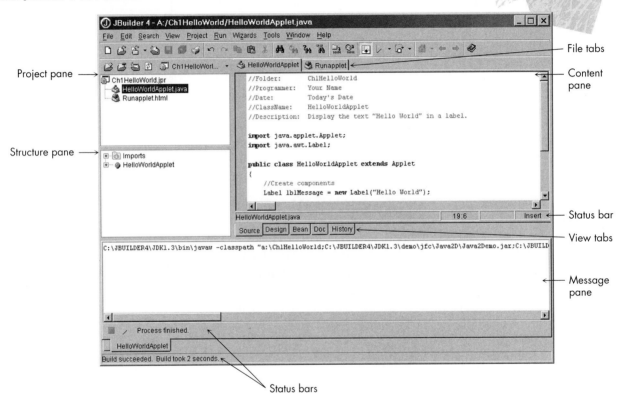

The right side of the IDE is called the Content pane. You use the Content pane to edit and display the code in your Java programs and html files. Notice the *File* tab at the top of the Content pane and the *File view* tabs along the bottom of the Content pane. Most of the time you will work on the *Source* tab of the class file you are working on.

JBuilder displays messages to you in the Message pane as well as the Status bars.

In most locations on the screen, you can right-click to display a context menu, also called a *shortcut menu*. Or you can point to an element and press F1 to display context-sensitive help.

Setting up JBuilder

It's best to set a few options before you begin your first applet:

- Select *Project / Default Project Properties / Code Style*. For *Braces* select *Next line*. And for *Event Handling* choose *Standard adapter* and click OK.

- Select *Tools / Editor Options* and select the *Editor* tab. Change the *Block indent* setting to 4. Then expand the entry for *Indent options* and make sure that all four options are selected: *Smart indent*, *Indent after brace*, *Use tab character*, and *Align closing curly brace* (Figure AJ.2). Click OK.

F i g u r e   A J . 2

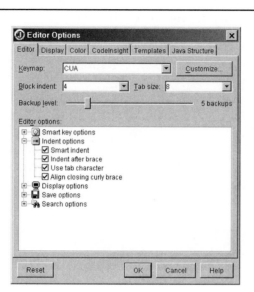

Select Tools / Editor Options to customize the JBuilder editor.

Writing the Chapter 1 HelloWorldApplet—Step by Step

In this step-by-step tutorial, you will create the HelloWorldApplet that appears in Chapter 1.

If you plan to write all of your programs on a single computer, you can set up a folder to hold your projects or allow JBuilder to use its default folder. In this tutorial you will create a project on diskette in the A: drive so that you can move the project from one computer to another. The instructions that follow are for a Windows system.

Create a Project

The first step is to create a new empty project.

STEP 1: Open JBuilder. Your screen should be similar to Figure AJ.3.

Trouble? If a project is already open, select *File / Close Projects* and close any open project(s).

STEP 2: Choose *File / New Project*, which opens the Project Wizard.

STEP 3: For *Project name*, type *Ch1HelloWorld*. Notice that the name also appears for *Project directory name*.

STEP 4: Change the Root path to *a:* and delete the entries for *Source directory name*, *Backup directory name*, and *Output directory name*. Deselect the check box for *Project directory is parent to source and output directories* (Figure AJ.4). Click *Next*.

Note that JBuilder wants to create multiple folders for the project. In order to simplify creating and running applets, we are going to use only one folder to hold all project files.

The JBuilder IDE with no project open.

Set up the paths for the new project.

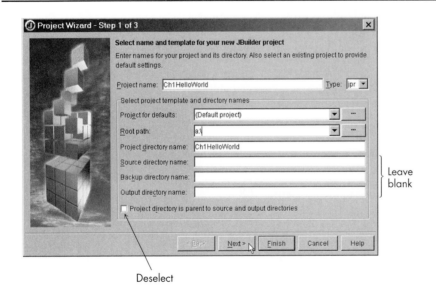

STEP 5: Step 2 of the wizard gives you a chance to verify that all paths are correct. Make sure that no extra levels of folders exist and that all folder names are the same (Figure AJ.5). If the entries are not right, you can

either edit this screen or click *Back* to return to the previous screen. Click *Finish* on this screen, or click *Next* and *Finish* on the next screen. (For now, we will ignore the project description entries.)

The project Ch1HelloWorld.jpr should appear in the Project pane.

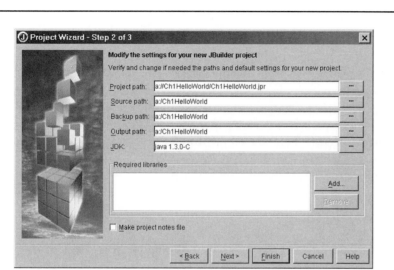

Figure AJ.5

Double-check the project paths before continuing.

Add a New Class to the Project

STEP 1: Choose *File / New Class*; the Class Wizard appears.

STEP 2: Delete the entry for *Package* and type *HelloWorldApplet* for *Class name*. For the Base class, you can either type the entry or click the ellipsis button and select *java.applet.Applet* from the list.

STEP 3: Make the *Options* match Figure AJ.6, deselecting all options except *Public*. Click OK.

Figure AJ.6

Set up the options for the new applet's class file.

Type in the Java Applet Code

The Content pane should show the beginning of your applet's source code. Click on the Source tab at the bottom of the Content pane if necessary to display the applet.

STEP 1: Insert blank lines at the beginning of the code and type the comment lines, pressing Enter at the end of each line.

STEP 2: Add a second import statement:

```
import java.awt.Label;
```

The JBuilder editor can help you select many entries from lists, rather than having to remember and type the entries. If a single entry pops up, you can accept it by pressing Enter or typing the next punctuation for the statement, such as a period or a semicolon. If a list pops up, use your arrow keys or mouse to select the correct entry, then press Enter or type the punctuation character to accept it.

STEP 3: Insert a new line between the curly braces and type the rest of the applet's code (Figure AJ.7).

F i g u r e   A J . 7

Type the applet's code.

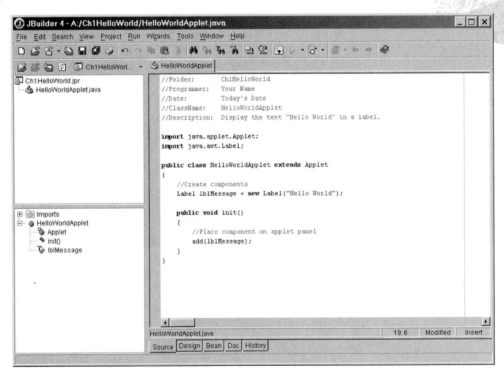

All the time you are typing, the smart editor is checking your code. You may see an Error folder pop up in the Structure pane. You can expand the folder's entries to see error messages, which indicate incorrectly formed statements. You can ignore the messages if you are still typing a line; otherwise, double-check your typing to determine the cause of the errors.

Create the HTML File

STEP 1: Click the Add Files / Packages button (with the green plus sign) above the Project pane, or select *Project / Add Files / Packages.* The Add Files or Packages to Project dialog box appears.

STEP 2: On the Explorer tab, select the drive and folder where you created your project (a:\Ch1HelloWorld). Then type *RunApplet.html* for the file name and click OK.

A dialog box will pop up telling you that the file does not exist and asking if you want to create it. Say OK.

STEP 3: Your new file RunApplet.html should appear in the Project pane. Double-click on its entry to make the (empty) file appear in the Content pane. Alternatively, you can click on the RunApplet.html tab at the top of the Content pane to switch files.

STEP 4: Click on the Source tab in the Content pane. Now you can use the editor to type the HTML code.

STEP 5: Type the Applet tag lines:

```
<applet code = HelloWorldApplet.class
        width  = 200
        height = 200>
</applet>
```

Note that capitalization and spacing are not important for HTML coding, but the class name is case-sensitive.

STEP 6: Click the Save All toolbar button or select *File / Save All.*

Compile and Run the Applet

You run an applet from the HTML file. The first time you run the applet, you must tell JBuilder which file to use.

STEP 1: Click the Run Project toolbar button or select *Run / Run Project.* The Runtime Properties dialog box appears. (This happens only the first time that you run a project.)

STEP 2: On the *Applet* tab select *HTML file* and click the ellipsis button. Locate your RunApplet.html file and click OK and OK again to select the file.

The applet first compiles, and if no errors are found, it executes.

Errors? If the compiler finds any errors, you will see the messages in the Message pane. You can double-click on an error message and the editor highlights the line that caused the error. However, sometimes the actual error is on the line preceding or following the highlighted line.

Correct any errors and execute again.

STEP 3: Your applet should appear in the Applet Viewer window. Stop execution by clicking the Close button on the viewer's window.

Save and Reload a Program

STEP 1: Save your project by either clicking the Save All toolbar button or selecting *File / Save All.* These commands are enabled if you have made any changes since the files were last saved or loaded.

STEP 2: Close the project by selecting the Close Project button above the Project pane or choosing File / Close Project. Note that both commands include the name of the project (*Close Project "Ch1HelloWorld.jpr"*).

If you are using shared computers, make sure to always close your project before closing JBuilder.

STEP 3: To open a saved project, you can use *File / Open Project* or *File / Reopen*.

Using the Object Browser

You can use the Structure pane to display information about your project or about any Java classes. For example, with your applet selected in the Project pane, the Structure pane shows the components and methods in the class. Click on the entry for *init()* and the `init` method appears highlighted in the Content pane (Figure AJ.8).

Click on init() in the Structure pane to display the `init` *method in the Content pane.*

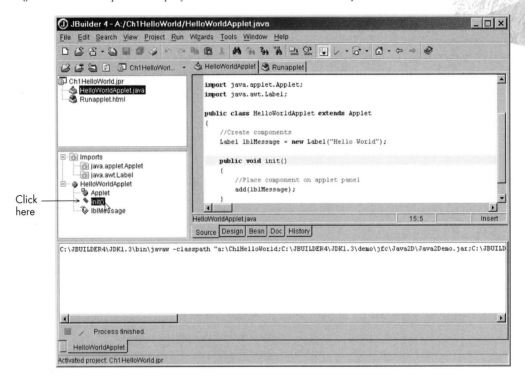

Click here

When your projects become much larger, you will find that the quickest way to locate a particular line of code is to click on its entry in the Structure pane.

You can also use the Structure pane to browse through Java classes and view constants and methods. For example, to view the definition of a Label class, double-click on *java.awt.Label* under *Imports*. Then expand the entry for Label and you will see all of the methods, variables, and constants that are defined in the Label class. If you select an entry from the list, you will see the source code for the Label class in the Content pane. The Content pane generates a new tab for any class that you open. You can close any tab by right-clicking the tab and choosing `Close` from the shortcut menu.

If you want to browse through Java classes that do not already appear in the Project pane, select *Search / Browse Classes*. You can select any Java class that is stored on your computer.

Changing the JDK Version

You may need to use a version of the JDK other than the one installed with JBuilder. As of this writing, JBuilder 4 Foundation installs with JDK version 1.3.0-C. Unfortunately, the printing methods in Chapter 11 do not work in this version of Java. You can print with earlier or later versions of the JDK, but not this one.

If you are using JBuilder 4 Professional or Enterprise, you can specify which version of the JDK you want to use for the compile. On the Project Properties dialog box, drop down the list for JDK and select a different version from the versions you have stored on your computer.

Microsoft Visual J++ 6.0

If you have used Microsoft Visual Basic or Visual C++, Visual J++ will feel very comfortable to you. And even if you haven't used one of Microsoft's development environments, if you have used Windows applications you will find using VJ++ very familiar.

The biggest drawback of using VJ++ is that its Java is nonstandard. VJ++ is based on Java 1.1, which means that you cannot use any 1.2 features, such as Swing components and JavaBeans. Instead, Microsoft has included support for the standard Windows components, which are different from the Java components. If you plan to write Java programs that run only on Windows, you can use the Windows components. But if your goal is to run cross-platform, to take advantage of Java's strengths, then you must avoid using any Microsoft components or extensions.

You can write and run most of the programs in this text using VJ++, with the exception of the Swing applets and applications (Chapter 7 and Chapter 10) and the JavaBean projects (Chapter 15). If you stick with AWT components, your applets can run in either browser on Windows and other operating systems.

VJ++ comes in two editions: the Standard edition and the Professional edition. In order to perform database operations, you must have the Professional edition. You can purchase VJ++ separately or as a component of Visual Studio. The Help files are integrated into the MSDN (Microsoft Developers Network), which is a two-CD package that comes with Visual Studio or can be purchased separately, or you can access the files from the Web.

The VJ++ Environment

Figure AV.1 shows the VJ++ environment. Note that the multiple windows can be moved, resized, hidden, and shown.

Writing the Chapter 1 HelloWorldApplet—Step by Step

In this step-by-step tutorial, you will create the HelloWorldApplet that appears in Chapter 1.

Create a Project

STEP 1: Open VJ++ from the *Programs* menu. The New Project dialog box appears (Figure AV.2).

Figure AV.1

The Visual J++ environment.

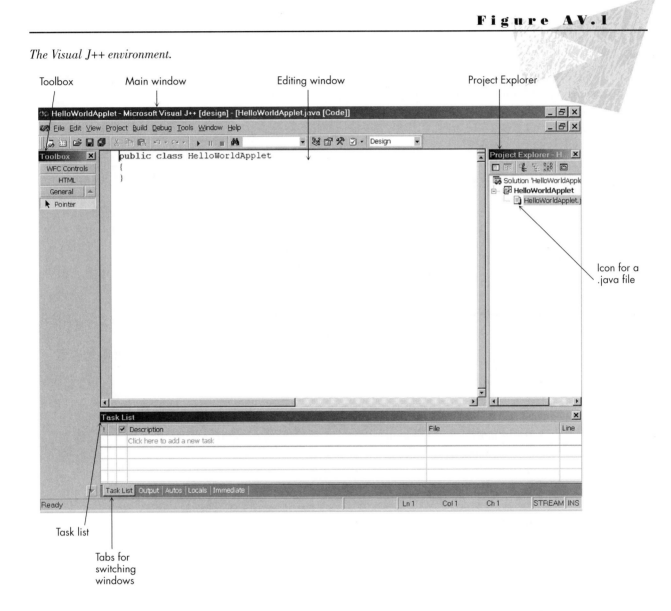

Toolbox Main window Editing window Project Explorer

Icon for a .java file

Task list

Tabs for switching windows

STEP 2: Select the icon for Empty Project that appears on the *New* tab. Enter the project name (HelloWorldApplet) and the location for the file. You can type in the name of a new folder; if the folder does not already exist, it will be created. Call your folder Ch1HelloApplet, to match the listing in Chapter 1. Click *Open*.

You have just created an empty project. The next step is to add a class to the project.

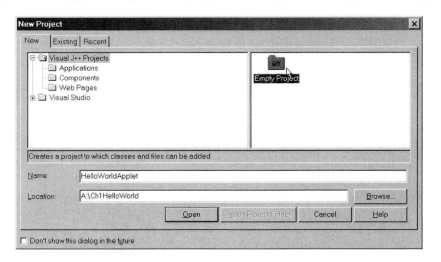

Figure AV.2

Begin a new project by selecting Empty Project. Select the folder name and enter the new project name.

Add a Class to the Project

STEP 1: From the *Project* menu select *Add Class*.

STEP 2: Make sure that the Class icon is highlighted (not ClassMain) and type the name for the class: HelloWorldApplet (no spaces). You don't need to add the .java extension; VJ++ will do it for you. Click *Open*.

Type in the Java Applet Code

STEP 1: In the Editing window, type the code for the HelloWorldApplet, pressing Enter at the end of each line (Figure AV.3).

Figure AV.3

Type the code for HelloWorldApplet in the Editing window.

```
//Folder:          Ch1HelloWorld
//Programmer:      Your Name
//Date:            Today's Date
//ClassName:       HelloWorldApplet
//Description:     Display the text "Hello World" in a label.

import java.applet.Applet;
import java.awt.Label;

public class HelloWorldApplet extends Applet
{
    //Create components
    Label lblMessage = new Label("Hello World");

    public void init()
    {
        //Size panel and place component on applet panel
        resize(200, 200);
        add(lblMessage);
    }
}
```

The VJ++ IntelliSense dynamic completion feature helps you type your code faster. When you type a period, the program quickly pops up a list of available entries. You can select an item from the list by pressing Enter or type a space or punctuation character, then continue with any more text on the line.

Be especially careful to note capitalization and punctuation. These two features trip up more Java programmers than any other.

Note that the Java editor is performing syntax checking all the time you are typing. When you are in the middle of a statement, the editor sees that as an error since the statement isn't complete. You can ignore its warnings until you finish each line. Then if you still see a warning red underline, check to see what's wrong. You can find a message corresponding to each of the red marks in the Task List window.

Compile and Run the Applet

STEP 1: Click the Start toolbar button (▶) or select *Debug / Start*. The applet will compile. If no errors are found, you will see the HelloWorldApplet Properties dialog box, asking how you want to run this class. VJ++ makes the assumption that you want to run HelloWorldApplet when the project runs, which is the correct assumption (Figure AV.4). Click OK. (Note that this dialog box appears only the first time you run the project.)

Figure AV.4

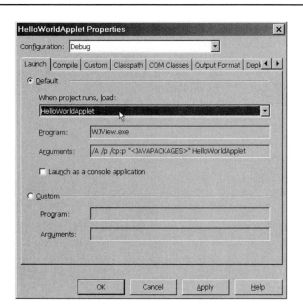

The project's Properties dialog box appears only the first time you run the project. You must select the class to run first. In this case, the project has only one class.

The Microsoft Applet Viewer should appear with your applet running. Check for errors. If you see a warning dialog box telling you the solution update failed, click the Cancel button. You will see warning error messages in the Task List at the bottom of the screen (Figure AV.5). Double-click on the red exclamation mark at the beginning of a line, and your cursor will jump to the line that caused the error. However, often the actual error occurs on a line that comes before the selected line. For example, if the message indicates that a semicolon is missing, look at the previous lines of code.

Figure AV.5

Any syntax errors found by the compiler appear in the Task List. Double-click on the exclamation mark to jump to the offending line.

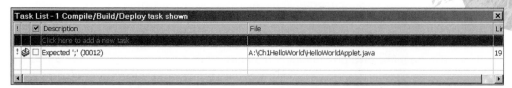

Correct any errors and execute again.

The Applet Viewer window should appear with your Hello World applet.

Note: If you see only a title bar for the Applet Viewer, resize its window to see the entire applet.

Save and Reload the Project

STEP 1: Select *File / Save All* to save the project and .java file.

STEP 2: Select *File / Close All* or *File / Exit* to exit VJ++.

Assuming that you saved the project in the Ch1HelloWorld folder on a diskette, you can reload the project from that diskette. The procedure is the same whether you are on the same computer or carry the diskette to another computer.

STEP 3: To load your saved program, start VJ++ if necessary and place your diskette in the drive.

STEP 4: Open the *File* menu. If you are on the same computer as the one you used to create the project, you should see the name of your project near the bottom of the *File* menu on the *Recently Used Files* list, where you can select it. Otherwise, choose *Open Project* from the *File* menu and browse to find your diskette, folder, and project. You can select either the .sln or .vjp file.

Add an HTML file

STEP 1: From the *Project* Menu, select *Add Web Page*. On the *New* tab in the *Add Item* dialog box, click to select the icon for Page and type a name for the file. Name the file RunApplet.htm (or RunApplet.html) and click *Open*.

STEP 2: Notice the tabs at the bottom of the Editing window for *Design*, *Source*, and *Quick View*. Click on *Source*. You will see a template for an HTML page.

STEP 3: Move your cursor to a line between the <BODY> and </BODY> tags.

STEP 4: Type the Applet tag lines:

```
<applet code = HelloWorldApplet.class
        width = 200
        height = 200>
</applet>
```

Note that capitalization and spacing are not important for HTML coding, but the class name is case-sensitive.

STEP 5: Save the file using the Save toolbar button or *File / Save RunApplet.htm*.

STEP 6: You can now open the HTML file in either Netscape or Internet Explorer. Your HelloWorldApplet should run when the page is opened.

Using the Object Browser

You can use the VJ++ Object Browser to view objects in any package. Select *View / Other Windows / Object Browser* to display the window (Figure AV.6). In the Classes list, click on any class name that you want to view. You can choose any existing Java class or your own class. In the Members list you can see the components and methods. Click on the name of a component to display information about its class at the bottom of the window. You can double-click on a component or method name to jump immediately to the Edit window with the corresponding section of code displaying.

The VJ++ Object Browser.

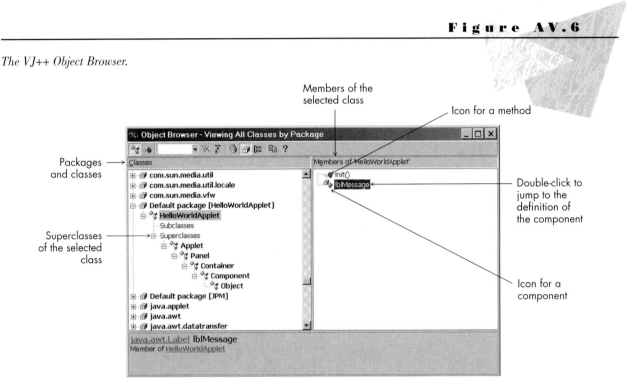

Notice that in the Classes list, you can expand the entries to see the subclasses and superclasses of any class. Click on any entry in the Classes list to see all members of the class in the Members list. Then click on the name of any member to see a description at the bottom of the window.

You can switch back and forth among open windows by pressing Ctrl + F6 or Ctrl + Tab, or making a selection from the Window menu.

BlueJ

BlueJ is considerably different from the other available IDEs. BlueJ was developed especially for teaching Java. Its error messages are easier to understand, it displays the project classes visually using UML notation, and it allows you to test parts of a project without having to run (or even write) the whole thing. You can download BlueJ for free from http://bluej.monash.edu/.

BlueJ has versions that run under Linux, Solaris, Windows 95/98, and Windows NT. At the time of this writing, a Macintosh version was being developed.

If you want to try using BlueJ, first download and install JDK 1.3 (although BlueJ will run with 1.1 or 1.2). Then download and install BlueJ, following the instructions you find on their Website. You can also download a tutorial and a user manual, both in .pdf format.

The BlueJ Environment

Figure AB.1 shows the BlueJ IDE. Its simplicity is a little misleading; it can really do most everything you need to do. The opening view shows the project classes visually.

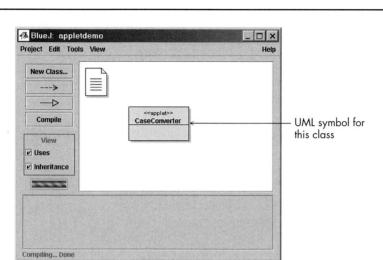

The BlueJ environment. Double-click the symbol for the applet's class to enter the editor.

BlueJ's Templates

BlueJ, like the other IDEs, allows you to begin a new class file using a template. But BlueJ's templates are customizable. You can edit a text file to make the applet template, class template, and HTML template exactly like you want it.

Writing the Chapter 1 HelloWorldApplet—Step by Step

In this step-by-step tutorial, you will create the HelloWorldApplet that appears in Chapter 1.

Begin a New Project

STEP 1: Open the BlueJ program and select *Project / New*. In the New Project dialog box (Figure AB.2), select the folder where you want the project to appear and name the project. BlueJ will create a new folder with the project name.

Add a Class to the Project

STEP 1: Click on the New Class button. In the Add New Class dialog box, type HelloWorldApplet (no spaces) and click Applet for Class Type. Click OK.

Note: For this first tutorial, you are going to use BlueJ's default applet template. In the future, you may want to replace the template. Move applet.tmpl from the BlueJ folder (Appendix A) on your student CD to BlueJ's lib folder (bluej/lib), or edit the file to suit your needs.

Select location for new project

Begin a new project using the New Project dialog box.

Enter the name of the new project

When your applet appears in the IDE, its symbol has slash marks (Figure AB.3). This means that the class has not been compiled. You will take care of that soon.

The slash marks on the applet's symbol indicate that the file has not been compiled since it was written or changed. Click the Compile button to compile.

Type in the Java Applet Code

STEP 1: Open the class in the editor by double-clicking on its icon, or you can right-click on the icon and select *Edit Implementation* from the popup shortcut menu.

STEP 2: In the Editing window, you will see code generated by the template. Delete all the extra lines so that you can follow the simple listing in Chapter 1. Figure AB.4 shows the file with the extra lines removed.

STEP 3: Move the cursor to the correct lines and type the rest of the applet code as it appears in Chapter 1 (Figure AB.5).

Be especially careful to note capitalization and punctuation. These two features trip up more Java programmers than any other.

The applet template file with the extra lines removed.

```
import java.applet.Applet;
import java.awt.*;

public class HelloWorldApplet extends Applet
{

    public void init()
    {
        // provide any initialisation necessary for your Applet

    }
}
```

Type the rest of the applet code.

```
//Folder:          Ch1HelloWorld
//Programmer:      Your Name
//Date:            Today's Date
//ClassName:       HelloWorldApplet
//Description:     Display the text "Hello World" in a label.

import java.applet.Applet;
import java.awt.*;

public class HelloWorldApplet extends Applet
{
    //Create components
    Label lblMessage = new Label("Hello World");

    public void init()
    {
        //Place component on applet panel
        add(lblMessage);
    }
}
```

Compile and Run the Applet

STEP 1: Click the Compile button at the top of the editor. The applet will compile. If no errors are found, you will see the message "Class compiled - no syntax errors" at the bottom of the window.

If the compiler identifies any error, it displays a message in the message area at the bottom of the screen and highlights the line in error. For more explanation of the error, click the question mark at the right end of the error message. You will have to identify and fix any errors and click Compile again, until it compiles without any errors (a clean compile).

STEP 2: Click the Close button in the upper-right corner of the window to return to the main window.

STEP 3: Point to the icon for your HelloWorldApplet and right-click. Select *Run Applet* from the shortcut menu.

STEP 4: In the Run Applet dialog box, change the Height to 200 (both Height and Width should be 200). Click OK.

STEP 5: The Applet Viewer should pop up with your applet running. Click the window's Close button when finished.

BlueJ automatically creates an HTML file with an applet tag when you run the applet. You can open the HTML file in a browser, such as Netscape or Internet Explorer, outside of BlueJ.

Save and Reload the Project

In BlueJ you don't have to initiate any command to save the project; it is saved automatically. Only one project can be open at a time. If you open a new project or exit the program, any unsaved classes are saved.

STEP 1: Select *Project / Close* to close the project.

STEP 2: To load your saved project, select *Project / Open*. Select your project name and click OK.

Viewing Java Classes and Help

BlueJ's Help menu allows you to view their tutorial, their user manual, or the Java class libraries, which are extremely useful for looking up the classes and their members. As originally configured, the menu choices take you to Web addresses. However, you can download the tutorial and user manual from the BlueJ site, http://bluej.monash.edu, and the Java class libraries from Sun's site, http://java.sun.com/j2se/1.3/docs.html. See the BlueJ user manual sections 8.1 and 8.3 for information on changing the configuration files to view the Help files from the local machine.

Assuming that you download the Java class library documentation from Sun and unzip it into the folder c:\jdk1.3\docs, the configuration command to enter for bluej.defs is

```
bluej.url.javaStdLib=file://c:/jdk1.3/docs/api/index.html
```

Creating and Compiling from the JDK

You can compile and run your Java program using the JDK from a system prompt.

Create and Compile the Program

STEP 1: Use your favorite text editor (Windows Notepad?) to write the Java program.

STEP 2: Save the file with an extension of .java.

If you are using a word processor, make sure to save as Text or Text Only.

Notepad tries to add .txt as the extension of saved files. In the Save As dialog box, make sure to change the *Files as type* entry to *All files (*.*)*, or you will get .txt added to your file name.

STEP 3: Go to the system prompt. In Windows, select *Start / Programs / MS-DOS Prompt.*

To make the following commands work, the folder that holds the JDK must be in the system path. The best way to accomplish this is to add the *path* statement to your Autoexec.bat file and reboot. You can also type the *path* command at the system prompt for a temporary change. If you installed JDK 1.3 in the default location, this is the statement to add the correct folder to the current path:

```
path c:\jdk1.3\bin;%path%
```

STEP 4: Change to the folder that contains your .java file, if necessary.

```
cd a:\Ch1HelloWorld
```

STEP 5: At the system prompt, type

```
javac filename.java
```

Note: This command is case-sensitive. It is important to spell and capitalize the name of your file exactly as you saved it.

STEP 6: Check for messages. No news is very good news—it means that the Java compiler did not find any syntax errors.

If you receive warning error messages, you must go back into the editor, locate and correct the problems, resave the file, then compile again.

The compiler-generated error messages display the line number of the problem line, the portion of the line causing the problem, and an explanation of the error. Use these messages as a rough guide—often a syntax error is actually caused by a problem in an earlier line, which makes the marked line incorrect.

When you compile with no error messages (a clean compile), the Java compiler generates a .class file. You can look in the folder with your .java file and see the compiled .class file, which contains the bytecodes. The .class file is the one that you execute in either a browser or the Applet Viewer.

Using Sun's Applet Viewer

To run your applet, you first must create an HTML file that has an applet tag. Use the sample in Chapter 1 or see the example earlier in this appendix for VJ++. Once you create an HTML file, you will generally make a copy of it for each project, modifying the class name and maybe the applet's height and width.

When you have an HTML file for your applet, you can view your applet's output by opening the HTML file in a browser, such as Netscape or Internet Explorer. Or you can use Sun's Applet Viewer program, which comes with the JDK.

To run Sun's Applet Viewer, you must be at the system prompt. The path must be set to include the folder that holds the JDK (C:\JDK1.3\bin is the default). The folder that holds the HTML file must be current (or in the path). The command is

```
appletviewer htmlFileName
```

For example, to run your RunApplet.html file, use this command:

```
appletviewer RunApplet.html
```

As with the compiler command, this command is case-sensitive. Make sure to capitalize the file name correctly.

Figure AJD.1 shows a nice clean compile and run of the Chapter 1 HelloWorldApplet.

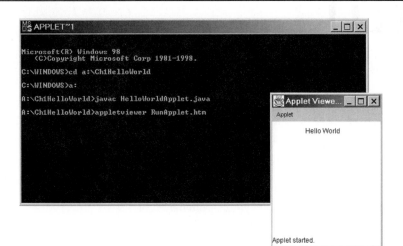

A clean compile and execution using the JDK javac compiler and applet viewer.

Getting Help

You can view the Java class libraries online at
http://java.sun.com/j2se/1.3/docs/api/index.html

If you want to be able to access the Java documentation while you are offline, you can download the documentation files from http://java.sun.com/j2se/1.3/docs.html. Unzip the file into the folder c:\jdk1.3\docs. Then add this URL to your browser's bookmarks or favorites list:

```
file://c:/jdk1.3/docs/api/index.html
```

B

Conventions and Standards

Adopting standards helps programmers, managers of programmers, future programmers that must modify and maintain programs, as well as instructors and lab personnel who help students locate program errors and evaluate student work.

Of course, you *must* follow the rules of Java. In addition, you *should* follow conventions and standards. Many conventions have been adopted by professional programmers. Other conventions have been proposed by Sun Microsystems and various programmer groups. An individual, a company, or an educational institution may generate others. Often an employer publishes a list of standards that all employees must follow.

This appendix lists the conventions used in this text.

Naming Conventions

Convention	Examples	Applies To
Use a prefix to indicate object or data type.	intCount lblMessage	variables objects
Capitalize the first letter of each word after the prefix.	setRate intCount strEmployeeName PayrollApplet	methods variables objects classes and interfaces
Use set and get prefix for methods that assign and retrieve values from private data.	setRate getName	methods
Use classname from extends clause as a suffix.	PayrollApplet	classes
Use able suffix on implemented interfaces	Sortable	interfaces
Use uppercase and underscores for constant (after data type prefix).	intLIMIT intNUMBER_QUESTIONS	primitive data with the keyword final

Prefixes

Name program variables and constants using the prefixes in Tables B.1 and B.2 for primitive data types and the wrapper classes.

Primitive Data Types

Data Type	Prefix	Example
boolean	bln	blnFound
char	chr	chrCode
double	dbl	dblVolume
int	int	intCount
float	flt	fltTotal

Wrapper Classes

Use uppercase for the prefix, except for strings.

Class	Prefix	Example
Boolean	Bln	BlnHide
Integer	Int	IntQuantity
Float	Flt	FltRate
String	str	strFormattedOutput

Name components using the prefixes in Table B.3.

Components

Component	Prefix	Example
Button	btn	btnOK
CheckBox	chk	chkBold
CheckBox (used in a group) (option button)	opt	optRed
Frame	frm	frmMain
Label	lbl	lblMessage
List	lst	lstSchools
Menu	mnu	mnuEdit
MenuBar	mnu	mnuMain
MenuItem	mnu	mnuPrint
PopupMenu	mnu	mnuLabel
TextArea	txa	txaReport
TextField	txt	txtName

Source Program Format

Your programs will be easier to follow if you consistently indent blocks, add extra spacing, and write good, consistent comments.

Indentation

- Indent all lines in a block, which is defined by opening and closing braces. Generally, about four spaces is best for a tab level.

  Example:

  ```
  {
      if (intCount = 0)
      {
          lblMessage.setText("No items to count");
      }
      else
      {
          lblCount.setText("Count = " + intCount);
          intSummary += intCount;
      }
  }
  ```

- Indent the lines within an if statement, even when not using braces.

  Example:

  ```
  if (intCount = 0)
      lblMessage.setText("No items to count");
  else
      lblMessage.setText("You had " + intCount + " items.");
  ```

Spacing

In Java, white space is free. You can add extra spaces between elements and extra blank lines without affecting program performance. Extra spaces can help improve the readability of your code.

- Include a blank line between methods.

- Use a blank line after the initial comments and between logical groups of statements.

Line Continuation

One statement can appear on multiple lines. In Java, a semicolon indicates the end of a statement. If you continue a statement to another line, indent the continuation line to indicate that it's part of the original statement.

Example:

```
lblMessage.setText
    ("This is a really big message, "
    + "which spans several lines");
```

Comments

Every class should begin with identifying comments that indicate, as a minimum:

- The class name

- The folder name

- The programmer name

- The date

- A description of the function of the class

You can use either the single-line comment method or the multiple-line method.

Examples:

```
//Class:        MyNewClass
//Folder:       MyFolder
//Programmer:   My Name
//Date:         1/1/01
//Description:  Make objects that do something.

/*
Class:          MyNewClass
Folder:         MyFolder
Programmer:     My Name
Date:           1/1/01
Description:    Make objects that do something.
*/

fltTotal += fltAmount           //Add current amount to total
```

Include a comment at the top of each method to describe the purpose of the method.

Example:

```
public void setName(String newName)
//Set the value of the Name property
{
    .....
}
```

APPENDIX

C

Java 1.0 Event Handling and Deprecated Methods

At the completion of this appendix, you will be able to . . .

1. Recognize early Java event handling routines.

2. Look up deprecated methods from earlier versions of Java.

Early versions of Java incorporated a different approach to handling events. The event processing was modified with Java 1.0 to better accommodate multiple platforms. At the time of this writing, the Macintosh systems still use the earlier methods of event handling.

In addition to events, many of the methods in various classes have been modified and renamed. You are discouraged from using the earlier syntax. These methods generate a message indicating that they are deprecated. This term means that they still work but may become obsolete in future versions of the JDK.

Event Handling Using the Action Method

Java 1.0 uses an `action` method for handling events. This method contains two arguments: the event and an object. Also notice in the following example that the return type for the `action` method is boolean. Therefore, the method must contain a `return` statement.

```
public boolean action(Event thisEvent, Object thisObject)
{
    // Handle events

    lblMessage.setText("Hello World");
    return true;
}
```

This Hello World applet displays a message when the user clicks the button.

```
// Hello World Applet to demonstrate Java 1.0 event handling

import java.applet.*;
import java.awt.*;

public class HelloWorld extends Applet
{
    //Create controls
    Button btnDisplay = new Button("      Display      ");
    Label lblMessage = new Label("              ");

    public void init()
    {
        //Place controls on the page

        add(lblMessage);
        add(btnHello);
    }

    public boolean action(Event thisEvent, Object thisObject)
    {
        // Handle events

        lblMessage.setText("Hello World");
        return true;
    }
}
```

Responding to Multiple Buttons

When you use the Java 1.0 event handling, the technique for determining which event triggered the method is also different. A `target` property of the class contains the name of the object causing the event.

```
public boolean action(Event thisCmd, Object thisObject)
{
    //Check which button was pressed

    if(thisCmd.target == btnEnglish)
        lblGreeting.setText("Hello");
    if(thisCmd.target == btnSpanish)
        lblGreeting.setText("Hola");
    if(thisCmd.target == btnFrench)
        lblGreeting.setText("Bonjour");

    return true;
}
```

Sample Program

This program has three command buttons. The `action` method uses an `if` to determine which command button was clicked. The Event argument holds a value indicating which command button was pressed.

```
//Folder:          ApxCEvents
//Programmer:      Bradley/Millspaugh
//Date:            6/2001
//Class Name:      multicmd
//Description:     Demonstrate event handling in Java prior to version 1.1.
//                 The user can click one of three buttons to
//                 select the language for the label.

import java.applet.*;
import java.awt.*;
import java.io.*;

public class multicmd extends Applet
{
    //Declare buttons and label
    Button btnSpanish = new Button("Spanish");
    Button btnEnglish = new Button("English");
    Button btnFrench = new Button("French");
    Label lblGreeting = new Label("              ");

    public void init()
    {
        // Add controls to the interface
        add(btnEnglish);
        add(btnSpanish);
        add(btnFrench);
        add(lblGreeting);
    }
```

```
public boolean action(Event thisCmd, Object thisObject)
{
    //Check which button was pressed

    if(thisCmd.target == btnEnglish)
        lblGreeting.setText("Hello");
    if(thisCmd.target == btnSpanish)
        lblGreeting.setText("Hola");
    if(thisCmd.target == btnFrench)
        lblGreeting.setText("Bonjour");
    return true;
}
}
```

Deprecated Methods

The following list contains many of the deprecated methods along with their newer versions. The changes to the Component class relate to the changes in event handling. Another significant change is in the use of the prefixes set and get.

The Date class, which is a part of the util package, contains many changes due to the demands for localization issues. The Calendar class is a new feature providing the formatting and calendar styles by country or region. All constructors for the Date class except for an empty argument list also have been deprecated.

Class	Deprecated Method	Replacement Method
java.awt.Component	action()	actionPerformed()
	bounds()	
	deliverEvent()	
	disable()	
	enable() enable(boolean)	setEnabled(boolean)
	getPeer()	
	gotFocus(Event, Object)	
	handleEvent()	
	hide()	setVisible(boolean)
	inside()	
	keyDown(Event, int)	KeyListener
	keyUp(Event, int)	KeyListener
	layout()	

continued

Class	Deprecated Method	Replacement Method
	locate(int, int)	setLocation(int, int)
	location()	setLocation(Point)
	lostFocus(Event, Object)	FocusListener
	minimumSize(Event, int, int)	MouseListener
	mouseDown(Event, int, int)	MouseListener
	mouseDrag(Event, int, int)	MouseListener
	mouseEnter(Event, int, int)	MouseListener
	mouseExit(Event, int, int)	MouseListener
	mouseMove(Event, int, int)	MouseListener
	mouseUp(Event, int, int)	MouseListener
	move(int, int)	setBounds()
	nextFocus()	FocusListener
	postEvent()	
	preferredSize()	
	reshape(int, int, int, int)	
	resize(Dimension)	setSize(Dimension)
	resize(int, int)	setSize(int, int)
	show() show(boolean)	setVisible(boolean)
	size()	
java.util.Date	getDate()	Calendar class
	getDay()	Calendar class
	getHours()	Calendar class
	getMinutes()	Calendar class
	getMonth()	Calendar class
	getSeconds()	Calendar class
	getTimezoneOffset()	Calendar class
	parse()	
	setDate()	Calendar class

continued

Class	Deprecated Method	Replacement Method
	setHours()	Calendar class
	setMinutes()	Calendar class
	setMonth()	Calendar class
	setSeconds()	Calendar class
	setYear()	Calendar class
	toGMTString()	
	toLocaleString()	
	UTC(int, int, int, int, int, int)	

D

Solutions to Feedback Questions

Chapter 1

Feedback 1.1

1. Java is a simple, object-oriented, robust, secure, portable, high-performance, architecturally neutral, interpreted, multithreaded, dynamic language.
2. Five levels of security: the rules of the language, the compiler, the verifier, the ClassLoader, and the Security Manager.
3. Java Development Kit—the language library.
   Java Virtual Machine—the interpreter.
   Just-in-time Compiler—translates code and stores for future access.

Feedback 1.2

1. ```
   import java.util.*;
   ```

2. ```
   Label lblCompanyName = new Label("TriState Industries");
   ```

3. ```
   /*  Class Name:    Java Class
       Programmer:    My Name Here
       Date:          01/01/01
       Description:   This is a wonderful program */
   ```

Feedback 1.3

1. ```
   lblMessage.setFont(fntBold);
   ```

2. ```
   setBackground(Color.gray);
   ```

3. ```
   lblMessage.setForeground(Color.darkGray);
   ```

Chapter 2

Feedback 2.1

1. ```
   Label lblCompany = new Label("Hello World", Label.CENTER);
   ```
2. Constructors vary in the argument list. When a constructor is called, the list of arguments and argument types determines the appropriate constructor.

Feedback 2.2

Note: The answers to the following may have different names for the variables, but make sure to use the proper data type and prefix.

1. ```
   int intSurveyCount;
   ```

2. ```
   long lngSurveyCount;
   ```

3. ```
   float fltBalance = 0.0f;
   ```

4. `String strVendor;`

5. `static float fltTransactionTotal;`
   The declarations should be inside a class but not within a method.

6. `float fltTransaction;`
   The declaration should appear at the top of the class—inside the class but not inside a method.

7. A local variable is used when it is needed only within a method. An instance variable is required when each object of the variable type needs a value for the variable and a class variable if every object shares a single value for the variable.

Feedback 2.3

1. `TextField txtLastName = new TextField(10);`
   `TextField txtFirstName = new TextField(10);`

2. `add(new Label("Last Name"));`
   `add(txtLastName);`
   `add(new Label("First Name"));`
   `add(txtFirstName);`

3. `txtLastName.requestFocus();`

4. `strLastName = txtLastName.getText();`
   `strFirstName = txtFirstName.getText();`

5. `txaClient.setText(strLastName + ", " + strFirstName + "\n");`

Feedback 2.4

1. The ActionListener interface contains methods that respond to user events. You add this to the class to provide for event-handling.

2.
```
public void actionPerformed(ActionEvent event)
{
//Triggered when the user clicks the button or presses the Enter
// key in any of the text fields
String strOutputLine; //Declare local variable

//Assign the text fields to variables
strLast = txtLastName.getText();
strFirstName = txtFirstName.getText();

//Concatenate the variables
strOutputLine = strLastName + ", " + strFirstName;

//Append the concatenated line to the output
txaOutput.append(strOutputLine + "\n");

//Clear the text fields
txtLastName.setText("");
txtFirstName.setText("");

//Place the cursor in the first text field
txtLastName.requestFocus();
}
```

3. Add the listener to the button such as:

```
btnProcess.addListener(this);
```

Feedback 2.5

1. By implementing an interface you are overriding the class. All methods in the class are originally abstract and must have new definitions even if the new method contains no statements.
2. `showStatus("Clear all entries");`

Chapter 3

Feedback 3.1

1. ```
MyLayout = new FlowLayout(FlowLayout.LEFT, 10, 5);
setLayout(MyLayout);
```

2. ```
public void init()
{
    //Set up the GridLayout Manager
    setLayout(new GridLayout(2,2));

    //Add the components
    add(new Label("Name:"));
    add(txtName);
    add(new Label("Phone:"));
    add(txtPhone);
}
```

3. `add("North", lblCompanyName);`

Feedback 3.2

(a) txtDescription
     gridwidth = REMAINDER   (Make component take the rest of the row.)
     fill = HORIZONTAL   (Make the component expand to fill the display area.)
(b) txtPartNumber
     anchor = WEST   (Left align in display area.)
(c) txtVendorCode
     gridwidth = REMAINDER   (Make component take the rest of the row.)
     fill = HORIZONTAL   (Expand to fill the display area.)
(d) lblDescription
     weight = 1   (Give the label column a relative weight of 1.)
     anchor = EAST   (Right align label in display area.)
(e) lblPartNumber
     anchor = EAST   (Right align label in display area.)
     gridwidth = 1   (Use one cell and go to the next row.)
     fill = NONE   (Do not fill display area. Must reset from previous component.)
(f) lblVendorCode
     anchor = EAST   (Right align label in display area.)

(g) btnOK

weighty = 1	(Make row full height—makes blank row appear.)
gridx = 3	(Place in fourth column.)
gridy = 3	(Place in fourth row.)
fill = HORIZONTAL	(Expand to fill the display area.)

Chapter 4

Feedback 4.1

1. `fltBonus = fltSales * .05f;`

2. `intPounds = intOunces / 16;`
   `intOunces = intOunces % 16;`

3. `intNum1 = 5 and intNum2 = 3.`
   (a) 17
   (b) 17
   (c) 1
   (d) 2

4. `dblAnswer = Math.pow(dblWidth, 3.0);`

Feedback 4.2

1. `intCount++;`

   or

   `++intCount;`

2. `intCount += 5;`
3. When the operator precedes the variable, it is a prefix operator and the math operation is performed before the remainder of the statement is processed. An operator following the variable is a postfix operation, which occurs after any other processing called for in the statement. The two statements do not produce the same output.

Feedback 4.3

1. `float fltAmount = Float.valueOf(txtAmount.getText()).floatValue();`

2. `int intNumber = Integer.valueOf(txtNumber.getText()).intValue();`

3. `lblTotalAmount.setText("" + fltTotalAmount);`

4. (a) float
   (b) float
   (c) int
   (d) long
   (e) long
   (f) double

Feedback 4.4

1. ```
//Format a float value to currency number format.
NumberFormat fmtCurrency = NumberFormat.getCurrencyInstance();
strFormat = fmtCurrency.format(fltNumber);
```

2. ```
NumberFormat fmtDecimal = NumberFormat.getInstance();
fmtDecimal.setMaximumFractionDigits(3);
```

3. ```
strFormat = fmtCurrency.format(fltTotalSales);
```

4. ```
lblCurrency.setText(strFormat);
```

Feedback 4.5

1. ```
try
{
    //Integer division. Zero for intSecond throws an exception.
    intResult = intFirst / intSecond;
    lblIntegerResult.setText(""+ intResult);
}

catch(ArithmeticException err)
{
    showStatus("Error in calculation");
}
```

2. ```
try
{
    //Get data from screen.
    //Invalid integer or blank throws an exception.
    int intNumber = Integer.valueOf(txtNumber.getText()).intValue();
}

catch(NumberFormatException err)
{
    showStatus("Invalid data entered.");
}
```

Feedback 4.6

1. ```
Float FltPrice = new Float(txtPrice.getText()); //Get string value
```

2. ```
fltAmountDue = FltPrice.floatValue() * IntQuantity.intValue();
```

Chapter 5

Feedback 5.1

1. (a) Any class that contains variables and at least one method demonstrates encapsulation by combining the data and actions into a single unit.

(b) The `extends` clause such as `extends Applet` provides for inheritance from another class.

2. (a) An object is similar to a variable except that the data type is a class. If btnCalculate is declared as type Button, it is a Button "object."

(b) An object is considered to be an instance of a class type.

(c) Instantiation is the declaration statement that creates a new object.

Feedback 5.2

1.
```
public class Product
{
     private String strDescription;
     private int intQuantity;
     private float fltCost;
}
```

2.
```
Product currentProduct = new Product();
```

3.
```
public void setCost(float fltNewCost)
{
     //Assign new value to the cost property
     fltCost = fltNewCost;
}
```

4.
```
currentProduct.setCost(Float.valueOf(txtCost.getText()).floatValue());
```

Chapter 6

Feedback 6.1

1. False, the values are not equivalent; the int will convert to a float.
2. True, A comes before J in the alphabet and the ASCII code, which makes J greater than A.
3. `(intNumberCorrect >= 90)`
4. (a) True, intCountOne is equal to intCountTwo.
   (b) True, intCountThree is a negative number.
   (c) True.
   (d) False.
   (e) False.
   (f) True.
   (g) False.
   (h) False.
5.
```
int intApples = Integer.valueOf(txtApples.getText()).intValue();
int intOranges = Integer.valueOf(txtOranges.getText()).intValue();
if(intApples > intOranges)
    lblMost.setText("Apples");
else
    lblMost.setText("Oranges");
```

6.
```
if(fltBalance > 0.0f)
{
    fltBalance = 0.0f;
    intCounter++;
}
```

Feedback 6.2

1. It's the frogs
2. It's the toads and the polliwogs
3. It's true

Feedback 6.3

1.
```
if(fltScore >= 85.0f)
        chrGrade = 'A';
else
        chrGrade = 'C';
```

2.
```
intQuota = (chrCode == '1') ? 1000: 2000
```

Feedback 6.4

1. Increment is after comparison
2. Not less
3. Nothing will display.
4. Limit exceeded

Chapter 7

Feedback 7.1

1.
```
Checkbox chkReturnCustomer = new Checkbox("Return Customer");
```

2.
```
Checkbox optMale = new Checkbox("Male", cbgSex, false);
Checkbox optFemale = new Checkbox("Female", cbgSex, false);
```

3.
```
if(optMale.getState())
```

Feedback 7.2

An ItemListener responds to clicks in option buttons and check boxes as they occur. It is usually preferable to use an ActionListener and wait for a button to be clicked.

Feedback 7.3

```
switch(intAisle)
{
    case 1:
        lblComment.setText("Books");
        break;
    case 2:
        lblComment.setText("Software");
        break;
    case 3:
        lblComment.setText("Toys");
        break;
    case else:
        lblComment.setText("General Merchandise");
}
```

Chapter 8

Feedback 8.1

```
boolean blnItemFound = false;    //Sets a boolean variable to show not found
int intItemIndex = 0;

//Loop as long as the item is not found and there are more items in the list
while(!blnItemFound && intItemIndex == lstItems.getItemCount())
{
    //Compare the input item with an element in the list
    if (txtNewItem.getText().equals(lstItems.getItem(intItemIndex)))
    {
        blnItemFound = true;        //Change the boolean if a match is found
    }
    intItemIndex ++;                //Increment the item count
}
if (blnItemFound)            //Test if no match was found
{
    lblMessage.setText("Item is in the list");
}
else
{
    lblMessage.setText("Item is not in the list");
}
```

Feedback 8.2

1. (a) Semicolons should separate the parts of the loop.
    (b) Cannot have a semicolon at the end of the first line.
2. (a) 3, 11
    (b) 9, 2
    (c) 6, 6.0f
    (d) 0, 5
3.  ```
    for(int intIndex = 0; intIndex < 20; intIndext += 2)
        txaNumbers.append( "" + intIndex + "\n");
    ```
    ```

4. 5
    4
    3
    2
    1
5. Infinite loop.

Feedback 8.3

1.  ```
    String strEmployees[] = {" Mary Jones", "Kim Le", "Jerry Altman",
    "Yvonne Gonzales");
    JComboBox cboEmployees = new JComboBox(strEmployees);
    ```

2.  ```
    cboEmployee.setEditable(true);
    ```

Chapter 9

Feedback 9.1

1. Invalid; 19 is the largest subscript for an array set to 20 elements.
2. Valid.
3. Invalid; 19 is the largest subscript for an array set to 20 elements.
4. Invalid; 30 is too large.
5. Valid.
6. Invalid; negative numbers not allowed.
7. Valid; a subscript must be an integer but Java will round.
8. Valid.

Feedback 9.2

1.  ```
    int intTemperature[3][5]
    ```

2.  ```
    for(int intIndex = 0; intIndex < 5; intIndex++)
        intTemperature[0][intIndex] = 0;
    ```

3.  ```
    for(int intIndex = 0; intIndex < 5; intIndex++)
        intTemperature[1][intIndex] = 75;
    ```

4.  ```
    for(int intColumnIndex = 0; intColumnIndex < 5; intColumnIndex++)
    {
        intTemperature[3][intColumnIndex] = intTemperature[0][intColumnIndex] +
            intTemperature[1][intColIndex];
    }
    ```

Chapter 10

Feedback 10.1

1.  ```
    Frame frmName = new Frame("Your Name");
    ```
    ```

2. With the WindowListener interface you must override all of the methods, but with an `extends` of the WindowAdapter class you can include only a `windowClosing` method.

3.
```
public void windowClosing(WindowEvent event)
{
    //Exit to the operating system
    System.exit(0);
}
```

Feedback 10.2

1.
```
Menu mnuInsert = new Menu("Insert");
MenuItem mnuInsertBreak = new MenuItem("Break");
MenuItem mnuInsertPageNumbers = new MenuItem("Page Numbers");
MenuItem mnuInsertDate = new MenuItem("Date and Time");
```

2. `mnuFrameMain.add(mnuInsert);`

3. `mnuInsert.addActionListener(this);`

4. `CheckboxMenuItem mnuInsertNormal = new CheckboxMenuItem("Normal", true);`

5. `mnuInsertBreak.setEnabled(false);`

Feedback 10.3

1. Each constructor requires the parent frame.
```
//Call the parent's constructor
super(frmParent, "About My Application", true);
```

2. `show();`

   `dispose();`

3. A dialog is not visible until you set the size and show the dialog.

4. Java only allows one `extends` class and a dialog requires the Dialog class.

Chapter 11

Feedback 11.1

1. The text will appear at an x location of 10 and a y location of 50; that is, 10 pixels from the left edge and 50 pixels down from the top.

2.
```
Font fntArial = new Font("Arial", Font.NORMAL, 14);
myGraphicObject.setColor(Color.blue);
myGraphicObject.setFont(fntArial);
myGraphicObject.drawString("Your Name", 145, 150);
```

3. In the `paint` method.

Feedback 11.2

1. `imgWinter = getImage(getDocumentBase(),"Winter.jpeg");`
2. `gr.drawImage(imgWinter, 50, 20, this);`
3. To display the image, pass the image to display, call the `repaint` function in the `event` method.
4. Call the `paint` method from an `update` method to avoid having the entire screen cleared for each paint.

Feedback 11.3

1. `AudioClip sndWelcome;`

2. `sndWelcome = getAudioClip(getDocumentBase(),"WelcomeHome.wav");`
   `sndWelcome.loop(); // or sndWelcome.play();`

Feedback 11.4

1. The `getPrintJob` method begins the print job, gives the job a name, and displays the Print dialog box to the user.

2. `myApplet.printAll();`

3.
```
private void printText()
{
    //Print text as a graphic
    PrintJob printer = getToolkit().getPrintJob(frmMain, "Print", null);
    if (printer != null)            //Print job not canceled by the user
    {
        //Create a Graphics object for printing
        Graphics grPrintPage = printer.getGraphics();
        grPrintPage.setFont(fntPlain);
        grPrintPage.drawString("Your Name", 100, 100);
        grPrintPage.dispose();          //Send the page to the printer
        printer.end();                  //End the print job
    }
}
```

4. The printer methods are declared in the Applet class.

Feedback 11.5

1. Threads allow multiple tasks to share processing time.
2. The `run` method.
3. There are multiple ways to create an animation. You can place an image on the screen and then move the image or use an animated .gif file.

Feedback 11.6

1. `ImageIcon imgHello = new ImageIcon("Hello.gif");`
2. `btnGreeting = new JButton(imgHello);`

Chapter 12

Feedback 12.1

1.
```
public interface Payroll
{
}
```

2. The methods in an interface must be overridden when the interface is implemented.

Feedback 12.2

1. A member class has one copy per instance; a static member class has only one copy for all intances. Therefore, you can use the static member class to keep summary information.
2. Local inner classes are closely related to local variables, which have local scope and can be used only within that method. A common use of a local inner class is to implement an event-handling interface or extend another class, such as a MouseAdapter or WindowAdapter.
3. An anonymous class is a local class that you define without giving it a name. You can declare an anonymous inner class as an expression, which may be an argument for a method call or assigned to a variable.

Chapter 13

Feedback 13.1

1.
```
System.out.println("Your Name");
```
2.
```
try
{
. . .
}

catch(ArithmeticException err)
{
    System.err.println("Arithmetic Error");
}
```

Feedback 13.2

1.
```
PayrollFile = new FileOutputStream("A:\Payroll.txt");
objPayroll = new ObjectOutputStream(PayrollFile);
objPayroll.writeObject(empCurrent);
```

2.
```
PayrollFile = new FileInputStream("A:\Payroll.txt");
objPayroll = new ObjectInputStream(PayrollFile);
empCurrent = (Payroll) objPayroll.readObject();
```

Feedback 13.3

```
1.  try
    {
        //Load the MicroSoft drivers
        Class.forName ("com.ms.jdbc.odbc.JdbcOdbcDriver");
    }

    catch (ClassNotFoundException error)
    {
        try
        {
                //Load the Sun drivers
                Class.forName ("sun.jdbc.odbc.JdbcOdbcDriver");
        }

        catch (ClassNotFoundException err)
        {
                //No drivers found
                System.err.println("Driver did not load properly");
        }
    }
```
```
2.  DriverManager.getConnection("jdbc:odbc:ABCInc");
3.  SELECT [First Name], [Phone] FROM Employee;
4.  ResultSet rsEmployees = cmdEmployees.executeQuery(
            "SELECT [First Name], [Phone] FROM Employee;");
```

Feedback 13.4

```
1.  cmdProducts.executeUpdate("Insert Into Products "
            + "([Part Number], Description, [Vendor Code]) "
            + "Values('"
            + txtPartNumber.getText() + "', '"
            + txtDescription.getText() + "', '"
            + txtVendor.getText() + "')");
```

```
2.  cmdProducts.executeUpdate("Update Products "
        + "Set [Part Number] = '" + txtPartNumber.getText() + "', "
        + "Description = '" + txtDescription.getText() + "', "
        + "[Vendor Code] = '" + txtVendor.getText() + "' "
        + "Where [Part Number] = '" + strPartNumber + "';");
```

```
3.  cmdProducts.executeUpdate("Delete from Products where [Part Number] = '"
        + txtPartNumber,getText() + "';");
```

Chapter 14

Feedback 14.1

1. `<Script language = JavaScript>`
2. `document.write("<b><i>Your Name</i></b>");`
3. Writes *Hello* in heading style 3.
4. `document.write("Browser " + navigator.appName);`
   `document.write("Version " + navigator.appVersion);`
   `document.write("OS      " + navigator.platform);`

Feedback 14.2

1. `<Input Type = "button" Value = "OK" Name = "btnOK"`
   `    onClick = "Calculate()">`
2. `<Input Type = "button" Value = "Urgent"`
   `    onClick = 'window.alert("Call Your Mother")'>`

Chapter 15

Feedback 15.1

1. The term JavaBean generally refers to components written to extend the Java language. You can compare JavaBeans to Microsoft's ActiveX components or COM. These components are self-contained and can be incorporated into applications or sometimes can run by themselves.
2. The Beanbox tool from Sun.
3. A property is a data field that contains a value. Examples are color, size, position, employee name, or hours. A method refers to the actions, such as `setColor`, `getEmployeeName`, or `calculateOvertime`.

   For a program to be built from a set of components, some visual and some not, the components must have a way to send messages to each other. The communication between components is called *event transmission*. A component that fires an event is called an *event source*; the component that catches the event is an *event listener*.

Feedback 15.2

1. RMI, CORBA, DCOM
2.

Service	Purpose
Event	Messaging for objects.
Life cycle	Create and update objects while keeping the location transparent.
Naming	Associate a name of an object with the network address.
Object querying	Allow queries by fields other than the object name.
Persistence	Store an object for later retrieval.
Properties	Store information about another object.
Transaction	Control the operation over multiple objects.

E

Creating JAR Files

Archiving Files

You can use the Java jar tool to create an **archive** file called a **Java ARchive (JAR)** file. A JAR file combines all of the files needed by an applet, application, or JavaBean into a single compressed file. A JAR file can contain the class files as well as any images, videos, or sound files that are needed by the program. The JAR file format is the newest type of archiving available for applets (programmers previously used zip files and Microsoft cab files).

If you create a JavaBean, you will need to create a JAR from the bean's class(es). As you learned in Chapter 15, to add a new bean to the BeanBox, you first must create a JAR.

You may also want to create a JAR for an applet. The JAR can contain all supporting classes and image and sound files. Since applets are frequently viewed over the Internet, you must make sure that all extra files for the multimedia are available and that the files are as compact as possible.

When an applet runs in a browser, a separate connection is made to retrieve each file, including each image and sound file. If your applet contains multiple files, it may require many Internet connections, which can take considerable time and resources. The browser retrieves the entire JAR file with one connection, and then can uncompress and use the files locally.

You create a JAR file from your working project. Then you can specify the JAR file name in the `archive` clause of the HTML `applet` tag:

```
<Applet archive = ArchiveDemo.jar
        code = Demo.class
        width = 400 height = 400>
```

The jar Tool

One of the tools in the JDK is the **jar tool**, which you can use to create and maintain JAR files. You run the jar tool from the operating system command line, in Windows called the *MS-DOS prompt*.

When you type the command to run the jar tool, you must specify the action that you want to perform (create a file, list the contents, update the file, or extract the contents). You may also include arguments to specify additional options, name the JAR file, specify an optional manifest file, and include the names of all individual files to include in the JAR file.

The jar Tool Command—General Format

```
jar c|t|u|x [f][m][v] [JARfileName ] [manifestFileName] [filesToInclude]
```

The first argument, shown in Table E.1, is required. It indicates *create*, *list*, *update*, or *extract*. The next group of arguments, shown in Table E.2, is optional.

Action Option	Purpose
c	Create an archive file. You must include the name of the archive file and the files to include.
t	List the contents of the named archive file.
u	Update the archive file. You must include the names of the files to include.
x	Extract the contents. Extracts only the files you name, or all files if none is named.

The jar Tool—Examples

```
//Create a new JAR called Ch12JAR.jar. Include the two named files
// (Ch11Image.class and Coffee.jpg)
// and show all compression information.
jar cfv Ch12JAR.jar Ch11Image.class Coffee.jpg

//List the contents of MyJarFile.jar, showing all compression information.
jar tvf MyJarFile.jar

//Update MyJarFile.jar by adding AdditionalImage.jpg
jar uf MyJarFile.jar AdditionalImage.jpg

//Create a new JAR called MyProject.jar. Include all class files and all
// .jpg files in the current folder.
jar cf MyProject.jar *.class *.jpg
```

Action	Purpose
f	Indicates that the file name specified should be used for the create, list, update, or extract operation. If f is not specified, the file name is expected to come from standard input. You must include the f if you include the JAR file name.
m	Specifies that a manifest file will be named on the command. A default manifest file is automatically created for all JAR files. Use this option only when you want to change the format of the manifest file by specifying your own template file. Needed for JavaBeans.
v	Verbose. Displays all compression information.

You can specify the arguments in any order. For example, `cfv` and `cvf` are equivalent. However, if you include both a JAR file name and a manifest file name, you must specify the `f` and `m` arguments in the same order as the file-names. For example, the following two statements are equivalent. Both create a new JAR called MyFile.jar, with a manifest file called MyManifest.txt, and include the file MyClass.class.

```
jar cvfm MyFile.jar MyManifest.txt MyClass.class
jar cmfv MyManifest.txt MyFile.jar MyClass.class
```

Creating a JAR file

Make sure that the folder holding the jar tool is in your system path. The program is usually located in the *bin* folder under the *jdk1.3* folder; your system may be set up differently.

You may need to edit your Autoexec.bat file, or type a command to temporarily change the path each time you execute. This command adds the jar tool's default folder to the system path in Windows:

```
path = %path%;c:\jdk1.3\bin
```

To go to the system prompt in Windows, use the *Start* menu, select *Programs* and *MS-DOS Prompt.* Then use MS-DOS commands to change to the drive and folder that hold the files you want to archive.

Example

```
a:
cd a:\Ch11Image
```

At the DOS prompt, you can just type `jar` and press the Enter key; you receive a listing of the various parameters (Figure E.1). *Note:* The jar directory must be in your path for this to work.

F i g u r e   E . 1

The Help screen for the **jar** *command, showing all parameters.*

Figure E.2 shows creating a JAR file and listing the contents of the file. The class and image files are in the current folder called Ch11Image on the A: drive.

Create a new JAR file called Ch11Jar.jar, which holds one .class file and one .gif file.

```
jar cfv Ch11Jar.jar ImageApplet.class Hello.gif
```

Read this command as: Create a new JAR file; the file name will follow; display verbose output; name the new JAR file Ch11Jar.jar; include ImageApplet.class and Hello.gif, both of which are in the current folder.

You can see the output of the command in Figure E.2, along with a second `jar` command to list the contents of the new JAR file. Notice in the figure that a manifest file is created by default.

Paths in JAR Files

It's best to store files in a JAR file with no path names, as in the previous example. If you specify a path to a file, the path name will be included with the file, which requires the exact paths when the files are extracted. For example, this command

```
jar cfv Ch11Jar.jar a:\Ch11Image\ImageApplet.class a:\Ch11Image\Hello.gif
```

stores the path (a:\Ch11Image) along with the file names in the JAR. When the file is unarchived and run, it *must* be stored in the named folder.

You can use the -C (uppercase) argument of the `jar` command to switch to a new folder. The file reference following the -C argument is stored without the path name. Note that the -C argument changes the folder for only the one following entry. For multiple files, you must include the -C for each (Figure E.3).

```
jar cfv a:Ch11Jar.jar -C a:\Ch11Image ImageApplet.class -C a:\Ch11Image Hello.gif
```

You can name a folder in place of a file, and the jar tool will include all files in the folder. An effective technique is to create a new folder, add all the files you want to include in the JAR, and set up the `jar` command to use all files in the folder. This command archives all files in the TempFolder folder. Notice the closing backslash, space, and period (Figure E.4).

```
jar cfv a:Ch12Jar.jar -C a:\TempFolder\ .
```

Creating a Manifest File

Generally you can allow the jar tool to create the default manifest file. But when you create a JAR file for a JavaBean, you must create your own manifest. A manifest file is simply text, which you can create with a text editor. If you use the Windows Notepad application, it's easy to create and edit the file if it has a .txt extension. However, the extension isn't required and you can call the file anything you want, as long as it's all one word.

This manifest file for a JavaBean is called Manifest.txt; it contains only two lines.

```
Name: CompanyBean.class
Java-Bean: True
```

Warning: You must end the last line with a carriage return (Enter Key), otherwise the jar tool ignores the file.

After you save the completed manifest file, you can create a JAR file that includes the manifest (Figure E.5).

F i g u r e   E . 5

Include a previously created manifest file in the JAR file for a JavaBean.

Additional Resources

You can find additional information on JAR files in Sun's tutorial, http://developer.java.sun.com/developer/Books/JAR/basics/.

Retrieving Files from a JAR

You can run an applet from a JAR by including the archive clause in the applet tag.

```
<Applet archive = Ch11Image.jar
        code = ImageApplet.class
        width = 400 height = 400>
```

When this applet runs, the JVM automatically decompresses the files. If the JAR contains multiple class files, all will be available for the applet. However, image files may not be so easy.

Retrieving Image Files from a JAR

Unfortunately, retrieving image files from a JAR requires changing your program. Java's getImage method cannot locate image files in a JAR. If your applet runs in Internet Explorer, you must use the getResource method; in Netscape you must use getResourceAsStream method. You can see both methods in the MovingImageApplet in the ImagesInJar folder.

Netscape Code

```
//Retrieve the image file (Netscape)
InputStream inpStr = getClass().getResourceAsStream("auto.gif");
byte[] buffer = new byte[inpStr.available()];
inpStr.read(buffer);
imgMove = Toolkit.getDefaultToolkit().createImage(buffer);
```

Internet Explorer Code

```
//Load image in Internet Explorer
URL url = getClass().getResource(strFileName);
imgMove = getImage(url);
```

Working with Dates and Functions

Working with Dates

In Chapter 2 you learned to retrieve the current system date and use the Calendar class for dates. This appendix expands on the coverage to give you more control of dates.

Prior to Java 1.1, the Date class was the only class for working with dates. However, the Date class cannot handle internationalization and locales. Most of the methods in the Date class have been deprecated in favor of methods in the Calendar class, which *can* handle internationalization.

The date in both the Date class and the Calendar class is held as a long data type, which represents the number of milliseconds since midnight GMT January 1, 1970. The Calendar class is actually an abstract class designed to work with Date objects. You can use the Calendar object to get the date and retrieve the various parts of the date according to the local calendar and time zone.

If you want to display the date or portions of the date, you don't want to display a number of milliseconds. The classes in java.text.DateFormat are designed to convert dates into human-understandable formats.

Retrieving the System Date and Time

You can use either of these statements to retrieve the current date. You should give preference to the Calendar method if you plan to display the date or work with any part of the date.

```
import java.util.Date
import java.util.Calendar
Date dateToday = new Date();
Calendar calToday = Calendar.getInstance();
```

Formatting the Date and Time for Display

Use the DateFormat class of the java.text package to format dates and times for display. The getDateInstance and getTimeInstance methods create an instance of the DateFormat class and retrieve the system settings for locale and default formats.

```
import java.text.DateFormat;

//Format today's date to match system default date format
DateFormat defaultDate = DateFormat.getDateInstance();
lblToday.setText(defaultDate.format(calToday.getTime()));

//Format time using the system-defined short date format
DateFormat shortTime = DateFormat.getTimeInstance(DateFormat.SHORT);
lblTime.setText(shortTime.format(calToday.getTime()));
```

Setting the Date

You can set the date in a Calendar object using the Calendar constants or numbers.

```
calDeadline.set(Calendar.YEAR, 2001);              //Set the year
calDeadline.set(Calendar.MONTH, Calendar.APRIL);   //Set the month
calDeadline.set(Calendar.MONTH, 3);                //Set month to April
calDeadline.set(Calendar.DAY, 15);                 //Set the day
calDeadline.set(2001, 3, 15);                      //Same as previous
```

Calculating with Dates

You can use the add method of the Calendar class to add to a specific element of a Calendar object.

```
calToday.add(Calendar.DATE, 30); //Add 30 days to the date
```

This statement adds 30 days to the date in calToday, incrementing the month as necessary. For example, 2/26/2001 (a nonleap year) + 30 = 3/28/2001.

Compare two dates using the boolean before and after methods of the Calendar object.

```
if (calToday.after(calDeadline))
   lblMessage.setText("Today is past the deadline.");
```

You cannot directly subtract one Calendar object from another. If you want to find the difference between two dates, you must use Date objects instead. This example retrieves two dates from screen components. The month names are stored in Choice components (chMonth1 and chMonth2); the day and year come from TextField components. The program creates Calendar objects, converts the Calendar objects to Date objects, calculates the difference, and displays the result in lblDifference. Note the conversion from milliseconds to days. (You can see this entire applet in APXFDates.)

```
//Calculate the difference between two dates
//Set up Calendar objects
Calendar calFirstDate = Calendar.getInstance();
Calendar calSecondDate = Calendar.getInstance();

//Set up first date
int intMonth = chMonth1.getSelectedIndex();
int intDay = Integer.valueOf(txtDay1.getText()).intValue();
int intYear = Integer.valueOf(txtYear1.getText()).intValue();
calFirstDate.set(intYear, intMonth, intDay);

//Set up second date
intMonth = chMonth2.getSelectedIndex();
intDay = Integer.valueOf(txtDay2.getText()).intValue();
intYear = Integer.valueOf(txtYear2.getText()).intValue();
calSecondDate.set(intYear, intMonth, intDay);

//Convert Calendar values to Date
Date dateFirst = calFirstDate.getTime();
Date dateSecond = calSecondDate.getTime();

//Find difference in milliseconds
long lngDifference = dateSecond.getTime() - dateFirst.getTime();
```

```
//Convert milliseconds to days and display result
lngDifference = lngDifference / (1000 * 60 * 60 * 24);
lblDifference.setText("" + lngDifference);
```

Math Functions and Constants

Java's Math class (java.lang.Math) provides many functions and constants that you can use to perform math operations, find the absolute value of a number, calculate a random number, round, convert to powers, and perform trig functions.

To refer to a function or constant in the Math class, you must include the class name. For example, to find the absolute value of intNumber, use this statement:

```
int intAbsolute = Math.abs(intNumber);
```

Constants

The Math class defines constants for E and PI.

```
public static final double E = 2.7182818284590452354;
public static final double PI = 3.14159265358979323846;
```

To use one of these constants, you must include the Math class name:

```
double dblArea = Math.PI * (dblRadius * dblRadius);
```

Absolute Value

The abs method returns the positive representation of both negative and positive numbers. The method can take int, long, float, and double arguments.

Method	Returns
Math.abs(int intNumber)	The absolute value of intNumber.
Math.abs(long lngNumber)	The absolute value of lngNumber.
Math.abs(float fltNumber)	The absolute value of fltNumber.
Math.abs(double dblNumber)	The absolute value of dblNumber.

Minimum and Maximum

The min and max methods return the lower or higher of the two supplied arguments. Both methods can take arguments of int, long, float, or double, but both arguments must be of the same data type.

Method	Returns
Math.min(int intNum1, intNum2)	The lower of the two integers.
Math.min(long lngNum1, lngNum2)	The lower of the two long values.
Math.min(float fltNum1, fltNum2)	The lower of the two float values.
Math.min(double dblNum1, dblNum2)	The lower of the two double values.
Math.max(int intNum1, intNum2)	The higher of the two integers.
Math.max(long lngNum1, lngNum2)	The higher of the two long values.
Math.max(float fltNum1, fltNum2)	The higher of the two float values.
Math.max(double dblNum1, dblNum2)	The higher of the two double values.

Rounding

You have several options for rounding. You can round a float to an int and round a double to a long. For double values, you can choose to always round up or always round down using the ceil and floor methods. The rint method rounds a double to the nearest integer value (but returns the value as a double).

```
int intNumberRounded = Math.round(fltNumber);
```

Method	Returns
Math.round(float fltNumber)	A rounded integer.
Math.round(double dblNumber)	A rounded float value.
Math.rint(double dblNumber)	A double representing the closest integer.
Math.floor(double dblNumber)	A double rounded down.
Math.ceil(double dblNumber)	A double rounded up.

Powers and Logarithms

You must be careful when using the sqrt, pow, and log methods; each of these methods has restrictions on the legal values. For example, it's illegal to calculate the square root of a negative number. You can either validate the value before calculating or check for isNaN (boolean is-not-a-number) on the result.

Check before calculating:

```
if (dblInput <= 0.0)
{
    lblResult.setText("Not a legal calculation");
}
    else
{
    dblResult = Math.sqrt(dblInput);
    lblResult.setText("" + dblResult);
}
```

Check after calculating:

```
dblResult = Math.sqrt(dblInput);
if (Double.isNaN(dblResult))
{
    lblResult.setText("Not a number");
}
else
{
    lblResult.setText("" + dblResult);
}
```

Method	Returns
`Math.sqrt(double dblNumber)`	A double square root. Argument must be >= 0.
`Math.pow(double dblNumber, double dblPower)`	A double; dblNumber raised to the power of dblPower. If dblNumber == 0.0, dblPower must be > 0. If dblNumber < 0.0, dblPower must be a whole number. Throws an ArithmeticException for violations.
`Math.log(double dblNumber)`	A double; the natural logarithm, where dblNumber >= 0.0. Throws an ArithmeticException for violations.
`Math.exp(double dblNumber)`	A double; the value of *e* raised to the power of dblNumber. The inverse of `log`.

Note: You can use exception handling to validate the results of these functions.

Trig Functions

The trig functions all take their angle values in radians and all return double values.

Method	Returns
`Math.sin(double dblAngle)`	A double; the sine of dblAngle.
`Math.cos(double dblAngle)`	A double; the cosine of dblAngle.
	continued

Method	Returns
`Math.tan(double dblAngle)`	A double; the tangent of dblAngle.
`Math.asin(double dblAngle)`	A double; the arcsine of dblAngle.
`Math.acos(double dblAngle)`	A double; the arccosine of dblAngle.
`Math.atan(double dblAngle)`	A double; the arctangent of dblAngle.
`Math.atan2(double dblCoordA, dblCoordB)`	A double; the theta in polar coordinates.

Random Numbers

You can generate pseudo-random numbers with the `random` method of the Math class, which generates a double number between 0.0 and 1.0 (exclusive). You can also use the java.util.Random class to generate float, long, int, boolean, and byte pseudo-random numbers.

```
double dblRandom = Math.random();
```

To generate integer numbers in a predetermined range, add a calculation.

```
//Generate integers between 0 and 9
int intRandom = (int) (10.0 * Math.random());
//Generate integers between 1 and 10
int intRandom = (int) (10.0 * Math.random()) + 1;
```

BigDecimal and BigInteger

You can use the BigDecimal and BigInteger classes from java.math to store and perform calculations with very large numbers. But the reason you are most likely to use the BigDecimal class is for decimal calculations. As you know, the Java float and double data types store numbers in floating-point notation, which is based on binary fractions. The binary floating-point values cannot hold decimal values (tenths and hundredths) exactly, so you see rounding errors when displaying values such as dollars and cents. When you need to calculate and display tenths and hundredths exactly accurately, use the BigDecimal class.

You can see an example applet using BigDecimal in APXFBigDecimal. This program is Ch4Payroll converted to use BigDecimal rather than float values.

Creating a BigDecimal Value

You can create BigDecimal values from a string of characters, from a double, from a BigInteger, or from a long, using the `valueOf` method.

```
import java.math.*;

//Create BigDecimal from a double
BigDecimal decPay = new BigDecimal(0.0d);

//Create BigDecimal from a string of characters
BigDecimal decRate = new BigDecimal(txtRate.getText());

//Create BigDecimal from a long value, setting 2 decimal positions
BigDecimal decLong = BigDecimal.valueOf(lngValue, 2);
```

Calculating with a BigDecimal Value

You cannot perform calculations on BigDecimal values with the normal math operators. Instead, you use the methods in the BigDecimal class.

```
decPay = decHours.multiply(decRate);      //Multiply hours * rate
```

Each of these methods returns a BigDecimal value:

Method	Returns
add(BigDecimal *decAddValue*)	The named value increased by decAddValue. Example: decResult = decValueOne.add(decValueTwo);
subtract(BigDecimal *decSubValue*)	The named value decreased by decSubValue. Example: decResult = decValueOne.subtract(decValueTwo);
multiply(BigDecimal *decMultValue*)	The named value multiplied by decMultValue. Example: decResult = decValueOne.multiply(decValueTwo);
divide(BigDecimal *decDivValue*, *intScale*)	The named value divided by decDivValue, with the specified number of decimal positions. Example: decResult = decValueOne.divide(decValueTwo, 2);

Setting the Scale and Rounding Big Decimal Values

You can use one of several methods for rounding. The setScale method sets the number of decimal positions and the rounding method.

```
//Round to two decimal positions
decPay = decPay.setScale(2, BigDecimal.ROUND_HALF_UP);
```

Rounding Constant	Action
ROUND_DOWN	Always round down.
ROUND_HALF_UP	Round up when last digit >= 5.
ROUND_HALF_DOWN	Round up when last digit > 5.
ROUND_UP	Always round up.

continued

Rounding Constant	Action
ROUND_CEILING	Round positive numbers up, negative numbers down.
ROUND_FLOOR	Round positive numbers down, negative numbers up.
ROUND_HALF_EVEN	Rounds to an even number. If the digit to the left of the decimal point is odd, behave as ROUND_HALF_UP; if it's even, behave as ROUND_HALF_DOWN.
ROUND_UNNECESSARY	Do not round.

More BigDecimal Methods

You may find these additional BigDecimal methods helpful.

Method	Returns
abs()	A BigDecimal; the absolute value of the named object. Example: `decAbsolute = decValue.abs();`
negate()	A BigDecimal; the negative of the named object. Example: `decNegate = decValue.negate();`
equals(Object decValueTwo)	A boolean; true if the value of the named BigDecimal is equal to the value of decValueTwo. Example: `blnEqual = decValueOne.equals(decValueTwo);`
compareTo(BigDecimal decValueTwo)	An int; -1 if the named value is less than decValueTwo, 0 if equal, 1 if greater than. Example: `intCompare = decValueOne.compareTo(DecValueTwo);`
signum()	An int; -1 if the named value is negative, 0 if 0, 1 if positive. Example: `intSign = decValueOne.signum();`
movePointLeft(int intNumberPositions)	Move the decimal point left the given number of positions. Example: `decNew = decMove.movePointLeft(2);`
movePointRight(int intNumberPositions)	Move the decimal point right the given number of positions. Example: `decNew = decMove.movePointRight(4);`
min(BigDecimal decValueTwo)	A BigDecimal; the smaller of the named value and the argument. Example: `decMin = decValueOne.min(decValueTwo);`
max(BigDecimal decValueTwo)	A BigDecimal; the larger of the named value and the argument. Example: `decMax = decValueOne.max(decValueTwo);`
intValue()	The named value converted to an int; may lose precision. Example: `intValue = decValue.intValue();`
longValue()	The named value converted to a long; may lose precision. Example: `lngValue = decValue.longValue();`

continued

Method	Returns
`floatValue()`	The named value converted to a float; may lose precision. Example: `fltValue = decValue.floatValue();`
`doubleValue()`	The named value converted to a double; may lose precision. Example: `dblValue = decValue.doubleValue();`
`toBigInteger()`	The named value converted to a BigInteger; may lose precision. Example: `bgiIntValue = decValue.toBigInteger();`

BigIntegers

BigIntegers are essentially the same as BigDecimals, without the decimal point. You can create a BigInteger or BigDecimal with as many digits as you need. The methods for the BigInteger class are essentially the same as those for BigDecimal, with the addition of a few more for converting to integer.

Method	Returns
`remainder(BigInteger bgiDivisor)`	A BigInteger; the remainder of dividing bgiDivisor into the named object. Example: `bgiRemainder = bgiValue.remainder(bgiDivisor);`
`divideAndRemainder(BigInteger bgiDivisor)`	A BigInteger array of 2; the result of the division and the remainder. Example: `BigInteger[] bgiResult = bgiValue.divideAndRemainder(bgiDivisor);`
`gcd(BigInteger bgiFactor)`	A BigInteger; the greatest common denominator of abs(named BigInteger) and abs(bgiFactor). Example: `bgiGcd = bgiValue.gcd(bgiFactor);`
`mod(BigInteger bgiDivisor)`	A BigInteger; the whole number result of the named value divided by bgiDivisor. Example: `bgiResult = bgiValue.mod(bgiDivisor);`
`modPow(BigInteger bgiPower)`	A BigInteger; the result of the named value raised to the power of bgiPower. Example: `bgiResult = bgiValue.modPow(bgiPower);`

The BigInteger class also has methods for bit manipulation, such as `and`, `or`, `xor`, `not`, `andNot`, `testBit`, `setBit`, `clearBit`, `flipBit`, `getLowestSetBit`, `bitLength`, and `bitCount`.

Methods for Working with Strings

The String class has many methods for working with string data. Although you cannot change a string's value once it is created, you *can* create new strings based on operations to existing strings.

Method	Returns
chrAt(int intIndex)	A char; the character at intIndex position (intIndex = 0 to length −1). Example: `chrOneChar = strString.chrAt(1);` Returns second character of string.
compareTo(String strStringTwo)	An int; −1 if the named string compares lower than strStringTwo, 0 if the strings compare equal, 1 if the second string compares higher (case-sensitive). Example: `intCompare = strStringOne.compareTo(strStringTwo);`
compareToIgnoreCase(String strStringTwo)	An int; −1 if the named string compares lower than strStringTwo, 0 if the strings compare equal, 1 if the second string compares higher. Ignores the case of the arguments. Example: `intCompare = strStringOne.compareToIgnoreCase(strStringTwo);`
concat(String strStringTwo)	A String; the concatenation of the named string and strStringTwo. Example: `strLongString = strStringOne.concat(strStringTwo);` Equivalent to `strLongString = strStringOne + strStringTwo`
endsWith(String strStringTwo)	A boolean; true if the named string ends with strStringTwo or if strStringTwo is an empty string. Example: `blnMatches = strStringOne.endsWith(strStringTwo);`
equals(String strStringTwo)	A boolean; true if the named string compares equal to strStringTwo (case-sensitive). Example: `blnSame = strStringOne.equals(strStringTwo);`
equalsIgnoreCase(String strStringTwo)	A boolean; true if the named string compares equal to strStringTwo. Ignores case of the arguments. Example: `blnSame = strStringOne.equalsIgnoreCase(strStringTwo);`
indexOf(String strSubstring)	An int; the index position within the named string where the first occurrence of the substring occurs. −1 if the substring is not found within the string. Example: `intIndex = strStringOne.indexOf(strSubstring);`
indexOf(String strSubstring, int intStartIndex)	An int; the index position within the named string where the first occurrence of the substring occurs, beginning at position intStartIndex. −1 if the substring is not found within the string. Example: `intIndex = strStringOne.indexOf(strSubstring, intStart);`
lastIndexOf(String strSubstring)	An int; the index position within the named string where the first occurrence of the substring occurs, starting at the end of the string and searching backward. −1 if the substring is not found within the string. Example: `intIndex = strStringOne.lastIndexOf(strSubstring);`
lastIndexOf(String strSubstring, int intStartIndex)	An int; the index position within the named string where the first occurrence of the substring occurs, beginning at position intStartIndex and searching backward. −1 if the substring is not found within the string. Example: `intIndex = strStringOne.lastIndexOf(strSubstring, intStart);`
length()	An int; the number of characters in the named string. Example: `intCount = strString.length();`
regionMatches(boolean blnIgnoreCase, int intToOffset, String strSubstring, int intOffset, int intLength)	A boolean; true if the two string regions match. Compares the named string, beginning with position intOffset, for a length of intLength, with strSubstring, beginning with position intToOffset. Example: `blnMatches = strStringOne.regionMatches(true, 0, strStringTwo, 0, 3);` Compares the first three characters of the two strings, ignoring case.

continued

Method	Returns
regionMatches(int intToOffset, String strSubstring, int intOffset, int intLength)	A boolean; true if the two string regions match. Compares the named string, beginning with position intOffset, for a length of intLength, with strSubstring, beginning with position intToOffset. Example: blnMatches = strStringOne.regionMatches(0, strStringTwo, 0, 3); Compares the first three characters of the two strings (case-sensitive).
replace(String strOldChar, String strNewChar)	A new String that replaces all occurrences of strOldChar with strNewChar. Returns the original string if strOldChar does not appear. Example: strNewString = strStringOne.replace('a', 'o');
startsWith(String strPrefix)	A boolean; true if the named string begins with the characters in strPrefix. Example: blnMatches = strStringOne.startsWith(strPrefix);
startsWith(String strPrefix, int intToOffset)	A boolean; true if the named string begins with the characters in strPrefix, beginning at position intToOffset. Example: blnMatches = strStringOne.startsWith(strPrefix, 2); Compares the beginning of strStringOne with the characters in strPrefix, beginning at the third character.
substring(int intBeginIndex)	A new string that consists of a substring of the named string, beginning with intBeginIndex position and continuing for the rest of the string. Example: strNewString = strStringOne.substring(2); Creates a new string from all characters of old string, beginning with the third character.
substring(int intBeginIndex, int intEndIndex	A new String that consists of a substring of the named string, beginning with intBeginIndex position and continuing until intEndIndex. Example: strNewString = strStringOne.substring(0, 2); Creates a new string from the first three characters of old string (position 0 through position 2).
toCharArray()	A new char array with as many elements as characters in the named string. Example: char[] charArray = strString.toCharArray();
toLowerCase()	A new String with all characters of the original string; any uppercase characters are converted to lowercase. Example: strNewString = strString.toLowerCase();
toUpperCase()	A new string with all characters of the original string; any lowercase characters are converted to uppercase. Example: strNewString = strString.toUpperCase();
trim()	A new String with any space characters from either end of the original string removed. Example: strNewString = strString.trim();
valueOf(boolean blnVariable)	A new String that holds "true" or "false", depending on the value of the argument. Example: strNewString = String.valueOf(blnVariable);
valueOf(char chrVariable) valueOf(char[] chrArray) valueOf(double dblVariable) valueOf(float fltVariable) valueOf(int intVariable) valueOf(long lngVariable) valueOf(Object objVariable)	A new String that holds the text value of the argument. Example: strNewString = String.valueOf(fltVariable);

APPENDIX

G

Debugging Java Programs

When your Java program gets a clean compile (no syntax errors) but doesn't run correctly, what do you do? The first step is usually to proofread the code and look for clues to what went wrong. You can also use debugging tools to help locate the error.

Each of the Java IDEs has built-in debugging tools. You can use these tools to help find and eliminate logic and run-time errors. The debugging tools also can help you to follow the logic of existing projects to better understand how they work.

The debugging tools that are the most helpful and easiest to understand for beginning programmers are

- Setting breakpoints—pausing execution of a program before a critical section. You can make sure that execution reaches a particular point and then perform the next two steps.

- Stepping through program execution—executing your program one line at a time so that you can watch what happens. You can see which branch of an `if` statement executes and watch loops execute multiple times. You can also choose to step into called methods and view the called statements execute one at a time, or step over, which allows the called method to execute quickly and then returns to the calling method.

- Examining the values of variables—displaying the current content of variables, to help determine why the program is producing unexpected results.

This appendix will demonstrate how to perform these three debugging techniques in Forté, JBuilder, VJ++, and BlueJ.

Note: The illustrations and examples in this appendix use Java language constructs from Chapters 6 and 7. You may want to postpone reading this section until completing Chapter 7.

Forté

You can use toolbar buttons, the *Debug* menu, or keyboard shortcuts to activate Forté's debugging tools. The first time you debug an applet or application, you must specify the debugger type. Right-click on the .java file name under Filesystems and choose *Properties*. Then click on the *Execution* tab, drop down the *Debugger* list, and choose *Applet Debugging* (Figure GF.1).

Breaking Program Execution

You can suspend execution of a program by setting a breakpoint in code; the program will halt execution when the breakpoint is reached.

Setting a Breakpoint

To set a breakpoint, the code must be displayed in the Edit window. Click in the line that you want to be the breakpoint and choose *Debug / Add/Remove Breakpoint,* or right-click and choose *Add/Remove Breakpoint* from the context menu. The chosen line appears shaded in blue (Figure GF.2).

Set up the class file for applet debugging.

A Forté breakpoint line is shaded in blue. The debugger stops before executing the marked line.

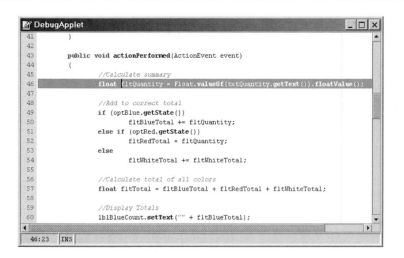

After setting a breakpoint, choose *Debug / Start Debugging* (or use F5, the keyboard shortcut). When the program reaches the breakpoint, it halts and displays the line, *before* executing the line.

You can click on the breakpoint line and execute the same command to toggle the breakpoint off.

Checking the Current Values of Expressions

When your program has halted during execution, you can quickly check the current value of a variable. In the window that shows the code, point to the name of the variable that you want to view; a small label pops up, similar to a ToolTip, which displays the current contents of the variable (Figure GF.3).

The steps for viewing the contents of a variable during run time are

- Break the execution (using a breakpoint).

- Point to the variable you wish to view. The current contents of the variable will pop up in a label.

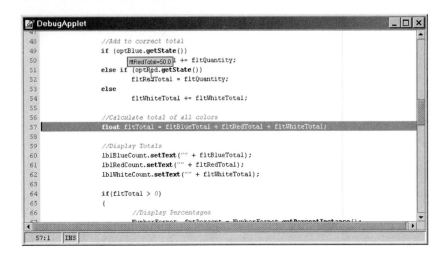

Setting Watch Variables

You can choose which variables to display in the *Watches* tab of the Debugger window. Forté displays the name, data type, and current value for any variable that is within scope. The properties of the variable appear in the Properties pane of the Debugger window (Figure GF.4). The easiest way to add a new watch variable is to click in the variable name in code, right-click, and select *Add Watch* from the context menu. You can also select **Add Watch** from the *Debug* menu.

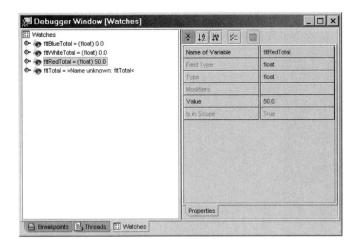

Stepping through Code

The best way to debug a project is to thoroughly understand what the project is doing every step of the way. Use the Trace Into and Trace Over commands to view every statement as it executes, line by line.

You step through code when the program is suspended at a breakpoint. You can set a breakpoint or choose one of the stepping commands at design time; the program will begin running and immediately transfer to single-stepping. As you execute the project by clicking a button, for example, the actionPerformed event occurs. Execution transfers to the `actionPerformed` method, the Code window for that method appears on the screen, and you can follow line-by-line execution.

The easiest way to single-step is to use the F7 keyboard shortcut for Trace Into. Repeatedly press F7 and watch as each line is highlighted and then executed. If you want to continue execution without stepping, choose the *Continue* command (from the *Debug* menu or by pressing Alt + F5).

Debugging Step-by-Step Tutorial for Forté

In this exercise you will learn to set a breakpoint, pause program execution, single-step through program instructions, display the current values in variables, and debug a project.

Test the Project

STEP 1: Open Forté.

STEP 2: Display the *Filesystems* tab of the Explorer window, if necessary. Right-click on *Filesystems* and select *Add Directory* from the context menu. In the Add Directory dialog box, select the ApxGDebugForte folder on your student CD.

STEP 3: Expand the Filesystems node and click to select the Debug Applet class icon.

STEP 4: Run the applet by selecting either *Build / Execute* or clicking the Execute toolbar button.

STEP 5: Enter color Blue, quantity 100, and press Enter or click on the Calculate button.

STEP 6: Enter another color Blue, quantity 50, and press Enter. Are the totals correct?

STEP 7: Enter color Red, quantity 30, and press Enter.

STEP 8: Enter color Red, quantity 10, and press Enter. Are the totals correct?

STEP 9: Enter color White, quantity 50, and press Enter.

STEP 10: Enter color White, quantity 100, and press Enter. Are the totals correct?

STEP 11: Stop execution. You are going to locate and correct the errors in the Red and White totals.

Break and Step Program Execution

STEP 1: Right-click on the DebugApplet Filesystems entry and choose *Properties*. In the Properties sheet, click on the *Execution* tab.

STEP 2: Drop down the list for *Debugger* and choose *Applet Debugging* (Figure GF.5). The next time you want to debug this project, the *Debugger* option should already be set. Close the Properties sheet.

STEP 3: Display the program code in the Editor and click in the first calculation line in the `actionPerformed` method. Right-click and choose *Add/Remove Breakpoint*. A breakpoint will be set on the selected line (Figure GF.6).

STEP 4: Choose *Start Debugging* from the *Debug* menu or press F5.

Trouble? If you receive a message that no `main` method was found, return to step 1 in this section.

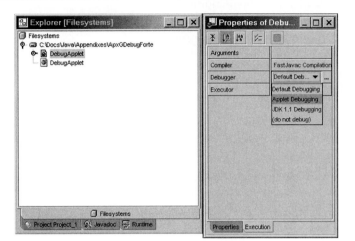

Select Applet Debugging *the first time you debug a program.*

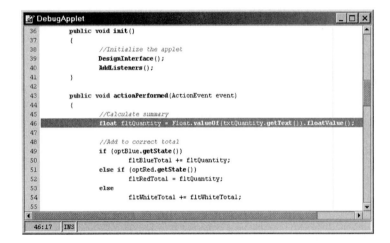

Set a breakpoint by right-clicking on the desired statement and selecting Add/Remove Breakpoint.

STEP 5: When the applet appears in the Applet Viewer, enter Red, quantity 30, and press Enter.

> The project transfers control to the `actionPerformed` method, stops when the breakpoint is reached, and highlights the current line.

> *Note:* The highlighted line has not yet executed.

STEP 6: Click in the Editor window to make it the active window. Press the F7 key, which causes Forté to execute the current program statement (the assignment statement). You need to press F7 two or three times to execute each program line.

> F7 is the keyboard shortcut for *Debug / Trace Into.*

STEP 7: Press F7 as many times as it takes to execute the statement. The highlight moves to the next statement (the `if` statement).

STEP 8: Press F7 twice; the condition (`optBlue.getState()`) is tested and found to be False.

STEP 9: Continue pressing F7 a few more times and watch the order in which program statements execute.

View the Contents of Variables

STEP 1: Scroll up if necessary and point to fltQuantity and pause. A label pops up showing the contents of that variable.

STEP 2: Point to fltRedTotal to see the current value of that total variable. This value looks correct, since you just entered 30, which was added to the total.

Continue Project Execution

STEP 1: Press Alt + F5, the keyboard shortcut for the *Debug / Continue* command to continue execution.

  Note: You will need to manually switch back and forth between the applet's window and the Forté debugging windows. Arrange the Editor window and the Applet Viewer window so that you can see part of each one. Then click in the Applet Viewer window to make it the active window (in front of the other window).

STEP 2: Enter color Red and quantity 10. When you press Enter, program execution again breaks at the breakpoint.

  The 10 you just entered should be added to the 30 previously entered for Red, producing 40 in the Red total.

STEP 3: Switch to the Editor window and use F7 to step through execution. Keep pressing F7 until the 10 is added to fltRedTotal. Display the current contents of the total. Can you see what the problem is?

  Hint: fltRedTotal has only the current amount, not the sum of the two amounts. The answer will appear a little later; try to find it yourself before going on.

Test the White Total

STEP 1: Press Alt + F5 to continue execution. Make the Applet Viewer the active window.

STEP 2: Enter color White, quantity 100, and press Enter.

STEP 3: When execution halts at the breakpoint, make the Editor the active window and press F7 to single-step execution until you get to the line that adds to the White total.

STEP 4: Point to each variable to see the contents. See if you can you spot the problem before continuing.

Correct the Red Total Error

STEP 1: Stop program execution by pressing Shift + F5 (or click on the Finish Debugging toolbar button or select *Debug / Finish Debugging*).

STEP 2: Locate this line:

```
fltRedTotal = fltQuantity;
```

This statement *replaces* the value of fltRedTotal with fltQuantity rather than *adding* to the total.

STEP 3: Change the line to read

```
fltRedTotal += fltQuantity;
```

Correct the White Total Error

STEP 1: Locate the line that adds to the White total.

```
fltWhiteTotal += fltWhiteTotal;
```

Of course, this adds fltWhiteTotal to itself rather than add the current quantity.

STEP 2: Edit the line to read

```
fltWhiteTotal += fltQuantity;
```

STEP 3: Press F5 to start debugging again. Test the program and check all totals. Each time the program stops at the breakpoint, press Alt + F5 to continue. Make sure to enter at least two quantities for each color to make sure the totals are accumulating correctly.

STEP 4: Halt execution with Shift + F5.

Remove the Breakpoint

STEP 1: Scroll if necessary to view the breakpoint line. Click in the breakpoint line, display the context menu, and select *Add/Remove Breakpoint,* or select *Debug / Add/Remove Breakpoint.*

STEP 2: Execute the applet again (*Build / Execute*). Test by entering another value and color. The applet will not stop this time since you removed the breakpoint.

STEP 3: Test thoroughly and then stop execution.

JBuilder 4 Foundation

Note: As this text went to press, JBuilder 5 was announced by Inprise/Borland. The Personal Edition of JBuilder 5, included on the text CD, is the upgrade to JBuilder 4 Foundation. Although it was too late to change the text, the instructions in this appendix and appendix A ("Using an IDE") should not change significantly.

You can use toolbar buttons, the *Debug* menu, or keyboard shortcuts to activate the JBuilder 4 Foundation debugging tools.

Breaking Program Execution

You can suspend execution of a program by setting a breakpoint in code; the program will halt execution when the breakpoint is reached.

Setting a Breakpoint

You set breakpoints in the code in the Content pane. You can click in the gray margin area to the left of a line to toggle a breakpoint on and off. Or you can click in the line that you want to be the breakpoint and choose *Run / Add Breakpoint,* or right-click and choose *Toggle Breakpoint* from the context menu. The chosen line appears shaded in red, with a large red dot in the gray margin (Figure GJ.1).

After setting a breakpoint, choose *Run / Debug Project* (or use Shift + F9, the keyboard shortcut). When the program reaches the breakpoint, it suspends execution and displays the line, *before* executing the line.

You can click on the breakpoint line and execute the same command to toggle the breakpoint off.

The Debugger User Interface

When you start a debugging session, JBuilder displays the Debugger at the bottom of the IDE (Figure GJ.2). The Session tab at the bottom of the Debugger shows the current debugging session. If you begin a new session without closing the first one, you might see multiple Session tabs. You can close a session by right-clicking the tab and selecting *Remove tab.*

Figure GJ.1

Click in the gray margin area to set a breakpoint in JBuilder. The large red dot indicates that a breakpoint has been set.

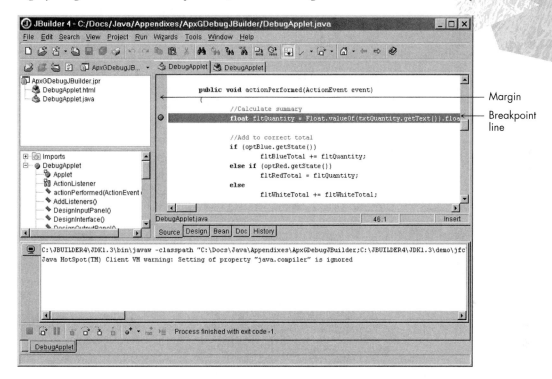

Figure GJ.2

JBuilder's Debugger.

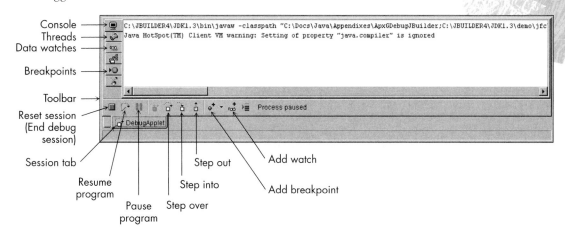

The vertical tabs along the left side of the Debugger display various views. The Console tab displays the system console and error messages in the right pane. The tab that you will use most is the Data watches tab, which displays the contents of any variables or expressions that you specify.

Checking the Current Values of Expressions

When your program is suspended during execution, it's usually helpful to check the current value of variables. The JBuilder Professional and Enterprise editions have a useful feature that allows you to point to any variable in code and the current content pops up in a ToolTip. In the Foundation edition you can still view the contents of variables, but you must set Watches rather than display ToolTips.

Setting Watch Variables

You can add Watch variables to display in the *Data watches* tab of the Debugger. JBuilder displays the name, data type, and current value for any variable that is within scope (Figure GJ.3). The easiest way to add a new Watch variable is to click in the variable name in code, right-click, and select *Add Watch* from the context menu. You can also right-click in the *Data watches* tab or select *Add Watch* from the *Run* menu; you will have to type the name of the variable into a dialog box.

F i g u r e   G J . 3

The Data watches pane displays the contents of Watch expressions.

Stepping through Code

The best way to debug a project is to thoroughly understand what the project is doing every step of the way. The stepping commands allow you to view each program line as it executes. Use the Step Over, Step Into, and Step Out commands to execute program statements one line at a time. You will use the Step Over command the most—it executes the next line of code without showing you the line-by-line execution of the Java methods you are executing. You will use Step Into when the line of code calls a method in your project and you want to see the execution of the method. Step Out resumes rapid execution until the current method finishes.

To step through code, execution must be suspended. The best way to choose the location at which to suspend execution is to set a breakpoint. You set a breakpoint where you would like to see what is happening, such as the first line of code inside the `actionPerformed` method. Then choose *Run / Debug project;* the project begins execution and displays the applet in the Applet Viewer. As you execute the applet by clicking a button on the UI, for example, the actionPerformed event occurs. Execution transfers to the `actionPerformed` method, the code for that method appears in the Content pane, and you can follow line-by-line execution.

The easiest way to single-step is to use the F8 keyboard shortcut for Step Over. Repeatedly press F8 and watch as each line is highlighted and then executed. If you want to continue execution without stepping, choose the *Resume Program* command (from the Debugger toolbar, from the **Run** menu, or by pressing F9).

Sometimes the debugger does step into Java library routines and show you lines that you don't want to see. Choose Step Out to finish the method and return to the calling method.

Debugging Step-by-Step Tutorial for JBuilder

In this exercise you will learn to set a breakpoint, pause program execution, single-step through program instructions, display the current values in variables, and debug a project.

Test the Project

STEP 1: Open JBuilder.

STEP 2: Select *File/Open Project* and open the ApxGDebugJBuilder.jpr project on your student CD.

STEP 3: Run the applet by either selecting *Run / Run Project* or clicking the Run Project toolbar button.

You are going to test the applet. It's a good idea to keep a piece of scratch paper showing the values you have entered and what values you expect for the totals.

STEP 4: Enter color Blue, quantity 100, and press Enter or click on the Calculate button.

STEP 5: Enter another color Blue, quantity 50, and press Enter. Are the totals correct?

STEP 6: Enter color Red, quantity 30, and press Enter.

STEP 7: Enter color Red, quantity 10, and press Enter. Are the totals correct?

STEP 8: Enter color White, quantity 50, and press Enter.

STEP 9: Enter color White, quantity 100, and press Enter. Are the totals correct?

STEP 10: Stop execution. You are going to locate and correct the errors in the Red and White totals.

Break and Step Program Execution

STEP 1: Display the program code in the Content pane and click in the gray margin to the left of the first calculation line in the `actionPerformed` method. A breakpoint will be set on the selected line (Figure GJ.4).

STEP 2: Choose *Debug Project* from the *Run* menu or press Shift + F9.

The Debugger will start and run the applet in the Applet Viewer. This process takes a little while.

STEP 3: When the applet appears in the Applet Viewer, enter Red, quantity 30, and press Enter.

The project transfers control to the `actionPerformed` method, stops when the breakpoint is reached, and highlights the current line.

Note: The highlighted line has not yet executed.

Click in the gray margin to the left of a line to toggle a breakpoint on and off.

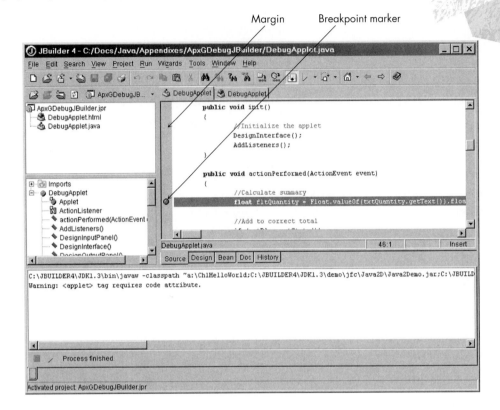

STEP 4: Arrange the Applet Viewer window and the JBuilder IDE window so that you can see part of each one. You will be switching back and forth between the two windows. Switch to the JBuilder window now.

STEP 5: Press the F8 key, which causes JBuilder to execute the current program statement (the assignment statement). F8 is the keyboard shortcut for *Step Over*. For some statements you must press F8 more than once to execute the entire line.

The highlight moves to the next statement (the if statement).

STEP 6: Press F8 again; the condition (optBlue.getState()) is tested and found to be False.

STEP 7: Press F8 again and watch the order in which program statements execute.

View the Contents of Variables

STEP 1: Scroll up if necessary and click on fltQuantity. Right-click and choose *Add Watch* from the context menu. The name fltQuantity should appear for Expression. Click OK.

STEP 2: Check the Debugger. If the *Data watch* tab is not selected, select it now. fltQuantity should appear in the *Watch* pane, along with its current value (30.0).

STEP 3: Add Watches for fltBlueTotal, fltRedTotal, and fltWhiteTotal. Check the value for fltRedTotal. This value looks correct, since you just entered 30, which was added to the total.

Continue Project Execution

STEP 1: Press F9, the keyboard shortcut for the *Resume program* command, to continue execution.

Then click in the Applet Viewer window to make it the active window (in front of the JBuilder window).

STEP 2: Enter color Red and quantity 10. When you press Enter, program execution again breaks at the breakpoint.

The 10 you just entered should be added to the 30 previously entered for Red, producing 40 in the Red total.

STEP 3: Switch to the JBuilder window and use F8 to step through execution. Keep pressing F8 until the 10 is added to fltRedTotal. Check the value of fltRedTotal in the *Watch* pane. Can you see what the problem is?

Hint: fltRedTotal has only the current amount, not the sum of the two amounts. The answer will appear a little later; try to find it yourself before going on.

Test the White Total

STEP 1: Press F9 to resume execution. Make the Applet Viewer the active window.

STEP 2: Enter color White, quantity 100, and press Enter.

STEP 3: When execution halts at the breakpoint, make JBuilder the active window and press F8 to single-step execution until you get to the line that adds to the White total.

STEP 4: Check the values of each variable in the Watch pane. See if you can spot the problem before continuing.

Note: If you begin stepping into code for Java library routines, you can select *Step out* to finish a method. You can close the tabs for extra classes by right-clicking on a tab and selecting the *Close* command.

Correct the Red Total Error

STEP 1: Stop program execution by pressing the red Reset Program button on the Debugger's toolbar (or select *Run / Reset Program* from the menu).

STEP 2: Locate this line:

```
fltRedTotal = fltQuantity;
```

This statement *replaces* the value of fltRedTotal with fltQuantity rather than *adding* to the total.

STEP 3: Change the line to read

```
fltRedTotal += fltQuantity;
```

Correct the White Total Error

STEP 1: Locate the line that adds to the White total.

```
fltWhiteTotal += fltWhiteTotal;
```

Of course, this adds fltWhiteTotal to itself rather than add the current quantity.

STEP 2: Edit the line to read

```
fltWhiteTotal += fltQuantity;
```

STEP 3: Press F9 to start debugging again. Test the program and check all totals. Each time the program stops at the breakpoint, press F9 to continue. Make sure to enter at least two quantities for each color, to make sure the totals are accumulating correctly.

STEP 4: Halt execution by pressing the Reset Program button.

Remove the Breakpoint

STEP 1: Scroll if necessary to view the breakpoint line. Click in the gray margin for the breakpoint line. The breakpoint should toggle off. You can also right-click in the breakpoint line and select *Toggle Breakpoint.*

STEP 2: Execute the applet again (*Run / Run Project* or F9). Test by entering another value and color. The applet will not stop this time, since you removed the breakpoint and are not debugging.

STEP 3: Test thoroughly and then stop execution.

Microsoft Visual J++

You can use toolbar buttons, the *Debug* menu, or keyboard shortcuts to activate Microsoft Visual Studio's debugging tools.

Breaking Program Execution

You can click on the Break toolbar button to pause execution. This places the project into break time at the current line. The disadvantage of this method is that you usually want to break at a particular point. To choose the location of the break, set a breakpoint in code; the program will halt execution when the breakpoint is reached.

Setting a Breakpoint

To set a breakpoint, make sure the Code window is displaying. Then place the cursor in the gray margin indicator area at the left edge of the Code window and click; a large red dot displays in the margin indicator (Figure GV.1). You can also set a breakpoint by placing the cursor on the line before which you want to break and clicking on the Insert Breakpoint button, or by choosing *Insert Breakpoint* from the *Debug* menu.

After setting a breakpoint, start (or restart) program execution. When the project reaches the breakpoint, it will halt, display the line, and go into break time.

You can click on the breakpoint's red dot to toggle it off, use *Remove Breakpoint* to turn off an individual breakpoint, or clear all breakpoints from the *Debug* menu.

Checking the Current Values of Expressions

You can quickly check the current value of an expression, such as a variable, a condition, or an arithmetic expression. During break time, display the Code window and point to the name of the expression that you want to view; a small label pops up, similar to a ToolTip, that displays the current contents of the expression (Figure GV.2). If you want to view the contents of an expression of more than one word, such as a condition or arithmetic expression, highlight the entire expression and then point to the highlighted area; the current value will display.

Click in the gray margin area to set a breakpoint in VJ++. The large red dot indicates that a breakpoint has been set.

The steps for viewing the contents of a variable during run time are

- Break the execution (using a breakpoint).

- Point to the variable or expression you wish to view. The current contents of the expression will pop up in a label.

Point to an expression and its current contents pops up in a label.

The Debug Windows

Microsoft VJ++ has several debugging windows you can choose from the *View* menu. When selecting multiple windows you will notice that they display on different tabs of two windows. The Watch and Output windows are on the same display area while Autos, Locals, Immediate, and Threads display on tabs in another window. You can separate the windows by dragging from the windows tab using your left mouse button.

Window	Purpose
Autos	Displays value and type of local variables as well as property values of components that are currently in scope.
Immediate	Executes commands immediately.
Locals	Displays the value and type of variables declared within the method currently executing.
Output	Displays current output results in console mode.
Threads	Shows each thread as it begins.
Watch	Displays values of selected fields.

The Autos Window The Autos Window contains three columns: Name, Value, and Type. In the Autos window you can check the value of a variable or object that is currently within the scope of the code that is executing. Objects are indicated with a plus sign. If you drill down on the sign, you can see the property settings of the object.

At a break in execution you can change the value of a variable by clicking in the Value column and typing in the new value.

The Locals Window The Locals window contains the same three columns as the Autos window but displays the names of all variables and objects in the current method. You can make changes to the values in this window by clicking on the Value column. The Locals window contains a drop-down list of methods so that you can see all methods that have executed and jump to the code for another method, if the method is within the current class. (Many methods that execute come from superclasses and the source is not available for display.)

The Immediate Window The Immediate window is used to display and change values. The Immediate window appears as a blank window. If you type a question mark and a variable name and press Enter, the current value of the variable is displayed. You can also drag the variable name from your code to the Immediate window. You can display the window by selecting it from the **View** menu or use the shortcut Ctrl + Alt + I. However, you likely will find that the other three debugging windows are easier to use.

The Watch Window You can choose which variables and expressions to display in the Watch window. The Name, Value, and Type columns are the same as for the Locals and Autos windows. Add variables and expressions to the Watch window by selecting *Debug / Add Watch*. Or you can drag a variable name or highlighted expression from the Code window to the Watch window.

Stepping through Code

The best way to debug a project is to thoroughly understand what the project is doing every step of the way. Use the Step Into and Step Over commands to view every statement as it executes, line by line.

You step through code at break time. You can set a breakpoint or choose one of the stepping commands at design time; the program will begin running and immediately transfer to break time. As you execute the project by clicking a button, for example, the actionPerformed event occurs. Execution transfers to the `actionPerformed` method, the Code window for that method appears on the screen, and you can follow line-by-line execution.

The easiest way to single-step is to use the F11 keyboard shortcut for Step Into. Repeatedly press F11 and watch as each line is highlighted and then executed. If you want to continue execution without stepping, choose the *Start* command (from the menu, from the toolbar button, or by pressing F5).

Debugging Step-by-Step Tutorial for Microsoft Visual J++

In this exercise you will learn to set a breakpoint; pause program execution; single-step through program instructions; display the current values in properties, variables, and conditions; and debug a project.

Test the Project

STEP 1: Open Microsoft VJ++.

STEP 2: Open the debugging project on your student CD. The project is found in the ApxGDebugVJ folder.

STEP 3: Run the project.

STEP 4: Enter color Blue, quantity 100, and press Enter or click on the Calculate button.

STEP 5: Enter another color Blue, quantity 50, and press Enter. Are the totals correct?

STEP 6: Enter color Red, quantity 30, and press Enter.

STEP 7: Enter color Red, quantity 10, and press Enter. Are the totals correct?

STEP 8: Enter color White, quantity 50, and press Enter.

STEP 9: Enter color White, quantity 100, and press Enter. Are the totals correct?

STEP 10: Stop execution. You are going to locate and correct the errors in the Red and White totals.

Break and Step Program Execution

STEP 1: Display the program code and click in the gray margin indicator area for the first calculation line in the `actionPerformed` method (Figure GV.3). A breakpoint will be set on the selected line.

Figure GV.3

Click in the gray margin to set the breakpoint.

```
public void actionPerformed(ActionEvent event)
{
    //Calculate summary
    float fltQuantity = Float.valueOf(txtQuantity.getText()).floatValue();
```

STEP 2: Close the Code window.

STEP 3: Run the project, enter Red, quantity 30, and press Enter.

> The project transfers control to the `actionPerformed` method, stops when the breakpoint is reached, places a yellow arrow in the margin for the current line, and enters break time.
>
> *Note:* The line with the selection arrow has not yet executed.

STEP 4: Press the F11 key, which causes VJ++ to execute the current program statement (the assignment statement). F11 is the keyboard shortcut for *Debug/Step Into.*

> The statement is executed and the yellow arrow moves to the next statement (the `if` statement).

STEP 5: Press F11 again; the condition (`optBlue.getState()`) is tested and found to be false.

STEP 6: Continue pressing F11 a few more times and watch the order in which program statements execute.

View the Contents of Properties, Variables, and Conditions

STEP 1: Scroll up if necessary and point to fltQuantity and view the contents of that variable.

STEP 2: Point to optBlue in the `if` statement; then point to optRed. The label that pops up shows the current state of the option button.

STEP 3: Point to fltRedTotal to see the current value of that total variable. This value looks correct, since you just entered 30, which was added to the total.

STEP 4: Locate the `if` statement and highlight the condition (within the parentheses). Then point to the highlighted text to view the result of the condition (Figure GV.4).

Figure GV.4

To display the result of a condition, highlight the condition and point to it.

```
if(fltTotal > 0)
{           fltTotal > 0 = true
    //Display Percentages
    NumberFormat  fmtPercent = NumberFormat.getPercentInstance();
    String strFormat = fmtPercent.format(fltBlueTotal/fltTotal);
    lblBluePercent.setText("" + strFormat);
```

Continue Project Execution

STEP 1: Press F5, the keyboard shortcut for the Start command, to continue execution.

> *Note:* You may have to click on the Applet Viewer in the task bar to make the applet's window come to the front.

STEP 2: Enter color Red and quantity 10. When you press Enter, program execution again breaks at the breakpoint. The 10 you just entered should be added to the 30 previously entered for Red, producing 40 in the Red total.

STEP 3: Use F11 to step through execution. Keep pressing F11 until the 10 is added to fltRedTotal. Display the current contents of the total. Can you see what the problem is?

   Hint: fltRedTotal has only the current amount, not the sum of the two amounts. The answer will appear a little later; try to find it yourself before going on.

Test the White Total

STEP 1: Press F5 to continue execution. If the applet does not reappear, click the Applet Viewer's toolbar button.
STEP 2: Enter color White, quantity 100, and press Enter.
STEP 3: When execution halts at the breakpoint, press F11 to single-step execution until you get to the line that adds to the White total.
STEP 4: Point to each variable to see the contents. See if you can spot the problem before continuing.

Correct the Red Total Error

STEP 1: Stop program execution by clicking on the End toolbar button or on the Applet Viewer's Close button.
STEP 2: Locate this line:

```
fltRedTotal = fltQuantity;
```

This statement *replaces* the value of fltRedTotal with fltQuantity rather than *adding* to the total.
STEP 3: Change the line to read

```
fltRedTotal += fltQuantity;
```

Correct the White Total Error

STEP 1: Locate the line that adds to the White total.

```
fltWhiteTotal += fltWhiteTotal;
```

Of course, this adds fltWhiteTotal to itself rather than add the current quantity.
STEP 2: Edit the line to read

```
fltWhiteTotal += fltQuantity;
```

STEP 3: Test the program again and check all totals. Each time the program stops at the breakpoint, press F5 to continue. Make sure to enter at least two quantities for each color, to make sure the totals are accumulating correctly.

Look at the Autos and Locals Windows

STEP 1: With the breakpoint still in the code, run the applet, enter a color and quantity, and press Enter. Using F11, step through a few lines of code.
STEP 2: Open the Locals and Autos debugging windows (*View / Debug Windows*). You can switch back and forth between the two windows using the tab on their window.

STEP 3: Investigate the values in both windows. Click on plus signs to drill down in the hierarchy and view properties of various objects.

STEP 4: With the Autos window displaying, single-step a few more lines in the program and notice what happens in the window.

Remove the Breakpoint

STEP 1: Scroll if necessary to view the breakpoint line. Click the red dot in the margin to remove the breakpoint.

STEP 2: Press F5 to continue execution. Test by entering another value and color. The applet will not stop this time, since you removed the breakpoint.

STEP 3: Test thoroughly and then stop execution.

BlueJ

BlueJ has a built-in debugger that allows breakpoints, single-stepping, and examining variables and objects during execution. Unfortunately, the debugging commands work only on applications, not applets.

To learn about debugging in BlueJ, display their tutorial (*Help* menu) and print out Section 6. The debugging tutorial takes only a short time and is very informative.

Glossary

For further reference, you can find a good Java glossary at http://mindprod.com/jgloss.html.

abstract class   A class that contains methods that must be overridden for implementation. Used as a superclass. Interface classes are automatically abstract; others may be declared as abstract.

abstract method   An empty method that must be overridden for implementation.

actionPerformed method   A method containing code to handle events for actions such as the click of a button.

add method   Method used to add components to a container.

addSeparator method   Method that adds a separation line to a menu.

anchor   Used in designing layouts. Specifies point of alignment.

animated .gif   An image file that contains animation.

anonymous class   An unnamed inner class.

append method   Adds text to a TextArea component.

applet   A program that runs in a browser.

application   A java program that can run alone without a browser.

application programming interface (API)   Set of standard packages included in the Java language. In general, refers to programming at the system level.

archive   A compressed file that holds all of the classes and other files needed for an applet, application, or bean. Called a JAR (Java ARchive) file.

argument   A value supplied to a call to a method.

arithmetic operator   Math operators for addition (+), subtraction (-), multiplication (*), division (/), and modulus(%).

array   A variable that stores a series of values.

assignment operator   An operator that assigns a value to a variable, can be combined with a math operator. (=, +=, −+, *=, /=, %=).

audio clip   A sound file.

AudioClip object   Java object that can hold a sound file.

AWT   Abstract windows toolkit, the package containing the components for a graphical user interface.

base class   A superclass from which another class may inherit.

Bean Development Kit (BDK)   Sun product that contains the BeanBox for testing JavaBeans.

BeanBox   An application for testing JavaBeans.

BeanInfo class   Specifies interface information for a JavaBean.

beans   Generic term for a component in Java; a JavaBean.

binding   Order in which operations occur, according to the precedence of the operators.

block   A set of statements enclosed in braces {}.

BorderLayout   A layout manager that is divided into segments for north, south, east, west, and center.

braces   Used to enclose a block of statements for methods, decisions, and loops. {}

break statement   A statement used to exit a loop, decision, or `case` statement.

business rule   Validation rule specific to the needs of an organization.

button   A visual component normally used to activate an action. Common examples are OK and Cancel.

bytecode   The compiled code in a class file; must still be

581

interpreted by the Java Virtual Machine on the destination system.

CardLayout A layout manager that simulates a tabbed-type screen. Multiple views are "stacked" on each other; only one view is visible at a time.

case statement Specifies the values within a `switch` statement; a decision-making statement for situations that depend on the value of a single variable.

casting Temporary conversion of a value into a different data type for use in assignments and calculations.

catch Statement used to handle exceptions.

certificate Determines authenticity of an applet.

CheckboxMenuItem A class to create menu item objects that can be checked.

Choice class A visual component that displays a drop-down list of choices. Methods are similar to the List class.

class A unit of code defining the data and actions, somewhat like a template from which objects may be created.

class variable A variable declared with the `static` keyword. Only one copy of the variable exists for all instances of the class.

client The user or receiver in a multisystem application.

Common Object Remote Broker Architecture (CORBA) Technique for implementing client/sever applications.

compile error An error detected by the compiler such as an ActionListener implemented with no `actionPerformed` method.

compiler A program used to translate source code into bytecode.

compound condition Multiple conditions combined with && (and) and/or || (or).

concatenation Joining string information. The plus sign (+) is used to concatenate text.

condition A comparison for decision making; uses relational operators (>, <, ==, !=, >=, <=).

conditional operator A three-part operator that can replace an `if` statement.

Connection object An object for connecting to a database.

constructor method A method that is automatically called when an object is instantiated.

Container A component that can hold other components and/or containers.

Content Pane The basic layer of a Swing container component.

critical section A block of statements containing a `synchronized` qualifier.

Data Source Name (DSN) System name used to refer to a database. Defined on the client machine.

data type Specifies the type of value to be stored in a variable or constant. May be used to indicate the return type for a method. Examples of data types are integer (int), floating point (float), and character (char).

declaration statement A statement that creates a variable, constant, or object.

decrement operator Subtracts one from a variable (--).

default statement Part of the case structure; the default is executed when none of the cases are true.

Delete SQL command for deleting records.

deprecated A method or variable that is not supported in newer versions of the JDK.

Dialog class Used to create window objects such as an About dialog or message box.

digital signature A JAR file providing security information about the developer of a program.

direct reference A reference to a specific position within an array.

display area The area in which a component displays; one or more cells in a GridBagLayout.

dispose method Unloads a frame to free memory.

document object Javascript object representing a Web page.

document object model Hierarchy of objects in JavaScript.

drawImage method Displays images; used in the `paint` method.

drawString method Displays text strings; used in the `paint` method.

element Single value from an array or list.

else Clause of an `if` statement that executes when the condition is false.

encapsulation OOP concept for combining data and actions into a single unit and hiding the properties and methods from other components.

end (AudioClip) method Available with audio clips to stop the sound file.

Enterprise JavaBeans Model for creating beans for a distributed multitier environment.

event An action that may be taken by the user, such as a click, drag, or key press. Events also can be triggered by an internal action, such as repainting the screen.

event listener The component that catches the event.

event source A component that fires an event.

event transmission Communication between components. The combination of an event source and an event listener.

exception object An object that is generated when an exception occurs; used for error handling.

executeQuery method Database method to execute an SQL statement.

executeUpdate method Database method to execute an SQL `Update` statement.

exponentiation Math operation of raising to a power.

extends Clause used to create a subclass from, or inherit from, another class.

FileInputStream A class to create an object to read from a data file.

FileOutputStream A class to create an object to write to a data file.

final Keyword used to define a constant.

FlowLayout Default layout manager for an applet. Components are positioned one after another in the sequence added to the container.

focus Positioning of the cursor on an individual component.

Font class A class for creating Font objects used in text display.

for loop A loop that usually contains a counter.

format method A method that formats numeric and date fields.

Frame A class for creating container objects that can hold a menu.

function Term for a method in JavaScript.

getAudioClip method Associates a sound file with an Audio-Clip object.

getCurrencyInstance method A formatting method for currency fields.

getDocumentBase method Returns the path of the current Web page.

getFloat method Database conversion method for retrieving a float value.

getGraphics method Provides access to draw methods.

getImage method Associates an image file with an image object.

getInstance method Defines a Calendar object for the current locale.

getInt method Database conversion method for retrieving an int value.

getItem method Returns an element from a list or choice component.

getItemCount method Returns the number of elements in a list or choice component.

getPercentInstance method A formatting method for percentage fields.

getSelectedIndex method Returns the index of the current item in a list or choice component.

getSelectedItem method Returns the value of the current item in a list or choice component.

getState method Returns the state (on or off) of a checkbox.

getString method Database conversion method for retrieving a String value.

getText method Returns the current string value of a text component.

GridBagConstraints An object that holds a set of properties to control the appearance of a component placed on a Grid-BagLayout.

GridBagLayout A layout manager that offers the greatest flexibility. Cells need not all be the same size.

GridLayout A layout manager that arranges components in rows and columns. All cells are the same size.

hierarchy Relationship of superclasses and subclasses.

IDE Integrated development environment. An application for developing programs that includes an editor, tools for running and debugging programs, and an object browser. May also include a graphical screen designer.

if statement Statement for testing conditions for decision making.

image file A .gif or .jpeg file, which holds a picture.

Image object An AWT object for holding image files (.gif or .jpeg).

implements A clause used to add an interface to a class.

import statement Gives access to java classes without the need to fully qualify the name. You can refer to Applet without using java.applet.Applet.

increment operator Adds one to a variable (++).

InfoBus Used to define the interface of components and pass data, including arrays and rows of a dataset, from one bean to another.

inheritance OOP concept allowing a subclass to be based on a superclass and contain all public and protected members of the superclass.

init method An applet method that runs once when an applet is created.

inner class A class declared inside of another class.

inner join SQL technique for combining data from multiple tables; contains only the records that have matching records in both tables.

Insert SQL command for adding a record.

Insets A constraint for layouts that controls the number of pixels between cells.

instance An object created from a class. Each object is referred to as an instance.

instance variable A variable declared in a class. Each instance of the class has its own copy of the variable.

instantiate To declare an object from a class.

interface Similar to a class. Contains methods that can be implemented by a class or added to another class with the `implements` clause. The Java solution for avoiding multiple inheritance.

Interface Design Language (IDL) Defines the interface for objects.

internationalization Developing an application/applet that can be executed in different countries.

interpreter A program that translates source code into machine code one line at a time.

introspection Process of determining the properties of an interface of a bean.

ItemListener An interface containing methods for handling actions caused by check box components.

itemStateChanged method A method that executes when the on/off state of a check box is changed.

iteration One execution of a block of statements within a loop construct.

Java Archive (JAR) A compressed file that holds all of the classes and other files needed for an applet, application, or bean. Created with Sun's jar application.

Java Database Connectivity (JDBC) Specific implementation of database connection for Java.

Java Development Kit (JDK) The Sun Microsystems product containing the language library.

Java Foundation Classes (JFC) Visual components; also referred to as Swing.

Java Native Interface (JNI) Allows Java programs to use methods that were created in another programming language.

Java Runtime Environment (JRE) The Sun Microsystems product needed to run a compiled Java program.

Java Virtual Machine (JVM) A virtual computer used to compile Java bytecode into the native code for a computer system.

JavaBeans Component technology for Java.

JComboBox A Swing component that can contain a list and a text component.

JList A Swing component for lists.

Join SQL technique for combining data from multiple tables; updateable.

just-in-time (JIT) compiler Stores the compiled version of a Java applet for future reference to that applet. Used to speed execution of Java by avoiding repeated interpretation of the bytecode to machine code.

keyboard shortcut   Key combination for button or menu actions. Example: Ctrl+X is frequently used for exit. Also called *hotkeys*.

label   A visual component that displays information; cannot be used for input.

Layout Manager   Classes used to control the screen design including FlowLayout (default), GridLayout, GridBagLayout, and CardLayout.

left join   SQL join that contains all records from the first table and only the matching records from the second table.

legacy code   Existing code.

lifetime   The length of time or portion of the program in which a variable or object continues to exist.

List class   An AWT component for displaying lists.

local inner class   An inner class declared inside a method.

local variable   A variable that is available only inside a block of statements. The declaration is inside of the block.

locale   Geographical location in which the program is run; used for internationalization.

logic error   An error in a program that does not halt execution but causes erroneous results in the output.

logical operator   The operators && (and), || (or), and ! (not); used to construct compound

conditions and to reverse the truth of a condition.

look and feel   Appearance of program output. Examples: Windows, Metal, Motif, Java, Mac.

loop   A block of statements that may execute multiple times.

loop (AudioClip method) Available with audio clips to continuously play the sound file.

main method   First method to be executed in an application.

MediaTracker   An audio visual class that can keep track of whether all images and sound clips have finished loading.

member class   An inner class; one copy exists for each instance of the outer class.

Menu class   Used to create the menu on a frame.

MenuBar class   Creates the top-level menu.

MenuItem class   Used to define the menu items (commands) to appear on a menu.

Metal   A look-and-feel style available in JFC.

method   Procedure or function containing programming instructions/actions.

modulus   An operator (%) that returns the remainder of a division calculation.

Motif   A look-and-feel style available in JFC.

MouseListener   An interface that contains the methods for mouse events.

multitasking   More than one process execute at the same time.

multithreading   More than one task within an application run simultaneously.

Navigator object   An object that contains properties with information about the platform and operating system.

nested class   An inner class. Has access to all instance and class variables and objects of the outer class or any other inner classes, including members declared as private.

nested if statement   A decision statement enclosed within another decision statement.

new keyword   Keyword for instantiating (creating) an object.

NumberFormat class   Class that declares the format styles for numeric fields.

object   An instance declared based on a class.

object-oriented programming (OOP)   Programming style that incorporates inheritance, encapsulation, and polymorphism.

Object Request Broker (ORB)   Calls methods from objects in any language.

object serialization   Stores the state of an object from one execution of an applet or application until the next time the program runs.

ObjectInputStream   Stream class for reading an object from a data file.

ObjectOutputStream   Stream class for writing an object to a data file.

Open DataBase Connectivity (ODBC) Technique used with databases for standardized connections.

override A method that contains the same return type and argument list as an existing class; the existing class is replaced.

overriding A method created to replace an existing method.

package Portion of the library such as the applet package. A group of files.

paint method Redraws the screen.

Panel A container used to hold visual components.

parameter List of elements on a method declaration specifying the argument types to be passed to the method.

persistence Storage of data for future access.

play method Available with audio clips to play the sound file once.

polymorphism Object-oriented concept providing a common naming structure for similar properties and methods of classes.

PopupMenu class A menu that can appear on a component or window, rather than in a menu bar. Pops up in response to a right-mouse click.

postfix An increment or decrement operator that follows an expression, the calculation occurs after the expression executes.

precedence Hierarchy or order of operations for evaluation of multiple operators in a single expression.

prefix An increment or decrement operator that precedes an expression; the calculation occurs before the expression executes.

primitive data type Elementary data type; does not include wrapper classes.

print method A system method for printing to the standard output device.

printAll method Prints the contents of the container.

PrintJob class Available in the Applet class for generating output to a printer.

println method A system method for printing to the standard output device and including a carriage return.

private Method and variable qualifier indicating that access exists only for members of the class (not for objects of the class).

Properties Sheet A dialog box that displays the property values of an object.

property A variable declared in a class that can be modified by an object of the class. The property may be public or a public method provided to allow access to a private variable.

protected Access type that acts like private but allows inheritance.

public Method and variable qualifier indicating access can be made by objects of the class.

radio button Option button; a visual component used to indicate a mutually exclusive list of options. Created in AWT by

using a group with Checkbox components.

readObject method Method for storing the contents of an object.

relational operator Operator for performing comparisons (<, >, ==).

Remote Method Invocation (RMI) Allows use of an object that exists on a different computer.

remove method Method that removes an element from a list component.

removeAll method Method that removes all elements from a list component.

repaint method Calls the `paint` method.

resize method Method for controlling the size of an element. Frequently used to initialize the size of an applet.

ResultSet object Contains the records returned from a database query.

return statement Statement that returns a value from a method. The return type on the declaration must match the data type of the value on the `return` statement.

right join SQL join that contains all records from the second table and only the matching records from the first table.

Runnable interface Used with threading.

run-time error A program error that occurs during execution.

scope Refers to the visibility of a variable or component within a class. The scope may be local or for the entire class.

scripting   A language used to create dynamic and interactive Web pages.

security   Language features to prevent an applet from doing damage to the host system. Includes digital signatures that ensure that an applet or component came unmodified from a reputable source.

semicolon   Punctuation used to indicate the termination of a statement.

Serializable interface   Facilitates object serialization, which saves and restores the properties of an object.

server   The system that contains the application or data in a multisystem environment.

setBackground method   Sets the background color of a container or component.

setEnabled method   Sets the enabled property of a visual component. A disabled component is visible but appears in a shaded color.

setFont method   Sets the font for a component or container.

setForeground method   Sets the foreground color of text for a component or container.

setLayout method   Assigns a layout manager to a container.

setMaximumFractionDigits method   Sets the maximum number of decimal positions to the right of the decimal point in formatting for display.

setMinimumFractionDigits method   Sets the minimum number of decimal positions to the right of the decimal point in formatting for display.

setText method   Assigns a text value to a text component, such as a label, text field, or text area.

setVisible method   Sets the visibility of a component. If visibility = false, the component or container does not appear.

showStatus method   Displays a message in the status bar of an applet.

source program   Program written in a programming language, prior to its compilation.

SQL Select statement   Selects fields and/or records from a database. Produces a ResultSet.

standard input device   The device set as the system default for input; generally the keyboard.

standard output device   The device set as the system default for output; generally the monitor.

state   Current setting of a field, such as true or false. For an object, the current values for all fields.

Statement object   Can be set to an SQL statement.

static member class   An inner class declared with the `static` keyword. The outer (containing) class has only one copy of the inner class.

stop method   Halts playing of a sound file for an audio clip.

stream   A series of bytes, used for transfer of data.

string literal   A text constant enclosed in quotes.

Structured Query Language (SQL)   An industy-standard language for navigating and updating databases.

subclass   A class that extends or inherits from another class.

submenu   A secondary menu that appears below a menu item.

subscript   Position of an element within an array.

subscripted variable   One element of an array.

superclass   A class from which another class inherits. Also called a *base class.*

Swing components   Visual components created from JFC (Java Foundation Classes).

switch statement   A case structure for making multiple decisions when all decisions are based on testing the same variable.

synchronized   Keyword that specifies that the method must not be executed by two threads at the same time. Required with threads.

table   An array.

table lookup   Searches of table data; may be direct or indirect reference.

tags   Embedded codes in HTML.

TextArea component   A text component that allows multiple lines of input or output.

TextField component   An AWT visual component for data entry.

this   Keyword that refers to the current object.

thread   A single process or task within a program.

ToolBox   A collection of components.

ToolTip   A definition or message that appears when the cursor pauses over a component.

try   Keyword that begins a block of code that will handle exceptions.

two-dimensional table   An array with rows and columns.

Update   An SQL command for making changes to database records.

update method   Can be overridden to customize a call to the `paint` method; used to avoid flickering in animation.

validation   Process of testing input data for reasonableness, valid character entry, or business rules.

variable   A memory location referred to by a name. The value of a variable can change during program execution.

Vector   A class that is similar to an array.

void   Keyword that specifies that a method does not return a value.

window object   JavaScript object that is created prior to displaying a page.

wrapper class   A class that extends the capability of a primitive data type. For example, the Float class holds a float data value and has methods for comparing to other objects, converting to other data types, and testing for numeric values.

write method   JavaScript method for displaying text on a Web page.

writeObject method   Output the state of an object; used for object serialization.

XML   A markup language for database information in Web pages.

Index

A